EDUCATIONAL MEASUREMENT

ADVISORY BOARD

EDUCATIONAL MEASUREMENT

From Foundations to Future

EDITED BY

Craig S. Wells
Molly Faulkner-Bond

THE GUILFORD PRESS
New York   London

Copyright © 2016 The Guilford Press
A Division of Guilford Publications, Inc.
370 Seventh Avenue, Suite 1200, New York, NY 10001
www.guilford.com

Printed in the United States of America

This book is printed on acid-free paper.

Last digit is print number: 9   8   7   6   5   4   3   2   1

Library of Congress Cataloging-in-Publication Data is available from the publisher.

ISBN 978-1-4625-2562-1

Prologue
A Ronference Retrospective

Stephen G. Sireci

Ronald K. Hambleton is one of the bravest persons I have ever met. He is not afraid to take on any psychometric challenge or educational research project, nor is he afraid to stand up for what he believes in or to defend those he loves. However, there is one thing that terrifies him. It is the "R" word (*retirement*). Most professors with a history of outstanding accomplishments enjoy a retirement party in their honor, which sometimes takes the form of a conference. Given that Ron was showing no signs of slowing down after 43 years of teaching at UMass, we decided, "Why wait for him to retire?" Thus, in 2012 the time seemed right to give those to whom he has given so much the opportunity to honor him through a conference that would feature many of the people who have been influenced by his teaching, mentorship, and collegiality. It was through this desire to acknowledge Ron's monumental contributions to countless individuals, and to the psychometrics field, that "Teach Your Children Well: A Conference to Honor Ronald K. Hambleton" (also known as "the Ronference") was born.

The Ronference was spectacular in so many ways, but clearly one way was the level of scholarship exhibited through the presentations and workshops. Rather than let our memories of the Ronference fade, this book immortalizes many of the important lessons and messages that were presented. It provides another way for us to honor Ron and thank him for the generous gifts of time and talent that he bestowed on so many of us over the years. The chapters in this book are written by Ronference participants who have been influenced by Distinguished University Professor Hambleton over the years. The work described in these chapters represents some of the most important developments in contemporary psychometrics, and the authors place these developments within the appropriate historical context. As the book was assembled, it became clear how incorporating the areas in which Ron has worked over his career accounts for the most significant developments in educational and psychological testing over the past half century. Thus, this book represents one of the most comprehensive compendiums of the past, present, and (predicted) future of the most important areas in psychometrics—most of which were inspired by Ron's work.

The 25 chapters in this book cover an incredible range of important topics in educational research and psychometrics, including a history of testing, item response theory, computer-based testing, reporting results from educational assessments, and testing special populations. The chapter authors represent teams of Ronference participants brought together to best cover these topics, as well as others with whom Ron has collaborated over the years. Continuing to adhere to the theme of collegiality that best characterizes Professor Hambleton, this book brings together the foremost experts in each topic area (from across the globe) so that each chapter provides comprehensive and insightful coverage.

The Ronference was held on November 9–10, 2012, and featured five workshops, 25 invited presentations, a poster session, and, of course, remarks from the guest of honor. (We almost had to add a third day to allow Ron to finish his remarks, but, alas, the conference space was rented for only 2 days.) None of those events would have been possible without the support of many individuals and organizations, but the first real step in organizing the conference was to secure funding. We approached the testing organizations that have made some of the most significant contributions to psychometric research and with which Ron has worked over the past several decades. I knew these organizations appreciated Ron's history of service and commitment to them and to the field. Staying true to the spirit of collegiality, these organizations generously agreed to support the conference. I would like to thank these sponsors for making the Ronference possible. Specifically, the organizations to be thanked are the American Institute of Certified Public Accountants, College Board, CTB, Educational Testing Service, Graduate Management Admissions Council, Medical Council of Canada, National Board of Medical Examiners, Pearson, and the University of Massachusetts Amherst College of Education. The individuals at these institutions who were instrumental in supporting the Ronference include Krista Breithaupt, Wayne Camara, Ida Lawrence, Christine McCormick, Craig Mills, Ron Nungester, Richard Patz, Gretchen Rossman, Larry Rudner, and Jon Twing. Others who were instrumental in pulling off the Ronference include Molly Faulkner-Bond and Emily Pichette (who organized just about everything), Peg Louraine (Ron's right-hand lady for years), Fernanda Gandara (who, along with Vahab Khademi, took photos), and virtually all of our Research in Educational Measurement and Psychometrics doctoral students (and alumni) at UMass Amherst. Of course, special thanks go to the person who enabled Ron to be what he has become: his wife and partner-for-life, Else Hambleton.

At the time of this writing, photos from the Ronference can be viewed at *http://tinyurl.com/hj55l2g*, and the conference website can still be viewed in archival form at *www.umass.edu/ronference*. Thankfully, much of the scholarship presented at the Ronference is contained within this book. Gratitude for making this book a reality is extended to Craig S. Wells and Molly Faulkner-Bond, who worked tirelessly getting some of the busiest professionals in the field to complete their chapters. If it were not for their tenacious dedication to this project, this seminal compendium would not exist. Thanks, Craig and Molly!

It is important to note that in addition to representing an outstanding scholarly contribution to the field, this book expresses an enormous amount of love and gratitude for the man who is responsible for the success of so many contributors to this book, and to so many readers of it. Ron may be best known for his research, but to those who know him well, it is clear he has not dedicated his career to psychometrics. Rather, he has dedicated his life to supporting others—to building and supporting the careers of all who are lucky enough to have interacted with him. And to those who have not met Ron, I know he has touched you and educated you through his writings. Long before I met Ron, I felt like I knew him through his books and journal articles. When I did meet him, his concern for my professional growth was immediately apparent. He has been an important mentor to me, and I know I am not alone in that regard. The testimonials at the Ronference dinner were heartwarming. It became clear that many of us credit Ron with the success we have achieved, and the illustrations of how he turned around the lives of so many were inspiring.

Like the Ronference itself, this book stands as a tribute to Ron Hambleton for all he has done for us as individuals, for us collectively, and for the fields of quantitative psychology, educational research, and psychometrics. Thanks, Ron, for so generously sharing yourself, for your scholarship, and for caring so deeply. Thank you for sharing your passion for research. Thank you for always being there to help out on a project, edit our writings, and give career advice. You have established one of the most successful psychometric doctoral programs in the world and have given us all a model of professionalism and mentorship that we strive to emulate. If we were to grade your career (thus far!) using the NAEP achievement levels, we would have to establish a new level above "Advanced"!

Enjoy the book! And "teach your children well." Just like Ron.

Editors' Note. Concomitant with the Ronference, the University of Massachusetts Amherst College of Education established the Ronald K. Hambleton Legacy Fund, a scholarship fund for doctoral students in psychometrics at UMass. If you would like to donate to this fund, visit *http://tinyurl/jdkpahd.*

Preface

This book has several goals, all of which stem from one man's work. As Stephen G. Sireci discusses in his Prologue, this book grew out of the proceedings of "Teach Your Children Well: A Conference Honoring Ronald K. Hambleton" (affectionately known as "the Ronference"). The purpose of that conference was to honor the achievements of Professor Hambleton, whose 40-plus-year career in educational measurement has touched the lives of individuals, organizations, states, and countries around the world through his teaching, research, and service.

One major motivation for this book was to encapsulate and build on, in more permanent form, some of the reflections and ideas presented at the conference. This motivation stemmed partially from our personal affection for Ron, but also, more importantly, from our belief that the contents of this particular career transcend the individual. Part of what has made Professor Hambleton such an influential scholar is his uncanny ability to identify promising new educational measurement topics when they are still nascent, and propel them to prominence through his attention and hard work. In this way, Ron Hambleton's career is a reflection of the field as a whole. Papers presented at the Ronference discussed topics ranging from K–12 teacher evaluation, to the application of item response theory (IRT) models to complex "21st-century" item types, to the current state of multilingual testing and test adaptation practices—all topics that directly relate to Professor Hambleton's work over the years, but also, coincidentally, to a wide-ranging sampling of critical topics in the educational measurement field. This is the essence of Ron Hambleton's unique eminence: What Ron studies, we all study, in large part because of him.

A second, more indirect theme of the Ronference was that of chronological perspective and the evolution of the measurement field over time. By compelling speakers to ground their presentations in the context of one man's long-spanning career, the conference also forced or inspired many speakers to discuss their work from a somewhat historical perspective. Even presentations that described cutting-edge developments such as automated test assembly were enhanced by the implicit requirement that the speakers consider these topics in the context of several decades of work, rather than just the latest iteration of the discussion.

This infusion of perspective serves the book's secondary goal, which is to try to encapsulate an element of Professor Hambleton's work in the classroom. Any of Ron's many students would likely attest that a major feature—and benefit—of his instruction is his rich knowledge of how psychometrics has evolved over time in terms of technology, ideas, personalities, and priorities. Even as he is revealing a new formula or recommending a recently published paper, his perspective always pans out, at some point, to a larger scale. How, for example, did the field's shift toward IRT in the 1980s and 1990s pave the way for current scholars to be wrestling with, say, automated test assembly algorithms? How much (or how little) do current challenges in computer-based testing resemble the challenges identified 30 years ago when the field was new? How should our summaries and discussions of the field as it currently stands—and will stand in the future—be tempered or enhanced by knowledge of how we got here?

This approach is one of the most valuable aspects of Ron Hambleton's teaching precisely because—to this point, at least—it comprises knowledge and information that go beyond what students and professionals can read in books. We are pleased and proud to include several chapters in this volume that engage these types of historical questions and perspective, as a prelude to the subsequent chapters that tackle key themes and issues in current and future practice. By grounding contemporary ideas in historical perspective, this book will help both new and seasoned scholars to develop a better perspective on how and why certain issues have gained prominence in the field—which may, in turn, help them discover novel applications, solutions, or evolutions that will propel educational measurement into its second century as a professional field. We believe that these historical chapters are a key part of what makes this book unique. And, by capturing this perspective in writing for the first time, even scholars who have not had the privilege of studying under Professor Hambleton directly will have access to some of the knowledge he brings based on his longevity as a scholar and a teacher.

Perhaps a shorter, more direct way of saying all this is to state that our goal for this book is to present an accessible, historically grounded overview of key measurement topics that will be of use and interest to a wide range of individuals. The heart of the book is organized into five major parts, each of which gives a past-to-future treatment of a major measurement topic over the course of several chapters. The topics—criterion-referenced testing (CRT), IRT, computer-based testing (CBT), cross-lingual and cross-cultural assessment, and accountability testing—have all been major foci of Professor Hambleton's work at some point in his career, but, again, are also important topics for measurement generally. These five sections are sandwiched by chapters that attempt to give a general overview of educational measurement's origins (in Part I) and its future (in Part VII). Each chapter is authored by one or more prominent scholars who, in addition to being major players in the field, are friends and colleagues of Ron Hambleton himself.

Of course, knowing Ron is not a prerequisite for finding value in this book. Taken together, we believe this collection of chapters provides a solid overview of these topics, and we believe there is something here for everyone: students, young scholars and professionals, policymakers, practitioners, and even seasoned experts who may appreciate the historical component documenting the field's progress. We have sought to create a book that is streamlined and focused, offering readers comprehensive introductions that provide enough background to establish a good working knowledge, without going so far into the weeds as to alienate or lose focus. Our aim is to land somewhere between a handbook, an introduction, and a reference manual—for example, to give enough information to help readers determine whether they want or need a dedicated volume on a given topic.

In function, we want this book to be accessible and to be used to solve practical problems. So in form, it is not so big that it must remain sitting on a shelf. These elements—practicality and utility—are perhaps the final pieces of our mission in creating this book. As Ron himself attests in the book's second chapter, his career has always focused on using his expertise in ways that are useful, and specifically useful for people who actually "do" education—that is, teachers, principals, and policymakers. The questions he takes up are questions whose answers can provide direct solutions for problems that exist in the world of education, not just in the theoretical realms of peer-reviewed academic journals. This book has been designed to reflect these values. Although, of course, we recognize the value of scholarship and academic publication, this book is not directly about either of those areas. Ultimately, the information here is meant to be used to educate, to stimulate, and to motivate readers on the topics it contains. If this book inspires even one conversation or action that leads to some kind of improvement in educational testing or practice—and, in truth, we hope it may inspire many—then we will consider it successful in its aims.

Acknowledgments

This book is a direct extension of the conference held to honor Ronald K. Hambleton in November 2012. In his Prologue, Stephen G. Sireci listed the many organizations and individuals who made that conference possible, and we must begin our acknowledgments by wholeheartedly echoing Steve's thanks to those groups. Without our conference sponsors and volunteers, the Ronference would not have happened, and this book would not exist. We will not repeat the list here, but we encourage readers to flip back a few pages and read (or reread) the Prologue to ensure that these generous people receive the attention they deserve for the work they did to make the Ronference happen. In addition to our sponsors, we would like to thank those who helped organize and run the conference, including Emily Pichette (Steve Sireci's assistant), the graduate students in the Research in Educational Measurement and Psychometrics (REMP) concentration at UMass, Peg Louraine (Ron's long-time assistant), and REMP faculty members April Zenisky, Lisa Keller, and Jennifer Randall. Without the funding provided by the aforementioned sponsors and the support of many individuals, the conference would not have been held and this book would not exist.

Second, we would like to thank the many impressive (and busy) individuals who contributed to this book as authors and coauthors. Their expertise and experience is our book's greatest asset, and, in most cases, the work they put in for us took place outside of their normal workdays and responsibilities. We are grateful that so many of them were willing to make time to write these chapters, engage with our edits and comments, and then wait patiently while we assembled the full manuscript. Sadly, as the book was going through the final copy editing, we learned that one of the great psychometricians, Bob Linn, passed away. In the words of Ron Hambleton himself, "Bob Linn was a very special mentor to many of us—he was patient, constructive, cooperative, and knowledgeable (seemingly, about everything), but always modest about his skills. In his research, he consistently wrote on the timely topics of the day over more than 50 years of his professional career, and to paraphrase a famous quote, 'when Bob Linn spoke, everyone listened.' His scholarship guided a generation of researchers, policymakers, educators, and students." We are greatly honored that Dr. Linn took the time and effort to contribute a chapter to the book. He will be missed deeply, but his ideas will continue to have a positive influence on the measurement and educational policy community.

Finally, we owe a deep debt of gratitude to three individuals in particular. First, we would like to thank Ronald K. Hambleton for his tireless commitment and dedication to the field of psychometrics through his research, teaching, and service, and for his inspiration and feedback regarding the contents of the book. Second, we would like to thank Stephen G. Sireci, who was primarily responsible for the conference held in honor of Ron, for his invaluable feedback on the content and structure of the book. Third, we are very grateful for the guidance, support, and feedback we received from C. Deborah Laughton, Publisher, Research Methods and Statistics, and the staff at The Guilford Press. C. Deborah's experience, knowledge, positive support, and patience were instrumental in the development and completion of the book.

Contents

PART I. THE ROOTS

1. A Brief History of Educational Testing and Psychometrics   3
    Kurt F. Geisinger and Betty Jean Usher-Tate

PART II. CRITERION-REFERENCED TESTS

2. Criterion-Referenced Testing: Advances over 40 Years   23
    Ronald K. Hambleton, April L. Zenisky, and W. James Popham

3. Standard Setting   38
    Mary J. Pitoniak and Gregory J. Cizek

4. Validity in the Making: From Evidence-Centered Design to the Validations
of the Interpretations of Test Performance   62
    **Barbara S. Plake, Kristen Huff, Rosemary R. Reshetar,
Pamela Kaliski, and Michael Chajewski**

5. Decision Consistency   74
    Kyung (Chris) T. Han and Lawrence M. Rudner

6. Applications of Generalizability Theory   89
    Brian E. Clauser and Jerome C. Clauser

PART III. ITEM RESPONSE THEORY

 7. A Brief History of and Introduction to Item Response Theory   107
       Molly Faulkner-Bond and Craig S. Wells

 8. Concepts and Methods in Research on Differential Functioning of Test Items: 126
       Past, Present, and Future
       H. Jane Rogers and Hariharan Swaminathan

 9. Understanding Two-Dimensional Models of Multidimensional   143
       Item Response Theory through Graphical Representations
       Terry A. Ackerman and Robert A. Henson

10. Testing Assumptions of Item Response Theory Models   162
       Craig S. Wells, Joseph Rios, and Molly Faulkner-Bond

PART IV. COMPUTER-BASED TESTING

11. The History of Computer-Based Testing   185
       Walter D. Way and Frederic Robin

12. Current Issues in Computer-Based Testing   208
       Craig N. Mills and Krista J. Breithaupt

13. The Future of Computer-Based Testing: Some New Paradigms   221
       April L. Zenisky and Richard M. Luecht

14. Design and Modeling Frameworks for 21st-Century   239
       Simulation- and Game-Based Assessments
       Alina A. von Davier and Robert J. Mislevy

PART V. CROSS-LINGUAL ASSESSMENT

15. Cross-Lingual Educational Assessment   259
       Avi Allalouf and Pnina Hanani

16. On Item Pools, Swimming Pools, Birds with Webbed Feet,   273
       and the Professionalization of Multilingual Assessment
       Fons J. R. van de Vijver and Ype H. Poortinga

17. Test Adaptation Standards for Cross-Lingual Assessment   291
       **José Muñiz, Paula Elosua, José-Luis Padilla,
       and Ronald K. Hambleton**

PART VI. ACCOUNTABILITY TESTING AND SCORE REPORTING

18. The History of Accountability in Educational Testing   307
   Robert L. Linn

19. Growth: Measurement, Meaning, and Misuse   318
   Lisa A. Keller, Kimberly F. Colvin, and Alejandra Garcia

20. Toward Improving the Reporting of Test Score Results: 335
   Lessons Learned from the Evolution of Reports
   from the National Assessment of Educational Progress
   April L. Zenisky, John Mazzeo, and Mary J. Pitoniak

21. Performance Assessment and Accountability: Then and Now   356
   Suzanne Lane

22. The History of Testing Special Populations: The Evolution of Fairness   373
   in Testing
   Jennifer Randall and Alejandra Garcia

23. English Learners and Accountability: The Promise, Pitfalls, and Peculiarity   395
   of Assessing Language Minorities via Large-Scale Assessment
   Molly Faulkner-Bond and Ellen Forte

24. Alternate Assessments for Students with Disabilities: 416
   Lessons from the National Center and State Collaborative
   Martha L. Thurlow and Rachel F. Quenemoen

PART VII. ONGOING DEBATES AND FUTURE DIRECTIONS

25. The Times They Are A-Changing, but the Song Remains the Same: 435
   Future Issues and Practices in Test Validation
   Stephen G. Sireci and Molly Faulkner-Bond

   Epilogue: A History of Ronald K. Hambleton   449
   Else Hambleton

   Glossary of Abbreviations   459

   Author Index   463

   Subject Index   475

   About the Editors   491

   Contributors   492

PART I

The Roots

CHAPTER 1

A Brief History of Educational Testing and Psychometrics

Kurt F. Geisinger and Betty Jean Usher-Tate

Testing as we know it in the 21st century, is the product of critical developments over two centuries in fields as diverse as mathematics, psychology, and sociology, and influences of varied cultures, historical events, and developments in technology. There are accounts of a "test-dominated society" in ancient China that date as far back as 2200 B.C.E. with a standardized system of examinations that was notoriously strict (DuBois, 1970; Galton, 1869; Suen & Wu, 2006; Thorndike & Lohman, 1990). The premise that "boys of promise are sure to be passed on from step to step, until they have reached the highest level of which they are capable" (Galton, 1869, p. 334) was clearly evident in the Chinese civil service that conducted formal proficiency testing. On the other hand, the era of the "modern" history of testing is often associated with Cattell's use of the term *mental test* in 1890 and with E. L. Thorndike's emphasis on the importance of standardization: "Every extrinsic condition influencing . . . ability should be alike for all" (Thorndike, 1904, p. 160).

In the history of university examination protocols, one may also consider two prominent 11th-century European universities that continue to be operational in the 21st century: the University of Bologna in Italy, founded in 1088, and the University of Oxford in the United Kingdom, founded in 1096. By 1219 and 1636, respectively, these universities had instituted the individual oral defense examinations to determine eligibility for degree conferral (DuBois, 1970), a practice still used around the world, primarily in graduate programs.

Travel and cross-cultural exposure often kindle profound change, as evidenced by early 18th-century travelers to Asia who witnessed the Chinese system of testing and the impact of paper production (DuBois, 1970; Suen & Wu, 2006). Subsequent advances in paper production heralded innovations with the printing press and movements toward written examinations and group testing in Europe. In 1548 the Society of Jesus opened the first Jesuit school in Messina, Sicily. Later, Jesuit schools were established across Europe, Asia, and Latin America (O'Malley, 2000) by Jesuit missionaries. An early Jesuit explained the purpose of their schools as being *institutio puerorum, reformatio mundi* (the proper education of youth will mean improvement for the whole world; O'Malley, 2000, p. 63). Jesuits are credited with the systematic use of written tests administered to groups both for placement and for postinstructional assessments. In 1599, they published the first test manual and educational standards, titled the *Ratio Studiorum* (DuBois, 1970; O'Malley, 2000). This document presented codes for administrative principles, curricular guidelines, and pedagogy for secondary and higher levels in education; it encapsulated the gold standard in education that has been used for about three centuries. The basis of testing rests on a long-established tradition tied both to education and the world of work.

The multiple-choice format has become the single most influential change or addition to test design for large-scale testing and postinstruction purposes. Prior to the 1900s, test items typically prompted narrative responses that were graded using time-consuming and inherently subjective processes. Frederick Kelly introduced the world to the multiple-choice test format for large-scale testing in 1914 (Davidson, 2011), and the format was readily embraced because it increased the comparability of scores and reduced both time and subjectivity in the scoring process while providing psychometricians with ample data for statistical analyses. Testing continues to evolve along with the type of instruments or technology we use to assess and the criteria against which we evaluate the test (Geisinger, 2000).

Early History of Psychometrics

One of the primary goals in testing is to differentiate individuals on the basis of skills, knowledge, qualities, or abilities; another may be to show how individuals are the same. Therefore, the impetus for early developments in psychometrics was conceptual and statistical advances that led to the systematization and quantification of individual differences based upon psychological testing. Most notable are the works of Sir Francis Galton, Karl Pearson, and Sir Ronald Fisher in the United Kingdom; Emil Kraepelin and Wilhelm Wundt in Germany; and James Cattell and Edward L. Thorndike of the United States. Charles Darwin published *Origin of Species* (1859) and Galton published *Hereditary Genius* (1869). Though others before Darwin and Galton had previously studied similar issues (e.g., Aristotle [*History of Animals*], Voltaire [*Traitéde Métaphysique*, 1734], Carl Linnaeus [*Systema Natural*], and Immanuel Kant [*Critique of Pure Reason*, 1781]), Galton was the first to treat the subject in a statistical manner and present numerical results, thereby introducing the "law of deviation from an average" into research discussions. The logic of testing follows the paradigm of experimental methodology; therefore, the variance in the test scores is considered reflective of interindividual differences, rather than any differences in test administration (Geisinger, 1994).

Sir Francis Galton

Galton was a prolific writer between 1849 and 1908, contributing 479 journal articles, 74 books and pamphlets, and 18 book chapters over the course of his career. He made major contributions to several genres in science—geography, meteorology, genealogy, eugenics, psychology, and statistics—and his empirical contributions in the study of individual differences, intelligence, and the mathematical science of correlation and regression were innovative and groundbreaking in his era (Tredoux, n.d.).

Pertinent contributions to psychological and educational research, Galton developed a first battery of tests used to study individual differences in psychological functions. He also developed the questionnaire as a form of assessment and invented a stopwatch for use in the investigation process. Galton's study of twins considered the effects of nature versus nurture. His interests in individual differences also spawned investigations that led to the use of fingerprints as a source of unique human identification (DuBois, 1970). In light of his pioneering methodologies for standard deviation, correlation, and regression, Galton has been described as the Father of Psychometrics; additionally, his direct association with the great minds of Pearson, Fisher, Spearman, and Cattell also significantly influenced psychometrics and statistics.

Later in his life, Galton founded the Eugenics Laboratory. Although eugenics has generally been rejected as an appropriate research topic on ethical grounds, Galton's professorship did lead to a number of positive advancements in psychometrics. His endowment established the Galton Professorship of Eugenics, which was first awarded to Karl Pearson, who had studied with Galton and was also a personal friend and associate.[1] Based on Galton's framework to describe the relationship between two variables, Pearson made further contributions to correlation methodology with his conception of the Pearson product–moment formula for linear correlation, which continues to be utilized today. The second individual to be offered the Galton Professorship—considered very prestigious at the time—was Sir Ronald Aylmer Fisher. Fisher made many contributions to research science, but was professionally renowned for introducing analysis of variance (ANOVA), the method of maximum likelihood estimation (MLE), and nonparametric statistics (Aldrich, 1997). Also affiliated with Galton's laboratory was Charles Spearman, who developed the methodology for factor analysis and various nonparametric statistics.

James McKeen Cattell

Near the end of the 19th century, a number of early psychology pioneers attempted to develop measures of intelligence. Galton (1883), who was extremely interested in the study of genius, believed that perception was the key to intelligence and that the speed of one's reaction to environmental stimuli was the way to measure intelligence. He also measured subjects' head size and used various verbal memory tasks and subjects' judgments of physical measurements such as weight, sound, and visual discrimination

---

[1] Among his many accolades as an eminent mathematical statistician, Pearson also authored three volumes of Galton's biographies between 1914 and 1930.

as approaches to measuring intelligence. Cattell, an American, was in correspondence with Galton while completing his doctorate in Leipzig under the tutelage of Wilhelm Wundt. Cattell's dissertation at Leipzig focused on reaction time, and many of his proposed intelligence tests related to speed of hand movement, speed of responses to sounds, time to name colors, memory tasks, pain sensitivity, discriminations of weight, and other measurements of physical judgments and reactions. Attempts made to validate these measures against success in college netted essentially null findings. When Cattell joined Galton at Cambridge, he helped to establish the first psychometrics laboratory. Cattell also taught cross-discipline courses on mental testing and extended the scope of mental tests beyond Galton's measures (Cambridge University, 2014). Based on his 1890 publication, Cattell is credited as the first to use the term *mental test* (DuBois, 1970; Minton, 1998). In 1921, Cattell founded a test publishing company, The Psychological Corporation, which continues to this day, now as part of Pearson Assessment.

Alfred Binet

Although Galton's influence in the development of statistical procedures is acknowledged in psychological testing, it is not as evident that Galton's and Cattell's work also set the stage for the contributions made by Alfred Binet. Binet was a Parisian who had earned a doctoral degree in experimental psychology and had also served as an attorney. As an experimental psychologist, Binet had worked with others on investigating suggestibility under hypnosis early in his professional career, and had taken an extreme position on the basis of weak evidence. Binet and his colleagues had also researched the effects of magnets on hypnosis. His research was criticized publicly as having very poor controls. In reaction to these criticisms, Binet strove to implement rigorous experimental methods throughout the remainder of his career. DuBois (1970) provided a listing of other psychologists (e.g., Ebbinghaus, Kraepelin) who also attempted, mostly unsuccessfully, to assess intelligence using physiologically oriented measures and word association tasks, forming a context for Binet's later work in this area.

The Parisian schools were among the first in the world that were publicly open to all pupils. An early result of the open-door policy was the failure of many students to succeed in the schools, and the issue was compounded by financial and other consequences to keeping these weaker students in school. Binet was charged with finding or developing measures that would help the schools identify those students who were unlikely to succeed in general classrooms. Working with his colleague Victor Henri, he used trial and error to find measures that would work in this regard. They tried some sensorimotor discrimination tasks akin to those of Galton and Cattell, and they also used some that were more aligned with mental functioning: remembering series of digits, performance of mental mathematics, making moral judgments, quality of handwriting, and so on. He also performed a number of experiments without elaborate equipment to test complex mental functions. As Thorndike and Lohman suggested, "These studies probably led Binet to the conviction . . . that the only way to study the nature of intelligence was to use complex tasks that manifestly required the application of intelligence for their completion" (Thorndike & Lohman, 1990, p. 6). Binet and Henri (1896) suggested 10 mental functions that composed intelligence: memory, attention, comprehension, suggestibility, aesthetic appreciation, moral judgment, willpower, motor skill, imagination, and imagery.

Binet published his first measure of intelligence (working with Theodore Simon) in 1905; its goal was to identify children considered intellectually disabled. This measure consisted of 30 tasks arranged in order of difficulty (Binet & Simon, 1905). Most of the tasks were the kinds of problems often encountered in schooling; it is clear that the measure was empirically based rather than based on an underlying belief of what comprised intelligence. The measure included tasks targeting memory, reasoning, comprehension, numerical facility, general knowledge, and comparisons of objects. There was a belief, however, that intelligence improved throughout the childhood years, so tasks became more difficult as a child aged. The scale was improved in 1908 with better instructions and subtests. Also in 1908, the notion of mental age was introduced as the raw score of Binet's examination. Mental age was found to be easily understood by the public with its focus upon judgment, comprehension, memory, and reasoning. An individual's intelligence was estimated to be the mental age divided by the chronological age. A 1911 test was also an improvement on the 1908 test, but Binet's untimely death that year essentially ended this effort in France.

Lewis M. Terman

Terman had become familiar with Binet's work while an undergraduate at Clark University. For his dissertation, he applied Binet's work, in English translation, to 14 students, seven who were bright and seven weak academically. Terman found that the intellectually gifted students excelled on intellectual functions but not motor ones. He sent information about his study to Binet, and it appears that Binet incorporated aspects of Terman's work into his 1908 scale (Thorndike & Lohman, 1990). Other American psychologists also translated (adapted) Binet's scales. Terman, however, studied his version with a relatively large sample (400 subjects). Using these data, Terman was effectively able to group tests by age level and to develop better instructions and answer forms. Since much of the work was performed while he worked at Stanford University, Terman's adaptation of Binet's instrument became known as the Stanford–Binet Intelligence Scales (Becker, 2003). This version propelled intelligence testing to a position where it was perceived as an essential component of modern educational practices.

Thus to recap, prior to the work of Galton, testing was very much administered individually and scores were interpreted without the empirical benefits of statistics. The subsequent work of Binet, Simon, and Terman paved the way for the assessment of cognition and for both individual and group assessment as acceptable formats or modes of delivery. Although at the time of Binet, all intelligence testing was performed individually, the *Industrial Revolution* was about to influence the format of testing intelligence too.

Large-Scale Assessment

Group Administered Intelligence Tests

In the early years of the 20th century, a number of researchers made attempts to develop group tests for various purposes. In general, the effort aimed to measure specific cognitive skills and aptitudes, including learning aptitudes (DuBois, 1970). Arthur Otis, who was a professor at Stanford University at the same time that Terman had studied and adapted Binet's individually administered intelligence test, began working on a group test that could fulfill the same or similar functions. Although he had not yet published this test as a group test of intelligence, it nevertheless became the model used for candidate selection or differentiation in World War I.

Under the leadership of the president of the American Psychological Association (APA), Robert Yerkes, psychologists of that era organized into multiple committees to help the war effort. It was decided that the government should employ intelligence tests to assess candidates for various Armed Forces positions (DuBois, 1970). Yerkes, whose background was in mental health, was the leading advocate for development of the group-administered mental tests. He proposed that tests be used to eliminate the mentally unfit (Thorndike & Lohman, 1990). Others on the committee recommended a classification model rather than a selection model—a dispute that was never fully resolved (Thorndike & Lohman, 1990; Von Mayrhauser, 1987). The frantic efforts, primarily during 1917, led to five forms of what became known as the Army Alpha, all built anew largely on the model of Otis's unpublished group intelligence test. In addition, a single form of the Army Beta was built for those subjects who could not read the test questions in English; the Beta was built on a model of testing that had been developed just prior to the war as an intelligence examination for subjects who were deaf (Pinter & Patterson, 1915, 1917). A negative evaluation of the use of these measures has been presented in Gould (1981).

Large-Scale Educational Testing in the United States

After the war, the testing movement had a new complexion; the focus was now on group-administered tests, based in large measure on the perceived benefit of this effort. During the first half of the 20th century, it was widely believed that intelligence was largely a genetically determined characteristic. The use of intelligence testing rapidly permeated the public schools of the United States, owing mostly to its perceived benefits, efficiency, trust in the fruits of science as beneficial, and the typical U.S. spirit of entrepreneurism (Thorndike & Lohman, 1990). Terman advocated that every child undergo group-administered intelligence testing each year and individualized testing for those who scored very high or low. During the 1919–1920 academic year it was estimated that a million children were given group-administered mental tests, and that number doubled for the 1920–1921 academic year (Terman et al., 1922).

Over the years, the proliferation of group-administered intelligence tests waned in schools as group tests of educational achievement increased. These were tests based upon what students learned, or perhaps should have learned, while in school. In the business of education, changes directly affect trends, supply, and demand, which likewise are reflective of politics, technological advances, and societal affairs. In the United States, for example, the shift toward large-scale testing and reliance on standardized tests for university admissions and school accountability was a response to growing needs, such as the increasing number of students applying to colleges for admission. Such tests were perceived as solutions to challenges reflecting the technology of the times (Lemann, 2003).

College Admission Tests

Initially, the College Entrance Examination Board was developed to help the Ivy League and Seven Sisters colleges deal with admissions decisions. Prior to the 1930s, most of the students who entered such colleges and universities were primarily attending boarding schools on the East Coast, and the examinations themselves were hand-scored essays based upon the curricula prevalent in these elite high school institutions. There was also a perception that these Ivy League-type universities had previously made most of their admissions decisions on the basis of qualities such as "character" (Lemann, 1999, 2003). After World War II, U.S. soldiers were given educational opportunities, thereby exponentially increasing the number of students applying for admission to colleges and universities and rendering the admissions process of the time inefficient. In addition, Harvard's president during 1933, James Conant, wanted to open Harvard to talented scholars from other parts of the country.

Conant wanted an intelligence test, based on the successes of the Army Alpha, to be the vehicle for identifying such promising scholars. During this same period, Carl Brigham, a Princeton psychologist, had been adapting a version of the Army Alpha to be used in college admissions, a test that became the Scholastic Aptitude Test (SAT). Starting in 1938, the member colleges of the College Entrance Examination Board began using the multiple-choice SAT in lieu of the previous essay tests for admissions purposes. In its inception, the SAT had two subtests (Verbal and Quantitative), both of which provided individual scores that were then summed for an overall score; however, both tests were essentially tests of reasoning and developed educational skills. Since high school grades were not standardized, it was believed that uses of a measure such as the SAT increased the comparability of the candidates for college admission.

Subsequent to the SAT's introduction, the College Board joined other higher education associations to form the Educational Testing Service (ETS), located in Princeton, New Jersey. Essentially, as soon as the development of the ETS occurred, an ETS office was also opened in Berkeley, California. When the University of California system decided to use the SAT as a systemwide admissions measure in the 1950s, they became the ETS's largest customer (Douglas, 2007). Over time, the SAT has evolved into the test currently published by the College Board with the assistance of the ETS and other testing entities.

Slightly later, American College Testing (ACT) was developed by E. F. Lindquist, a psychometrician and professor at the University of Iowa. The ACT was conceptualized for dual purposes: as a high school achievement test and for college admissions (Lemann, 1999; Thorndike & Lohman, 1990). This measure originally consisted of four tests: English, Mathematics, Social Studies, and Natural Sciences. Some 30 years later, in 1989, two of the tests were made less achievement oriented and more tests of generic educational skills: the Social Studies test became a Reading section (focusing upon Social Studies reading), and the Natural Sciences test was transformed into the Science Reasoning test.

Although the SAT was built on an intelligence testing model whereas the ACT was built more to represent achievement tests and learning in the schools, over the years, the two tests have become more similar. In fact, a number of steps have occurred that make both tests even more like tests of educational achievement than tests of ability. For example, in 2005, a required essay test was added to the SAT, vocabulary was deemphasized, and the Verbal test became a test of critical reading. When the SAT added a required essay test, ACT instead offered an optional Writing Test. Subsequent to No Child Left Behind (NCLB) legislation, a number of states began using the ACT as their high school achievement measure. In 2011, approximately 1.67 million students took the ACT and 1.66 million took the SAT. Although most 4-year colleges and universities require the scores from standardized tests in their admissions process, almost all institutions place more emphasis on other factors of evaluation such as class rank, grade-point average (GPA), and extracurricular activities.

Developments in Psychometrics

Several thematic trends have affected the quantitative underpinnings of educational and psychological testing. The first of these was the development of correlational and ANOVA statistics that emerged from the work of Galton, Pearson, Spearman, and Fisher, among others, which we discussed in the first section of this chapter. Without these developments, psychometrics would never have advanced to the field that it is today. Indeed, it continues to be hard to imagine any psychometric work today that does not employ these statistics as part of the underlying models and as part of the analytic procedures. Other trends centered on the development of classical test theory, item response theory (IRT), and response to changes, including technology and educational reform.

Classical Test Theory

The development of classical test theory was in many ways an outgrowth of the initial development of correlational statistics. As illustrated in Equation 1.1, classical test theory posits that an examinee's observed score on a test is composed of two components: the examinee's actual achievement or proficiency on the tested construct (e.g., third-grade mathematics) and random error, which occurs due to nonproficiency variables such as testing conditions, mistakes, lucky guesses, etc.

$$X = T + E \qquad (1.1)$$

Although psychometricians cannot know an examinee's actual true score (T), they can estimate the amount of error in an examinee's score (E) and use this information, along with the observed score (X), to make judgments about the examinee's proficiency (Guilford, 1954; Gulliksen, 1950; Mosier, 1940).

This model of the understanding of test scores is based upon three assumptions (Guilford, 1954): (1) the mean of all error components equals zero; (2) the correlation between true scores and error scores is zero in principle (because error scores are randomly distributed around the individual's true score); and (3) error scores across different testing are also uncorrelated. This model continues to be heavily used today in our understanding of the reliability of test scores. Reliability is best considered as the consistency, stability, and accuracy of test scores. The third assumption is especially relevant when considering test–retest, alternate-forms, and split-half[2] reliability analyses. When considering classical reliability approaches to test interpretation, we generally are concerned with the likelihood that an examinee would score the same or similarly upon retesting. Once these three assumptions follow, it can be concluded that total test variance is composed of only two components: true variance and error variance. The reliability coefficient is thus defined as the ratio of true variance to total variance, or the proportion of total variance that is true variance. This conception easily handled many testing situations in a world in which most testing was performed using paper-and-pencil testing forms, such as Army Alpha, the SAT, and the ACT.

Reliability

Using classical test theory, a variety of approaches to analyzing split-half reliability was developed, in general depending upon the assumptions that were held (i.e., equal variances across the two test halves). Such coefficients were useful in a time before machines that scored test papers composed of objectively scored items (that were later scanned). Those scoring tests often used punch sheets (answer keys) that were laid on top of a test sheet. Holes existed where correct answers could be found. It was common to have a scoring sheet for the odd-numbered questions and one for the even-numbered questions. One could then compare these half-test scores as well as add them together to get the total score. However, to detect a form of cheating, one also had to check that examinees did not answer more than one option. Nevertheless, conceiving of error

---

[2] *Split-half reliability* is an estimate of the accuracy of test scores by comparing two relatively equivalent components of a test, often the scores based upon the odd and even items composing a test.

scores as the differences between odd and even halves of the test provided (where questions were generally ordered in terms of their difficulty level, progressing from easy to hard throughout the test) permitted the psychometricians to estimate the reliability of a test that had only a single form and single administration.

More elaborate approaches to considering the reliability of single forms of tests emerged shortly after the classical psychometric model was conceptualized. Among the articles that were critical in this approach were those of Kuder and Richardson (1937), Hoyt (1941), and Cronbach (1951). Kuder and Richardson considered tests composed of dichotomously scored questions. They demonstrated how *internal consistency reliability*[3] could be conceived; how it could be affected by test length and interitem correlations, especially the former; and provided some basic formulae for computing it. Hoyt followed their article with a demonstration of how the classical model of testing could be conceptualized from an ANOVA approach, where total test variance could be decomposed into variance attributable to examinees (true variance), items, and error (differences in performance across items). The resultant Hoyt coefficient was identical to the primary coefficient (known as KR-20) identified by Kuder and Richardson. Cronbach wrote the article on reliability that is probably the most frequently cited in the history of educational and psychological testing. In this article he proposed a reliability coefficient called *coefficient alpha*. This index was also equivalent to KR-20, but it was a generic formula that could estimate the reliability of a test composed of some dichotomously scored questions and others that are polytomously scored. In general, coefficient alpha conceptualizes true variance as consistency across items. That is, item intercorrelations lead to true variance; a lack of correlations across items could be perceived as error.

Generalizability

Generalizability theory can be perceived as an extension of classical test theory (CTT) and not as an independent contribution (Brennan, 2001, 2011). Originally conceived by Cronbach and his colleagues (Cronbach, Gleser, Nanda, & Rajaratnam, 1972), it was an extension of the ANOVA approaches to reliability. Whereas CTT perceives error as random and undifferentiated, generalizability theory attempts to categorize error into discernable components. For example, in a situation where a group of students takes different test forms on different days of the week, and those test forms are scored by different raters, a generalizability study could differentiate sources of variance attributable to forms, raters, and days. These three variables (forms, raters, days) are considered to be facets of the design. Having such information allows one to understand and predict the dependability of measures given across these different facets. The use of generalizability theory continues to advance (Brennan, 2001; Shavelson & Webb, 1991) (see also Clauser & Clauser, Chapter 6, this volume).

---

[3]This term refers to the consistency of performance across the items composing a test.

Item Response Theory

Another major development in psychometrics was the development of IRT, first known as *latent trait theory*, which could be used in the analysis of both categorical data and binary dichotomous data. IRT provided more information than CTT because it afforded a means of estimating item difficulty and identifying associations between items and the underlying construct, thus reducing the number of items in a scale. The historical roots of IRT came from psychophysical scaling (Mosier, 1940), latent structure analysis (Lazarfeld, 1959), and Guttman (1944) scaling—what Guttman called the *item trace line* is now called the *item characteristic curve* (Weiss & Yoes, 1991). In 1952, Fred Lord wrote a dissertation, also published as a *Psychological Monograph,* which laid out the theoretical foundations of IRT. Some perceive the true "coming out" of IRT as the publication of Birnbaum's development of the three-parameter IRT logistic model in Lord and Novick's seminal *Statistical Theories of Mental Test Scores* (1968). Lord's earlier work (e.g., 1953) focused upon the two-parameter model with the two parameters being item difficulty and item discrimination. The three-parameter model added a third parameter to address the possibility that an examinee answers an item correctly by chance, sometimes called a *guessing* or *pseudo-guessing parameter.* Many in testing have also found considerable benefit with a one-parameter model, where the only item parameter is its difficulty. This model was first proposed by the Danish mathematician Georg Rasch (1960), and continues to be called the *Rasch model.* Ben Wright has had significant influence in extending this model to many testing problems (e.g., Wright & Stone, 1979). (See also Faulkner-Bond & Wells, Chapter 7, this volume, for a more in-depth discussion of the history of IRT.)

One aspect that has been argued for IRT is that the item parameter values are invariant across subpopulations (Wright & Panchepakesan, 1969). When the invariance property is met, some difficult testing concerns are far less thorny. Among the testing issues considerably aided by IRT are equating forms, using computer-adaptive tests, having conditional standard errors of measurement throughout the distribution of test scores, and constructing tests with well-planned psychometric qualities—all of which we discuss in the next section. Most IRT models assume an underlying unidimensional structure (Hambleton & Swaminathan, 1984), meaning that the only influences driving examinee performance is ability on a single target construct (e.g., mathematics achievement). However, within recent decades, multidimensional IRT (MIRT) has also become available (Reckase, 1985, 1997). Many of the IRT models have been developed for objectively scored test items, partial-credit responses, and Likert-type items.

Developments in Testing

The Criterion-Referenced Testing Movement

Until the early 1960s, large-scale educational testing was typically what we now call *norm-referenced testing.* Like intelligence tests, educational tests were seen as fundamentally conforming to a normal curve, and scores were based upon where a test taker falls along an established continuum. Scores were often interpreted as percentile ranks. In the 1960s, the alternative method that emerged was criterion-referenced (see also Hambleton, Chapter 2, this volume): "Criterion-referenced tests provide a basis for assessing the performance of examinees in relation to well-defined domains of content rather than in relation to other examinees" (Hambleton & Rogers, 1991, p. 3). By the late 1980s, Hambleton and Rogers reported, over 900 articles had appeared in the published literature on the topic, and early writers on this topic "were interested in an approach to testing that would provide information necessary for making a variety of individual and programmatic decisions arising with specific objectives, skills and competencies" (p. 4).

As Popham and Husek (1969) and Hambleton and Rogers (1991) pointed out, the classical and even IRT approaches to test construction were based upon norm-referenced approaches that were not compatible with this type of decision making. Specifically, whereas norm-referenced test construction prioritizes the use of highly discriminating items that will spread examinees along the ability distribution, criterion-referenced tests need to be based upon carefully delineated domains of content, competencies, standards, and objectives as well as the ability to succeed in the subsequent instructional sequence (Geisinger, 2012). This close tie to the content places different emphases in the test construction phase of assessment. Test construction for criterion-referenced tests need not be based upon item discrimination statistics, or even place emphasis upon them (Geisinger, 2012).

One of the major uses for criterion-referenced tests is to make a decision about what scores constitute mastery and nonmastery of the content domain (i.e., cut scores). For this reason, criterion-referenced tests became relevant to licensure and certification testing as well. Given the nature of those types examinations, it became incumbent on testing professionals to determine ways of setting passing or cut scores, and whole books have now been written on this topic (e.g., Cizek, 2012; Cizek & Bunch, 2007; see also Pitoniak & Cizek, Chapter 3, this volume). As a result of criterion-referenced tests, other psychometric aspects of testing also changed. For example, there was less concern with test score reliability and more focus on the reliability of mastery classifications. Hambleton and Pitoniak (2010) summarized the many psychometric changes that were necessitated by the different goals and orientation of criterion-referenced tests.

Educational Reform and Statewide Testing

In 1983, President Ronald Reagan delivered his "A Nation at Risk" address in which he noted 13 testing-related indicators of educational risk, such as alarming rates of functional illiteracy and the progressive decline in SAT scores. In addition, he pointed out rapid advancement in computers, technology, and robotics (National Commission on Excellence in Education, 1983). More large-scale testing and adequate yearly progress (AYP) reports ensued. There was increased public debate about standards, equity, political platforms, and demands to improve educational standards. Between 1976 and 1998, 17 states implemented high-stakes high school graduation exams (Amrein & Berliner, 2002). Educational reform debates were likely the impetus for the No Child Left Behind Act (NCLB) of 2001 under President George W. Bush. Shortly after NCLB came into effect, the number of states instituting statewide tests, in one form or another, increased to fulfill accountability requirements.

With the proposed 2010–2011 A Blueprint for Reform: The Reauthorization of the Elementary and Secondary Education Act (ESEA) and Race-to-the-Top funds, President Barack Obama premised the reform movement with this statement: "Every child in America deserves a world-class education" (Duncan & Martin, 2010, p. 1). State-mandated tests have proliferated to multiple grade levels and subject areas in K–12 public education. States use test scores as the primary measure of performance in accountability systems because they are cost-effective and convenient (Strecher & Barron, 2001, p. 259). In consideration of implications and unintended consequences of large-scale or statewide testing as an accountability measure, Anne Anastasi's (1989) position still holds: "All too often, the decision-making responsibility is shifted to the test. The test user loses sight of the fact that tests are tools, serving as valuable aids to the skilled practitioner, but useless or misleading when improperly used" (pp. 471–472).

Need for Equating

Because statewide testing has "mushroomed" in scope, importance, and visibility, and because states are required under NCLB to demonstrate year-to-year improvements in test scores, and also because testing has taken increased significance throughout society, the need for equating and establishing comparability of scores has become even more critical. "Equating is a statistical process that is used to adjust scores on test forms so that the scores on the forms can be used interchangeably" (Kolen & Brennan, 2004, p. 2); this process is important because, even when test construction practices are followed rigorously, differences in scores across forms often occur. Given that states need to show year-to-year gains and the same test forms cannot be used for multiple years, equating test forms has become increasingly prevalent and critical in importance. Many test programs such as statewide achievement tests, intelligence tests, the SAT, and the ACT require multiple equivalent forms of the same tests. The need for additional test forms is necessitated by the ever-growing test security concerns, litigation, the need to provide regular testing periods so that individuals can take a test more than once meaningfully, and the goal of ensuring fairness to examinees regardless of the form that they complete (Kolen & Hendrickson, 2013).

In the 1980s, there were relatively few tests requiring equating and therefore there were probably only a handful of psychometricians with expertise in this subspecialty. Research on concerns related to equating has exploded in the past 20–30 years as the requirements of equating in actual application have become clear, practical issues apparent, and unusual situations encountered. Equating has become even more challenging as many tests have come to be administered by computer, and many of these tests are themselves adaptively administered to different individuals, making the idea of a form, per se, somewhat passé.

Computer-Adaptive Testing

Computer-based assessments have certain advantages over paper-based applications in their capacity for immediate data entry, ease of scoring, and almost immediate plotting of results and changes over time when applicable (Cella, Gershon, Lai, & Choi, 2007, p. 135). In the latter part of the 20th century, earliest iterations of the computer-based testing (CBT) were essentially static or fixed; in other words, paper-based tests (PBTs) were converted to electronic platform for administration. Later, some CBTs evolved to include multimedia or interactive media components. With advancement in technology and increased access to personal computers, CBT improved in item formats, use of interactive technology, scoring capacity, linkage to data banks, and access to the Web or Internet. Limitations existed with this testing platform, many of which were quickly overcome. One of the greatest current challenges to accommodation solutions has been in the area of providing certain content for the visually impaired (e.g., graphs and figures).

The computer-adaptive testing (CAT) platform takes CBT to another level of sophisticated technological algorithms. Unlike the ordinary CBT where each test form is predetermined, CAT adjusts to the ability level, aptitude, or cognitive status of the examinee so the items exposed to each examinee are not predetermined. This examinee-specific targeting means, in turn, that CAT technology can also shorten the test by requiring fewer items for accurate classification or ability estimation (Cella et al., 2007; Wu, Kuo, & Yang, 2012). The fundamental CAT platform is based on an item bank in which each item is coded for content and item characteristics (at a typical minimum, item difficulty, and item discrimination). Therefore, after the examinee responds to the initial item, an algorithm selects subsequent items from the item bank dependent on accuracy of a prior response while conforming to the test blueprint for item content and distribution. This form of assessment has been applied to a number of large-scale testing environments that are considered high stakes, such as certification, licensure exams, and college admissions. Additionally, CAT has also been applied on smaller scales in health-related quality-of-life surveys (Cella et al., 2007, p. 135). Some CATs are designed using "testlets" (sections) to assure content coverage of test blueprints.

Test preparation for CAT can involve some fundamental differences from preparation for a paper-based administration. For example, examinees are encouraged to review their responses and edit if they see fit when taking a test on paper or even with some computer-based administrations. However, CAT platforms often do not permit the use of the back button (you may not revise) because ability is reestimated after each item, and subsequent items are supplied accordingly. An experimental study conducted by Hays and colleagues (2010) regarding *next*, *back*, and *auto* advance in a CAT environment showed very little differences in missing data, reported scores, or internal consistency reliability between individuals with access to next and back buttons and those with only auto advance. What was notably different, however, was the increase in time for those who had the next and back button options. In the very recent past, a compromise in the computer-based testing model became relatively prevalent:

multistage testing (MST). In this model a test is composed of several stages or parts. All examinees begin with the same first set of items, and the examinees are essentially triaged or routed based upon their performances on the first and subsequent stages to easier or harder sets.

Conclusions

Whereas the history of testing can be traced over three millennia, modern testing is less than 150 years old. Much like the world predicted in the book *Future Shock* (Toffler, 1970), changes seem to be coming faster and faster, perhaps driven in large measure recently by technology. When Lord first conceived of IRT, there were no computers or software capable of analyzing such data. Today, any microcomputer can handle such software, and we are now at the advent of high-stakes testing routinely administered on tablets or other electronic media. We have come a long way in educational testing in just over a century. From helping to make schooling more efficient with intelligence and admissions tests, we have moved to an era where accountability and the equitable distribution of resources are key concerns, with test scores being used as a means to quantify achievement and determine value added of a teacher's and a school's effectiveness. The future of testing, however, must rely on its past for guidance. We should not "jump into" testing practices because they seem reasonable on their face; we must learn from the early explorations in intelligence testing to remind ourselves that what may seem obvious and apparent may not be valid, once research results are available. And we must parallel our technological and psychometric developments with those for the content and psychological processes of what we are measuring, and use both within the context of best professional practices.

REFERENCES

Aldrich, J. (1997). R. A. Fisher and the making of maximum likelihood 1912–1922. *Statistical Science, 12*(3), 162–176.

Amrein, A. L., & Berliner, D. C. (2002). High-stakes testing, uncertainty, and student learning. *Education Policy Analysis Archives, 10*(18), 1–74.

Anastasi, A. (1989). Ability testing in the 1980s and beyond: Some major trends. *Public Personnel Management, 18*(4), 471–485.

Becker, K. A. (2003). *History of the Stanford–Binet intelligence scales: Content and psychometrics* (Stanford–Binet Intelligence Scales, Fifth Edition Assessment Service Bulletin No. 1). Itasca, IL: Riverside.

Binet, A., & Henri, V. (1896). La psychologie individuelle. *L'Année Psychologique, 2*, 411–465.

Binet, A., & Simon, T. (1905). Methodes nouvelles pour le diagnostic du niveau intellectual des anoramaux. *L'Année Psychologique, 11*, 191–211.

Birnbaum, A. (1968). Test scores, sufficient statistics, and the information structures of tests. In F. M. Lord & R. M. Novick (Eds.), *Statistical theories of mental test scores* (pp. 425–435). Reading, MA: Addison-Wesley.

Brennan, R. L. (2001). *Generalizability theory*. New York: Springer-Verlag.

Brennan, R. L. (2011). Generalizability theory and classical test theory. *Applied Measurement in Education, 24*, 1–21.

Cattell, J. M. (1890). Mental tests and measurement. *Mind, 15*, 373–382.

Cella, D., Gershon, R., Lai, J. S., & Choi, S. (2007). The future of outcomes measurement: Item banking, tailored short-forms, and computerized adaptive assessment. *Quality of Life Research, 16*, 133–141.

Cizek, G. J. (Ed.). (2012). *Setting performance standards: Concepts, methods, and perspectives* (2nd ed). Mahwah, NJ: Erlbaum.

Cizek, G. J., & Bunch, M. B. (2007). *Standard setting: A guide to establishing and evaluating performance standards on tests*. Thousand Oaks, CA: Sage.

Cronbach, L. J. (1951). Coefficient alpha and the internal structure of tests. *Psychometrika, 16*, 167–188.

Cronbach, L. J., Gleser, G. C., Nanda, H., & Rajaratnam, N. (1972). *The dependability of behavioral measurements: Theory of generalizability for scores and profiles*. New York: Wiley.

Davidson, C. (2011). Where did standardized testing come from anyway? Retrieved from *www.hastac.org/blogs/cathy-davidson/2011/09/02/where-did-standardized-testing-come-anyway*.

Douglas, J. A. (2007). *The conditions of admission: Access, equity, and the social contract of public universities*. Stanford, CA: Stanford University Press.

DuBois, P. H. (1970). *A history of psychological testing*. Boston: Allyn & Bacon.

Duncan, A., & Martin, C. (2010). *ESEA blueprint for reform*. Washington, DC: U.S. Department of Education, Office of Planning, Evaluation and Policy Development.

Galton, F. (1869). *Hereditary genius: An inquiry into its laws and consequences*. London: Macmillan.

Galton, F. (1883). *Inquiries into the human faculty and its development*. London: Macmillan.

Geisinger, K. F. (1994). Cross-cultural normative assessment: Translation and adaptation issues influencing the normative interpretation of assessment instruments. *Psychological Assessment, 6*(4), 304–312.

Geisinger, K. F. (2000). Psychological testing at the end of the millennium: A brief historical review. *Professional Psychology: Research and Practice, 31*(2), 117–118.

Geisinger, K. F. (2012). Norm- and criterion-referenced testing. In H. Cooper (Ed.), *APA handbook of research methods in psychology: Vol. 1. Foundations, planning, measures, and psychometrics* (pp. 371–393). Washington, DC: American Psychological Association.

Gould, S. J. (1981). *The mismeasure of man*. New York: Norton.

Guilford, J. P. (1954). *Psychometric methods* (2nd ed.). New York: McGraw-Hill.

Gulliksen, H. (1950). *Theory of mental tests*. New York: Wiley.

Guttman, L. (1944). A basis for scaling qualitative data. *American Sociological Review, 9*, 139–150.

Hambleton, R. K., & Pitoniak, M. (2010). Setting performance standards. In R. L. Brennan (Ed.), *Educational measurement* (4th ed., pp. 433–470). Westport, CT: Praeger.

Hambleton, R. K., & Rogers, H. J. (1991). Advances in criterion-referenced measurement. In R. K. Hambleton & J. N. Zaal (Eds.), *Advances in educational and psychological testing* (pp. 3–43). Boston: Kluwer.

Hambleton, R. K., & Swaminathan, H. (1984). *Item response thoery: Principles and applications*. New York: Dorsey.

Hays, R. D., Bode, R., Rothrock, N., Riley, W., Cella, D., & Gershon, R. (2010). The impact of next and back buttons on time to complete and measurement reliability in computer-based surveys. *Quality of Life Research, 19,* 1181–1184.

Hoyt, C. (1941). Test reliability estimated by analysis of variance. *Psychometrika, 6,* 153–160.

Kolen, M. J., & Brennan, R. L. (2004). *Test equating, scaling, and linking: Methods and practices.* New York: Springer.

Kolen, M. J., & Hendrickson, A. B. (2013). Scaling, norming, and equating. In K. F. Geisinger (Ed.), *APA handbook of testing and assessment in psychology* (Vol. 1, pp. 201–222). Washington, DC: American Psychological Association.

Kuder, G. F., & Richardson, M. W. (1937). The theory of estimation of test reliability. *Psychometrika, 4,* 151–160.

Lazarfeld, P. F. (1959). Latent structure analysis. In S. Koch (Ed.), *A study of a science* (Vol. 3, pp. 476–542). New York: McGraw-Hill.

Lemann, N. (1999). *The big test: The secret history of the American meritocracy.* New York: Farrar, Straus & Giroux.

Lemann, N. (2003). A history of admissions testing. In R. Zwick (Ed.), *Rethinking the SAT: The future of standardized testing in university admissions* (pp. 5–14). New York: Routledge Falmer.

Lord, F. M. (1952). *A theory of test scores* (Psychometric Monographs, No.7). Richmond, VA: Psychometric Corporation.

Lord, F. M. (1953). The relation of test score to the trait underlying the test. *Educational and Psychological Measurement, 13,* 517–548.

Lord, F. M., & Novick, M. (1968). *Statistical theories of mental test scores.* Reading, MA: Addison-Wesley.

Minton, H. L. (1998). Introduction to: "New methods for the diagnosis of intellectual level of subnormals." Alfred Binet & Theodore Simon (1905). (C. D. Green, Compiler). Toronto, Ontario, Canada: York University. Retrieved from *http://psychclassics.yorku.ca/Binet/intro.htm.*

Mosier, C. I. (1940). Psychophysics and mental test theory: Fundamental postulates and elementary theorems. *Psychological Review, 47,* 355–366.

National Commission on Excellence in Education. (1983, April 26). A nation at risk. Retrieved from *www2.ed.gov/pubs/NatAtRisk/risk.html.*

O'Malley, J. W. (2000). How the first Jesuits became involved in education. In V. J. Daminuco (Ed.), *The Jesuit ratio studiorum: 400th anniversary perspectives* (pp. 56–74). New York: Fordham University Press.

Pinter, R., & Patterson, D. G. (1915). The Binet scale and the deaf child. *Journal of Educational Psychology, 6,* 201–210.

Pinter, R., & Patterson, D. G. (1917). *A scale of performance tests.* New York: Appleton.

Popham, W. J., & Husek, T. R. (1969). Implications of criterion-referenced measurement. *Journal of Educational Measurement, 6,* 1–9.

Rasch, G. (1960). *Probabilistic models for some intelligence and attainment tests.* Copenhagen: Danish Institute for Educational Research.

Reckase, M. D. (1985). The difficulty of items that measure more than one ability. *Applied Psychological Measurement, 15,* 146–178.

Reckase, M. D. (1997). The past and future of multidimensional item response theory. *Applied Psychological Measurement, 21,* 25–36.

Shavelson, R., & Webb, N. M. (1991). *Generalizability theory: A primer.* Newbury Park, CA: Sage.

Strecher, B. M., & Barron, S. (2001). Unintended consequences of test-based accountability when testing in "milepost" grades. *Educational Assessment, 7*(4), 259–281.

Suen, H. K., & Wu, Q. (2006). The keju examination system of China from a modern psychometric perspective. In H. F. Liu (Ed.), Selected anthology of the International Conference on Imperial Examinations, Xiamen, China. Retrieved from *http://suen.ed.psu. edu/~hsuen/pubs/Xiamen%20paper%20final2.pdf.*

Terman, L., Dickson, V. E., Sutherland, A. H., Franzen, R. H., Tupper, C., & Fernald, G. (1922). *Intelligence tests and school reoganization.* Yonkers, NY: World Book.

Thorndike, E. L. (1904). *An introduction to the theory of mental and social measurements.* New York: Science Press.

Thorndike, R. M., & Lohman, D. F. (1990). *A century of ability testing.* Chicago: Riverside.

Toffler, A. (1970). *Future shock.* New York: Bantam Books.

Tredoux, G. (Ed.). (n.d.). Collected works. Retrieved 2014 from *galton.org.*

Von Mayrhauser, R. T. (1987). The manager, the medic, and the mediator: The clash of professional styles and the wartime origins of group mental testing. In M. M. Sokal (Ed.), *Psychological testing and American society* (pp. 128–157). New Brunswick, NJ: Rutgers University Press.

Weiss, D. J., & Yoes, M. E. (1991). Item response theory. In R. K. Hambleton & J. N. Zaal (Eds.), *Advances in educational and psychological testing* (pp. 69–95). Boston: Kluwer.

Wright, B. D., & Panchepakesan, N. (1969). A procedure for sample-free item analysis. *Educational and Psychological Measurement, 29,* 23–48.

Wright, B. D., & Stone, M. H. (1979). *Best test design.* Chicago: MESA Press.

Wu, H. M., Kuo, B. C., & Yang, J. M. (2012). Evaluating knowledge structure-base adaptive testing algorithms and system development. *Educational Technology and Society, 15*(2), 73–88.

PART II

Criterion-Referenced Tests

Criterion-Referenced Testing
Advances over 40 Years

Ronald K. Hambleton, April L. Zenisky, and W. James Popham

When one of us (RKH) took on his first, and what turned out to be his only, university position, Dwight Allen, his dean, suggested that he do some practical research after first looking at American schools to identify some important measurement problems. The dean argued, too, that it would be much more of a contribution to the field of education to find at least adequate solutions to the important assessment problems in American schools than to be the researcher who derived the "99th derivation of the KR-20 (Küder & Richardson, 1937) statistic based on weaker assumptions." Dean Allen argued that with enough publications, like the KR-20 derivation, tenure would be guaranteed at the University of Massachusetts (UMass), but no difference in American education would result from the publications.

In 1969 and 1970 when he began his professional career at UMass, a major paradigm shift in assessment was about to take place: The shift from strictly norm-referenced testing to a balance between criterion-referenced testing and norm-referenced testing in educational assessment. Prior to 1969 and for many years after too, measurement textbooks instructed teachers in how to construct norm-referenced tests for classroom use. Tests should contain items that were not too hard and not too easy (i.e., with p-values[1] between, say, .20 and .80). A normal distribution of scores was one of the criteria for judging the quality of a test. Reliability assessment was focused on the consistency of scores over parallel forms. "Grading on the curve" was a concept of which every teacher was well aware. There was little or no focus on the construction of tests to assess what children were actually learning and what knowledge and skills

---

[1]In classical test theory, p-values are a measure of difficulty that represents the proportion of examinees who answered an item correctly. The values range from 0 (i.e., no one answered correctly; very difficult) to 1 (i.e., everyone answered correctly; very easy).

they might have acquired; instead the focus was on constructing tests to discriminate among students in the reference group of interest, and, accordingly, score interpretations were normative.

What was clear to many educators in 1969 was that improvements might come if we could articulate what were important educational outcomes (i.e., behavioral objectives), and then teach to them, and assess the extent to which those outcomes were achieved on a student-by-student basis. The measurement focus would be on constructing content-valid assessments, and looking at the performance of students in relation to the expectations of instruction, rather than in relation to one another. Reliability might be assessed by looking at the consistency of resulting mastery–nonmastery decisions. No one at the time expressed this desired paradigm shift in measurement philosophy better than Popham and Husek (1969).

Criterion-referenced testing (CRT) is currently such a defining component of the large-scale, high-stakes assessment landscape, both in the United States and elsewhere, that it is hard to imagine a time when it wasn't. But that was indeed the case in 1969, a time when the mindset guiding testing practices was focused primarily on spreading examinees out along a proficiency spectrum to establish the distribution of test takers from low to high—a task particularly well suited to norm-referenced tests. This era of testing was exemplified in the United States by the widespread use of the Scholastic Aptitude Test (SAT) for undergraduate university admissions for both traditional students and also veterans of World War II and Korea under the G.I. Bill, and consequently, a high degree of weight was afforded to the value of norm-referenced tests in the public's view. In fact, a long-time colleague from a major testing company once told one of us (RKH) that he had been assigned to keep an eye on the development of CRT for his test publishing company until the concept "died."

In a way, this emerging approach to testing had received an unintended boost about 10 years prior from an unlikely source: the public's reaction to the 1957 launch of the *Sputnik* rocket by the Soviets. Now regarded as a watershed moment in American education, the seeming loss of the "space race" rocked American complacency about the adequacy of its science and mathematics education practices. *Sputnik*, and its aftermath of extensive research and school evaluations (e.g., see Project Talent), led to a refocusing on education through both legislative and instructional means, including a redefinition of what students needed to know to ensure the competitiveness of the United States in the global economy. The situation was understood as follows: America was perhaps no longer the best, and to be better, its students would have to know *more* (in terms of content). Hence, the seeds of educational reform, educational outcomes, and standards were further sown.

The term *criterion-referenced testing* is credited to Robert Glaser (1963) in his brief (three pages!) paper titled "Instructional Technology and the Measurement of Learning Outcomes," which appeared in *American Psychologist*. He wrote:

> In large part, achievement measures currently employed in education are norm referenced. This emphasis upon norm-referenced measures has been brought about by the preoccupation of test theory with aptitude, and with

selection and prediction problems; norm-referenced measures are useful for this kind of work in correlational analysis. However, the imposition of this kind of thinking on the purposes of achievement measurement raises some question, and concern with instructional technology is forcing us toward the kind of information made available by the use of criterion-referenced measures. We need to behaviorally specify minimum levels of performance that describe the least amount of end-of-course competence the student is expected to attain, or that he needs in order to go on to the next course in a sequence. (p. 520)

In this article, Glaser's words had the effect of completely reframing the underpinnings of the work being done among psychologists and psychometricians to measure student achievement. By focusing on the degree of competence independent of how other examinees did, the primary interpretation of test results was transformed from an emphasis on rank-ordering examinees along a continuum to one that prioritized an independent evaluation of knowledge and skills of each individual. Hambleton (1974) described the types of educational programs that were being designed around specified learning outcomes and CRT to assess and to monitor student achievement. These educational programs became known as *individually prescribed instruction* (IPI). Glaser and Nitko (1971) provided an excellent source for learning more about these programs and the development of CRT.

The goal of the present chapter is to reflect on the CRT movement from the time of Glaser's paper in 1963 to the present by highlighting a selection of papers that have proven to be key in developing the ideas and practices of CRT to the present day. The selection of papers is reflective of the perspective of one of us (RKH), an active researcher from the 1970s to today in guiding the field of psychometrics through this transition from a norm-referenced world to one that uses a balance of CRT and norm-referenced tests. A secondary goal of this chapter is to briefly look forward in this area and enumerate some of the remaining problems and emerging challenges for CRT. For broader reviews of the CRT literature between 1963 and 1994, readers are referred to Berk (1984) and Popham (1978a, 1994). For reviews of other related topics, there are numerous chapters and books (see, e.g., Hambleton & Pitoniak, 2006, and Cizek, 2012, on setting performance standards; van der Linden, 1991, 1997, on applications of decision theory to CRT; and Shrock & Coscarelli, 2007, for practical aspects of CRT).

Those Heady Early Years: Developments Fast and Furious

Once Glaser's ideas were published, research and practice reflecting this change in approach soon followed. Hambleton (1994) reported that from 1971 to 1979, he counted more than 1,600 contributions to the criterion-referenced testing literature. These contributions were on every topic from "Do we need CRT at all?" to debates about the advantages and disadvantages of norm-referenced tests and CRT; to best ways to describe learning outcomes; and on technical topics such as defining and estimating reliability and validity, setting performance standards, and reporting scores.

In 1972, Popham introduced the notion of framing criterion-referencing as connected to "objectives," specifically, those instructional objectives that are *measurable*. The strategy espoused by Popham here was to utilize systems analysis principles in the design of highly quantitative educational accountability systems, with objectives defined and prioritized. To Popham, this strategy represented a departure from prior practices, for which educational goals were loose and nonmeasurable more often than not, in his estimation. In this systems approach, criterion-referenced measures for output appraisal flow logically from carefully defined goals to provide evidence of knowledge and skills relative to those goals.

Hambleton and Swaminathan and their students at the time (James Algina, Linda Cook, Doug Coulson, Dan Eignor, and Janice Gifford) picked up the challenges from Robert Glaser and Jim Popham and began their own program of research on many technical aspects of criterion-referenced testing CRT that spanned about 15 years. As was often the case in UMass research (this was true, too, about their work in the areas of item response theory [IRT] and test adaptation methodology), they began with the notion that the concept of study (e.g., reliability estimation) may not be ultimately useful to educators, but whatever value the concept has would depend on the existence of methods for applying that concept successfully.

Hambleton and his colleagues were influenced early in their work by Melvin Novick from American College Testing (ACT), known internationally for his test theory research. Novick highlighted for them the potential role of Bayesian estimation and decision theory. Bayesian estimation offered the potential for better measurement information because so often CRT were short, and it further offered the potential of prior and collateral information that could strengthen criterion-referenced measurements. Decision theory was likewise attractive because CRT was all about mastery and nonmastery decision making, and so it made sense to reconceptualize criterion-referenced measurement problems in terms of decisions, false-positive and false-negative error rates, and the seriousness of those error rates. Don Mellenbergh, Wim van der Linden, and others picked up similar ideas about the same time, and ultimately they produced a full theory of criterion-referenced measurement in decision theory terms (e.g., see van der Linden & Mellenbergh, 1977, and van der Linden, 1997, for applications to standard setting and other areas).

Hambleton and Novick (1973) also laid out their own formulation of Bayesian estimation of CRT scores and decision making. Swaminathan, Hambleton, and Algina (1974) followed up that work with specific details and examples. (For a full review of all of their work, see Hambleton, Swaminathan, Algina, & Coulson, 1978.) The basic idea was that information about test quality (i.e., score reliability) and group performance (the mean) could be used in mastery estimation to produce a posterior belief distribution about each examinee's true mastery or proficiency. With values for false-positive and false-negative error rates that must be set, decisions could be made to minimize the loss function preferred by the tester. For example, as with many certification and licensure exams, the preference may be to take false-positive errors more seriously and weight them higher than false-negative errors.

The flaw with the Hambleton–Novick formulation was that, to some extent, the Bayesian examinee estimates of proficiency are dependent on the group of examinees from whom the estimates were obtained. Low-performing examinees, relative to the members in their group, would have their estimates increased. High-performing examinees would have their scores lowered. Quite simply, this is unacceptable in a measurement framework where examinee scores are being interpreted in relation to a domain of content and one or more performance levels. High-performing examinees would be furious with the strategy and argue that the approach is unfair to them—and they would be correct. It is true that, on average, the Bayesian proficiency estimates would be closer to true examinee scores than to their observed scores, but at the individual level, the scores would be biased and therefore they could not be justified in high-stakes situations.

The UMass work on this line of research was discontinued. At the same time, and in hindsight, there would appear to be considerably more merit for the use of Bayesian methods in the context of diagnostic testing where mastery/nonmastery decisions about examinees are less consequential and often the number of test items is very limited, and so the extra information available would seem to be valuable. A brief review of many testing initiatives currently in place to enhance the utility of subtest scores highlights the fact that prior and collateral sources of information are being used regularly (e.g., see Sinharay, Haberman, & Puhan, 2007).

Aiming for Consistency:
The Evolution of Reliability Assessment

Popham and Husek (1969) initially suggested that the KR-20 formula could be used to assess the reliability of criterion-referenced test CRT scores. Soon after, however, it was noted that with no pressure on test developers to maximize or even focus on test score variance, it would be quite possible for classical test score reliability to sink to zero or near zero despite the merits of the test itself. One of the first to consider the problem was Livingston (1972), and he addressed the limited score variance problem with CRTs by focusing on true score variability and test score variability in relation to the passing score for the test. This "Livingston approach" was viewed as an extension of classical reliability since if the test score mean were substituted for the passing score, the classical reliability estimate would result. The approach suggested by Livingston did resolve the problem of low test score variance but did not address a related primary question: If examinees are being assigned to, say, one of two performance categories (e.g., masters and nonmasters, or passers and failers), using two parallel forms of a CRT, how consistent would the *classifications* be? In other words, because of the way in which the CRT scores were being used, a decision theory approach to reliability seemed in order. Also, a similar approach could be used to assess the validity of CRT scores by looking at the similarity between decisions made on the basis of the test and decisions (i.e., classifications) using a criterion measure. These ideas were introduced in Hambleton and Novick (1973), and further developed by Swaminathan and colleagues (1975).

There really were two problems with parallel form approaches to the estimation of decision consistency. First, parallel-form reliability estimation required that a second form be developed, which was time-consuming and costly, and most inconveniently, required that examinees take time to complete a second form with minimal time and learning between the two test administrations. These requirements were often unrealistic, much the same as they are with norm-referenced tests. The concept of decision consistency was correct, but what was needed was something akin to classical split-half reliability estimation. Both Huynh (1976) and Subkoviak (1976) developed highly successful single-administration estimates of decision consistency for binary-scored test items, and followed up with practical advances such as software and look up tables to speed up computation. Many years later, Livingston and Lewis (1995) provided a practical solution for the case with both binary and polytomously scored items in the same test.

The second problem was that in considering the number of correct decisions or classifications as a criterion for judging the reliability of CRT scores, no consideration was given to the number of correct classifications due to chance factors alone. After all, on the second administration of a test, every examinee must be classified somewhere, and some of those classifications, even if made at random, would be correct. Consider an extreme case—flipping a coin to make a mastery–nonmastery decision. A parallel form estimate of decision consistency would be expected to be .50, and all the agreement observed would be due to chance! The answer was that the decision consistency estimate needed to be corrected for chance agreement, and this was done through the use of Cohen's kappa statistic (Swaminathan et al., 1975). The main advantage of using decision consistency and kappa estimates to describe reliability is that they were consistent with the way CRTs were being used. Also, the approach was easily extendable to the assessment of validity, and decisions that were binary or polytomous (e.g., today it is common to assign examinees on state achievement tests to four categories, often labeled "failing," "basic," "proficiency," and "advanced").

For a complete and balanced review of the development of reliability indices for CRTs and binary and multicategory decision making, and with binary and polytomously scored item-level data, readers are referred to Haertel (2006) and to the important work of Huynh, Subkoviak, Brennan, and Kane, Livingston, and Lewis that Haertel cites in his review. Han and Rudner's chapter in this volume also provides an in-depth introduction to many of the methods described briefly here.

What became clear too through this process of developing an approach to reliability in the criterion-referenced measurement framework was that full reporting of criterion-referenced reliability information would necessarily have to include information about the performance levels, the examinee score distribution, as well as the estimates of decision consistency, kappa, and the single-administration estimation method that was used. Even the consistency of classifications can be reported for true proficiency states. Currently, just about every technical manual for a state testing program contains this information.

Standard Setting: Debates and Advances

By the middle of the 1970s, many companies had set up systems to promote behavioral objectives and associated CRTs. Small collections of behavioral objectives along with short pretests and posttests to measure the objectives were put in place in many school districts around the country. Hambleton (1974) wrote about several of the more popular ones, but there were many. Standard setting around these tests was easy to do but hard to defend when challenges came: Decisions were binary (i.e., pass or fail) and a candidate was required to answer at least three of four items, or four of five items, for example, that measured an objective. Minimum competency tests by states were also being introduced, but again, without much sophistication in setting performance standards. The only standard-setting methods in place in the early 1970s included the methods by Nedelsky (1954), Angoff (1971), and Ebel (1972), as well as two methods from industrial/organizational psychology: the contrasting groups method and the borderline group method. None of these methods was much used, however. One of us (RKH) recalls being called by a state test director and asked to offer a standard-setting method over the telephone, but in no more than 15 minutes because that was all the time she had available.

Passing scores were, for the most part, arbitrary, and most everyone agreed (see Glass, 1978). But dispute over the particular meaning of the word *arbitrary* was a key point in the paper by Glass (1978) and the reactions of several researchers, including two of us (Hambleton, 1978; Popham, 1978). Glass dismissed the efforts of researchers to set performance standards by arguing that the methods used were arbitrary in the sense of being "mindless and capricious" (p. 297). Popham agreed that far too much of the standard setting in the past had been poorly carried out, but despite the role of judgment in standard setting, he argued that highly consistent and defensible standards could and should be set. Although few accepted the conclusions of Glass, his harsh remarks were a major stimulus to numerous researchers who aspired to generate "highly consistent and defensible standards" (e.g., see Cizek, 2012). This paper by Glass and the resulting reactions of critics constituted a turning point in standard-setting research.

Standard-setting methods are always going to be judgmental at some level and therefore controversial, but because CRTs began to be used in American schools for promotion and graduation, consequences of flawed decisions were serious, and so research on new methods, improvements in methodology, and validity initiatives became important. Many researchers, including Livingston and Zieky (1982), produced booklets describing procedures to follow in setting and validating performance standards. Possible guidelines for setting performance standards were offered later, methods were catalogued, and many comparative studies of methods were carried out. The period of the 1980s was marked by a steady stream of papers that moved the field forward. For an excellent review of these developments, see the chapters by Jaeger (1989) and Popham (1997).

The next major set of advances in standard setting came in the 1990s, following the decision by the National Assessment Governing Board (NAGB) in 1989 to set "achievement levels" on the reporting scales of the National Assessment of Educational Progress (NAEP). In its time this was a highly controversial decision by NAGB and resulted in a major battle between NAGB and the National Center for Education Statistics (NCES), with scholars lined up on both sides; the controversy went on for more than 5 years. One of us (RKH) was responsible for designing and carrying out the study to set performance standards on the 1990 NAEP in mathematics (Hambleton & Bourque, 1991). The study led to major criticism, and the mantra was born: "The standards were fatally flawed." For a general accounting of the flavor of that and subsequent debates, see Pellegrino, Jones, and Mitchell (1999) and Hambleton, Brennan, and colleagues (2000). But there was a positive value to the battle, in that it resulted in many significant advances in the methodology for setting performance standards, and there was no question that the many critics of NAGB's choice to implement such standards were quite influential in the methods that were developed and evaluated. Among the most important advances emerging at this time:

1. A strong emphasis on the development of clear and detailed descriptions of the performance levels.
2. The need to field-test, in experimental designs when possible, new methods prior to their use in major studies.
3. The desirability of compiling procedural, internal, and validity evidence to support the resulting performance standards (e.g., see Kane, 1994).
4. The desirability of conducting parallel investigations to assess the consistency of performance standards.
5. The development of standard-setting methods to accommodate new forms of assessment such as writing samples and performance tasks.
6. The value of formative and summative assessments of the standard-setting process itself (through surveys and direct observation by third parties to the studies).
7. The importance of planning the composition of a standard-setting panel in advance of a study, and then strategically sampling to ensure that the desired composition of a panel could be achieved.
8. Providing meaningful feedback to panelists, including impact data, during the process.

Of course, not all of these advances were due strictly to the NAEP standard-setting work, but their value was substantiated through the ambitious NAEP standard-setting research agenda. The important book edited by Cizek (2012) provides several highly influential chapters that were an outgrowth of the NAEP standard-setting research.

Today, the NAEP standards remain, and are an integral part of, NAEP score reporting. The research itself quickly spread to state assessment programs and credentialing examinations. Pitoniak and Cizek (Chapter 3, this volume) provide an overview of standard-setting methods and procedures in use today.

CRT in the Spotlight: Test Score Reporting

Although so many of the advances in testing that have occurred with respect to CRT are somewhat technical in nature and therefore happen behind the scenes in the area of test development, one critical effect of the widespread use of CRT is perhaps most readily apparent in the domain of reporting test results to examinees and other stakeholders. For the bulk of the 20th century, under the norm-referenced paradigm, reporting test scores was predicated on the primary reporting goal of differentiating examinees from one another along the ability scale. Thus, although examinees would receive test scores, the key information for interpretation of those scores was often couched in terms of percentiles or percentile ranks. Such normative comparisons define achievement as a step removed from specific knowledge and skills and instead frame performance in relative terms based on observed distributions of examinees. With the advent of CRT, however, reporting practices were opened to a whole new world of score meaning. The prominence of normative comparisons dropped (though they were not eliminated in many cases) in favor of reporting documents that highlighted what examinees knew and could do relative to absolute standards. As a matter of orientation, this shift has the effect of focusing test users on the relationship between individual examinees and the knowledge, skills, and abilities being assessed, and reporting efforts in a CRT framework consequently must address that information in some way in communicating about test performance.

Early work in the area of CRT certainly had an impact on reporting, but among the earliest papers devoted to results on reporting within a CRT approach came in a report by Mills and Hambleton in 1980. A key point made by these authors was the differentiation of reporting methods used with norm-referenced tests from those that were appropriate for criterion-referenced tests, noting that such different testing purposes require different reporting systems. CRT score reporting systems necessitated certain specifications, such as information needs, a testing program built to be consistent with those needs, audience identification, proper test selection, and proper test construction. Design considerations for the reports themselves must focus on physical features, the reporting of normative information, the choice of performance standards, and test score interpretations. In many ways, this report very much set the stage for the reporting efforts that followed and the reports that are in operational use today.

In the years that followed the Mills and Hambleton paper, with the increasingly widespread use of CRT, more and more agencies sought to incorporate strategies for criterion-referenced reporting in a range of testing contexts, with varying success. Among the many reporting approaches that emerged in operational testing at this time were achievement levels, performance-level descriptors, criterion-referenced domain scores, item-level reporting, and scale anchoring/item mapping. NAEP, again, was a particular thought leader in this area throughout the 1980s and 1990s (see Zenisky, Mazzeo, & Pitoniak, Chapter 20, this volume).

With the emergence of so many new reporting strategies to root performance in the construct of interest, the time was likewise ripe for the development of evaluations investigating the interpretability and usability of score reports. This work was led most notably by studies on NAEP reporting (e.g., Hambleton & Slater, 1994; Wainer, Hambleton, & Meara, 1999). Key findings from this era indicated that although well-constructed graphical displays aided users in understanding test performance, too often the users lacked context for interpreting results, and many displays were attempting to convey too much information (and hence were too convoluted for their intended audiences). On this latter point, another significant takeaway from this research was the importance of differentiating the reporting needs and interests for different user groups (examinees, families, educators, policymakers, etc.). Other work at this time focused on the public reporting of test results, in light of the emerging shift to CRT in large-scale educational assessments, with research by Hambleton and Meara (1999) on newspaper coverage of NAEP results and work by Hambleton, Impara, and colleagues (2000) delving into newspaper accounts of results associated with the Maryland School Performance Assessment Program. In both of these cases, the criterion-referenced nature of the assessments lent itself to interesting findings about student performance, but again there was much misunderstanding of results (and indeed, the tests themselves) present in media accounts.

The publication in 2004 of the seminal study in reporting by Goodman and Hambleton signaled the next major advance in CRT results reporting research. This article, which wholly filled one issue of *Applied Measurement in Education*, detailed an evaluation of individual student score reports and interpretive guides from 11 U.S. states, two Canadian provinces, and three U.S.-based norm-referenced tests used in K–12 education. The research described in that paper marked the most comprehensive review of individual reports to date that was widely available to the research community (rather than a conference paper or technical report), and was particularly influential in synthesizing promising features across the reports studied and also in identifying the problematic elements of reports. Promising features discussed by Goodman and Hambleton included features to promote *readability* (headers, highlight sections, graphical displays, reports for different audiences, and personalization), features to *add meaning*, the use of *performance levels*, and *diagnostic information*. On the flip side, some issues uncovered included providing too much information, providing too little information about test purpose, lack of information about score precision, the use of statistical jargon, and some additional general design problems. In terms of sparking research and practice in the area of reporting, this paper offered clear guidance on the issues in then-current reports, and also numerous directions for future study.

The reporting problems detailed in Goodman and Hambleton (2004) identified not only issues with reports but likewise revealed challenges in how reports were conceptualized, developed, and disseminated in operational testing. In 2008, Hambleton and Zenisky gave a keynote address at the Sixth Conference of the International Test

Commission in Liverpool in which they laid out the basic principles for what is now known as their model of *score report development* (Hambleton & Zenisky, 2013; Zenisky & Hambleton, 2012). In its general form, this model reinforces the notion that the process of developing score reports cannot be left until all other test development activities are nearly completed; rather, score reporting is integrally connected to test purpose and use, and so the process begins with careful reflection on the needs of specific intended user groups and a review of report examples and relevant literature, followed by report development and, critically, field-testing of reports with stakeholders. Field testing is envisioned as a feedback loop, whereby data gathered informs reports, and field testing may then be repeated. Finally, report development does not end with the operational production of reports but rather a continual monitoring of use and understanding in a maintenance phase.

More recent work in the area of results reporting in the CRT context has focused on technological tools for communicating test results (Zenisky & Hambleton, 2013). Most U.S. states now host Web links on state department of education webpages that allow site visitors to access anonymized databases of student performance to carry out descriptive analyses of test results in aggregate, and more advanced tools such as the NAEP Data Explorer support more sophisticated techniques such as regression analyses. These publicly available data analysis mechanisms hold a great deal of promise in terms of putting data out there to make test scores and other accompanying results more accessible to stakeholders in terms of understanding what examinees know and can do in the CRT framework that predominates assessment practices. As we look ahead to testing practices in the coming years, however, challenges remain. For many test users, the meaning that can be ascribed to test results is too often too disconnected or imprecise. The displays that are provided to different users must be improved to deliver clear and readily relatable information. The technology-based tools that give enormous flexibility to users in terms of access must be built carefully and offer appropriate guidance for users, as such tools have much promise, but also leave open the door to misinterpretation and misunderstanding in a different way than static reporting practices.

Conclusions and Looking Ahead

CRT theory and practices are now firmly entrenched in current assessment practices. Over the past 45 years we have seen the following:

1. A change from many test publishers completely rejecting the concept of CRT to a situation where now they are competing with each other for hundreds of millions of dollars' worth of contracts for delivering these tests to every state in the country, and many countries around the world. Also, over 1,000 credential agencies in the United States are now using criterion-referenced assessments for making pass–fail decisions.

2. These tests have moved from measuring behavioral objectives to now focusing on measuring highly detailed descriptions of learning outcomes.

3. A shift from paper-and-pencil modes of test administration to computer-administered tests and from linear to new test designs such as fully adaptive tests and multistage tests has taken place.

4. These tests have shifted from almost exclusive reliance on multiple-choice test items to the use of many new item types, such as writing samples, performance tasks, and numerous new item types made possible by the computer (e.g., multiple true–false).

5. From development of items, one at a time, to assessment engineering with the capability of using item specifications and computers to generate large numbers of items in a highly cost effective way (e.g., see Zenisky & Luecht, Chapter 13, this volume).

6. From binary scored unidimensional test items to polytomously scored unidimensional and multidimensional test items.

7. From binary scored items and binary decisions at the test score level to polytomously scored items and multicategory performance classifications.

8. From the use of the KR-20 formula to assess score reliability to single-administration estimates of decision consistency and decision accuracy.

9. From several methods for setting a single performance standard on a test score made up of binary-scored test items of the same item type to more than 20 methods (with variations) for setting multiple performance standards on a test score consisting of both binary-scored and polytomously scored items, often in multiple-item formats.

10. Focus has shifted from the compilation of primarily content validity evidence to support the various uses of CRT scores and decisions to a much more comprehensive approach to the compilation of empirical evidence.

11. From simple reports of student performance on a set of behavioral objectives and possibly an overall binary decision (pass or fail) based on test scores, in principle, the field is moving to more scientifically designed reports, with specific reports for potential users of the information that are understandable and useful (e.g., see reports being designed for the Partnership for Assessment of Readiness for College and Careers [PARCC] and Smarter Balanced), and where considerable attention is given to test score report design and validation.

We conclude with the hope that in the coming years focus will center on efforts to validate the scores and decisions from CRTs—to date, this lack of validation work is a serious shortcoming in the field. Also, despite the big effort to improve test score report design in recent years, much more research is needed to ensure that users can fully understand the score reports they receive, and can use these reports in meaningful ways to improve curriculum and instruction, and help more students achieve their potential.

REFERENCES

Angoff, W. (1971). Scales, norms, and equivalent scores. In R. L. Thorndike (Ed.), *Educational measurement* (pp. 508–597). Washington, DC: American Council on Education.

Berk, R. A. (Ed.). (1984). *A guide to criterion-referenced test construction.* Baltimore: Johns Hopkins University Press.

Cizek, G. J. (Ed.). (2012). *Setting performance standards: Foundations, methods, and innovations* (2nd ed.). New York: Routledge.

Ebel, R. (1972). *Essentials of educational measurement* (2nd ed.). Englewood Cliffs, NJ: Prentice-Hall.

Glaser, R. (1963). Instructional technology and the measurement of learning outcomes. *American Psychologist, 18,* 519–521.

Glaser, R., & Nitko, A. J. (1971). Measurement in learning and instruction. In R. L. Thorndike (Ed.), *Educational measurement* (pp. 625–670). Washington, DC: American Council on Education.

Glass, G. V. (1978). Standards and criteria. *Journal of Educational Measurement, 15,* 237–261.

Goodman, D. P., & Hambleton, R. K. (2004). Student test score reports and interpretive guides: Review of current practices and suggestions for future research. *Applied Measurement in Education, 17,* 145–220.

Haertel, E. (2006). Reliability. In R. L. Brennan (Ed.), *Educational measurement* (pp. 65–110). Westport, CT: American Council on Education/Praeger.

Hambleton, R. K. (1974). Test and decision-making procedures for selected individualized instructional programs. *Review of Educational Research, 44,* 371–400.

Hambleton, R. K. (1978). On the use of cut-off scores with criterion-referenced tests in instructional settings. *Journal of Educational Measurement, 15,* 177–290.

Hambleton, R. K. (1994). The rise and fall of criterion-referenced measurement. *Educational Measurement: Issues and Practice, 13*(4), 21–26.

Hambleton, R. K., & Bourque, M. L. (1991). *Initial performance standards for the 1990 NAEP Mathematics Assessment* (Technical Report). Washington, DC: National Assessment Governing Board.

Hambleton, R. K., Brennan, R. L., Brown, W., Dodd, B., Forsythe, R. A., Mehrens, W. A., et al. (2000). A response to "Setting Reasonable and Useful Performance Standards" in the National Academy of Sciences' grading the Nation's Report Card. *Educational Measurement: Issues and Practice, 19,* 5–13.

Hambleton, R. K., Impara, J., Mehrens, W., & Plake, B. S., with Pitoniak, M. J., Zenisky, A. L., & Smith, L. F. (2000). *Psychometric review of the Maryland School Performance Assessment Program* (Final Report). Baltimore: Abell Foundation.

Hambleton, R. K., & Meara, K. (1999). *Newspaper coverage of NAEP results: 1990 to 1998* (Laboratory of Psychometric and Evaluation Research Report No. 355). Amherst, MA: University of Massachusetts, School of Education.

Hambleton, R. K., & Novick, M. R. (1973). Toward an integration of theory and method for criterion-referenced tests. *Journal of Educational Measurement, 10,* 159–170.

Hambleton, R. K., & Pitoniak, M. J. (2006). Setting performance standards. In R. L. Brennan (Ed.), *Educational measurement* (pp. 433–470). Westport, CT: American Council on Education/Praeger.

Hambleton, R. K., & Slater, S. C. (1994). NAEP state reports in mathematics: Valuable information for policy-makers. *New England Journal of Public Policy, 10*(1), 209–222.

Hambleton, R. K., Swaminathan, H., Algina, J., & Coulson, D. (1978). Criterion-referenced testing and measurement: A review of technical issues and developments. *Review of Educational Research, 48*, 1–47.

Hambleton, R. K., & Zenisky, A. L. (2008, July). *Reporting test scores in more meaningful ways: Some new findings, research methods, and guidelines for score report design.* Keynote address presented at the Sixth Conference of the International Test Commission, Liverpool, UK.

Hambleton, R. K., & Zenisky, A. L. (2013). Reporting test scores in more meaningful ways: Some new findings, research methods, and guidelines for score report design. In K. F. Geisinger (Ed.), *APA handbook of testing and assessment in psychology* (pp. 479–494). Washington, DC: American Psychological Association.

Huynh, H. (1976). On the reliability of decisions in domain-referenced testing. *Journal of Educational Measurement, 13*, 253–264.

Jaeger, R. M. (1989). Certification of student competence. In R. L. Linn (Ed.), *Educational measurement* (pp. 485–514). New York: Macmillan.

Kane, M. (1994). Validating the performance standards associated with passing scores. *Review of Educational Research, 64*, 425–461.

Küder, G. F., & Richardson, M. W. (1937). The theory of the estimation of test reliability. *Psychometrika, 2*(3), 151–160.

Livingston, S. A. (1972). Criterion-referenced applications of classical test theory. *Journal of Educational Measurement, 9*, 13–26.

Livingston, S. A., & Lewis, C. (1995). Estimating the consistency and accuracy of classifications based on test scores. *Journal of Educational Measurement, 32*, 179–197.

Livingston, S. A., & Zieky, M. J. (1982). *Passing scores: A manual for setting standards of performance on educational and occupational teests.* Princeton, NJ: Educational Testing Service.

Mills, C. N., & Hambleton, R. K. (1980). *Guidelines for reporting criterion-referenced test score information* (Laboratory of Psychometric and Evaluation Research Report No. 100). Amherst, MA: University of Massachusetts, School of Education.

Nedelsky, L. (1954). Absolute grading standards for objective tests. *Educational and Psychological Measurement, 14*, 3–19.

Pellegrino, J. W., Jones, L. R., & Mitchell, K. J. (1999). *Grading the Nation's Report Card: Evaluating NAEP and transforming the assessment of educational progress.* Washington, DC: National Academy Press.

Popham, W. J. (1972). Objectives-based management strategies for large educational systems. *Journal of Educational Research, 66*(1), 4–9.

Popham, W. J. (1978). As always provocative. *Journal of Educational Measurement, 15*(4), 297–300.

Popham, W. J. (Ed.). (1994). Honoring Robert Glaser's work on criterion-referenced testing (Special issue). *Educational Measurement: Issues and Practice, 13*(4), 5–30.

Popham, W. J. (1997). The criticality of consequences in standard-setting: Six lessons learned the hard way by a standard-setting abettor. In M. L. Bourque (Ed.), *Proceedings of achievement levels workshop* (pp. 107–112). Washington, DC: National Assessment Governing Board.

Popham, W. J., & Husek, T. (1969). Implications of criterion-referenced measurement. *Journal of Educational Measurement, 6*, 1–9.

Shrock, S. A., & Coscarelli, W. C. (2007). *Criterion-referenced test development* (3rd ed.). San Francisco: Pfeiffer.

Sinharay, S., Haberman, S. J., & Puhan, G. (2007). Subscores based on classical test theory: To report or not to report. *Educational Measurement: Issues and Practice, 26*(4), 21–28.

Subkoviak, M. J. (1976). Estimating the reliability from a single administration of criterion-referenced test. *Journal of Educational Measurement, 13*, 265–276.

Swaminathan, H., Hambleton, R. K., & Algina, J. (1974). A Bayesian decision-theoretic procedure for use with criterion-referenced tests. *Journal of Educational Measurement, 12*, 87–98.

van der Linden, W. J. (1991). Applications of decision theory to test-based decision making. In R. K. Hambleton & J. Zaal (Eds.), *Advances in educational and psychological testing* (pp. 129–156). Boston: Kluwer.

van der Linden, W. J. (1997). Decision theory in educational testing. In J. P. Keeves (Ed.), *Educational research, methodology, and measurement: An international handbook* (2nd ed., pp. 725–730). Oxford, UK: Elsevier Science.

van der Linden, W. J., & Mellenbergh, G. J. (1977). Optimal cutting scores using a linear loss function. *Applied Psychological Measurement, 1*, 593–599.

Wainer, H., Hambleton, R. K., & Meara, K. (1999). Alternative displays for communication of NAEP results: A redesign and validity study. *Journal of Educational Measurement, 36*, 301–335.

Zenisky, A. L., & Hambleton, R. K. (2012). Developing test score reports that work: The process and best practices for effective communication. *Educational Measurement: Issues and Practice, 31*(2), 21–26.

Zenisky, A. L., & Hambleton, R. K. (2013). From "Here's the story" to "You're in charge": Developing and maintaining large-scale online test and score reporting resources. In M. Simon, M. Rousseau, & K. Ercikan (Eds.), *Improving large-scale assessment in education* (pp. 175–185). New York: Routledge.

CHAPTER 3

Standard Setting

Mary J. Pitoniak and Gregory J. Cizek

The purpose of educational measurement is to provide information about individuals and groups, and this information is often used to facilitate decision making. In addition to discrete test scores, other results yielded by a test may include the classifications of examinees into categories. The process used to operationally define these categories as points on the score scale is called *standard setting*, which is the focus of this chapter. Specifically, this chapter is designed to familiarize the reader with the key concepts related to standard setting, to describe the steps that typically comprise standard-setting procedures, to review some common methods used to set standards, to highlight some challenges often encountered when setting standards, and to suggest some issues for future consideration. Because of length restrictions, this chapter can provide only an overview of key points and is not intended to enable the reader to conduct a standard-setting study without additional resources. Throughout the chapter, the reader is referred to relevant references for more information, with the most detailed procedural information being found in Cizek and Bunch (2007) and Zieky, Perie, and Livingston (2008).

It should be noted that, as with other areas of educational measurement, it is important to follow professional guidelines for standard setting, including the *Standards for Educational and Psychological Testing* (American Educational Research Association, American Psychological Association, & National Council on Measurement in Education [AERA, APA, & NCME], 2014). Several of these standards address issues relevant to the setting of performance standards, such as providing detailed description of the qualifications and experience of the panelists involved in the setting of performance standards and how the panelists went about their tasks; documenting the rationale for setting performance standards and the basis for setting them; providing external evidence to support the validity of test score interpretations associated with the performance category descriptions; designing a process whereby panelists can optimally use the knowledge that they have to influence the standard setting; and, for credentialing tests, placing standards in the context of knowledge and skills rather than adopting a straight normative approach to obtain a prespecified pass rate.

What Is Standard Setting?

The term *standard setting* is a shorthand expression for the process of establishing the specified levels of performance that an examinee must attain in order to be classified into one of two or more performance categories. More simply, standard setting is the process of establishing cut scores on examinations; those cut scores are used to create performance categories into which examinees are classified. Such categories—and the cut scores used to derive them—do not exist a priori; the categories are typically social constructions and must be derived by procedures that rely on human judgment.

For some examinations—particularly in the areas of professional licensure and certification—it is often the case that only a single cut score is needed to create two categories such as *Pass–Fail*, or *Award Certification–Deny Certification*. In other contexts, multiple cut scores may be needed to create more than two categories that have been mandated by a policy. For example, three cut scores are used to create the four familiar categories of *Below Basic*, *Basic*, *Proficient*, and *Advanced* that have become commonly used to denote differing degrees of student achievement in K–12 educational testing in the United States.

As a technology in the field of psychometrics, standard setting has been defined as "the proper following of a prescribed, rational system of rules or procedures resulting in the assignment of a number to differentiate between two or more states or degrees of performance" (Cizek, 1993, p. 100). The system of rules or procedures may be one of various acceptable procedures used to identify the one or more points on a test score scale that correspond to the levels of performance necessary for examinees to be classified into a given performance level. But standard setting is not only a technical matter. As Cizek has observed, "Standard setting is perhaps the branch of psychometrics that blends more artistic, political, and cultural ingredients into the mix of its products than any other" (2001, p. 5). As a process that relies on judgment, the primary aim of modern standard setting is to devise and implement systematic, reproducible procedures that enable participants in the standard-setting process to bring to bear their judgments in such a way as to translate the participants' conceptual notions regarding levels of performance or the policy positions of authorizing entities into specific locations on a test score scale. It is these translations (see Figure 3.1) that define the categories.

The process of determining cut scores is not only technical, social, and political, but obviously consequential as well. Standard setting has important consequences for test takers, for the entities responsible for testing programs, and for society generally. On tests used for credentialing test takers, cut scores are typically one component in a larger process that can permit or deny the right of candidates to practice a profession

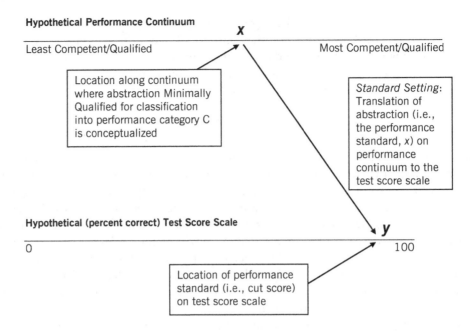

FIGURE 3.1. The relationship between performance standard and cut score. From Cizek (2012b). Copyright 2012 by Routledge. Adapted by permission.

of their choosing in order to advance highly qualified practice in a profession and to protect the public. In student testing, classifications into performance categories can influence whether students are permitted to graduate from high school and can also provide important information for policymakers considering changes to educational approaches.

Key Concepts in Standard Setting

As is described later in this chapter, a variety of procedures exists for obtaining the cut scores that define performance categories on tests. However, although the actual procedures can vary widely, there are elements common to most of the most frequently used standard-setting methods. In this section, some foundational concepts common to many standard-setting procedures are introduced and defined.

● *Content standards.* In American elementary and secondary education, *content standards* refer to collections of specific statements, typically organized by grade level and subject area, that describe in detail what students in K–12 settings should be taught (Cizek, 2012b). Similar compendia of the knowledge, skills, and abilities (KSAs) deemed necessary for licensure or certification are also created for credentialing testing programs via job analysis or role delineation studies (additional information on job analyses can be found in Raymond & Luecht, 2013; Tannenbaum, 1999; Tannenbaum, Robustelli, & Baron, 2008).

• *Standards-referenced tests.* SRTs are tests developed to measure examinees' acquisition of content standards, and are a key component of what have come to be known as *standards-based assessment systems* (Cizek, 2012a).

• *Performance standards.* Performance standards are levels of achievement on a test necessary for an examinee to be classified into one of the ordered categories that result when cut scores are established (Cizek, 2012b).

• *Cut scores.* Cut scores are the actual points on the score scale that operationalize the performance standards (Cizek, 2012b).

• *Performance-level labels.* Performance standards are typically described by *performance-level labels* (PLLs), which are short descriptions of the categories (Egan, Schneider, & Ferrara, 2012). There may be as few as two performance levels (e.g., with PLLs such as *Pass* and *Fail*) or several performance levels (e.g., with PLLs such as *Beginning, Intermediate, Advanced*, and *Distinguished*). PLLs are created and used to serve as shorthand summaries of what the categorical assignment represents. In educational settings, they are used to describe achievement at a given grade level or in a subject, to describe degrees of progress across educational levels, to inform decisions about the placement/promotion/retention/graduation of students, to inform inferences and actions related to evaluations of educators, and to provide information to the public about the monitoring and performance of public institutions. In credentialing, terms such as *Minimally Competent* may be used to describe practitioners who are deemed qualified to practice safely and effectively, with those in the *Not Minimally Competent* level not possessing these KSAs. Through the use of these descriptive labels, the process of setting performance standards is not only consequential for the affected stakeholders in the process, but has substantial communication value and power in diverse contexts (see Egan et al., 2012).

• *Performance-level descriptors.* PLLs are often accompanied by longer elaborations intended to more fully describe what placement in a category indicates about what an examinee knows and/or can do. These elaborations are referred to as *performance-level descriptors* (PLDs) (Egan et al., 2012). PLDs consist of one to several paragraphs that describe the KSAs that an examinee at a given performance level would be expected to have mastered.

• *Panelists.* All standard setting relies, at least in part, on judgments to establish cut scores. Often, one or more groups of participants are empaneled to provide judgments about specific aspects of the standard-setting process. In addition to their number and representativeness, the qualifications of the panelists to make the required judgments are an important consideration (Hambleton & Pitoniak, 2006).

• *Rounds.* Standard-setting procedures often solicit multiple judgments from participants, wherein the participants provide ratings or other data and have the opportunity to reconsider their judgments in rounds or iterations of the judgment process used for a particular standard-setting method (Hambleton, Pitoniak, & Copella, 2012).

• *Feedback*. Various kinds of information are provided to standard-setting panelists to assist them in making their judgments. Collectively, these sources are called *feedback* and typically consist of three different kinds of information: (1) normative feedback, (2) reality feedback, and (3) impact feedback. These types of feedback are described later in the chapter (see also Cizek & Bunch, 2007).

• *Borderline examinee*. Many of the common standard-setting methods require participants to conceptualize a hypothetical test taker, often termed the *borderline examinee* (Pitoniak & Morgan, 2011), whose level of knowledge and skill places him or her just barely into a performance category (e.g., just barely Passing, just barely Proficient). Participants then make judgments about the estimated performance of the "just barely" examinee, or a group of similar examinees. In some applications, the target/borderline examinee is also referred to as a *minimally qualified candidate, minimally competent examinee,* or *target examinee.*

• *Vertical articulation*. In some standard-setting contexts, it is not a single cut score that is needed, but a system of cut scores that spans several areas or levels. Perhaps the most common of these applications is K–12 achievement testing where, for example, participants are asked to recommend a series of Proficient cut scores on mathematics tests administered across grades 3 through 8. Once initial cut scores are recommended at the individual grade levels, a process called *vertical articulation* (or *vertical moderation*) is employed to smooth out inordinate or unreasonable fluctuations in the system of cut scores across the grades (see Cizek, 2005; Cizek & Agger, 2012).

Steps for Setting Performance Standards

In this section, several steps common to conducting a standard-setting process are described. Although there are different methods for setting performance standards, as described in a later section of the chapter, most contemporary methods share a set of common steps. It is important to follow these steps in order to support the validity of the interpretations that will be made from the classification of examinees into performance levels.

With most methods, the expertise of a panel of qualified participants is a foundation of the standard-setting process. Some of the common steps are completed in advance of the actual standard-setting session, others during the session, and some after the session has concluded. It is also worth noting that although the steps are listed as discrete parts of the process, some of the activities—such as collection of ratings, provision of feedback, and gathering of panelists' evaluations of the process—occur iteratively across the session. The following list of common steps has been adapted from those contained in Hambleton and Pitoniak (2006; see also Hambleton et al., 2012; Pitoniak & Morgan, 2011; Tannenbaum & Katz, 2013).

Before the Standard-Setting Session

Step 1: Choose an Appropriate Standard-Setting Method

The choice of an appropriate standard-setting method is a first step, and the method should align with the nature and purpose of the test as well as the policy aims of the organization responsible for setting the performance standards (Kane, 2001; Reckase, 2000). Among the issues to be considered is the number of cut scores that will be needed—a number that should be guided by the test design and length. For example, a short test may not be able to support more than one cut score. (Ideally, issues such as these would be considered when developing the test specifications, before the test is even created.) Taking into account this information, a decision is made about the specific standard-setting method to be used. Numerous methods exist, and most may be modified or adapted to a specific assessment situation, though none is ideal for all uses. The features of several methods are described later in the chapter; within this section some issues to be kept in mind during the decision-making process are described.

The item formats that comprise the test are an important factor to consider when choosing a method. Item formats range from selected response (SR) and constructed response (CR) to interactive scenario-based or performance tasks. A test may contain one or a mixture of these formats. A standard-setting method must be selected that has been designed for use with the item formats included in the test on which performance standards will be set. A second factor for consideration is whether test-related information (e.g., item-level performance data and overall test-level data that may be used to estimate the impact of a given cut score) will be available at the time of the standard-setting session; the availability of such data is a necessary component of some standard-setting methods.

The degree to which the panelists are familiar with the intended population of test takers is also important. If an examinee-centered method such as the contrasting groups method (described later in this chapter) is used, panelists need to have personal knowledge of specific students for whom test scores are available, whereas with a test-centered method such as Angoff (1971), a more general knowledge of the KSAs of the target population is sufficient. An additional important factor is the availability of resources that a given method employs, such as time, materials, and analytic expertise (e.g., knowledge of item response theory [IRT]). Attention should also be paid to the extent to which a given standard-setting method has been evaluated through research and is professionally defensible.

The availability of a qualified and experienced facilitator should also be considered. If a standard-setting method has not been widely used and a knowledgeable facilitator cannot be obtained, it may be better to choose a more common method for which a seasoned facilitator can be located.

Step 2: Choose a Panel

A qualified and representative panel of participants is a cornerstone of an effective standard-setting session. The purpose of the test and the content that is measured will guide the specification of panelist qualifications. Panelists must be knowledgeable about the population being tested (e.g., fourth-grade students, physicians) and the KSAs (e.g., mathematics, anatomy) that the examinees must demonstrate in order to be classified into different categories.

It is important that the panel also be sufficiently large, representative, and diverse, because these qualities will increase the dependability, generalizability, and validity of the interpretations to be made from the standard-setting results. Targets should be established for relevant panel attributes such as demographic and other characteristics, and the degree to which those targets are met should be documented. The appropriate size of the panel depends in part on the method chosen, but in general a panel should have at least 10 to 15 members (Raymond & Reid, 2001). Larger panels of 20 to 30 individuals may be desirable to ensure broader representation and more stable results; in some cases the panels are divided into subpanels of fewer members, providing an opportunity to examine replicability of cut scores across equivalent panels. Other characteristics that may be taken into account when determining target panel composition include role (e.g., practitioner, educator, public representative), gender, race, and geographic region. (See Loomis, 2012, for a description of the panelist selection process for the National Assessment of Educational Progress.)

Step 3: Develop PLDs

As noted earlier, PLDs describe what an examinee in a given category should know or be able to do. PLDs expand upon the PLLs and relate directly to the performance standards. It is important that they distinguish clearly between one level and the next, be written in positive terms and clear and concise language, and focus on achievement. The PLDs should be written before the standard-setting process, ideally at the beginning of the test development process so that they are a fully integrated aspect of test design and development (see Bejar, Braun, & Tannenbaum, 2007; Hendrickson, Huff, & Luecht, 2010; Plake, Huff, & Reshetar, 2010; Plake et al., Chapter 4, this volume). Additional information about best practices for writing PLDs can be found in Egan et al. (2012) and Perie (2008).

At the Standard-Setting Session

Step 4: Train Panelists

Although panelists are often sent orientation materials in advance of the standard-setting session, the bulk of the training typically takes place once they arrive. Panelist knowledge of the purpose, design, and content of the test should not be assumed, and this information should be provided during the meeting (Skorupski & Hambleton, 2005). In addition to familiarizing the panelists with the general content covered by the test, the facilitator should have them take all or part of the test on which they will set standards under conditions that are as close as possible to the actual operational testing conditions. After completing the test-taking exercise, private self-scoring of their responses by the panelists helps them gain an appreciation of the level of challenge presented by the test. The concept of a cut score and the actions that will be taken as a result of the cut scores being set in the current situation must be carefully explained. A thorough review of the standard-setting method, with ample time for practice, is also an essential part of training.

Step 5: Define the Borderline Examinee

A key component of most standard-setting methods is the concept of a borderline examinee. As described earlier in this chapter, the borderline examinee represents the person who is just good enough to be in a given performance level. That is, the examinee possesses *just enough* of the relevant KSAs to be classified into a given performance level. There will be a borderline examinee associated with each cut score being set; for example, if there are three cut scores separating examinees into Below Basic, Basic, Proficient, and Advanced, there will be three borderline examinee conceptualizations, one for the examinee who is just barely at the Basic level, one for the examinee who is just barely at the Proficient level, and one for the examinee who is just barely at the Advanced level.

After thoroughly reviewing the PLDs, the panelists should be guided through the process of defining the borderline examinee. The facilitator should stress that the borderline is not the average examinee within the level, nor the best, but instead the one who is just good enough to be classified in the level. A record of the panelists' discussion that contains a summary of the KSAs of the borderline examinee(s) should be preserved; this description should be posted or distributed to panelists for their use throughout the session.

Step 6: Collect Ratings

Once panelists have been trained in the standard-setting method, the first round of ratings is collected. The type of rating depends on the method being used, but in general it is a judgment about the performance of the borderline examinee in relation to the items on the test. For example, in the Angoff (1971) method, panelists provide, for each item, an estimate of the probability that a borderline examinee will get the item correct. For the bookmark method, the panelist indicates the point in an ordered item booklet where the borderline examinee has at least a specified probability (e.g., .67) of answering an SR item correctly or of obtaining a given score point or higher on a CR item. Further information about types of item ratings is provided in a later section of this chapter.

Although the collection of ratings is listed as only one step, ratings are typically provided two or more times during a standard-setting session, with specific kinds of information provided and discussion conducted between rounds (see Step 7). At least two rounds are generally recommended, with three rounds often being optimal (Zieky et al., 2008).

Step 7: Provide Feedback and Conduct Discussion

After ratings are collected, summary information describing the ratings is provided to the panelists. Types of information will vary depending on the method and how it is implemented in a given study (Reckase, 2001). In general, however, three types of feedback are provided: normative, reality, and impact. *Normative feedback* consists of data about the range of the panelists' ratings at the item and/or overall test level. *Reality data* provide an indication of actual examinee performance on the test. *Impact feedback* gives the panelists an idea of the impact of the panel-recommended cut score, specifically the percentage of examinees who would be classified into each performance level if the panel's recommended cut scores were implemented. Timing of the presentation of these data will vary by study, but generally normative feedback is presented after each round, reality data after the second and third rounds, and impact data after the third (or final) round. Research on the effects of feedback is mixed (Mee, Clauser, & Margolis, 2013; Reckase, 2001), but such information is usually seen as an effective means of providing reference points for panelists as they review and potentially revise their judgments (Zieky et al., 2008).

Step 8: Obtain Recommended Cut Scores

At the end of each round of ratings, panelists' judgments are combined to obtain a cut score for each performance level. The manner in which they are combined depends on the method, but in general the ratings are averaged by taking either the mean or the median. Panelists may be shown the overall cut score(s) after each round; in nearly all cases, their recommended cut score(s) are shown to them before the session has ended. It is important to stress to panelists that the outcome of the session is one or more recommended cut score(s), and that the policymaker is responsible for setting the operational cut score(s).

Step 9: Conduct Panelist Evaluations

It is critical to collect feedback about the standard-setting process from the panelists, preferably several times during the session. Panelists are asked to absorb a lot of information and to perform an unfamiliar task; their understanding of what they are taught and being asked to do should be documented. Among the input that panelists are asked to provide on the evaluation form are their views of the adequacy of the training, the time allotted for different activities, their understanding of the rating task, and the feedback provided to them. It is also important to ask them at the end of the session about their confidence in the resulting cut score and whether they view it as reasonable. A thorough discussion of the role of evaluations in the standard-setting process and samples of evaluation forms is provided by Cizek (2012a).

After the Standard-Setting Session

Step 10: Compile Validity Evidence and Prepare Technical Documentation

The standard-setting process is not complete after the session has ended. A key part of the process is compiling evidence to support the validity of interpretations made from the categorization of examinees into levels, and documenting that evidence and other technical information. Validity evidence can be classified into three types: procedural, internal, and external (Kane, 1994, 2001; see also Hambleton & Pitoniak, 2006). *Procedural evidence* includes the degree to which the procedures were designed and carried out in a systematic and thorough fashion. *Internal evidence* may consist of data about the replicability of the standard and intrapanelist and interpanelist consistency. *External evidence* includes differences in standards achieved by different standard-setting methods (if applicable), and the degree to which classifications resulting from the cut scores align with other evidence and appear reasonable. Panelist evaluation data are another relevant source of procedural and external validity evidence. Technical documentation should include summaries of all available validity evidence as well as detailed information about panelist qualifications, procedures, ratings, and panelist feedback. (See Hambleton et al., 2012, for a detailed list of criteria for evaluating a standard-setting study.)

Step 11: Make Recommendation to Policymaker

As noted earlier, the panel-recommended cut score is not necessarily the final, operational cut score. The policymaker has the responsibility for reviewing the recommendation, including validity evidence, and making the final decision. It is important that those conducting the standard-setting session carefully prepare understandable and clear information to guide the policymaker's decision.

Methods for Setting Performance Standards

The choice of a standard-setting method should be made carefully after consideration of several factors. As noted in the previous section about steps for standard setting, these factors include the purpose of the test and the types of items that comprise it, the capabilities of the staff who will be conducting the study and how those mesh with the resources required by the method, and evidence for the validity of the method.

Given space limitations, not all of the available methods are described in this section. The focus is on methods that have been in use for longer periods of time, and those that are currently used most frequently.

Methods can be classified according to different taxonomies. Historically, the simplest classification has been that of *test-centered* versus *examinee-centered* methods (e.g., Livingston & Zieky, 1982). In the former, panelists make judgments about test questions, whereas in the latter the focus is on the examinees. Although this classification system is useful, as methods have proliferated it has become helpful to use a broader schema. For example, Hambleton and Pitoniak (2006) describe a taxonomy in which methods are classified into four types depending on the types of ratings provided: (1) test items and scoring rubrics, (2) candidates, (3) candidate work, and (4) score profiles. In this chapter each method is placed into one of these four categories.

Modified Angoff Method

The modified Angoff method is a test-centered standard-setting approach. It was first mentioned by William Angoff in his 1971 chapter in the second edition of *Educational Measurement* (pp. 508–597), though in a later reprint of the chapter he credited Ledyard Tucker with conceiving the original idea (Angoff, 1984, pp. 9–10). Two variations of the rating task are actually described in Angoff's chapter; in the more commonly used approach, described in a footnote, panelists are asked to estimate the probability that the borderline candidate will answer each item correctly. The method described in chapter text, in which panelists indicate instead whether the borderline candidate would answer the item correctly or not, is a less commonly used variant now known by terms including the *yes–no method* (Impara & Plake, 1997; Plake & Cizek, 2012) and the *item score string estimation method* (Loomis & Bourque, 2001).

The word *modified* is generally attached to any description of the Angoff (1971) method, given its very brief description in the original text. These most typical modifications include many of the steps described earlier in this chapter, such as formulating a definition of the borderline examinee and going through several iterations of ratings, with discussion and feedback taking place in between rounds. For the rating task as applied to multiple-choice items, panelists are often told to visualize either one borderline examinee and estimate the probability that he or she will get the item correct, or 100 borderline examinees and estimate the proportion that will get it correct. In either case the ratings may technically range from 0 to 1, and the panelist's overall cut score is obtained by summing the item-level ratings. The panel cut score is calculated by averaging the panelist cut scores, either through use of the mean, trimmed mean, or median. A similar method may also be used with CR items, where the panelists are asked to estimate the score that the borderline examinee would obtain on the task; in such cases the method may be termed the *extended Angoff method* (Hambleton & Plake, 1995) or the *mean estimation method* (Loomis & Bourque, 2001), depending on the type of rating that is being provided (see also Plake & Cizek, 2012).

The modified Angoff method is one of the most widely used approaches, though since the introduction of the bookmark method (described in the next section), it has been used more in licensing and certification than in educational contexts (Plake & Cizek, 2012). The method also has one of the most extensive research bases (e.g., see Brandon, 2004; Hurtz & Auerbach, 2003). As Plake and Cizek note, "it has been the object of a greater degree of scholarly inquiry, professional scrutiny, and comparative research than any other method" (p. 197). Scrutiny has included reviews of the Angoff method's use with the National Assessment of Educational Progress (NAEP), where it was subjected to harsh criticism as being "fundamentally flawed" (Pellegrino,

Jones, & Mitchell, 1999) for asking panelists to complete a nearly impossible cognitive task (Shepard, Glaser, Linn, & Bohrnstedt, 1993). However, the use of the method in NAEP has also been defended by policymakers and psychometricians. For example, Hambleton and colleagues (2000) presented a rebuttal to Pellegrino and colleagues (1999) and reviewed evidence that they felt refuted the report and supported the credibility of the Angoff standard-setting method as implemented for NAEP.

Bookmark Method

In 1996, Lewis, Mitzel, and Green introduced a "new IRT-based standard setting procedure" (p. 1). The method takes advantage of the feature of IRT, in which the latent trait (i.e., the examinee's ability) and item difficulty are on the same scale (Hambleton, Swaminathan, & Rogers, 1991). In this test-centered standard-setting approach, items (often an intact test form) are ordered by their IRT-estimated difficulty, ranging from easiest to hardest, in what is termed an *ordered item booklet* (OIB). Whereas an SR item occurs once in the booklet, a CR item will occur once for every nonzero score point, along with a copy of the scoring rubric and a sample response for that score point. Also used in this method is an item map—ordered in the same way as the item booklet—that lists, for each item, its location (page number) in the OIB, its scale location (i.e., its difficulty level on the reporting scale), an indication of the item's position in the original test booklet, and its content categorization.

The task for the panelist is to review the OIB, making note of the KSAs required by the item, and to place a bookmark on the first item that the borderline examinee is not likely to answer correctly with a given level of probability. *Likelihood* is not left as a vague concept, but is defined in terms of a *response probability* (RP) criterion. In most implementations of the bookmark method, an RP criterion of .67 is used; that is a 2/3 likelihood that the borderline examinee will answer correctly (Lewis, Mitzel, Mercado, & Schulz, 2012; Mitzel, Lewis, Patz, & Green, 2001). Once the bookmark is set, the scale score associated with that item can be identified. Each panelist's performance standard is obtained by taking the IRT item location value of the item immediately preceding the bookmark (although Reckase, 2006, has suggested using the IRT-based value that is the midpoint between that for the bookmarked item and the preceding item). The panel's performance standard is then obtained by calculating the mean or, most often, median of the panelists' scale score performance standard. There are several rounds of ratings, as with other methods, with normative and impact data being presented between rounds (reality data are already present from the beginning of the method since the items are ordered by difficulty).

Cizek and Bunch (2007) describe several advantages of the bookmark method, including the relative ease with which both SR and CR items can be reviewed together during the session, straightforward materials preparation, and the use of IRT, which is likely employed in the test development and analyses components of the assessment. They also note that the task is likely to be understandable by panelists since it is conceptually similar to judgments they may make on a daily basis. Challenges that may arise when using the method include a mismatch between the difficulty of the test and the abilities of the examinees, gaps in the OIB, and use with field-test data when the operational item parameter estimates may be different and result in a different item ordering. Compared to the Angoff method, research on the bookmark method is rather limited (Karantonis & Sireci, 2006), and one implementation that capitalized on a procedural error raises issues about what the panelists are actually doing while going through the booklet (Davis-Becker, Buckendahl, & Gerrow, 2011).

Contrasting Groups Method

The contrasting groups method is an approach to standard setting in which the rating task focuses more directly on examinees, as opposed to test items; in fact, in the contrasting groups method panelists may not see the test items at all. Instead, using the PLDs, they classify known examinees directly into a performance level. Obviously, in order to do this task the panelist must have personal knowledge of the examinees' levels of knowledge and skill. For that reason, the panelists are generally teachers who rate their students. (The term *panelists* is a bit of a misnomer since the individuals doing the rating are not necessarily convened in person in a group setting.)

As an example, panelists may be asked to place students into one of four categories: Below Basic, Basic, Proficient, or Advanced. Several different approaches may be taken with these ratings in order to calculate cut scores; for the sake of simplicity, calculation of one cut score, the one dividing Basic from Proficient, is described here. The simplest way to calculate the cut scores would be to plot two test score distributions— one for the students placed into the Basic level, and one for the students placed into Proficient. The point at which these distributions cross is the cut score. In practice, this approach may not work if the score distributions are irregular, in which case smoothing of the distributions may be needed. Other approaches are more analytical. For example, the score scale could be divided into intervals, with the percentage of examinees at Basic and Proficient levels calculated; the point at which 50% of the examinees are rated as Proficient is the cut score dividing the two levels (Livingston & Zieky, 1982). Alternatively, a cut score can be calculated that results in the fewest number of "false-positive" errors (i.e., classifying a Basic student as Proficient) and "false-negative" errors (i.e., classifying a Proficient student as Basic) or some weighted combination of the two types of errors; logistic regression can be applied in this type of approach to use the continuous total test score to predict the probability of being in a performance category (Livingston & Zieky, 1989; Sireci, Rizavi, Dillingham, & Rodriguez, 1999; Sireci, Robin, & Patelis, 1999).

Advantages of the contrasting groups approach are that it uses the ratings of panelists about actual students with whom they are familiar. Therefore, it may be viewed as a simpler, more straightforward cognitive task than those involving a probability or likelihood. Also, ratings may be collected before the test is administered, which may be a logistical benefit in terms of timing. Challenges include potential difficulties in locating enough panelists to provide ratings on a sufficient number of students to enable the calculation of a cut score. In addition, panelists' ratings may be biased by the intrusion of characteristics other than KSAs—for example, the "halo effect," whereby a panelist rates a student as Proficient because of likeability or other personal characteristics rather than the student's KSAs.

Body of Work Method

The body of work (BoW) method involves the rating of examinees' work, and does not require personal knowledge of the examinees themselves. This method is best suited for tests comprised mostly or completely of CR items. Panelists are given samples of sets of work from the pool of examinees who took the test, and are then asked to place each of these sets into one of the performance levels. The nature of the placement, or sorting, procedure may vary across rounds. As described in Kingston, Kahl, Sweeney, and Bay (2001) and Kingston and Tiemann (2012), the first round involves rangefinding, in which work samples from across the score distribution are provided in order that panelists can classify a range of work. The second round involves pinpointing, where panelists are provided a set of work samples that have scores in the range of the cut scores determined during the first round of range finding. However, the BoW method may also be implemented without pinpointing; instead, range finding is done during each round (see Measured Progress, 2012). In either approach, once the BoWs are sorted into levels, cut scores are then calculated using logistic regression (Kingston et al., 2001; Kingston & Tiemann, 2012) or averaging techniques (Morgan & Hardin, 2009; Olson, Mead, & Payne, 2002).

An advantage of the BoW method is that panelists review samples of student work, a task with which educators are familiar. It also allows for a review of the overall performance of an examinee rather than focusing on the performance of individual items or sections of an assessment (Hambleton, 1998). A challenge of the method is that it involves a lot of materials preparation, which may be particularly difficult in logistical terms if a pinpointing round is used, since that range is determined during the meeting. However, use of a computer-based rating system can alleviate some of those difficulties (Measured Progress, 2012).

Common Challenges in Standard Setting and How to Address Them

As with any group meeting in which participants are assigned a task, a standard-setting session will likely have its share of challenges. Both thorough preparation and on-the-spot strategies are needed in order to address these challenges successfully. As described in Zieky and colleagues (2008), potential challenges include criticisms of test items, issues with panelists, security breaches, and use of PLDs. Within this section, several challenges and accompanying solutions described by Zieky et al. are outlined.

Criticisms of Items

The standard-setting session may be the first time that panelists see actual test items or tasks, and they are often eager to point out what they perceive as flaws. This can become overly time-consuming and distract from the purpose of the session. Therefore, it is important to clearly describe the purpose of the session in the meeting invitation and during the meeting orientation. The process for test development should also be described so that panelists are aware of all of the quality-control steps through which the items have already passed. It can be helpful to specifically note that panelists understandably often want to discuss how to improve the item rather than perform the rating task, but that the role of the facilitator is to keep the panelists focused on the task at hand. That said, discussion of item characteristics and perceived flaws is inevitable, often occurring right after the panelists have taken the test. Although it is important to give panelists a chance to share their opinions because they would likely otherwise be frustrated, the focus should be directed back to the rating task. Providing a preprinted form on which panelists can record their comments can also help them feel that their voices have been heard and that they can move on to the rating task. It is important, however, to stress that the rating must be provided on the item as it appears in the session materials. If the panelist believes that the item is miskeyed or confusing, his or her rating should reflect that view, unless it is the relatively rare case where the item is clearly flawed, in which case all panelists should be told not to rate it. It is also beneficial to have a subject-matter expert present at the session to be able to answer questions and hear feedback, though again the discussion should be quickly steered away from item critique to the rating task.

Issues with Panelists

On occasion, panelist behavior may present challenges. For example, a panelist may arrive with a predetermined opinion about the test or assessments in general, such as "Tests harm children, and therefore the cut score should be low" or "The country is in decline because children aren't learning enough, and therefore the cut score should be high." Such panelists may be unwilling to follow procedures and fully engage in the task other than to engineer their ratings to achieve a specific outcome. They may do this quietly or attempt to monopolize discussion in order to influence others' opinions. Rather than not understanding the process, they are trying to subvert it.

Approaches to handling issues with panelists must be agreed upon before the meeting starts so that objections cannot be raised that a panelist was treated a certain way because of stated viewpoints rather than a refusal to engage in the process. An advance decision on who has the power to make decisions about how to handle such panelist behavior is key, whether it be a policymaker, the facilitator, or other staff. Possible actions include allowing the panelist to stay but removing the panelist's ratings from the data used to calculate the cut score, or removing the panelist from the standard-setting session. The latter is rarely done, and only when a panelist is being truly disruptive to the process. Excluding a panelist's extreme ratings can be problematic; one way to address this possibility in advance is to use a median or trimmed mean to obtain the panel's cut score. However, it is important to inform panelists of this approach at the beginning of the meeting. It is often the case that a panelist with extreme views will gradually move more toward the mean of the other panelists' through discussion and feedback, rendering facilitator actions unnecessary. It is also important to note that if a panelist appears to be following the procedures but has a different opinion, the panelist should not be viewed as uncooperative, and the panelist's ratings should be treated the same as other panelists'.

Security Concerns

Test security is an issue throughout the test development and administration process, and standard setting is no exception. It is important to stress the importance of confidentiality to panelists, and to have them sign a nondisclosure agreement before they are given any test materials; any consequences of such disclosure should be made clear (e.g., disclosure of secure NAEP materials is subject to a large fine). To help prevent unauthorized removal of test materials, materials should be numbered, assigned to specific participants, and signed in and out at the beginning and end of each day. Materials should not be left unattended, and it can be useful to have a separate room in which materials are locked at the end of each day, with hotel or other location staff being directed not to enter the room.

Use of PLDs

PLDs serve as a basis for the definition of the borderline examinee and are thus a key component of the standard-setting process. Best practice calls for the PLDs to be written well in advance of the standard-setting session, ideally during the test development process, so that the items are clearly linked to the PLDs (Bejar et al., 2007; Hendrickson et al., 2010; Plake et al., 2010). Reviews by stakeholders during the PLD drafting process are also helpful to ensure that the descriptions are clear to those who will use the test results.

The creation of clearly defined PLDs will facilitate their use by panelists; vague PLDs can undermine the standard-setting process. In either case, panelists may want to revise the PLDs and/or have a different understanding of their meaning. Generally, revision of PLDs is not undertaken at the standard-setting session; however, particularly strong opinions on needed changes may be forwarded to policymakers for their review. The charge of the standard-setting panel—to set cut scores—should be made clear at the beginning of, and throughout, the meeting as needed, as was described in the previous section on criticism of test items.

To help ensure common understanding of the meaning of the PLDs, ample time should be taken to review and concretize them in terms of specific behaviors. This point is particularly important when it comes to the description of the borderline examinee, that person who is just good enough to be in the level described by the overall PLD for that level. The borderline examinee description should contain examples of the specific knowledge and skills possessed by the borderline examinee—not vague concepts that can be understood differently by different panelists. For example, instead of noting that a borderline Basic examinee can do subtraction, the description may indicate that that examinee can compute the difference of two four-digit numbers. The detailed descriptions of the borderline examinees should be made available to panelists when they are making their ratings to facilitate maintenance of a common understanding of what that examinee should know and be able to do.

The Road Ahead

The theory and practice of setting performance standards has evolved dramatically over the last 50 years. One particularly noticeable change has been a shift from norm-referenced standard setting (i.e., basing cut scores on relative performance within a group) to criterion- or standards-referenced standard setting, in which cut scores are more grounded in judgments about the level of knowledge or skill necessary for classifying an examinee into a certain performance level. The practice of standard setting continues to evolve, perhaps at an even greater rate than previously. In part, the evolution appears to center around three enduring tensions in the standard-setting field. In this section, the three enduring tensions are presented and some implications of those tensions described.

Norm-Referenced versus Standards-Referenced Standard Setting

As just indicated, a broad shift has occurred across many applications from norm-referenced to criterion- or standards-referenced standard setting. Previously, it was not uncommon to adopt what have been called *relative standards*. That is, a cut score was established relative to, or dependent upon, the performance of some group. For example, a norm-referenced or relative approach to standard setting might result in requiring examinees to score at or above the 75th percentile, or at or above some number of standard deviations away from average performance on the examination. As late as the 1970s, norm-referenced methodologies dominated as the preferred standard-setting approach; in a 1976 article focused primarily on standard setting in licensure and certification contexts, Andrew and Hecht reported that "at present, the most widely used procedures for selecting . . . pass–fail levels involve norm-referenced considerations in which the examination standard is set as a function of the performance of examinees in relation to one another" (p. 45; see also Meskauskas, 1986).

A shift to what have been called more *absolute standards* (see Jaeger, 1989) has occurred, however, and the resulting performance standards are referenced to a criterion level or anchored in the content standards covered by a test.

At least, that is what we say.

One of the enduring tensions in standard setting appears to be the extent to which there is complete comfort in totally embracing so-called "absolute" standards. Nearly all contemporary standards-based standard setting incorporates at least some norm-referencing influence. These influences are evident in the use of *reality feedback* (i.e., the actual performance of examinees on the items or tasks being evaluated) or *impact feedback* (i.e., typically consisting of information about the percentage of the examinee group that would be classified into a performance level, e.g., Passing, if a certain cut score were adopted). Furthermore, when planning a standard-setting activity, there is routinely much discussion about *when* impact data should be provided to participants, with the realization that providing participants with the impact information early in the process will exert a stronger norm-referencing influence than later in the process.

It may not be possible—or even desirable—for the participants in a standard-setting procedure to be uninfluenced by their own conceptions of norms for examinee performance, no matter how a specific standard-setting process is configured. This might explain why the field of psychometrics continues to wrestle with how best to incorporate norm-referenced information into procedures that are—at least ostensibly—intended to focus exclusively on content considerations. It seems difficult to conceive of either alternative: how participants could recommend standards based on either (1) content considerations without reference to the nature and characteristics of the examinee population, or (2) consideration of the nature and characteristics of the examinee population without reference to test content. Nonetheless, the relative roles and influence of each kind of information continue to be contested in modern standard-setting practice.

Content-Referenced versus Policy-Referenced Standard Setting

Similar to the tension regarding if, how, when, and to what extent normative information should be considered in the standard-setting process, a recent tension has arisen about the appropriate timing and influence of providing policy-referenced information in the standard-setting process. Traditionally—and perhaps admittedly oversimplifying the process—a typical standard-setting procedure is conducted with participants focusing primarily on content considerations and deriving recommended cut scores that would then be communicated to a board, agency, or other policy body that had that authority to accept, reject, or modify the recommended performance standards.

More recently, a trend can be discerned in standard-setting procedures that are being designed to give greater priority to the intentions of policymakers—essentially by reversing the sequence in the standard-setting process such that the policy body weighs in *first*, typically by providing initial boundaries or recommendations for cut scores, with subsequent content-focused panels working within these policy guidelines.

There are several examples of these innovative procedures (e.g., see Haertel, Beimers, & Miles, 2012; O'Malley, Keng, & Miles, 2012; Phillips, 2012). In one of the most commonly used approaches described by O'Malley and colleagues (2012), policymakers first establish "neighborhoods" within which subsequently empanelled subject-matter experts are directed to examine content bands to identify potential cut score recommendations. Figure 3.2 provides an illustration of the empirical evidence (e.g., high school grades, SAT scores) that was used by policymakers in Texas to help

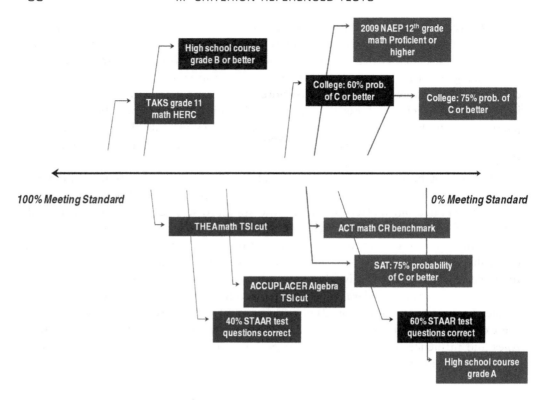

FIGURE 3.2. Evidence-based standard setting.

derive three "neighborhoods" to be used by content panels for recommending cut scores for a statewide testing program.

The chapter describing the method presented by O'Malley and colleagues (2012) is appropriately titled "From Z to A" to reflect the radical reordering of the typical sequence of standard setting. The slate of new standard-setting methods that has been proposed along these lines illustrates the tension related to which starting point for standard setting should be assumed. More research is needed on these emerging approaches to ascertain how well participants in these procedures are able to perform their tasks, as well as the effect(s) of these approaches on the resulting cut scores.

Present-Referenced versus Future-Referenced Standard Setting

A final tension has to do with the temporal focus of the criterion in standard setting. For nearly all of the history of standard setting in achievement testing contexts, the focus has been on the present level of KSAs of the test takers. Accordingly, most of the current standard-setting methods were developed to set cut scores that best differentiated between *current* levels of KSAs within a specified population of examinees. For example, standard setting for high school exit examinations has typically focused on establishing a performance standard for what students should know at a given time point in order to graduate. Standard setting for licensure and certification examinations has typically focused on establishing a performance standard reflecting what a candidate should know at the time of entry-level credentialing. As such, the validation effort for these approaches has routinely—and appropriately—focused on content-based sources of validity evidence.

At least in the context of standard setting for K–12 achievement testing, the focus has shifted in many situations to not only what a student has mastered at a given time point, but has expanded to include the ability to make desired inferences about future performance (Cizek, 2012b). This expanded focus is clearly evident in the assessments being developed by two major consortia (and in many discrete state-level testing programs) to gauge not only mastery of Common Core State Standards, but also to permit inferences based on student performance on those assessments about students' likelihood of success in postsecondary contexts (a.k.a. *college and career readiness*).

This shift to include additional inferential aims that are anchored in the future has substantial implications for standard-setting practice. As a starting point, it is clear that, at least in the short term, some tension will exist regarding which inferential claim should be the primary focus of validation efforts. If the present-oriented claim is privileged, content-based evidence would seem most relevant. However, if the future-oriented claim is privileged, a substantial shift in standard-setting validation would be warranted from more content-based evidentiary sources to more predictive validity-focused strategies.

Conclusion

Placement of examinees into performance levels is a common—and often necessary and desirable—practice in both standards-based student assessment and in licensure and certification. Important decisions are made on the basis of these categorizations, and it is therefore critical that the methods by which the performance standards are set be thoughtfully designed and implemented.

Within this chapter the basic concepts and procedures for standard setting have been reviewed, along with challenges and future directions. Because standard setting is a judgmental process—not a purely psychometric one—it is essential that all aspects of the standard-setting session be carefully planned with an understanding of the many factors at play. The information presented here, and that in the other resources cited herein, can facilitate these efforts.

REFERENCES

American Educational Research Association, American Psychological Association, & National Council on Measurement in Education. (2014). *Standards for educational and psychological testing.* Washington, DC: Authors.

Andrew, B. J., & Hecht, J. T. (1976). A preliminary investigation of two procedures for setting examination standards. *Educational and Psychological Measurement, 36,* 45–50.

Angoff, W. H. (1971). Scales, norms, and equivalent scores. In R. L. Thorndike (Ed.), *Educational measurement* (2nd ed., pp. 508–597). Washington, DC: American Council on Education.

Angoff, W. H. (1984). *Scales, norms, and equivalent scores.* Princeton, NJ: Educational Testing Service.

Bejar, I. I., Braun, H. I., & Tannenbaum, R. J. (2007). A prospective, progressive, and predictive approach to standard setting. In R. Lissitz (Ed.), *Assessing and modeling cognitive development in school* (pp. 31–63). Maple Grove, MN: JAM Press.

Brandon, P. R. (2004). Conclusions about frequently studied modified Angoff standard-setting topics. *Applied Measurement in Education, 17,* 59–88.

Cizek, G. J. (1993). Reconsidering standards and criteria. *Journal of Educational Measurement, 30*(2), 93–106.

Cizek, G. J. (2001). (Ed.) *Setting performance standards: Concepts, methods, and perspectives.* Mahwah, NJ: Erlbaum.

Cizek, G. J. (2005). Adapting testing technology to serve accountability aims: The case of vertically-moderated standard setting. *Applied Measurement in Education, 18*(1), 1–10.

Cizek, G. J. (2012a). The forms and functions of evaluations of the standard setting process. In G. J. Cizek (Ed.), *Setting performance standards: Foundations, methods, and innovations* (2nd ed., pp. 165–178). New York: Routledge.

Cizek, G. J. (2012b). An introduction to contemporary standard setting. In G. J. Cizek (Ed.), *Setting performance standards: Foundations, methods, and innovations* (2nd ed., pp. 3–14). New York: Routledge.

Cizek, G. J., & Agger, C. A. (2012). Vertically moderated standard setting. In G. J. Cizek (Ed.), *Setting performance standards: Foundations, methods, and innovations* (2nd ed., pp. 467–484). New York: Routledge.

Cizek, G. J., & Bunch, M. (2007). *Standard setting: A practitioner's guide to establishing and evaluating performance standards on tests.* Thousand Oaks, CA: Sage.

Davis-Becker, S. L., Buckendahl, C. W., & Gerrow, J. (2011). Evaluating the bookmark standard setting method: The impact of random item ordering. *International Journal of Testing, 11,* 24–37.

Egan, K. L., Schneider, M. C., & Ferrara, S. F. (2012). Performance level descriptors: History, practice and a proposed framework. In G. J. Cizek (Ed.), *Setting performance standards: Foundations, methods, and innovations* (2nd ed., pp. 79–106). New York: Routledge.

Haertel, E. H., Beimers, J., & Miles, J. (2012). The briefing book method. In G. J. Cizek (Ed.), *Setting performance standards: Foundations, methods, and innovations* (2nd ed., pp. 283–300). New York: Routledge.

Hambleton, R. K. (1998). Setting performance standards on achievement tests: Meeting the requirements of Title I. In L. Hansche (Ed.), *Handbook for the development of performance standards: Meeting the requirements of Title I* (pp. 87–114). Washington, DC: Council of Chief State School Officers.

Hambleton, R. K., Brennan, R. L., Brown, W., Dodd, B., Forsyth, R. A., Mehrens, W. A., et al. (2000). A response to "Setting reasonable and useful performance standards" in the National Academy of Sciences' *Grading the Nation's Report Card. Educational Measurement: Issues and Practice, 19*(2), 5–14.

Hambleton, R. K., & Pitoniak, M. J. (2006). Setting performance standards. In R. L. Brennan (Ed.), *Educational measurement* (4th ed., pp. 433–470). Westport, CT: Praeger.

Hambleton, R. K., Pitoniak, M. J., & Copella, J. (2012). Setting performance standards. In G. Cizek (Ed.), *Setting performance standards: Theory and applications* (2nd ed., pp. 47–76). New York: Routledge.

Hambleton, R. K., & Plake, B. S. (1995). Using an extended Angoff procedure to set standards on complex performance assessments. *Applied Measurement in Education, 8,* 41–55.

Hambleton, R. K., Swaminathan, H. R., & Rogers, J. (1991). *Fundamentals of item response theory.* Thousand Oaks, CA: Sage.

Hendrickson, A., Huff, K., & Luecht, R. (2010). Claims, evidence, and achievement-level descriptors as a foundation for item design and test specifications. *Applied Measurement in Education, 23,* 358–377.

Hurtz, G. M., & Auerbach, M. A. (2003). A meta-analysis of the effects of modifications to the Angoff method on cutoff scores and judgment consensus. *Educational and Psychological Measurement, 63,* 584–601.

Impara, J. C., & Plake, B. S. (1997). Standard setting: An alternative approach. *Journal of Educational Measurement, 34*(4), 353–366.

Jaeger, R. M. (1989). Certification of student competence. In R. L. Linn (Ed.), *Educational measurement* (pp. 485–514). New York: Macmillan.

Kane, M. (1994). Validating the performance standards associated with passing scores. *Review of Educational Research, 64,* 425–461.

Kane, M. (2001). So much remains the same: Conception and status of validation in setting standards. In G. Cizek (Ed.), *Standard setting: Concepts, methods, and perspectives* (pp. 53–88). Mahwah, NJ: Erlbaum.

Karantonis, A., & Sireci, S. G. (2006). The bookmark standard setting method: A literature review. *Educational Measurement: Issues and Practice, 25*(1), 4–12.

Kingston, N. M., Kahl, S. R., Sweeney, K., & Bay, L. (2001). Setting performance standards using the body of work method. In G. J. Cizek (Ed.), *Standard setting: Concepts, methods, and perspectives* (pp. 219–248). Mahwah, NJ: Erlbaum.

Kingston, N. M., & Tiemann, G. C. (2012). Setting performance standards on complex assessments: The body of work method. In G. Cizek (Ed.), *Setting performance standards: Theory and applications* (2nd ed., pp. 201–223). New York: Routledge.

Lewis, D. M., Mitzel, H. C., & Green, D. R. (1996, June). Standard setting: A bookmark approach. In D. R. Green (Chair), *IRT-based standard setting procedures utilizing behavioral anchoring.* Symposium presented at the Council of Chief State School Officers National Conference on Large-Scale Assessment, Phoenix, AZ.

Lewis, D. M., Mitzel, H. C., Mercado, R. L., & Schulz, E. M. (2012). The bookmark standard setting procedure. In G. J. Cizek (Ed.), *Setting performance standards: Foundations, methods, and innovations* (2nd ed., pp. 225–253). New York: Routledge.

Livingston, S. A., & Zieky, M. J. (1982). *Passing scores: A manual for setting standards of performance on educational and occupational tests.* Princeton, NJ: Educational Testing Service.

Livingston, S. A., & Zieky, M. J. (1989). A comparative study of standard-setting methods. *Applied Measurement in Education, 2,* 121–141.

Loomis, S. C. (2012). Selecting and training standard setting participants: State of the art policies and procedures. In G. J. Cizek (Ed.), *Setting performance standards: Foundations, methods, and innovations* (2nd ed., pp. 107–134). New York: Routledge.

Loomis, S. C., & Bourque, M. L. (2001). From tradition to innovation: Standard setting on the National Assessment of Educational Progress. In G. J. Cizek (Ed.), *Standard setting: Concepts, methods, and perspectives* (pp. 175–217). Mahwah, NJ: Erlbaum.

Measured Progress. (2012). *Developing achievement levels on the National Assessment of Educational Progress in writing grades 8 and 12 in 2011: Process report.* Dover, NH: Author. Retrieved from *www.nagb.org/content/nagb/assets/documents/publications/ALS_Process_Report_9-21-12_Final_Panelist_Names_Redacted.pdf.*

Mee, J., Clauser, B. E., & Margolis, M. J. (2013). The impact of process instructions on judges' use of examinee performance data in Angoff standard setting exercises. *Educational Measurement: Issues and Practice, 32*(3), 27–35.

Meskauskas, J. A. (1986). Setting standards for credentialing examinations: An update. *Evaluation and the Health Professions, 9,* 187–203.

Mitzel, H. C., Lewis, D. M., Patz, R. J., & Green, D. R. (2001). The bookmark procedure: Psychological perspectives. In G. J. Cizek (Ed.), *Standard setting: Concepts, methods, and perspectives* (pp. 249–281). Mahwah, NJ: Erlbaum.

Morgan, D. L., & Hardin, E. (2009). *Setting cut scores with WritePlacer®* (College Board Special Report). New York: The College Board. Retrieved from *http://professionals.collegeboard.com/profdownload/writeplacer-setting-cut-scores.pdf.*

Olson, B., Mead, R., & Payne, D. (2002). *A report of a standard setting method for alternate assessments for students with significant disabilities* (Synthesis Report 47). Minneapolis: University of Minnesota, National Center on Educational Outcomes. Retrieved from *http://education.umn.edu/NCEO/OnlinePubs/Synthesis47.html.*

O'Malley, K., Keng, L., & Miles, J. (2012). From Z to A: Using validity evidence to set performance standards. In G. J. Cizek (Ed.), *Setting performance standards: Foundations, methods, and innovations* (2nd ed., pp. 301–322). New York: Routledge.

Pellegrino, J. W., Jones, L. R., & Mitchell, K. J. (1999). Setting reasonable and useful performance standards. In *Grading the Nation's Report Card* (pp. 162–184). Washington, DC: National Academy of Sciences.

Perie, M. (2008). A guide to understanding and developing performance-level descriptors. *Educational Measurement: Issues and Practice, 27*(4), 15–29.

Phillips, G. W. (2012). The benchmark method of standard setting. In G. J. Cizek (Ed.), *Setting performance standards: Foundations, methods, and innovations* (2nd ed., pp. 323–346). New York: Routledge.

Pitoniak, M. J., & Morgan, D. L. (2011). Setting and validating cut scores for tests. In C. Secolsky & D. B. Denison (Eds.), *Handbook on measurement, assessment, and evaluation in higher education* (pp. 343–381). New York: Routledge.

Plake, B. S., & Cizek, G. J. (2012). Variations on a theme: The modified Angoff, extended Angoff, and yes/no standard setting methods. In G. J. Cizek (Ed.), *Setting performance standards: Foundations, methods, and innovations* (2nd ed., pp. 181–199). New York: Routledge.

Plake, B. S., Huff, K., & Reshetar, R. (2010). Evidence-centered assessment design as a foundation for achievement-level descriptor development and for standard setting. *Applied Measurement in Education, 23,* 342–357.

Raymond, M. R., & Luecht, R. M. (2013). Licensure and certification testing. In K. F. Geisinger (Ed.), *APA handbook of testing and assessment in psychology: Vol 3. Testing and assessment in school psychology and education* (pp. 391–414). Washington, DC: American Psychological Association.

Raymond, M. R., & Reid, J. B. (2001). Who made thee a judge?: Selecting and training participants for standard setting. In G. J. Cizek (Ed.), *Standard setting: Concepts, methods, and perspectives* (pp. 119–157). Mahwah, NJ: Erlbaum.

Reckase, M. D. (2000). *The evolution of the NAEP achievement levels setting process: A summary of the research and development efforts conducted by ACT.* Iowa City, IA: ACT. Retrieved from *www.ealta.eu.org/conference/2008/docs/colloquium/Reckase%20 MD%202000%20The%20evolution%20of%20the%20NAEP.pdf.*

Reckase, M. D. (2001). Innovative methods for helping standard-setting participants to perform their task: The role of feedback regarding consistency, accuracy, and impact. In G. J. Cizek (Ed.), *Setting performance standards: Concepts, methods, and perspectives* (pp. 159–173). Mahwah, NJ: Erlbaum.

Reckase, M. D. (2006). A conceptual framework for a psychometric theory for standard setting with examples of its use for evaluating the functioning of two standard setting methods. *Educational Measurement: Issues and Practice, 25*(2), 4–18.

Shepard, L. A., Glaser, R., Linn, R., & Bohrnstedt, G. (1993). *Setting performance standards for student achievement.* Stanford, CA: National Academy of Education.

Sireci, S. G., Rizavi, S., Dillingham, A., & Rodriguez, G. (1999). *Setting performance standards on the ACCUPLACER Elementary Algebra Test* (Center for Educational Assessment Research Report No. 368). Amherst: University of Massachusetts, Center for Educational Assessment.

Sireci, S. G., Robin, F., & Patelis, T. (1999). Using cluster analysis to facilitate standard setting. *Applied Measurement in Education, 12,* 301–325.

Skorupski, W., & Hambleton, R. K. (2005). What are panelists thinking when they participate in standard-setting studies? *Applied Measurement in Education, 18,* 233–255.

Tannenbaum, R. J. (1999). Laying the groundwork for a licensure assessment. *Journal of Personnel Evaluation in Education, 13,* 225–244.

Tannenbaum, R. J., & Katz, I. R. (2013). Standard setting. In K. F. Geisinger (Ed.), *APA handbook of testing and assessment in psychology: Vol 3. Testing and assessment in school psychology and education* (pp. 455–477). Washington, DC: American Psychological Association.

Tannenbaum, R. J., Robustelli, S. L., & Baron, P. A. (2008). Evidence-centered design: A lens through which the process of job analysis may be focused to guide the development of knowledge-based test content specifications. *CLEAR Exam Review, 19,* 26–33.

Zieky, M. J., Perie, M., & Livingston, S. (2008). *Cutscores: A manual for setting standards of performance on educational and occupational tests.* Princeton, NJ: Educational Testing Service.

CHAPTER 4

Validity in the Making

From Evidence-Centered Design to the Validations of the Interpretations of Test Performance

Barbara S. Plake, Kristen Huff, Rosemary R. Reshetar,
Pamela Kaliski, and Michael Chajewski

Score interpretations are the foundation of test validation. As specified in the *Standards for Educational and Psychological Testing* (American Educational Research Association, American Psychological Association, & National Council on Measurement in Education, 2014), "Validity refers to the degree to which evidence and theory support the interpretations of test scores entailed in the proposed uses of tests" (p. 11). Therefore, it is essential that all steps in the test design and development process support the intended interpretations of test scores. The purpose of this chapter is to document a process that is intended to (1) build validity of score interpretations into the test design and development process, and (2) serve as a mechanism for validating whether the intended score interpretations can be supported by test performance. We accomplish these goals in two major sections: First, we focus on a process to articulate intended score interpretations through the development of performance-level descriptors (PLDs); second, we present a methodology to verify that test scores support these intended test score interpretations. Both of these efforts were part of the redesign effort for the College Board's Advanced Placement (AP) program. This effort comprised multiple studies. In regard to the development of PLDs, the approach described here was used to articulate PLDs for multiple AP examinations. The AP Environmental Science examination was then used in a second study to examine how well the cut scores set for this AP examination supported the intended interpretations articulated in the PLDs for the examination.

Developing PLDs

If test score interpretations are to serve as the foundation for a validity argument, an obvious place to start building both an assessment and its validity argument is by articulating intended score interpretations. In this chapter we focus on tests whose intended score interpretations are articulated through PLDs (also referred to as *achievement-level descriptors*, ALDs), although the methodology identified could be generalized to other applications so long as there is a clear statement of the intended score interpretations for proposed test uses.

PLDs serve many important functions in educational testing. Primarily they serve as a means for interpreting test scores to help test users understand what examinees are able to do based on their test performance. Another important function of PLDs is in the area of standard setting when subject-matter experts use these performance descriptors to anticipate how examinees are expected to perform on the test questions, which in turn helps inform where to place the cut scores so examinees are appropriately classified into performance categories (see Pitoniak and Cizek, Chapter 3, this volume, for more information on the standard-setting process and its use of PLDs).

Typically, PLDs are determined through judgmental procedures that involve subject-matter experts and curriculum specialists who are familiar with an assessment's context, content, and examinee population. These experts review the learning objectives or standards that form the basis of the measurement targets for the examination program and, through discussion and iteration, identify the knowledge and skills that differentiate performance along the continuum within the scope of the assessment design. For example, NAEP distinguishes performance across four primary categories: Below Basic, Basic, Proficient, and Advanced. Advanced Placement examinations distinguish performance across five primary categories (1 = No Recommendation, 2 = Possibly Qualified, 3 = Qualified, 4 = Well Qualified, and 5 = Extremely Well Qualified). Once PLDs are drafted, there is often a series of reviews to ensure that they appropriately capture the characteristics of examinees in the relevant performance categories. There are multiple approaches for developing PLDs; when PLDs are developed within an evidence-centered design framework, the connection between the PLD and the intended score interpretations is explicit.

Use of Evidence-Centered Design to Create PLDs

Evidence-centered design (ECD) is a test development strategy that takes into account at the design phase the claims or score interpretations that are intended to be supported for the test scores (Mislevy, Steinberg, & Almond, 2003). ECD encompasses a set of practices that are not rote but rather are shaped by the particular circumstances of the implementation. In other words, the particulars of how ECD is used in practice will differ depending on the intended purpose and use of the assessment as well as the constraints of both the development process and the operational assessment. Examples of factors that can shape the "look and feel" of ECD in practice include whether an assessment is being designed from scratch or ECD practices are being incorporated into an ongoing development process, whether the targets of measurement are pre-defined or need to be articulated as part of the design process, the number and type of tasks, etc.

For the purposes of this chapter, examples are drawn from the implementation of ECD for the AP redesign project (Huff, Steinberg, & Matts, 2010). In brief, ECD was a useful design approach for AP to meet three goals: (1) Leverage contemporary research findings about how students learn and incorporate deep conceptual knowl-edge in the design of the assessment, to minimize the measurement of decontextual-ized declarative knowledge and more clearly communicate to teachers and students the targets of measurement for the exam; (2) provide specific guidelines for item writing and form assembly to improve construct equivalence across forms; and (3) structure a comprehensive validity argument to support meaningful inferences from the examina-tion scores.

For the AP redesign process, ECD was implemented as a set of iterative activi-ties that each resulted in useful artifacts. The three general activities were domain analysis, domain modeling, and the development of the assessment framework. The *domain analysis* resulted in an articulation of the content and skills that were valued in the domain. The *domain model* consisted of (1) the claims about students' perfor-mances based on the assessment; (2) the observable evidence (in terms of student work) required to support each claim; and (3) the PLDs, which described how the claims and evidence were expressed across the underlying performance continuum. The *assess-ment framework* was comprised of the task models and form assembly specifications.

The primary purpose of the AP Examination Program is to reliably classify exam-inees into one of five performance, or achievement, levels. Institutions of higher edu-cation make policy decisions about placement and credit based on the achievement levels. As such, AP developed PLDs relatively early in the ECD process for the purpose of informing item writing. This practice is recommended by many practitioners and theorists (see Huff & Plake, 2010, for a review), though implemented by few. Plake, Huff, and Reshetar (2010) provide a comprehensive description of how PLDs were developed from claims and evidence statements for AP. Briefly, claims and evidence statements, which form the basis of the ECD domain model (see Ewing, Packman, Hamen, & Clark, 2010), were categorized according to the score qualification defini-tions that serve as the basis of AP score reporting. The claims and evidence statements assigned to each performance category served as the basis for the performance descrip-tion for that category. The claims and evidence statements also served as the basis for item features that were varied during the construction process to create similar items from a template (i.e., task models; Huff, Alves, Pellegrino, & Kaliski, 2013).

As indicated above, PLDs serve a critical role in the test design and development process. Furthermore, they serve a critically important role in standard setting, where cut scores are determined to categorize examinee performance into the performance categories defined by the PLDs. In the ECD approach to test design and develop-ment, PLDs are developed prior to standard setting and are used to inform item writ-ing; however, the PLDs may need to be adjusted by the standard-setting panelists to focus on the most salient knowledge and skills that distinguish performance for the examinee who is "just barely" achieving each performance level. With ECD the actual methodology for setting the performance standards (e.g., modified Angoff, bookmark; see Pitoniak & Cizek, Chapter 3, this volume, for brief descriptions of different methodologies) will not need to be modified, but, as we demonstrate in this chapter, the strength of the inferences that can be made about student performance when PLDs are used both at the beginning of the design process (to inform test design and item writing) and at the end (to set the performance standards) is a distinct advantage.

Verifying that Test Scores Support Intended Test Score Interpretations

As mentioned previously, in this chapter we present two sets of studies. In the first set (see above), we described how ECD was used to create PLDs for several AP examinations. In this section, we present a study that investigated how well the scores from the AP Environmental Science (APES) examination aligned with the PLDs for that examination.

In any context, once cut scores are set based on the test content and the PLDs, examinees whose test scores fall within the boundaries for these performance categories are given score reports that use PLD language to describe what they know and are able to do. Therefore, in order for these score reports and interpretations to be valid and appropriate, it is essential that the test scores do in fact represent what these examinees are expected to be able to do based on their test scores. There are two sources of invalidity that need to be addressed: (1) Do the test scores for examinees classified into performance-level categories reflect the expectations articulated in the PLDs? (2) Does the test fully reflect the content as represented in the PLDs? A critical but often overlooked step in gathering validity evidence is to examine empirical evidence for the PLDs to support the examination's interpretation/use argument (Kane, 2013).

Context for APES PLD Validation

Beginning in 2011, the AP Examination Program introduced panel-based standard-setting procedures. In March 2011, a panel was convened to create the PLDs for APES that were used as the starting reference point during the standard-setting meeting. For each of the AP scores, a set of nine cognitive processes, six quantitative skills, and three scientific processes that students at that level would be able to demonstrate were identified. The PLDs were then created that combined these cognitive processes, quantitative skills, and scientific processes in meaningful ways to describe what students who scored in the five AP performance categories know and are able to do. The standard setting meeting for the APES Examination was conducted with a separate panel of 15 subject-matter experts who provided recommendations regarding the cut scores using a modified Angoff procedure (Angoff, 1971; see also Pitoniak & Cizek, Chapter 3, this volume). Following the standard setting conducted in June 2011, final cut scores—a minimum number of required points to obtain each of the AP scores

2 through 5—were adopted by the AP program and applied to the main form of the 2011 examination. The scores on other forms (e.g., alternate forms) of the 2011 examinations were equated to the main form, and the equated cut scores were applied to those forms.

This study explored analytical methods and systematic procedures for gathering subject-matter experts' evaluations to examine the validity of PLDs that were created for the mixed-format 2011 APES Examination and used as the input for standard setting on the same examination. This study, therefore, investigated how well test scores for examinees classified into performance-level categories reflected the expectations based on the PLDs. This study served as a validity check on both the PLDs as well as on the cut scores used to classify examinees into these performance categories.

Past Research on PLD Validation

A number of studies have addressed the fundamental question of how to interpret scores on tests in terms of what examinees know and are able to do. Some of these studies use a scale anchoring methodology because, for the tests used in these studies, there are no performance categories to apply in interpreting test performance. In one such application, Gomez, Noah, Schedl, Wright, and Yolkut (2007) used a scale anchoring procedure for interpreting ranges of scores on the TOEFL iBT reading test. Scale anchoring has also been applied to the National Assessment of Educational Progress (Beaton & Allen, 1992) and Trends in International Mathematics and Science Study (Kelly, 2002). Basically this approach looks for items that differentiate performance on the score continuum, identifying items that are hard for lower-performing students but are less difficult for higher-ability students. This differentiation can be quantified either through classical statistics, such as the proportion of students, conditional on scale score, who answered the item correctly, or through item response theory (IRT) approaches, based on item difficulty parameter values at varying proficiency levels. Thus, scale anchoring can be used to create PLDs.

Once cut scores are adopted and applied to an examination, PLDs can be validated by examining the performance of examinees who have been classified into performance categories and verifying that those students are indeed demonstrating performance on the examination items that matches the descriptions of performance in the PLDs (Plake et al., 2010; Schneider, Huff, Egan, Gaines, & Ferrara, 2013). Toward this end, the item selection techniques used for scale anchoring have been applied to examinations with PLDs and cut scores (Kerbel & Perie, 2013). These examinations, however, have been comprised exclusively of multiple-choice (MC) test questions.

The APES Examination used for this study was first offered in 1998. In 2011, over 98,000 students took the exam. A total of 95,642 students took the main form of the APES Examination, and this form was used for the standard setting. A total of 3,914 students took an alternate form of the exam, which is administered to students who are unable to take the main form of the examination due to scheduling conflicts or other irregularities. Items from the main and alternate examination were used to form a pool of eligible items from which items were selected for the PLD validation study. Each examination contained 100 dichotomously scored MC items and four 11-point (0–10) analytically scored constructed response (CR) items. For the main form, one of the 100 MC items was dropped from scoring, so the resulting exam form included 99 scored MC items.

In March 2012, five subject-matter experts participated in a 1.5-day PLD validation meeting. All participants were faculty at 4-year institutions of higher education from around the country and had experience with APES in the year prior to the PLD validation meeting. Two were panelists at the meeting where PLDs were written and at a meeting to pilot standard-setting methodology; two were panelists at the same meeting to pilot standard-setting methodology; and one was a panelist at the June 2011 standard-setting meetings.

PLD Validation Study Design

There are three general steps in conducting PLD validation studies: (1) Prepare materials for panelist review; (2) conduct the PLD validation meeting; and (3) if needed, update the PLDs and/or revise the test design. These steps are discussed next.

Prepare Materials

To prepare packets, exemplar items for each performance category were selected that showed differentiation in test performance across adjacent performance categories. First, items (both MC and CR) were classified into performance categories based on how examinees who had been classified into the five AP score categories (based on their test scores) performed on these items. The statistical procedures for mapping MC items and CR item scores to AP score categories 1–5 incorporated IRT and classical test theory (CTT) methods and are detailed in a paper by Chajewski and Kaliski (2013). The three-parameter logistic (3PL) IRT model was used to calibrate the MC items, and the generalized partial credit model (GPCM) was used for the CR items. Cut scores resulted from the operational standard setting for the five performance levels used in the AP program. MC items were classified into performance categories based on two criteria: location and probability. For the location criterion, items were classified into performance categories based on the relationship of their item difficulty (b) parameter values to the proficiency-based value (θ) of the cut scores. For the probability criterion, a response probability of .67 was employed to determine the θ-value corresponding to the probability of responding to an item correctly 67% of the time. This value was again compared to the θ-based cut score to assign the MC item to a performance category.

When items were reviewed for selection to be considered by the PLD review committee, MC items were denoted as *concordant* if the assignment to performance categories was consistent between the location and probability methods, or as *discordant* if the assignment was inconsistent across these methods. The resulting scale score bundles of MC items contained 43, 43, 21, 36, and 30 items each for AP levels 1 through 5, respectively. Within each bundle, MC items were given psychometric recommendations of "preferred," "OK," or "not preferred." The criteria for these recommendations were based on the IRT probability and location classifications combined with CTT percent correct statistics (Chajewski & Kaliski, 2013). From the subset of items that showed promising differentiation in performance across adjacent performance categories, 15 items from each bundle were selected by an environmental science expert to ensure full coverage of the content specifications within each performance category.

For the CR items, the information for panelists included the number of score points most likely to be obtained by examinees at each AP score level, along with notation of which rubric points test takers at each level most often obtained. The methodology to determine the number of score points most likely for each AP level are described next.

For each CR item, each score point was given a theta value based on the calibrations from the GPCM. It should be noted that the APES Examination is comprised of four CR items, each of which has an analytical scoring rubric. Similar to the MC classification process, both location and probability criteria were applied to these score points for each of the four CR items. In addition, a third approach was used based on the item's step function. The corresponding location of the probability maximum was classified using the AP cut score theta intervals in the same fashion as the MC location parameter was used. For the step function approach, the region across the θ scale where the item characteristic curve (ICC) of each response option had the highest probability was determined. This region was referred to as the step for that score point and evaluated in conjunction with the theta ranges for each AP score 1 through 5 (see Figure 4.1). From the step function procedure, a score can be classified as (1) "complete inclusion" when it is associated with one and only one specific AP performance category; or (2) "majority membership" if the step function covers multiple AP performance categories—then the one for which the majority of the step function falls into would be designated as the performance category for that score point. Whereas some scores may be unclassifiable under the inclusion criterion, because their intervals cross AP cut score boundaries, the majority membership method will always provide a classification. After CR score values were assigned to score categories, they were then designated as *concordant* or *location*. If a CR item score was concordantly classified to an AP scale score by the location method and the majority step function criterion, the item score was said to be concordant. If a given score point on a CR item did not have a step in the step function (i.e., did not occupy any unique place along the latent trait scale), the score point was classified solely based on the *location* method.

To determine which score points were most likely at each PLD level (1–5), responses from 300 examinees were rescored for each item. Scorers noted which rubric points each examinee received. Frequency data were analyzed to determine the relative difficulty of the individual rubric points. This information was combined with the classification information described above to prepare materials for the panelists' review.

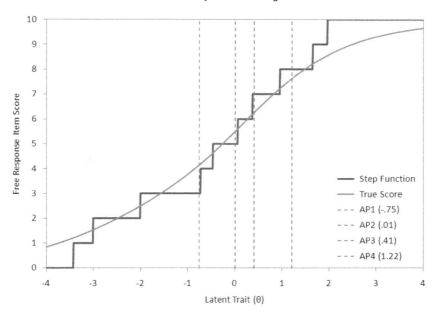

FIGURE 4.1. Main form CR question four-step function for free response item scores.

Conduct the PLD Review Meeting

The MC item bundles and the CR information described above were reviewed by the five subject-matter experts. At the meeting panelists worked on one PLD level at a time in order of highest (5) to lowest (1). For each PLD level, they first worked individually and reviewed each MC and CR item. Panelists were given worksheets with the list of items by PLD level, and space to note for each item whether they agreed that the MC item or CR item score point was represented by the PLD in which it was classified. If yes, they were asked to note which aspect of the PLD showed evidence of alignment. They were also given space for other comments. Each panelist kept a list of items that were marked "no" for revisiting later in the meeting. At that time, they were asked which PLD (if any) they believed the item matched. For each PLD level, they also answered two general questions: (1) Are there any skills/bullet points in the PLD that were *not* represented by this set of items? (2) What are the general skills represented in these items that are consistent with the PLD? Panelists conducted their evaluation tasks independently, and then group discussion about their ratings was held to elicit more detail.

Table 4.1 summarizes the panelists' review results for the MC items. An item was classified as not fitting or "no" in this table if three or more raters thought it did not fit with the assigned PLD. The table notes which skill levels the panelists believed were represented by the items when they were not consistent with their assigned PLDs. Panelists generally agreed with CR point classifications, with 1 point in PLD 2 and 2 points in PLD 1 rated "no."

Category (AP level)	Number of "no" items[a]	Comments
TABLE 4.1. Panelists' Review Results for MC Items (15 per Category)		
5	4	Should be 4 or 3
4	1	Should be 3
3	7	Should be 4
2	9	Most should be 3, a couple 2
1	9	Should be 2

[a]Three or more raters selected "no."

Update PLDs and/or Revise Test Design

A content review of the raters' agreement and disagreement with statistical AP level classifications and their commentary was conducted to determine patterns that would guide recommendations for revisions to PLDs and for improving item writing to target PLDs. A few key points are worth noting. First, as panelists tried to apply the PLDs to specific questions on the APES Examination, they experienced difficulty in applying descriptors that included language that assumes an inherent understanding of student performance over time rather than in one instance on one question. Some examples of this language in PLDs are "struggles to . . . ," "inconsistently uses . . . ," "interprets most . . . ," "usually demonstrates. . . . " It is possible that panelists may have found it difficult to determine the appropriate PLD in a single instance of one MC item, since these terms would be best applied in a frame of reference of how a student would perform holistically on all the MC items of similar difficulty throughout the examination. It should be noted that the PLDs were developed to support both test design and the course curricula. Therefore the language in some of the PLDs is intended to support teachers' observations of student achievement over time, which is consistent with language such as "usually demonstrates," "inconsistently uses," etc.

In other instances, PLD statements were perhaps too broad or not defined with enough specificity for panelists to apply. Language in this category included "use of basic terminology/vocabulary" and "subject-specific principles that relate to foundational knowledge." Panelists would need to interpret what basic or foundational levels were in these cases.

Also, some questions seem to reflect different PLD levels; for example, a question may require a very basic quantitative skill as well as a higher cognitive processing skill. Overall, it seemed some of the panelists may have rated the MC questions only based on the ease or difficulty of the content or concept in the stem of the question and did not include in their rating any assessment of how difficult the associated distracters may be for students. Some specific distracters are included in the MC questions because they are common misconceptions and therefore can influence how students perform on that particular item. Finally, as expected, some specific PLD statements were difficult to apply to any question on the MC section of the AP exam and could be assessed only with CR questions.

The primary utility of the packets of MC and CR items chosen to be illustrative of examinee performance at varying performance categories was to provide subject-matter experts with information about how examinees who are classified into performance-level categories actually perform on the assessment. Because the cut scores that form the basis for setting these performance categories were informed by the PLDs, and the PLDs articulate what examinees are expected to know and be able to do based on how they perform on the test, it then follows to examine empirically the kinds of tasks and items on the test that are representative of how examinees in the performance-level category do on that test. When congruence is found between what is specified in the PLDs and what is seen in the examinees' test performance, validity evidence is provided for the PLDs and for the test. However, when there is a mismatch, then it is important to examine both the PLDs for missing skills that are seen in the items characteristic of the performance of examinees in the performance categories and the test blueprint and development processes to ensure that the test is a valid reflection of the performance expectations as articulated in the PLDs.

This study was the first to use a mixed-format examination in a PLD validation effort. The item selection strategy focused on representative MC items that examinees in the five performance categories were able to answer correctly, or the typical number of score points they were able to earn on CR components, allowing the PLD review committee to consider how well aligned the PLDs were to actual examinee test performance.

Although this study used a mix of IRT and CTT approaches for classifying the MC items into performance categories, it is feasible to do the classification within either psychometric model. In order to address the challenges to panelists in classifying single MC items, panelists could review and give feedback about packets of items that represented what test takers at each AP level "can" and "can't" do. We also received comments that it would be helpful for panelists to receive performance information on the distracter selections.

Since the properties of CR questions and rubrics differ across exams, the analyses and materials prepared for the CR evaluation tasks will need to be customized. For analytically scored CR questions, information about relative order of difficulty for test takers to obtain specific points seemed to be helpful to the panelists in understanding how examinees performed on these tasks. However, many exams use holistic scoring rubrics, so these data are not applicable. In addition, the score distributions within and across performance levels need to be considered in any approach. It is expected that creativity and flexibility are warranted when applying a PLD validation effort with examinations that have CR tasks.

Discussion

In articulating a validity argument, claims are made about what examinees are expected to know and be able to do, based on how they perform on the test. In this chapter, we present two ways to consider validity of score interpretation in test design and development. The first approach is to use ECD to develop the PLDs. By building the intended score interpretations into the test design, a foundation to support score interpretations is created. With the PLDs in place, the table of specifications can reflect the intended score interpretations, and item writers will have guidance on how to develop items with those interpretations in mind. Moreover, these PLDs serve as an important communication device to inform test users how to interpret scores on a test, particularly those that have performance-level categories as part of the scoring paradigm.

Building on the foundations for valid score interpretations from the use of ECD in creating the PLDs, these PLDs will then be used in setting cut scores that are used, in turn, to classify examinees based on their test performance. A critical but often overlooked step in gathering validity evidence is to examine the empirical evidence that supports the claims about examinee performance made in the PLDs. Therefore, the second approach for gathering validity evidence is through examining how well the cut scores support the intended score interpretations.

Taken together, these two approaches bring validity front and center in the test design and development process. Validity is based on the degree to which evidence can be presented to support test score interpretations for their intended uses. In order for test scores to support intended interpretations, the test must represent the construct it intends to measure. This is where ECD provides valuable evidence because the test is designed to support the intended claims about examinee performance. Because ECD is an early first step in the test design and development process, intended score interpretations govern all steps in the test development, from test specifications through test content. By using ECD as a framework for developing the PLDs, there is a direct connection between the intended score interpretations and the articulation of the PLDs.

Then, by using these PLDs as the foundation for standard setting, the connection from intended score interpretations continues to the setting of the cut scores that determine performance category assignments of examinees. Closing the loop on test interpretations then results from examining whether these score interpretations are empirically supported by connecting examinee performance with the intended score interpretations articulated by the PLDs. By using this comprehensive application of ECD from the beginning stages of test design and development, through the generation of PLDs that are used consistently in setting cut scores, and then through a validation process of these cut scores, a coherent argument to support the intended interpretations of test score can be articulated. Thus, through this systematic process, making an argument for validity is the overriding consideration throughout the test design and implementation, thereby supporting the score interpretations for their intended use.

REFERENCES

American Educational Research Association, American Psychological Association, & National Council on Measurement in Education. (2014). *Standards for educational and psychological testing.* Washington, DC: Authors.

Angoff, W. H. (1971). Scales, norms, and equivalent scores. In R. L. Thorndike (Ed.), *Educational measurement* (2nd ed., pp. 508–560). Washington, DC: American Council on Education.

Beaton, A. E., & Allen, N. L. (1992). Interpreting scales through scale anchoring. *Journal of Educational Statistics, 17,* 191–204.

Chajewski, M., & Kaliski, P. K. (2013, April). *Item selection methodology for validation of scale score performance level descriptors.* Paper presented at the annual meeting of the National Council on Measurement in Education, San Francisco, CA.

Ewing, M., Packman, S., Hamen, C., & Clark, A. (2010). Representing targets of measurement. *Applied Measurement in Education, 23,* 325–341.

Gomez, P. G., Noah, A., Schedl, M., Wright, C., & Yolkut, A. (2007). Proficiency descriptors based on a scale-anchoring study of the new TOEFL iBT reading test. *Language Testing, 24*(3), 417–444.

Huff, K. L., Alves, C., Pellegrino, J., & Kaliski, P. (2013). Using evidence-centered design task models in automatic item generation. In M. Gierl & T. Haladyna (Eds.), *Automatic item generation* (pp. 102–118). New York: Informa UK Limited.

Huff, K. L., & Plake, B. S. (2010). Innovations in setting performance standards for K–12 test-based accountability. *Measurement: Interdisciplinary Research and Perspective, 8*(2), 130–144.

Huff, K. L., Steinberg, L., & Matts, T. (2010). The promises and challenges of implementing evidence-centered design in large-scale assessment. *Applied Measurement in Education, 23*(4), 310–324.

Kane, M. T. (2013). Validating the interpretations and uses of test scores. *Journal of Educational Measurement, 50*(1), 1–73.

Kelly, E. (2002). Application of the scale anchoring method to interpret the TIMSS achievement scales. In D. F. Robitaille & A. E. Beaton (Eds.), *Secondary analysis of the TIMSS data* (pp. 375–390). London: Kluwer Academic.

Kerbel, A., & Perie, M. (2013, April). *One year after standard setting: Validating the PLDs.* Paper presented at the annual meeting of the National Council on Measurement in Education in San Francisco, CA.

Mislevy, R. J., Steinberg, L. S., & Almond, R. G. (2003). On the structure of educational assessments. *Measurement: Interdisciplinary Research and Perspectives, 1,* 3–7.

Plake, B. S., Huff, K., & Reshetar, R. (2010). Evidence-centered assessment design as a foundation for achievement-level descriptor development and for standard setting. *Applied Measurement in Education, 23*(4), 342–357.

Schneider, M. C., Huff, K. L., Egan, K. L., Gaines, M., & Ferrara, S. (2013). Relationships among item cognitive complexity, contextual demands, and item difficulty: Implications for achievement-level descriptors. *Educational Assessment, 18*(2), 99–121.

CHAPTER 5

Decision Consistency

Kyung (Chris) T. Han and Lawrence M. Rudner

When a test is based on a continuous scale or a discrete interval scale, the consistency of the test score can be explained under the concept of test reliability. In classical test theory (CTT), an individual's observed test score (X) is defined as the sum of his/her true score (T) and an error term (E), and the test reliability index typically is defined by the correlation of X and T (ρ_{XT}). The term *true score* (T) in CTT, despite how it may sound, has little bearing on an individual's trait but is simply an expected value (= mean)[1] of an individual's score distribution when the individual is tested repeatedly with a large number of strictly parallel test forms. This is just a conceptual definition of T, however, and not observable in practice. Repeatedly testing the same individual with a large number of strictly parallel test forms is impossible in the real world, and is simply treated as a mathematical abstract (Lord, 1980). Rather, the test reliability index is computed as $\sqrt{\rho_{XX'}}$, where X' is an observed score from a test form that is strictly parallel to X (see Allen & Yen, 1979, for details).

There are many types of tests that involve different decisions based on their scores: for example, pass–fail (e.g., credentialing exams), accept–reject (e.g., admissions tests and recruiting tests), diagnosed–none (e.g., mental health tests), mastery–nonmastery (e.g., certification exams), proficiency profiles (e.g., educational tests), personality profiles (e.g., psychological tests), and others. When a test score is used as the sole criterion to decide an examinee's classification with a cut score(s)—as in a criterion-referenced test (CRT)—or when the ultimate outcome itself is an examinee's classification, as in the measurement decision theory (Rudner, 2009), the concept of *test reliability* is viewed under the notion of *decision consistency* or *classification consistency*

---

[1] Another way to view the true score is to define it as an unknown, not directly observable latent trait with a fixed parameter value. This view is more common in modern test theories based on item response theory (IRT).

(Hambleton & Novick, 1973; American Educational Research Association, American Psychological Association, & National Council of Measurement in Education [AERA, APA, & NCME], 2014).

Like the concept of test reliability in CTT, the most direct approach for measuring decision consistency is to administer parallel tests to the same individuals and then to evaluate the level of congruence in decisions across two administrations. Hambleton and Novick (1973) first proposed such an approach. As Table 5.1 illustrates, in a test designed to make a mastery–nonmastery decision for a certification purpose, the observed proportion of agreement P is the sum of the percentage of examinees who were classified as master (p_{11}) or nonmaster (p_{00}) based on both test forms X and X'. In the example shown in Table 5.1, $P = 0.45 + 0.35 = 0.80$. When there are more than two categories, the observed proportion of agreement P is the sum of all percentage values on the diagonal, which can be expressed simply as

$$P = \sum_{i=0}^{k-1} p_{ii} \tag{5.1}$$

where k is the number of categories.

Swaminathan, Hambleton, and Algina (1974) pointed out, however, that the observed proportion of agreement P did not separate out the percentage of examinees classified into the same category just by chance. They suggested using Cohen's (1960) kappa (κ) coefficient to remove the chance effect from P and to filter in only the contribution of the test to decision consistency measure. The mathematical expression of Cohen's coefficient κ is as follows:

$$\kappa = \frac{P - P_s}{1 - P_s} \tag{5.2}$$

where

$$P_s = \sum_{i=0}^{k-1} p_{i \cdot} p_{\cdot i} \tag{5.3}$$

In Table 5.1, $P_s = 0.5 \cdot 0.4 + 0.5 \cdot 0.6 = 0.5$, and, therefore, $\kappa = (0.8 - 0.5)/(1 - 0.5) = 0.6$.

TABLE 5.1. Illustration of Decisions Involving Two Categories		Test X		Marginal proportion
		Master	Nonmaster	
Test X'	Master	0.45 (p_{11})	0.15 (p_{01})	0.60 ($p_{\cdot 1}$)
	Nonmaster	0.05 (p_{10})	0.35 (p_{00})	0.40 ($p_{\cdot 0}$)
Marginal proportion		0.50 ($p_{1 \cdot}$)	0.50 ($p_{0 \cdot}$)	1.00 ($p_{\cdot \cdot}$)

The proportion of agreement P and Cohen's κ are closely related because κ is essentially a function of P given the proportion of chance agreement. An increase or decrease in P, however, does not necessarily translate directly into κ. As the literature suggests, there are several factors that can heavily influence each index differently— for example, test length, location of cut score, and score variability. Berk (1980), in his discussion on P and κ, pointed out that κ was too sensitive and increased with test length and test variability, and could result in an index value that might be misleading or too complex to interpret and understand intuitively. More importantly, κ's correction for chance assumes that the rates of two decision categories across the two test administrations stay exactly the same. Although this might be a reasonable assumption for some test applications where the rates of categorical decisions are fixed—for example, the top 20% of test takers are classified as "pass" and the bottom 80% are classified as "fail" in every administration—the correction for chance makes little sense when the proportion of decision categories varies across test administration, as occurs in typical CRT (Berk, 1980; Livingston & Wingersky, 1979). Therefore, choosing between P and κ as an index of decision consistency should ultimately be based on how cut scores are derived and interpreted. Berk suggested that test developers provide all available information, such as test length, cut score, and proportions of decision categories, as well as decision consistency indices.

Once P or κ is chosen as the decision consistency index, the next step is deciding how to compute the index. The most direct approach for computing P and κ is to observe frequencies of decision categories from two test administrations to the exact same test-taker group as described in Hambleton and Novick (1973) and Swaminathan and colleagues (1974). The direct observation approach, however, is neither practical nor completely feasible for most operational test programs because of the requirement for two test administrations. Instead, more practical approaches have been developed to estimate the decision consistency indices based on a single test administration. The following sections of this chapter briefly describe CTT-based methods to estimate decision consistency indices with a single test administration, as well as other methods based on item response theory (IRT). The latter part of this chapter covers measurement decision theory (MDT), which, by design, yields the test outcome that is of categorical decision without setting a cut score(s). Lastly, we compare the CTT, IRT, and MDT-based methods for computing decision consistency via a simulation study.

CTT Approaches

With a given cut score C, Equation 5.1 can be rewritten using the probability term instead of observed proportions of frequencies:

$$\text{Prob}_c = \frac{\sum_{i=1}^{M} \text{Prob}_c^{(i)}}{M} \tag{5.4}$$

where M is the number of test takers and $\text{Prob}_c^{(i)}$ is the coefficient of agreement for person i, which can be expressed as

$$\text{Prob}_c^{(i)} = \text{Prob}(X_i \geq C, X_i' \geq C) + \text{Prob}(X_i < C, X_i' < C) \tag{5.5}$$

By assuming that X and X' for each person i are independently distributed and are identically binomial in form, Subkoviak (1976) showed that Equation 5.5 can be simplified further to

$$\text{Prob}_c^{(i)} = [\text{Prob}(X_i \geq C)]^2 + [1 - \text{Prob}(X_i \geq C)]^2 \tag{5.6}$$

where

$$\text{Prob}(X_i \geq C) = \sum_{X_i=C}^{n} \binom{n}{X_i} \theta_i^{X_i} (1-\theta_i)^{n-X_i} \tag{5.7}$$

with n being the total number of items (i.e., test length) and θ_i being person i's true score (i.e., true probability of answering each item correctly, assuming all items are indifferent in terms of probability). For estimating θ_i, Subkoviak used the regression equation described in Lord (1965):

$$\hat{\theta} = \alpha_{21}\left(\frac{X_i}{n}\right) + (1-\alpha_{21})\left(\frac{\mu}{n}\right) \tag{5.8}$$

where μ is the mean observed score and α_{21} is the KR-21 reliability index, which is

$$\alpha_{21} = \frac{n}{n-1}\left(1 - \frac{\mu(n-\mu)}{n\sigma^2}\right) \tag{5.9}$$

Subkoviak's (1976) single-test administration approach reportedly has a tendency to result in conservative estimates of decision consistency compared with parallel test administration approaches. Lee, Brennan, and Wan (2009) later extended Subkoviak's approach using a multinomial model (Lee, 2007) for a test with polytomous items, and a compound multinomial model (Lee, 2007) for a test with items that differ in the number of score categories. Computer software (MULTI-CLASS; Lee, 2008) is available for the multinomial approaches.

Huynh (1976) also proposed a single-test administration approach using a binomial model. Unlike Subkoviak (1976), however, who used the point estimate on the true score for each individual as the probability for binomial density function, which he then averaged across individuals, Huynh followed Lord's (1965) strong true score models and imposed a beta density on the true score for raw score point x. For the marginal density of score x,

$$f(x) = \binom{n}{x} B(\alpha + x, n + \beta - x) / B(\alpha, \beta) \tag{5.10}$$

where B is the beta function, and its two parameters α and β are computed based on the first two moments of the test score distribution as follows:

$$\alpha = \left(-1 + \frac{1}{\alpha_{21}}\right)\mu \tag{5.11}$$

and

$$\beta = -\alpha + \frac{n}{\alpha_{21}} - n \tag{5.12}$$

The sum of Equation 5.10 below C is the marginal proportion below the cut score, and the sum of Equation 5.10 from C to the highest raw score point is the marginal proportion at and above the cut score. To obtain the proportion of decision agreement, a bivariate beta-binomial distribution with joint density is computed as

$$f(x, x') = \binom{n}{x}\binom{n}{x'} B(\alpha + x + x', 2n + \beta - x - x') / B(\alpha, \beta) \tag{5.13}$$

where x and x' are observed scores from parallel test forms X and X', respectively (Keats & Lord, 1962). So, for example, if the number of decision categories (k) is two, the estimated proportion agreement P (Equation 5.1) can be computed by

$$P = \sum_{i=0}^{k-1} p_{ii} = \sum_{x,x'=0}^{c-1} f(x, x') + \sum_{x,x'=c}^{n} f(x, x') \tag{5.14}$$

Peng and Subkoviak (1980) investigated this using a simple normal approximation of the beta-binomial distributions and found that the alternative resulted in reasonably accurate estimates on decision consistency indices. Hanson and Brennan (1990) compared the performance of the two-parameter beta-binomial method (Huynh, 1976) with the four-parameter version of the beta-binomial approach and the four-parameter beta compound binomial approach (Hanson, 1991). In the four-parameter beta-binomial methods, the beta density function in Equation 5.10 is revised as

$$B^*(\alpha, \beta, l, u) = \frac{(-l + x)^{a-1}(u - x)^{\beta-1}}{(u - 1)^{\alpha+\beta-1} B(\alpha, \beta)} \tag{5.15}$$

where l and u are parameters specifying the lower and upper bound of the beta distribution, respectively (Lord, 1965). In their investigation, Hanson and Brennan (1990) found that the two-parameter beta-binomial models often did not adequately fit to the observed score distribution, whereas the four-parameter model more often showed a better fit.

Livingston and Lewis (1995) proposed a framework for estimating decision consistency and accuracy[2] using the four-parameter beta-binomial model (Hanson & Brennan, 1990). In the first step of their framework, they computed the *effective test length,* which refers to the number of discrete, dichotomously scored, locally independent, and equally difficult test items necessary to produce total scores having the same precision (Livingston & Lewis, 1995, p. 180). The effective test length, n^*, can be computed by

---

[2]Decision accuracy indicates how accurately people are classified based on their test score X, compared to their true classes. The decision accuracy is very important and closely related with decision consistency, but this chapter mainly focuses on the decision consistency.

$$n^* = \frac{(\mu_x - l)(\mu_x + u) - r\sigma_x^2}{\sigma_x^2(1 - r)} \qquad (5.16)$$

where r is the test reliability coefficient. Once n is computed, the observed test scores are rescaled to a new scale that extends from 0 to n^* by

$$x^* = \frac{(x - l)}{(u - l)} n^* \qquad (5.17)$$

This rescaling procedure makes it possible not only to handle tests featuring just dichotomous items but also tests that consist of polytomous items, differently weighted dichotomous items, or a mixture of dichotomous and polytomous items. Based on the rescaled observed scores, the distribution of proportional true scores can be estimated using the four-parameter beta-binomial model (Equation 5.15; Hanson & Brennan, 1990). For each true score level (Livingston & Lewis, 1995, proposed 100 score levels between 0 and 1 with an interval of 0.01), one can construct a binomial distribution with parameters n and t_i, with t_i being the midpoint of the interval. Using cumulative probability distributions at each true score level and the cut score mapped onto the scale of x^*, one can then estimate a conditional distribution of the two-way classification on x and x'. A computer software program, BB-CLASS (Brennan, 2004), can handle both the Hanson and Brennan (1990) and Livingston and Lewis (1995) models.

IRT-Based Approaches

In IRT, person i's latent trait parameter θ_i often is treated as conceptually equivalent to a true score in CTT. If a test score is estimated based on the θ scale, its standard error of estimation (*SEE*) when giving the test items to a random person at the corresponding θ can be computed by the inversed square root of the test information function (Lord & Novick, 1968); that is, $SEE(\theta) = 1/\sqrt{\sum_{i=1}^{n} I(\theta)}$, where $I(\theta)$ represents item information at each θ value.

Rudner (2001, 2005) suggested procedures to estimate expected decision accuracy indices by assuming that the distribution for examinee's θ estimate is normally distributed; that is, $N(\theta, SEE(\theta))$. Based on that assumption, Rudner (2001) computed the probability of having an observed $\hat{\theta}_i$ above the cut score (θ_c) given true θ_i (i.e., true positive probability), which is the area under the normal curve, $N(\theta, SEE(\theta))$, and to the right of

$$z = (\theta_c - \theta_i)/SEE(\theta_i) \qquad (5.18)$$

The true negative probability can be determined the same way by computing the area below the cut score. The sum of true positive probability and true negative probability is the decision accuracy index value. That is,

$$P_A = \int_{\theta_i = \theta_c}^{\infty} \text{Prob}(\hat{\theta} \geq \theta_c \mid \theta_i) g(\theta_i) d\theta_i + \int_{\theta_i = -\infty}^{\theta_c} \text{Prob}(\hat{\theta} < \theta_c \mid \theta_i) g(\theta_i) d\theta_i \qquad (5.19)$$

where $g(\theta_i)$ is the density of θ. For calculating the decision consistency index, the probability that person i falls into the same category on two independent administrations of parallel forms can be computed using $\text{Prob}(\hat{\theta} \geq \theta_c \mid \theta_i) \cdot \text{Prob}(\hat{\theta} \geq \theta_c \mid \theta_i)$ for cases above the cut score and $\text{Prob}(\hat{\theta} < \theta_c \mid \theta_i) \cdot \text{Prob}(\hat{\theta} < \theta_c \mid \theta_i)$ for cases below the cut score (Lee, Hanson, & Brennan, 2002). Thus, the decision consistency index can be computed as

$$P = \int_{\theta_i = -\infty}^{\infty} \left[\text{Prob}(\hat{\theta} \geq \theta_c \mid \theta_i)^2 + \text{Prob}(\hat{\theta} < \theta_c \mid \theta_i)^2 \right] g(\theta_i) d\theta_i \qquad (5.20)$$

Lee (2010) proposed procedures for computing decision accuracy and consistency indices for tests with cut scores that were set either on the summed score scale or on the scale score scale. Lee used the recursive algorithm developed by Lord and Wingersky (1984) to compute the conditional summed score distribution given θ. Computer software tools—Classify (Wheadon & Stockford, 2014) and IRT-CLASS (Lee & Kolen, 2008)—are available to the public for Lee's procedures. Another software tool, cacIRT (Lathrop, 2014), is an **R** package that can handle both the Lee (2010) and Rudner (2001, 2005) approaches.

One IRT-based approach that is becoming more widely used in practice involves construction of a classification decision table (e.g., Table 5.1) based on simulated data. Assuming one knows the θ distribution, a large number (e.g., 10,000) of individuals' true θ values can be generated, following the known θ distribution. A large number of randomly selected θ estimates from real data can be used as well, if available. Then, assuming the availability of item parameter estimates, two sets of simulation studies can be conducted to produce a pair of score estimates on the θ scale for each individual, concluding with the construction of a classification table given the cut scores (θ_c). The decision consistency indices can be directly computed via Equations 5.1 to 5.3. The simulation-based approach is useful especially when the aforementioned analytic methods are infeasible or inappropriate due to, for example, complexity of test design (e.g., computerized adaptive testing), decisions based on composite score scale, and/or violations of assumptions such as the equal item difficulty for CTT-based approaches (Hyunh, 1976).

As Hambleton and Jones (1993) pointed out, $SEE(\theta)$ can be considered in classical measurement terms to derive a corollary to reliability at a given theta value. The standard error of measurement (SEM) is used to describe the level of precision of true score estimates with

$$SEM = S_x \sqrt{1 - r_{xx}} \qquad (5.21)$$

Rearranging Equation 5.21, when a scale has a mean of zero and a standard deviation of one, as is common with IRT scales, reliability at any given theta value becomes (when $SEE(\theta) \leq 1$)

$$r_{xx} = \sqrt{1 = SEE(\theta)} \qquad (5.22)$$

MDT Approach

MDT,[3] a Bayesian alternative to IRT and CTT, provides a model to compute the likelihoods or probabilities of group memberships (i.e., mastery, classification, or latent states) for individual examinees based on their item responses, a priori item p-values conditioned on group membership, and possibly a priori population classification proportions. If the decision rule is to classify each examinee into the most likely group for that individual, which is a reasonable rule, then the mean probability aggregated over each individual's classified group is a measure of expected decision accuracy. Melsa and Cohn (1978) present an excellent overview of measurement decision theory. An interactive tutorial for the MDT model presented in this chapter can be found at *http://edres.org/mdt*.

Often credited to Wald (1939, 1947, 1950) and perhaps first applied to measurement by Cronbach and Gleser (1957), MDT is now widely used in agriculture, computing, and engineering, as it provides a simple model for the analysis of categorical data. Applied to measurement, decision theory requires only one key assumption: that the items are independent. Thus, there is no need for the tested domain to be unidimensional, nor is there any need for examinee ability to be normally distributed. In addition, one can be less concerned with the fit of the data to a theoretical model, as is the case with IRT or most latent class models. Few pilot-test examinees are needed and, with very few items, classification accuracy can exceed that of IRT.

Given these features, it is surprising that MDT has not attracted wider attention within the measurement community. Key articles in the mastery testing literature of the 1970s employed decision theory (Hambleton & Novick, 1973; Huynh, 1976; van der Linden & Mellenbergh, 1978) and should be reexamined in light of today's measurement problems. Lewis and Sheehan (1990) and others used decision theory to adaptively select testlets and items. Kingsbury and Weiss (1983), Reckase (1983), and Spray and Reckase (1996) have used decision theory to determine when to stop testing. Most such research to date has applied decision theory to testlets or test batteries or as a supplement to IRT and specific latent class models. Notable articles by Macready and Dalton (1977), Vos (1999), and Welch and Frick (1993) illustrate the less prevalent item-level application of decision theory examined here.

The first component of the MDT model is the set of $k = 1, 2, \ldots, K$ possible mastery states, that take on values m_k. In the case of pass–fail testing, there are two possible states, and therefore $K = 2$. The second component of MDT is a set of N precalibrated items for which the probability of each possible observation, usually right or wrong, given each mastery state, is known a priori. Individual responses to the set of items form the model's third component. Each item is considered to be a discrete random variable stochastically related to the mastery states and realized by observed values z_N. Each examinee has a response vector, **z**, composed of $z_1, z_2, \ldots, z_N$.

The last component is the decision space. One can form any number of D decisions based on the data. Typically, one wants to determine the mastery state and there

---

[3] Based on Rudner (2009). Russian, Ukrainian, and French versions can be found at *http://edres.org/mdt*.

will be $D = K$ decisions. With adaptive or sequential testing, a decision to continue testing will be added, and thus there will be $D = K + 1$ decisions.

Following Bayes's theorem, the MDT model is

$$P(m_k | \mathbf{z}) = cP(\mathbf{z} | m_k)P(m_k) \tag{5.23}$$

where $P(m_k)$ is the probability of a randomly selected examinee having a mastery state m_k, and $\mathbf{z}$ is an individual's response vector $z_1, z_2, \ldots, z_N$, where $z_i \in (0,1)$ and c is a normalizing constant.

The posterior probability $P(m_k | \mathbf{z})$ that the examinee is of mastery state m_k given his or her response vector, $\mathbf{z}$, is equal to the product of a normalizing constant (c), the probability of the response vector given m_k, and the prior classification probability. For each examinee, there are K probabilities, one for each mastery state.

In the case of two-group mastery testing, Equation 5.23 yields two normalized probabilities for each individual: The first is the probability the individual is a master; the second is the probability the individual is a nonmaster. The key prior information includes the probabilities of a correct (and therefore incorrect) response for each item for masters and the corresponding probabilities for nonmasters.

If desired, the probabilities of a randomly selected individual being a member of group m_k, $P(m_k)$ can be estimated in a variety of ways, including from prior testing, transformations of existing scores, existing classifications, and judgment. In the absence of information, equal priors can be assumed. To be properly applied, however, the use of unequal priors needs to be based on information about the tested individual. Applying group priors to individuals in the absence of additional information is a form of statistical stereotyping. On average, there is an improvement in decision making, but that does not necessarily hold for the individual. For example, consider two groups of examinees in which one group has a consistently higher pass rate. The use of unequal priors would give an advantage to every member of that group regardless of his or her ability or degree of test preparation. The use of equal priors for most practical situations is advised.

Without a simplifying assumption, the probabilities of the observed response vector for each mastery state, $P(\mathbf{z} | m_k)$, can be problematic. The frequency of each exact response vector will be low. By assuming local independence, however,

$$P(\mathbf{z} | m_k) = \prod_{i=1}^{N} P(z_i | m_k) \tag{5.24}$$

The probability of the response vector is equal to the product of the conditional probabilities of the item responses. In MDT, the local independence assumption is also called the "naive Bayes" assumption. Presuming the local independent assumption is true, one can proceed with analysis.

The normalizing constant in the formula (Equation 5.23)

$$c = \frac{1}{\sum_{k=1}^{K} P(\mathbf{z} | m_k)P(m_k)} \tag{5.25}$$

ensures that the sum of the posterior probabilities equals 1.0. Equation 5.25 presents the probabilities of an individual belonging to each group $k = 1, 2, \ldots, K$. That is, the formula (Equation 5.25) yields an estimate of the accuracy of the classification for each individual. If each decision is denoted d_k and code $d_k = 1$ for the most likely group k, and set $d_k = 0$ for all less likely groups, then the expected decision accuracy can be expressed as

$$Pa = \sum_{i=1}^{N} \sum_{k=1}^{K} d_k P(m_k \mid \mathbf{z}) \tag{5.26}$$

Following Lee, Hanson, and Brennan (2002), classification consistency typically is defined as the probability that an examinee will be classified into the same category on independent administrations of two parallel forms of a test. Thus the expected accuracy for an individual is $P(m_k \mid \mathbf{z}) \cdot P(m_k \mid \mathbf{z})$, and using the notation from Equation 5.26, the expected consistency for the test is

$$P = \sum_{i=1}^{N} \sum_{k=1}^{K} d_k P(m_k \mid \mathbf{z})^2 \tag{5.27}$$

Equations 5.26 and 5.27 are MDT corollaries to IRT Equations 5.19 and 5.20.

Examples

To illustrate these decision consistency and decision accuracy statistics, a dataset containing 3,000 records was developed based on the IRT parameters for 20 randomly selected items from a grade 8 National Assessment of Educational Progress (NAEP) mathematics assessment. Two thousand random records were set aside for calibrating the models and the remaining 1,000 were used to calculate actual and expected decision accuracy and consistency. Thetas were normally distributed, N(0,1). The mean a, b, and c parameters were .86, –.10, and .11, respectively. The KR-21 reliability for the validation data set, Equation 9, was .816. The cut score was set at $\theta = -0.295$, which is the 28.4th percentile. The number-correct score corresponding to $\theta = -0.295$ is 11, which was the cut score used for CTT-based approaches.

For the CTT-based approach, the actual decision accuracy of the 1,000 records was computed by comparing the true classification based on the known true θ values and the individuals' classifications based on their number-correct scores. These values are presented in Table 5.2. The decision accuracy of the 20-item test was 0.90 (= 0.593 + 0.307 from Table 5.2). For the decision consistency estimation, four different methods were conducted: the Hanson and Brennan (1990) procedure with the two-parameter (2P/HB) beta-binomial method and the four-parameter (4P/HB) beta-binomial method, and the Livingston and Lewis (1995) procedure with the two-parameter (2P/LL) beta-binomial method and the four-parameter (4P/LL) beta-binomial method. As reported in Table 5.3, all four methods resulted in similar expected decision consistency index values between 0.821 and 0.840. The four-parameter beta-binomial methods showed slightly higher estimates than the two-parameter methods. As for the

TABLE 5.2. Actual Decision Accuracy of the 20-Item Test (Based on 1,000 Records)

		True θ		
		Master (θ ≥ −0.295)	Nonmaster (θ < −0.295)	Marginal proportion
Test X	Master (X ≥ 11)	0.593	0.079	0.672
	Nonmaster (X < 11)	0.021	0.307	0.328
Marginal proportion		0.614	0.386	1.000

expected decision accuracy, the estimates were slightly underestimated compared with the actual decision accuracy, but not by much.

For IRT, because the thetas in the calibration sample were known, it was possible to compare the true thetas against the cut score to determine the true mastery state. The items were calibrated from the calibration sample by estimating theta and item parameters simultaneously with thetas forced to a normal distribution. The resulting calibrated item parameters were then used to estimate thetas in the validation sample. Generated thetas greater than the cut score were classified as true masters. Calibrated thetas greater than the cut score were classified as observed masters. A comparison of true and observed classifications revealed a validation sample accuracy of .88.

Figure 5.1 shows the information function, $I(\theta)$, for the 20 sample test questions. Information is fairly peaked around $\theta = 0.0$ and is respectable for a 20-item test in the −0.5 to 0.5 range. From Equation 5.22, the standard error at the cut score of −.295 is .377 and the reliability at the cut score is .858. With this knowledge, one can expect there to be a high degree of accuracy and consistency. Because of the standard errors of theta estimation around the cut score, however, one also can expect a number of false positives and false negatives.

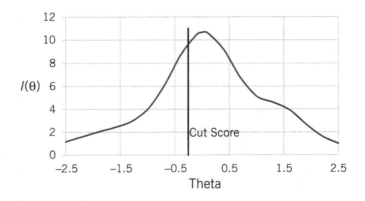

FIGURE 5.1. Information function for the sample 20-item test.

TABLE 5.3. Actual and Expected Accuracy and Expected Consistency for a Sample 20-Item Test

	Accuracy		Expected consistency
	Actual	**Expected**	
CTT (2P/HB)	.900	.876	.832
CTT (4P/HB)	.900	.880	.837
CTT (2P/LL)	.900	.872	.821
CTT (4P/LL)	.900	.886	.840
IRT	.880	.901	.829
MDT	.881	.941	.887

From the results shown in Table 5.3, it can be seen that, for this test, the IRT and MDT approaches were similar in terms of their actual accuracy: The estimated IRT accuracy was close to actual, whereas MDT was overestimated. On repeated trials, one could expect better consistency from MDT.

Summary and Conclusions

One common approach to classification testing is to design a test that measures a broad range of abilities, define a cut score, and then compare individual scores against the cut scores. When the goal is simple classification, such an approach can be extremely inefficient. Items are used to refine ability estimates that are some distance from the cut score.

This chapter outlined three models—CTT, IRT, and MDT—for estimating psychometric data when the specific goal is to classify examinees. Classification accuracy and decision consistency can readily be evaluated in all three models.

For IRT, accuracy and consistency can be estimated from the item parameters, a given cut score, and an expected theta score distribution. This method is extremely powerful. Often the expected score distribution can be estimated from prior experience. Thus expected accuracy and consistency for an IRT-based examination can easily be part of the test design process. A second major application of IRT could involve adjusting the length of a test to meet target expected accuracy.

For MDT, accuracy and consistency can be estimated from a single administration. This, too, is powerful. The data from a single past administration can easily be used to identify the top performing items in terms of their ability to separate examinees into the desired groups, and again, to adjust the length of a test to meet target expected accuracy. We strongly suspect that it is possible to estimate accuracy and consistency from the MDT item conditional probabilities. That task remains open for future research.

REFERENCES

Allen, M. J., & Yen, W. M. (1979). *Introduction to measurement theory*. Prospect Heights, IL: Waveland Press.

American Educational Research Association, American Psychological Association, & National Council of Measurement in Education. (2014). *Standards for educational and psychological testing*. Washington, DC: Authors.

Berk, R. A. (1980). A consumers' guide to criterion-referenced test reliability. *Journal of Educational Measurement, 17*(4), 323–349.

Brennan, R. L. (2004). *Manual for BB-CLASS: A computer program that uses the beta-binomial models for classification consistency and accuracy* (CASMA Research Report No. 9). Iowa City: University of Iowa.

Cohen, J. (1960). A coefficient of agreement for nominal scales. *Educational and Psychological Measurement, 20*, 37–46.

Cronbach, L. J., & Gleser, G. C. (1957). *Psychological tests and personnel decisions*. Urbana, IL: University of Illinois Press.

Hambleton, R. K., & Jones, R. W. (1993). An NCME instructional module on comparison of classical test theory and item response theory and their applications to test development. *Educational Measurement: Issues and Practice, 12*(3), 38–47.

Hambleton, R. K., & Novick, M. (1973). Toward an integration of theory and method for criterion-referenced tests. *Journal of Educational Measurement, 10*(3), 159–170.

Hanson, B. A. (1991). *Methods of moments estimates for the four-parameter beta compound binomial model and the calculation of classification consistency indexes* (Research Report 91-5). Iowa City, IA: ACT.

Hanson, B. A., & Brennan, R. L. (1990). An investigation of classification consistency indexes estimated under alternative strong true score models. *Journal of Educational Measurement, 27*, 345–359.

Huynh, H. (1976). On the reliability of decisions in domain-referenced testing. *Journal of Educational Measurement, 13*, 253–264.

Keats, J. A., & Lord, F. M. (1962). A theoretical distribution for mental test scores. *Psychometrika, 27*, 59–72.

Kingsbury, G. G., & Weiss, D. J. (1983). A comparison of IRT-based adaptive mastery testing and a sequential mastery testing procedure. In D. J. Weiss (Ed.), *New horizons in testing: Latent trait test theory and computerized adaptive testing* (pp. 257–283). New York: Academic Press.

Lathrop, Q. (2014). cacIRT: Classification accuracy and consistency under item response theory. Retrieved from *http://cran.r-project.org/web/packages/cacIRT*.

Lee, W. (2007). Multinomial and compound multinomial error models for tests with complex item scoring. *Applied Psychological Measurement, 31*, 255–274.

Lee, W. (2008). *MULT-CLASS: A computer program for multinomial and compound-multinomial classification consistency and accuracy (Version 3.0)* [Computer software]. Iowa City: University of Iowa, Center for Advanced Studies in Measurement and Assessment. Available at *www.education.uiowa.edu/centers/casma/computer-programs*.

Lee, W. (2010). Classification consistency and accuracy for complex assessments using item response theory. *Journal of Educational Measurement, 47*(1), 1–17.

Lee, W., Brennan, R. L., & Wan, L. (2009). Classification consistency and accuracy for complex assessments under the compound multinomial model. *Applied Psychological Measurement, 33*(5), 374–390.

Lee, W., Hanson, B. A., & Brennan, R. L. (2002). Estimating consistency and accuracy indices for multiple classifications. *Applied Psychological Measurement, 26,* 412–432.

Lee, W., & Kolen, M. J. (2008). *IRT-CLASS: A computer program for item response theory classification consistency and accuracy (Version 2.0)* [Computer software]. Iowa City: University of Iowa, Center for Advanced Studies in Measurement and Assessment. Available at *www.education.uiowa.edu/centers/casma/computer-programs.*

Lewis, C., & Sheehan, K. (1990). Using Bayesian decision theory to design a computerized mastery test. *Applied Psychological Measurement, 14*(2), 367–386.

Livingston, S. A., & Lewis, C. (1995). Estimating the consistency and accuracy of classifications based on test scores. *Journal of Educational Measurement, 32,* 179–197.

Livingston, S. A., & Wingersky, M. S. (1979). Assessing the reliability of tests used to make pass/fail decisions. *Journal of Educational Measurement, 16*(4), 247–260.

Lord, F. M. (1965). A strong true-score theory, with applications. *Psychometrika, 30,* 239–270.

Lord, F. M. (1980). *Applications of item response theory to practical testing problems.* Mahwah, NJ: Erlbaum.

Lord, F. M., & Novick, M. R. (1968). *Statistical theories of mental test scores.* Reading, MA: Addison-Wesley.

Lord, F. M., & Wingersky, M. S. (1984). Comparison of IRT true-score and equipercentile observed-score "equatings." *Applied Psychological Measurement, 8,* 453–461.

Macready, G., & Dalton, C. M. (1977). The use of probabilistic models in the assessment of mastery. *Journal of Educational Statistics, 2*(2), 99–120.

Melsa, J. L., & Cohn, D. L. (1978). *Decision and estimation theory.* New York: McGraw-Hill.

Peng C.-Y. J., & Subkoviak, M. J. (1980). A note on Huynh's normal approximation procedure for estimating criterion-referenced reliability. *Journal of Educational Measurement, 17,* 359–368.

Reckase, M. D. (1983). A procedure for decision making using tailored testing. In D. J. Weiss (Ed.), *New horizons in testing: Latent trait test theory and computerized adaptive testing* (pp. 237–255). New York: Academic Press.

Rudner, L. M. (2001). Computing the expected proportions of misclassified examinees. *Practical Assessment Research and Evaluation, 7*(14). Available at *http://pareonline.net/getvn.asp?v=7&n=14.*

Rudner, L. M. (2005). Expected classification accuracy. *Practical Assessment Research and Evaluation, 10*(13). Available at *http://pareonline.net/getvn.asp?v=10&n=13.*

Rudner, L. M. (2009). Scoring and classifying examinees using measurement decision theory. *Practical Assessment Research and Evaluation, 14*(8). Available at *http://pareonline.net/getvn.asp?v=14&n=8.*

Spray, J. A., & Reckase, M. D. (1996). Comparison of SPRT and sequential Bayes procedures for classifying examinees into two categories using a computerized test. *Journal of Educational and Behavioral Statistics, 21*(4), 405–414.

Subkoviak, M. J. (1976). Estimating reliability from a single administration of a criterion-referenced test. *Journal of Educational Measurement, 13,* 265–276.

Swaminathan, H., Hambleton, R. K., & Algina, J. (1974). Reliability of criterion referenced tests: A decision-theoretic formulation. *Journal of Educational Measurement, 11,* 263–267.

van der Linden, W. J., & Mellenbergh, G. J. (1978). Coefficients for tests from a decision-theoretic point of view. *Applied Psychological Measurement, 2,* 119–134.

Vos, H. J. (1999). Applications of Bayesian decision theory to sequential mastery testing. *Journal of Educational and Behavioral Statistics, 24*(3), 271–292.

Wald, A. (1939). A new formula for the index of cost of living. *Econometrica, 7*(4), 319–331.

Wald, A. (1947). *Sequential analysis.* New York: Wiley.

Wald, A. (1950). *Statistical decision functions.* New York: Wiley.

Welch, R. E., & Frick, T. (1993). Computerized adaptive testing in instructional settings. *Educational Technology Research and Development, 41*(3), 47–62.

Wheadon, C., & Stockford, I. (2014). Classify: Classification accuracy and consistency under IRT models. Retrieved from *http://cran.r-project.org/web/packages/classify.*

CHAPTER 6

Applications of Generalizability Theory

Brian E. Clauser and Jerome C. Clauser

Classical test theory provides a framework for answering practical questions about test scores. For nearly a century it has served as the cornerstone of item analysis, equating, and measures of score reliability. As powerful as classical test theory is for solving assessment problems, the framework is limited because it is based on the notion that observed scores are composed of two components: one representing the examinee's true score and a second component representing an undifferentiated source of error ($X = T + E$). This approach may be completely appropriate in the simple condition in which a group of examinees responds to a set of test items. There are, however, a wide range of practical situations in which this approach is not applicable.

Consider a test in which each examinee completes a set of tasks and each task is scored by two judges. In this situation, the classical test theory model begins to break down. Reliability still may be conceptualized as the correlation between scores from two forms of the test, but the definition of a test form is much less clear. A second form could be composed of different tasks scored by the same judges, or it could be different tasks scored by different judges. Similarly, if an evaluator wants to increase the reliability of the resulting scores, he or she either could increase the number of tasks or the number of judges per task. Because the classical test theory framework does not differentiate between measurement error associated with the judgments and error associated with the sampling of tasks, it provides a less-than-satisfactory approach to this problem. It also is readily apparent that adding judges to the assessment design only scratches the surface of potential complexity. The same two judges could score all tasks, or different judges could be assigned to different tasks. The same judges could score all examinees, or different examinees could be scored by different judges. It even may be the case that different examinees complete different sets of tasks. Each of these choices has implications for the conceptualization and estimation of score reliability.

Generalizability theory was developed to support inferences in the face of exactly this type of complexity.

Generalizability theory is a framework for understanding and interpreting observed scores. The focus of the theory is on assessing the precision of scores, but because evaluating reliability in the context of complex assessment settings requires the evaluator to make thoughtful decisions about what represents a second form of the assessment (or what represents a replication of the assessment procedure), the framework pushes the evaluator to consider precision more broadly, and to incorporate aspects of score interpretation that typically might be considered issues of validity (Kane, 1982). The theory allows the evaluator to understand how different aspects of the measurement procedure contribute to measurement error. As discussed in the previous paragraph, this point has been extremely important in evaluating performance assessments in which expert judges are used to score tasks.

Generalizability theory also provides a framework for assessing measurement error in contexts where the score of interest is for an aggregate examinee group (e.g., a classroom or a school). The approach provides flexible procedures for assessing measurement error when tests are constructed using stratified sampling, as may be the case when tests are built from a table of specifications. Generalizability theory also allows the evaluator to assess error in circumstances in which the value of interest is not a score for an individual examinee or an aggregate, but the grand mean. One area where this approach is important is in assessing the precision of the estimated cut score derived from an Angoff standard-setting exercise (see Pitoniak & Cizek, Chapter 3, this volume).

This chapter clearly is not intended as an exhaustive guide to generalizability theory. Instead, the aim is to provide a conceptual introduction, some analytic basics to support the conceptual understanding, and some examples of less common applications that hopefully will encourage readers to consider how generalizability theory can be used to better understand their own practical measurement problems.

Concepts, Terminology, and Key Equations

Fundamentally, generalizability theory is an approach to conceptualizing and breaking down observed scores into components representing different aspects of the measurement procedure. The simplest model includes the *object of measurement*, which typically is the examinee, and one additional factor (referred to as a *facet*) such as items; each person responds to multiple items. With this model, scores can be broken down into components associated with (1) variability in examinee proficiency, (2) variability in item difficulty, and (3) a residual term that includes the systematic interaction between persons and items as well as the effects of other factors that are not included in the design. As suggested previously, the basic concept can be expanded in numerous ways. One common design includes persons, tasks, and raters. For example, each person completes a set of tasks, and each task is scored by multiple raters. Observed scores from this design can be broken down into components representing (1) variability in the proficiency of the examinees, (2) variability in the difficulty of the tasks, (3) variability in the stringency of the raters, (4) an interaction between raters and tasks (representing the tendency of individual raters to give higher scores for specific tasks), (5) an interaction between raters and examinees (representing the tendency of individual raters to give higher scores to specific examinees), (6) an interaction between persons and tasks (representing the tendency of individuals to perform better on specified tasks), and (7) a residual term that includes the three-way interaction.

In the generalizability theory literature, these estimates of variability are referred to as *variance components*. Variance components can potentially be estimated for each facet of the design and for all of the associated interactions. The potential to estimate variance components depends on the design used to collect the data. Facets of the design may be "crossed" or "nested." For example, if each examinee responds to the same sample of items, the design is crossed (typically written $p \times i$, persons crossed with items). With this design it is possible to estimate the variance components for persons (p), items (i), and persons crossed with items (pi). If each examinee responds to a separate set of items, items are nested in person (written $i:p$). With this design, the item effect and the interaction term are confounded. This means that it will only be possible to estimate a variance component for persons and one for items nested in persons.

Table 6.1 presents an example of results from a generalizability analysis using a simple $p \times i$ design (examinees or persons crossed with items). For this study, each examinee responded to the same set of computer-based patient management items delivered as part of a medical licensing examination. This produced three variance components: persons, items, and persons-by-items. Complete details are available in the original publication (Clauser, Margolis, & Swanson, 2002). Table 6.1 presents results for a "single observation"—in this context, that means for a score based on a single item. This is the basic input for estimating measurement error in generalizability theory. Of course, the variance components of interest are those based on scores produced using more than one item. This adjustment to the variance components for single observations is conceptually linked to a concept from statistics, the standard error of the mean:

$$SEM = \frac{\sigma}{\sqrt{n}} \tag{6.1}$$

TABLE 6.1. Variance Components for Persons-Crossed-with-Items Design

Source of variance	Single observation	5 items	10 items	20 items
Person (P)	0.1917	0.1917	0.1917	0.1917
Item (I)	0.3160	0.0632	0.0316	0.0158
PI	1.0898	0.2180	0.1090	0.0545

or the square of that value

$$SEM^2 = \frac{\sigma^2}{n} \qquad (6.2)$$

This equation links precision to sample size. In a like fashion, the contribution that the variance components make to measurement error varies as a function of sample size. In addition to variance components for single observations, Table 6.1 provides estimated components for tests of 5, 10, and 20 tasks. The table shows that the contribution to error variance decreases as the test length increases. Changing the test length does not impact the estimated person variance component.

Table 6.2 provides estimated variance components for a person-crossed-with-task-crossed-with-raters design ($p \times t \times r$). For this study, each examinee completed the same set of performance tasks (the tasks were computer-delivered patient management problems). Unlike the example in Table 6.1 where the tasks were scored using an automated scoring system, each of these tasks was scored by the same panel of raters. This crossed design results in seven estimated variance components, as described previously: persons, raters, tasks, person-by-task, person-by-rater, task-by-rater, and the residual term. Again, the table provides results for a "single observation"; in this context, that means for a score based on a single task scored by a single rater. The table also presents results for a score based on 10 tasks with two raters per task and 20 tasks with one rater per task. This allows for comparison of the score precision for two designs that require the same number of ratings or the same amount of rater time. For these conditions, the variance components are reduced as a function of the sampling for that component. For the condition with 10 tasks and two raters per task, the task component is divided by 10, the rater component is divided by 2, the person-by-task component is divided by 10, the person-by-rater component is divided by 2, and the rater-by-task and the residual term are divided by 20 (the product of 10 and 2). Similarly, when scores are based on 20 tasks each scored by one rater, the task and person-by-task components are divided by 20, the rater and person-by-rater components are divided by 1 (and so unchanged), and the rater-by-task and the residual term

TABLE 6.2. Variance Components for Persons-Crossed-with-Task-Crossed-with-Rater Design

Source of variance	Single observation	10 tasks and 2 raters	20 tasks and 1 rater
Person	0.5159	0.5159	0.5159
Task	0.4181	0.0418	0.0209
Rater	0.0179	0.0090	0.0179
PT	1.8165	0.1817	0.0908
PR	0.0029	0.0015	0.0029
TR	0.0948	0.0047	0.0047
PTR	0.6368	0.0318	0.0318

are divided by 20 (the product of 20 and 1). More detail about the specifics of the study can be found in the original publication by Clauser, Swanson, and Clyman (1999).

Absolute and Relative Error

Having adjusted the variance components as a function of the sampling design used as part of the measurement procedure, an estimate of the expected error variance for the scores can be produced by summing the individual variance components. The square root of this value is the standard error for the associated score. However, one additional decision is required before this estimate can be produced: The evaluator must decide which variance components will contribute to measurement error. In the generalizability literature, two types of error are commonly discussed: absolute error and relative error. *Absolute error* will include all of the variance components (except the object of measurement, typically the person), and *relative error* will include only interaction effects that include the person effect. In a design in which examinees respond to items, relative error will include only the residual term; absolute error will include both the residual term and the variance component for items:

$$\sigma_{\delta}^2 = \frac{\sigma_{pi}^2}{n_i} \tag{6.3}$$

represents the relative error variance, and

$$\sigma_{\Delta}^2 = \frac{\sigma_i^2}{n_i} + \frac{\sigma_{pi}^2}{n_i} \tag{6.4}$$

represents the absolute error variance. The corresponding equations for the two-facet design presented in Table 6.2 are

$$\sigma_{\delta}^2 = \frac{\sigma_{pt}^2}{n_t} + \frac{\sigma_{pr}^2}{n_r} + \frac{\sigma_{ptr}^2}{n_{tr}} \tag{6.5}$$

and

$$\sigma_{\Delta}^2 = \frac{\sigma_t^2}{n_t} + \frac{\sigma_r^2}{n_r} + \frac{\sigma_{tr}^2}{n_{tr}} + \frac{\sigma_{pt}^2}{n_t} + \frac{\sigma_{pr}^2}{n_r} + \frac{\sigma_{ptr}^2}{n_{tr}} \tag{6.6}$$

respectively.

The terminology suggests the appropriate interpretation of these error terms; relative error is viewed as appropriate for making decisions about the relative standing or rank ordering of examinees, and absolute error is appropriate for making decisions about performance with reference to the sampled domain. In Equation 6.3, each examinee has responded to the same set of items. The assumed random sampling of those items will impact the mean score for the examinee sample, but it will not impact the interpretation of scores used to compare examinees because all examinees have responded to the same items. Variability in the mean difficulty across randomly equivalent sets of items—or, more to the point, a deviation of the sample mean from the mean for all items in the universe of potential items—will impact interpretations in which the test score is intended to reflect the proportion of material in the domain that the examinee has mastered. The same logic is reflected in Equations 6.5 and 6.6. If all examinees are scored on the same set of tasks scored by the same raters, the difficulty of the specific set of items and the stringency of the specific set of raters does not impact comparisons about examinees; there is a level playing field. Similarly, the rater-by-task interaction—the extent to which some raters tend to be more stringent in evaluating some tasks—does not impact the relative standing of examinees. By contrast, if decisions are to be made about an examinee's mastery of a domain defined by the universe of potential tasks and raters, all of the sources of error included in Equation 6.6 must be considered. This potential pool from which tasks or raters are sampled typically is referred to as the *universe of admissible observations.*

Using the equations for absolute and relative measurement error and the estimated variance components from Tables 6.1 and 6.2, it is straightforward to evaluate how the measurement error will vary as a function of sample size. Figure 6.1 shows the absolute and relative measurement error for tests ranging from 5 to 50 tasks, based on the values from Table 6.1. This type of information allows the evaluator to determine the test length required to achieve a predetermined level of precision. Figure 6.2 shows the absolute measurement error for tests ranging from 5 to 20 tasks scored by one, two, or four judges. This figure not only shows the level of resources needed to achieve an identified level of precision, but it allows for comparison of strategies that require more or less testing time as opposed to more or less time from expert judges. Resources are always limited, and the potential to use generalizability theory to assess the efficiency of a test administration design can be important.

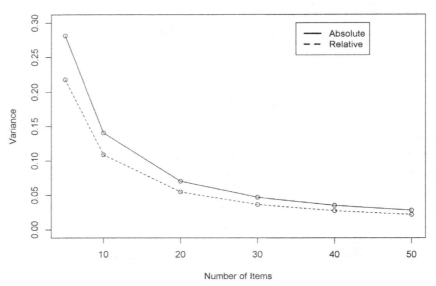

FIGURE 6.1. Absolute and relative measurement error for tests of different lengths.

Error Variance by Number of Items

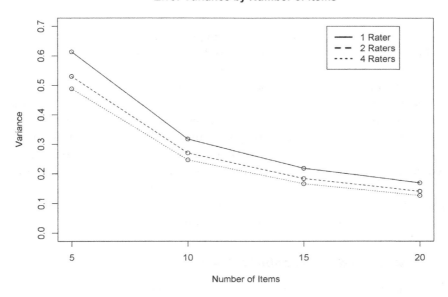

FIGURE 6.2. Absolute measurement error for different task and rater configurations.

Nested Designs

For the results presented in Tables 6.1 and 6.2 and Figures 6.1 and 6.2 it has been assumed that crossed designs will be used. The simplicity of this design is attractive, but sometimes nesting is unavoidable. When large numbers of examinees are tested, it may be impractical to have the same judges score all of them. In this case examinees may be nested in judges. When examinees are tested on different days, it may be appropriate to administer different tasks to different examinees. The concept of nested versus crossed designs has been introduced, as has the concept of absolute versus relative error variance. In considering how nesting impacts estimated score precision, it is worth noting how these concepts interact. As noted, for the single-facet design, if items are nested in persons rather than crossed, the variability associated with item sampling is confounded by the person-by-item interaction and the residual variance. In this case,

$$\sigma_\delta^2 = \frac{\sigma_{i:p}^2}{n_i} = \frac{\sigma_i^2}{n_i} + \frac{\sigma_{pi}^2}{n_i} = \sigma_\Delta^2 \tag{6.7}$$

It should be clear from Equation 6.7 that the term *confounded* is not meant to imply simply that the item effect and the residual term cannot be analytically separated within the data collection design. With the nested design the error variance associated with between-person comparisons is actually larger. It should also be clear that interpreting nested designs requires random sampling. Estimating the person variance component would be impossible if each examinee sees a different set of items without the assumption that those sets of items are randomly equivalent.

G Studies and D Studies

The issue of crossed versus nested designs also provides a convenient segue to consideration of the distinction between G studies and D studies. *G studies* are based on datasets that support estimation of variance components and conclusions about the most effective and efficient designs for collecting data to support decisions about individuals. *D studies* are used to draw conclusions about individuals. In principle, the same dataset can support both studies, but sometimes it may be useful to implement more elaborate data collection for the G study than ultimately may be used for the D study. Depending on the specific conditions, the measurement precision associated with the crossed design and that associated with the nested design may differ. If G study data were collected with a crossed design, it will be possible to estimate the expected D study measurement precision for either design. If the data were collected with a nested design, the expected precision with a crossed design will not be known.

Generalizability and Dependability Coefficients

To this point much of the conceptual essence of generalizability theory has been described. One aspect that has not been described is the concept of *generalizability coefficients*. This is a concept that connects generalizability theory to much of the early history of both statistics and test theory. The generalizability coefficient provides an estimate of the squared correlation between the observed score and the universe score. The *universe score* is the score that an examinee would be expected to receive if the samples were infinite—that is, if the examinee's score were measured without error. This score is conceptually similar to the concept of true score in classical test theory. This coefficient also provides an estimate of the correlation between two independent measurement events based on sampling from the same universe of admissible observations. For the person-by-items design, the generalizability coefficient takes the following form:

$$E\hat{\rho}^2 = \frac{\sigma^2(p)}{\sigma^2(p) + \sigma^2(pi) / n_i} \tag{6.8}$$

With this design, the generalizability coefficient directly parallels the true-score theory framework for reliability. Gulliksen (1950, p. 23) defines the correlation between the observed score and true score as

$$r_{xt} = \frac{s_t}{s_x} \tag{6.9}$$

Because $s_x^2 = s_t^2 + s_e^2$, squaring both sides of Equation 6.9 produces

$$r_{xt}^2 = \frac{s_t^2}{s_t^2 + s_e^2} \tag{6.10}$$

This direct parallel with true score theory only holds for the simple, one-facet design. For example, with the two-facet design discussed previously, the generalizability coefficient is

$$E\hat{\rho}^2 = \frac{\sigma^2(p)}{\sigma^2(p) + \dfrac{\sigma^2_{pt}}{n_t} + \dfrac{\sigma^2_{pr}}{n_r} + \dfrac{\sigma^2_{ptr}}{n_{tr}}} \tag{6.11}$$

More generally, the coefficient can be defined as

$$E\hat{\rho}^2 = \frac{\sigma^2(p)}{\sigma^2(p) + \sigma^2(\delta)} \tag{6.12}$$

As is evident in Equation 6.12, the error term in the generalizability coefficient represents relative error. In keeping with the distinction between absolute and relative measurements, generalizability theory also provides a coefficient based on absolute error. This is referred to as the *dependability coefficient* and is defined as

$$\Phi = \frac{\sigma^2(p)}{\sigma^2(p) + \sigma^2(\Delta)} \tag{6.13}$$

These coefficients are important because they provide a direct conceptual link to the true score theory framework, but as Cronbach, Linn, Brennan, and Haertel (1997) point out, they are not as directly useful in interpreting scores as are the related estimates of the standard error.

Variance Components

The definitions and equations that have been presented so far provide much of the basis for generalizability theory, but some comment about the definition of variance components is needed (although some readers certainly will be familiar with the concept from the study of statistics). Keeping this discussion at the conceptual level, first it is necessary to understand that although the variance component for persons and the variance of person mean scores are related, they are not the same. Based on the equations provided by Brennan (2001a, pp. 26–27), the estimate of the variance component for persons in the persons-by-items design is

$$\hat{\sigma}^2(p) = \frac{MS(p) - MS(pi)}{n_i} \tag{6.14}$$

where p represents persons, i represents items, and MS refers to mean square. The variance component for the residual is

$$\hat{\sigma}^2(pi) = MS(pi) \tag{6.15}$$

and the mean square for persons is the variance of the person means

$$MS(p) = \frac{n_i \sum_p (\bar{X}_p - \bar{X})^2}{n_p - 1} \tag{6.16}$$

Substituting Equations 6.15 and 6.16 into Equation 6.14 results in

$$\hat{\sigma}^2(p) = \frac{\sum_p (\overline{X}_{pi} - \overline{X})^2}{n_p - 1} - \frac{\hat{\sigma}^2(pi)}{n_{ij}} \tag{6.17}$$

So it is apparent that the variance component for persons (or by extension, for any other effect) will be smaller than the estimated variance of the means for that effect. This is because the variance of the observed means will include the impact of additional random error; the variance component is an estimate of the variability of the expected mean scores measured without sampling error.

The estimated variance components that form the basis for generalizability theory are defined in the framework of analysis-of-variance procedures. They do not, however, require the distributional assumptions that support significance testing within that framework. Generalizability theory does assume random sampling. This is a much weaker assumption, but strictly speaking, it often may be far-fetched. The theoretical universe often consists of tasks that could be developed using the guidelines that were used to develop the specific tasks that were used in the analysis. As during the developmental phase of an assessment program, these tasks may be the only ones that exist, and they clearly were not selected randomly from an infinite universe. The credibility of this approach rests on the credibility of the belief that the initial tasks, developed as part of a pilot project, will be representative of the complete pool of tasks that would subsequently support operational testing.

Table 6.3 presents the equations for variance components for the persons-by-items design and for the persons-by-task-by-raters design. These equations are based on the typical sums-of-squares equations that are the basis for analysis of variance; the table also includes the equations for sums of squares required for the same designs. These

TABLE 6.3. Variance Components Equations

Source of variance	Sums of squares	Expected mean squares
Person	$T(p) - T(\mu)$	$\sigma^2(pi) + n_i\sigma^2(p)$
Item	$T(i) - T(\mu)$	$\sigma^2(pi) + n_p\sigma^2(i)$
PI	$T(pi) - T(p) - T(i) - T(\mu)$	$\sigma^2(pi)$
Person	$T(p) - T(\mu)$	$\sigma^2(ptr) + n_r\sigma^2(pr) + n_r\sigma^2(pt) + n_t n_r\sigma^2(p)$
Task	$T(t) - T(\mu)$	$\sigma^2(ptr) + n_p\sigma^2(tr) + n_r\sigma^2(pt) + n_p n_r\sigma^2(t)$
Rater	$T(r) - T(\mu)$	$\sigma^2(ptr) + n_p\sigma^2(tr) + n_t\sigma^2(pr) + n_p n_t\sigma^2(r)$
PT	$T(pt) - T(p) - T(t) - T(\mu)$	$\sigma^2(ptr) + n_r\sigma^2(pt)$
PR	$T(pr) - T(p) - T(r) - T(\mu)$	$\sigma^2(ptr) + n_t\sigma^2(pr)$
TR	$T(tr) - T(t) - T(r) - T(\mu)$	$\sigma^2(ptr) + n_p\sigma^2(tr)$
PTR	$T(ptr) - T(pt) - T(pr) - T(tr) + T(p) + T(t) + T(r) - T(\mu)$	$\sigma^2(ptr)$

provide an example; tables with additional designs are available in Brennan (2001a). Estimation of variance components is easily accomplished using specialized software. Brennan has provided a suite of programs for this purpose; mGENOVA is the most widely applicable (Brennan, 2001b). The EDUG software provides a potentially useful alternative. It is also possible to estimate variance components using many of the currently popular statistical software packages.

To this point much of the conceptual basis of generalizability theory has been covered. The chapter continues with brief presentations on the application of generalizability theory to two settings that go beyond simply examining the precision of a test score. The first of these applications is evaluating the stability of results from a standard-setting exercise; the second describes the extension of univariate generalizability theory to multivariate applications.

Evaluating Standard-Setting Results within a Generalizability Theory Framework

One essential part of the validity argument for tests that are used to make classification decisions is evidence to support the credibility of the cut score. A central part of that argument is evidence that if the standard-setting procedure was replicated, the results would be similar across replications. As Kane (2001) stated, "No matter how well designed the standard setting study and no matter how carefully implemented, we are not likely to have much faith in the outcome if we know that the results would be likely to be very different if the study were repeated" (pp. 70–71). Generalizability theory provides a useful framework for evaluating the stability or replicability of estimated cut scores (e.g., Brennan, 1995; Camilli, Cizek, & Lugg, 2001; Clauser, et al., 2009; Hambleton, Pitoniak, & Copella, 2012; Kane, 2001). The examples discussed in this chapter focus on evaluating the results of standard-setting exercises that use the Angoff method, although the analytic approach may be more broadly applicable.

As Pitoniak and Cizek discussed in Chapter 3 (this volume), when content experts are asked to make judgments as part of the Angoff (1971) standard-setting method, they are told to estimate the probability that a minimally proficient examinee (i.e., a person who just crosses the threshold of having enough of the knowledge or skills that the test is intended to measure) will correctly answer each of the items used in the exercise. The expected score for a minimally proficient examinee will be the sum (or average) of those estimated proportions across the sample of items. Although differential weighting may be used (Clauser, Clauser, & Hambleton, 2014), typically results will simply be averaged across judges and items. In this case, the measure of variability of interest in evaluating the stability of the resulting cut score will be a measure of the error associated with the grand mean; that is, the mean across all judges and items. This design is different than the typical application of generalizability theory in that none of the facets of the design represents the object of measurement. Depending on the specifics of the situation, all of the variance components might contribute to measurement error.

Table 6.4 provides an example of the results of a generalizability analysis from a standard setting in which three independent panels of judges reviewed the same set of items. The design can be described as items crossed with judges nested in panels: $i \times (j: p)$. The results include variance components for (1) *item*, representing the variability in judged item difficulty across the sample of items; (2) *panels*, representing the variability in panel stringency after accounting for the variability in stringency across judges; (3) *judges nested in panels*, representing variability in the stringency within panels; (4) *items by panel*, representing a tendency for individual panels to view specific items as being relatively more difficult; and (5) *items by judges nested in panels*, which includes the systematic tendency for individual judges to view specific items as being relatively more difficult, and the residual variance associated with effects that are not included in the design.

As with the previous analyses, Table 6.4 provides variance components for a single observation as well as results for alternative D study designs. These include (1) a design with 10 judges in each of three panels with all judges reviewing the same 75 items, (2) a design with one panel of 30 judges with all judges reviewing the same 75 items, and (3) a design with 10 judges in each of three panels with each panel reviewing a different sample of 75 items. The values in parentheses represent the denominators for estimating the D study variance components. These designs are intended to show how the precision of the estimate changes across a set of designs that holds the total number of judgments constant. If all of the variance components are viewed as contributing to error, the performance of the designs can be interpreted based on the penultimate row for each design, representing the total error variance. Some authors have suggested that the item component should not be viewed as contributing to estimation error (e.g., Clauser, Swanson, & Harik, 2002). If this is the case, the appropriate error estimates are those from the final row of Table 6.4. (The issues are discussed in greater detail in Clauser, Margolis, & Clauser, 2014.)

The results demonstrate that increasing the number of judges or items improves the precision of the estimated cut score. This finding is directly analogous to the results

TABLE 6.4. Variance Components for Judges-Nested-in-Panels-Crossed-with-Items Design

Source of variance	Single observation	3 panels, 10 judges, 75 items	1 panel, 30 judges, 75 items	3 panels, 10 judges, 225 items
Item	40.0178	0.5336 (75)	0.5336 (75)	0.1779 (225)
Panel	24.7626	8.2542 (3)	24.7626 (1)	8.2542 (3)
Judge: Panel	48.8754	1.6292 (30)	1.6292 (30)	1.6292 (30)
I × P	1.6571	0.0074 (225)	0.0221 (75)	0.0074 (225)
I × J:P	166.8347	0.0741 (2250)	0.0741 (2250)	0.0741 (2250)
Total error	282.1476	10.4985	27.0216	10.1428
Non-item error	242.1298	9.9649	26.4880	9.9649

showing that increasing the number of tasks or judges leads to more precise scores. As with the previous example, these results allow for constructing efficient data collection designs. The present results also suggest that collecting judgments from multiple panels may be advantageous, even when the total number of judges is held constant. (See Clauser et al., 2014, for a more complete discussion.)

Multivariate Generalizability Analysis and Correlated Error

Cronbach, Gleser, Nanda, and Rajaratnam (1972) viewed the univariate generalizability theory model that has been discussed to this point as a special case of the more general multivariate model. With this approach, multiple levels are defined for a fixed facet in the analysis. One common context where this is appropriate is in performing analyses of tests that are constructed using stratified sampling procedures. For example, a licensing test for physicians might be constructed to ensure that each form included specified numbers of items from common disciplines such as internal medicine, surgery, obstetrics, psychiatry, neurology, and so forth. This approach clearly would violate the random sampling assumption for the typical univariate generalizability analysis. In this context, discipline is viewed as a fixed facet, and each test form will have items sampled from each level of the fixed facet. The various levels are defined in advance and scores from these multiple disciplines will be correlated, but the level of correlation likely will vary across levels (in this example, disciplines).

To support interpretations across levels of the fixed facet, the multivariate model will include analyses resulting in variance components that are equivalent to those that would be produced if a univariate analysis were completed for each level. The multivariate model also includes covariance terms. When multiple-choice items are sampled from strata representing content categories, it may be reasonable to assume that performance on items from one category will be related to performance on another category based on examinee proficiency; that is, it will be assumed that error for scores from one category will be uncorrelated with error in scores from another category. Another example in which this type of model is appropriate is when tests are constructed using prespecified numbers of items with different formats (e.g., multiple-choice items and short essays). Again, it may be reasonable to assume that measurement error from one format will be independent of error from another format.

Table 6.5 provides an example of a multivariate analysis of a test comprising multiple-choice items and computer-delivered patient management simulations. The values on the diagonal in the upper portion of the table represent the person (or universe score) variance for the two formats separately. The value on the lower, off-diagonal is the covariance term. The value on the upper, off-diagonal (*in italics*) is referred to as the universe score correlation; this is the correlation between the proficiencies measured by the two formats. Including the covariance term in the model makes it possible to estimate the generalizability coefficients for a composite score across conditions in which the relative number of items included from each format changes. Because there are no covariance terms for the item facet or the person-by-item interaction term, the

TABLE 6.5. Multivariate Single Observation Variance Components

Source of variance	Simulation	MCQ
Person (P)	0.1917	*0.6931*
	0.0200	0.0045
Item (I)	0.3160	0.0259
PI	1.0898	0.1712

Note. The value in italics is the universe–score correlation.

error variance for the composite score is a simple weighted composite of the error terms.

Multivariate models also are useful for understanding error in performance assessments in which each task is evaluated on multiple dimensions; the results might be viewed as a profile rather than a composite. For example, Table 6.6 provides a generalizability analysis from a clinical skills examination in which examinees interact with a series of standardized patients (actors trained to portray the part of real patients). Each patient interaction is scored on four dimensions. Because the same interaction produces multiple scores, it is not reasonable to conclude that error in one score will be independent of error in another score. As with the previous table, the values on the diagonal represent variance components from univariate analyses of each of the scores representing levels of the fixed facet. Unlike the previous example, there are covariance terms for each facet of the model. These covariances allow for

TABLE 6.6. Multivariate Clinical Skills Variance Components

Source of variance	Data gathering	Interpersonal skills	English proficiency	Documentation
Person	**0.003**	*0.479*	*0.180*	*0.691*
	0.034	**2.015**	*0.595*	*0.570*
	0.010	0.956	**1.281**	*0.433*
	0.014	0.331	0.200	**0.167**
Task	**0.007**	*0.152*	*0.108*	*0.098*
	0.017	**1.754**	*0.218*	*0.045*
	0.003	0.101	**0.122**	*0.116*
	0.004	0.026	0.018	**0.196**
PT	**0.012**	*0.207*	*0.035*	*0.181*
	0.048	**4.268**	*0.196*	*0.085*
	0.002	0.246	**0.368**	*0.011*
	0.017	0.149	0.006	**0.719**

appropriate estimation of the error variance for a composite score. The covariances also make it possible to estimate the correlation between error terms for the multiple scores. Consider the task term for the interpersonal skills score and the data-gathering score. The positive correlation (.152) between these terms indicates that tasks that tend to produce higher data-gathering scores also produce very modestly higher interpersonal skills scores. (For more details, see the original publication by Clauser, Harik, & Margolis, 2006.)

These examples provide a sense of some of the potential applications of multivariate generalizability theory. The potential to use this technology to understand composite and profile scores goes far beyond what can be described in the chapter.

Conclusions

Given the flexibility and the range of applications of generalizability theory, it is reasonable to ask why relatively few researchers write about it and why there are so relatively few papers in the literature. One reason may be that a considerable investment may be required to master the tools of generalizability theory. In addition, generalizability theory requires that the evaluator give thoughtful consideration to the facets of the assessment that may contribute to error. In the introduction to their foundational monograph on generalizability theory, Cronbach and colleagues (1972) noted: "The reader is certain to gain far more from his third reading of most sections than from his first or second" (p. 4). Given the complexities of generalizability theory, this chapter has provided only the basics. It is hoped that this introduction will be of use, but interested readers may want more comprehensive references as they explore generalizability theory. Brennan (2001a) provides an excellent resource. Cronbach and colleagues also is an essential reference for anyone who is serious about understanding generalizability theory.

REFERENCES

Angoff, W. H. (1971). Scales, norms, and equivalent scores. In R. L. Thorndike (Ed.), *Educational measurement* (2nd ed., pp. 508–600). Washington, DC: American Council on Education.

Brennan, R. L. (1995). Standard setting from the perspective of generalizability theory. In M. L. Bourque (Ed.), *Joint conference on standard setting for large-scale assessments* (pp. 269–287). Washington, DC: NCSE-NAGB.

Brennan, R. L. (2001a). *Generalizability theory.* New York: Springer-Verlag.

Brennan, R. L. (2001b). *Manual for mGENOVA.* Iowa City: Iowa Testing Programs, University of Iowa.

Camilli, G., Cizek, G. J., & Lugg, C. A. (2001). Psychometric theory and the validation of performance standards: History and future perspectives. In G. J. Cizek (Ed.), *Setting performance standards: Concepts, methods, and perspectives* (pp. 445–475). Mahwah, NJ: Erlbaum.

Clauser, B. E., Harik, P., & Margolis, M. J. (2006). A multivariate generalizability analysis of data from a performance assessment of physicians' clinical skills. *Journal of Educational Measurement, 43,* 173–191.

Clauser, B. E., Margolis, M. J., & Swanson, D. B. (2002). An examination of the contribution of the computer-based case simulations to the USMLE Step 3 examination. *Academic Medicine (RIME Supplement), 77*(10), S80–S82.

Clauser, B. E., Mee, J., Baldwin, S. G., Margolis, M. J., & Dillon, G. F. (2009). Judges' use of examinee performance data in an Angoff standard-setting exercise for a medical licensing examination: An experimental study. *Journal of Educational Measurement, 46*(4), 390–407.

Clauser, B. E., Swanson, D. B., & Clyman, S. G. (1999). A comparison of the generalizability of scores produced by expert raters and automated scoring systems. *Applied Measurement in Education, 12,* 281–299.

Clauser, B. E., Swanson, D. B., & Harik, P. (2002). A multivariate generalizability analysis of the impact of training and examinee performance information on judgments made in an Angoff-style standard-setting procedure. *Journal of Educational Measurement, 39,* 269–290.

Clauser, J. C., Clauser, B. E., & Hambleton, R. K. (2014). Increasing the validity of Angoff standards through analysis of judge-level internal consistency. *Applied Measurement in Education, 27,* 19–30.

Clauser, J. [C.], Margolis, M., & Clauser, B. (2014). An examination of the replicability of Angoff standard setting results within a generalizability theory framework. *Journal of Educational Measurement, 51,* 127–140.

Cronbach, L. J., Gleser, G. C., Nanda, H., & Rajaratnam, N. (1972). *The dependability of behavioral measurements: Theory of generalizability for scores and profiles.* New York: Wiley.

Cronbach, L. J., Linn, R. L., Brennan, R. L., & Haertel, E. (1997). Generalizability analysis for performance assessments of student achievement or school effectiveness. *Educational and Psychological Measurement, 57,* 373–399.

Gulliksen, H. (1950). *Theory of mental tests.* New York: Wiley.

Hambleton, R. K., Pitoniak, M. J., & Copella, J. M. (2012). Essential steps in setting performance standards on educational tests and strategies for assessing the reliability of results. In G. J. Cizek (Ed.), *Setting performance standards: Foundations, methods, and innovations* (2nd ed., pp. 47–76). New York: Routledge.

Kane, M. T. (1982). A sampling model for validity. *Applied Psychological Measurement, 6,* 125–160.

Kane, M. T. (2001). So much remains the same: Conception and status of validation in setting standards. In G. Cizek (Ed.), *Standard setting: Concepts, methods, and perspectives* (pp. 53–88). Mahwah, NJ: Erlbaum.

PART III
Item Response Theory

A Brief History of and Introduction to Item Response Theory

Molly Faulkner-Bond and Craig S. Wells

> Any operational definition of ability, for present purposes, must consist
> of a statement of a relationship between ability and item responses.
> —LORD (1952, p. 4)

If one were to stop people on the street and ask them how they think tests are scored, many individuals would probably say something to the effect of, "Add up the number of correct answers" or "Tally the points." They would be expressing the idea of deriving a test score by counting the number of items an examinee answered correctly (or points the examinee earned, if some items are worth more than 1 point each) and using this sum as a representation of the examinee's achievement. More correct responses lead to higher scores, and higher scores lead us to conclude that the examinee is relatively more capable. This "number correct" approach is central to classical test theory (CTT) and feels very logical, besides.

These same individuals might be surprised (and perhaps alarmed) to learn that many, if not most, large-scale assessments are not, in fact, scored this way—not exactly. Rather, large-scale or standardized assessments today are often scored using item response theory (IRT), a statistical method for estimating an examinee's achievement or proficiency on a construct of interest using the pattern of item responses. As the convoluted phrasing of the preceding sentence suggests, although IRT does produce test scores, it doesn't do so in a way that looks or feels like "scoring" an examinee's answers in the traditional and intuitive way described in the first paragraph. Instead, IRT asks a slightly different question—something more like, "What is the ability level of this examinee that maximizes the likelihood of observing his or her item response pattern?" In an IRT framework, one focuses on examinee performance at the item level—rather than the test level—and conceives of this performance as an interaction between characteristics of the item (e.g., how difficult it is) and characteristics of the examinee (e.g., how capable he or she is on whatever skill the item is measuring). An implication of this approach is that not all items are "worth the same," and indeed, the very value of what items are worth will vary from examinee to examinee and item to item. These ideas may make some sense conceptually, but again, it is not how many people would probably talk about test scores, if you asked them.

As this introduction suggests, IRT is considerably more complex than CTT, both to explain and to execute. Given these drawbacks, one could very reasonably ask how or why it is so widely used. Although test developers may seem like an odd bunch of individuals, one would hope they are not so bizarre as to prefer an unnecessarily complicated approach to scoring when a simpler alternative can do the trick just as well. And indeed, it turns out they are not simply masochists: Despite its tradeoffs, IRT provides a number of extremely helpful advantages over CTT that make it a preferable scoring model in many, if not most, standardized assessment circumstances. These advantages essentially revolutionized the testing field in the 20th century, making it possible not only to improve existing testing practices, but also to take testing in entirely new directions that simply were not possible with CTT alone.

This chapter tells the story of not only how, but also why, IRT has become so widely used and appreciated in the testing world. After first introducing the basics of what IRT is and how it works, we discuss some of the major breakthroughs that made this theory and its widespread use possible. In particular, we argue that, for IRT to rise to prominence the way it has, three types of critical advancement were necessary. First, a conceptual articulation was necessary to describe a different way of thinking about achievement and ability, beyond the number correct approach. Second, someone needed to translate that articulation into a system of computational formulas or equations. Third, that system of formulas needed to be solvable—not just theoretically, but literally, maybe just pragmatically, and ultimately solved. In case it isn't clear, that final step involves not only mathematics, but also, it turns out, technology and computing power.

This framework suggests a clean linear development of one idea building from the next, but of course, science does not work this way: Although all of these milestones were eventually reached for IRT, the ideas and discussions that made such developments possible were concurrent, dynamic, iterative, and multidimensional. Also, as with all scientific advancements—and indeed, as with science itself—IRT was born from a variety of individuals and fields that were working independently of one another on problems that either happened to be very similar in form, or which seemed unrelated until they were brought together by the right people in the right moment. This chapter also takes a more conceptual approach to this conversation, rather than focusing too closely on the details of particular mathematical challenges in this story. For those who are interested in a more technical treatment of this history, Bock (1997) provides an excellent summary.

What Is IRT?: Overview and Formulas

All IRT models define the probability of a positive response as
a mathematical function of item properties, such as difficulty,
and examinee properties, such as ability level.
—HAMBLETON, VAN DER LINDEN, AND WELLS (2010, p. 24)

Before telling the story of how IRT came to be, it is important to start by explaining what IRT is. Thus, in this section, we provide a basic introduction to the most important concepts and formulae of IRT. This treatment is necessarily brief and incomplete; interested readers are referred, however, to any of many texts on this topic, including Hambleton, Swaminathan, and Rogers (1991); van der Linden and Hambleton (1997); Yen and Fitzpatrick (2006); and de Ayala (2009), for more information.

IRT Concepts and Assumptions

Conceptually, IRT is a probabilistic theory that describes an examinee's performance on a test item as the result of interactions between characteristics of the examinee and the item. Rather than focus on whether the examinee answered an item correctly or incorrectly, IRT focuses on the probability that a particular examinee with a particular ability level would get a particular item right, given that item's particular characteristics. As we will show in the formulae that follow, different IRT models differ primarily in which item characteristics they posit as relevant for this purpose; obviously there are tradeoffs to both inclusion and exclusion of different characteristics.

On the examinee side, however, many popular IRT models posit that only one characteristic is or can be relevant: the examinee's ability on the underlying construct of interest. In simpler terms, this means that IRT is premised on the assumption that whether or not an examinee gets, say, a mathematics item correct or incorrect is driven only by the examinee's ability in mathematics—not, for example, by the examinee's reading skills, or by whether the examinee is feeling rushed or anxious. This assumption of *unidimensionality* is critical to IRT, and must be vigilantly checked and safeguarded by test makers and users.[1]

A related assumption is that the examinee's response to each item is independent of his or her response to any other item. At its core, this assumption is driven by the same commitment to unidimensionality—it requires, again, that (on the examinee's side of things) only the student's ability drives his or her response to each item—but in practice this also means that items cannot depend on or influence one another in the course of a test. For instance, the fact that an examinee answered item #6 correctly should have no bearing on whether he or she answers item #7 correctly after controlling for the examinee's proficiency. Dependencies, however, can potentially occur due to, for example, a shared reading passage, an inadvertent giveaway in one item for the

---

[1]Technically, multidimensional IRT (MIRT) models are possible and have gained increased attention in the field in recent years. MIRT is not discussed in this chapter, but interested readers are referred to Ackerman & Henson, Chapter 9 on MIRT in this volume.

other, etc. This assumption, called *local independence*, also must be checked to ensure it holds. If it does hold, however, then local independence makes it possible to calculate the probability of an examinee's full set of responses by simply multiplying the probability of his or her response to each item as one large product, as in Equation 7.1:

$$P(U_1, U_2, ..., U_n | \theta) = P(U_1 | \theta)P(U_2 | \theta)...P(U_n | \theta)$$

(7.1)

This equation essentially says that the probability of an examinee with a certain ability (θ), giving the particular sequence of responses that he or she has given on a test (e.g., correct, incorrect, correct, correct, incorrect), is simply the product of the probability of that examinee for giving each response in that sequence. It is also important to note that all the quantities in Equation 7.1 are conditional on an examinee's estimated ability on the construct of interest (θ), meaning the probability values change as θ changes. The θ value for an examinee that produces the highest probability value is an estimate IRT can produce of the examinee's ability.

A third assumption of many IRT models is that the underlying item response function that defines the probability of correctly answering an item follows a specific shape. For example, many of the models that are applied to dichotomously scored items use a logistic function that looks like an *S*-shaped curve. If the true item response function does not follow an *S*-shape curve, then the model will provide inaccurate predictions of the probability of answering an item correctly and, more importantly, the attractive features and applications of IRT may not be available. Fortunately, there are many techniques available for checking the shape assumption (as well as unidimensionality and local independence; see Wells, Rios, & Faulkner-Bond, Chapter 10, this volume for a description of methods used to check IRT model assumptions).

IRT Models

The question, then, which IRT models attempt to answer is, What is that probability? What is the probability that an examinee with a certain ability level (θ) would answer an item with certain characteristics correctly? How does this probability change or vary for examinees with different levels of ability? Several methods have been developed to estimate this relationship; the three simplest and most common are summarized next. These models all assume the same basic form of the relationship between examinee and item characteristics—a logistic function—meaning they agree with respect to the third question posed above (about how the probability changes for different ability levels). But they differ in what types of item characteristics are presumed to have an impact on this function's shape and, by extension, on an examinee's response.

The One-Parameter Logistic Model

The one-parameter logistic (1PL) model conceives the examinee–item relationship in the simplest terms by positing that only one item characteristic plays a role in the interaction: the *item's difficulty*. The model estimates the probability that an examinee's ability takes on a certain quantity with the logistic function in Equation 7.2, where θ represents the examinee's ability and b represents the item's difficulty:

$$P(\theta) = \frac{e^{(\theta - b_i)}}{1 + e^{(\theta - b_i)}} \tag{7.2}$$

As in all IRT formulae, these two quantities are placed on the same single scale representing the range of ability on the latent trait of interest (e.g., mathematics proficiency), and the distance between their locations on this common scale is what drives the probability value. The exponents in the equation will be largest when the examinee's ability exceeds the difficulty of the item, and larger exponents will lead the overall quantity to asymptotically approach 1 (which signifies certainty that the examinee would answer the item correctly).

The Two-Parameter Logistic Model

The two-parameter logistic (2PL) model introduces a second item characteristic into the probability equation: *item discrimination* (a), meaning how well the item differentiates between more and less capable examinees on the construct (similar to point-biserial estimates in CTT). The 2PL formula is shown in Equation 7.3, and is identical to the 1PL equation save for the addition of the new a-parameter. In this equation, lower a-values (i.e., less than 1) will mute the impact of the ability–difficulty relationship, whereas higher a-values—indicating items with higher discrimination—will increase its impact and the resulting probability estimate.

$$P(\theta) = \frac{e^{a_i(\theta - b_i)}}{1 + e^{a_i(\theta - b_i)}} \tag{7.3}$$

The Three-Parameter Logistic Model

Finally, the three-parameter logistic (3PL) model incorporates both discrimination (a) and difficulty (b) parameters, as well as a *pseudo-guessing parameter* (c) to account for the possibility that an examinee might get an answer correct even if he or she has very low ability and is simply guessing or using misinformation to solve the problem. The 3PL equation is

$$P(\theta) = c_i + (1 - c_i) \frac{e^{a_i(\theta - b_i)}}{1 + e^{a_i(\theta - b_i)}} \tag{7.4}$$

where $P(\theta)$ is examinee ability as defined above and a, b, and c are defined as above. In Equation 7.4, higher c-values will deflate the quantity on the right side of the equation, leading to lower ability estimates than items with lower guessing parameters, all other things equal. Although the *c*-parameter is estimated empirically and may take on a range of values, it often is closely related to the number of response options in each item—for instance, for multiple-choice items with four options, *c*-values are likely to be around 0.25, since each examinee has a one in four chance of choosing the right option simply by chance.

The 3PL model is typically only appropriate for selected response items, such as multiple-choice format, where the examinee has a finite, predetermined set of response options from which to choose. Since many tests in the 20th century used these types of items, however, the development of a model appropriate for this format was critical to IRT's relevance in the testing world. In other words, the development of the 3PL model was a major, important turning point for IRT, as the next section discusses, because it made the model appropriate and useful for scoring the types of tests and items that were already widely in use (and continue to be to this day).

Polytomous and Multidimensional Models

The three models presented here are designed for dichotomous (right–wrong) items and unidimensional tests, both of which have been the norm in large-scale standardized testing in the 20th century. Models also exist, however, for polytomous items with more than one response category (e.g., see Nering & Ostini, 2010), as well as for multidimensional models where performance is driven by more than one underlying ability (e.g., see Reckase, 2009; see also Ackerman & Henson, Chapter 9, this volume). We do not present formulas for these more complex models in this chapter, but they resemble the models presented above and are based on the same form and framework.

Advantages and Disadvantages of IRT

Regardless of the number of parameters, response categories, or dimensions, all IRT models pose certain costs and benefits for those who use them. Although a full discussion of these factors is beyond the scope of this chapter, some of the primary points are summarized briefly to enhance the historical conversation that follows.

Advantages of IRT

The major benefit of any IRT model over CTT is the property of *invariance* for item characteristics and examinee ability parameters. *Parameter invariance* means that the values of item difficulty (and discrimination or guessing, if applicable) and examinee ability are not dependent on the particular examinees (in the former case) or items (in the latter) on which such values were initially based. Although one may use a particular sample (of items or persons) to estimate parameters initially, the property of parameter invariance means that once these have been estimated, they are interpretable and applicable in more general terms: That is, we have a general estimate of an examinee's "ability" on the construct of interest, independent of any particular test, and we have a general estimate of an item's difficulty, independent of any particular group of students. Were we to administer the same items to a different group of examinees, we would not expect their item characteristics to fluctuate beyond sampling error, nor would we expect examinee ability estimates to change were they administered a different set of items.

Invariance is a highly desirable property for many reasons. For one thing, it allows one to meaningfully compare examinees who did not take the same test. For another—on the flipside—it allows one to administer different tests or items to different examinees based on their ability and still produce comparable scores. But perhaps the most basic benefit is that invariance essentially solves a central anxiety for test developers and users: namely, the question of whether one would draw the same conclusions about examinees had one used a different set of items to evaluate them (and vice versa, with items). To the extent that inferences about examinees are test- or context-dependent, they may be inappropriate as a basis for decision making, particularly in high-stakes contexts.

Coincidentally, item and examinee characteristics derived through CTT are not invariant, and therefore are wont to cause precisely this anxiety among measurement experts. For this reason, the task of developing stable assessments and scales with consistent, known properties is a perennial focus of psychometricians and educational psychologists. Indeed, as we argue in the next section, the pursuit of this critical scaling feature is perhaps the one thing that many of the disparate researchers whose work contributed to the birth of IRT had in common with one another.

Disadvantages of IRT

There are two primary disadvantages to IRT. The first is conceptual: Unlike CTT, which requires few and weak assumptions about the distribution of content of examinee ability, IRT requires stronger assumptions. Specifically, unidimensionality, local independence, and the shape of the item response function assumptions must be satisfied for the invariance property to hold. If they are violated, then the item and examinee parameters produced cannot necessarily be trusted as accurate or invariant. These assumptions may be unpalatable in some testing situations, and also may have limiting effects on the test construction or construct definition. However, it is useful to note that the IRT posits falsifiable models in that the assumptions are testable. Therefore, an important part of developing a score scale using IRT is to assess the assumptions of the IRT model (see Wells, Rios, & Faulkner-Bond, Chapter 10, this volume, for a description of methods that assess IRT model assumptions).

Second, from a more pragmatic standpoint, IRT may be considered complicated. If one is starting to build a new assessment from scratch, then all of the variables in an IRT model—that is, all of the characteristics of examinees and items—are unknown and must be estimated. This estimation requires complex statistical methods, particularly when all parameters are unknown, and also large samples of students and items to return stable estimates. These facts, in turn, also mean that IRT requires a considerable amount of computing power (whether human or digital) to produce examinee and item parameter estimates.

The Development of IRT

That is why a new theory, however special its range of application, is seldom or never just an increment to what is already known. Its assimilation requires the reconstruction of prior theory and the re-evaluation of prior fact, an intrinsically revolutionary process that is seldom completed by a single man and never overnight.
—KUHN (1996, p. 7)

IRT's inception required developing and convening all the key concepts introduced in the preceding section—invariance, local independence, item characteristics (difficulty, discrimination, and pseudo-guessing), examinee ability—into a solvable mathematical form that appropriately models the relationship between examinee ability and item responses. To spoil the ending: The general consensus is that these components were all brought together successfully for the first time in Birnbaum's (1968) chapters in Lord and Novick's *Statistical Theories of Mental Test Scores* (e.g., see Bock, 1997; Hambleton et al., 2010). The four most seminal chapters in this volume (Chapters 17–20), authored by Alan Birnbaum and building on earlier work done by Frederic M. Lord, introduced precisely these concepts: (1) a logistic model to represent the relationship between examinee and item characteristics; (2) the incorporation of item characteristics, including guessing, in the formulation of the logistic model; and (3) maximum likelihood estimation as a means to solve for item and examinee parameters based on the observed data (Bock, 1997, p. 25). In the abridged history of IRT, one might simply state that Lord and Novick's book marks the official invention of the method, and call it a day.

As always, of course, there is more to the story. For one thing, obviously, Lord and Birnbaum did not work in a vacuum; their work drew on earlier concepts, techniques, and ideas that made their important breakthroughs of the 1950s and 1960s possible. For another, the conceptual introduction of IRT, though important, was more of a first step than a culmination. Although the ideas had all been connected successfully, it would take many more years and thinkers to translate these ideas into practical, usable tools that could be implemented on a large scale. This is not to detract from the important contributions of Lord and Birnbaum, nor to suggest that they were explicitly aware of every piece of work on which their own work drew. Rather, the discussion of others' work—before, during, and after the careers of these two—is meant simply to provide a richer context for understanding and appreciating the impact and enormity of the transition to IRT as it took place.

The balance of this chapter recounts some specific important breakthroughs that made IRT (1) literally possible, in terms of its mechanics; and (2) appealing as an alternative to CTT. As stated previously, these breakthroughs are grouped according to whether they were conceptual, mathematical, or technological in nature.

Conceptual Advances: Thurstone's Scaling, Lord's Theory, and Rasch's Measurement

Hopefully it is clear by this point that IRT represents a fundamentally different way of thinking about examinee ability and performance compared to CTT. This section describes when and in what context these ideas underlying IRT first appeared in the social sciences. Although this summary is necessarily brief and incomplete, we focus on three watershed thinkers and manuscripts, which other writers have also agreed were important turning points in IRT's development (e.g., see Bock, 1997; Engelhard, 1984; Hambleton et al., 2010; Wright & Masters, 1982).

Perhaps the earliest glimmer of IRT can be traced to a 1925 manuscript by Louis Thurstone in which he proposed a scaling method for the Stanford–Binet test of children's intelligence (Bock, 1997). Thurstone's goal was to develop a scaling method that was appropriate for an instrument administered to a diverse population (children of various ages) who would be expected to vary in their performance as a function of an observed characteristic (chronological age). In such a scenario, items were typically easier for older students and more difficult for younger students, which raised the question of how one might determine what an item's "real" difficulty level was, and, by extension, how one might use this information to make inferences about the intelligence of students at different ages.

To address this challenge, Thurstone proposed a method of establishing an item's "par" based on the age at which 50 percent of examinees would be expected to answer it correctly. He calculated these values based on the observed proportions of students at each age who actually got the item correct—for example, if 41% of 5-year-olds answered the item correctly, and 53% of 6-year-olds answered it correctly, one could calculate the age between 5 and 6 associated with 50%—and then showed that one could use these "age at par" values to create a scale for the items. Since the items were scaled based on an age value, and since all examinees also had a chronological age, this put items and students on the same scale. This common scale, in turn, facilitated inferences and interpretations about examinee performance based on the examinee's age and the age-at-par scale values of the items he or she answered correctly and incorrectly.

In the same paper, Thurstone also created a seminal graphic in which he took a sample of items from the instrument and plotted the proportion of children at various ages (between 3 and 15) who answered each item correctly. For all of the items plotted, the proportions increased as a function of age, creating S-shaped curves that ascended from left (younger ages; fewer correct answers) to right (older ages; more correct answers). These empirical curves essentially mapped out the conditional probability that an examinee would get any particular item correct as a function of his or her age. Thurstone was also careful to note that the curves were neither linear nor parallel—two important considerations in IRT.

Bock (1997) has argued that "modern IRT-based item analysis and test scoring owe more to the scale concept of Binet's clinical assessment of intelligence in children than to classical test theory based on the number-correct score" (p. 22); and indeed, it may be clear to readers already that Thurstone's key ideas in this paper are strikingly similar to the central foundational concepts underlying IRT. In particular, rather than focus on the number of items a student answered correctly, Thurstone attended to the particular items that a student answered, and the relationship between the items' age-at-par (an item characteristic) and the students' chronological age (a student characteristic). In addition, by scaling items based on their "age at par values," he introduced the idea of placing items and examinees on the same scale or continuum—a major feature and advantage of IRT. All of these ideas were marked departures from current practice in Thurstone's time.

Obviously, there are some key differences between Thurstone's model and modern IRT as well. Most notably, the use of an observed variable, age, as the common scaling factor and driver of student performance on the assessment (rather than a latent variable, such as ability) is a major shortcoming, as it limits the model's use to constructs and populations where such an observed variable exists and functions in this way (consider, e.g., that the same methods proposed here likely would not work on an adult population, since age could not be used to group or rank adults according to their expected levels of intelligence). Thurstone also stopped short of developing a general equation for his probability curves, and focused instead on using the mean and standard deviation of distributions of students at different ages to establish his scale (and these means and standard deviations relied, again, on his ability to group students according to their scale values a priori using the observed age variable).

Due, in part, to some of these shortcomings, it took a while before the ideas introduced in Thurstone's paper reappeared in the measurement conversation and took hold. From a conceptual standpoint, the next—and arguably, most important—step for IRT was Frederic Lord's 1952 monograph "A Theory of Test Scores." In this manuscript, Lord introduced a method he called *latent trait theory*, which is based on the starting principle that "any operational definition of ability . . . must consist of a statement of a relationship between ability and item responses" (p. 4). This type of relationship, again, is one of the defining characteristics of IRT. Although Thurstone and Lord were not in direct conversation with one another—in particular, Lord was responding directly to shortcomings in CTT, whereas Thurstone was not—both authors were motivated by a desire to achieve measurement invariance, and their methods in these two manuscripts have many similarities (that were observed and discussed by Samejima, 1962).

Ultimately, however, it is the differences between Lord and Thurstone that make history. In particular, Lord's manuscript offered two key innovations over Thurstone's work. First, he shifted to a latent trait as the driver of performance; although he was not necessarily responding to Thurstone, he likely would have recognized Thurstone's use of age as the Trojan horse that it was. Rather than assign examinees their scale values a priori, Lord realized that this is actually the central question measurement is usually asking: "What *is* this examinee's value on our scale of interest?" Second, Lord also recognized that a general function was necessary to capture the relationship between this latent variable and observed performance. Thus, whereas Thurstone had drawn descriptive probability curves but stopped short of fitting a general equation to them, Lord took the necessary next step and chose the normal ogive model (which we discuss briefly in the next section on mathematical breakthroughs) for this purpose. Coincidentally, this model also produced S-shaped curves for conditional probability; Lord followed after Tucker (1946) and called these "item characteristic curves."

There is one more key conceptual milestone in the birth of IRT. In 1960, Danish mathematician Georg Rasch produced a manuscript, *Probabilistic Models for Some*

Intelligence and Attainment Tests, in which he proposed a measurement model that was functionally equivalent to the one-parameter latent trait model Lord had proposed in his work. Rasch's model sought to characterize achievement based only on the distance between examinee ability and item difficulty—the only factors he believed should matter in determining an examinee's score—on a common scale (Rasch, 1960). This focus on location differences between examinees and items on a common scale has clear parallels to Thurstone's scaling work; indeed, Engelhard (1984) argues that despite the obvious surface similarity to Lord's work, Rasch's work is actually a closer conceptual relative to Thurstone's 1925 work in terms of motivation and conceptualization.

In addition, whereas Lord sought to empirically derive and demonstrate the relationship between underlying ability and performance, Rasch began by asserting what he believed this relationship *should* be, and then developed his model to meet this conceptual criterion. Rasch was, moreover, careful to specify that his measurement model was constitutive in nature—that is, any scenario in which his model did not hold should not be considered true measurement. To this day, these fundamental differences in orientation persist between users of the Rasch model and users of the multiparameter (e.g., 2PL and 3PL) models in Lord's tradition.

Mathematical Advances: Models and Estimation Methods

A second arm of the IRT development story pertains to the development of particular mathematical formulations that made it possible to pin down the conceptual ideas of psychometricians such as Thurstone, Lord, and Rasch into quantitatively solvable problems. For this part of the conversation, we can once again see the first glimmers in Thurstone's 1925 manuscript, where he acknowledges near the end that "a refined statistical method [for his scaling approach] . . . would be to fit an equation to the curve for each test question and then to ascertain the point [on the age scale] at which the curve intersects the 50 per cent level" (p. 445). At the time, Thurstone acknowledged that "this [method] would be rather laborious"—which, given the state of mathematics and computing in 1925, was true.

The idea, however, stuck. Indeed, contemporary IRT is undergirded by two important mathematical processes: (1) some kind of function to characterize the probabilistic relationship between an examinee's ability and his or her response to an item (i.e., a probabilistic equation fit to the curve for each test question); and (2) some method of identifying the best set of estimates for examinee and item characteristics, given this function and the observed set of responses. Today, the model is typically based on a logistic function, and the parameters are estimated using the maximum likelihood (ML) estimation or a fully Bayesian framework. How did these come to be the methods of choice? This section attempts to describe the journey from there to here.

An important intermediary step in the mathematical development of IRT is the establishment of the principle of local independence, which was described earlier in this chapter. Local independence is essentially the means by which one moves from the item level to the test level in IRT, and it is particularly critical for developing estimates of examinee ability. Its development has been attributed to sociologist Paul Lazarsfeld (Bock, 1997), who introduced the principle in a chapter he contributed to a 1950 U.S. War Department volume, *Measurement and Prediction*. Lazarsfeld's focus in the article was dichotomous survey data, and he essentially showed that, provided with an estimate for the underlying latent variable (θ), and a suitable function to model the probability of getting a particular response given that estimate, one could calculate the probability of a set of responses conditioned on this variable by multiplying them. Lazarsfeld had landed on local independence, but, according to Bock (1997) he struggled to articulate an appropriate function to calculate his probabilities, and therefore stalled in his pursuits.

The first item response function arguably came from Lord in his 1952 latent trait theory manuscript where he proposed using the normal ogive model to represent the relationships between examinees and items (Hambleton, 2012; Lord, 1952). In simplest terms, this was a calculus-based model that used integration to produce a cumulative normal distribution to represent the distribution of probabilities for an examinee's ability estimate. Unfortunately, the math required to estimate the parameters proved problematic, which led psychometricians such as Birnbaum to look for alternative models to represent the item response function.

Birnbaum was working for the U.S. military in the late 1950s, and had read and been inspired by Lord's work. Perhaps not surprisingly, however, he found the calculus associated with the normal ogive model cumbersome and intractable, and thus set out to find a simpler alternative. He proposed a logistical model, which (for any readers for whom this may be unfamiliar) is essentially a way of estimating the likelihood that a subject will land in one of two states (in this case, correct or incorrect on a given item) as a function of his or her value on some other variable (e.g., proficiency in math).

As the previous sentence makes clear, logistic regression expresses a relationship between only discrete variables—that is, variables that have a finite set of possible values. Birnbaum's critical innovation was to recast the ability variable in IRT from a continuous one (meaning it could take on any one of an infinite set of values between $-\infty$ and ∞) to a discrete one (meaning it is restricted to a finite list of possible values). By "binning" possible ability estimates into a finite set of values, Birnbaum was able to escape the need for integral calculus, and instead used a probability-driven estimation method (which, though still a chore in the 1950s, was considerably more manageable).

Although Birnbaum was not the first person to make this transition from a normal ogive to logistic model—Bock (1997) credits this innovation to Ronald Fisher and Frank Yates (1938)—he can be credited with bringing this innovation into the world of testing and measurement. Birnbaum can also be thanked for the incorporation of the pseudo-guessing c-paramater, although Bock notes that this, too, first appeared elsewhere, in David Finney's (1952) toxicology work using the probit model. As stated earlier, the incorporation of the c-parameter was critical to IRT's widespread adoption, since multiple choice has long been a preferred item format for large-scale testing. Birnbaum and Lord's mutual inspiration of, and collaboration with, one another throughout the 1950s and 1960s was highly productive for the field of testing, and produced the 1-, 2-, and 3PL models that are still widely used today.

Armed with local independence and a logistic function to characterize the probability relationship between ability and item response, the remaining mathematical necessity was an estimation method that could zero in on values for examinee ability and item characteristics that maximize the likelihood of the observed data from a test administration. A natural candidate for this job was the maximum likelihood approach—which, as Bock noted, was introduced in the same year as Thurstone's scaling method, in Ronald Fisher's (1925) article "Theory of Statistical Estimation"—but there were challenges to overcome.

First, those wishing to use maximum likelihood estimation (MLE) had to solve the problem that all of the desired parameters in the IRT models (i.e., examinee ability, item difficulties, item discriminations, item guessing parameters) are typically unknown, and must be estimated. Lord (1953) provided the general framework for simultaneously estimating item and person parameters via MLE using the normal ogive model. However, the computational work was impractical, especially considering the lack of computer power at the time. Fortunately, Birnbaum (1968) presented a simpler approach that jointly estimated the item and person parameters, a method known as *joint maximum likelihood estimation* (JMLE). JMLE is an iterative, two-stage procedure. In the first stage, the item parameters are estimated via MLE wherein the person parameters are treated as known (standardized raw scores are used to begin the process). In the second stage, the person parameters are estimated via MLE, treating the item parameters as known. The process continues until the change in the likelihood between successive iterations is sufficiently small.

Although the development of JMLE was a breakthrough that allowed IRT models to be applied in practice, JMLE item parameter estimates had an unattractive quality in that they need not be consistent as the sample size increases. The problem with JMLE is that as the sample size increases, the number of parameters (i.e., person parameters) that need to be estimated also increases. Bock and Lieberman (1970) developed an estimation method, marginal maximum likelihood estimation (MMLE), for estimating item parameters that removes the "nuisance" ability parameter from the likelihood function by integrating over the ability distribution. Unfortunately, Bock and Lieberman's solution was computationally intensive and impractical primarily because it required inverting the information matrix for all items.

Bock and Aitkin (1981) further developed MMLE by implementing the expectation-maximization (EM) algorithm, a technique designed for MLE when missing data are present (Dempster, Laird, & Rubin, 1977). The EM algorithm is also a two-step, iterative procedure. In the E-step, we find the "expected" proportion correct at discrete (quadrature) points along the θ scale. The M-step estimates the item parameters by maximizing the likelihood function using the "expected" proportion correct. One of the advantages of the EM algorithm is that it allows for piecewise estimation, where only sections of the overall information matrix need to be inverted at any given time. In IRT, for example, this could allow for estimation of items independently of one another, rather than all at once (Bock, 1989, 1997). By breaking this task down into smaller, more manageable steps, the EM algorithm solved the matrix inversion problem, making it possible for the first time to program and calculate IRT parameter estimation from start to finish (Bock & Aitkin, 1981).

Although MMLE solved the problem of obtaining item parameter estimates that are consistent, there still remained a problem of item and person parameter estimates that are deviant in some datasets. For example, it was difficult to estimate the ability parameter for examinees with atypical item responses. The solution to this problem came from using Bayesian estimation methods. Swaminathan and Gifford (1982, 1985a, 1985b) first introduced Bayesian estimation in the context of JMLE. Mislevy (1986) extended the Bayesian approach to MMLE, which was appealing because it capitalized on the attractive properties of MMLE over JMLE. The Bayesian approach incorporates prior distributions on the item and/or parameters with the likelihood function from the data to obtain "reasonable" parameter estimates. The prior distribution for a particular parameter essentially specifies the probabilities for specific values for a parameter. For example, a common prior distribution for the item difficulty parameter is a normal distribution with mean equal to zero and a standard deviation of 2—therefore, values near zero have a higher probability than values far from zero. Incorporating prior distributions allowed parameters that are difficult to estimate to have "reasonable" estimates.

Technical Advances: Software and Computing Power

The third key piece of the IRT puzzle was developing the programs and algorithms to actually do the math represented in the method's formulas with actual data. This was not a trivial accomplishment, and indeed, as previous sections have suggested, the field stalled more than once as statisticians worked to either simplify complex computations or develop other new ways of solving their conceptual formulae. Thus, part of the history of IRT is also the history of computing; the method truly became a viable tool for test development and scoring when users finally had both the methods and the computational means to produce ability estimates and item parameters in a reasonable amount of time and with a reasonable amount of effort.

IRT software has generally evolved symbiotically with the estimation methods described in the final paragraphs of the preceding section: As new estimation methods were established, they were programmed, and as programming power increased, new estimation methods and software became possible. Based on this relationship, it should come as no surprise that certain individuals—most notably R. Darrell Bock—played important roles in both the mathematical and the technical advances, as the citations in this section and the one preceding it make clear.

Perhaps the earliest instance of an IRT estimation program occurred when Bock and Lieberman (1970) successfully programmed Lord's normal ogive IRT model on a computer. After this breakthrough, early computer programs such as LOGIST (Wingersky, Barton, & Lord, 1982) and BICAL (Wright & Mead, 1978), as well as the Rasch modeling software package WinSteps (Linacre, 2015), used JMLE. As the next generation of estimation emerged with MMLE and Bayesian estimation, these approaches to item and person parameter estimation were incorporated into the next generation of commercially available IRT estimation programs: BILOG (Mislevy & Bock, 1982) and later PARSCALE (Muraki & Bock, 1991). The availability of these programs made IRT a practical option for large-scale assessment for the first time, and this fact in turn secured IRT's foothold as a widely used method in educational testing for decades to follow.

Today, the combination of increased computing power and more/better coding languages and platforms has allowed psychometricians to develop increasingly sophisticated algorithms for IRT estimation over the years. New commercial software packages such as IRTPRO (Cai, Thissen, & du Toit, 2011) and flexMIRT (Cai, 2013) have incorporated updates in modeling and estimation based on recent developments, allowing for better and more flexible model implementation. More notably, widespread use of the open-source *R* programming language (R Core Team, 2014) has allowed psychometricians to code their own routines without purchasing commercial pacakges; *R* also allows psychometricians to share and collaborate quickly and affordably, which has helped spur development and simulations to improve IRT in many ways.

Coda: Extensions and Refinements to Concepts, Math, and Technology

The (hi)story told here has primarily focused on the build up to (unidimensional, dichotomous item) IRT's most basic and important firsts: the first articulation of the model, the first articulation of the math, and the first time it was successfully run on a computer. These key moments were all culminations of a sort, but they were also beginnings: Since the 1960s, psychometricians and mathematicians have worked tirelessly to improve, extend, and innovate the basic IRT models described here. The final section of this chapter briefly summarizes a handful of the many important contributions that have followed in the footsteps of the breakthroughs discussed to this point.

First, most notably, the period around Lord and Novick's 1968 volume was marked by a flurry of activity to develop appropriate models for polytomous items (i.e., items with more than one response category), following in both Lord's and Rasch's separate traditions. Hambleton and colleagues (2010) offer a detailed account of this period and the models it produced, including the rating scale model (Rasch, 1961; Wright & Masters, 1982), the graded response model (Samejima, 1969), the nominal response model (Bock, 1972), the partial credit model (Masters, 1982), and the generalized partial credit model (Muraki, 1992).

Secondly, multidimensional models, to address when more than one latent ability drives examinee performance, also appeared very quickly in the literature (McDonald, 1967), although they did not take hold in the field until much closer to the 21st century, perhaps due to computing and estimation challenges. Ackerman and Henson (Chapter 9, this volume) present an excellent introduction to MIRT and demonstrate some of this method's potential. A related family of IRT models are those known as *diagnostic cognitive models* (DCM) or *cognitive diagnostic assessment* (CDA), which aim to produce items and assessments that provide information about an examinee's misconceptions based on his or her response (Leighton & Gierl, 2007; Rupp, Templin, & Henson, 2010; Samejima, 1994; Tatsuoka, 1983). DCM/CDA models typically do not function as intended on unidimensional assessments, though more recent work has suggested that multidimensional assessments designed to provide diagnostic information can do so (Bradshaw, Izsák, Templin, & Jacobson, 2014).

More complex models such as DCM/CDA and MIRT are made possible, in part, by advances in estimation techniques, pointing to a third front for IRT expansion. Although MMLE is a powerful estimation method, its disadvantage is that it is difficult to apply to very complicated models. To solve this problem, a fully Bayesian estimation framework was adopted in the form of Markov chain Monte Carlo (MCMC) estimation. Bayesian estimation generally requires fewer and more flexible assumptions about the underlying ability distribution, and generally follows a two-stage, iterative procedure. In the first stage, each examinee's ability parameter is sampled from its posterior distribution, conditioned on the current item parameter values and previous ability parameter values. In the second stage, each item's parameters are sampled from its posterior distribution, conditioned on the current ability parameters and previous item parameter values. Often, a decision rule is used to determine whether to accept or reject the new parameter values at each stage. After an initial large number of iterations, the Markov chain will have converged to the underlying joint posterior distribution. The item parameter estimates are based on, for example, the mean of each parameter's marginal distribution.

Although the theory for MCMC estimation had been available for many years (see Metropolis, Rosenbluth, Rosenbluth, Teller, & Teller, 1953; Metropolis & Ulam, 1949), it was not until powerful computers became widely available that it became a feasible estimation method. The application of MCMC estimation to IRT, especially the development of software such as BUGS (Lunn, Thomas, Best, & Speigelhalter, 2000; Thomas, 1994), has allowed psychometricians to estimate parameters in complicated models that otherwise would be only theoretically interesting.

Conclusion

Perhaps one of the greatest joys of being a student of Ronald K. Hambleton is hearing him recount his stories and experiences of IRT's birth in the 1960s, 1970s, and 1980s. While introducing formulas and statistical concepts, Professor Hambleton can't resist sprinkling in personal anecdotes about conversations he had with Fred Lord or Fumiko Samejima during the exciting period when they, and many others, were working furiously to bring this method to life. There are many chapters and manuscripts that will introduce readers to the basics of IRT; the goal of this chapter is to try to contextualize these important moments by incorporating them into a larger narrative of individuals and their contributions over the years. Inevitably, this chapter has not touched on every important moment or manuscript in IRT's history, but hopefully the events described here have helped to give the uninitiated reader a sense of where this scoring method came from, and why it is so important to the field of assessment. The remaining chapters in this section discuss how IRT currently is being used in the field, as well as how it may advance psychometrics into new and better territory in the future.

REFERENCES

Birnbaum, A. (1968). Some latent trait models and their use in inferring an examinee's ability. In F. M. Lord & M. R. Novick (Eds.), *Statistical theories of mental test scores* (pp. 397–479). Reading, MA: Addison-Wesley.

Bock, R. D. (1972). Estimating item parameters and latent ability when responses are scored in two or more nominal categories. *Psychometrika, 37*, 29–51.

Bock, R. D. (1989). Measurement of human variation: A two-stage model. In R. D. Bock (Ed.), *Multilevel analysis of educational data* (pp. 319–342). San Diego, CA: Academic Press.

Bock, R. D. (1997). A brief history of item response theory. *Educational Measurement: Issues and Practice, 16*(4), 21–33.

Bock, R. D., & Aitkin, M. (1981). Marginal maximum likelihood estimation of item parameters: Application of an EM algorithm. *Psychometrika, 46*(4), 443–459.

Bock, R. D., & Lieberman, M. (1970). Fitting a response model for n dichotomously scored items. *Psychometrika, 35*(2), 179–197.

Bradshaw, L., Izsák, A., Templin, J., & Jacobson, E. (2014). Diagnosing teachers' understandings of rational numbers: Building a multidimensional test within the diagnostic classification framework. *Educational Measurement: Issues and Practice, 33*(1), 2–14.

Cai, L. (2013). *flexMIRT: Flexible multilevel item factor analysis and test scoring* (Version 2) [Windows]. Chapel Hill, NC: Vector Psychometric Group.

Cai, L., Thissen, D., & du Toit, S. H. C. (2011). *IRTPRO: Flexible, multidimensional, multiple categorical IRT modeling* (Version 2.1) [Windows]. Lincolnwood, IL: Scientific Software International.

de Ayala, R. J. (2009). *The theory and practice of item response theory.* New York: Guilford Press.

Dempster, A. P., Laird, N. M., & Rubin, D. B. (1977). Maximum likelihood from incomplete data via the EM algorithm. *Journal of the Royal Statistical Society: Series B (Methodological), 39*(1), 1–38.

Engelhard, G., Jr. (1984). Thorndike, Thurstone, and Rasch: A comparison of their methods of scaling psychological and educational tests. *Applied Psychological Measurement, 8*(1), 21–38.

Finney, D. J. (1952). *Probit analysis: A statistical treatment of the sigmoid response curve* (2nd ed.). New York: Cambridge University Press.

Fisher, R. A. (1925). Theory of statistical estimation. *Proceedings of the Cambridge Philosophical Society, 22*, 699–725.

Fisher, R. A., & Yates, F. (1938). *Statistical tables for biological, agricultural and medical research.* Oxford, UK: Oliver & Boyd.

Hambleton, R. K. (2012, October). *The story of D in IRT models.* Instructional presentation, University of Massachusetts Amherst, Amherst, MA.

Hambleton, R. K., Swaminathan, H., & Rogers, H. J. (1991). *Fundamentals of item response theory.* Newbury Park, CA: Sage.

Hambleton, R. K., van der Linden, W. J., & Wells, C. S. (2010). IRT models for the analysis of polytomously scored data: Brief and selected history of model building advances. In M. L. Nering & R. Ostini (Eds.), *Handbook of polytomous item response theory models* (pp. 21–42). New York: Routledge.

Kuhn, T. S. (1996). *The structure of scientific revolutions* (3rd ed). Chicago: University of Chicago Press.

Leighton, J. P., & Gierl, M. J. (Eds.). (2007). *Cognitive diagnostic assessment for education: Theory and applications.* New York: Cambridge University Press.

Linacre, J. M. (2015). *Winsteps Rasch measurement computer program* (Version 3.90.0). Beaverton, OR: Winsteps.com.

Lord, F. M. (1952). A theory of test scores. *Psychometrika Monograph 7*(17).

Lord, F. M. (1953). An application of confidence intervals and of maximum likelihood to the estimation of an examinee's ability. *Psychometrika, 18,* 57–75.

Lord, F. M., & Novick, M. R. (Eds.). (1968). *Statistical theories of mental test scores.* Reading, MA: Addison-Wesley.

Lunn, D. J., Thomas, A., Best, N., & Speigelhalter, D. (2000). WinBUGS—a Bayesian modeling framework: Concepts, structure, and extensibility. *Statistics and Computing, 10,* 325–337.

Masters, G. N. (1982). A Rasch model for partial credit scoring. *Psychometrika, 47*(2), 149–174.

McDonald, R. P. (1967). Some applications of a unified theory of weighting. *Australian Psychologist, 2*(1).

Metropolis, N., Rosenbluth, A. W., Rosenbluth, M. N., Teller, A. H., & Teller, E. (1953). Equations of state calculations by fast computing machines. *Journal of Chemical Physics, 21,* 1087–1092.

Metropolis, N., & Ulam, S. (1949). The Monte Carlo method. *Journal of the American Statistical Association, 44,* 335–341.

Mislevy, R. J. (1986). Bayes modal estimation in item response models. *Psychometrika, 51,* 177–195.

Mislevy, R. J., & Bock, R. D. (1982, July). *Implementation of the EM algorithm in the estimation of item parameters: The BILOG computer program.* Paper presented at the Item Response Theory and Computerized Adaptive Testing Conference, Wayzata, MN.

Muraki, E. (1992). A generalized partial credit model: Application of an EM algorithm. *Applied Psychological Measurement, 16*(2), 159–176.

Muraki, E., & Bock, R. D. (1991). *PARSCALE: Parametric scaling of rating data* (Version 1). Chicago: Scientific Software International.

Nering, M. L., & Ostini, R. (Eds.). (2010). *Handbook of polytomous item response theory models.* New York: Routledge.

Rasch, G. (1960). *Probabilistic models for some intelligence and attainment tests.* Copenhagen: Danmarks Paedegogiske Institut.

Rasch, G. (1961). On general laws and the meaning of measurement in psychology (pp. 321–333). Paper presented at the Proceedings of the Fourth Berkeley Symposium on Mathematical Statistics and Probability: Volume 4. *Contributions to biology and problems of medicine.* Berkeley: University of California Press. Retrieved from *http://projecteuclid.org/euclid.bsmsp/1200512895.*

R Core Team. (2014). *R: A language and environment for statistical computing.* Vienna, Austria: R Foundation for Statistical Consulting. Retrieved from *www.R-project.org.*

Reckase, M. (2009). *Multidimensional item response theory.* New York: Springer.

Rupp, A. A., Templin, J., & Henson, R. A. (2010). *Diagnostic measurement: Theory, methods, and applications*. New York: Guilford Press.

Samejima, F. (1962). Theoretical correspondence between Lord's theory and Thrustone's theory. *Japanese Journal of Psychology, 33*(2), 84–97.

Samejima, F. (1969). Estimation of latent ability using a response pattern of graded scores. *Psychometrika Monograph Supplement, 34*(4, Pt. 2), 1–100.

Samejima, F. (1994, April). *Cognitive diagnosis using latent trait models*. Paper presented at the annual meeting of the National Council of Measurement in Education, New Orleans, LA.

Swaminathan, H., & Gifford, J. A. (1982). Bayesian estimation in the Rasch model. *Journal of Educational Statistics, 7*, 175–191.

Swaminathan, H., & Gifford, J. A. (1985a). Bayesian estimation in the two-parameter logistic model. *Psychometrika, 50*, 349–364.

Swaminathan, H., & Gifford, J. A. (1985b). Bayesian estimation in the three-parameter logistic model. *Psychometrika, 51*, 589–601.

Tatsuoka, K. K. (1983). Rule space: An approach for dealing with misconceptions based on item response theory. *Journal of Educational Measurement, 20*(4), 345–354.

Thomas, A. (1994). BUGS: A statistical modeling package. *RTA/BCS Modular Languages Newsletter, 2*, 36–38.

Thurstone, L. L. (1925). A method of scaling psychological and educational tests. *Journal of Educational Psychology, 16*(7), 433–451.

Tucker, L. R. (1946). Maximum validity of a test with equivalent items. *Psychometrika, 11*, 1–13.

van der Linden, W. J., & Hambleton, R. K. (1997). *Handbook of modern item response theory*. New York: Springer Science & Business Media.

Wingersky, M. S., Barton, M. A., & Lord, F. M. (1982). *LOGIST user's guide*. Princeton, NJ: Educational Testing Service.

Wright, B. D., & Masters, G. N. (1982). *Rating scale analysis: Rasch measurement*. Chicago: Mesa Press.

Wright, B. D., & Mead, R. J. (1978). BICAL: Calibrating items and scales with the Rasch model (Research Memorandum 23A). Chicago: Statistical Laboratory, Department of Education, University of Chicago.

Yen, W. M., & Fitzpatrick, A. R. (2006). Item response theory. In R. L. Brennan (Ed.), *Educational measurement* (4th ed., pp. 111–153). Westport, CT: Praeger.

CHAPTER 8

Concepts and Methods in Research on Differential Functioning of Test Items
Past, Present, and Future

H. Jane Rogers and Hariharan Swaminathan

Differential item functioning of test items (DIF) has been a topic of enduring interest and vigorous psychometric research for the last 40 years. Over that time, methods for investigating DIF have evolved rapidly, from simple comparisons of proportion correct across groups to sophisticated multilevel mixture modeling of item responses. The issue itself has been reframed in various ways, most notably with the transition from the use of the term *bias* to that of *differential functioning* (Holland & Thayer, 1988) and the further distinction of DIF from impact. DIF has been conceptualized equivalently, but usefully differently, as a threat to validity, as undesired multidimensionality, and as lack of measurement invariance. Our goal in this chapter is to broadly outline that conceptual and methodological development, provide a picture of where the field stands today, and identify emerging areas of research.

There are several excellent books/chapters that review the history of research on test and item bias and capture the state of the art at the time they were written (Berk, 1982; Camilli, 2006; Camilli & Shepard, 1994; Cole & Moss, 1989; Holland & Wainer, 1993; Penfield & Camilli, 2007). We will not attempt to improve on them and will be more general in our discussion; we focus on methods and issues that remain important today and those that have emerged in the years since the last major review. We apologize in advance to researchers and authors whose work we have not noted; given space limitations, we have focused on broad trends. We note at the outset that along with his many other contributions to educational measurement, Ron Hambleton has made a considerable contribution to the literature on DIF since the 1980s through dozens of presentations and publications. We cite here only his empirical research publications: Rogers and Hambleton (1989); Hambleton and Rogers (1989, 1991); Hambleton and Jones (1994); Mazor, Clauser, and Hambleton (1992, 1994); Clauser,

Mazor, and Hambleton (1991, 1993, 1994); Mazor, Hambleton, and Clauser (1998); Allalouf, Hambleton, and Sireci (1999); Zenisky, Hambleton, and Robin (2003).

A Condensed History of Research on DIF

Zumbo (2007) described three generations of DIF research. In his view, the first generation was centered on concept development; the second focused on statistical methods for identifying DIF; and the third and present generation is concerned with explanations for DIF and the integration of DIF investigations into the modern practice and uses of testing. Zumbo notes that his view does not imply distinct historical periods or a linear progression of research. We agree that, as in most fields of research, development proceeds on several fronts simultaneously, and it is difficult to precisely identify points in time where thinking and practice changed significantly. We also agree with Zumbo in his description of the evolution of DIF research, but we see a somewhat different set of transitions that can also be captured in three general periods or phases. Somewhat irreverently, we would call these phases (1) "We have a problem: Let's get to work" (developing methods); (2) "Hmm . . ." (searching for meaning); and (3) "Aha! Let's model it!" (combining methods and meaning). We describe each of these phases in the remainder of this chapter, with particular focus on the third and current phase.

Phase 1: Defining and Operationalizing DIF

Recognition of the issue of bias in tests and test items began to emerge during the first half of the 20th century, with the focus mainly on cultural and socioeconomic differences on intelligence tests (Camilli, 1993). Attention to the question of bias in IQ and achievement tests increased in the late 1960s during the civil rights era, when education was seen by differing groups as both a means for, and a barrier to, social change (Camilli & Shepard, 1994; Cole, 1993). At this time, IQ tests were widely used for selection and placement decisions, and in this context, test bias was defined as differential predictive validity (Shepard, 1982). In the early 1970s, interest in the psychometric community turned to methods for detecting bias at the item level, and research continued energetically for the next 20 years or so. In the validity framework, item bias was viewed as a problem of construct validity.

Early statistical methods for detecting item bias treated bias as an item-by-group interaction, flagging items for which the difference in difficulty between groups was unexpectedly large. The analysis of variance (ANOVA) method of Cardall and Coffman (1964) and the transformed item difficulty method of Angoff (1972) are the most well-known methods of this type. By the end of the 1970s, it was recognized that these methods were flawed due to their inability to properly account for mean differences in performance between groups, although Camilli and Shepard note that these methods continued to be used through the early 1980s. Scheuneman's (1975) chi-square method was among the first to match examinees on a measure of the trait being measured before examining group differences in performance. As item response theory (IRT) became established as a viable measurement framework during the 1970s, item bias was more precisely defined in psychometric terms as a difference between groups in item characteristic curves (Lord, 1977).

During the early phase of the evolution of the study of test and item bias, when the rhetoric of testing opponents was particularly strong, there was considerable discussion in the psychometric literature around definitions of test and item bias and test fairness. These discussions, along with more current views, are thoughtfully analyzed by Shepard (1982) and Camilli (1993, 2006). What is clear from these chapters is that it is not possible to formulate a simple, all-purpose definition of test and item bias that reflects both public and psychometric understandings. This realization ultimately resulted in a turn away from the use of the term *bias* for technical purposes. The legal settlement in 1984 known as the *Golden Rule settlement* (described in Camilli & Shepard, 1994, pp. 30–33), in which *bias* was effectively defined as mean group differences in performance, was instrumental in this turn. The term *differential item functioning*, introduced by Holland and Thayer (1988) as a more accurate representation of the target of statistical procedures, was readily adopted by the psychometric community because it was amenable to a clear conceptual and operational definition. The widely accepted definition of DIF is that an item shows DIF in a population if individuals at the same level of the trait(s) measured by the test but belonging to different subgroups have unequal probabilities of a given response to the item. This definition distinguishes DIF from *impact*, defined as mean differences in performance across groups on the dimension intended to be measured. Another distinction had also become established by this time with respect to the type of DIF: uniform versus nonuniform (Mellenbergh, 1982; Scheuneman, 1975). *Uniform DIF* occurs when one group has a consistent advantage over the other across the trait continuum; *nonuniform DIF* occurs when the size and possibly direction of the difference between groups changes across the trait continuum.

The relabeling of the statistical concept of item bias allowed psychometricians to continue apace with developing new and better methods for detecting DIF, with the caveat that these methods could only be used to detect differential performance across groups, and that the determination of bias required extrastatistical judgment. Although the definition of DIF naturally places detection methods within an IRT framework, other more practically useful methods were developed due to the sample size requirements for, and estimation issues encountered with, IRT methods. By the early 1990s, a number of methods for detecting DIF in dichotomously scored items had emerged as the main contenders: the Mantel–Haenszel (MH) procedure (Holland & Thayer, 1988); logistic regression (Swaminathan & Rogers, 1990); SIBTEST (Shealy & Stout, 1993b); the standardization (STD) procedure (Dorans & Kulick, 1986); and a set of IRT-based procedures, including Lord's (1980) chi square, Raju's (1988) area method, and the likelihood ratio test (Thissen, Steinberg, & Wainer, 1993). These methods have been comprehensively reviewed by earlier authors (Camilli, 2006; Penfield & Camilli, 2007). All have advantages and deficiencies of one kind or another, and despite exhaustive comparisons too numerous to cite, none has been declared the clear winner in all situations. The logistic regression procedure is the most flexible, as it easily accommodates multiple groups and multiple conditioning variables (e.g., Mazor et al., 1998). The MH procedure can be obtained as a special case of the logistic regression procedure (Swaminathan & Rogers, 1990). The MH procedure is currently the most widely used approach for assessing DIF in statewide assessments, followed by the STD procedure. Sinharay and Dorans (2010) report that the MH and STD procedures are used in concert at Educational Testing Service (ETS): Whenever an item is flagged for DIF by the MH procedure, its STD P-DIF value (Dorans & Kulick, 1986) is examined. If the P-DIF value is sufficiently small, it is concluded that the DIF flag is in error.

Phase 2: Interpreting DIF

During the 1990s, research on new methods for detecting DIF slowed, as the body of accumulated research revealed how little congruence there was between statistical and judgmental methods, and how little knowledge had been gained that would inform the development of DIF-free tests (hence, the "Hmm . . ." phase). Skaggs and Lissitz (1992) expressed frustration with the lack of consistency in results found within and across DIF procedures. Scheuneman (1987) anticipated this state of affairs several years in advance, remarking that

> at one time an orderly progression of research was envisioned as follows: (a) Devise procedures for reliably detecting those items that are performing differently for the groups of interest; (b) examine the items and identify causes for this differential performance; (c) develop procedures for modifying these items so that the differential performance is reduced or eliminated where appropriate; and (d) develop guidelines for item writers so that future items are free from such biases. At present this field of research . . . cannot be said to have moved much beyond the first step in this process. Perusal of much of the recent literature in this area would almost suggest that the methodological work, so essential to progress before the fourth step can be attained, has become an end in itself. (pp. 97–98)

As the interest in and perceived need for new statistical methods waned in the 1990s, research on DIF took several different directions. In one direction, existing methods were extended or modified to accommodate polytomously scored items, which were becoming increasingly common in large-scale assessments (Chang, Mazzeo, & Roussos, 1996; Dorans & Schmitt, 1991; Rogers & Swaminathan, 1993; Welch & Hoover, 1993; Zwick, Donoghue, & Grima, 1993). Potenza and Dorans (1995) and Penfield and Lam (2000) provide useful reviews of these procedures. These extensions also allow the application of DIF methods to personality and attitude measures, although applications in these areas have been relatively recent (e.g., Azocar, Arean, Miranda, & Munoz, 2001; Bolt, Hare, Vitale, & Newman, 2004; Orlando & Marshall, 2002).

In another direction, in an attempt to give greater meaning to DIF results, attention turned to the use of effect size measures, rather than significance tests, for identifying

DIF. Holland and Thayer (1988) had led the way in this area with their use of the common log-odds ratio index associated with the MH procedure. A classification scheme was developed at ETS in the early 1990s for labeling items as showing negligible, moderate, or large DIF (Zieky, 1993). Although the STD procedure had always been used descriptively rather than inferentially at ETS, its item discrepancy index came to be regarded as an effect size measure at around this time, and cutoffs were suggested for classifying DIF as warranting item review (Dorans & Holland, 1993). For the SIBTEST procedure, the numerator of the test statistic is taken as an effect size measure; Roussos and Stout (1996b) proposed guidelines for interpreting the effect size that would produce results consistent with those from the ETS classification. Effect size measures were developed later for the logistic regression procedure (Jodoin & Gierl, 2001; Monahan, McHorney, Stump, & Perkins, 2007; Zumbo, 1999). As DIF procedures for polytomous items were developed, effect size measures for those methods were also introduced: Dorans and Schmitt (1991) for the STD method; Camilli and Congdon (1999) for the ordinal Mantel procedure; Zumbo (1999) and Penfield and Algina (2003) for ordinal logistic regression; and Kim, Cohen, Alagoz, and Kim (2007) and Steinberg and Thissen (2006) for ordinal IRT models.

A third direction for DIF research that gained momentum in the 1990s was in the area of explanation of DIF effects and confirmatory DIF analyses. Zumbo (2007) considers this period the beginning of the third generation of DIF research. As Roussos and Stout (1996a, p. 360) noted, "Attempts at understanding the underlying causes of DIF using substantive analyses of statistically identified DIF items have, with a few exceptions, met with overwhelming failure. . . . Only limited progress has occurred . . . but so far few general principles for guiding item writing have been developed." Some early studies of the causes of DIF are described in Scheuneman (1987), Scheuneman and Gerritz (1990), Schmitt and Dorans (1990), and O'Neill and McPeek (1993). Schmitt, Holland, and Dorans (1993) suggested systematic approaches for exploratory and confirmatory studies of DIF. Rogers and Swaminathan (1998) took a different approach, proposing a hierarchical model that allows for exploration of factors that explain variation in DIF effects across schools, districts, or other units of organization.

Research in the area of explaining DIF was furthered by its reconceptualization as *undesired multidimensionality*. Although implicit in the construct invalidity view of DIF, this conceptualization began to appear explicitly in the early 1990s (e.g., Ackerman, 1992; Camilli, 1992; Roussos & Stout, 1996a; Shealy & Stout, 1993a). Under this view, DIF was regarded as a result of group differences on a secondary, nuisance dimension. Shealy and Stout used this view of DIF to develop the DIF detection procedure implemented in the SIBTEST computer program (Shealy & Stout, 1993b). They conceived of a valid subtest measuring only the intended construct and a suspect, "studied" subtest consisting of one or more items measuring a common nuisance dimension. Differential item or bundle functioning is indicated if, after conditioning on valid subtest score, there are mean differences between groups on the studied subtest. The original SIBTEST procedure assumed that the mean differences on the studied subtest were in the same direction for all valid subtest scores (unidirectional DIF). Li and Stout (1996) provided an extension for "crossing" DIF.

Roussos and Stout (1996a) proposed using the Shealy and Stout framework for testing hypotheses about DIF by creating subtests consisting of items with characteristics that were hypothesized to cause DIF. If there was a single nuisance dimension, these items would act in concert to create DIF "amplification," though each item separately might show only small DIF. On the other hand, incorrectly bundling items measuring several different nuisance dimensions might result in cancellation of the DIF. Douglas, Roussos, and Stout (1996) discussed procedures for identifying suspect bundles. Banks (2013), in a comprehensive review of peer-reviewed research on differential bundle functioning (DBF), found 15 peer-reviewed applications of the SIBTEST procedure for confirmatory investigations of DIF. The majority of these studies investigated male–female DIF in mathematics tests. Banks notes that effect sizes are lacking for interpreting the results of these studies.

Raju, van der Linden, and Fleer (1995) proposed an alternative procedure for investigating differential functioning of items and tests (DFIT) that can be used to investigate causes of DIF. This approach uses IRT item parameters from separate group calibrations to calculate true scores for focal group examinees on all or subsets of items. True scores are calculated using both sets of item parameters, and the sum of squared differences across the focal group is taken as a measure of differential test functioning. Raju et al. proposed a chi-square test of significance for the DFIT statistic. Conceptually, this procedure is a generalization of the area method for DIF in single items. Banks (2013) found only one peer-reviewed application of the DFIT approach for confirmatory investigation of DIF.

Phase 3: Unifying DIF Research through Latent Variable Modeling

In the later 1990s, research on DIF entered a new phase, with more complex modeling. Arising from changes in the measurement landscape that had begun in the preceding decade, the concept of DIF as a lack of measurement invariance began to take hold. On one front, structural equation modeling (SEM) was becoming widely used in the arena of educational and psychological research as advances were made in computing technology and software. Groundwork had been laid in the 1980s for factor analysis of categorical outcomes such as item scores by Muthén and Christoffersson (1981) and Muthén (1984). On another front, there was increasing interest in and need for test adaptation across languages to allow for cross-cultural comparisons. Hambleton (1994), under the aegis of the International Test Commission, developed the first set of guidelines for adapting educational and psychological tests. A psychometric issue of major concern in this area was ensuring measurement equivalence of adapted tests. The SEM framework, multigroup confirmatory factor analysis (MG-CFA) in particular, provided a comprehensive approach to assessing measurement equivalence that was unavailable within IRT (see van de Vijver & Poortinga, Chapter 16, this volume). Although it had long been recognized that item response models (without lower asymptote parameters) were nonlinear factor analysis models (e.g., Takane & de Leeuw, 1987), little use had been made of the commonality of frameworks prior to this time. Despite the fact that the IRT likelihood ratio test (Thissen et al., 1993) does provide a test of metric and scalar invariance at the item level, it was generally regarded as a test of equality of item parameters rather than of measurement equivalence/invariance. The utility of SEM procedures for assessing measurement equivalence of adapted tests made it clear that DIF could be viewed as lack of measurement invariance and tested using SEM procedures.

The MG-CFA approach to DIF can be implemented in two different ways, which may be termed *forward* and *backward procedures* (Kim & Yoon, 2011). In the forward procedure, parameters are estimated separately for all groups, with only minimal constraints for identification and scaling purposes. Parameters for one item at a time are then constrained to be equal and a chi-square difference statistic is calculated to test for invariance. In the backward procedure, parameters are initially constrained to be equal across groups and then constraints are released item by item; the chi-square difference statistic is again used as a test of invariance.

In the early 2000s, studies comparing the SEM and IRT frameworks for investigating DIF began to appear (e.g., Meade & Lautenschlager, 2004; Stark, Chernyshenko, & Drasgow, 2006); most of these early studies used linear CFA models, which are not appropriate for categorical outcomes. More recently, systematic comparisons of the MG-CFA approach with categorical outcomes and IRT approaches have been conducted (e.g., Kim & Yoon, 2011). Kim and Yoon found high false-positive rates for the backward MG-CFA procedure when DIF items were present among the indicators of the latent variable.

The increasing use of SEM, especially through the software package Mplus (Muthén & Muthén, 1998–2014), led to other approaches to modeling and testing DIF. An approach discussed considerably earlier by Muthén (1985, 1988) that had been largely ignored by psychometricians drew fresh interest in the 2000s. This method is based on the MIMIC (multiple-indicator, multiple-cause) model, which extends item response models by incorporating covariates. The covariates of interest in a DIF context are grouping variables such as sex and ethnicity/race. The MIMIC model specifies indirect effects of the covariates on the response through the latent variable as well as direct effects on the item scores. In other words, the model states that item score variance is explained both by the latent variable and group membership, which means that group membership predicts item score after controlling for the latent variable. Hence, the test of the direct effect of group on item score is a test of uniform DIF; a likelihood ratio test is used for this purpose. The model also allows group mean differences on the latent variable (impact).[1]

Although Gallo, Anthony, and Muthén (1994) implemented the MIMIC model for DIF in the context of age DIF in a depression scale, and Muthén, Kao, and Burstein (1991) applied it to study DIF associated with opportunity to learn, the approach did not enter mainstream DIF research until quite recently. Finch (2005) compared the MIMIC model for DIF with the MH and SIBTEST procedures for detecting uniform DIF in dichotomous items through a simulation study, and found that the MIMIC

---

[1]The logistic regression procedure (Swaminathan & Rogers, 1990) can be viewed as an observed variable version of the MIMIC model approach with respect to testing for uniform DIF.

model procedure had high Type I error rates for short tests when the data were generated with a three-parameter IRT model, but was less affected by contamination of the anchor items than the MH and SIBTEST procedures. Woods (2009) compared the MIMIC and MG-CFA approaches for detecting uniform DIF using simulated two-parameter and ordinal response data, concluding that the MIMIC model approach works better in small samples.

Woods and Grimm (2009) extended the MIMIC model approach for DIF by incorporating an interaction between the trait and group membership, thereby allowing for a test of nonuniform DIF. This model is the latent variable version of the logistic regression model for nonuniform DIF (Swaminathan & Rogers, 1990). Woods and Grimm provided a path diagram for this model with dichotomous items; Figure 8.1 shows a modified version for a single DIF item across two groups (one dichotomous group membership variable). In this figure, items 1 through 4 are anchor items, assumed to be DIF-free, that are used as indicators of the latent trait intended to be measured (θ). The relationship between the trait and item responses is through the latent response variables Y_j, with α_j representing item discrimination. The thresholds, τ_j, determine the observed 1/0 responses to the items. Responses to item 5 are influenced by θ, group membership, and the interaction of θ and group, denoted by the solid ellipse. A nonzero value of β_1 represents group differences on the thresholds (uniform DIF), and a nonzero value of β_2 represents group differences in the discrimination parameters (nonuniform DIF).

Figure 8.2 shows a path diagram for DIF as unintended multidimensionality based on the description by Bolt and Stout (1996). Here, items 1 through 4 (Y1–Y4) are pure indicators of the trait intended to be measured (θ), while items 5 through 7 (Y5–Y7) additionally measure a nuisance dimension η. Differential bundle functioning occurs when $E_R(\eta \mid \theta) \neq E_F(\eta \mid \theta)$. Differences between groups in the conditional mean of η given θ are evidenced by nonzero values of γ_2. Finch (2012) presented a similar figure. The SIBTEST procedure is a nonparametric version of this model, in which true score

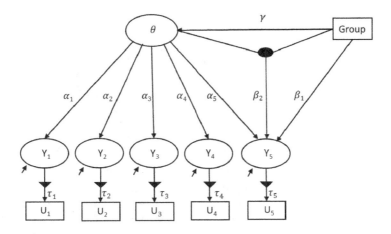

FIGURE 8.1. MIMIC model for DIF in a single item.

on the valid subtest represents θ and studied subtest score represents η. The models in Figures 8.1 and 8.2 have the flexibility to accommodate multiple groups and multiple covariates.

There are several models for DIF within the IRT framework that resemble the MIMIC model in Figure 8.2. These models allow for local item dependence due to common stimulus material, but most assume that DIF is present only with respect to the primary dimension. Wang, Bradlow, Wainer, and Muller (2008) proposed and demonstrated a method using the testlet response model of Bradlow, Wainer, and Wang (1999). The testlet model includes a person-specific testlet parameter that is essentially an individual's value on a testlet-specific dimension (equivalent to η in Figure 8.2) operating in addition to the primary dimension. The nuisance dimension is assumed to be uncorrelated with the primary dimension ($\gamma_1 = 0$). Wang et al. assumed that there were no mean differences between groups on either dimension for the dataset they analyzed. Similar to a concurrent calibration equating design, Wang et al. treated all items but the studied item as anchor items (i.e., DIF-free) and constrained their parameters to be equal across groups; they treated the studied item as a unique item in the two groups and estimated its parameters separately. This procedure is computer-intensive, requiring a separate run for each item. Although Wang and colleagues specified a two-parameter model for the items, they tested for DIF only in the difficulty parameter (i.e., uniform DIF).

Fukuhara and Kamata (2011) proposed a bifactor model for DIF with a similar structure to the Wang et al. model. The testlet model is a special case of the bifactor model that constrains discriminations on the testlet dimension to be proportional to the primary dimension discrimination parameters. Fukuhara and Kamata further generalized the Wang et al. model by allowing for mean differences between groups on the primary dimension (impact). In addition, the method specifies that the mean DIF magnitude for the set of items is zero, and hence does not require specification of a set of DIF-free anchor items. A further advantage of the approach over the Wang et al. approach, according to the authors, is that it permits DIF testing on all items

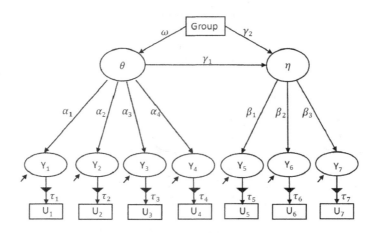

FIGURE 8.2. MIMIC model for differential bundle functioning.

simultaneously. Jeon, Rijmen, and Rabe-Hesketh (2013) presented an even more general multigroup bifactor model in which the assumption of uncorrelated general and specific dimensions is relaxed (but specific dimensions are uncorrelated with each other conditional on the general dimension), and means, variances, and correlations among dimensions are permitted to vary across groups. The models in both of these studies allowed only for uniform DIF. Both studies reported that ignoring local item dependence when it is present can result in biased estimates of DIF leading to incorrect DIF identification, and that modeling it appropriately improves accuracy of DIF detection.

Beretvas and Walker (2012) presented a multilevel formulation of the testlet model that can be used to test for DIF in testlets or subsets of items suspected of sharing a common source of DIF. Under a multilevel formulation, items are nested within individuals; item effects can be treated as random across people, and second-level predictors such as sex or ethnicity/race can be included, providing the capacity to model DIF. Under Beretvas and Walker's formulation, the testlet effect is decomposed into a person-specific random effect and a fixed testlet effect that reflects the testlet's contribution to item difficulty. The testlet effect can then be modeled as a function of the demographic variables, allowing testlet differential functioning to be identified. Beretvas and Walker argue that the separation of differential item functioning from differential testlet functioning allows the source of differential functioning to be identified as item-specific or as testlet-specific, and may permit detection of effects that would be missed under the SIBTEST approach.

Another avenue of research on methods for detecting DIF that has recently been explored is the use of mixture modeling, in which the causal DIF variable is treated as latent rather than observed. The premise of this approach is that individuals within manifest groups, such as sex or race/ethnicity groups, are not necessarily homogeneous with respect to the true causal DIF variable(s), which is presumed to have a cognitive basis. Skaggs and Lissitz (1992) argued persuasively that there is a fundamental flaw in looking for DIF between groups based on "highly visible external characteristics" (p. 239) that may have little relationship to the cognitive processes involved in responding to test items. In the mixture model, the same parametric item response model is assumed to hold within latent classes (DIF groups), but item parameters are permitted to differ across latent classes. Latent class membership is estimated simultaneously with the item parameters. Observed covariates hypothesized to be related to latent class membership may be included in the model. Estimation can be carried out using Mplus or using a Bayesian approach in a program such as WinBUGS. Several studies have explored the use of mixture models in the DIF context (de Ayala, Kim, Stapleton, & Dayton, 2002; DeMars & Lau, 2011; Lu & Jiao, 2009; Samuelsen, 2005). The findings to date indicate that despite its intuitive appeal, the mixture model approach for DIF is problematic, even in large sample sizes. Adequate estimation of latent class membership and item parameters requires relatively large numbers of DIF items that induce consistent patterns of differential performance between the latent groups. DeMars and Lau note that, in practice, there will typically be only a few DIF items in a test, and these may reflect several different nuisance dimensions. Despite these issues, this approach, along with the other SEM approaches, indicates the potential of modern statistical modeling to explain DIF effects.

Other Recent Developments in DIF Research

The rising popularity and accessibility of Bayesian methods using Markov chain Monte Carlo (MCMC) estimation procedures over the last decade has provided yet another means for investigating DIF. Several approaches that take advantage of MCMC estimation have been proposed. Although all of these have used an IRT framework, the general approach could be applied within the latent variable modeling framework described above. A particular advantage of Bayesian procedures with MCMC estimation is that inference about parameters does not require standard error estimates based on asymptotic theory. Wang and colleagues (2008) used an MCMC method to estimate parameters for their testlet model; after obtaining draws from the posterior distribution of all estimated parameters, they computed the difference between the item difficulty estimates in the groups of interest for a given item in each draw from the posterior distribution. The distribution of these differences represents the posterior distribution of the uniform DIF effect. Wang et al. suggested computing a "Bayesian *p*-value" (p. 369) by obtaining the posterior probability that the DIF effect is greater than zero. Also using a Bayesian approach with MCMC estimation, Rogers, Swaminathan, and Sen (2011) implemented a unidimensional two-parameter IRT version of their logistic regression procedure for DIF. Under this approach, uniform and nonuniform DIF parameters are estimated directly rather than constructed after estimation. Rogers et al. used the draws from the posterior distributions of the parameters to construct 95% credibility intervals for the true values of the uniform and nonuniform DIF effects.

Soares, Gonçalves, and Gamerman (2009) ambitiously presented an integrated Bayesian model for DIF analysis. One of the features of this approach is that an item does not have to be identified as DIF-free or suspect prior to the analysis. The status of the item can be estimated along with other parameters in the model. The model includes parameters for both uniform and nonuniform DIF and allows the inclusion of covariates to model the DIF parameters as a function of item characteristics. The model is heavily parametrized, and Soares and colleagues note that identification problems may require restricting some parameters or using more informative prior distributions. Specifying at least one anchor (DIF-free) item may be necessary for the procedure to converge. Large sample sizes improve the performance of the procedure. Soares et al. point out that one of the advantages of this model is that it yields proficiency estimates that are naturally purified. This approach is promising and shows the power of Bayesian procedures for estimating parameters of very complex and general models.

A Taxonomy of DIF Procedures

Table 8.1 provides a classification of procedures for investigating DIF across groups. Procedures can be classified according to the nature or treatment of the response variable and the conditioning variable. The response variable may be discrete, as in dichotomous or polytomous item responses, or continuous, as in a testlet, bundle, or test score. The conditioning or matching variable may be observed or latent and discrete (categorical) or continuous. The table shows how the procedures discussed in this chapter relate to each other. The procedures in parentheses were not discussed

TABLE 8.1. A Taxonomy of Procedures for Investigating Differential Response Functioning

Conditioning/ matching variable		Response variable	
		Discrete	Continuous
Observed	Discrete	MH, SIBTEST, STD	SIBTEST
	Continuous	Logistic regression	(Linear regression, path analysis)
Latent	Discrete	(Latent class models)	(Latent profile analysis)
	Continuous	IRT, SEM	SEM

explicitly in this chapter. The case of a continuous response variable and an observed continuous conditioning variable is the case of differential predictive validity; the case where the conditioning variable is latent and discrete has not, to our knowledge, been studied in the context of DIF.

Conclusion

As should be clear from this chapter, differential functioning of items and item sets continues to be a topic of great interest in the measurement community. The distribution of research between methods and substantive explanations, however, remains heavily skewed toward methods, with increasingly complex models being developed. It is noteworthy that it is easier to develop and estimate multigroup multilevel nonlinear latent variable models than it is to derive substantive explanations for DIF. Perhaps the fourth phase of DIF research will be a return to the "Hmm . . ." phase. Developments in cognitive psychology and other fields, in combination with powerful modeling techniques, may improve our understanding of DIF. Given the remarkable evolution of the field over the last 40 years, it is difficult to predict where the field will be in 10 or 20 years from now. However, if the past is a predictor of the future, there are many developments yet to come.

REFERENCES

Ackerman, T. A. (1992). A didactic explanation of item bias, item impact, and item validity from a multidimensional perspective. *Journal of Educational Measurement, 29,* 67–91.

Allalouf, A., Hambleton, R. K., & Sireci, S. G. (1999). Identifying the causes of DIF in translated verbal items. *Journal of Educational Measurement, 36*(3), 185–198.

Angoff, W. H. (1972, September). *A technique for the investigation of cultural differences.* Paper presented at the annual meeting of the American Psychological Association, Honolulu, HI.

Azocar, F., Arean, P., Miranda, J., & Munoz, R. F. (2001). Differential item functioning in a Spanish translation of the Beck Depression Inventory. *Journal of Clinical Psychology, 57,* 355–365.

Banks, K. (2013). A synthesis of the peer-reviewed differential bundle functioning research. *Educational Measurement: Issues and Practice, 32*(1), 43–55.

Beretvas, S. N., & Walker, C. M. (2012). Distinguishing differential testlet functioning from differential bundle functioning using the multilevel measurement model. *Educational and Psychological Measurement, 72*(2), 200–223.

Berk, R. A. (Ed.). (1982). *Handbook for detecting biased test items.* Baltimore: Johns Hopkins University Press.

Bolt, D. M., Hare, R. D., Vitale, J. E., & Newman, J. P. (2004). A multigroup item response theory analysis of the Psychopathy Checklist—Revised. *Psychological Assessment, 16,* 155–168.

Bolt, D. M., & Stout, W. (1996). Differential item functioning: Its multidimensional model and resulting SIBTEST detection procedure. *Behaviormetrika, 23*(1), 67–95.

Bradlow, E. T., Wainer, H., & Wang, X. (1999). A Bayesian random effects model for testlets. *Psychometrika, 64,* 153–168.

Camilli, G. (1992). A conceptual analysis of differential item functioning in terms of a multidimensional item response model. *Applied Psychological Measurement, 16,* 129–147.

Camilli, G. (1993). The case against item bias detection techniques based on internal criteria: Do item bias procedures obscure test fairness issues? In P. W. Holland & H. Wainer (Eds.), *Differential item functioning* (pp. 397–418). Hillsdale, NJ: Erlbaum.

Camilli, G. (2006). Test fairness. In R. L. Brennan (Ed.), *Educational measurement* (4th ed., pp. 221–256). Westport, CT: American Council on Education/Praeger.

Camilli, G., & Congdon, P. (1999). Application of a method of estimating DIF for polytomous test items. *Journal of Educational and Behavioral Statistics, 24,* 323–341.

Camilli, G., & Shepard, L. (1994). *Methods for identifying biased test items.* Newbury Park, CA: Sage.

Cardall, C., & Coffman, W. E. (1964). A method for comparing the performance of different groups on the same items of a test. *Research and Development Reports, 9,* 64–65. Princeton, NJ: Educational Testing Service.

Chang, H., Mazzeo, J., & Roussos, L. A. (1996). Detecting DIF for polytomously scored items: An adaptation of the SIBTEST procedure. *Journal of Educational Measurement, 33,* 333–353.

Clauser, B. E., Mazor, K. [M.], & Hambleton, R. K. (1991). The influence of test homogeneity on the identification of DIF test items using the Mantel–Haenszel procedure. *Applied Psychological Measurement, 15*(4), 353–359.

Clauser, B. [E.], Mazor, K. [M.], & Hambleton, R. K. (1993). The effects of purification of the matching criterion on the identification of DIF using the Mantel–Haenszel procedure. *Applied Measurement in Education, 6,* 269–280.

Clauser, B. [E.], Mazor, K. M., & Hambleton, R. K. (1994). The effects of score group width on the Mantel–Haenszel procedure. *Journal of Educational Measurement, 31*(1), 67–78.

Cole, N. S. (1993). History and development of DIF. In P. W. Holland & H. Wainer (Eds.), *Differential item functioning* (pp. 25–30). Hillsdale, NJ: Erlbaum.

Cole, N. S., & Moss, P. A. (1989). Bias in test use. In R. L. Linn (Ed.), *Educational measurement* (3rd ed., pp. 201–220). Phoenix, AZ: American Council on Education/Macmillan.

de Ayala, R. J., Kim, S., Stapleton, L. M., & Dayton, C. M. (2002). Differential item functioning: A mixture distribution conceptualization. *International Journal of Testing, 2,* 243–276.

DeMars, C. E., & Lau, A. (2011). Differential item functioning detection with latent classes: How accurately can we detect who is responding differentially? *Educational and Psychological Measurement, 71*(4), 597–616.

Dorans, N. J., & Holland, P. W. (1993). DIF detection and description: Mantel–Haenszel and standardization. In P. W. Holland & H. Wainer (Eds.), *Differential item functioning* (pp. 35–66). Hillsdale, NJ: Erlbaum.

Dorans, N. J., & Kulick, E. (1986). Demonstrating the utility of the standardization approach to assessing unexpected differential item performance on the Scholastic Aptitude Test. *Journal of Educational Measurement, 23*, 355–368.

Dorans, N. J., & Schmitt, A. J. (1991). *Constructed response and differential item functioning: A pragmatic approach* (Research Rep. No. 91-47). Princeton, NJ: Educational Testing Service.

Douglas, J., Roussos, L., & Stout, W. F. (1996). Item bundle DIF hypothesis testing: Identifying suspect bundles and assessing their DIF. *Journal of Educational Measurement, 33*, 465–484.

Finch, W. H. (2005). The MIMIC model as a method for detecting DIF: Comparison with Mantel–Haenszel, SIBTEST, and the IRT likelihood ratio. *Applied Psychological Measurement, 29*(4), 278–295.

Finch, W. H. (2012). The MIMIC model as a tool for differential bundle functioning detection. *Applied Psychological Measurement, 36*(1), 40–59.

Fukuhara, H., & Kamata, A. (2011). A bifactor multidimensional item response theory model for differential item functioning analysis on testlet-based items. *Applied Psychological Measurement, 35*, 604–622.

Gallo, J. J., Anthony, J. C., & Muthén, B. O. (1994). Age differences in the symptoms of depression: A latent trait analysis. *Journal of Gerontology: Psychological Sciences, 49*, 251–264.

Hambleton, R. K. (1994). Guidelines for adapting educational and psychological tests: A progress report. *European Journal of Psychological Assessment, 10*(3), 229–244.

Hambleton, R. K., & Jones, R. W. (1994). Comparison of empirical and judgmental procedures for detecting differential item functioning. *Educational Research Quarterly, 18*(1), 21–36.

Hambleton, R. K., & Rogers, H. J. (1989). Detecting potentially biased test items: Comparison of the IRT area and Mantel–Haenszel methods. *Applied Measurement in Education, 2*, 313–334.

Hambleton, R. K., & Rogers, H. J. (1991). Evaluation of the plot method for identifying potentially biased test items. In P. L. Dann, S. H. Irvine, & J. M. Collis (Eds.), *Computer-based human assessment* (pp. 307–330). Boston: Kluwer.

Holland, P. W., & Thayer, D. T. (1988). Differential item functioning and the Mantel–Haenszel procedure. In H. Wainer & H. I. Braun (Eds.), *Test validity* (pp. 129–145). Hillsdale, NJ: Erlbaum.

Holland, P. W., & Wainer, H. (Eds.). (1993). *Differential item functioning*. Hillsdale, NJ: Erlbaum.

Jeon, M., Rijmen, F., & Rabe-Hesketh, S. (2013). Modeling differential item functioning using a generalization of the multiple-group bifactor model. *Journal of Educational and Behavioral Statistics, 38*(1), 32–60.

Jodoin, M. G., & Gierl, M. J. (2001). Evaluating Type I error and power rates using an effect size measure with the logistic regression procedure for DIF detection. *Applied Measurement in Education, 14*, 329–349.

Kim, E. S., & Yoon, M. (2011). Testing measurement invariance: A comparison of multiple-group categorical CFA and IRT. *Structural Equation Modeling, 18*, 212–228.

Kim, S.-H., Cohen, A. S., Alagoz, C., & Kim, S. (2007). DIF detection and effect size measures for polytomously scored items. *Journal of Educational Measurement, 44*, 93–116.

Li, H., & Stout, W. F. (1996). A new procedure for detection of crossing DIF. *Psychometrika, 61*(4), 647–677.

Lord, F. M. (1977). A study of item bias, using item characteristic curve theory. In Y. H. Poortinga (Ed.), *Basic problems in cross-cultural psychology* (pp. 19–29). Amsterdam: Swets & Zeitlinger.

Lord, F. M. (1980). *Applications of item response theory to practical testing problems*. Hillsdale, NJ: Erlbaum.

Lu, R., & Jiao, H. (2009, April). *Detecting DIF using the mixture Rasch model*. Paper presented at the annual meeting of the National Council on Measurement in Education, San Diego, CA.

Mazor, K. M., Clauser, B., & Hambleton, R. K. (1992). The effect of sample size on the functioning of the Mantel–Haenszel statistic. *Educational and Psychological Measurement, 52*, 443–451.

Mazor, K. M., Clauser, B., & Hambleton, R. K. (1994). Identification of non-uniform differential item functioning using a variation of the Mantel–Haenszel procedure. *Educational and Psychological Measurement, 54*(2), 284–291.

Mazor, K. M., Hambleton, R. K., & Clauser, B. E. (1998). Multidimensional DIF analyses: The effects of matching on unidimensional subtest scores. *Applied Psychological Measurement, 22*(4), 357–367.

Meade, A. W., & Lautenschlager, G. J. (2004). A comparison of item response theory and confirmatory factor analytic methodologies for establishing measurement equivalence/invariance. *Organizational Research Methods, 7*, 361–388.

Mellenbergh, G. J. (1982). Contingency table models for assessing item bias. *Journal of Educational Statistics, 7*(2), 105–118.

Monahan, P. O., McHorney, C. A., Stump, T. E., & Perkins, A. J. (2007). Odds ratio, delta, ETS classification, and standardization measures of DIF magnitude for binary logistic regression. *Journal of Educational and Behavioral Statistics, 32*(1), 92–109.

Muthén, B. O. (1984). A general structural equation model with dichotomous, ordered categorical, and continuous latent variable indicators. *Psychometrika, 49*, 115–132.

Muthén, B. O. (1985). A method for studying the homogeneity of test items with respect to other relevant variables. *Journal of Educational Statistics, 10*, 121–132.

Muthén, B. O. (1988). Some uses of structural equation modeling in validity studies: Extending IRT to external variables. In H. Wainer & H. Braun (Eds.), *Test validity* (pp. 213–238). Hillsdale, NJ: Erlbaum.

Muthén, B. O., & Christoffersson, A. (1981). Simultaneous factor analysis of dichotomous variables in several groups. *Psychometrika, 46*, 407–419.

Muthén, B. O., Kao, C., & Burstein, L. (1991). Instructionally sensitive psychometrics: An application of a new IRT-based detection technique to mathematics achievement test items. *Journal of Educational Measurement, 28*, 1–22.

Muthén, L. K., & Muthén, B. O. (1998–2014). *Mplus: Statistical analysis with latent variables* [Computer software]. Los Angeles: Author.

O'Neill, K. A., & McPeek, W. M. (1993). Item and test characteristics that are associated with differential item functioning. In P. W. Holland & H. Wainer (Eds.), *Differential item functioning* (pp. 255–276). Hillsdale, NJ: Erlbaum.

Orlando, M., & Marshall, G. N. (2002). Differential item functioning in a Spanish translation of the PTSD checklist: Detection and evaluation of impact. *Psychological Assessment, 14*, 50–59.

Penfield, R. D., & Algina, J. (2003). Applying the LiuéAgresti estimator of the cumulative common odds ratio to DIF detection in polytomous items. *Journal of Educational Measurement, 40*, 353–370.

Penfield, R. D., & Camilli, G. (2007). Differential item functioning and item bias. In C. R.

Rao & S. Sinharay (Eds.), *Handbook of statistics: Psychometrics* (Vol. 26, pp. 125–167). Amsterdam: Elsevier.

Penfield, R. D., & Lam, T. C. M. (2000). Assessing differential item functioning in performance assessment: Review and recommendations. *Educational Measurement: Issues and Practice, 19*(3), 5–15.

Potenza, M. T., & Dorans, N. J. (1995). DIF assessment for polytomously scored items: A framework for classification and evaluation. *Applied Psychological Measurement, 19*(1), 23–37.

Raju, N. S. (1988). The area between two item characteristic curves. *Psychometrika, 53*, 495–502.

Raju, N. S., van der Linden, W. J., & Fleer, P. F. (1995). IRT-based internal measures of differential items and tests. *Applied Psychological Measurement, 19*, 353–368.

Rogers, H. J., & Hambleton, R. K. (1989). Evaluation of computer simulated baseline statistics for use in item bias studies. *Educational and Psychological Measurement, 49*, 355–369.

Rogers, H. J., & Swaminathan, H. (1993). A comparison of the logistic regression and Mantel–Haenszel procedures for detecting differential item functioning. *Applied Psychological Measurement, 17*, 105–116.

Rogers, H. J., & Swaminathan, H. (1998, August). *A multilevel approach for investigating DIF*. Paper presented at the annual meeting of the American Psychological Association, San Francisco, CA.

Rogers, H. J., Swaminathan, H., & Sen, R. (2011, May). *Assessing factorial invariance in nonlinear latent variable models*. Paper presented at the Modern Modeling Methods Conference, Storrs CT.

Roussos, L. A., & Stout, W. F. (1996a). A multidimensionality-based DIF analysis paradigm. *Applied Psychological Measurement, 20*, 355–371.

Roussos, L. A., & Stout, W. F. (1996b). Simulation studies of the effects of small sample size and studied item parameters on SIBTEST and Mantel–Haenszel Type I error performance. *Journal of Educational Measurement, 33*, 215–230.

Samuelsen, K. M. (2005). *Examining differential item functioning from a latent class perspective*. Unpublished doctoral dissertation, University of Maryland, College Park, MD.

Scheuneman, J. D. (1975, April). *A new method of assessing bias in test items*. Paper presented at the annual meeting of the American Educational Research Association, Washington, DC.

Scheuneman, J. D. (1987). An experimental, exploratory study of causes of bias in test items. *Journal of Educational Measurement, 24*(2), 97–118.

Scheuneman, J. D., & Gerritz, K. (1990). Using differential item functioning procedures to explore sources of item difficulty and group performance characteristics. *Journal of Educational Measurement, 27*, 109–131.

Schmitt, A. P., & Dorans, N. J. (1990). Differential item functioning for minority examinees on the SAT. *Journal of Educational Measurement, 27*(1), 67–81.

Schmitt, A. P., Holland, P. W., & Dorans, N. J. (1993). Evaluating hypotheses about differential item functioning. In P. W. Holland & H. Wainer (Eds.), *Differential item functioning* (pp. 281–316). Hillsdale, NJ: Erlbaum.

Shealy, R., & Stout, W. F. (1993a). An item response theory model for test bias and differential item functioning. In P. W. Holland & H. Wainer (Eds.), *Differential item functioning* (pp. 197–239). Hillsdale, NJ: Erlbaum.

Shealy, R., & Stout, W. F. (1993b). A model-based standardization approach that separates true bias/DIF from group differences and detects test bias/DIF as well as item bias/DIF. *Psychometrika, 58*, 150–194.

Shepard, L. A. (1982). Definitions of bias. In R. A. Berk (Ed.), *Handbook for detecting biased test items*. Baltimore: Johns Hopkins University Press.

Sinharay, S., & Dorans, N. J. (2010). Two simple approaches to overcome a problem with the Mantel–Haenszel statistic: Comments on Wang, Bradlow, Wainer, and Muller (2008). *Journal of Educational and Behavioral Statistics, 35*(4), 474–488.

Skaggs, G., & Lissitz, R. W. (1992). The consistency of detecting item bias across different test administrations: Implications of another failure. *Journal of Educational Measurement, 29*(3), 227–242.

Soares, T. M., Gonçalves, F. B., & Gamerman, D. (2009). An integrated Bayesian model for DIF analysis. *Journal of Educational and Behavioral Statistics, 34*(3), 348–377.

Stark, S., Chernyshenko, O. S., & Drasgow, F. (2006). Detecting differential item functioning with confirmatory factor analysis and item response theory: Toward a unified strategy. *Journal of Applied Psychology, 91*, 1291–1306.

Steinberg, L., & Thissen, D. (2006). Using effect sizes for research reporting: Examples using item response theory to analyze differential item functioning. *Psychological Methods, 11*, 402–515.

Swaminathan, H., & Rogers, H. J. (1990). Detecting differential item functioning using logistic regression procedures. *Journal of Educational Measurement, 27*, 361–370.

Takane, Y., & de Leeuw, J. (1987). On the relationship between item response theory and factor analysis of discretized variables. *Psychometrika, 52*, 393–408.

Thissen, D., Steinberg, L., & Wainer, H. (1993). Detection of differential item functioning using the parameters of item response models. In P. W. Holland & H. Wainer (Eds.), *Differential item functioning* (pp. 67–114). Hillsdale, NJ: Erlbaum.

Wang, X., Bradlow, E. T., Wainer, H., & Muller, E. S. (2008). A Bayesian method for studying DIF: A cautionary tale filled with surprises and delights. *Journal of Educational and Behavioral Statistics, 22*, 363–384.

Welch, C., & Hoover, H. D. (1993). Procedures for extending item bias techniques to polytomously scored items. *Applied Measurement in Education, 6*, 1–19.

Woods, C. M. (2009). Evaluation of MIMIC-model methods for DIF testing with comparison to two-group analysis. *Multivariate Behavioral Research, 44*, 1–27.

Woods, C. M., & Grimm, K. J. (2009). Testing for nonuniform differential item functioning with multiple indicator multiple cause models. *Applied Psychological Measurement, 35*(5), 339–361.

Zieky, M. (1993). Practical questions in the use of DIF statistics in test development. In P. W. Holland & H. Wainer (Eds.), *Differential item functioning* (pp. 337–348). Hillsdale, NJ: Erlbaum.

Zenisky, A. L., Hambleton, R. K., & Robin, F. (2003). Detection of differential item functioning in large-scale state assessments: A study evaluating a two-stage approach. *Educational and Psychological Measurement, 63*(1), 51–64.

Zumbo, B. D. (1999). *A handbook on the theory and methods of differential item functioning (DIF)*. Ottawa, Ontario, Canada: Directorate of Human Resources Research and Evaluation, Department of National Defense.

Zumbo, B. D. (2007). Three generations of DIF analyses: Considering where it has been, where it is now, and where it is going. *Language Assessment Quarterly, 4*(2), 223–233.

Zwick, R., Donoghue, J. R., & Grima, A. (1993). Assessment of differential item functioning for performance tasks. *Journal of Educational Measurement, 30*, 233–251.

CHAPTER 9

Understanding Two-Dimensional Models of Multidimensional Item Response Theory through Graphical Representations

Terry A. Ackerman and Robert A. Henson

Over the past several years there has been a growth of interest in multidimensional item response theory (MIRT) models, especially diagnostic classification models (DCM) (Rupp, Templin, & Henson, 2010). These new MIRT models take a different approach in the type of information they provide. Specifically, instead of providing ability estimates along latent continuums, the DCM provide information about whether examinees have achieved a predesignated level of competency on each trait being measured. The purpose of this chapter is to examine graphical representations of four particular two-dimensional MIRT models to illustrate how different aspects of each model can be represented.

Graphical representations (GR) can provide greater insight for measurement specialists and item/test developers about an item. Specifically, graphs can be used to show the general relationship between the latent ability (or abilities) and the observed outcome, most commonly the probability of a correct response. GRs can also be used to quickly present the value of an item. For example, the "value" of an item (or test) can be expressed through indices such as Fisher's information or Kullback–Leibler information. In addition, when using multidimensional models, GRs also can provide a link between quantitative analyses of the multiple dimensions and substantive interpretations of the score scale and thereby inform the test development process.

We examine the compensatory logistic model, the noncompensatory logistic model, a noncompensatory diagnostic model (DINA), and a compensatory diagnostic model (CRUM/GDM). We first provide a foundational background by reviewing the unidimensional perspective of the models and how things change as a second dimension is added. The DCMs (also referred to as *cognitive diagnosis models*) are briefly

143

introduced, and because DCMs are not typically discussed in the context of a single attribute but instead usually have several attributes, we discuss them only as multidimensional models. After discussing the models, three particular aspects of GRs are discussed: item representation, item information, and composite score representation.

The Models

Most practitioners are familiar with the two-parameter logistic (2PL) model given as

$$P_{ij} = \frac{1.0}{1.0 + e^{-1.7a_i(\theta_j - b_i)}} \tag{9.1}$$

where a_i represents the degree to which item i can discriminate or distinguish between levels of θ, the latent trait or ability; and b_i denotes the difficulty level of the item. This model can easily be expanded to include two latent abilities. However, when multiple skills are considered, there are many ways in which the interaction with the characteristics can be modeled. Although we focus on four such models, more multidimensional approaches exist (van der Linden & Hambleton, 1997).

A direct extension of the 2PL unidimensional model is the two-dimensional compensatory model, which can be expressed as

$$P_{ij} = \frac{1.0}{1.0 + e^{-(a_{1i}\theta_{1j} + a_{2i}\theta_{2j} + d_i)}} \tag{9.2}$$

where a_{1i} and a_{2i} represent the discrimination parameters for item i on dimension one and two, respectively; and θ_{1j} and θ_{2j} denote the latent abilities for examinee j. In this model, because item difficulty for each dimension is indeterminate, we have just one overall difficulty parameter for item i, denoted d_i. This model is described as *compensatory* because the abilities weighted by the item's respective discrimination parameters are additive in the logit. Thus, being "low" on one ability can be compensated by being "high" on the other ability. This aspect is illustrated later in the chapter. Note further, although it is not discussed in this chapter, the three-parameter logistic (3PL) MIRT model also has just one guessing or "c" parameter, following the assumption that guessing is modeled according to the overall probability of a correct response and is not broken down for each dimension.

Another way to express the interaction between the two traits is in a noncompensatory fashion as shown in the noncompensatory MIRT model given as

$$P_{ij} = \left[\frac{1.0}{1.0 + e^{-1.7(a_{1i}\theta_{1j} - b_{1i})}} \right]\left[\frac{1.0}{1.0 + e^{-1.7(a_{2i}\theta_{2j} - b_{2i})}} \right] \tag{9.3}$$

In this model, for a given item i, each dimension has a discrimination parameter, a_{1i} and a_{2i}, as well as a difficulty parameter, b_{1i} and b_{2i}. Also θ_{1j} and θ_{2j} denote the latent abilities on the two dimensions for examinee j. Notice also that this model is essentially the product of two 2PL unidimensional IRT models, one for each dimension.

The multiplicative nature of this model also implies that being "low" on one dimension cannot be compensated by being "high" on the other dimension. That is, the overall probability of correct response is never greater than the largest probability of the two dimensions. For example, if the first dimension (θ_1) component were 0.20, even if the second dimensional component (θ_2) were 1.0, the overall probability of correct response would only be 0.20.

Distinct from the previous models discussed, DCMs assume that ability can be based on a mastery profile α_j. The mastery profile is a multidimensional indicator vector of the attributes (or skills) an examinee has mastered or has not mastered. The DCM that is most similar to the MIRT model presented in Equation 9.2 is a two-dimensional compensatory diagnostic model (CGUM/GDM), which was first referred to as the *Compensatory RUM*. Using the notation presented in Rupp and colleagues (2010), this model can be expressed as

$$P_{ij} = \frac{1.0}{1.0 + e^{-1.7(\lambda_{1i}\alpha_{1j} + \lambda_{2i}\alpha_{2j} + \lambda_{0i})}} \tag{9.4}$$

where λ_{1i} and λ_{2i} are the discrimination parameters for item i on the first and second dimensions, α_{1j} and α_{2j} denote the two latent dichotomous abilities for examinee j, and, λ_{0i} represents the difficulty parameter for item i. Note that this model is very similar to the compensatory model given in Equation 9.2. The difference between the two models is that there are only two values of the latent attributes in a and the overall interpretation of the intercept. As opposed to defining an "average" difficulty of the item, λ_{0i} is related to the probability of a correct response for someone who has not mastered any of the measured attributes.

The final model is the noncompensatory diagnostic model called DINA (the deterministic inputs, noisy, "AND-gate" model; Junker & Sijtsma, 2001). In contrast to the compensatory model, DINA divides examinees into only two groups. The first group has mastered all measured attributes by the item ($\eta_{ij} = 1$) and thus should correctly respond to the item, and a second group that has not mastered at least one of the measured items ($\eta_{ij} = 0$) and should miss the item. Given the groups defined by η_{ij}, the probability of correct response to item i for person j can be written as

$$P_{ij} = (1 - s_j)^{\eta_i} g_j^{(1-\eta_i)} \tag{9.5}$$

where s_j is referred to as the "slip" parameter and specifies the probability that an examinee who should answer the item correctly "slips up" and misses the item. The parameter g_j represents the probability that an examinee correctly "guesses" (i.e., the guessing parameter) the answer when in fact he or she is expected to miss the item.

Illustrations of Theoretical Background

An interesting graphical perspective that many practitioners and researchers rarely see is that of the unidimensional 2PL model and its two-dimensional extension. Although many practitioners are familiar with the item characteristic curve (ICC), few understand the theoretical underpinning that motivates the model. For item i, Y_i' represents the latent variable that determines an examinee's performance on item i for which there is no guessing. There is also a threshold, γ_i, such that if an examinee is above this threshold, he or she would be expected to get the item correct. That is, if $Y_i' > \gamma_i$, then the response to item i (denoted u_i) is 1. The ICC can be thought of as the regression of a latent variable of an artificially dichotomized response, u_i, onto the θ-scale. This regression is assumed to be linear, and the conditional distribution of Y_i' is normally distributed and homoscedastic. This relationship can also be thought of in terms of the biserial correlation, $\rho_{i\theta}$. To the extent to which the raw score approximates the latent θ, the IRT a_i and b_i parameters can be expressed as

$$a_i = \frac{\rho_{i\theta}}{\sqrt{1-\rho_{i\theta}^2}} \tag{9.6}$$

$$b_i = \frac{\gamma_i}{\sqrt{1-\rho_{i\theta}^2}} = \frac{z(p_i)}{\sqrt{1-\rho_{i\theta}^2}} \tag{9.7}$$

where $\rho_{i\theta}$ represents the biserial correlation, γ_i is the threshold one needs to achieve to respond correctly to item i, and $z(p_i)$ represents the z-value associated with the proportion correct value. Illustrations relating the biserial correlation and threshold and conditional distributions to the ICC are displayed in Figure 9.1.

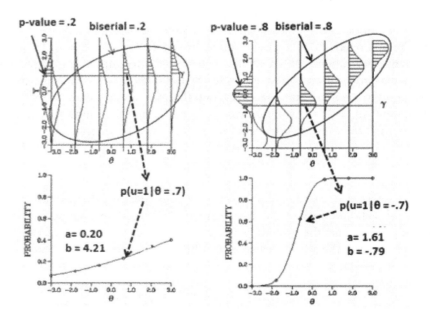

FIGURE 9.1. A diagram illustrating the theoretical motivation for the ICC of a very difficult item with low discrimination, and an easy item with high discrimination.

The item shown on the left in Figure 9.1 is a very low discriminating item with a biserial correlation (r_{bis}) of .2, $a = 0.2$, and a high threshold (i.e., a very difficult item) with p-value $=.2$ and $b = 4.21$. Note that the p-value is the proportion of the marginal distribution above the threshold γ. The item shown on the right has the opposite configuration: high discrimination with $r_{bis} = .8$, $a = 1.61$, and a lower threshold (i.e., an easy item) with p-value $= .8$ and $b = -0.79$. The high biserial is portrayed by the narrow ellipse, the low biserial by a wider ellipse. This is equivalent to illustrating different values of a Pearson product–moment correlation in which one would sketch an ellipse enclosing a hypothetical bivariate distribution of values in a scatter plot: the higher the correlation, then the more linear the relationship and thus the narrower the ellipse. Drawn within each ellipse are the conditional normal ogive curves that follow directly from the assumption of simple linear regression. The proportion of the conditional distribution above the threshold line, γ, indicated by the cross-hatched area in the conditional distribution, corresponds to the proportion of those examinees at the given level of proficiency who are expected to get the item correct. This proportion of the conditional distribution lying above the threshold for a given θ is also expressed by the normal ogive IRT model formula, in which the integration is of the conditional normal curve (Hambleton & Swaminathan, 1985).

$$p_i(u = 1 \mid \theta) = \int_{-\infty}^{a(\theta-b)} \frac{1}{\sqrt{2\pi}} \exp\left(-\frac{1}{2}t^2\right) dt \qquad (9.8)$$

It can also be seen that in both figures, the proportion of the marginal distribution lying above the threshold corresponds to the p-value or the proportion of examinees that would be expected to answer the item correctly.

Two-Dimensional Extension

When extending the unidimensional model to the multidimensional model, one soon realizes that conceptually things become more complicated to illustrate. Like its unidimensional counterpart, the two-dimensional model is based upon the assumption that for each item i there is some threshold τ_i, such that the scored response to item i, u_i, can be broken down into a dichotomy of a correct and incorrect response.

In the two-dimensional case, the threshold is actually a threshold plane, and at each (θ_1, θ_2) location in the latent ability plane there is a conditional normal curve. The area beyond the threshold plane in each normal conditional distribution, as in the unidimensional case, corresponds to the probability of a correct response for examinees possessing this two-dimensional composite of proficiency. This relationship is graphically illustrated in Figure 9.2. Although more complicated, the concept is a direct extension of the unidimensional case. To simplify the extension to the two-dimensional case, each graph in Figure 9.2 is broken down into progressive steps illustrating the construction of the item response surface (IRS). Beginning in the upper left are the three-dimensional axes (θ_1, θ_2 and Y [the propensity to answer the given item correctly]). To the right of the axes the regression plane, defined by $Y = a_1\theta_1 + a_2\theta_2$, has

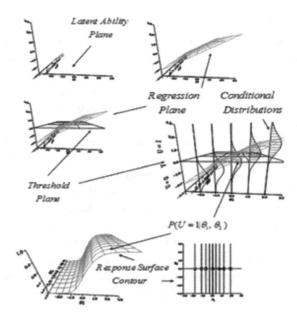

FIGURE 9.2. Graphical display illustrating the underlying motivation for a two-dimensional response surface.

been added. In Figure 9.2, $a_1 = 0$. These threshold planes correspond to the regression lines shown in Figure 9.1. The threshold plane now appears in the center left of each figure. In each case the threshold has been set to correspond to a p-value of .5. In the center right of Figure 9.2, a row of conditional normal distributions has been added. The cross-hatched portion above the threshold plane corresponds to the proportion of examinees at this location (θ_1, θ_2) expected to answer the item correctly. The conditional normals are only drawn in a row where $\theta_2 = -3$. When taken in concert, these proportions will form the item characteristic surface (ICS) shown at the bottom left of Figure 9.2. The corresponding contour is plotted in the lower right.

One important issue that practitioners need to consider, but is not discussed in this chapter, is how the correlation between the multiple latent abilities affects each item's parameter estimates. This is discussed from a factor analytic approach by Ackerman (2005) and from a logistic approach by Smith (2002).

Item Representation

In unidimensional models there are many concepts that can be easily displayed because there is only a single latent measure of ability and outcome. As a result, representation of the functional relationship between this latent ability and an outcome can be easily graphed in a two-dimensional plot.

Compensatory and Noncompensatory Items

Because the compensatory and noncompensatory items are based upon a continuous two-dimensional latent space, researchers can graphically represent the probability of a correct response for examinee j on item i for all θ_{1j}, θ_{2j} combinations as a response surface. This surface is the two-dimensional analog to the unidimensional ICC. An example of such a surface for a compensatory item with parameters $a_1 = 1.80$, $a_2 = .08$, and $d = 0.95$ from four different perspectives is shown in Figure 9.3.

An example of a response surface for the noncompensatory model with parameters of $a_1 = 2.0$, $a_2 = .9$, $b_1 = .6$, and $b_2 = .5$ is shown from four different perspectives in Figure 9.4. The effect of the multiplicative nature of this model can be seen by the curving of the surface.

The response surfaces are not very helpful in that only one can be examined at a time, unlike their unidimensional ICC counterparts. A more helpful representation would be to construct a contour plot for each surface. Such plots illustrate the equi-probability contours of the response surface. Representations of such plots are shown in Figure 9.5 for two items from the compensatory model and one item from the non-compensatory model. The x- and y-axes represent the scales for θ_1 and θ_2. The A, B, and C in each graph represent hypothetical examinees. The contour plot on the left of Figure 9.5 illustrates an item that discriminates only among levels of θ_1 with parameters $a_1 = 1.5$, $a_2 = 0$, and $d = 0.3$. Notice that examinees A and B, who have the same θ_1 value of about −1 and differ greatly on their θ_2 abilities, have exactly the same probability of a correct response of .2. That is, even though there is a huge discrepancy in their θ_2 values, there is no compensation when an item is distinguishing between levels of proficiency on only one ability. Notice also that examinees B and C, who have the same θ_2 ability but differ greatly on their θ_1 abilities, do have different probabilities of correct response: −.2 for B and .8 for C. Also note that the larger the a-parameter

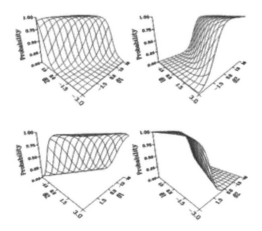

FIGURE 9.3. An example of a compensatory model item characteristic surface.

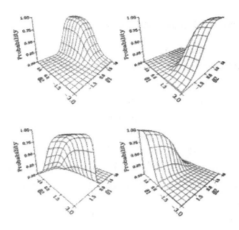

FIGURE 9.4. An example of a noncompensatory response surface.

values, the steeper the response surface and the closer together the equiprobability contours.

The middle contour plot in Figure 9.5 represents an item that is measuring both θ_1 and θ_2 equally. That is, $a_1 = a_2 = 1.0$. In this case, examinees A and B have opposite "profiles." That is, examinee A is low on θ_1 but high on θ_2. Examinee B is high on θ_1 and low on θ_2. However, due to the compensatory nature of this model, both examinees have the same probability of a correct response of .5. Thus, compensation in this model is maximal when both dimensions are measured equally well. (This is also why some researchers refer to this model as a *partially compensatory model*, because the degree of compensation is a function of the discrimination parameters. As seen in the contour plot on the left of Figure 9.5, when only one latent trait is being measured, there is no compensation.)

The contour plot also helps one to see the difference between the compensatory and noncompensatory models. The curving around of the response surface is much

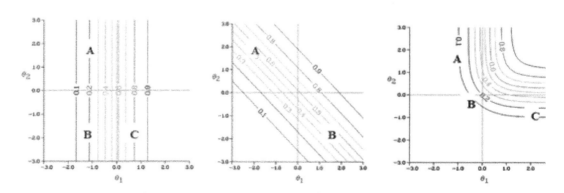

FIGURE 9.5. A contour plot for compensatory and noncompensatory items.

more noticeable when viewed in terms of contours. The contour plot for the noncompensatory model with parameters $a_1 = 1.2$, $a_2 = 1.1$, $b_1 = -.60$, and $b_2 = .50$ is displayed on the right in Figure 9.5. Notice also in this contour plot that subjects A, B, and C all have approximately the same probability of a correct response, even though their ability profiles are quite distinct. That is, examinee A is high on θ_2 and low on θ_1, examinee B is low on θ_1 and low on θ_2, and examinee C has the opposite profile of examinee A and is low on θ_2 and high on θ_1. Clearly in this case, there is no compensation; being high on one ability offers no compensation for examinees who are low on the other ability.

Although contours are an improvement over response surfaces, practitioners can examine only one item at a time with this method. Therefore, an attractive way of presenting many items is to illustrate items for these models using vectors. Following the work of Reckase (1985), Reckase and McKinley (1991), Ackerman (1994b, 1996) and Ackerman, Gierl, and Walker (2003), an item can be represented as a vector where the length of the vector, MDISC, is a function of the discrimination of the item:

$$\text{MDISC} = \sqrt{\left(a_1^2 + a_2^2\right)} \tag{9.9}$$

The vector is orthogonal to and lies on the $p = .5$ equiprobability contour. All vectors lie on a line that passes through the origin of the θ_1–θ_2 coordinate system. Because discrimination parameters are constrained to be positive, vectors can lie in only the first and third quadrants. The distance from the origin to the tail of vector, D, is equal to

$$\text{D} = \frac{-d}{\text{MDISC}} \tag{9.10}$$

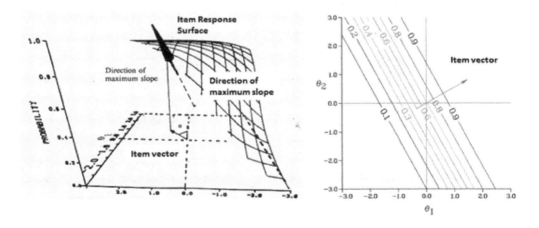

FIGURE 9.6. An item vector shown in relationship to its corresponding response surface.

The angular direction of the vector with the θ_1-axis, α, can be obtained using the formula

$$\alpha = \cos^{-1}\left(\frac{a_1}{\text{MDISC}}\right) \tag{9.11}$$

Note that the angular direction is a function of the ratio of the a_1 parameter with MDISC. If $a_2 = 0$, then the vector will lie along the θ_1-axis. If $a_1 = a_2$, the vector will lie at a 45-degree angle. An example of an item vector in relationship to a response surface is illustrated in Figure 9.6 on page 151.

The image on the right in Figure 9.6 is a vector that is imposed upon a contour plot of an item. The parameters for this item are $a_1 = 1.8$, $a_2 = 1$, and $d = 0.8$. Note that the more discriminating an item is, the closer together the equiprobability contours and the longer the vector.

Item vectors can be color-coded according to content. When this is done, practitioners can answer several different questions: Are items from a certain content area more discriminating or more difficult? Do different items from different content areas measure different ability composites? How similar are the vector profiles for different yet "parallel" forms? An example illustrating the use of vectors is shown in Figure 9.7. The plot on the left of Figure 9.7 is for a 101-item test with three categories of items.[1] Notice how items for each content area tend to lie within a relatively narrow sector. The plot on the right of Figure 9.7 illustrates how vectors can be used to examine the confounding of discrimination and difficulty.

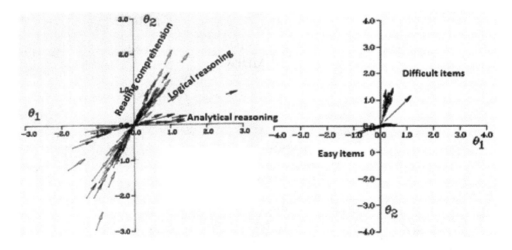

FIGURE 9.7. Item vectors for a 101-item test with three contents and a 20-item test with a confounding of difficulty and dimensionality.

---

[1]Although Figure 9.7 is in black and white, it is common and advantageous to use color-coding based on content area for ease of interpretation and visual inspection.

Vector representation for the noncompensatory model has not been as well developed. This is an area that needs to be studied more in the future.

Compensatory and Noncompensatory Diagnostic Model

The item representation is quite different for the two diagnostic models. Specifically, when using the MIRT models presented first with continuous ability, a smooth surface was plotted to represent the ICC. However, in the case of diagnostic models an examinee's ability is represented as a set of classes, where each class is defined by mastery or nonmastery of a set of skills. Therefore, there will not be a smooth surface in the ICC for diagnostic modeling. Instead it is better represented as a bar plot. Figure 9.8 provides examples of such bar plots for the DINA and CRUM. Notice that each profile indicated along the x-axis and the y-axis represents the probability of a correct response. Although this same plot could have been represented using a three dimensional plot (the x- and y-axes could have been mastery of each attributes), no additional information would have been provided. In addition, typical diagnostic models have more than just two attributes, in which case the figures easily extend to incorporate more profiles, although interpretation can become more complicated.

Two limitations of such a method are that the "shape" of the graph cannot be easily described because the ordering of classes is somewhat arbitrary. However, one recommendation is to order the classes based on the number of mastered attributes from low to high, as is done in these sample plots shown in Figure 9.8. In addition, the number of classes increases exponentially with the number of attributes.

Contour plots could also be constructed in simple cases where only two dimensions are being measured. However, in these cases they would not prove to be as useful as was the case when continuous abilities were used. A contour plot for two attributes would create a simple two-by-two grid where each square contains the corresponding probability of a correct response for each combination of mastery–nonmastery. For this reason we do not include additional contour plots for diagnostic models.

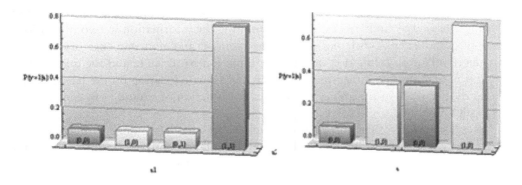

FIGURE 9.8. Item representations for the noncompensatory DINA and compensatory RUM models.

Unlike the models presented previously, bar plots do not naturally allow for the presentation of several items on the same plot. Vector plots used to summarize what is being measured by several items on a single plot, however, are more difficult to conceptualize for diagnostic models. Nevertheless, these plots could be reproduced when using a compensatory model. Recall that the CRUM has weights (discrimination parameters) for each attribute. As a result, these weights could be plotted as coordinates that could be used to indicate what is being measured and to what degree. However, the interpretation would be limited to substantive meanings. For example, when using a continuous model, the vector's location was related to the ability combinations that resulted in a probability of a correct response equal to .50. For diagnostic models, only a finite number of probabilities are possible, and so it is unlikely that a probability of .50 would ever be predicted by the model.

Vector plots for the DINA model could also be determined in this case, but may not be overly informative. The DINA model can either rely on only a single attribute or measure both in the two-attribute example. However, if both attributes are measured, the DINA model assumes that each attribute is measured equally. Thus, for the DINA model, these vectors would point in only one of three directions: only along the x-axis, only along the y-axis, or only at a 45-degree angle (i.e., between the two axes). Future research should consider alternative vector representations for diagnostic models and explore their usefulness.

Item Information

In this section, item information—that is, how well an item can distinguish between levels of proficiency—is explored graphically. From a two-dimensional perspective practitioners would need to know how well an item can measure various composites through the latent ability plane.

Information Representation for the Compensatory Logistic Model

Unlike the unidimensional IRT model in which the Fisher information function yields a unimodal curve that indicates how precisely each ability along the latent continuum is being assessed by an item or a test, determining the information in two dimensions is more complicated. With both the compensatory and noncompensatory models, information is both a function of the discrimination parameters and the direction or composite of skills being measured. That is, for a single location on the latent ability plane, the accuracy of the ability estimation is a function of what $\theta_1 - \theta_2$ composite is being measured.

Representation of test information for these two models is done through a series of vectors (Ackerman, 1994a). The latent ability plane is broken up into a 49-point grid, that is, a seven by seven grid from $\theta_1, \theta_2 = -3.0$ to $+3.0$ in increments of 1. At each of the 49 θ_1, θ_2 combinations, the amount of information is estimated from 0 to

90 degrees in 10-degree increments. The length of each information vector for the compensatory model, given as vector $I(\theta_1, \theta_2)$, is given by the formula

$$I(\theta_1, \theta_2) = (\cos\alpha)^2 Var(\hat{\theta}_1 \mid \theta_1, \theta_2) + (\sin\alpha)^2 Var(\hat{\theta}_2 \mid \theta_1, \theta_2)$$
$$+ (2\sin 2\alpha)Cov(\hat{\theta}_1, \hat{\theta}_2 \mid \theta_1, \theta_2)$$

(9.12)

where α is defined in Equation 9.11.

A "clamshell" plot (see Figure 9.9) can be used to examine the test information, especially to address questions such as these: If the test is measuring different content, how do the information profiles compare across the different content areas? Is the information profile similar across "parallel" forms? The plots shown in Figure 9.9 were created for the items shown previously on the right in Figure 9.7. Note that with this test there is a confounding of difficulty and dimensionality: Easy items measure θ_1 and difficult items measure θ_2. It is as though the authors added a second dimension to make the items more difficult. The maximum information appears to be provided around the origin. Along the θ_1-axis the maximum information is in the θ_2 direction, and along the θ_2-axis the maximum information is in the θ_1 direction. Very little information is provided about the extreme abilities in the first and third quadrants.

Multiple categories can be easily compared in the test information plots by using two different colors, one for each content area. At each of the 49 latent ability locations, the color representing the content area that provides the most information is used.

One final representation of test information is a number plot. In this type of plot, the information is computed for each composite direction from 0 to 90 degrees in 1-degree increments at each of the 49 points. The number representing the direction having the maximum information is indicated. The size of the font used to represent

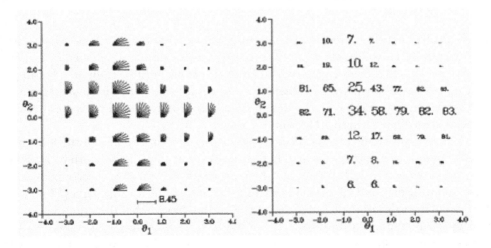

FIGURE 9.9. Test information vectors displayed as "clamshell" plots and as a "number plot" in which the angular direction of the maximum information is displayed.

the number is a function of the amount of information. An example of such a plot is displayed in the plot on the right in Figure 9.9. In this diagram it is clear that the composite that is being best measured changes drastically depending on the location in the latent ability plane. This creates a problematic inconsistency as one moves throughout the ability plane about which composite is being best measured.

Information Representation for the Diagnostic Models

Whereas Fisher's information is quite common in IRT models that assume continuous abilities in one or more dimensions, it is not applicable in diagnostic models. For Fisher's information to be computed, the ICC must be a continuous and smooth function or surface. DCMs define ability based on the mastery or nonmastery of attributes and thereby define classes. As a result, an alternative to Fisher's information must be used. Chang and Ying (1996) discuss the use of Kullback–Liebler information (KLI) as an alternative to Fisher's information in IRT. KLI was described as a global approach to information, whereas Fisher's information is described as a local measure of information. The advantage of KLI is that it is defined even when the ICC is not a continuous smooth function or surface, and so it can be used when the underlying model is a DCM (Henson & Douglas, 2005).

Specifically, the KLI can be used to measure the "discrimination" (or distance) between two different attribute patterns α_j and α_k as an indication of how different the response is expected to be between them. Notice that if the expected responses are different, then this item helps differentiate between the two different attribute patterns. The KLI between these two different attribute patterns is

$$\text{KLI}\left(\alpha_j, \alpha_k\right) = \sum_{x=0}^{1} P\left(x \mid \alpha_j\right) \ln\left(\frac{P(x \mid \alpha_j)}{P(x \mid \alpha_k)}\right) \tag{9.13}$$

where $P(x \mid \alpha)$ is the probability of a response x, given that the examinee has the attribute pattern α. However, the KLI only provides the discrimination power (or information) between two attribute patterns, and thus this value must be computed for all possible pairs of attribute patterns. Where this value is large, the item is most informative, and where this value is small, the item does not discriminate well between those two respective attribute patterns (Henson & Douglas, 2005).

Henson and Douglas (2005) suggested storing the information of the KLI for all possible pairwise comparisons in a matrix; however, it can also be plotted (see Figure 9.10) to provide a visual display of which attribute patterns are discriminated by a given item. In Figure 9.10, attribute patterns are along the x- and y-axes. The z-axis represents the value of the KLI for that combination. Notice that the values when comparing attribute pattern {0,0} to {1,1} are the largest, indicating that these two attribute patterns are highly discriminated. In contrast, the KLI is 0 when comparing any attribute pattern to itself. Finally, attribute patterns that differ by mastery of only one attribute have mild discrimination. Thus, the KLI plot can be interpreted in a similar way as Fisher's information is used in IRT with continuous latent variables.

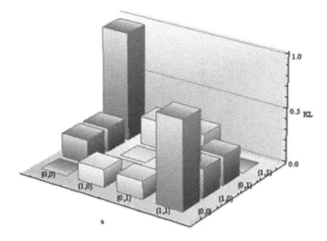

FIGURE 9.10. An example of an item's discrimination through all pairwise KLI.

Multidimensional Relationship with a Composite Score

It is quite common for practitioners to report a single score for test results even though the test is truly multidimensional. In this case it is important to examine how the multidimensional nature of a test maps into a unidimensional composite.

True Score Representation for the Compensatory Logistic Model

Only the compensatory model is discussed in this section, although the noncompensatory extension closely follows. In unidimensional IRT the true score representation allows practitioners to relate the latent ability scale to the expected number-correct scale. In the two-dimensional case this translates to relating the latent ability plane to the expected number correct surface. This is achieved by summing the probability of correct responses to all of the test items at each point in the latent ability plane and then using this information to create a true score surface. This process is illustrated in Figure 9.11. In this plot the equal expected score contours are shown on the latent ability plane. Every θ_1, θ_2 combination that lies on the same contour would be expected to achieve the same number correct score. This representation is for the 20-item test noted above, in which easy items measured θ_1 and difficult items measured θ_2. Above the latent ability plane is the true score surface.

The contour is important from a practitioner's perspective when cut scores are set to determine licensure or certification. Such plots indicate the different combinations of θ_1, θ_2 that would be expected to successfully meet the cut score, giving more insight into what combinations of skills would be represented by examinees who passed.

One interesting comparison that can be created is the difference between two contour surfaces. Such a plot, shown in Figure 9.12, can help practitioners examine the degree of parallelism between the two test forms. That is, if two tests were truly

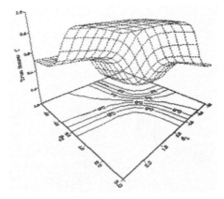

FIGURE 9.11. An example of a true score surface and corresponding contours.

parallel, examinees would have the same expected score on each form. In Figure 9.12 the difference in surface and corresponding contours are illustrated for two 40-item math tests. Where the surface lies above the no-difference plane, examinees would be expected to achieve a higher score on Form A. Conversely, where the surface dips below the no-difference plane, examinees would be expected to score higher on Form B. Thus, examinees near the origin would be expected to score slightly higher on Form A. One would also need to consider the standard error of the differences in order to accurately determine the magnitude of those differences.

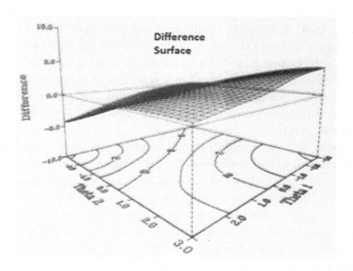

FIGURE 9.12. A surface plot indicated the difference between the true score surface of Form A minus the true score surface of Form B.

Conditional Estimation for the Compensatory Logistic Model

A final graphical analysis is one that allows practitioners to visualize the consistency of an observed number-correct score scale. In this analysis, the θ_1, θ_2 centroids for each number-correct score are plotted on the latent ability plane. This is where the $(\overline{\theta}_1, \overline{\theta}_2)$ are for each raw score. An example of such plots for the two tests displayed in Figure 9.7 are shown in Figure 9.13. In this figure, the number-correct score is located at the position of its corresponding $(\overline{\theta}_1, \overline{\theta}_2)$ centroid. This is an ideal situation because the centroids are linear, meaning the composite being measured does not change throughout the observable score scale. Practitioners should be concerned when this plot is not linear, such as when there is a confounding of difficulty and dimensionality. This could occur when easy items are measuring one skill and difficult items are measuring another skill.

Another interesting arrangement is to plot the centroids for different content categories. On the left in Figure 9.13 are four plots for the 101-item test: one for each of the three different content areas and then the total test. Somewhat amazingly, the three content areas are measuring quite different composites, yet when all three are combined, the plot becomes linear. Clearly this situation would have implications for equating. That is, should the test be equated by content or as a single test? Also displayed in this picture are ellipses around the numbers for each score category. Normally these would be color-coded. If $\sigma^2_{\theta 1} > \sigma^2_{\theta 2}$ (i.e., θ_2 is being measured more accurately), the ellipse is one color, and if $\sigma^2_{\theta 1} < \sigma^2_{\theta 2}$ (i.e., θ_1 is being measured more accurately), the ellipse is a different color.

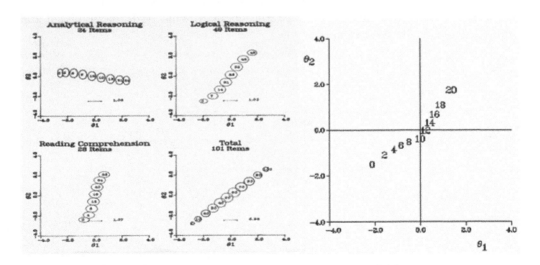

FIGURE 9.13. Centroid plot for the 101-item test for each of the three categories and the total test and for the 20-item test.

Conditional Analyses from a DCM Perspective

An analogous situation to the centroid plot in a diagnostic model is to create a likelihood graph of each raw score category for each pattern of mastery. Such a graph is shown in Figure 9.14. For a test that is measuring only two attributes, there are actually four possible profiles of mastery (0,0), (0,1), (1,0), and (1,1). A graph indicating the likelihood of each possible score on a 31-item test is displayed for each of the four attribute patterns. As would be expected, the complete mastery case (1,1) has the largest likelihood for the higher-level score categories.

Discussion

In this chapter four different models were illustrated: the compensatory and noncompensatory logistic models and their diagnostic counterparts, the noncompensatory diagnostic model and the compensatory diagnostic model. Graphical illustrations of four different psychometric analyses were examined. These include item representation, test information, true score representation, and conditional representation. By examining these illustrations, practitioners should begin to better understand the similarities and differences among the four models.

Too often researchers and testing practitioners immerse themselves in statistical analyses to understand their assessment results. Hopefully this chapter has helped to illustrate how graphical analyses can also provide a great deal of insight into what items and the test as a whole are measuring when the test data are truly multidimensional. This information should cross-validate descriptive statistics, statistical analyses, as well as the tables of specification. Equally important, one should never overlook the substantive analyses and relate the actual items to what both the graphical and numerical results are indicating.

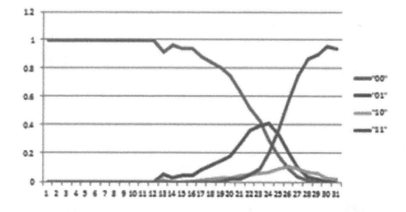

FIGURE 9.14. Likelihood curves for each score possibility for each attribute profile is displayed.

ACKNOWLEDGMENT

It is with sincere gratitude that we would like to thank Dr. Hambleton for all of the feedback and inspiration he has provided. Truly, the field of IRT would not be where it is today without his insightful and seminal contributions.

REFERENCES

Ackerman, T. A. (1994a). Creating a test information profile in a two-dimensional latent space. *Applied Psychological Measurement, 18*, 257–275.

Ackerman, T. A. (1994b). Using multidimensional item response theory to understand what items and tests are measuring. *Applied Measurement in Education, 7*, 255–278.

Ackerman, T. A. (1996). Graphical representation of multidimensional item response theory analyses. *Applied Psychological Measurement, 20*(4), 311–330.

Ackerman, T. A. (2005). Multidimensional item response theory modeling. In J. McArdle & A. Maydeu-Olivares (Eds.), *Festschrift for Rod McDonald* (pp. 3–25). Hillsdale, NJ: Erlbaum.

Ackerman, T. A., Gierl, M., & Walker, C. (2003). Using multidimensional item response theory to evaluate educational and psychological tests. *Educational Measurement, Issues, and Practice, 22*, 37–53.

Chang, H., & Ying, Z. (1996). A global information approach to computerized adaptive testing. *Applied Psychological Measurement, 20*, 213–229.

Hambleton, R. K., & Swaminathan, H. (1985). *Item response theory: Principles and applications*. Dordrecht, The Netherlands: Kluwer-Nijhoff.

Henson, R., & Douglas, J. (2005). Test construction for cognitive diagnosis. *Applied Psychological Measurement, 29*(4), 262–277.

Junker, B., & Sijtsma, K. (2001). Cognitive assessment models with few assumptions, and connections with nonparametric item response theory. *Applied Psychological Measurement 25*(3), 258–272.

Reckase, M. D. (1985). The difficulty of test items that measure more than one ability. *Applied Psychological Measurement, 9*, 401–412.

Reckase, M. D., & McKinley, R. L. (1991). The discrimination power of items that measure more than one dimension. *Applied Psychological Measurement, 14*, 361–373.

Rupp, A. A., Templin, J., & Henson, R. A. (2010). *Diagnostic measurement: Theory, methods, and applications*. New York: Guilford Press.

Smith, J. (2002). *Some issues in item response theory: Dimensionality assessment and models for guessing*. Unpublished doctoral dissertation, University of South Carolina, Columbia, SC.

van der Linden, W., & Hambleton, R. (1997). *Handbook of modern item response theory*. New York: Springer.

CHAPTER 10

Testing Assumptions of Item Response Theory Models

Craig S. Wells, Joseph Rios, and Molly Faulkner-Bond

tem response theory (IRT) is a powerful scaling technique that uses a mathematical model to depict the probability of a correct response given item and person parameters. The attractive features and many of the applications of IRT (e.g., computerized adaptive testing) rely on the invariance property in which the item parameter values retain the same values regardless of the ability distribution, and the person parameters retain the same values regardless of the items administered to the examinee (Embretson & Reise, 2000; Hambleton, Swaminathan, & Rogers, 1991). However, it is important to note that the invariance property only holds when the assumptions of the specific IRT model are satisfied (Bejar, 1983; Bolt, 2002; Hambleton et al., 1991; Swaminathan, Hambleton, & Rogers, 2007; Wells & Keller, 2010). Therefore, the model assumptions play an important role in the valid application of IRT models. As a result, assessing the assumptions of an IRT model is an important endeavor in any situation where that model is applied—for example, when developing and maintaining a stable score scale. There are three basic assumptions underlying the most popular IRT models: dimensionality, local independence, and functional form or shape of the item characteristic curve (ICC). The purpose of this chapter is to describe methods for testing the assumptions of IRT models.

Before we describe the methods for assessing IRT model assumptions, it is important to note that these model assumptions are not strictly satisfied in real data (Hambleton et al., 1991). For example, several IRT models, such as the three-parameter logistic (3PL) model, assume that test data are unidimensional, which indicates, strictly speaking, that the test is measuring only one latent variable. However, because several cognitive and personality factors as well as test-taking behavior influence performance, it is unrealistic to expect any test to measure only one latent variable (Hambleton et al., 1991). Fortunately, unidimensionality does not need to be *strictly* satisfied for the model to be useful (Harrison, 1986). Therefore, when examining IRT model assumptions, the goal is to determine if the assumptions are satisfied enough so that the model is useful for a given purpose. Ron Hambleton, whose research in this area influenced many of the techniques that we describe, was fond of the famous quote by George Box, "Essentially, all models are wrong, but some are useful" (Box & Draper, 1987, p. 424). We wholeheartedly endorse this perspective and its influence on assessing model assumptions. We also would like to express our gratitude to Professor Hambleton for his dedication to the psychometric field, his immense contributions to the measurement literature, and for providing guidance to practitioners with the goal of supporting the appropriate use of IRT in educational assessment.

Assessing Dimensionality and Local Independence

The dimensionality assumption indicates the number of underlying latent variables that the assessment is intended to measure. Although for the most popular IRT models applied to dichotomously scored data (e.g., 3PL model), it is assumed that the data are unidimensional, there are several multidimensional IRT models available that posit more than one latent variable. Local independence states that for a given IRT proficiency estimate, the joint probability of correct responses is the product of the probability of a correct response for each item (Chen & Thissen, 1997; Hambleton et al., 1991). That is,

$$P\left(\mathbf{U}_j \middle| \theta_j\right) = \prod_{i=1}^{n} P\left(u_{ij} \middle| \theta_j\right) \tag{10.1}$$

where $\mathbf{U}_j$ is the vector of item responses for examinee j and u_{ij} is the item response on item i for examinee j. Essentially, local independence implies that once the variability in the latent variable is "partialled out" or "controlled for," then the items are uncorrelated. The dimensionality and local independence assumptions are conceptually equivalent in that if the dimensionality assumption is satisfied, then local independence is satisfied.

Several techniques have been developed to assess test dimensionality and local independence. The purpose of this section is to provide a brief description of some of the most popular methods employed to assess test dimensionality and local independence. For more detailed descriptions of the methods, the reader is referred to Hattie (1985), Tate (2003), and Svetina and Levy (2014).

Confirmatory Factor Analysis

A popular technique to assess dimensionality and local independence is confirmatory factor analysis (CFA). CFA examines the hypothesized relationships between indicators and the latent variables that the indicators are purported to measure (Brown, 2006; Kline, 2015). A basic feature of CFA is that the models are specified by the test developer a priori using theory and often previous empirical research. Therefore, the researcher must explicitly specify the number of underlying latent variables and which items load on the specific latent variables.

CFA assesses dimensionality by verifying the number of underlying latent variables and the pattern of item-to-factor relationships. For example, if the hypothesized unidimensional structure is incorrect, the CFA model will provide poor fit to the data because the observed intercorrelations among the items will not be accurately reproduced by the model parameter estimates. If a CFA model with only one latent variable fits the data well, then that supports the use of an IRT model that assumes unidimensionality. If a CFA model with multiple latent variables fits the data well (and sufficiently better than the CFA model with one latent variable), then that supports the use of a multidimensional IRT model.

CFA can be used to assess local independence by examining the correlation of residuals between items. If the correlations are not small, then that is evidence the item pair is correlated even after controlling for (or partialling out) common variance due to the latent variable. A test developer can specify a priori the residuals to be correlated based on, for example, items that share a common stimulus (e.g., items associated with a reading passage). Modification indices, which provide information about specific misfit within a model, can also indicate pairs of items in which residuals should be correlated.

To examine the dimensionality and local independence of a test, the CFA model is evaluated for model fit and the magnitude of the factor loadings and correlations among the latent variables are examined. Model fit determines if the hypothesized model can reproduce the observed covariance matrix (i.e., covariance matrix for the indicators) using the model parameter estimates. If the model is specified incorrectly, then the model will not fit the data well. Although there are several approaches to assess model fit, such as hypothesis testing, the most common method uses goodness-of-fit indices. There are a plethora of goodness-of-fit indices available for a researcher to use to judge model fit (see Bollen, 1989; Hu & Bentler, 1999). It is advisable to use a few of the indices in evaluating model fit. Some of the more commonly used indices are the comparative fit index (CFI), the Tucker–Lewis index (TLI), the root mean square error of approximation ($RMSEA$), and the standardized root mean square residual ($SRMR$). Suggested cutoff values are available to help researchers determine if the model provides adequate fit to the data (e.g., see Hu & Bentler, 1999).

When evaluating dimensionality, it is common to compare the fit of several nested models. For example, the test developer may compare the fit of a one-factor model to a multifactor model where the latent variables are defined by the specific content subdomains or strands. If the fit for the one-factor model is much worse than the fit for the multifactor model, this serves as evidence that the unidimensionality assumption is not tenable. Although there is a hypothesis test based on the difference in chi-square statistics of the two models that can be used to compare the fit of nested models, it tends to be statistically significant because test developers often use very large sample sizes, and the null hypothesis being tested is false because real data are not strictly unidimensional. To address this problem, we can compare goodness-of-fit indices between nested models. For example, we can compare CFI values for the two models:

ΔCFI = CFI_F − CFI_C, where CFI_F and CFI_C are the CFI values for the full (in this case, the multifactor model) and compact (one-factor) model. Although values of ΔCFI greater than 0.01 have been proposed to indicate sufficiently worse fit (Cheung & Rensvold, 2002), more research is needed in this area to understand the distributional properties of ΔCFI.

Bifactor Model

The bifactor model is a multidimensional model that represents the hypothesis that several latent variables, each indicated by a subset of indicators, account for unique variance above and beyond the variance accounted for by one common latent variable that is based on all indicators. More specifically, this model is composed of one *general* and multiple *specific* factors. The general factor can be conceptualized as the target construct a measure was originally developed to assess (e.g., proficiency in mathematics), and accounts for the common variance among all indicators. In contrast, specific factors pertain to only a subset of indicators that are highly related in some way (e.g., by content subdomain, item type, or local dependence on a shared prompt), and account for the unique variance among a subset of indicators above and beyond the variance accounted for by the general factor. Within the bifactor model, each indicator loads on the general factor *and* on one, and only one, specific factor. As the specific factors are interpreted as the variance accounted for above and beyond the general factor, an orthogonal (uncorrelated) assumption is made for the relationships between the general and specific factors. Furthermore, the covariances among the specific factors are set to 0 to avoid identification problems (Chen, Hayes, Carver, Laurenceau, & Zhang, 2012). The residual variances of the indicators are interpreted as the variance unaccounted for by either the general or specific factors. Figure 10.1 provides an example of a bifactor model for a hypothetical math test with three content domains.

To test dimensionality and local independence, a test developer can examine the specific factors independently from the general factor. For example, if a proposed specific factor did not account for a substantial amount of variance above and beyond the general factor, one would observe small and nonsignificant factor loadings on the specific factor, as well as a small amount of variance of the specific factor in the bifactor model. These findings would indicate that the hypothesized specific factor does not provide unique variance beyond the general factor and thus provides support for unidimensionality and the use of a unidimensional IRT model. An appealing feature of the bifactor model is the ability to directly examine the strength of the relationship between the specific factors and their respective indicators. Such an assessment provides a researcher with information regarding the appropriateness of using particular items as indicators of the specific factors. If a relationship is weak, one can conclude that the item may be appropriate solely as an indicator of the general factor.

A limitation of the bifactor model is that it requires a restrictive assumption beyond orthogonality, which is that each indicator loads on one general factor *and* on one, and only one, specific factor. Allowing items to cross-load on multiple specific factors may lead to questionable item parameter estimates. Such a restriction

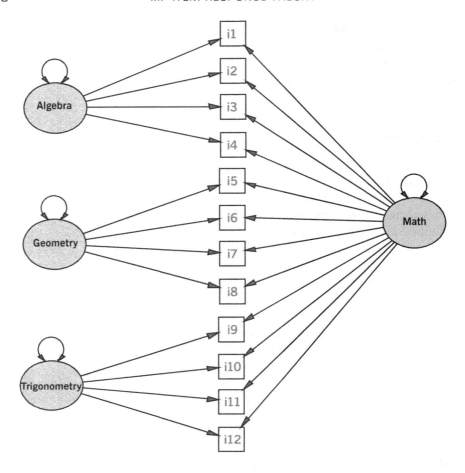

FIGURE 10.1. Example of a bifactor model for a hypothetical math test with three content domains.

on the structure of the multidimensionality may limit the application of the bifactor model. However, this is one of the major reasons why Reise (2012) promoted the use of exploratory bifactor analysis, which allows for indicators to cross-load on specific factors (for a detailed discussion of exploratory bifactor analysis, see Jennrich & Bentler, 2011). Such analyses would allow researchers to better understand the structure of the data before applying confirmatory procedures, which is particularly vital with the restrictive assumptions that are inherent in the confirmatory canonical bifactor model.

Exploratory Factor Analysis

In the event that CFA or the bifactor model does not provide a reasonable solution, then a practitioner may prefer to use an approach, such as exploratory factor analysis (EFA), that allows the data to suggest the dimensionality structure. Historically, EFA has been a popular method for assessing dimensionality. However, given its limitations, along with the advances in parameter estimation methods, software, and the theory for confirmatory methods such as CFA and the bifactor model, EFA today is more typically used as an alternative when confirmatory methods fail to provide a satisfactory solution. EFA's primary goal is to identify the appropriate number of latent variables that can reproduce the observed relationships among the items. The technique is data driven in that the practitioner uses descriptive statistics to determine the appropriate number of latent variables and the pattern of factor loadings.

When using EFA, practitioners are presented with two major decisions. First, one must decide on the rotation method to simplify and clarify the data structure (Costello & Osborne, 2005). In general, there are two classes of rotation methods: (a) orthogonal and (b) oblique. Orthogonal rotation produces uncorrelated factors, whereas oblique rotation allows for correlated factors. In general, it is recommended that an oblique rotation be applied, particularly when analyzing data from the social sciences, as it is generally expected that dimensions are correlated. The decision to apply an orthogonal rotation should be strongly supported by substantive research as any knowledge concerning dimensional correlations would be forfeited (Fabrigar, Wegener, MacCallum, & Strahan, 1999).

The second issue is that practitioners must decide on the criteria for determining the number of latent variables (i.e., factor retention). Several procedures have been developed to determine factor retention, such as Kaiser's eigenvalue-greater-than-1 rule (K1; Kaiser, 1960), Cattell's (1966) scree plot, the minimum average partial (MAP) test (Velicer, 1976), and parallel analysis (PA; Horn, 1965). Among these methods, K1 tends to be the least accurate (Velicer & Jackson, 1990); the scree plot, although useful in some cases, is criticized for being overly subjective and relying too heavily on experience to interpret appropriately (Zwick & Velicer, 1986); MAP underestimates when the number of items per component are low (Zwick & Velicer, 1986); and PA is the most accurate and robust across many conditions (Zwick & Velicer, 1986). Tran and Formann (2009) also found that PA performed well with binary data when employing tetrachoric correlations for analysis. For a step-by-step guide on how to apply PA, the reader is referred to Hayton, Allen, and Scarpello (2004).

Although EFA is an effective method for assessing test dimensionality when a confirmatory approach has failed, it has several limitations. First, the sample size required to obtain accurate dimensionality results must be sufficiently large. In a simulation study, Costello and Osborne (2005) found that the stability of accurate dimensionality assessment in EFA required 20 examinees per item, but that in practice, nearly 79% of 303 studies reviewed did not meet such a criterion. Second, EFA is unable to incorporate correlated residuals, which may have a deleterious effect on determining the number of factors. The third limitation, which applies to exploratory procedures in general, lies in the need to justify the dimensions obtained with theoretical knowledge. That is, besides requiring each dimension to be comprised of at least five or more strongly loaded items (where loadings $\geq .50$ are typically considered strong; Costello & Osborne, 2005), as well as obtaining a solution in which all dimensions provide adequate reliability, a researcher must provide substantive support for score interpretation. Put more simply "Theoretical knowledge is more relevant than a statistical measure" (Beavers et al., 2013, p. 11).

Nonparametric Conditional Covariance-Based Procedures

From an IRT perspective, *dimensionality* can be defined as the minimum number of latent variables necessary to satisfy local independence (Stout, 1990). Assuming the ICC is monotonic, defining the "minimum number" of dimensions is largely based on the stringency of the local independence assumption, which has led to two different definitions of dimensionality: (1) strict and (2) essential dimensionality (Tate, 2003). Strict dimensionality requires the *strong principle of local independence*—that is, after conditioning on the latent variables, statistical independence of item responses is obtained for all subsets of items across all thetas (ability estimate) within the ability continuum (de Ayala, 2009). In contrast, essential dimensionality only necessitates the *principle of essential local independence*—that is, upon conditioning on a fixed value of theta, the average absolute value of covariances converges to zero as the test length increases (Burg, 2007). In practical terms, strict dimensionality would dictate that practitioners report scores for *all* dominant and construct-irrelevant or nondominant dimensions that would completely account for the item covariances. Essential dimensionality would suggest that the number of dimensions for a test would be comprised only of all dominant dimensions that account for the majority of item covariances and are not greatly impacted by the presence of smaller dimensions. However, as noted by Stout and colleagues (1996), the strong principle of local independence is nearly impossible to attain in practice. As a result, when assessing dimensionality, we are most concerned with meeting the assumption of essential local independence.

The procedures within this category of dimensionality methods differ from parametric linear factor analytic procedures in that they (1) do not assume a parametric form of the ICC; (2) do not depend on the analysis of tetrachoric correlations used in weighted least squares (WLS) estimation for CFA and the bifactor model, which can be problematic (Schweizer, Ren, & Wang, 2014); and (3) evaluate dimensionality based on conditional item pair covariances. Specifically, testing for unidimensionality is equivalent to testing that across all item pairs and all values of the unidimensional latent variable, the conditional covariance is zero (assumption of weak local independence; Stout et al., 1996). Within this category of nonparametric procedures, the number correct is substituted for values on the unidimensional latent variable scale. Therefore, when unidimensionality holds, the conditional covariance of items i and l should be near zero when conditioning on a number-correct score (excluding items i and l) on the test of interest for all items and number correct scores. Two popular procedures of this type include (1) DIMTEST and (2) the dimensionality evaluation to enumerate contributing traits (DETECT).

DIMTEST is a procedure developed by Stout (1987) in which the conditional covariance of two clusters of test items (either dichotomous or polytomous) is evaluated explicitly for hypothesis testing of the unidimensionality assumption. A test statistic,

T, is implemented in the DIMTEST software program (Stout, Douglas, Junker, & Roussos, 1993), which aggregates the conditional covariance among a set of items referred to as the assessment subtest (AT), conditioned on the remaining items, which forms the partitioning test (PT; Svetina & Levy, 2014). The null hypothesis of essential unidimensionality is then evaluated based on the T statistic's associated p-value. Although this procedure has been shown to perform adequately with both dichotomous and polytomous items (e.g., Hattie, Krakowski, Rogers, & Swaminathan, 1996; Nandakumar, 1993), one of its main criticisms lies in deciding how to partition the AT (Linacre, 1994). Stout and colleagues (1996) suggest that one way of partitioning AT should be based on expert opinion related to test content, test structure, or cognitive considerations that results in AT items being dimensionally homogeneous (see Tate, 2003, for a review of additional partitioning approaches). Additionally, the number of AT items should be equal to at least 3 and at most one-third of the PT items, which should be at least 15. Violations to these restrictions on test length as well as to additional sample size restrictions have been shown to negatively impact the performance of DIMTEST. As an example, researchers have demonstrated decreased power when the total test length is less than 25 items and the sample size is less than 500 (e.g., Finch & Habing, 2007; van Abswoude, van der Ark, & Sijtsma, 2004).

DETECT is a nonparametric conditional covariance-based EXPLORATORY procedure that does not employ a hypothesis test, but is rather an estimation procedure (Stout et al., 1996) that can be used to assess test dimensionality (Jasper, 2010; Nandakumar & Ackerman, 2004). DETECT identifies the total number of dominant dimensions underlying a set of test items by finding mutually exclusive, homogeneous item clusters (Gierl, Leighton, & Tan, 2006). The DETECT index is computed by summing covariances between item pairs for all items on the test, conditioned on the observed scores of the remaining items. A DETECT index exists for each distinct item cluster partitioning, and as a result, an algorithm is applied to conduct multiple partitions of the data to maximize the DETECT index, which increases as the partitioning more closely resembles the true item cluster. Therefore, the number of clusters identified will indicate the number of dominant dimensions, assuming a simple structure. To assess if items are clustered into homogeneous and separate clusters, DETECT also provides a measure to approximate the degree of simple structure in the optimal partition, referred to as r_{max}.

Zhang and Stout (1999) demonstrated the utility of the DETECT procedure in correctly identifying the appropriate number of dimensions and item partitioning for multidimensional compensatory models under different levels of dimensions, number of examinees, and number of items. Similar positive results were observed by Gierl, Leighton, and Tan (2006) when examining the correct identification rates for DETECT with multidimensional complex data structures. Specifically, the authors found that DETECT worked well with as many as 50% complex structure items when the intersubdomain correlations were equal to or less than .60. However, Svetina (2013) found that DETECT performed poorly when dimensions were non-compensatory and complex item structures were present.

Additional Measures for Assessing Local Independence

In addition to using CFA or the bifactor model to examine possible local dependencies among sets of items, there are several statistics based on IRT that are available: X^2 (Chen & Thissen, 1997), G^2 (Bishop, Fienberg, & Holland, 1975; Chen & Thissen, 1997), the absolute value of mutual information difference (AMID; Tsai & Hsu, 2005), the model-based covariance (Reckase, 1997; see Levy & Svetina, 2010, for a test-level adaptation), conditional interitem correlations (Huynh & Ferrara, 1994), and the Jackknife Slope Index (Edwards & Cai, 2011), to name a few. One of the most popular IRT methods is Yen's (1984) Q_3 statistic, which, similar to the method employed in CFA, examines the correlated residuals, but using an IRT model. The residual for item i and examinee j, denoted d_{ij}, is computed by taking the difference between the item response on item i for examinee j from the model-based estimate, P_{ij}, for the same item and examinee (i.e., $d_{ij} = u_{ij} - P_{ij}$). Yen's Q_3 has a bias of $-1/(n-1)$ where n equals the number of items. For a more thorough review and comparative analyses of local dependence indices, the reader is referred to Chen and Thissen (1997); Ip (2001); Kim, de Ayala, Ferdous, and Nering (2007); Levy, Mislevy, and Sinharay (2009); and Liu and Maydeu-Olivares (2013).

Assessing the Shape of ICCs

IRT models assume that the underlying ICC follows the same shape specified by the parametric model (e.g., S-shaped function defined by the 3PL model). Testing the shape assumption requires obtaining an empirical ICC in which the shape is not constrained by the model, but rather is influenced primarily by the observed data. The empirical ICC is intended to be a proxy for the underlying ICC. If the underlying shape of the ICC follows the same shape specified by the parametric model, then we expect the empirical ICC to be close to the model-based ICC given sampling error.

Traditional Approaches

One way of obtaining an empirical ICC is to compute the observed proportion correct for examinees who have been placed into intervals along the θ scale. A common method of obtaining the observed proportions implemented in practice is as follows. First, the IRT model (e.g., 3PL model) is selected and then the item and ability parameters are estimated. Second, the θ scale is divided into intervals in which the examinees are placed based on their IRT proficiency estimate. The width of each interval and the number of intervals are dictated by the sample size and the variability in the sample with respect to the proficiency estimates; that is, more intervals can be used for larger sample sizes, presuming the variability in the proficiency estimates is sufficiently large. The number of intervals typically ranges from 8 to 10, but as many as 30 intervals can be used for very large sample sizes (e.g., $N > 50,000$). Third, once the examinees have been placed into their respective interval, the observed proportion correct, denoted p_{ig}, for item i in subgroup (i.e., interval) g can be computed by dividing the number of examinees who answered the item correctly by the number of examinees in the subgroup.

The difference between the observed proportions (p_{ig}) and the model-based predictions (denoted P_{ig}) are referred to as *raw residuals* (denoted r_{ig} and computed as $p_{ig} - P_{ig}$) and provide the basis for evaluating model fit via a summary statistic (e.g., Yen's Q_1; Yen, 1981) and graphical displays. There are a few ways of computing P_{ig}. For example, it can be based on the probability of a correct response at the midpoint of the interval. Another method is to use the average of the probabilities for all examinees within the respective subgroup.

One of the challenges in interpreting model fit using raw residuals is that their magnitude is partly influenced by sampling error (i.e., we expect the raw residuals to fluctuate more for subgroups with smaller sample sizes). To address this limitation, the residuals are often standardized by dividing the raw residuals by their respective standard error. The *standardized residual* (*SR*) for item i and subgroup g is computed as

$$SR_{ig} = \frac{p_{ig} - P_{ig}}{\sqrt{\dfrac{P_{ig}(1 - P_{ig})}{N_g}}} \tag{10.2}$$

where N_g represents the sample size for subgroup g. When the model fits the data, we expect the standardized residuals to be relatively small and randomly distributed around zero along the θ scale.

The *SR*s for an item can be combined to produce a summary statistic to assess model fit. For example, the sum of the squared *SR*s (SR^2), which was initially developed by Yen (1981) and is denoted Yen's Q_1, has been treated in practice as an approximate chi-square distributed statistic, $\sum_g SR_{ig}^2 \approx \chi_i^2$. However, Yen's Q_1 has several drawbacks. First, the degrees of freedom for the test statistic are unclear, making it difficult to know which chi-square distribution to use (Orlando & Thissen, 2000; Stone & Zhang, 2003). Second, grouping examinees into the intervals based on IRT proficiency estimates, which contain error, influences the distribution of the test statistic (Orlando & Thissen, 2000; Stone, 2000; Stone & Hansen, 2000; Stone, Mislevy, & Mazzeo, 1994; Stone & Zhang, 2003). Third, it is unclear if the residuals used to compute Yen's Q_1 follow a specific distribution (e.g., Gaussian) when the model fits (Haberman, Sinharay, & Chon, 2013). Because of these limitations, Yen's Q_1 has exhibited inflated Type I error rates in simulation research (Dodeen, 2004; Orlando & Thissen, 2000) and cannot be recommended to evaluate model fit by itself.

In response to these limitations, further summary statistics have been developed. For example, Orlando and Thissen (2000) computed the residuals by defining the groups based on raw scores instead of classifying examinees into intervals based on their IRT proficiency estimates. The summary statistic was computed the same as

Yen's Q_1. Simulation studies have exhibited reasonably controlled Type I error rates (Orlando & Thissen, 2000). Haberman and colleagues (2013) developed a fit statistic that is based on a comparison of two estimates of the ICC, in which they provided a theoretical proof that the SRs follow an asymptotically standard normal distribution. Simulation results, however, indicated that for the residuals to be asymptotically normally distributed required very large samples for moderate test lengths; otherwise, the Type I error rate was inflated, especially for longer tests (e.g., 40 items) and smaller sample sizes (e.g., 4,000 examinees). Another limitation of the study is that the authors did not examine the Type I error rate when assessing the fit of the 3PL model, which is a commonly used model.

Even though there have been improvements on developing a summary statistic for assessing model shape that has controlled Type I error rates, one serious drawback remains: Rejecting the point-null hypothesis being tested allows one to conclude only that the model does not fit perfectly. In fact, nearly every item would be statistically significant with very large sample sizes, since no parametric model would be able to represent the underlying ICC perfectly (Wainer & Thissen, 1987). In other words, since mathematical models such as parametric IRT models are a simplification of reality, they cannot be reasonably expected to represent reality entirely. Therefore, every model will misfit to a certain degree. However, even a misfitting model can be useful. As a result, the goal of evaluating model fit is to determine if the model provides a reasonable approximation to the data so that it is still useful for its intended purpose. Graphically displaying the residual information, which is described below, helps accomplish this goal.

Using graphical displays provides the information regarding model fit in a visually appealing way such that a practitioner can easily and quickly judge if the model provides a reasonable fit. One of the simplest methods of displaying model fit information graphically is to plot the observed proportions along with the ICC. Figure 10.2a provides an example of an ICC from the 3PL model based on real data from a multiple-choice test with 10,000 examinees. The y-axis represents the probability of a correct response and the x-axis represents the θ scale. The solid line represents the model-based ICC and the points about the line represent the observed proportion correct for each subgroup. Given that the points are close to the ICC and they appear to be randomly distributed about it, the graph indicates that the model provides a reasonable fit. To aid interpretation, we added confidence bands based on three standard errors. The equation for the standard error is given in the denominator of Equation 10.2. When the confidence band covers the ICC for most of the intervals, then that is evidence supporting a reasonable model fit.

It is also informative to plot the SRs. Figure 10.2b illustrates a plot of the SRs for each of the subgroups. The x-axis represents the θ scale and the y-axis represents the SR. The dotted and dashed lines at two and three SRs, respectively, help visually identify parts of the ICC that the parametric model may not represent accurately. For models that provide reasonable fit, the SRs are expected to be randomly distributed around 0 and within two to three standardized values.

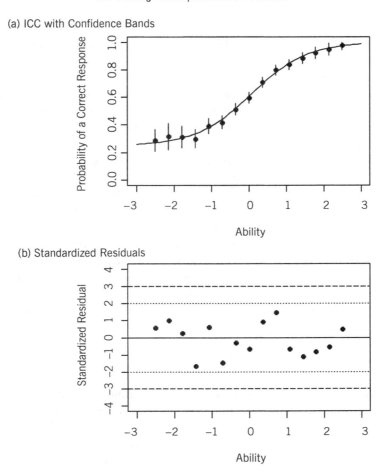

FIGURE 10.2. Graphical display of model fit using observed proportions and standardized residuals.

Nonparametric Approach

A second way of obtaining an observed ICC is to use a nonparametric IRT technique, such as kernel smoothing, to represent the observed data. Nonparametric IRT in the form of kernel smoothing has been shown to offer a promising tool for evaluating the shape of parametric models (Douglas & Cohen, 2001; Liang & Wells, 2009; Liang, Wells, & Hambleton, 2014; Lord, 1970; Wells & Bolt, 2008). Essentially, the shape assumption is assessed by comparing estimates of a nonparametric ICC against the estimates based on the parametric model of interest. The nonparametric ICC has fewer restrictions imposed on the shape of the ICC; therefore, if the parametrically based ICC differs from the nonparametric ICC, then the parametric model may be incorrect. Lord (1970) first introduced this method for the purpose of determining if empirically estimated ICCs follow a specific logistic form. Since Lord (1970), there have been advancements in the methods for obtaining a nonparametrically based ICC (Douglas, 1997; Eubank, 1988; Hardle, 1991; Ramsay, 1991).

Kernel smoothing (Ramsay, 1991) is a popular method of modeling an ICC non-parametrically. The essential principle underlying kernel smoothing, termed *local averaging*, is useful in estimating an ICC because, for a dichotomous item response, the probability of a correct response can be depicted as an average response for examinees close to a particular ability parameter value. Kernel-smoothed estimates of the probability of a correct response for item i are obtained for a set of Q evaluation points, denoted x_q, defined along the θ scale (e.g., $x_1 = -3.00$, $x_2 = -2.88, \ldots, x_{50} = 2.88$, $x_{51} = 3.00$, where $Q = 51$). An estimate of ability is provided for each examinee j by, for example, converting the rest score (i.e., total score excluding the item being modeled) to a standard score. We obtain the standard score to represent $\hat{\theta}_j$ by transforming each examinee's empirical percentile of the total score distribution into the corresponding value from the ability distribution (Ramsay, 1991). For example, if the ability distribution follows the standard normal distribution, then an examinee with a rest score at the 95th percentile would receive $\hat{\theta}_j$ of 1.645.

The kernel-smoothed ICC for item i and evaluation point q is estimated as follows:

$$\hat{P}_{non,iq} = \sum_{j=1}^{N} w_{jq} u_{ij} \tag{10.3}$$

where w_{jq} represents the weight assigned to each examinee at each evaluation point; N indicates the number of examinees; and u_{ij} is the response by examinee j on item i (i.e., 0 or 1). Weights are assigned to each examinee with respect to each evaluation point; therefore, each examinee receives Q weights. The weight for examinee j increases as the evaluation point moves closer to $\hat{\theta}_j$ and decreases toward zero as the evaluation point moves further away from $\hat{\theta}_j$. The weight for examinee j at evaluation point x_q can be calculated as

$$w_{jq} = \frac{K\left(\dfrac{\hat{\theta}_j - x_q}{h}\right)}{\displaystyle\sum_{j=1}^{N} K\left(\dfrac{\hat{\theta}_j - x_q}{h}\right)} \tag{10.4}$$

where x_q refers to evaluation point q, and $\hat{\theta}_j$ is the proficiency estimate for examinee j. Two other important components of the formula are h and K. The value h is referred to as the bandwidth or smoothing parameter because it controls the amount of bias and variance in the estimated ICC; h is often set equal to $1.1*N^{-.2}$ so as to produce a smoothed function with small bias and variance. K is referred to as the kernel smoothing function. K is always greater than or equal to zero and approaches zero as $\hat{\theta}_j$ moves away from a particular evaluation point, x_q. Two commonly used kernel functions are the Gaussian [$K(u) = \exp(-u^2)$] and uniform [$K(u) = 1$ if $|u| \leq 1$, else 0]. Given the previous information, it is apparent that the further an examinee is from the evaluation point, the less weight that examinee has in determining $\hat{P}_{non,iq}$, especially compared to an examinee who has a $\hat{\theta}$ equal to the evaluation point of interest, since the density for a Gaussian, for instance, is largest at $u = 0$.

The nonparametric approach based on kernel smoothing is similar to using the observed proportions previously described, in that both the nonparametric IRT model and the observed proportions are intended to be proxies for the underlying ICC. In fact, Douglas (1997) showed that for medium-length tests and medium sample sizes, the underlying ICC can be consistently estimated using nonparametric ICCs under a set of weak assumptions. An advantage of using nonparametric IRT to represent the underlying ICC is that the kernel-smoothed estimates are not influenced by the parametric model, in comparison to the previous methods where examinees are placed into intervals based on their IRT model ability parameter estimate. One of the disadvantages of grouping examinees into intervals based on the respective IRT model's ability parameter estimate is that the observed proportions are influenced by the parametric model (Molenaar & Hoijtink, 1990). This is an unattractive feature because the observed data may not be accurately representing the underlying ICC. The nonparametric approach does not suffer this drawback because the raw scores are used to represent the ability parameter estimate.

Once the nonparametric ICC is obtained, the next step is to estimate the ICC for the respective parametric model. There are several ways of obtaining the parametric ICC that can be compared to the nonparametric ICC. One method, illustrated by Douglas and Cohen (2001) for the two-parameter logistic (2PL) model, finds the item parameter estimates by regressing the logit $\hat{P}_{non,iq}$ onto the evaluation points. A second method that has been shown to be effective via simulation studies (Liang & Wells, 2009; Liang et al., 2014; Wells & Bolt, 2008) is an analytic solution that implements the maximum likelihood estimation (MLE) developed by Bolt (2002). It is important to note that for this method to be appropriate, the proficiency distribution must be defined in the same manner for both the nonparametric and parametric ICCs (Douglas & Cohen, 2001). For example, if the standard normal distribution is used to obtain the nonparametric ICC, then the proficiency distribution must be defined in the same manner when estimating the parametric ICC.

Figure 10.3 illustrates the nonparametric approach for a dichotomous item from a large-scale assessment. The solid line represents the kernel-smoothed ICC and the vertical lines represent the confidence bands based on three standard errors for each smoothed estimate. The standard error for item i and evaluation point q is computed as follows:

$$\hat{P}_{non,iq} \pm 3 * \sqrt{\sum_{j=1}^{N} w_{jq}^2 \hat{P}(\theta_j) \left[1 - \hat{P}(\theta_j)\right]} \tag{10.5}$$

where $\hat{P}(\theta_j)$ represents the probability of examinee j correctly answering item i based on the smoothed ICC. The dashed and dotted lines shown in Figure 10.3 represent the

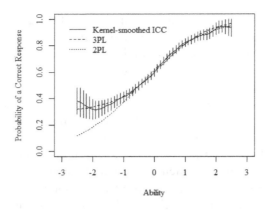

FIGURE 10.3. Comparison of kernel-smoothed ICC to the 3PL and 2PL models.

best-fitting response functions for the 3PL and 2PL models, respectively. It appears that the 3PL model provides a reasonable fit since the model-based estimates are very close to the nonparametric ICC. In comparison, the 2PL model ICC diverges from the nonparametric curve beyond the confidence bands in several places throughout the ability scale, indicating that this model does not provide an adequate fit.

Douglas and Cohen (2001) proposed a statistic to summarize the difference between the nonparametric and parametric response functions, referred to as the *root integrated squared error* (*RISE*). A discrete approximation of the *RISE* statistic for a dichotomously scored item is computed as follows:

$$RISE_i = \sqrt{\frac{\sum_{q=1}^{Q}\left(\hat{P}_{iq} - \hat{P}_{non,iq}\right)^2}{Q}} \qquad (10.6)$$

where $\hat{P}_i$ and $\hat{P}_{non,iq}$ represent points on the ICC for the model-based and nonparametric methods, respectively. A parametric bootstrapping method was adopted to approximate the significance level for each item. The bootstrapping procedure entails simulating M datasets (e.g., $M = 500$) under the condition that the parametric model fits and sampling N θ's from the standard normal distribution. The statistic *RISE* is calculated for each simulated dataset, producing a sampling distribution for *RISE*. The *p*-value associated with the observed *RISE* statistic for each item, based on the original data, is determined by the proportion of *RISE*s from the simulated data that were greater than the observed *RISE* value. The parametric bootstrapping procedure and *RISE* have exhibited controlled (or slightly deflated) Type I error rates and adequate power to detect model misfit (Liang & Wells, 2009; Liang et al., 2014; Wells & Bolt, 2008). However, items that are identified as misfitting should be examined graphically to determine if the misfit is non-negligible.

Summary and Conclusions

Testing the dimensionality, local independence, and ICC shape assumptions plays an important role in the valid application of IRT models. The purpose of the present chapter was to describe several approaches for assessing model assumptions with the understanding that the assumptions will always be violated to a certain degree when using real data. Therefore, the goal in testing the assumptions is to determine if the assumptions are satisfied well enough for the model to be useful.

Although there are several effective techniques that can be used to assess IRT assumptions, there is still room for improvement and further research. For example, the Bayesian approach of posterior predictive model checking (PPMC) developed by Guttman (1967) and applied to IRT by Sinharay (2005) and Sinharay, Johnson, and Stern (2006) offers a promising framework for assessing IRT model assumptions. The challenge in implementing PPMC is that it relies on the computationally and time-intensive Markov chain Monte Carlo (MCMC) estimation, which is difficult to implement routinely in large-scale assessments. However, as computers become more powerful, it may be possible in the near future to apply the Bayesian approach operationally.

Although there are a plethora of methods available for assessing model assumptions, there is a lack of research and theory on the robustness of the models in the face of assumption violations. For example, how much multidimensionality or local dependencies can exist in test data before unidimensional models are no longer useful? How much error can we tolerate when violating the shape assumption? Further research on the robustness of IRT models can provide useful information that we can use when assessing IRT model assumptions.

REFERENCES

Beavers, A. S., Lounsbury, J. W., Richards, J. K., Huck, S. W., Skolits, G. J., & Esquivel, S. L. (2013). Practical considerations for using exploratory factor analysis in educational research. *Practical Assessment, Research, and Evaluation, 10*(7). Available at *http://pare-online.net/getvn.asp?v=10&n=7.*

Bejar, I. I. (1983). Introduction to item response models and their assumptions. In R. K. Hambleton (Ed.), *Applications of item response theory* (pp. 1–23). Vancouver, BC: Educational Research Institute of British Columbia.

Bishop, Y. M. M., Fienberg, S. E., & Holland, P. W. (1975). *Discrete multivariate analysis: Theory and practice.* Cambridge, MA: MIT Press.

Bollen, K. A. (1989). *Structural equations with latent variables.* New York: Wiley.

Bolt, D. M. (2002). A Monte Carlo comparison of parametric and nonparametric polytomous DIF detection methods. *Applied Measurement in Education, 15*, 113–141.

Box, G. E. P., & Draper, N. R. (1987). *Empirical model building and response surfaces.* New York: Wiley.

Brown, T. A. (2006). *Confirmatory factor analysis for applied research* (2nd ed.). New York: Guilford Press.

Burg, S. S. (2007). *An investigation of dimensionality across grade levels and effects on vertical linking for elementary grade mathematics achievement tests* (Unpublished doctoral dissertation). University of North Carolina at Chapel Hill, Chapel Hill, NC.

Cattell, R. B. (1966). The scree test for the number of factors. *Multivariate Behavioral Research, 1*, 245–276.

Chen, F. F., Hayes, A., Carver, C. S., Laurenceau, J. P., & Zhang, Z. (2012). Modeling general and specific variance in multifaceted constructs: a comparison of the bifactor model to other approaches. Journal of Personality, 80(1), 219–251.

Chen, W. H., & Thissen, D. (1997). Local dependence indexes for item pairs using item response theory. *Journal of Educational and Behavioral Statistics, 22*(3), 265–289.

Cheung, G. W., & Rensvold, R. B. (2002). Evaluating goodness-of-fit indexes for testing measurement invariance. *Structural Equation Modeling: A Multidisciplinary Journal, 9*(2), 233–255.

Costello, A. B., & Osborne, J. W. (2005). Best practices in exploratory factor analysis: Four recommendations for getting the most from your analysis. *Practical Assessment, Research, and Evaluation, 10*(7). Available at *http://pareonline.net/getvn.asp?v=10&n=7.*

De Ayala, R. J. (2009). *Theory and practice of item response theory.* New York: Guilford Press.

Dodeen, H. (2004). The relationship between item parameters and item fit. *Journal of Educational Measurement, 41*, 261–270.

Douglas, J. (1997). Joint consistency of nonparametric item characteristic curve and ability estimation. *Psychometrika, 62*, 7–28.

Douglas, J., & Cohen, A. S. (2001). Nonparametric item response function estimation for assessing parametric model fit. *Applied Psychological Measurement, 25*, 234–243.

Edwards, M. C., & Cai, L. (2011, July). *A new procedure for detecting departures from local independence in item response models.* Paper presented at the annual meeting of the American Psychological Association, Washington, DC. Retrieved from *http://faculty.psy.ohio-state.edu/edwards/documents/APA8.2.11.pdf.*

Embretson, S. E., & Reise, S. P. (2000). *Item response theory for psychologists.* Mahwah, NJ: Erlbaum.

Eubank, R. L. (1988). *Spline smoothing and nonparametric regression.* New York: Marcel Dekker.

Fabrigar, L. R., Wegener, D. T., MacCallum, R. C., & Strahan, E. J. (1999). Evaluating the use of exploratory factor analysis in psychological research. *Psychological Methods, 4*(3), 272–299.

Finch, H., & Habing, B. (2007). Performance of DIMTEST- and NOHARM-based statistics for testing unidimensionality. *Applied Psychological Measurement, 31*(4), 292–307.

Gierl, M. J., Leighton, J. P., & Tan, X. (2006). Evaluating DETECT classification accuracy and consistency when data display complex structure. *Journal of Educational Measurement, 43*(3), 265–289.

Guttman, I. (1967). The use of the concept of a future observation in goodness-of-fit problems. *Journal of the Royal Statistical Society B, 29*, 83–100.

Haberman, S. J., Sinharay, S., & Chon, K. H. (2013). Assessing item fit for unidimensional item response theory models using residuals from estimated item response functions. *Psychometrika, 78*, 417–440.

Hambleton, R. K., & Han, N. (2005). Assessing the fit of IRT models to educational and psychological test data: A five-step plan and several graphical displays. In R. R. Lenderking & D. A. Revicki (Eds.), *Advancing health outcomes research methods and clinical applications* (pp. 57–77). McLean, VA: Degnon Associates.

Hambleton, R. K., Swaminathan, H., & Rogers, H. J. (1991). *Fundamentals of item response theory.* Newbury Park, CA: Sage.

Hardle, W. (1991). *Smoothing techniques with implementation in S.* New York: Springer-Verlag.

Harrison, D. (1986). Robustness of IRT parameter estimation to violations of the unidimensionality assumption. *Journal of Educational Statistics, 11,* 91–115.

Hattie, J. (1985). Methodology review: Assessing unidimensionality of tests and items. *Applied Psychological Measurement, 9,* 139–164.

Hattie, J., Krakowski, K., Rogers, H. J., & Swaminathan, H. (1996). An assessment of Stout's index of essential unidimensionality. *Applied Psychological Measurement, 20*(1), 1–14.

Hayton, J. C., Allen, D. G., & Scarpello, V. (2004). Factor retention decisions in exploratory factor analysis: A tutorial on parallel analysis. *Organizational Research Methods, 7*(2), 191–205.

Horn, J. L. (1965). A rationale and test for the number of factors in factor analysis. *Psychometrika, 30*(2), 179–185.

Hu, L. T., & Bentler, P. M. (1999). Cutoff criteria for fit indexes in covariance structure analysis: Conventional criteria versus new alternatives. *Structural Equation Modeling, 6*(1), 1–55.

Huynh, H., & Ferrara, S. (1994). A comparison of equal percentile and partial credit equating for performance assessments composed of free responses items. *Journal of Educational Measurement, 31,* 125–141.

Ip, E. H. S. (2001). Testing for local dependency in dichotomous and polytomous item response models. *Psychometrika, 66*(1), 109–132.

Jasper, F. (2010). Applied dimensionality and test structure assessment with the START-M mathematics test. *International Journal of Educational and Psychological Assessment, 6*(1). Available at *https://docs.google.com/file/d/0ByxuG44OvRLPZjUybDMtY2xYbVE/edit.*

Jennrich, R. I., & Bentler, P. M. (2011). Exploratory bi-factor analysis. *Psychometrika, 76*(4), 537–549.

Kaiser, H. F. (1960). The application of electronic computers to factor analysis. *Educational and Psychological Measurement, 20,* 141–151.

Kim, D., De Ayala, R. J., Ferdous, A. A., & Nering, M. L. (2007, April). *Assessing relative performance of local item dependence (LID) indexes.* Paper presented at the annual meeting of the National Council on Measurement in Education, Chicago, IL.

Kline, R. B. (2015). *Principles and practice of structural equation modeling* (4th ed.). New York: Guilford Press.

Levy, R., Mislevy, R. J., & Sinharay, S. (2009). Posterior predictive model checking for multidimensionality in item response theory. *Applied Psychological Measurement, 33*(7), 519–537.

Levy, R., & Svetina, D. (2010, May). *A framework for characterizing dimensionality assessment and overview of current approaches.* Paper presented at the annual meeting of the National Council on Measurement in Education, Denver, CO.

Liang, T., & Wells, C. S. (2009). A model fit statistic for generalized partial credit model. *Educational and Psychological Measurement, 69,* 913–928.

Liang, T., Wells, C. S., & Hambleton, R. K. (2014). An assessment of the nonparametric approach for evaluating the fit of item response models. *Journal of Educational Measurement, 28*(2), 115–129.

Linacre, J. M. (1994). Sample size and item calibrations stability. *Rasch Measurement Transactions, 7*(4), 328.

Liu, Y., & Maydeu-Olivares, A. (2013). Local dependence diagnostics in IRT modeling of binary data. *Educational and Psychological Measurement, 73*(2), 254–274.

Lord, F. M. (1970). Item characteristic curves estimated without knowledge of their mathematical form: A confrontation of Birnbaum's logistic model. *Psychometrika, 35*, 43–50.

Molenaar, I. W., & Hoijtink, H. (1990). The many null distributions of person fit indices. *Psychometrika, 55*, 75–106.

Nandakumar, R. (1993). Assessing essential unidimensionality of real data. *Applied Psychological Measurement, 17*, 29–38.

Nandakumar, R., & Ackerman, T. (2004). Test modeling. In D. Kapling (Ed.), *The SAGE handbook of quantitative methodology for the social sciences* (pp. 93–106). Thousand Oaks, CA: Sage.

Orlando, M., & Thissen, D. (2000). Likelihood-based item-fit indices for dichotomous item response theory models. *Applied Psychological Measurement, 24*(1), 50–64.

Ramsay, J. O. (1991). Kernel smoothing approaches to nonparametric item characteristic curve estimation. *Psychometrika, 60*, 323–339.

Reckase, M. D. (1997). A linear logistic multidimensional model. In W. J. van der Linden & R. K. Hambleton (Eds.), *Handbook of modern item response theory* (pp. 271–286). New York: Springer-Verlag.

Reise, S. P. (2012). The rediscovery of bifactor measurement models. *Multivariate Behavior Research, 47*, 667–696.

Schweizer, K., Ren, X., & Wang, T. (2014). A comparison of confirmatory factor analysis of binary data on the basis of tetrachoric correlations and of probability-based covariances: A simulation study. In R. E. Millsap, D. M. Bolt, L. A. van der Ark, and W.-C. Wang (Eds.), *Quantitative psychology research: The 78th annual meeting of the Psychometric Society* (pp. 272–292). New York: Springer.

Sinharay, S. (2005). assessing fit of unidimensional item response theory models using a Bayesian approach. *Journal of Educational Measurement, 42*(4), 375–394.

Sinharay, S., Johnson, M. S., & Stern, H. S. (2006). Posterior predictive assessment of item response theory models. *Applied Psychological Measurement, 30*, 298.

Stone, C. A. (2000). Monte Carlo based null distribution for an alternative goodness-of-fit statistic in IRT models. *Journal of Educational Measurement, 37*, 58–75.

Stone, C. A., & Hansen, M. A. (2000). The effect of errors in estimating ability on goodness-of-fit tests for IRT models. *Educational and Psychological Measurement, 60*, 974–991.

Stone, C. A., Mislevy, R. J., & Mazzeo, J. (1994, April). *Classification error and goodness-of-fit in IRT models.* Paper presented at the annual meeting of the American Educational Research Association, New Orleans, LA.

Stone, C. A., & Zhang, B. (2003). Assessing goodness of fit of item response theory models: A comparison of traditional and alternative procedures. *Journal of Educational Measurement, 40*, 331–352.

Stout, W. F. (1987). A nonparametric approach for assessing latent trait dimensionality. *Psychometrika, 52*, 589–617.

Stout, W. F. (1990). A new item response theory modeling approach with applications to unidimensional assessment and ability estimation. *Psychometrika, 55*, 293–326.

Stout, W. F., Douglas, J., Junker, B., & Roussos, L. (1993). *DIMTEST manual.* Unpublished manuscript available from W. F. Stout, University of Illinois at Urbana–Champaign, Champaign. IL.

Stout, W. F., Habing, B., Douglas, J., Kim, H. R., Roussos, L., & Zhang, J. (1996). Conditional covariance-based nonparametric multidimensionality assessment. *Applied Psychological Measurement, 20*, 331–354.

Svetina, D. (2013). Assessing dimensionality of noncompensatory multidimensional item response theory with complex structures. *Educational and Psychological Measurement, 73*(2), 312–338.

Svetina, D., & Levy, R. (2014). A framework for dimensionality assessment for multidimensional item response models. *Educational Assessment, 19*(1), 35–57.

Swaminathan, H., Hambleton, R. K., & Rogers, H. J. (2007). Assessing the fit of item response theory models. In C. R. Rao & Sinharay (Eds.), *Handbook of statistics: Vol. 26. Psychometrics* (pp. 683–718). Amsterdam: North Holland.

Tate, R. (2003). A comparison of selected empirical methods for assessing the structure of responses to test items. *Applied Psychological Measurement, 27*(3), 159–203.

Tran, U. S., & Formann, A. K. (2009). Performance of parallel analysis in retrieving unidimensionality in the presence of binary data. *Educational and Psychological Measurement, 69*, 50–61.

Tsai, T. H., & Hsu, Y. C. (2005, April). *The use of information entropy as a local item dependence assessment.* Paper presented at the annual conference of the American Educational Research Association, Montreal, Quebec, Canada.

van Abswoude, A. A., van der Ark, L. A., & Sijtsma, K. (2004). A comparative study of test data dimensionality assessment procedures under nonparametric IRT models. *Applied Psychological Measurement, 28*(1), 3–24.

Velicer, W. F. (1976). Determining the number of components from the matrix of partial correlations. *Psychometrika, 41*, 321–327.

Velicer, W. F., & Jackson, D. N. (1990). Component analysis versus common factor analysis: Some issues in selecting an appropriate procedure. *Multivariate Behavioral Research, 25*(1), 1–28.

Wainer, H., & Thissen, D. (1987). Estimating ability with the wrong model. *Journal of Educational and Behavioral Statistics, 12*, 339–368.

Wells, C. S., & Bolt, D. M. (2008). Investigation of a nonparametric procedure for assessing goodness-of-fit in item response theory. *Applied Measurement in Education, 21*(1), 22–40.

Wells, C. S., & Keller, L. A. (2010, May). *Effect of model misfit on parameter invariance.* Paper presented at the annual meeting of the National Council on Measurement in Education, Denver, CO.

Yen, W. M. (1981). Using simulation results to choose a latent trait model. *Applied Psychological Measurement, 5*, 245–262.

Yen, W. M. (1984). Effects of local item dependence on the fit and equating performance of the three-parameter logistic model. *Applied Psychological Measurement, 8*(2), 125–145.

Zhang, J., & Stout, W. (1999). The theoretical DETECT index of dimensionality and its application to approximate simple structure. *Psychometrika, 64*(2), 213–249.

Zwick, W. R., & Velicer, W. F. (1986). Comparison of five rules for determining the number of components to retain. *Psychological Bulletin, 99*(3), 432–442.

PART IV
Computer-Based Testing

CHAPTER 11

The History of Computer-Based Testing

Walter D. Way and Frederic Robin

Today, technology touches almost everything we do. From communication to transportation to entertainment, computers and electronic devices are ubiquitous and utilized in a variety of situations. Although trends indicate an ever-increasing reliance on digital media, some changes are not as quick and pervasive as one might expect. For example, sales of electronic books exploded between 2009 and 2012, but leveled off in 2013 to about 30% of all books sold in the United States. One explanation for this slowing growth (Carr, 2013) is that e-books may be better suited to some types of books (e.g., genre fiction) than others (e.g., nonfiction and literary fiction) and to certain reading situations (travel) than others (e.g., lying on the couch at home). Thus, it is not obvious that e-books will completely supplant traditional print books, and the answer to this question may well depend on whether they come to be seen by consumers as superior to print across a variety of reading situations.

Although not as dramatic or recent an innovation, some parallels can be drawn to the use of computer-based testing (CBT), which, like e-books, has not yet supplanted the traditional print-based approach to testing. Perhaps no trend in testing and measurement has been touted as long or as loudly as CBT. The roots of CBT and its derivative methods, such as adaptive testing, go back more than 100 years to the work of famed psychologist Albert Binet (cf. *www.iacat.org/content/first-adaptive-test*). Twenty-five years before the writing of this chapter, Bunderson, Inouye, and Olsen (1989) described four generations of computerized educational measurement, noting, "The changes brought about by the wide availability and low cost of new technological delivery system alternatives are moving testing from its delivery through paper-and-pencil and printed booklets to delivery through on-line computer work-stations" (p. 402). Why this trend did not proceed at the trajectory that many expected in 1989 is one interesting part of the history of CBT.

What Is CBT?

In its broadest sense, CBT includes not just tests administered on computers or work-stations but also tests delivered by other devices, including smartphones, tablets, and other electronic devices (Davey, 2005). In England, CBT is known as electronic assessment or "e-assessment," and is defined as "the end-to-end electronic assessment processes where ICT [information and communication technology] is used for the presentation of assessment activity and the recording of responses" (Busuttil-Reynaud & Winkley, 2006, p. 4). Both of these definitions anticipate the possible continued evolution of digital technology in the delivery of tests and suggest that the *computer* in CBT may eventually become a misnomer.

The advantages of CBT are relatively obvious when one compares CBT with the test preparation, administration, and scoring processes involved in traditional paper-based testing. CBT eliminates the need for printing, shipping, collecting, and tracking physical test books and answer documents. This makes the administration process more efficient and more secure. In addition, CBT provides more flexibility in administration, particularly in admissions, certification/licensure, and placement programs where individuals can schedule testing at times convenient to them. Because of the efficiencies in administration, CBT provides a faster turnaround of scores and score reports, particularly when tests consist of machine-scored items. When items can be precalibrated, dynamic administration models such as computerized adaptive testing (CAT) are possible, which can increase the efficiency and accuracy of measurement (Weiss, 1982). A variety of dynamic models is available to support CBT (cf. Folk & Smith, 2002; Luecht & Sireci, 2011); we discuss some of these models later in this chapter.

Perhaps the most compelling advantage of CBT is the ability to administer technology-enhanced items and tasks that better measure what test takers know and can do. Relatively early innovations in this area included simulations that were developed for licensure tests in medicine (Melnick & Clauser, 2006) and architecture (Bejar & Braun, 1994). More recently, efforts in developing technology-enhanced items have focused on the use of templates to describe the interaction between a test taker and the item or task presented, the response data that result, and the approach for scoring the responses (Haertel et al., 2012; Parshall & Harmes, 2007). Such templates are designed to encourage efficiency and consistency in the development of technology-enhanced items.

In this chapter we trace the history of CBT, focusing on three aspects: (1) how CBT has evolved to the point it is at today; (2) the major methodological implications of the shift to CBT; and (3) the major policy implications of the shift to CBT that will persist into the future. In recounting this history, we identify some of the prominent players and applications, and some of the successes and challenges associated with these efforts. We are grateful for the opportunity to contribute to this volume in honor of Dr. Hambleton. He has been keenly interested in CBT throughout his career and his many contributions to testing theory and practice have contributed—both directly and indirectly—to CBT's growth.

Evolution of CBT

Origins of CBT

It is obvious and somewhat trite to point out that the evolution of CBT has followed the evolution of computer use in education and society in general. Although true, there are other threads to the history of CBT worthy of mention. As previously noted, Binet's work in intelligence testing is credited as being a precursor to adaptive testing (Binet & Simon, 1912). In the 1920s, Sidney Pressey, an educational psychology professor at Ohio State University, developed a machine to administer test items to students in his introductory courses (Pressey, 1926, 1927). Pressey was an early advocate of the "programmed teaching" movement, which was later popularized by B. F. Skinner in the late 1950s and early 1960s (Skinner, 1958, 1961). Benjamin (1988) traced a history of teaching machines and devoted much of that article to the work of Pressey and Skinner.

Neither Pressey's nor Skinner's teaching machines were computers, per se; however, the programmed instruction movement soon embraced the concept of *computer-assisted instruction* (CAI). An early cited example of CAI was the IBM Teaching Machines project (Benjamin, 1988). This project included a high-speed computer connected with a typewriter, which allowed the computer to present problems to the student by way of the typewriter. The student, in turn, typed answers, which were transmitted to the computer for checking.

A better-known CAI system that began in the early 1960s was PLATO (Programmed Logic for Automatic Teaching Operations; Pagliaro, 1983). PLATO was initiated at the University of Illinois at Urbana–Champaign and later developed by Control Data Cooperation (CDC). PLATO was a small system throughout a lengthy developmental period during the 1960s, supporting only a single classroom of terminals. About 1972, PLATO began a transition to a new generation of mainframes that would eventually support up to 1,000 users simultaneously. In 1976, the system was purchased by CDC, which began to commercialize it. One of CDC's early successes was a partnership with the National Association of Security Dealers (NASD) to develop the first "on-demand" proctored CBT system, beginning in about 1978 (Zara, 2006). CDC's online testing business grew slowly until 1990, when it was spun off as one of several companies that built testing centers to support CBT for licensure, certification, and academic admissions programs that had begun in the late 1980s.

A Golden Age for CAT Research

The evolution toward CBT also began to gain momentum through theoretical and empirical research related to adaptive testing, which at the time took on various alternate terms, such as *sequential testing, branched testing, individualized measurement, tailored testing, programmed testing,* and *response-contingent testing* (Weiss & Betz, 1973). A number of important papers emerged in the late 1960s and early 1970s that began to provide a theoretical foundation for adaptive testing, including Birnbaum's (1968) presentation of latent trait models, Owen's (1969) introduction of a Bayesian

CAT procedure, several seminal papers by Lord (1970; 1971a, 1971b, 1971c, 1971d) on flexilevel testing, and work by Weiss and his colleagues at the University of Minnesota examining branching strategies in adaptive testing (Weiss, 1976).

The availability of CAI and platforms such as PLATO garnered the interest of the military, which was looking for efficient methods of training and assessing the aptitudes of recruits for placement into specialty areas. One extremely promising area for achieving this was CAT, and military-sponsored funding fueled what might be considered a golden age for CAT research. An early example of this work was a study by Hansen, Johnson, Fagan, Tan, and Dick (1974) examining the utility of a computerized adaptive measurement system in an Air Force technical training environment. To accomplish the study, testing procedures were programmed in the TUTOR language used to support the PLATO system at the University of Illinois. The conclusions from this study were very optimistic: "Adaptive testing offers the potential for time savings of up to 50%. Furthermore, it was found that a very flexible computer system to drive the adaptive testing strategies could be relatively easily developed" (Hansen et al., 1974, p. 2).

The military further encouraged research on CAT by sponsoring a series of conferences beginning in 1975 (Clark, 1976; Weiss, 1978, 1980, 1985). These conferences brought together leading researchers from military and academic circles, and the proceedings document a remarkable breadth and depth of adaptive testing research and theoretical work. It is of particular note for those interested in the history of CBT that—as of this writing—the proceedings from all four conferences can be found on the Internet.

The military's investment in CAT culminated in the development of the CAT version of the Armed Services Vocational Aptitude Battery (CAT-ASVAB), which was first proposed in 1976, the same year it was determined that a single-classification battery would be administered to applicants to the Army, Air Force, Navy, and Marine Corps (Defense Manpower Data Center, 2006). A feasibility project was funded in 1979, and psychometric evaluation proceeded along with the development and validation of an experimental CAT-ASVAB version between 1979 and 1983. A large-scale validation study was conducted between 1983 and 1985 to address the comparability of CAT and paper-and-pencil versions of the ASVAB (Segall, Moreno, Kieckhaefer, Vicino, & McBride, 1997). The results of this research were positive, leading to the operational development and implementation of the CAT-ASVAB between 1985 and 1990, and a smoothly running operational program since that time.

Two other trends also impacted the evolution of CBT in the 1980s. The first trend was the explosion in application and acceptance of item response theory (IRT) across a wide variety of test settings. This trend was facilitated in the academic community by several textbooks devoted to IRT (Hambleton & Swaminathan, 1985; Hulin, Drasgow & Parsons, 1983; Lord, 1980). In addition, major test publishers began using IRT to scale and equate tests (Hicks, 1983; Lenke & Rentz, 1982; Yen, 1983). As the principles of IRT became better known, its promise as a means of supporting CBT applications began to be broadly appreciated.

Also during the 1980s, microcomputers became widely available and their use in supporting CBT was fulfilled. For example, the CAT-ASVAB project was significantly boosted by the realization that the microcomputer industry had advanced to the point where off-the-shelf equipment could be utilized rather than contracted mainframe hardware and software. Haney (1985) described a pilot by the Portland Public School system to use microcomputers and a Rasch-based adaptive testing system. Educational Testing Service (ETS) used microcomputers to implement a CAT for the College Board to be used for college-level placement (Ward, 1988; Ward, Kline, & Flaugher, 1986). ETS also embarked on a project with the National Council of Architects to administer their Architects Registration Exam using microcomputers and a computerized mastery testing model (Lewis & Sheehan, 1990). Carlson and von Davier (2013) provide a historical review of ETS's contributions to IRT, a number of which addressed applications to CBT.

By the beginning of the 1990s, a number of large-scale testing programs were poised to implement CAT and other applications of CBT. There were many reasons to be optimistic that CBT would soon supplant traditional paper-and-pencil testing. The use of IRT and statistical methodology to support CAT had matured, and the technology to deliver CBT appeared to be within reach. Supported by a number of methodological refinements, CBT clearly expanded in the 1990s. However, the explosion in CBT and CAT applications that was expected did not quite materialize.

CAT Implementation and Challenges

In the late 1980s, ETS proposed to convert the Graduate Record Examination (GRE) to a CAT format. The development and supporting research proceeded in two phases: first, establishing the comparability of the CBT version with the paper-and-pencil GRE, and second, establishing the comparability of the adaptive testing model with the original linear model (Mills, 1999). In addition, ETS researchers embarked on significant work in developing a CAT item selection algorithm that would simultaneously balance not only psychometric goals but a variety of other constraints related to content, item format, items delivered within sets or passages, and exposure of test items (Stocking & Swanson, 1993).

The GRE CAT was introduced in 1993 and made available on a continuous basis. Issues with the test were encountered almost immediately. During the second half of 1994, 22 employees of Stanley H. Kaplan, a test preparation company, took the GRE CAT and proved that questions on a CAT could be memorized by test takers and passed on to others who had not yet taken the examination. Kaplan brought its findings to ETS's attention. ETS responded by bringing suit to Kaplan but also by pulling back on the availability of CAT administrations and significantly increasing item development (*Educational Testing Service, et al. v. Stanley H. Kaplan, Educational Center, LTD.*, 1997).

A second issue that arose with the GRE CAT concerned the policy that ETS implemented to score examinees who did not complete the test. Initially, ETS required students to respond to at least 80% of the CAT to receive a score. If this minimum threshold was met, the resulting score was based on the maximum likelihood estimate of ability for those questions answered by the test taker (Slater & Schaeffer, 1996). In essence, the 80% rule did not penalize test takers for not completing the test. Once the rule became known, rates of incomplete CATs increased and scores also increased, particularly for the GRE Analytical section, which was known to be speeded (Bridgeman & Cline, 2000). To counter this trend, ETS implemented a new method for scoring incomplete CATs called *proportional scoring* (Schaeffer et al., 1998). Proportional scoring imposed a penalty on test takers for unanswered items that, on average, appeared to be more severe than assuming they guessed at random on items but less severe than assuming that they answered items incorrectly (Mills & Steffen, 2000).

Although proportional scoring appeared to address comparability concerns of the CAT with the paper-and-pencil GRE, it did not address the issues associated with the speeded GRE Analytical CAT. This issue came to a head when a test taker received an extremely low score on the CAT and subsequently increased from the 3rd percentile to the 84th percentile on the GRE Analytical section upon retesting with the paper-and-pencil test. In response to the complaint, ETS removed the CAT score from the student's record and reimbursed the CBT test fees (Mayfield, 1999). Issues with speededness and other irregularities in CAT results subsequently led to a policy by ETS to cancel scores and offer free retests to some GRE CAT test takers with anomalous results (Carlson, 2000).

In the 1990s, ETS implemented CAT for many of their most prominent large-scale testing programs, including the GRE, the Test of English as a Foreign Language (TOEFL), the Praxis Professional Assessments for Beginning Teachers, and the Graduate Management Admission Test (GMAT). The decision to pursue CAT for these programs was bold, but operational challenges similar to those encountered by GRE were also present. Wainer and Eignor (2000) and Wainer (2000) summarized some of the ongoing issues, including maintaining security in the face of continuous testing, the massive test development efforts needed to limit item exposure, and increased costs of administration compared with paper-and-pencil testing. Based on these outcomes, it is probably not a coincidence that other large scale admissions testing programs, such as the SAT and ACT assessments and Law School Admissions Test (LSAT), all chose to maintain their programs in paper-and-pencil format through the 1990s and 2000s, despite initial research and development efforts focused on computerizing the tests.

CBT Expansion, Refinement, and More Challenges

Although ETS's forays into CAT produced mixed results, there was a number of successful CBT programs launched in the 1990s and early 2000s. One of the most fruitful areas for CBT implementation was certification and licensure. An advantage that computer-based certification and licensure testing has over admissions testing is a control and tracking of test takers that is not possible in admissions testing. This control and tracking serves to reduce concerns related to test security under continuous testing conditions. An early example of an adaptive test for licensure was the National Council on Nursing Licensure's Examinations for Registered and Practical Nurses (NCLEX-RN and NCLEX-PN). These examinations were computerized in 1994 using a variable-length CAT procedure based on the Rasch model. This approach reduced testing time for nursing candidates from 2 days conducted at a limited number of testing centers in major cities two times per year, to as little as 90 minutes at computer centers within a half hour's drive at almost any day or time desired (Zara, 1999). As Breithaupt, Mills, and Melican (2006) described, prominent examples of CBT innovations were introduced by the National Council of Architects Registration Boards (NCARB), the United States Medical Licensing Examination (USMLE), and the American Institute of Certified Public Accountants (AICPA). In addition, CBT certification programs were established by many companies in the information technology industries, including Microsoft, Novell, Cisco, Hewlett–Packard, and others. The success of these programs supported the expansion of vendors that maintained CBT centers across the globe, most notably Prometric and Pearson VUE. Each of these CBT vendors were soon supporting hundreds of customers in delivering CBTs around the world.

In educational testing within the United States, applications of CBT also began to spring up as state testing programs expanded to meet the requirements of the No Child Left Behind (NCLB) Act of 2001. Successful applications of CAT in educational settings had been established in 1990s (cf. Kingsbury & Houser, 1999), and the increased testing requirements of NCLB seemed ripe for CAT applications. However, controversy quickly arose related to the use of CAT in the context of the NCLB. Specifically, the U.S. Department of Education's final regulations stipulated that all of the items administered in a CAT used for NCLB accountability purposes must be developed to measure grade-level standards. This stipulation derailed efforts in several states to introduce CAT as part of their assessment programs because CAT item development efforts were not targeted within each grade to the specific grade-level standards (Trotter, 2003). The interpretation taken by many, as summarized in an *Education Week* article, was that CAT did not comply with NCLB:

> But the upshot, for now, is that computer adaptive tests are left out of the federal law, along with the public attention and federal money for test development that come with it. And the developers of adaptive tests feel they are missing out on what may be the greatest precollegiate testing boom in history. (Trotter, 2003, p. 18)

Because of this controversy, most states avoided the pursuit of CAT for their NCLB testing programs. Eventually, the U.S. Department of Education revised their position on adaptive testing, and led by Oregon, which received departmental approval for a CAT program in 2007, several states had developed and implemented CAT for their NCLB testing programs by the late 2000s.

Another impediment to large-scale applications of CBT in U.S. state testing programs was a lack of infrastructure in schools to support comprehensive testing of students annually. Unlike the CBT model deployed for licensure and admissions testing, where vendors maintain fully equipped testing centers that accommodate test takers by appointment, in K–12 schools are fully responsible for CBT administration. Way and McClarty (2012) summarized some of the challenges associated with K–12 CBT initiatives, noting the significant level of state funding needed to support one state's implementation of CBT (Virginia) and concluding that insufficient computer infrastructure almost guaranteed that most state-level applications of CBT would require supporting dual-mode testing (e.g., CBT and paper-and-pencil testing) for some time.

Despite these challenges, recent educational reforms in the United States have all but guaranteed a continued expansion of CBT for school-based testing. The American Recovery and Reinvestment Act of 2009 included $350 million in competitive grants that were awarded in 2010 to two state consortia for the design of comprehensive new assessment systems (U.S. Department of Education, 2010). Both consortia used the funds to develop assessments primarily designed for CBT administration (although dual-mode administration will still be supported). As of this writing, both consortia have implemented operational administrations of what can be characterized as a "next generation" of assessments.

Methodological Implications of the Shift to CBT

CBT has opened up a tremendous range of possibilities for the assessment of new and existing constructs. However, as has been made apparent in the previous section, progress in CBT implementations in the past 30 years has been hindered by practical issues in critical areas such as test security and sustainability. In hindsight, one can see the new and extraordinary demands that were made of the pioneering CAT programs and a lack of experience with the methodological implications of such demands as the principal reasons for the difficulties encountered. Nevertheless, a tremendous amount of research and experience was gained, which provided a solid foundation for the new implementations that have recently taken place (Yan, von Davier, & Lewis, 2014) and the new development to come (Bartram & Hambleton, 2006; Way et al., 2010).

Early Large-Scale CAT Programs

As indicated earlier, for tests measuring a broad range of traits or abilities, it has long been known that gains in measurement efficiency could be obtained if the test could be adapted to the test taker. To achieve such radical advances as cutting testing time by half and making tests available on demand in many more locations, new designs and methodologies in nearly all aspects of testing were developed, including (1) test assembly and scoring, (2) item banking and item and item pool[1] development, and (3) secure test delivery.

---

[1] *Item bank* refers to the total set of items the program has ready for administration or in development and that is stored and managed using an item banking system. *Item pool* refers to a subset of items from the item bank that is made available for test assembly.

Test Assembly and Scoring

Traditional test assembly typically relies on both test specifications and human expertise to produce and validate up to a handful of forms per year (Schmeiser & Welch, 2006). However, when new test forms need to be created in real time and/or in large numbers, this approach is not feasible. Instead, the human expertise has to be fully captured and exercised through a fully automated test assembly system (Swanson & Stocking, 1993; Theunissen, 1985; van der Linden & Boekkooi-Timminga, 1989). Such a system typically includes the following components:

1. A comprehensive set of *assembly specifications* in the form of content and measurement constraints or targets and associated loss functions.[2]

2. An *optimization function* to evaluate the relative value of each possible alternative selection.[3]

3. An item *exposure control* algorithm[4] to ensure test security.

4. A *scoring algorithm* to estimate the test taker's provisional and final scores.

5. An *item selection algorithm* to decide on the next item to deliver.

For example, Stocking and Swanson (1993) described the initial development of the test assembly system developed to support the CAT GRE program. Working in collaboration with the program's content and measurement experts, they found that up to 97 content constraints and targets, large numbers of enemy constraints,[5] and maximum information targets at several points covering the reported score scale range would be needed to fully capture the desired test specifications. They then determined optimization function weights to produce desirable tradeoffs between the content and measurement target losses than might occur. To lower maximum item exposure and thus improve test security, they implemented Hetter and Sympson's (1997) randomization scheme that limits the probability of selection for the items that would otherwise tend to be selected the most often. For scoring, they chose to implement a maximum likelihood estimation (MLE) IRT algorithm (Hambleton, Swaminathan, & Rogers, 1991; Lord, 1980). Finally, they implemented an efficient adaptive selection algorithm that not only accounts for the selections already made and the next selection to be

---

[2]We use the term *constraints* for specifications that are not allowed to be violated (e.g., the number of items to be delivered is equal to the test length, in the case of fixed length test); we use the term *target* for specifications that allow for some deviation from the attribute or value specified, with some loss incurred. Losses can be specified to be proportional to the deviation from the target or to be a fixed value.

[3]Typically, the *combined loss function* is specified as a weighted sum of the content and measurement losses.

[4]These algorithms use real-time random processes to determine if an item is or is not available for assembly (Hetter & Sympson, 1997; Stocking & Lewis, 1998).

[5]*Enemy constraints* are used to prevent the selection of more than one instance of items or collections of items that should not be present in the same test. For example, items may provide clues to one another, are derived from the same parent, share too closely related stimuli, etc.

made, but also accounts for the likely contribution of the future selections until the specified fixed test length is reached.[6]

Item Banking and Item and Item Pool Development

Of course, the degree to which a test assembly system can be successful in meeting all of the assembly specifications does, to a large extent, depend on the size and quality of the available item pool. Unfortunately, when the test program's goals and assembly specifications are as demanding and complex as that of the CATs described here, item development capability may fall short of actual needs. In the highly constrained CAT GRE example discussed above, Stocking and Swanson (1993) found that an item pool including as many as 518 items was needed to produce appropriate 27-item tests.[7] Logically, they expected highly informative items or items with content attributes that were in relative short supply in the item pool to be used at a higher rate than other items. However, testing simulations showed very lopsided results, with some items used in as many tests as the exposure control mechanism would allow and some not used at all. Later, as a result of the Kaplan incident described earlier, it became clear that more frequent rotation of item pools and more constraining exposure control than initially thought were required to ensure test security. Consequently, larger item resources than expected were needed. Thus, for high-stakes CAT programs to remain sustainable over time, more advanced capabilities were developed out of necessity to support item development and make better use of each item, including item banking, item pretesting and IRT calibration, automated pool assembly, and quality assurance and validation.

Although the use of item banking systems to manage item development and item availability was not new, their capabilities were greatly expanded to facilitate the authoring of existing and new item types and to handle the greatly expanded item metadata[8] required for automated pool assembly. Once items have been authored, the next step is to collect pretest data to determine their IRT parameters, which will be used later to score the operational tests in which they will be selected. To obtain accurate IRT parameters, the pretest items are embedded within the operational test or included in unannounced sections delivered along with the operational tests (Wainer & Mislevy, 1990). Once successfully calibrated, the pretest items can be included in item pools.

A readily available item pool is one that includes all the operational items in the item bank. However, technological limitations and the tendency of item selection algorithms to overuse some items make that choice ineffective, if not impossible, especially as the size of the bank grows. Instead, pool assembly strategies are implemented to

---

[6]Most programs decide on fixed test length. The NCLEX is one example of variable test length where testing stops only when the desired measurement target is reached.

[7]Tests that satisfied all constraints and, if not met, came close enough to meeting the specified content, measurement, and exposure targets.

[8]Item metadata typically include the item development status (e.g., in development or ready for operational use), its content attributes, measurement characteristics, etc.

provide collections of items that are sufficient for the adaptive test assembly needs (Flaugher, 1990; Way, Steffen, & Anderson, 2002). Then, once a new pool has been assembled, it is necessary to conduct extensive test assembly simulations to make sure it provides the resources the adaptive assembly algorithm requires in order to produce appropriate tests for all test takers. Again, as Stocking and Swanson (1993) demonstrated, this step is particularly important because CATs are the result of real-time interactions between test-taker responses and test assembly, which may result in substandard tests when test takers respond in unexpected ways and/or the item pool is in short supply of items with particular characteristics.

Secure Test Delivery

Traditional testing programs typically administer one test form to large groups of test takers a few times a year. To protect test security, each form may be used once or a few times before being discarded. However, when tests are delivered on demand, it becomes an economic necessity that items be reused across many forms before being discarded. Unfortunately, although item-level adaptive testing does prevent test takers from copying from each other during test administration and typically incorporates methods to control the exposure of the most popular items in the pool, early CAT programs proved vulnerable to simple memorization and sharing strategies, such as the ones employed by the Kaplan coaching company in 1994, and subsequently to informal groups that shared items as the Internet's reach grew. The CAT GRE program responded to the security threats by shortening the time any pool would be actively used, devising new rules limiting item use across pools, and by progressively increasing the size of its item bank and implementing more comprehensive item exposure control (Stocking & Lewis, 1998; Way & Steffen, 1998; Way et al., 2002).

Continued Evolution of CBT

The significant challenges faced by the early CAT programs did not diminish CBT's appeal to test users and researchers. As a result, methodological improvements have been proposed in all aspects of CAT, including item exposure control, scoring, pool and test assembly specifications, and selection algorithms. These advances have been documented in many research papers and presentations and in comprehensive theoretical and applied books and review papers (e.g., Drasgow, Luecht, & Bennett, 2005; Mills, Potenza, Fremer, & Ward, 2002; van der Linden & Glas, 2000). But despite these advances, effective tradeoffs between measurement efficiency for all test takers and test security have remained difficult to achieve for large-scale on-demand CAT testing programs (Davey & Nering, 2002; Robin, Steffen, & Liang, 2014).

Thus, in the early 2000s alternative CBT designs, such as linear on the fly tests (LOFTs), computerized sequential testing (CST), and multistage testing (MST) began to receive more attention (Davey, 2011; Hendrickson, 2007; Luecht & Sireci, 2011). With MST, in particular, it was found that gains in measurement efficiency could still be large in comparison to pencil-and-paper tests. MST could also retain desirable pencil-and-paper test features such as the ability to implement comprehensive quality control of any new test form before it is to be administered, and the option for test takers to review and change their responses to any item within a test section (Luecht & Clauser, 2002). As a result, testing programs such as the Uniform CPA Exam (Breithaupt, Zhang, & Hare, 2014), the GRE revised General Test (Robin et al., 2014), and the National Assessment of Educational Progress (NAEP; Oranje, Mazzeo, Xu, & Kulick, 2014) have implemented, or are in the process of implementing, new MST designs, rather than pursuing CAT.[9]

Improvements in computer and Internet technologies continue to play a critical role in the evolution of CBTs by pushing the limits of what is practically feasible (Bennett, 2006). Internet-based testing (iBT) delivery platforms are now used by large-scale testing programs. Such systems are not only opening up the possibility of using wireless devices such as tablets and smartphones, they also allow for better use of item resources and more secure on-demand testing through much faster rotation of larger numbers of item pools, MSTs, or linear tests (Ariel, Veldkamp, & van der Linden, 2004; Robin et al., 2014; Way, 1998). Improved technologies are also (1) supporting further developments of item formats and tasks that can expand the content domains that can be measured; (2) facilitating the collection and use of richer response data; (3) making possible the use of natural language-processing systems to machine-score constructed responses that could only be scored by human raters otherwise (Bennett, 2011); and (4) providing tools for increasing the accessibility of standardized tests to test takers with disabilities.

Evolution of Items and Tasks

Very early on, the potential of computers (now, more broadly, *human-system interfaces*) to considerably expand the measureable content domains and the recordable response behaviors had been recognized. However, the development of this potential has been very gradual and the room for improvements remains large. Besides the availability of the technical know-how, many of the challenges identified by Bennett and Ward (1993) remain. One challenge has been, and in many cases remains, the need to maintain comparability across modes of administrations when a paper-based test (PBT) version of the test is still required. Another is the ability to score more complex tasks such as essays or tasks involving a more or less open-ended series of responses. Yet another is to avoid construct irrelevant differential functioning across subgroups as test taker populations are becoming increasingly diverse.

For more information, Mislevy and Haertel (2006); Sireci and Zenisky (2006); Parshall, Harmes, Davey, and Pashley (2010); Bennett (2011); and Haertel and colleagues (2012) provide comprehensive methodological frameworks and extensive reviews of research, development, and implementations of innovative item formats.

---

[9]It could be argued that MST is actually a form of CAT since MSTs are adaptive, just in a different way. One could distinguish between "traditional" CAT and MST by thinking of the former as "item adaptive" and the latter as "multistage" (T. Davey, personal communication, February 24, 2014).

Automated Scoring of Complex Item Types

One benefit of CBT is that it permits the collection of data to support the application of automated scoring for item types that have traditionally required human evaluation. Applications of automated scoring of writing began in the mid-1960s (Page, 2003). Since that time, advances in artificial intelligence and computing technology, paired with research over several decades, have yielded a number of systems in which computers assign scores to constructed response items. Areas where automated scoring has been employed include mathematical responses, short content responses, spoken responses, and simulation-based tasks. Both the availability and acceptance of automated scoring systems have grown substantially in recent years, with year-over-year expansion of operational use in both high- and low-stakes assessments (Shermis & Burstein, 2003; Williamson, Mislevy, & Bejar, 2006).

CBT and Item Response Times

CBT also provides a mechanism to routinely record the time taken to answer each item on a test, which is not practical in conventional paper-and-pencil testing. A number of researchers have explored various ways of modeling item response times and using them to support CBT applications (Schnipke & Scrams, 2002; van der Linden, 2009b; Wang & Hanson, 2005). One obvious research application of item response time is as a contributing factor in test performance. However, most conventional tests measure constructs that do not explicitly incorporate speed of response, which limits the usefulness of this line of research. Nonetheless, researchers have explored promising applications with item response times to assist with conventional and adaptive test selection (van der Linden, 2011), monitoring test-taker motivation (Wise, Bhola, & Yang, 2006), and in detecting aberrant responses that might suggest security breaches (van der Linden, 2009a; van der Linden & Guo, 2008).

Policy Implications of the Shift to CBT

Although there are numerous policy implications of the shift from traditional paper testing to CBT, in this section we focus on four in particular. One obvious implication of the shift to CBT for policymakers is the alignment between how computers and technology are used for instruction or in practice and how they are used for assessments. This issue is most prominent in educational testing but can certainly be a consideration in other areas. A related implication concerns the infrastructure needed to support CBT, especially in situations where testing is not centrally supported through vendor-managed testing centers. A third important implication relates to test takers with disabilities and the challenges in providing accommodations to standard CBT processes that are consistent with how these individuals access instruction or work-related materials. A final implication of the shift to CBT assessments is the rapid changes in the technology available in schools and the workplace, and how these changes impact the assessment process.

Matching Assessment with Instruction and Practice

An early example of the challenge of matching assessment with practice in CBT was the architectural design simulations developed by the ETS in the early 1990s (Bejar & Braun, 1994). These simulations provided an interface for the testing candidate to use in solving architectural design problems. However, this interface was designed specifically for the assessment and differed from the primary tool used in practice by architects in the field, a software package called AutoCAD®. As a result, the researchers had to take special care to develop their design tool to have features that were as close to AutoCAD's features as possible. They also had to provide readily available tutorials so that candidates could become familiar with the interface before they sat down for the design assessments that were part of the Architects Registration Exam.

A more recent example of the importance of matching instruction and assessment is in the area of writing. It seems reasonable to assume that students who engage in word processing in their everyday schoolwork will perform better when they take a writing test online. On the other hand, students with little exposure to word processing in their daily instruction are less likely to perform as well on a computer-administered extended writing task. In this case, assessing students in a manner that is consistent with how they are instructed may be more important than establishing comparability between a paper and online version of the test. A recent NAEP writing online study supported this commonsense view (Horkay, Bennett, Allen, Kaplan, & Yan, 2006).

Although writing is an obvious example where aligning instructional practices with assessment matters, as assessment opportunities utilizing technology-enhanced item types increase, it will also matter whether and how students are taught the associated underlying material in the classroom. For example, performance on a complex algebra II problem that utilizes an equation editor may depend not only on students' understanding of the tools offered in the CBT testing interface, but also on students' exposure to similar classroom experiences with solving these types of problems in an online environment.

Developing Sufficient CBT Infrastructure

As previously mentioned, large-scale CBT initiatives in K–12 settings in the United States were hampered into the first 10 years of the 21st century because of uneven infrastructure for supporting CBT in the schools. Dean and Martineau (2012) recently summarized a survey of state implementation of technology in assessment. Although they reported at least some online testing initiatives or plans in 44 of 50 states, they also concluded that few states had undertaken large-scale assessments or comprehensively implemented technology-enhanced items into their assessments. This is likely to change with the implementation of the Common Core State Standards assessments, but there is still a need for individual states to further invest in technology to support both instruction and assessment. Such investments are beginning to be made; for example, in 2013 and 2014 the legislature in Michigan provided $95 million to support district technology improvements, professional development, and other strategies that will assist online testing implementations. It seems reasonably safe to predict that similar state-level investments will help to fuel the comprehensive transition to CBT in K–12 settings.

Assessing Individuals with Disabilities

The decade from 2000 to 2010 saw significant evolution in the policies and practices associated with testing students with disabilities (SWDs) in the United States, and part of these efforts addressed CBT in relation to SWDs (Thompson, Thurlow, & Moore, 2003; Thompson, Thurlow, Quenemoen, & Lehr, 2002; Thurlow, Lazarus, Albus, & Hodgson, 2010). The Common Core State Standards assessments developed in the early 2010s also included a particular focus on testing accommodations and accessibility tools for SWDs (cf. Laitusis, Buzick, Stone, Hansen, & Hakkinen, 2012).

Despite maturing policies addressing accessibility tools and accommodations, one emerging technological challenge for CBT is the need to support students in using preferred assistive technology when they test. For example, visually disabled students may utilize a variety of devices in the classroom, such as screen readers, screen magnifiers, auditory and tactile devices, and Braille printers. Advocates for these students demand that the CBT systems be capable of supporting these same assistive devices. Moreover, today's CBT systems are required to integrate a number of established and emerging technologies to create a seamless user experience across various browsers and devices and to support federally mandated content accessibility guidelines. Addressing these technical challenges to making CBT universally accessible will require continued research and development from vendors, and may have implications for policies regarding allowable accommodations for testing.

Assessment under Rapid Change

At this juncture in the history of CBT, the rapid advances in technology available for instruction and assessment are creating pressures for constant change. CBT has always provided increased flexibility as compared to traditional paper-and-pencil testing, such as the ability to revise the content of the test on the fly. But in today's environment, there is a need for CBT to take this flexibility a step further, for example, by utilizing principles of responsive design to optimize the experience of test takers across various computers and devices, and to support increasingly advanced assistive technologies for SWDs. In general, CBT has evolved to the point where the large-scale testing experience is transitioning from one of standardization to one of personalization (Way, Davis, Keng, & Strain-Seymour, 2016). Such rapid change associated with CBT is exciting, but it can also be disconcerting. Certainly, the task of building CBT assessments that produce scores to support intended inferences in a reliable and fair manner—and that are comparable over time—will be more challenging than ever.

Conclusions

The history of CBT is rich and varied, with roots that harken back to the early 20th century. Although it is interesting that it has taken CBT longer to mature than many would have predicted, there are many indications that a tipping point has been reached. In this chapter, we have examined the evolution of CBT from its beginning to current times. We have also pointed out a number of major implications of the shift to CBT for testing methodologies as well as testing policies.

As the use of computers and related personal technologies for administering and scoring tests becomes more and more commonplace, one yet unanswered question is the impact on the long-standing approaches to standardized testing that have been dominant in the United States for nearly 100 years. There are certainly signs that something more is yet to come. Consider this recent assertion from a group of experts recently commissioned to deliberate and provide recommendations on the future of assessment in education:

> Technologies available today and innovations on the immediate horizon can be used to access information, create simulations and scenarios, allow students to engage in learning games and other activities, and enable collaboration among students. Such activities make it possible to observe, document and assess students' work as they are engaged in natural activities—perhaps reducing the need to separate formal assessment for accountability from learning in the moment. Technologies certainly will make possible the greater use of formative assessment that, in turn, has been shown to significantly impact student achievement. Digital activities also may provide information about noncognitive abilities—such as persistence, creativity and teamwork—that current testing approaches cannot. (Gordon Commission, 2013, p. 11)

It is not a stretch at this point to say that after what has been a reasonably long incubation period, as of this writing CBT is mature enough to be the preferred assessment approach, at least in the United States. There are, of course, a variety of different testing applications, including psychological testing and assessment, workplace testing and credentialing, and educational testing and assessment. The impact of technology on these different testing applications will no doubt vary considerably. Nonetheless, with only a little speculation, one might easily say that although the future of testing may be what we are today calling CBT, for at least some assessment applications, what we are calling CBT may become something quite different.

REFERENCES

Ariel, A., Veldkamp, B. P., & van der Linden, W. J. (2004). Constructing rotating item pools for constrained adaptive testing. *Journal of Educational Measurement, 41,* 345–359.

Bartram, D., & Hambleton, R. K. (2006). *Computer-based testing and the Internet: Issues and advances.* Chichester, UK: Wiley.

Bejar, I. I., & Braun, H. (1994). On the synergy between assessment and instruction: Early lessons from computer-based simulations. *Machine-Mediated Learning, 4,* 5–25.

Benjamin, L. T. (1988). A history of teaching machines. *American Psychologist, 43,* 703–712.

Bennett, R. (2006). Inexorable and inevitable: The continuing story of technology and assessment. In D. Bartram & R. K. Hambleton (Eds.), *Computer-based testing and the Internet: Issues and advances* (pp. 77–89). Chichester, UK: Wiley.

Bennett, R. (2011). CBAL: *Results from piloting innovative K–12 assessments* (Research Report RR-11–23). Princeton, NJ: Educational Testing Service.

Bennett, R. E., & Ward, W. C. (Eds.). (1993). *Construction versus choice in cognitive measurement: Issues in constructed responses, performance testing, and portfolio assessment.* Hillsdale, NJ: Erlbaum.

Binet, A., & Simon, T. (1912). *A method of measuring the development of intelligence in young children* (C. H. Town, Trans.). Lincoln, IL: Courier Company. Retrieved from *https://archive.org/details/39002011125441.med.yale.edu.*

Birnbaum, A. (1968). Some latent trait models and their use in inferring an examinee's ability. In F. M. Lord & M. R. Novick, *Statistical theories of mental test scores* (pp. 397–479). Reading, MA: Addison-Wesley.

Breithaupt, K. J., Mills, C. N., & Melican, G. J. (2006). Facing the opportunities of the future. In D. Bartram & R. K. Hambleton (Eds.), *Computer-based testing and the internet* (pp. 219–251). West Sussex, UK: Wiley.

Breithaupt, K. J., Zhang, O. Y., & Hare, D. R. (2014). The multistage testing approach to the AICPA Uniform Certified Public Accounting Examinations. In D. Yan, A. A. von Davier, & C. Lewis (Eds.), *Computerized multistage testing: Theory and applications* (pp. 343–354). Boca Raton, FL: Chapman & Hall/CRC.

Bridgeman, B., & Cline, F. (2000). *Variations in mean response times for questions on the computer-adaptive GRE General Test: Implications for fair assessment* (Research Report RR-00–7). Princeton, NJ: Educational Testing Service.

Bunderson, C. V., Inouye, D. K., & Olsen, J. B. (1989). The four generations of computerized testing. In R. Linn (Ed.), *Educational measurement* (3rd ed.). New York: American Council on Education/Macmillan.

Busuttil-Reynaud, G., & Winkley, J. (2006). E-assessment glossary (Extended). *Higher Education Funding Council for England.* Retrieved from *www.jisc.ac.uk/uploaded_documents/eAssess-Glossary-Extended-v1–01.pdf.*

Carlson, J. E., & von Davier, M. (2013). *Item response theory* (R&D Scientific and Policy Contributions Series SPC-13–05; Research Report 13–28). Princeton, NJ: Educational Testing Service.

Carlson, S. (2000). *Online GRE flunks in rating some students.* Retrieved from *http://chronicle.com/article/Online-GRE-Flunks-in-Rating/106764.*

Carr, N. (2013, January 1). *Will Gutenberg laugh last?* [Blog post]. Retrieved from *www.roughtype.com/?p=2296.*

Clark, C. K. (1976). *Proceedings of the first conference on computerized adaptive testing.* Washington, DC: U.S. Government Printing Office. [ERIC Document ERIC Number: ED126110]

Davey, T. (2005). Computer-based testing. In B. S. Everitt & D. Howell (Eds.), *Encyclopedia of statistics in behavioral science.* West Sussex, UK: Wiley.

Davey, T. (2011). *Practical considerations in computer-based testing.* Princeton, NJ: Educational Testing Service.

Davey, T., & Nering, M. (2002). Controlling item exposure and maintaining item security. In

C. N. Mills, M. T. Potenza, J. J. Fremer, & W. C. Ward (Eds.), *Computer-based testing: Building the foundation for future assessments* (pp. 165–191). Mahwah, NJ: Erlbaum.

Dean, V., & Martineau, J. (2012). A state perspective on enhancing assessment and accountability systems through systematic implementation of technology. In R. W. Lissitz & H. Jiao (Eds.), *Computers and their impact on state assessments* (pp. 55–77). Charlotte, NC: Information Age.

Defense Manpower Data Center. (2006). *ASVAB technical bulletin No. 1: CAT-ASVAB forms 1 and 2.* Monterey, CA: Author.

Dragsow, F. R., Luecht, R. M., & Bennett, R. (2005). Technology and testing. In R. L. Brennan (Ed.), *Educational measurement* (4th ed., pp. 471–515). Washington, DC: American Council on Education/Praeger.

Educational Testing Service, et al. v. Stanley H. Kaplan, Educational Center, LTD, 965 F. Supp. 731 (D. Maryland 1997).

Flaugher, R. (1990). Item pools. In H. Wainer (Ed.), *Computerized adaptive testing: A primer* (pp. 41–63). Hillsdale, NJ: Erlbaum.

Folk, V. G., & Smith, R. L. (2002). Models for delivery of CBTs. In C. Mills, M. Potenza, J. Fremer, & W. Ward (Eds.), *Computer-based testing: Building the foundation for future assessments* (pp. 41–66). Mahwah, NJ: Erlbaum.

Gordon Commission on the Future of Assessment in Education. (2013). A public policy statement. Retrieved from *www.gordoncommission.org/rsc/pdfs/gordon_commission_public_policy_report.pdf.*

Haertel, G. D., Cheng, B. H., Cameto, R., Fujii, R., Sanford, C., Rutstein, D., et al. (2012, May). *Design and development of technology enhanced assessment tasks: Integrating evidence-centered design and universal design for learning frameworks to assess hard to measure science constructs and increase student accessibility.* Paper presented at the ETS Invitational Research Symposium on Technology Enhanced Assessments, Princeton, NJ.

Hambleton, R. K., & Swaminathan, H. (1985). *Item response theory: Principles and applications.* Boston: Kluwer-Nijhoff.

Hambleton, R. K., Swaminathan, H., & Rogers, H. J. (1991). *Fundamentals of item response theory.* Newbury Park, CA: Sage.

Haney, W. (1985). Making tests more educational. *Educational Leadership, 43*(2), 4–13.

Hansen, D. N., Johnson, B. F., Fagan, R. L., Tan, P., & Dick, W. (1974). Computer-based adaptive testing models for the Air Force technical training environment Phase I: Development of a computerized measurement system for Air Force technical training. *JSAS Catalogue of Selected Documents in Psychology, 5,* 1–86 (MS No. 882). AFHRL Technical Report 74-48. [ERIC Document Reproduction No. ED 094 759]

Hendrickson, A. (2007). An NCME instructional module on multi-stage testing. *Educational Measurement: Issues and Practice, 26*(2), 44–52.

Hetter, R. D., & Sympson, J. B. (1997). Item exposure control in CAT-ASVAB. In W. A. Sands, B. K. Waters, & J. R. McBride (Eds.), *Computerized adaptive testing, from inquiry to operation* (pp. 141–144). Washington, DC: American Psychological Association.

Hicks, M. M. (1983). True score equating by fixed b's scaling: A flexible and stable equating alternative. *Applied Psychological Measurement, 7,* 255–266.

Horkay, N., Bennett, R. E., Allen, N. L., Kaplan, B., & Yan, F. (2006). Does it matter if I take my writing test on computer?: An empirical study of mode effects in NAEP. *Journal of Technology, Learning, and Assessment, 5*(2). Retrieved December 11, 2007, from *www.jtla.org.*

Hulin, C. L., Drasgow, F., & Parsons, C. K. (1983). *Item response theory: Application to psychological measurement*. Homewood, IL: Dow Jones–Irwin.

Kingsbury, G. G., & Houser, R. L. (1999). Developing computerized adaptive tests for school children. In F. Drasgow & J. B. Olsen-Buchanan (Eds.), *Innovations in computer-based assessment* (pp. 93–116). Mahwah, NJ: Erlbaum.

Laitusis, C., Buzick, H., Stone, E., Hansen, E., & Hakkinen, M. (2012, June). Smarter Balanced Consortium: Literature review of testing accommodations and accessibility tools for students with disabilities. Retrieved from *www.smarterbalanced.org/wordpress/wp-content/uploads/2012/08/Smarter-Balanced-Students-with-Disabilities-Literature-Review.pdf*.

Lenke, J. M., & Rentz, R. R. (1982, March). *The use of the Rasch model in the development of the Stanford Achievement Test*. Paper presented at the annual meeting of the National Council on Measurement in Education, New York City.

Lewis, C., & Sheehan, K. (1990). Using Bayesian decision theory to design a computerized mastery test. *Applied Psychological Measurement, 14*, 367–386.

Lord, F. M. (1970). Some test theory for tailored testing. In W. H. Holtzman (Ed.), *Computer-assisted instruction, testing, and guidance* (pp. 139–183). New York: Harper & Row.

Lord, F. M. (1971a). Robbins–Monro procedures for tailored testing. *Educational and Psychological Measurement, 31*, 3–31.

Lord, F. M. (1971b). The self-scoring flexilevel test. *Journal of Educational Measurement, 8*, 147–151.

Lord, F. M. (1971c). Tailored testing: An application of stochastic approximation. *Journal of the American Statistical Association, 66*, 707–711.

Lord, F. M. (1971d). The theoretical study of the measurement effectiveness of flexilevel tests. *Educational and Psychological Measurement, 31*, 805–813.

Lord, F. M. (1980). *Applications of item response theory to practical testing problems*. Hillsdale, NJ: Erlbaum.

Luecht, R. M., & Clauser, B. E. (2002). Test models for complex CBT. In C. Mills, M. Potenza, J. Fremer, & W. Ward (Eds.), *Computer-based testing: Building the foundation for future assessments* (pp. 67–88). Mahwah, NJ: Erlbaum.

Luecht, R. M., & Sireci, S. G. (2011). *A review of models for computer-based testing* (Research Report 2011-12). New York: College Board.

Mayfield, K. (1999, September 1). An e-hurdle to grad school. Retrieved from *http://archive.wired.com/culture/lifestyle/news/1999/09/21531*.

Melnick, D., & Clauser, B. (2006). Computer-based testing for professional licensing and certification of health professionals. In D. Bartram & R. K. Hambleton (Eds.), *Computer-based testing and the Internet* (pp. 163–185). West Sussex, UK: Wiley.

Mills, C. N. (1999). Development and introduction of a computer adaptive Graduate Record Examination General Test. In F. Drasgow & J. B. Olson-Buchanan (Eds.), *Innovations in computerized assessment* (pp. 117–135). Mahwah, NJ: Erlbaum.

Mills, C. N., Potenza, M. T., Fremer, J. J., & Ward, W. C. (Eds.). (2002). *Computer-based testing: Building the foundation for future assessments*. Mahwah, NJ: Erlbaum.

Mills, C. N., & Steffen, M. (2000). The GRE computer adaptive test: Operational issues. In W. J. van der Linden & C. A. W. Glas (Eds.), *Computerized adaptive testing: Theory and practice* (pp. 75–99). Dordrecht, The Netherlands: Kluwer.

Mislevy, R. J., & Haertel, G. D. (2006). Implications of evidence-centered design for educational testing. *Educational Measurement: Issues and Practice, 25*(4), 6–20.

Oranje, A., Mazzeo, J., Xu, X., & Kulick, E. (2014). A multistage testing approach to group-score assessments. In D. Yan, A. A. von Davier, & C. Lewis (Eds.), *Computerized multistage testing: Theory and applications* (pp. 371–390). Boca Raton, FL: Chapman & Hall/CRC.

Owen, R. J. (1969). *A Bayesian approach to tailored testing* (Research Report 69–92). Princeton, NJ: Educational Testing Service.

Page, E. B. (2003). Project essay grade: PEG. In M. D. Shermis & J. Burstein (Eds.), *Automated essay scoring: A cross-disciplinary perspective* (pp. 43–54). Mahwah, NJ: Erlbaum.

Pagliaro, L. A. (1983). The history and development of CAI: 1926–1981, an overview. *The Alberta Journal of Educational Research, 29*(1), 75–84.

Parshall, C. G., & Harmes, J. C. (2007). Designing templates based on a taxonomy of innovative items. In D. J. Weiss (Ed.), *Proceedings of the 2007 GMAC conference on computerized adaptive testing.* Retrieved from *www.psych.umn.edu/psylabs/CATCentral.*

Parshall, C. G., Harmes, J. C., Davey, T., & Pashley, P. J. (2010). Innovative item types for computerized testing. In W. J. van der Linden & C. A. W. Glas (Eds.), *Elements of adaptive testing* (pp. 215–230). New York: Springer.

Pressey, S. L. (1926). A simple apparatus which gives tests and scores—and teaches. *School and Society, 23*(586), 373–376.

Pressey, S. L. (1927). A machine for automatic teaching of drill material. *School and Society, 25*(645), 549–552.

Robin, F., Steffen, M., & Liang, L. (2014). GRE(r) Revised General Test (Admission Test). In D. Yan, A. A. von Davier, & C. Lewis (Eds.), *Computerized multistage testing: Theory and applications* (pp. 325–342). Boca Raton, FL: Chapman & Hall/CRC.

Schaeffer, G. A., Bridgeman, B., Golub-Smith, M. L., Lewis, C., Potenza, M. T., & Steffen, M. (1998). *Comparability of paper-and-pencil and computer adaptive test scores on the GRE General Test* (Research Report 98–38). Princeton, NJ: Educational Testing Service.

Schmeiser, C. B., & Welch, C. J. (2006). Test development. In R. L. Brennan (Ed.), *Educational measurement* (4th ed., pp. 307–353). Washington, DC: American Council on Education/Praeger.

Schnipke, D. L., & Scrams, D. J. (2002). Exploring issues of examinee behavior: Insights gained from response-time analyses. In C. N. Mills, J. J. Fremer, & W. C. Ward (Eds.), *Computer-based testing: Building the foundation for future assessments* (pp. 237–266). Hillsdale, NJ: Erlbaum.

Segall, D. O., Moreno, K. E., Kieckhaefer, W. F., Vicino, F. L., & McBride, J. R. (1997). Validation of the experimental CAT-ASVAB system. In W. A. Sands, B. K. Waters, & J. R. McBride (Eds.), *Computerized adaptive testing: From inquiry to operation* (pp. 103–114). Washington, DC: American Psychological Association.

Shermis, M. D., & Burstein, J. (2003). *Automated essay scoring: A cross disciplinary perspective.* Mahwah, NJ: Erlbaum.

Sireci, S. G., & Zenisky, A. L. (2006). Innovative item formats in computer-based testing: In pursuit of improved construct representations. In S. M. Downing & T. M. Haladyna (Eds.), *Handbook of test development* (pp. 329–347). Mahwah, NJ: Erlbaum.

Skinner, B. F. (1958). Teaching machines. *Science, 128,* 969–977.

Skinner, B. F. (1961). Why we need teaching machines. *Harvard Educational Review, 31,* 377–398.

Slater, S. C., & Schaeffer, G. A. (1996, April). *Computing scores for incomplete GRE computer adaptive tests.* Paper presented at the meeting of the National Council on Measurement in Education, New York City.

Stocking, M. L., & Lewis, C. (1998). Controlling item exposure conditional on ability in computerized adaptive testing. *Journal of Educational and Behavioral Statistics, 23,* 57–75.

Stocking, M. L., & Swanson, L. (1993). A method for severely constrained item selection in adaptive testing. *Applied Psychological Measurement, 17,* 277–292.

Swanson, L., & Stocking, M. L. (1993). A model and heuristic for solving very large item selection problems. *Applied Psychological Measurement, 17,* 151–166.

Theunissen, T. J. J. M. (1985). Binary programming and test design. *Psychometrika, 50,* 411–420.

Thompson, S. J., Thurlow, M., & Moore, M. (2003). *Using computer-based tests with students with disabilities* (Policy Directions No. 15). Minneapolis: University of Minnesota, National Center on Educational Outcomes. Retrieved from *http://education.umn.edu/ NCEO/OnlinePubs/Policy15.htm.*

Thompson, S. J., Thurlow, M. L., Quenemoen, R. F., & Lehr, C. A. (2002). *Access to computer-based testing for students with disabilities* (Synthesis Report 45). Minneapolis: University of Minnesota, National Center on Educational Outcomes. Retrieved from *http://education.umn.edu/nceo/OnlinePubs/Synthesis45.html.*

Thurlow, M., Lazarus, S. S., Albus, D., & Hodgson, J. (2010). *Computer-based testing: Practices and considerations (Synthesis Report 78).* Minneapolis: University of Minnesota, National Center on Educational Outcomes.

Trotter, A. (2003, May 8). A question of direction. *Educational Week.* Retrieved from *www. edweek.org/media/ew/tc/archives/TC03full.pdf.*

U.S. Department of Education. (2010, April 9). Overview information: Race to the Top Fund Assessment Program: Notice inviting applications for new awards for fiscal year (FY) 2010. *75 Federal Register,* 18171–18185.

van der Linden, W. J. (2009a). A bivariate lognormal response-time model for the detection of collusion between test takers. *Journal of Educational and Behavioral Statistics, 34,* 378–394.

van der Linden, W. J. (2009b). Conceptual issues in response-time modeling. *Journal of Educational Measurement, 46,* 247–272.

van der Linden, W. J. (2011). Test design and speededness. *Journal of Educational Measurement, 48,* 44–60.

van der Linden, W. J., & Boekkooi-Timminga, E. (1989). A maximum model for test design with practical constraints. *Psychometrika, 54,* 237–248.

van der Linden, W. J., & Glas, C. A. W. (Eds.). (2000). *Computerized adaptive testing: Theory and practice.* Boston: Kluwer.

van der Linden, W. J., & Guo, F. (2008). Bayesian procedures for identifying aberrant response-time patterns in adaptive testing. *Psychometrika, 73,* 365–384.

Wainer, H. (2000). *CATs: Whither and whence* (Research Report 00-12). Princeton, NJ: Educational Testing Service.

Wainer, H., & Eignor, D. E. (2000). Caveats, pitfalls, and unintended consequences of implementing large-scale computerized testing. In H. Wainer (Ed.), *Computerized adaptive testing: A primer* (2nd ed., pp. 271–299). Hillsdale, NJ: Erlbaum.

Wainer, H., & Mislevy, R. J. (1990). Item response theory, item calibration and proficiency estimation. In H. Wainer (Ed.), *Computerized adaptive testing: A primer* (pp. 65–102). Hillsdale, NJ: Erlbaum.

Wang, T., & Hanson, B. A. (2005). Development and calibration of an item response model that incorporates response time. *Applied Psychological Measurement, 29,* 323–339.

Ward, W. C. (1988). The College Board computerized placement tests: An application of computerized adaptive testing. *Machine-Mediated Learning, 2,* 271–282.

Ward, W. C., Kline, R. G., & Flaugher, J. (1986). *College Board computerized placement tests: Validation of an adaptive test of basic skills* (Research Report 86–29). Princeton, NJ: Educational Testing Service.

Way, W. D. (1998). Protecting the integrity of computerized testing item pools. *Educational Measurement: Issues and Practice, 17*(4), 17–27.

Way, W. D., Davis, L. L., Keng, L., & Strain-Seymour, E. (2016). From standardization to personalization: The comparability of scores based on different testing conditions, modes, and devices. In F. Drasgow (Ed.), *Technology and testing: Improving educational and psychological measurement* (pp. 260–284). New York: Routledge.

Way, W. D., & McClarty, K. L. (2012). Standard setting for computer-based assessments: A summary of mode comparability results and considerations. In G. J. Cizek (Ed.), *Setting performance standards: Foundations, methods, and innovations* (2nd ed., pp. 451–466). New York, NY: Routledge.

Way, W. D., & Steffen, M. (1998, April). *Strategies for managing item pools to maximize item security.* Paper presented at the meeting of the National Council on Measurement in Education, New Orleans, LA.

Way, W. D., Steffen, M., & Anderson, G. S. (2002). Developing, maintaining, and renewing the item inventory to support CBT. In C. N. Mills, M. T. Potenza, J. J. Fremer, & W. C. Ward (Eds.), *Computer-based testing: Building the foundation for future assessments* (pp. 143–164). Mahwah, NJ: Erlbaum.

Way, W. D., Twing, J. S., Camara, W., Sweeney, K., Lazer, S., & Mazzeo, J. (2010). Some considerations related to the use of adaptive testing for the Common Core Assessments. Retrieved from *www.ets.org/s/commonassessments/pdf/AdaptiveTesting.pdf.*

Weiss, D. J. (1976). Adaptive testing research at Minnesota: Overview, recent results, and future directions. In C. L. Clark (Ed.), *Proceedings of the first conference on computerized adaptive testing* (pp. 24–35). Washington, DC: U.S. Civil Service Commission.

Weiss, D. J. (1978). *Proceedings of the 1977 computerized adaptive testing conference.* Minneapolis: University of Minnesota, Department of Psychology, Computerized Adaptive Testing Laboratory.

Weiss, D. J. (1980). *Proceedings of the 1979 computerized adaptive testing conference.* Minneapolis: University of Minnesota, Department of Psychology, Computerized Adaptive Testing Laboratory.

Weiss, D. J. (1982). Improving measurement quality and efficiency with adaptive testing. *Applied Psychological Measurement, 6,* 473–492.

Weiss, D. J. (1985). *Proceedings of the 1982 computerized adaptive testing conference.* Minneapolis: University of Minnesota, Department of Psychology, Computerized Adaptive Testing Laboratory.

Weiss, D. J., & Betz, N. E. (1973, February). *Ability measurement: Conventional or adaptive?* (Research Report 73-1). Minneapolis: University of Minnesota, Department of Psychology, Psychometric Methods Program.

Williamson, D. M., Mislevy, R. J., & Bejar, I. I. (Eds.). (2006). *Automated scoring of complex tasks in computer-based testing.* Mahwah, NJ: Erlbaum.

Wise, S. L., Bhola, D. S., & Yang, S. (2006). Taking the time to improve the validity of low-stakes tests: The effort-monitoring CBT. *Educational Measurement: Issues and Practice, 25*(2), 21–30.

Yan, D., von Davier, A. A., & Lewis, C. (2014). *Computerized multistage testing: Theory and applications*. Boca Raton, FL: CRC Press.

Yen, W. M. (1983). Use of the three-parameter logistic model in the development of a standardized achievement test. In R. K. Hambleton (Ed.), *Applications of item response theory* (pp. 123–141). Vancouver, British Columbia, Canada: Educational Research Institute of British Columbia.

Zara, A. R. (1999). Using computerized adaptive testing to evaluate nurse competence for licensure: Some history and a forward look. *Advanced Health Science Education: Theory and Practice, 4*, 39–48.

Zara, A. R. (2006). Online assessment distribution models for testing programs: Lessons learned from operational experience. In S. Howell, M. Hricko, & D. D. Williams (Eds.), *Online assessment and measurement: Case studies from higher education, K–12 and corporate* (pp. 196–205). Hershey, PA: Information Science.

CHAPTER 12

Current Issues
in Computer-Based Testing

Craig N. Mills and Krista J. Breithaupt

The current era of computer-based testing (CBT) began in the early 1990s with the computerization of Novell's certified network engineer (CNE) examination in 1990 (Luecht & Sireci, 2011), the Graduate Record Examinations (GRE) General Test in 1992 (Mills & Stocking, 1996), Praxis 1, also in 1992 (Parkerson & Parkerson, 2008), and two nursing examinations for the National Council on Nursing Licensure's Examinations (NCLEX) in 1994 (Zara, 1994). These developments were followed by the introduction of three additional programs, the Armed Services Vocational Aptitude Battery (ASVAB), the Graduate Management Admission Test (GMAT), and the Architects Registration Exam (ARE) in 1997. In 1999 the U.S. Medical Licensing Examination was first offered on computer (Luecht & Sireci, 2011). Since that time, CBT has become a major testing industry. The two largest providers of CBT delivery in established test centers, Prometric and Pearson VUE, together administer tests in over 15,000 test centers around the globe (Prometric, 2014). Prometric reports administering over 10 million tests per year.

The purpose of this chapter is to provide a brief overview of the current state of CBT. It begins with a discussion of some of the reasons testing programs transition their tests from paper to computer. Some of the more popular test administration models are then briefly reviewed along with some of the common considerations associated with the development and administration of CBTs. The third section discusses areas in which advances are being made.

Why Programs Choose CBT

There are many reasons testing programs implement CBT. These include increasing accuracy and efficiency of measurement, convenience, speed of reporting results, increasing access to resource information and tools, the capability of assessing complex skills, and examinee experience.

Accuracy

Many testing programs use some form of computerized-adaptive testing (CAT). Most traditional tests are designed to provide information across a fairly wide spectrum of ability. As a result, many examinees encounter questions that are either too hard or too easy for them. CAT attempts to limit the administration of items that are too hard or too easy by using information about an examinee's responses and item response theory (IRT) statistics about previously administered items to select subsequent ones (Yen & Fitzpatrick, 2006). This method allows the test to be better matched to an individual's proficiency and, as a result, can provide a more precise estimate of an examinee's ability than a traditional test of the same length. Similarly, the adaptive process can be used to shorten tests and testing time. Since the test is more closely aligned with an examinee's proficiency, a given level of precision can be obtained with fewer test items than on a traditional fixed-form paper-based test (Parshall, Spray, Kalohn, & Davey, 2002).

Convenience

Most CBTs are offered more frequently than their paper-and-pencil counterparts, allowing examinees to take tests at times and in locations that fit their schedules. The Uniform CPA Examination (CPA Exam), for example, was administered in paper-and-pencil format on only 2 days twice a year. The computerized version is available 6 days a week, 8 months of the year (Mills, 2011). In addition, CBTs are available in a variety of settings, such as "brick and mortar" dedicated test centers, training sites, and even remotely proctored individual sites such as homes or offices.

Speed of Reporting Results

Many CBT programs report results in the test center immediately upon completion of the test administration (Davey, 2011), thereby giving examinees immediate feedback on their performance. In the case of certification and licensure examinations, faster score reporting can reduce the time required to grant the certificate or license.

Access to Resource Information and Tools

Testing programs may want to provide examinees with access to resource materials (e.g., regulations, standards, supplemental information, spreadsheets) that would be impractical to provide in a paper-and-pencil environment. CBTs can include these types of resources relatively easily. Computerization also allows incorporation of commonly used tools such as spreadsheets, computer-aided design software, and more (Breithaupt, Mills, & Melican, 2006).

Assessment of Complex Skills

Many testing programs want to test skills that are difficult or impossible to assess in paper-and-pencil formats. The American Institute of Certified Public Accountants (AICPA), for example, wanted to assess CPA candidates' ability to identify relevant accounting standards. As accounting standards become more complex and as different companies report under different standards (e.g., Generally Accepted Accounting Principles, International Financial Reporting Standards), aspiring CPAs need to be able to quickly locate and interpret standards rather than memorize them. Step 3 examinations in the U.S. Medical Licensing Examination (USMLE) present complex case simulations that include activities such as taking a patient history, conducting a physical examination, ordering medical procedures, completing patient notes, and managing a patient over time (Clauser, Margolis, & Case, 2006).

Examinee Experience

Adaptive testing presents tests to examinees that are better matched to their ability level than traditional tests. For lower-ability candidates this adaptive feature can result in a more enjoyable testing experience since they are not presented with a large number of difficult test questions. For higher-ability examinees, however, the tests may seem harder, because these examinees are used to encountering substantial numbers of questions that are easy for them. Regardless of ability, examinees tend to prefer computer-administered tests to paper tests (Pope, Breithaupt, & Zumbo, 2010). Among the features that may influence examinees' preference for CBTs are elimination of the need to take tests in large venues such as auditoriums and convention centers, the ability to easily mark items for review, access to onscreen testing aids and resources, and the presentation of a single item at a time. The preference for CBTs will likely increase given that computers, tablets, and smartphones are ubiquitous to students. In fact, the recent emphasis on educational standards designed to ensure that students are college and career ready has triggered the rapid adoption of computer-based assessments in state assessments across the country.

Test Administration Models in Use

There are numerous test administration models available for CBT. This section briefly summarizes a few of the more common ones: linear fixed form, linear on the fly (LOFT), multistage adaptive testing, and CAT.

Linear Fixed Form

Perhaps the simplest form of CBT is the administration of a traditional test of fixed length in computer format. Most programs that choose this model still have to make relatively substantial changes to their programs. For example, it is often the case that a transition to CBT is in response to a desire to provide more testing dates or locations (or both) to candidates. In either case, it is likely that the program will have to produce more test items than it did in the past to address the security concerns that come with increased exposure of test forms (Way, Steffan, & Anderson, 2002). For smaller programs or those in highly competitive markets, the additional expense can be challenging, particularly if the test or the certification that comes from passing it is optional. The higher expense can be particularly difficult in the first few years of CBT since it is common for candidate volumes to decrease following a switch to CBT (regardless of administration model).

Linear on the Fly

An alternative to fixed forms that can provide some additional benefits is the assembly of a unique form for each examinee at the time of administration. Given an item bank of sufficient size, LOFT can generate a unique test for each examinee by sampling items within each constraint in the test specification. Depending on the size of the item bank, the potential for two examinees to see very similar tests can be greatly reduced. The typical LOFT test is the same length as the fixed linear form. A significant body of research has developed to define rules used by the test administration software for item selections (e.g., Stocking & Lewis, 1998). Problems persist related to overuse of some items or unequal exposure of content within the available item bank (Breithaupt & Hare, 2016). Some examples of this administration format are the certification examinations offered by MicroSoft© (Microsoft, 2014).

Some elements of adaptive testing can be incorporated into a LOFT design. If prior information is known about the examinee (e.g., prior test scores, course grades), that information can be used to build a linear test with measurement precision maximized near the ability level that the prior information suggests is appropriate for the examinee. Van der Linden (2005) discusses several assembly methods appropriate for assembling LOFT designs, some of which consider the ability profiles of typical examinee populations, with examples such as the Test of English as a Foreign Language (TOEFL) examinations.

Multistage Adaptive Testing

A multistage test (MST) typically administers multiple sets of items, called *testlets*, to examinees. Each testlet is a linear form. However, upon completion of each testlet, the examinee's performance on that testlet is used to select the next testlet adaptively. A common multistage adaptive design is a 1–3–3 model in which a testlet of moderate difficulty is administered in the first stage. Depending on performance on the first testlet, a second testlet that is easy, moderately difficult, or hard is administered. Upon completion of the second testlet, the examinee's performance is again considered and a decision is made whether the final testlet will be easy, moderately difficult, or hard. A 1–3–3 design is useful when there is a desire to have similar precision across the score scale. A comprehensive overview of MST designs is available from Yan, von Davier, and Lewis (2014).

The CPA Exam uses a 1–2–2 multistage design (Breithaupt et al., 2006). Since the CPA Exam is a licensing examination, the primary goal is to achieve accurate measurement near the cut score. Although failing candidates are provided with some information about their performance relative to passing candidates, there is not a need for as much precision in the score for low-scoring examinees as there is near the cut. As a result, there are no easy testlets. Therefore, the CPA Exam has only four possible routes for an examinee: moderate, hard, hard; moderate, moderate, moderate; moderate, hard, moderate; and moderate, moderate, hard. In practice, most of the examinees follow the first two routes.

Computerized Adaptive Testing

Although some LOFT tests and most MSTs have adaptive features, the term *CAT* is usually reserved for tests in which the test adapts following the examinee's response to each question (Luecht & Sireci, 2011). Following the administration of an initial item, the adaptive algorithm selects the next question from the item pool that is deemed to be the next "best" item. Subsequent items are selected according to the algorithm until a stopping rule is reached. The stopping rule can be based on test length (all examinees receive the same number of questions), measurement precision (the error associated with the examinee's ability estimate falls below some target) or a combination of the two.

Item Selection

Different models exist for determining which item will be selected for administration. Early research into CAT focused on selecting the most informative item based on the current ability estimate (e.g., Lord, 1971). This approach results in the most precise estimate of ability, but ignores very real requirements about the range of content to be covered and other features of the test. Accordingly, most CATs today seek to satisfy a large number of constraints.

One item selection technique is to satisfy content constraints sequentially. In this case, each content area in the blueprint can be considered to be a testlet. Item selections are made only from the first content area in the test blueprint until the desired number of items has been administered from that area. Items are selected one at a time, based on which item would be the most informative of the available items in the content area. Thus, the adaptation is limited to that which is possible in the first content area. Once the content constraint has been satisfied for the first area, items are selected only from the second content area until that constraint has been met. Item selection continues until all content constraints have been met. This technique has the advantage of ensuring that all examinees receive content-balanced tests, but it risks degrading measurement precision if the items available within each content area do not have difficulties that range across the ability scale. As the test progresses, this problem can be exacerbated if, for example, the examinee is performing poorly and the content in one of the remaining areas is relatively difficult.

A second technique is to use the test specifications and the constraints they represent as a target, but not a requirement. These heuristic models, such as the weighted deviations model, acknowledge that they will not satisfy all constraints, but attempt to produce tests where the constraint violations are minimized, particularly for the more important constraints (Stocking & Lewis, 1998). As in the first technique, the next item selected is the most informative given the constraints; however, the entire pool of items is considered during item selection.

An alternative item selection method makes use of "shadow tests," developed by van der Linden (2005) and designed to produce a test that optimally meets all constraints. In effect, the item selection based on shadow tests is a two-step process. After each question is administered, the algorithm identifies the items that would best complete the entire test given the constraints. From this virtual or shadow test, the best item is selected for administration. Following the administration of that item, a new virtual test (one item shorter than the prior one) is defined, and the best item from that test is administered. This process continues with progressively shorter shadow tests from which to select items until the test is complete and the constraints are all met.

Although shadow tests are a very strong design, their construction and subsequent item delivery rules can be computationally intensive. Some practitioners have referred to this optimization-based selection of items as elegant, but impractical (e.g., Luecht, 1998). However, with increased computer power and the availability of more powerful optimization solvers, we believe that shadow testing is feasible and will begin to gain traction in large volume testing programs where item exposure, construction of large numbers of comparable test forms, and tailored testing are challenging.

Stopping Rules

CATs can be either fixed or variable in length. The stopping rule for a fixed-length CAT is straightforward. The test continues until the required number of items has been administered, the allotted time expires, or the examinee exits the test. The stopping rules for variable-length CATs are based primarily on the desired precision associated with the ability estimate. As items are administered, the error associated with the ability estimate decreases. The error can decrease quickly if the examinee performs consistently across the majority of the items, which also results in a relatively shorter test. However, if the examinee is inconsistent, relatively more items will be needed to reach the required level of precision. As with fixed-length testing, there is also a maximum test length in variable tests. If the maximum test length is reached, the test is terminated even if the desired precision has not been reached. Variable-length tests are also terminated if time expires or the examinee exits the test.

Stopping rules for variable-length tests can be quite complex, particularly in a decision-making context. The NCLEX, for example, is a variable-length CAT. The specifications for that test require that at least a minimum number of items be administered (Kingsbury & Zara, 1991). The total number of items administered in NCLEX cannot exceed a set maximum number of items. Once the requisite minimum number of items has been administered, the test ends if the error band associated with the examinee's ability estimate does not include the cut score. If the maximum number of items has been administered, the pass–fail decision is based on completed items. However, if time expires, the responses to completed items are reviewed and the pass–fail decision is made.

Test Assembly

Tests are typically built to meet a blueprint or a set of test specifications. There is usually a large number of requirements in a test blueprint. These may include content coverage, psychometric specifications, item formats, word count, administrative requirements, and more. When many forms of the test are required (e.g., for security needs), the task of assembling multiple equivalent forms for both concurrent and subsequent test appointments becomes exceedingly difficult, if not impossible, for traditional manual construction of forms by expert panels. Therefore, automated test assembly (ATA) mechanisms that employ mathematical optimization procedures have been developed (Breithaupt, Zhang, & Hare, 2014; van der Linden, 2005). The item selection heuristics and algorithms previously described for CAT are examples of ATA occurring during test administration. ATA is also routinely used for non-CAT assessments such as MSTs, fixed forms, and LOFT (e.g., Breithaupt & Hare, 2007; Breithaupt et al., 2014).

Security

Although the convenience of being able to offer tests on numerous occasions is an attractive feature of CBT, it does create some issues, most notably the risk that examinees will communicate with one another about the test content. If test content becomes widely known, test validity is diminished (e.g., Gao, Tay, & Drasgow, 2009). Testing programs use a variety of techniques to prevent and detect cheating. With regard to sharing information (preknowledge), programs often use multiple versions of their tests simultaneously and can randomize the order of item presentations. Short administration windows act as another deterrent. Programs also control item exposure (the number of times an item can be administered within a certain period of time). In addition, many programs rotate available item sets (pools) from the item bank frequently over time (Veldkamp & van der Linden, 2010). All of these security procedures can be used with programs that make use of ATA algorithms.

Preknowledge isn't limited to examinees sharing test content with one another. There are many coaching and test preparation services that sell practice materials with items purported to be actual live test questions over the Internet. These "brain dump" sites both solicit and distribute such items. It is hard to combat any form of collusion or test preparation service operating on the Internet because even when their Internet service providers (ISPs) shut down in response to legal action taken by the testing program, they can easily reopen under a different name. For this reason, some testing companies employ security monitoring services that continually search the Web for suspicious activity regarding the sale of test items for their programs.

Another very common variety of cheating is proxy testing whereby an imposter poses as a legitimate examinee and takes the test on his or her behalf. The use of biometric identifiers such as fingerprint images, palm prints, or retina scans are seen by many as effective deterrents to proxy testing. Once a person has provided biometric data, the data can be stored and checked each time the individual takes a test or even each time he or she leaves and enters the testing room. Biometric data will not necessarily eliminate proxy testing, but using it does prevent a single professional test taker from taking the same test for different people. Once the biometric data are associated with an individual, the system will flag the association of those data with another individual. Although biometric information is a very useful tool, data privacy laws in many countries can complicate the implementation of biometric procedures and can place limits on how the data can be used.

Despite the efforts programs make to deter cheating, some cheating will always occur, especially for high-stakes tests (e.g., Gao et al., 2009). Cheating is a major concern in high-stakes testing in grades K–12. Recent accountability efforts often include the performance of students in the evaluation of teacher effectiveness. This is a highly controversial use of test results, and there have been instances of teachers and others modifying students' test responses in an effort to improve the results. For this reason, forensic analysis is becoming increasingly important. Much of the forensic work has been done with respect to paper-based tests and involves measures such as large score gain analysis for retakers, unusual answer similarity between individuals or groups of test takers, handwriting analysis, and analysis of erasures and evidence that more than one person marked an answer document. Cohen and Wallack (2006) provide an excellent overview of security issues in paper-based and computerized test administrations.

Log files from computer-delivered tests contain a wealth of information not available with paper tests. Available data include time spent on items, changes to answers, number of visits to an item, whether or not items are marked for review, and more. Rapid responding can be evidence of preknowledge or evidence that the examinee is focusing most of his or her time on a small set of questions in order to memorize them while ignoring most of the items on the test (possibly because other examinees have been given instructions to memorize them). Changes in item performance can also be monitored over time. If items become easier or the time examinees spend on them becomes shorter, it may be an indication that the item has been compromised and should be removed from the pool.

Current Developments and Challenges

There are a number of exciting newer developments in CBT. These include increased flexibility in testing locations, artificial intelligence/automated scoring of examinee-produced responses, efficient and integrated item inventory management, item development, calibration, and interoperability and open-source platforms.

Increased Flexibility in Testing Locations

Some practical challenges exist in the model of secure test delivery in dedicated test centers for high-stakes examinations. The demand for more flexibility in the test-taker experience and more accessibility to a global population of test takers has forced testing programs to expand their services and to consider assessments that might be securely provided outside the traditional test centers. Interest in remote or online proctoring is increasing, and numerous companies are now offering such services. See Foster and Layman (2013) for a summary of several leading providers of online proctoring services. An increased emphasis on validated competencies and the increasing use of "badges," such as those that can be issued through Mozilla's Open Badges initiative, as well as demands for greater convenience, including massively open online course (MOOC) offerings, are likely to drive continued demand for remote proctoring services.

Another development that will likely affect testing locations is the increasing requirement that tests be device independent. Although this is not a significant concern for licensure and certification programs, the variety of devices in use in K–12 education have created requirements that state and district tests be available not only on computers, but also on other digital devices (Dean & Martineau, 2012).

Artificial Intelligence/Automated Scoring

Increased demands for complex assessment tasks result in the use of more questions in which an examinee is required to supply an answer rather than select one from a list provided in the test. Examples of such items include essays, graphs, and other technology-enhanced items (TEI; Scalise & Wilson, 2006). The widespread use of CBTs in the assessments that have developed in connection with the Common Core State Standards has resulted in the need to address device independence, accessibility, translation, automated scoring of non-objective assessments, and TEI. Zenisky and Sireci (2013) discuss how these item types can assist with measurement of higher-order thinking. Such items can be difficult to score consistently, efficiently, and accurately. Human scoring is widely used, but little is known about the quality of human scoring (Williamson, Mislevy, & Behar, 2006). Bennett and Zhang (2016) describe some advantages of automated scoring with respect to consistency, objectivity, efficiency, cost, and other factors while acknowledging that there are still aspects of automated scoring that do not perform as well as humans. Williamson also reviews different types of automated scoring and gives examples of available software systems for it.

Efficient and Integrated Item Inventory Management, Item Development, and Calibration

Several case studies in the literature illustrate the practical use of discrete optimization for distinct models of computer-delivered high-stakes examinations. It is our belief, however, that real progress in the future may occur via research on the broader problems of large item pool planning, inventory management, and deliberate long-term supply-chain analyses where banking, assembly, and inventory management are fully integrated (Luecht, 2016). This means we will need shorter item development timelines and some mechanisms with which to improve and automate the steps involved in the test development, delivery, and scoring process. It may be fair to note that the needs of the largest testing programs typically drive development and innovation among the commercial providers of systems supporting computerized test delivery. As more state assessment programs and influential large-volume testing programs incorporate innovative items and demand greater control over pool rotation and content updates to ongoing test administrations, test delivery vendors will need to develop systems that accommodate these demands. We will begin to see effective solutions when a range of vendors compete to achieve greater interoperability across systems and when automation in test assembly is supported seamlessly by item banking and by test publishing and delivery system designs and workflows.

It seems inevitable that we will need to take advantage of more efficient item writing, automated scoring, and precalibration or real-time calibration of pilot items. Important advances are being made in the use of evidence-centered design to specify assessment tasks and in automated item generation (AIG) to develop the items. Gierl and Haladyna (2013) offer an evaluation of developments for AIG. These developments will lead to a need for technologies and methods for item banking that use real-time or synchronous exposure data and/or immediate calibration of pilot items to drive more subtle test and item pool design in future assessments. The ability to easily and rapidly update test specifications and to obtain and update statistically calibrated item data for pilot items will also likely be needed.

Interoperability and Open-Source Platforms

The Smarter Balanced Assessment Consortium (SBAC) and Partnership for Assessment of Readiness for College and Careers (PARCC) have developed large item banks for use by their member states. As different states (and their vendors) deploy these item banks in different administration and delivery systems, interoperability becomes a requirement. Several interoperability standards are available, including the sharable content object reference model (SCORM), the schools interoperability framework (SIF), and the question and test interoperability (QTI) specification (Way, Davis, Keng, & Srain-Seymour, 2016). Interoperability is especially important in state-based assessments in order to give states the ability to maintain continuity in their testing programs when they work with multiple delivery vendors or decide to change vendors. There is a similar need for flexibility in certification and licensure programs, but to date, there has not been a demand from test sponsors for interoperability. It seems inevitable that testing programs will soon demand interoperability for item banking software, assembly, and scoring systems. Drasgow, Luecht, and Bennett (2006) describe a vision for interoperability in testing programs as a system or systems for comprehensive inventory planning, test development, publishing, delivery, and scoring.

Similarly, most CBTs are delivered through proprietary test delivery engines. As a result, it is difficult for test sponsors to deploy their tests through multiple vendors, to change vendors, or ensure that different engines produce the same results in a given situation. One open-source engine is the Open Assessment Technologies (TAO) platform. TAO has been used internationally in the Program for International Student Assessment (PISA) 2012 administration and is the platform chosen for the 2015 PISA as well. TAO is also used to deliver the Common Core alternate assessments field tests developed by the National Center and State Consortium (NCSC). SBAC released an open source platform for use by its member states in 2015.

Discussion

This chapter has discussed a number of the current issues in CBT. We began with a brief explanation of the growth of CBT, summarized a number of reasons programs implement it, explained commonly used test administration models, and discussed some of the issues currently being addressed. The implications of these developments are interesting to contemplate.

The assessment landscape is changing quickly. In K–12 educational settings, organizations are responding to the need for nationally equivalent Common Core assessments, and the emphasis on test content development may have peaked. The availability of large banks of pretested items and their associated statistics holds the promise of allowing states to access large numbers of high-quality items from which to build their assessments. Although there will be a need for ongoing item development and pretesting, it will likely be at a lower level than in the past. For much of that item development, automated item generation will make the process more efficient and economical. Interoperability between test development and delivery vendors will mean that state boards of education and other test sponsors will have greater flexibility in obtaining items from multiple sources and using those items to build tests customized to their specific needs. The growing acceptability of open-source platforms for test development and administration will reduce the value of proprietary test delivery engines and platforms. Demands for more flexible test administrations and device independence will threaten the dominance of traditional test center administration models.

These changes will likely result in increased emphasis on other aspects of the measurement process. These will include the development of stronger, more easily understood models of score interpretation and analysis; further development of evidence-centered design concepts to test design and to set performance standards or cut scores; more strategic selection of test administration models; and the development of more clearly defined objectives for learning activities suitable for both individuals and groups.

REFERENCES

Bennett, R. E., & Zhang, M. (2016). Validity and automated scoring. In F. Drasgow (Ed.), *Technology and testing* (pp. 143–173). New York: Routledge.

Breithaupt, K., & Hare, D. R. (2007). Automated simultaneous assembly of multistage testlets for a high-stakes licensing examination. *Educational and Psychological Measurement, 67*(1) 5–20.

Breithaupt, K., & Hare, D. R. (2016). Automated test assembly. In F. Drasgow (Ed.), *Technology in testing* (pp. 128–141). New York: Routledge.

Breithaupt, K., Mills, C. N., & Melican, G. (2006). Facing up to opportunities of the future. In D. Bartram & R. K. Hambleton (Eds.), *Computer-based testing and the Internet: Issues and advances* (pp. 219–251). West Sussex, UK: Wiley.

Breithaupt, K., Zhang, O., & Hare, D. R. (2014). Multistage testing approach to the AICPA Uniform Certified Public Accounting Examinations. In D. Yan, A. von Davier, & C. Lewis (Eds.), *Computerized multistage testing: Theory and applications* (pp. 343–354). Boca Raton, FL: CRC Press.

Clauser, B. E., Margolis, M. J., & Case, S. (2006). Testing for licensure and certification in the professions. In R. L. Brennan (Ed.), *Educational measurement* (4th ed.). Westport, CT: Praeger.

Cohen, A. S., & Wallack J. A. (2006). Test administration, security, scoring and reporting. In R. L. Brennan (Ed.), *Educational measurement* (4th ed., pp. 355–386). Westport, CT: Praeger.

Davey, T. (2011). *Practical considerations in computer-based testing.* Princeton, NJ: Educational Testing Service.

Dean, V., & Martineau, J. (2012). A state perspective on enhancing assessment and accountability systems through systematic implementation of technology. In R. W. Lissitz & H. Jiao (Eds.), *Computers and their impact on state assessments* (pp. 55–78). Charlotte, NC: Information Age.

Drasgow, F., Luecht, R. M., & Bennett, R. E. (2006). Technology and testing. In R. L. Brennan (Ed.), *Educational measurement* (4th ed., pp. 471–515). Westport CT: Praeger.

Foster, D., & Layman, H. (2013). Online proctoring systems compared. Available at *www.caveon.com/blog2/wp-content/uploads/2013/03/Online-Proctoring-Systems-Compared-Mar-13-2013.pdf.*

Gao, J., Tay, L., & Drasgow, F. (2009). Conspiracies and test compromise: An evaluation of the resistance of test systems to small scale cheating. *International Journal of Testing, 9*(4), 283–309.

Gierl, M. J., & Haladyna, T. M. (2013). *Automatic item generation theory and practice.* New York: Routledge.

Kingsbury, G. C., & Zara, A. (1991). Procedures for selecting items for computerized adaptive tests. *Applied Measurement in Education, 2,* 359–375.

Lord, F. M. (1971). Robbins–Munro procedures for tailored testing. *Educational and Psychological Measurement, 31,* 2–31.

Luecht, R. M. (1998). Computer-assisted test assembly using optimization heuristics. *Applied Psychological Measurement, 22,* 224–236.

Luecht, R. M. (2016). Computer-based test delivery models, data, and operational implementation issues. In F. Drasgow (Ed.), *Technology and testing* (pp. 179–205). New York: Routledge.

Luecht, R. M., & Sireci, S. G. (2011). *A review of models for computer-based testing.* Research Report 2011-12. New York: College Board.

Microsoft. (2014). Exam policies and FAQ. Retrieved September 17, 2014, from *www.microsoft.com/learning/en-ca/certification-exam-policies.aspx#exam_basics.*

Mills, C. N. (2011, October 4). *The Uniform Certified Public Accountant Examination*. Paper presented at the annual meeting of the International Association for Computer Adaptive Testing, Pacific Grove, CA.

Mills, C. N., & Stocking, M. L. (1996). Practical issues in large-scale computerized adaptive-testing. *Applied Measurement in Education, 9*, 287–304.

Parkerson, D. H., & Parkerson, J. A. (2008). *The American teacher: Foundations of education*. New York: Routledge.

Parshall, C. G., Spray, J. A., Kalohn, J. C., & Davey, T. (2002). *Practical considerations in computer-based testing*. New York: Springer.

Pope, G., Breithaupt, K., & Zumbo, B. (2010, July). *A survey of test taker beliefs and experiences: A social psychology of assessment and testing*. Invited presentation at the 7th International Test Commission Conference, Hong Kong, China.

Prometric. (2014). About Prometric. Retrieved September 10, 2014, from *www.prometric.com/en-us/about-prometric/pages/global-network-strength.aspx*.

Scalise, K., & Wilson, M. (2006). Analysis and comparison of automated scoring approaches: Addressing evidence-based assessment principles. In D. M. Williamson, R. J. J. Mislevy, & I. I. Bejar (Eds.), *Automated scoring of complex tasks in computer-based testing* (pp. 373–401). Mahwah, NJ: Erlbaum.

Stocking, M. L., & Lewis, C. (1998). Controlling item exposure conditional on ability in computerized adaptive testing. *Journal of Educational and Behavioral Statistics, 23*, 57–75.

van der Linden, W. J. (2005). *Linear models for optimal test design*. New York: Springer.

Veldkamp, B. P., & van der Linden, W. J. (2010). Designing item pools for computerized adaptive testing. In W. J. van der Linden & C. A. W. Glass (Eds.), *Computerized adaptive testing: Theory and practice* (pp. 149–163). Dordrecht, The Netherlands: Kluwer.

Way, W. D., Davis, L., Keng, L., & Srain-Seymour, E.(2016). From standardization to personalization: The comparability of scores based on different testing conditions, modes, and devices. In F. Drasgow (Ed.), *Technology and testing* (pp. 261–283). New York: Routledge.

Way, W. D., Steffan, M., & Anderson, G. (2002). Developing, maintaining, and renewing inventory to support CBT. In C. N. Mills, M. T. Potenza, J. J. Fremer, & W. C. Ward (Eds.), *Computer-based testing: Building the foundation for assessments* (pp. 143–164). Mahwah, NJ: Erlbaum.

Williamson D. M., Mislevy R. J. J., & Bejar I. I. (Eds.). (2006). *Automated scoring of complex tasks in computer-based testing*. Mahwah, NJ: Erlbaum.

Yan, D., von Davier, A., & Lewis, C. (2014). *Computerized multistage testing: Theory and applications*. Boca Raton, FL: CRC Press.

Yen, W. M., & Fitzpatrick, A. R. (2006). Item response theory. In R. L. Brennan (Ed.), *Educational measurement* (4th ed., pp. 111–153). Westport, CT: Praeger.

Zara, A. R. (1994, March). *An overview of the NCLEX/CAT beta test*. Paper presented at the meeting of the American Educational Research Association, New Orleans, LA.

Zenisky, A., & Sireci, S. (2013, April). *Innovative items to measure higher-order thinking*. Paper presented at the annual meeting of the National Council on Measurement in Education, San Francisco, CA.

CHAPTER 13

The Future
of Computer-Based Testing
Some New Paradigms

April L. Zenisky and Richard M. Luecht

The past few decades have been exciting for measurement professionals, especially for anybody involved in computer-based testing (CBT) research, development, or implementation. Since the early 1990s, we have experienced the operational implementation of computerized adaptive testing (CAT) for programs such as the College Board's ACCUPLACER, the Armed Services Vocational Aptitude Battery (ASVAB), the Graduate Management Admission Test (GMAT), and the National Council on Nursing's Licensure's Examinations (NCLEX). More recently, adaptive multistage testing (MST; Zenisky, Hambleton, & Luecht, 2010) applications have emerged as alternatives to item-level CAT, including the Uniform Certified Public Accountants (CPA) Examination and the latest rendition of the Graduate Record Examination (GRE). In fact, a Web search of research citations on terms such as *computer* and *testing* is likely to produce over 500,000 hits. It seems reasonable to assume that there is probably no part of the testing industry that has not considered some type of CBT applications for their own assessment purposes.

The first large-scale computerized tests largely utilized technology in a rather limited way, as a mechanism for administration. In those early days, agencies copied their paper-based test forms into software for computer-based administration, and one by one multiple-choice test questions flashed on examinees' screens, in a prescribed sequence. As quaint and perhaps mundane as that may sound now, those small steps opened the door for the later innovations that comprise so much of what is commonplace in the computerized tests of today.

For example, the past 20 years have seen expanded use of automated test assembly (ATA) in operational settings at many testing organizations. ATA employs mathematical optimization heuristics and algorithms to very quickly construct multiple test forms that meet sometimes complex test content and statistical specifications (e.g., Drasgow, Luecht, & Bennett, 2006; Luecht, 1998; van der Linden, 1998, 2005; van der Linden & Boekkooi-Timminga, 1989). ATA allows test developers to simultaneously build large numbers of parallel fixed CBT forms as well as for linear on the fly tests (LOFTs) and MSTs (Luecht, 2012b, 2012c; Luecht & Sireci, 2011). The use of ATA has also led to other practical benefits, such as optimized item bank inventory planning to guide future item writing.

Perhaps some of the most exciting innovations have emerged in terms of test development and the introduction of *technology-enhanced items* (TEIs; Koch, 1993; Parshall, Harmes, Davey, & Pashley, 2010; Sireci & Zenisky, 2006; Zenisky & Sireci, 2002). Today, common CBT variations on the selected response (SR) or short-answer (SA) item type themes include (1) multiple-response items requiring the examinee to select two or more responses from a list; (2) short-answer, fill-in-the-blank items; (3) "hot spot" items that require using a mouse to select a designated graphical area on a digital image or a picture; (4) computerized essays; (5) proofing and text insertion items; (6) look-up items that require examinees to select information from reference charts, graphics, or other exhibits; (7) ordered response formats where examinees select the appropriate sequence or priorities for multiple steps or options; (8) inclusion of digital animations or audio or video stimuli; and (9) graphical modeling formats that require candidates to use a graphical interface or draw on grid (e.g., plotting a line corresponding to a linear equation).

Moving beyond technology-enhanced SR and SA items, we have also seen the development of various types of realistic performance-based simulations. Examples include the design architecture simulations developed for the National Council of Architect Registration Boards (NCARB) examination, the computerized case simulations used on the U.S. Medical Licensing Examination involving complex medical simulations that require management of a patient's case over some period of time (Clyman, Melnick, & Clauser, 1995), and the accounting simulations used on the Uniform CPA Examination (Devore, 2004). There remain many unresolved research and operational cost/implementation issues that limit the widespread adoption of complex simulations, but there is no denying that these types of performance-based assessments have advanced the measurement sciences in important and fundamental ways (Drasgow et al., 2006; Luecht & Clauser, 2002).

Distributed online scoring is another area where technology has helped to significantly reduce score processing time and costs. Online scoring networks (OSNs) have been effectively used since the mid-1990s to manage the large-scale human scoring needs required by written essays and other types of constructed response (CR) items (Drasgow et al., 2006). Secure Internet portals provide a way to assign and digitally distribute CR data 24 hours a day, 7 days a week to human scorers located almost anywhere in the world. Online training and real-time statistical monitoring capabilities further provide powerful ways to ensure quality control (QC) for the scoring process.

So, as far as testing has come in this technology-enhanced era, the question that is our focus at present is, what comes next? The remainder of this chapter explores five of the more promising technology-oriented aspects of testing: (1) assessment engineering and principled test design, (2) automatic item generation, (3) gaming and advanced simulation techniques, (4) automated essay scoring, and (5) automated speech recognition.

Assessment Engineering and Principled Test Design

Mislevy (1996) lucidly articulated an important call for a new evidence-based assessment paradigm—one that focuses on establishing a strong cognitive basis for assessment; also see Hornke and Habon (1986); Irvine (2002); Mislevy (2006); Mislevy, Steinberg, and Almond (2002, 2003); Nichols (1994); Snow and Lohman (1989); and Whitely (1976). It is not merely a call for more consideration of cognition in the assessment enterprise, and it is most certainly not a call to merely adopt cognitive item coding taxonomies as part of the test assembly process. Rather, Mislevy's call is to design evidence-based *validity* into the assessment development process from the onset (also see Kane, 2006). It is important to understand the implications of this new paradigm.

In the past, item design and item writing activities have been considered to be art forms carried out by subject-matter experts (SMEs) (Haladyna, 2004; Schmeiser & Welch, 2006; Wesman, 1971). Despite the growing sophistication of our quantitative psychometric procedures (e.g., Kolen & Brennan, 2014; van der Linden & Hambleton, 1997), item creation and test design activities have largely remained in the hands of test developers—that is, SME item writers and test editors. In fact, assessment design typically incorporates two rather distinct systems of test specifications: (1) the content blueprint and, to a lesser extent, the so-called "cognitive" categories (e.g., Anderson & Krathwohl, 2001; Bloom, Engelhart, Furst, Hill, & Krathwohl, 1956; Marzano, 2001; Webb, 1997); and (2) statistical targets such as an average item difficulty, a minimum reliability coefficient, or an item response theory (IRT) test information target (van der Linden, 2005). ATA developments (mentioned earlier) have largely grown out of the need to more comprehensively reconcile these two systems of test specifications by using optimization heuristics and algorithms to select the items from an item bank that simultaneously satisfy both types of specifications.

The dependence on empirically estimated item and test score scale characteristics comes at a price. We need large, motivated, and representative samples of examinees to estimate every statistical quantity used in the test assembly process. That need never dissipates or goes away, which is why test security risks of item exposure remain high and item development costs go up (Luecht, 2005). In fact, given limited testing seat capacities, CBTs often realize substantially increased item production demands, higher costs, and complex item inventory planning systems (e.g., Way, Steffen, & Anderson, 2001).

In addition, it is difficult to fully understand what a particular score scale is really telling us about the supposed *construct* being measured when the scale itself is largely constructed to merely maximize the intercorrelations between the items (i.e., to maximize a reliability coefficient), subject to also balancing the content according to some established blueprint (e.g., Cronbach, 1957; Green, 1988). As Messick (1994) suggested, rather than running factor analyses or other types of dimensionality analyses after the test forms are built, it would seem more important and fruitful to build validity into the scale and to better understand the cognitive nature of the construct from the onset.

Luecht (2006, 2012b, 2013) has suggested adopting a highly structured, integrated test design and development framework that borrows iterative design and QC principles from industrial engineering and manufacturing. Not coincidentally, this framework is called *assessment engineering* (AE). AE begins with a detailed, evidence-articulated *vision* for a particular scale called a *construct map* (cf. Wilson, 2005). Using a domain-specific language, or *task model grammar* (TMG), detailed cognitive task models are then constructed and mapped by their complexity requirements along the scale to specify the nature and amount of measurement information needed. Figure 13.1 shows a potential *task model map* (TMM) for a "normal" proficiency distribution. Easier task models are shown to the left; more difficult ones to the right. The TMG specifies whether each task model (i.e., each dot in Figure 13.1) is more or less complex because of the specific skills required by the task, the level of content or information density, or some other manipulated feature of each task model specification.

The individual task models are comprised of (1) one or more required cognitive actions or mental procedures, (2) one or more static knowledge components (data or other information to be manipulated using the actions), (3) levels of content, (4) the complexity of the context in which the task is to be presented, and (5) any auxiliary tools or resources available for working on the task. The TMG documents the complexity of each of these components. The knowledge objects (sometimes called *declarative knowledge* by cognitive scientists) can differ in quantity or in complexity for a given task model. Objects can also be linked or networked together to form more complex objects by specifying relations between two or more objects that vary in type. More actions and/or knowledge components, more complex actions and/or knowledge objects, more complex relationships between the knowledge objects, and higher information density are all usually hypothesized to increase the difficulty of the task model. These vaiables provide a great deal of flexibility in designing the task models. Those hypotheses about complexity can further be empirically verified by experimentally manipulating the task characteristics in systematic ways. Once verified, item generation templates can be created to replicate the conditions of each task model experiment.

The task model templates are subsequently used to manufacture all of the items in a particular task model family. This use of templates can range from highly structured item forms and guidelines for human item writers to use (e.g., Case & Swanson, 2001) to automatic item generation (e.g., Bejar, 2002; Embretson, 1996; Embretson & Yang, 2006; Gierl & Haladyna, 2012; Gorin & Embretson, 2012). Engineering becomes relevant at two levels. First, the creation of one or more item generation templates per task model ensures a consistent item design that taps the same intended content and

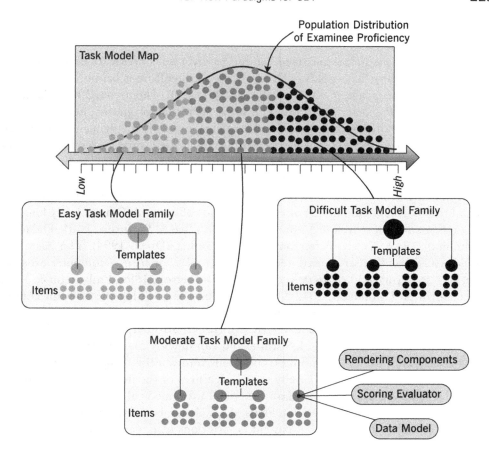

FIGURE 13.1. A sample task model (task models and templates) for an item bank.

cognitive complexity as specified by the task model. Item writers are not allowed to modify a task model's required complexity components. Second, IRT calibrations and related statistical residual analyses can be used as QC mechanisms aimed at maintaining the operating characteristics of each task model family of items.

This strong QC-oriented perspective on item design ensures that all items within a family perform as statistical *isomorphs*—that is, the items are completely interchangeable within families (Bejar, 2002; Bejar, Lawless, Morley, Wagner, Bennett & Revuelta, 2003; Bejar & Yocom, 1991; Irvine, 2002). AE still uses IRT or other data-appropriate measurement models for purposes of calibrating and item families and scoring the examinees (e.g., using a hierarchical calibration framework devised by Geerlings, Glas, and van der Linden, 2011). But the psychometric model of choice and hierarchical calibration process serve primarily as part of the engineering QC system (see Luecht, 2012a, 2012b, 2012c; Shu, Burke & Luecht, 2010).

Automatic Item Generation

In order to build such assessments as outlined above, test developers need test items, and often, quite large item pools. The psychometric literature is brimming with guidance on item development (Case & Swanson, 1988, 2001; Haladyna, 2004; Haladyna & Rodriguez, 2013; Osterlind, 1989), but for some testing programs, item needs simply outstrip traditional approaches to writing items, typically involving a cadre of item writers on retainer and extensive item editing and review procedures (Baranowski, 2006). Without sacrificing quality—an unacceptable tradeoff in high-stakes testing—one strategy that agencies have turned to is that of automatic item generation (AIG), which uses algorithms, neural net models, and possibly natural language-processing capabilities to generate hundreds or even thousands of items. AIG has a fairly long history in assessment research (e.g., Bormuth, 1970; Case & Swanson, 2001; Haladyna & Shindoll, 1989; Hively, Patterson & Page, 1968; LaDuca, 1994). The basic idea behind AIG is to use a structured item writing template or *shell*, a computer program or script—sometimes called an *item generator* (Embretson, 1996; Embretson & Yang, 2006; Gorin & Embretson, 2012)—and a database containing the relevant content instantiations used by the item generator to produce a very large number of items. Automatic item generators such as IGOR (Mortimer, Stroulia, & Yazdchi, 2012) use sophisticated natural language algorithms and can quickly manufacture hundreds or even thousands of items—including translations into multiple languages. *Item cloning* is a special case of AIG, whereby surface features of the items are systematically changed. A very simple example of an item shell for a medical examination (Case & Swanson, 1988, 2001) is presented in Figure 13.2. A database used by the item generator might contain a large array of patient descriptions (e.g., gender, age, occupation),

A (*client description*) has a (*type of issue and constraint*).

Which of the following (*strategies*) is most likely to be effective in this situation?

A. _____
B. _____
C. _____
D. _____

Database of *strategy* options

(*Strategy option #1 & reference to plausible issue type + constraint*)
(*Strategy option #2 & reference to plausible issue type + constraint*)
:
(*Strategy option #n & reference to plausible issue type + constraint*)

FIGURE 13.2. Template for item shell.

another array of injuries and locations, and a database table that contains plausible structures associated with each injury/location.

AIG has been feasibly demonstrated in a number of contexts (Bejar et al., 2003; Bejar & Yocom, 1991; Embretson & Yang, 2006; Gierl & Lai, 2012; Gorin & Embretson, 2012; Irvine, 2002; Meisner, Luecht, & Reckase, 1993). The largest challenge facing AIG is not item production, but rather, producing items that maintain a prescribed set of specified statistical characteristics (Geerlings et al., 2011; Luecht, 2012a; Shu et al., 2010) or mechanisms for predicting those item characteristics (Gorin & Embretson, 2012). Ongoing research to link strong cognitive models or related specifications to definable features and entries for each item family remains a challenge. As noted in the prior section, AE can also incorporate AIG (Luecht, 2012a, 2012b).

Gaming and Advanced Simulations

In thinking about emerging forms of assessment, one area of considerable promise is that of e-assessment and the gamification of testing. Technology-based games have long engaged children and adults alike, particularly capturing the public's attention beginning in the 1970s with the introduction of home video game consoles from companies such as Magnavox, Coleco, Nintendo, and Atari and the introduction of video arcades. These highly interactive games, developed for amusement purposes, are largely defined by three elements: first, the presentation of a goal; second, the use of clear feedback to the player about progress relative to that goal; and third, the constant adjustment of the game given player action to a level just beyond a player's current proficiency (Pausch, Gold, Skelly, & Thiel, 1994)—the latter a condition striking in its similarity to the premise of adaptive testing.

More recently, the term *serious games* has come into use to describe virtual environments in which the goal of interest is predicated on a goal of education or training (Shute, Ventura, Bauer, & Zapata-Rivera, 2008), where content is presented as players become immersed in the activity of the game and this game-play results in a quantifiable outcome (Shute, 2011). A natural extension of serious games is into the realm of assessment by embedding assessment activities such as simulations, collaboration environments, virtual worlds, games, and cognitive tutors into games to use the player's actions as indicators of knowledge or skill. In some ways, some current testing applications are beginning to incorporate some elements of gaming in their implementation, along the lines of the simulations on the Architect Registration Examination and the Uniform CPA Examination referenced earlier. However, the tenets of serious gaming go well beyond what is typically done in those simulations at present to create truly highly immersive environments.[1]

---

[1] One approach to understanding the integration of technology and assessment is provided by DiCerbo and Behrens (2012), who presented a continuum ranging from (1) computerized administration of linear or adaptive tests, (2) simulated-based performance assessments, (3) game-based stealth assessments, to (4) the accumulation of information from multiple assessments across levels 1, 2, and 3. In this section we look to levels 3 and 4 in the DiCerbo and Behrens framework as the future of game-based assessment.

Why gamification, though? The promise of this approach in testing is threefold. Current assessment methods are very, very good at assessing many educational and job-based constructs that have long been of interest, but those are largely defined by a traditional perspective of achievement and knowledge, assessed in a static space. Emerging approaches to measurement using games-based principles are able to develop scenarios that more nimbly assess the higher-order skills that predominate current conversations about what students should know and be able to do in the 21st century, and what should be assessed (Fu, Zapata-Rivera, & Mavronikolas, 2014; Rosen, 2014). So, the first potential of gamification in testing is that constructs such as problem solving, collaboration, communication, and information literacy may well be more readily adapted into these gamified scenarios because of the interactive and responsive elements inherent in the environment.

From a design perspective this shift in the nature and availability of constructs for testing has enormous implications for test development and analysis. Fu and colleagues (2014) note that one key difference between traditional and game-based assessment lies in the data. Historically, assessment development has considered "the answer" to be paramount and built development, delivery, scoring, and reporting systems on the notion that the outcome generated by the test taker is what matters (whatever form that may take, from the selection of an option in a multiple-choice question to the synthesis of an essay—anywhere in the vein of the seven categories of item formats conceptualized by Bennett, Ward, Rock, and LaHart [1990], including multiple-choice, selection/identification, reordering/rearrangement, substitution/correction, completion, construction, and presentation). In the present day, however, data from game-based simulations is different in both qualitative and quantitative ways, as it not only details the final outcome of the assessment activity embedded in the game but also produces enormous amounts of process-related data, ranging from software object access counts to response latency information. Every action taken can be viewed as data, but the challenge remains to distill data elements such as time stamps, click-streams, and all other actions taken in meaningful and actionable information. Scalise (2013) has referenced the information gathered through TEIs as "semi-amorphous"; considerable work is ongoing to data-mine these data elements from traditional assessment perspectives (Almond, Deane, Quinlan, Wagner, & Sydorenko, 2012; Bouchet, Harley, Trevors, & Azevedo, 2013; Kerr & Chung, 2012) as well as to conceptualize new paradigms (Fu et al., 2014) in the realms of scaling and data mining.

The third consideration that makes gamification so attractive as an emerging strategy for measurement is, quite simply, the potential for it to influence a seismic shift in the nature of tests. Beyond cosmetic changes, and more than statistical adjustments, the gamification of assessment is predicated on a very different perspective on measurement. The traditional view of items as discrete data points would be replaced by an interconnected, organic performance—for example, the implications for how we might look at local independence are quite significant. Interestingly, the conceptualization of assessment as embedded in an immersive simulation in an evolving environment harkens to the idea of *authentic assessment* (a term that came into vogue about 30 years ago to describe the direct examination of examinee performance in contrast to the use of simplified and/or indirect items as proxies; per Wiggins, 1990). Characterizing some assessments as authentic (and thus, others are "inauthentic") was—and still is—very divisive language, but in this context speaks to (1) how novel this approach is, especially for large-scale, high-stakes assessment; and (2) the extent to which gamification represents a new paradigm for the testing industry, not only from the side of test development but also relative to the examinee experience on a fundamental level.

Automated Scoring

The automated scoring of test items that require examinees to generate a response is an idea that has been around for a long time, but was limited in its operational use on a large scale due to technical challenges of implementation. Scoring essays and other text-based responses was pioneered by systems such as Project Essay Grade (Page, 1994), e-rater (Burstein, Kukich, Wolff, Lu, & Chodorow, 1998), and latent semantic analysis (Landauer, Foltz, & Laham, 1998), and expert systems analysis and mental modeling approaches had found early use in the evaluation of computer programs (Braun, Bennett, Frye, & Soloway, 1990) and architectural design tasks (Bejar, 1991).

In recent years, however, the research on these systems has continued, and advancements in delivery and analysis have fostered assessment development and administrative environments where many such systems are now in use. Williamson, Xi, and Breyer (2012) characterized current approaches to automated scoring as falling into two broad categories: simulation-based methods and response-type systems. The simulation-based methods align with the realistic computerized scenarios in place for tests such as the Uniform CPA Examination, the Architect Registration Examination, and the U.S. Medical Licensing Examination. In their paper, Williamson and colleagues noted that the automated systems in place for these exams tend to be highly specific to these individual tests and sometimes even to particular task types within those tests.

In contrast to simulation-based systems, response-type systems are built to handle specific item types. Text processors that handle written responses of varying lengths (a category that includes e-rater) comprise the most well known of these systems, but it should be noted that other responses for which systems have been built include spoken responses and graphical modeling, among other tasks. Task-specific systems can generally be framed in a consistent way (Williamson, Xi, & Breyer, 2012), beginning with the delineation of specific features that are valued in the response. A features identification system is then built to evaluate the extent to which such features are present or absent in examinee work, culminating in the implementation of a statistical methodology used to compute some type of score.

However, automated scoring, although full of promise, has never been without detractors. A considerable body of research on this topic has operated from the assumption that human scorers are the gold standard to which machine scoring must be held. In fact, this assumption is the cornerstone of a validity argument in support of machine-based systems. For example, Higgins and Heilman (2014) noted that some form of evaluating computer–human agreement has been used in nearly all validation studies of automated scoring. As the use of automated scoring systems has continued to grow, however, concern has likewise increased about the extent to which such systems can be "gamed" or otherwise manipulated by examinees to produce artificially high ratings of performance (e.g., producing relatively verbose responses and using multisyllablic vocubulary). Some research has looked into this issue, such as by recruiting experts to create work samples that might receive higher than deserved scores from the engines (Higgins & Heilman, 2014; Powers, Burstein, Chodorow, Fowles, & Kukich, 2001). One strategy that has been suggested over the years is to replace high-frequency words with less common synonyms. This method was studied in Bejar (2013).

Higgins and Heilman (2014) developed a four-step strategy to evaluate the extent to which automated scoring systems are vulnerable to compromise. With a scoring method specified, their steps are:

1. *Hypothesis.* Here, it is necessary to identify potential gaming strategies that might be employed in a specific scoring context, perhaps based on research, knowledge of the details of the scoring engine, or even anecdotal evidence.

2. *Simulation.* The strategies identified above must be operationalized so that they can be modeled via computer.

3. *Optimization.* The function to be optimized is typically the highest possible score, so the task here is to find the best combination of strategies for improving test takers' scores.

4. *Evaluation.* An evaluation metric to be used in ranking conjoined gaming strategies.

This empirical approach of Higgins and Heilman offers a compelling data-based approach to address the validity concerns about automated scoring that have emerged over the years.

However, concerns remain. A recent study by Liu and colleagues (2014) evaluated c-rater[TM] in the context of complex CR science items, and found that the magnitude of agreement between humans and c-rater was sufficiently adequate in aggregate, but certain issues were found that completely precluded the elimination of human scoring. Examples of these challenges included incomplete or inaccurate arguments in writing samples, the presence of non-normative ideas, a grammatical concern about pronoun resolution, and the sample size of the training sets used to build the automated scorer.

This area of automated scoring is essential to the innovations described earlier in this chapter related to gamification as well as the expansion of CR items in large-scale, high-stakes testing applications. In the United States the push is on to measure higher-order thinking skills as described in the Common Core State Standards (Common Core State Standards Initiative, 2010a, 2010b), a curriculum which is heavily weighted toward the demonstration of knowledge and skills through the generation of answers. If the use of novel test and item formats to measure both traditional and emerging constructs of interest is to catch on, the measurement methods, including scoring strategies such as automated scoring, must likewise address the technical and operational challenges that persist.

Automated Speech Recognition

Automated speech recognition (ASR) is a technology that may yet offer a new opportunity for the measurement of many constructs. Speech recognition software has been implemented in a range of specialized nonassessment contexts (e.g., dictation of health care documentation, word processing applications, therapeutic treatment of brain injury, military systems, gaming, navigation, and language learning, just to mention a few applications) and has found mainstream use with the inclusion of natural language user interface technology in many models of smartphones and tablets, in the form of personal digital assistants such as Apple, Inc.'s "Siri." The technology of ASR itself is quite advanced, incorporating algorithms such as neural networks, dynamic time warping, and more recently and most commonly, hidden Markov models (Rabiner, 1989). One important distinction to make in ASR systems is that some are characterized as speaker-dependent (meaning that system must be trained to recognize the cadences and speech patterns of a specific intended user, but once such training has occurred, the system is quite accurate for that user), whereas other systems are speaker-independent (and as such must be prepared to handle a greater range of vocabulary, speech patterns, adverse noise, and acoustical signals across the possible user base). These are considerations that have implications for the use of ASR in testing scenarios.

Of course, the concept of oral assessment independent of technology has a long history in education and psychology, and ASR has already found some application in testing, primarily in the domain of language testing. This is simply logical: Rather than asking examinees about their proficiency in speaking a particular language, assessment in this context should evaluate their proficiency directly, and ASR can offer a mechanism for doing so in a technology-rich environment. A related use for ASR is in psychological testing, as in the diagnosis of deficiencies in voice, speech, and language, such as occur in childhood apraxia (e.g., Hosom, Shriberg, & Green, 2004). It should be noted, too, that the use of speech recognition is an assistive technology element of test accommodation practices, and accordingly, can be viewed as a critical component of a universally designed assessment (Thurlow, Lazarus, Albus, & Hodgson, 2010).

On their own, ASR assessments do exist, but at present they are rather simplistic for the most part, using directed prompts to collect isolated speech samples without the benefit of interactions with an interlocutor (e.g., Balogh, Barbier, Bernstein, Suzuki, & Harada, 2005; Bernstein & Cheng, 2007). The item formats drawing on ASR tend to be limited to sentence repetition or short-answer verbal responses consisting of words and simple phrases. With the implementation and operational challenges in some testing environments being what they are, the technological complications associated with ASR for assessment purposes are nontrivial. Extensive and dedicated training with numerous and rich examples of responses from an appropriate examinee sample will typically improve the speech recognizer, but assembling the training samples is no small endeavor. In order for the speech input to be of high enough quality to be used for evaluation, the relevant acoustic *signal* needs to be distinguished from ambient noise, and the signal needs to be further parsed as "speech" comprised of lexical and syntactic components. In addition to the many regional and dialectical patterns of speech, ASR often needs to deal with the less than formal structures of spoken language, not to mention tonal qualities and other aspects of speech that imply meaning. Even the simplest ASR applications require rather sophisticated "engines" to merely process the speech samples, and to do so accurately and efficiently (Saini & Kaur, 2013). Then, and only then, the ASR engine needs to actually score the examinees' responses relative to analytical or holistic scoring rubrics that are often normalized relative to a large, normative body of speech samples in terms of fluency and articulation features of speech (e.g., Price, Fisher, Bernstein, & Pallett, 1988).

Even with these caveats and technical considerations, the potential does exist, however, for ASR to bring about significant change in educational and psychological testing on the level of the other innovations discussed in this chapter. An example of this is potential change found in the work of Clark, Martinez-Garza, Biswas, Luecht, and Sengupta (2012). They framed their approach to mitigating challenges encountered in operationalizing game-based performance in terms of a model termed the *explanation dialog model*, student explanations become assessment data of interest, and these explanations can be evaluated using adaptive testing strategies as well as ASR. As the testing experience continues to develop toward more interactive, more engaging, and more naturalistic evaluations of knowledge, skills, and abilities, what is more natural than speech as a response action? If examinees can simply say their choice, or action, or answer, intermediary actions such as clicking on a selected response or typing a response into an input box may come to be viewed as more removed or indirect—and perhaps may someday be viewed as leading to less valid inferences than ASR-based items.

Closing Thoughts:
Reflection on Our Foundations and the Future

Despite lingering assumptions to the contrary, amid stereotypes of number-two pencils and paper test booklets, the field of psychometrics today is anything but stagnant. General advances in technology and numerous related fields such as machine learning, natural language processing, and human–computer interaction have opened doors to the possibility that tests in the future will look and function very differently from current practices. However, implementation of the innovations described here—on any scale—would not be feasible without the foundational research in psychometrics that has already occurred and which has set the stage for what is to come.

In so very many ways, the legacy of Ronald K. Hambleton (to whom this volume is dedicated) has been instrumental—a pioneering architect of this evolving assessment landscape in which we find ourselves working. His research contributions to criterion-referenced testing, computerized assessment, and IRT, among innumerable other topics, have helped to lay the psychometric groundwork for current and future generations of test developers to continue to push the envelope with regard to fundamental conceptualizations of what tests are, what they look like, how they function, and how we manage the data. Over his career, Ron has both endorsed and been an catalyst of change, but always backed by careful research and even more careful questioning, to connect innovations and ideas with their practical implications in operational testing. The prognosis for the future of CBT is bright, indeed, built on a solid foundation, with many of the bricks carefully laid by Ron Hambleton.

REFERENCES

Almond, R., Deane, P., Quinlan, T., Wagner, M., & Sydorenko, T. (2012). *A preliminary analysis of keystroke log data from a timed writing task* (Research Report, ETS RR-12–23). Princeton, NJ: Educational Testing Service.

Anderson, L. W., & Krathwohl, D. R. (Eds). (2001). *A taxonomy for learning, teaching, and assessing: A revision of Bloom's taxonomy of educational objectives.* New York: Addison Wesley Longman.

Balogh, J., Barbier, I., Bernstein, J., Suzuki, M., & Harada, Y. (2005). A common framework for developing automated spoken language tests in multiple languages. *JART Journal, 1*(1), 67–79.

Baranowski, R. A. (2006). Item editing and editorial review. In S. M. Downing & T. M. Haladyna (Eds.), *Handbook of test development* (pp. 349–357). Mahwah, NJ: Erlbaum.

Bejar, I. I. (1991). A methodology for scoring open-ended architectural design problems. *Journal of Applied Psychology, 76,* 522–532.

Bejar, I. I. (2002). Generative testing: From conception to implementation. In S. H. Irvine & P. C. Kyllonen (Eds.), *Item generation for test development* (pp. 199–220). Mahwah, NJ: Erlbaum.

Bejar, I. I. (2013, April). *Gaming a scoring engine: Lexical and discourse-level construct-irrelevant response strategies in the assessment of writing.* Paper presented at the meeting of the National Council on Measurement in Education, San Francisco, CA.

Bejar, I. I., Lawless, R. R., Morley, M. E., Wagner, M. E., Bennett, R. E., & Revuelta, J. (2003). A feasibility study of on-the-fly item generation in adaptive testing. *Journal of Technology, Learning, and Assessment, 2*(3). Available at *http://ejournals.bc.edu/ojs/index.php/jtla/article/view/1663/1505.*

Bejar, I. I., & Yocom, P. (1991). A generative approach to the modeling of isomorphic hidden-figure items. *Applied Psychological Measurement, 15*(2), 129–137.

Bennett, R. E., Ward, W. C., Rock, D. A., & LaHart, C. (1990). *Toward a framework for constructed-response items* (RR-90-7). Princeton, NJ: Educational Testing Service.

Bernstein, J., & Cheng, J. (2007). Logic and validation of fully automatic spoken English test. In M. Holland & F. P. Fisher (Eds.), *The path of speech technologies in computer assisted language learning: From research toward practice* (pp. 174–194). Florence, KY: Routledge.

Bloom, B. S., Engelhart, M. D., Furst, E. J., Hill, W. H., & Krathwohl, D. R. (1956). Taxonomy of educational objectives: The classification of educational goals. In *Handbook I: Cognitive domain.* New York: David McKay.

Bormuth, J. R. (1970). *On a theory of achievement test items.* Chicago: University of Chicago Press.

Bouchet, F., Harley, J. M., Trevors, G. J., & Azevedo, R. (2013). Clustering and profiling students according to their interactions with an intelligent tutoring system fostering self-regulated learning. *Journal of Educational Data Mining, 5*(1), 104–145.

Braun, H. I., Bennett, R. E., Frye, D., & Soloway, E. (1990). Scoring constructed responses using expert systems. *Journal of Educational Measurement, 27,* 93–108.

Burstein, J., Kukich, K., Wolff, S., Lu, C., & Chodorow, M. (1998, April). *Computer analysis of essays.* Paper presented at the NCME symposium on automated scoring, San Diego, CA.

Case, S., & Swanson, D. (1988). *Constructing written test questions for the basic and clinical sciences* (2nd ed.). Philadelphia: National Board of Medical Examiners.

Case, S., & Swanson, D. (2001). *Constructing written test questions for the basic and clinical sciences* (3rd ed.). Philadelphia: National Board of Medical Examiners.

Clark, D. B., Martinez-Garza, M., Biswas, G., Luecht, R. M., & Sengupta, P. (2012). Driving assessment of students' explanations in game dialog using computer-adaptive testing and hidden Markov modeling. In D. Ifenthaler, D. Eseryel, & X. Ge (Eds.), *Assessment in game-based learning: Foundations, innovations, and perspectives* (pp. 173–200). New York: Springer.

Clyman, S. G., Melnick, D. E., & Clauser, B. E. (1995). Computer-based case simulations. In E. L. Mancall & P. G. Bashook (Eds.), *Assessing clinical reasoning: The oral examination and alternate methods* (pp. 139–149). Evanston, IL: American Board of Medical Specialties.

Common Core State Standards Initiative. (2010a). Common Core State Standards for English language arts and literacy in history/social studies, science, and technical subjects. Retrieved from *www.corestandards.org/assets/CCSSI_ELA%20Standards.pdf.*

Common Core State Standards Initiative. (2010b). Common Core State Standards for mathematics. Retrieved from *www.corestandards.org/assets/CCSSI_Math%20Standards.pdf.*

Cronbach, L. J. (1957). The two disciplines of scientific psychology. *American Psychologist, 12,* 671–684.

Devore, R. N. (2004). *Considerations in the development of accounting simulations.* AICPA Technical Report Series Two. Jersey City, NJ: AICPA.

DiCerbo, K. E., & Behrens, J. T. (2012). Implications of the digital ocean on current and future assessment. In R. Lissitz & H. Jiao (Eds.), *Computers and their impact on state assessment: Recent history and predictions for the future* (pp. 273–306). Charlotte, NC: Information Age.

Drasgow, F., Luecht, R. M., & Bennett, R. E. (2006). Technology and testing. In R. L. Brennan (Ed.), *Educational measurement* (4th ed., pp. 471–515). Washington, DC: American Council on Education (ACE)/Praeger.

Embretson, S. E. (1996). Multidimensional latent trait models in measuring fundamental aspects of intelligence. In I. Dennis & P. G. C. Tapsfield (Eds.), *Human abilities, their nature and measurement.* Hillsdale, NJ: Erlbaum.

Embretson, S. E., & Yang, X. (2006). Automatic item generation and cognitive psychology. *Handbook of Statistics, 26,* 747–768.

Fu, J., Zapata-Rivera, D., & Mavronikolas, E. (2014). *Statistical methods for assessments in simulations and serious games* (ETS RR-14-12). Princeton, NJ: Educational Testing Service.

Geerlings, H., Glas, C. A. W., & van der Linden, W. J. (2011). Modeling rule-based item generation. *Psychometrika, 76*(2), 337–359.

Gierl, M., & Haladyna, T. M. (2012). *Automatic item generation.* New York: Taylor-Francis/Routledge.

Gierl, M., & Lai, H. (2012). The role of item models in automatic item generation. *International Journal of Testing, 12,* 273–298.

Gorin, J. S., & Embretson, S. E. (2012). Using cognitive psychology to generate items and predict item characteristics. In M. J. Gierl & T. M. Haladyna (Eds.), *Automatic item generation: Theory and practice* (pp. 136–156). New York: Taylor-Francis/Routledge.

Green, B. F. (1988). Construct validity of computer-based tests. In H. Wainer & H. Braun (Eds.), *Test validity* (pp. 77–86). Hillsdale, NJ: Erlbaum.

Haladyna, T. M. (2004). *Developing and validating multiple-choice test items* (3rd ed.). New York: Routledge.

Haladyna, T. M., & Rodriguez, M. C. (2013). *Developing and validating test items.* New York: Routledge.

Haladyna, T. M., & Shindoll, R. R. (1989). Item shells: A method of writing effective multiple-choice items. *Evaluation and the Health Professions, 12,* 97–104.

Higgins, D., & Heilman, M. (2014). Managing what we can measure: Quantifying the susceptibility of automated scoring systems to gaming behavior. *Educational Measurement: Issues and Practice, 33*(3), 36–46.

Hively, W., Patterson, H. L., & Page, S. H. (1968). A "universe-defined" system of arithmetic achievement tests. *Journal of Educational Measurement, 5,* 275–290.

Hornke, L. F., & Habon, M. W. (1986). Rule-based item bank construction and evaluation within the linear logistic framework. *Applied Psychological Measurement, 10,* 369–380.

Hosom, J.-P., Shriberg, L., & Green, J. R. (2004). Diagnostic assessment of childhood apraxia of speech using automated speech recognition (ASR) methods. *Journal of Medical Speech–Language Pathology, 12*(4), 167–171.

Irvine, S. H. (2002). Item generation for test development: An introduction. In S. H. Irvine & P. C. Kyllonen (Eds.), *Item generation for test development* (pp. 3–34). Mahwah, NJ: Erlbaum.

Kane, M. T. (2006). Validation. In R. L. Brennan (Ed.), *Educational measurement* (4th ed., pp. 18–64). Washington, DC: American Council on Education (ACE)/Praeger.

Kerr, D., & Chung, G. K. (2012). Identifying key features of student performance in educational video games and simulations through cluster analysis. *Journal of Educational Data Mining, 4*(1), 144–182.

Koch, D. A. (1993). Testing goes graphical. *Journal of Interactive Instruction Development, 5,* 14–21.

Kolen, M., & Brennan, R. (2014). *Test equating, scaling, and linking: Methods and practices* (3rd ed.). New York: Springer Verlag.

LaDuca, A. (1994). Validation of a professional licensure examination: Professions theory, test design, and construct validity. *Evaluation in the Health Professions, 17,* 178–197.

Landauer, T. K., Foltz, P. W., & Laham, D. (1998). An introduction to latent semantic analysis. *Discourse Processes, 25*(2–3), 259–284.

Liu, O. L., Brew, C., Blackmore, J., Gerard, L., Madhok, J., & Linn, M. C. (2014). Automated scoring of constructed-response science items: Prospects and obstacles. *Educational Measurement: Issues and Practice, 33*(2), 19–28.

Luecht, R. M. (1998). Computer-assisted test assembly using optimization heuristics. *Applied Psychological Measurement, 22,* 224–336.

Luecht, R. M. (2005). Some useful cost–benefit criteria for evaluating computer-based test delivery models and systems. *Journal of Applied Testing Technology,* 7(2). Available at *www.testpublishers.org/journal.htm.*

Luecht, R. M. (2006, May). *Engineering the test: From principled item design to automated test assembly.* Paper presented at the annual meeting of the Society for Industrial and Organizational Psychology, Dallas, TX.

Luecht, R. M. (2012a). Automatic item generation for computerized adaptive testing. In M. Gierl & T. Haladyna (Eds.), *Automatic item generation* (pp. 196–216). New York: Taylor-Francis/Routledge.

Luecht, R. M. (2012b). An introduction to assessment engineering for automatic item generation. In M. Gierl & T. Haladyna (Eds.), *Automatic item generation.* New York: Taylor-Francis/Routledge.

Luecht, R. M. (2012c). Operational CBT implementation issues: Making it happen. In R. Lissitz & H. Jiao (Eds.), *Computers and their impact on state assessments: Recent history and predictions for the future* (pp. 105–130). Charlotte, NC: Information Age.

Luecht, R. M. (2013). Assessment engineering task model maps, task models and templates as a new way to develop and implement test specifications. *Journal of Applied Testing Technology, 14.* Available at *www.testpublishers.org/journal-of-applied-testing-technology.*

Luecht, R. M., & Clauser, B. E. (2002). Test models for complex CBT. In C. Mills, M. Potenza, J. Fremer, & W. Ward (Eds.), *Computer-based testing* (pp. 67–88). Mahwah, NJ: Erlbaum.

Luecht, R. M., & Sireci, S. G. (2011). *A review of models for computer-based testing.* Research report 2011–2012. New York: College Board.

Marzano, R. J. (2001). *Designing a new taxonomy of educational objectives.* Thousand Oaks, CA: Corwin Press.

Meisner, R., Luecht, R. M., & Reckase, M. D. (1993). *Statistical characteristics of items generated by computer algorithms* (ACT Research Report Series, RR-93-9). Iowa City, IA: ACT.

Messick, S. (1994). The interplay of evidence and consequences in the validation of performance assessments. *Educational Researcher, 32*(2), 13–23.

Mislevy, R. J. (1996). Test theory reconceived. *Journal of Educational Measurement, 33,* 379–416.

Mislevy, R. J. (2006). Cognitive psychology and educational assessment. In R. L. Brennan (Ed.), *Educational measurement* (4th ed., pp. 257–306). Washington, DC: American Council on Education.

Mislevy, R. J., Steinberg, L. S., & Almond, R. G. (2002). On the role of task model variables in assessment design. In *Item generation for test development* (pp. 97–128). Mahwah, NJ: Erlbaum.

Mislevy, R. J., Steinberg, L. S., & Almond, R. G. (2003). On the structure of educational assessments. *Measurement: Interdisciplinary Research and Perspectives, 1,* 3–66.

Mortimer, T., Stroulia, E., & Yazdchi, M. V. (2012). IGOR: A web-based automatic item generation tool. In M. Gierl & T. Haladyna (Eds.), *Automatic item generation* (pp. 217–230). New York: Taylor-Francis/Routledge.

Nichols, P. (1994). A framework for developing cognitively diagnostic assessments. *Review of Educational Research, 64*, 575–603.

Osterlind, S. J. (1989). *Constructing test items.* Boston: Kluwer.

Page, E. B. (1994). Computer grading of student prose, using modern concepts and software. *Journal of Experimental Education, 62*(2), 27–142.

Parshall, C. G., Harmes, J. C., Davey, T., & Pashley, P. (2010). Innovative items for computerized testing. In W. J. van der Linden & C. A. W. Glas (Eds.), *Computerized adaptive testing: Theory and practice* (2nd ed., pp. 215–230). Norwell, MA: Kluwer.

Pausch, R., Gold, R., Skelly, T., & Thiel, D. (1994). What HCI designers can learn from video game designers. In C. Plaisant (Ed.), *Conference companion on human factors in computing systems* (pp. 177–178). New York: ACM Press.

Powers, D., Burstein, J., Chodorow, M., Fowles, M., & Kukich, K. (2001). *Stumping e-rater: Challenging the validity of automated essay scoring* (Research Report No. 01-03). Princeton, NJ: Educational Testing Service.

Price, P., Fisher, W. M., Bernstein, J., & Pallett, D. S. (1988). The DARPA 1,000–word resource management database for continuous speech recognition. In *Proceedings of International Conference on Acoustics, Speech and Signal Processing* (ICASSP-88) (Vol. 1, pp. 651–654).

Rabiner, L. R. (1989). A tutorial on hidden Markov models and selected applications in speech recognition. *Proceedings of the IEEE, 77*(2), 257–286.

Rosen, Y. (2014). Thinking tools in computer-based assessment: Technology enhancements in assessments for learning. *Educational Technology, 54*(1), 30–34.

Saini, P., & Kaur, P. (2013). Automatic speech recognition: A review. *International Journal of Engineering Trends and Technology, 4*(2), 132–136.

Scalise, K. (2013, September). *Virtual performance assessment and games: Potential as learning and assessment.* Paper presented at the invitational research symposium on science assessment, Washington, DC.

Schmeiser, C. B., & Welch, C. J. (2006). Test development. In R. L. Brennan (Ed.), *Educational measurement* (4th ed., pp. 307–353). Washington, DC: American Council on Education (ACE)/Praeger.

Shu, Z., Burke, M., & Luecht, R. M. (2010, April). *Some quality control results of using a hierarchical Bayesian calibration system for assessment engineering task models, templates, and items.* Paper presented at the annual meeting of the National Council on Measurement in Education, Denver, CO.

Shute, V. J. (2011). Stealth assessment in computer-based games to support learning. In S. Tobias & J. D. Fletcher (Eds.), *Computer games and instruction* (pp. 503–524). Charlotte, NC: IAP Information Age.

Shute, V. J., Ventura, M., Bauer, M., & Zapata-Rivera, D. (2008). *Monitoring and fostering learning through games and embedded assessments* (ETS RR-08-69). Princeton, NJ: Educational Testing Service.

Sireci, S. G., & Zenisky, A. L. (2006). *Innovative item formats in computer-based testing: In pursuit of improved construct representation.* Mahwah, NJ: Erlbaum.

Snow, R. E., & Lohman, D. F. (1989). Implications of cognitive psychology for educational measurement. In R. L. Linn (Ed.), *Educational measurement* (3rd ed., pp. 263–331). New York: American Council on Education/Macmillan.

Thurlow, M., Lazarus, S. S., Albus, D., & Hodgson, J. (2010). *Computer-based testing: Practices and considerations* (Synthesis Report 78). Minneapolis, MN: University of Minnesota, National Center on Educational Outcomes.

van der Linden, W. J. (1998). Bayesian item-selection criteria for adaptive testing. *Psychometrika, 63,* 201–216.

van der Linden, W. J. (2005). *Linear models for optimal test design.* New York: Springer.

van der Linden, W. J., & Boekkooi-Timminga, E. (1989). A maximin model for test design with practical constraints. *Psychometrika, 54,* 237–247.

van der Linden, W. J., & Hambleton, R. K. (1997). *Handbook of modern item response theory.* New York: Springer.

Way, W. D., Steffen, M., & Anderson, G. S. (2001). Developing, maintaining, and renewing the item inventory to support CBT. In C. N. Mills, M. T. Potenza, J. J. Fremer, & W. W. Ward (Eds.), *Computer-based testing: Building the foundation for future assessments* (pp. 143–164). Mahwah, NJ: Erlbaum.

Webb, N. (1997). *Criteria for alignment of expectations and assessments on mathematics and science education.* Research Monograph No. 6. Washington, DC: CCSSO.

Wesman, A. G. (1971). Writing the test item. In R. L. Thorndike (Ed.), *Educational measurement* (2nd ed., pp. 99–111). Washington, DC: American Council on Education.

Whitely, S. E. (1976). Solving verbal analogies: Some cognitive components of intelligence test items. *Journal of Educational Psychology, 68,* 234–242.

Wiggins, G. (1990). The case for authentic assessment. *Practical Assessment, Research & Evaluation, 2*(2). Retrieved from *http://PAREonline.net/getvn.asp?v=2&n=2.*

Williamson, D. M., Xi, X., & Breyer, F. J. (2012). A framework for the evaluation and use of automated scoring. *Educational Measurement: Issues and Practice, 31*(1), 2–13.

Wilson, M. (2005). *Constructing measures: An item response modeling approach.* Mahwah, NJ: Erlbaum.

Zenisky, A., Hambleton, R. K., & Luecht, R. M. (2010). Multistage testing: Issues, designs, and research. In W. J. van der Linden & C. E. W. Glas (Eds.), *Elements of adaptive testing* (pp. 355–372). New York: Springer.

Zenisky, A. L., & Sireci, S. G. (2002). Technological innovations in large-scale assessment. *Applied Measurement in Education, 15*(4), 337–362.

CHAPTER 14

Design and Modeling Frameworks for 21st-Century Simulation- and Game-Based Assessments

Alina A. von Davier and Robert J. Mislevy

n this chapter we consider the meaning, the current use, and the potential future of simulation- and game-based assessments (SGBAs). In the overview we give readers a sense of (1) what SGBAs are, (2) why these types of assessments are important, (3) how and why they initially rose to prominence, and (4) how they are currently used. In the next section we outline the structure of SGBAs from the game and assessment design perspectives. Next we briefly discuss the data, data analysis, and psychometrics considered for SGBAs. Then we discuss the validity and fairness issues surrounding SGBAs and their uses. We conclude the chapter with a discussion of the future research directions and the limitations of SGBAs.

In this chapter we make a distinction between simulation-based assessments (SBAs) and game-based assessments (GBAs). Although both SBAs and GBAs may be very useful for the assessment of new constructs, the simulations are especially useful at the end of a curriculum unit where they can provide a realistic environment for the synthesis of the learned material. Whereas the game aspects of GBAs, such as competitiveness and entertainment, may increase the motivation and engagement of some test takers, they also may contribute to the variance in test takers' performances. Our attention has therefore been on GBA as formative assessment. More research

The idea for this chapter originated at the 2012 Ronference, and although the topics of simulation- and game-based assessments were not explicitly presented at the gathering, they were on everyone's mind as instantiations of 21st-century assessments. In the time since the Ronference, Robert Mislevy led the efforts in writing a primer on game-based assessments (Mislevy et al., 2014) and a chapter on game-based assessments for a National Council on Measurement in Education volume on technology in assessment (Mislevy et al., 2015). In this period of time, Alina von Davier became the leader of the new research center at Educational Testing Service, the Computational Psychometrics Research Center, and she outlined a comprehensive research agenda around the psychometrics in support of the new generation assessments. This chapter is a synthesis of our recent experiences with the simulation- and game-based assessments.

needs to be conducted on the risk of construct irrelevance introduced by these game aspects. From this perspective, SBAs are more similar to traditional assessments than to GBA. On other aspects, SBAs and GBAs are similar. For example, depending on the complexity of the simulations, the psychometric models considered for both types of assessments may be similar.

Here we primarily focus on computerized SGBAs because the computerized instantiations facilitate telemetry data collection and storage as they are nuanced later in this chapter. However, if other devices for data collection are available, then performance-based tasks, board games, teamwork, and other types of real-life activities can, in principle, be incorporated in the subsequent discussion. Examples of devices are Kinect for Windows (2014) and Kinect Software Development Kit (SDK; 2014), which capture and save time-stamped multimodal data (video, audio, movement, and position in space).

An Overview of SGBAs

Researchers had identified the potential of games for education by the 1980s (e.g., Malone, 1981). As technology has advanced, a renewed interest has emerged around simulations and games as tools for instruction and assessment. Observers have pointed out that some game components, and sometimes a lack of instructional design, may not induce knowledge transfer and may introduce construct-irrelevant variance (Mislevy et al., 2014). More recently, the idea of combining games and assessment emerged in the context of formative assessments (Baker & Delacruz, 2008).

Critics of the current high-stakes testing point out that contemporary, traditional summative assessment practices too often lack actionable information, providing only static snapshots rather than student progress over time, and raise validity issues with the fact that the traditional tests do not reflect the way people learn and work (Darling-Hammond et al., 2013). Fairness and equity concerns are also expressed. Hence, the next generation of assessments should encompass features to improve upon the current system. For example, the new assessments should provide actionable diagnostic information. However, in order to be able to say more about a test taker, one needs a richer input and a closer connection to instructional options. To gain both this input and connection, some tests may become part of learning and assessment systems in which the data collection will be more comprehensive and able to exploit additional information about the test takers that can be used to estimate their skills. Examples of these additional data are time information, keystroke data, multimodal data (e.g., eye-tracking facial features and the position of the head and body), and data about the test taker's behavior concerning the revisions and changes of responses. Ideally, such testing systems of the future will also assess test takers adaptively over a period of time, and the tests will be less obtrusive.

New assessments will leverage digital advances to assess a wider range of competencies more effectively than traditional assessments. Two ways to leverage technology are to include rich tasks, simulations, or games, and to merge them with assessments into SGBAs. For example, a test may include a simulation of a chemistry lab and measure students' strategies for experimentation; learning about land use planning can be embedded in a cooperative game that simulates the work that actual planners do (Beckett & Shaffer, 2005).

SGBAs are of interest because, if built appropriately, they may create an organic link among teaching, learning, and assessment: They can become a coupled system, in which teaching, learning, and assessment co-occur. As such the assessments are embedded (or linked to) a curriculum and a learning progression and include several teaching strategies, for example, by direct knowledge sharing or indirectly by including "quests" with problems to solve, and by providing access to resources. They could also include several assessment strategies, such as traditional multiple-choice (MC) items embedded in quizzes, complex tasks, simulation challenges, etc.—all of which could take place at a predetermined point in time (summative) or along the way for diagnostic purposes (formative). Moreover, this type of assessment can be adaptive, making the next task dependent on the performance on previous performances. This adaptive feature is particularly useful for formative assessments, where the focus is on providing feedback and helping the test taker move to the next level.

Any assessment should be developed around specific, well-defined constructs and should have a clearly stated purpose. This is also true for SGBAs. If the need is to test the constructs from Common Core State Standards (CCSS) and Next Generation Science Standards (NGSS), then any assessment of these constructs should be aligned with CCSS and NGSS (although caution should be given to the drop-from-the-sky type of test uses; see Gorin & Mislevy, 2003).[1] Table 14.1 (Mislevy et al., 2014) lists ways that SGBAs might be used—that is, as *assessment use cases*. Evidence from work processes inside the simulation or game is captured in data streams (Shute, 2011). In more complex and interactive simulations and games, players choose how to move through the game space, investigate situations, and meet goals. Features of sequences and partial solutions can provide evidence about players' understanding of the context, strategy use, and metacognitive skills. Identifying and interpreting such data are exciting challenges to assessment designers and psychometricians.

When we think about assessment design, there are three kinds of data that are of interest, and SGBAs can make improvements in collecting each of them.

1. *Data about the test taker.* SGBAs can capture test takers' responses, timing data, steps in a solution, paths taken in an investigation, etc. This is possible because a computer platform enables us to capture much more information.

2. *Data about situations.* SGBAs make it possible to present situations that can elicit performances that provide direct evidence about a wider range of aspects of capabilities. For example, a less constrained problem-solving environment enables test takers to construct models or explanations (see, e.g., Mislevy et al., 2014).

---

[1]This opinion is not shared by all those who design GBA. For example, Jakl and Gibson (2013) promote the idea of a bottom-up approach, in which the relevant features of the construct are discovered from the data, and the system requires only a set of preliminary, potentially relevant evidentiary features with which to start.

TABLE 14.1. Use Cases for Assessment in Games

Use Case	Description
Information for internal game purposes	Many recreational games already assess players, at least implicitly. They gather information about what players are doing well and what they are not, to adjust the pace or difficulty to optimize engagement. A GBA can similarly allow adaption or provide feedback to optimize learning or information about players.
Formative assessment: Information for students	A GBA can provide information to students as they play or at the end of challenges. Some information could be organized around details of players' actions and their results, or, in serious games, around standards or learning objectives.
Formative assessment: Information for teachers	Teachers working with multiple students can be provided with summaries of students' progress with respect to challenges or learning objectives, so as to keep a class on pace, lead classroom discussion on key concepts, or trigger follow-up with certain students.
Information for designers	If many students are playing a game, information about aspects of play such as feature usage, heightened or decreased engagement, sticking points, and pacing can be gathered and explored to improve play and improve learning.
End-of-course assessment	End-of-course assessments might use games as a source of information to evaluate learning.
Large-scale accountability assessment	In large-scale accountability tests, states administer assessments based on grade-level standards. Stakes for students, teachers, and/or schools might be attached to the results. Game-based tasks could be contemplated for such assessments.
Large-scale educational surveys	Educational surveys such as the National Assessment for Educational Progress administer samples of tasks to samples of students in order to provide a snapshot of what students in a population are able to do. Game-based tasks could also be contemplated for these assessments.

Note. From Mislevy et al. (2015). Copyright © Educational Testing Service. All rights reserved.

3. *Data about the matching of students and tasks, or the contextualization.* Well-designed SGBAs are examples of situated learning environments in which learning and assessment are inseparable from the context (Owen & Halverson, 2013). With SGBAs, we can design rich, interactive tasks that are deeply contextualized. When the tasks are properly matched with students who have been working on these types of tasks, and matched with what will be done with the information, it is possible to collect stronger, more useful, evidence for contextualized assessment use cases. When not matched, the same tasks can actually work worse in drop-in-from-the-sky use cases (see Gorin & Mislevy, 2013) because there are many more possibilities of construct-irrelevant variance, and the potential matchup to instructional options may not be as good. For example, simulations that address inquiry strategies in the context of electric circuits will be particularly meaningful for students who have studied circuits, but troublesome to students who have no experience with them. This is a

variant of the low-generalizability problem associated with performance tasks, intensively researched in the 1980s (e.g., Dunbar, Koretz, & Hoover, 1991; Linn, 1994; Ruiz-Primo & Shavelson, 1996). These data features match our understanding of the tests of the future: One form of new-generation assessments will be comprehensive adaptive learning and testing systems that work in sync with the curriculum and teachers' strategies.

We can build on experience in performance assessment. It is interesting to see how the arguments for computer-based SGBAs are foreshadowed in Ryans and Frederiksen's (1951) chapter on performance assessment in the first edition of *Educational Measurement*, along with useful design strategies. Substantial advantages can be seen, however, in the use of technology to present interactive environments, capture performance data, and use automated scoring processes to overcome some of the thorny problems that "low-tech" performance assessment faced historically. For example, the National Board of Medical Examiners designs computer-simulated patient management cases, identifies key features of candidates' widely varying solution paths, and creates scoring algorithms that combine expert judgment and psychometric modeling (Margolis & Clauser, 2006).

The Structure of SGBAs

SGBAs are complex, and creating them brings together content experts, game developers, and psychometricians. The designers are trying to simultaneously achieve the following purposes (Mislevy, Behrens, DiCerbo, Frezzo, & West, 2012):

1. The game design contains the design of tasks and simulations, plus the game aspects, such as competition and entertainment.

2. The instructional design contains key concepts and capabilities in the target domain.

3. The assessment design identifies the construct(s) to be assessed and the test use, the evidence needed to assess that particular construct(s), the theory that relates this evidence to the construct and to the claims one wants to make based on the test results, and the incorporation of evidence rules in the task design.

4. In addition, the assessment design contains links to the measurement design; that is, whether the underlying test is adaptive or linear, how long should a task be to be reliable, how many dimensions are measured, and which assessment use(s) are being supported (see Table 14.1).

5. The data collection, management, and analysis refer to the collection in a log file of process data of all the actions of a test taker/game player during the session; the structure imposed on these data that would allow for exploratory analyses, such as descriptive statistics; and the various sets of data analysis that need to be performed.

All these domains have their own language for describing the goals and the design-under-constraints challenges they face. They have their own methods for evaluating tradeoffs and crafting solutions to balance them. SGBA designers must tackle all of them jointly in the same artifact. This is particularly challenging when goals, constraints, and solutions conflict across domains.

At the same time, an SGBA is a holistic experience from the perspective of the student/test taker, with the playing, learning, and performance blended. A good SGBA design feels seamless to a player, yet provides game-play situations and player actions that at once serve the goals of play, learning, and assessment.

SGBA Design

We refer only briefly to evidence-centered design (ECD) here, given that it is a well-known approach to assessment design. The interested reader is referred to Mislevy, Steinberg, and Almond (2003) on the ECD framework and to Mislevy (2013) and Mislevy and colleagues (2014) on its application to SGBAs. ECD is used to organize the elements of assessment arguments in assessment in general, and in SGBAs in particular. It also clarifies the roles psychometric methods play in assessments that operationalize those arguments (also see Levy, 2012; Shute, Ventura, Bauer, & Zapata-Rivera, 2009).

In this subsection we introduce the concepts and the language used by game designers. Salen and Zimmerman (2004) and Owen and Halverson (2013), among many others, provide details. Throughout this chapter, we provide examples from two SGBAs. *SimCityEDU: Pollution Challenge!* is a game-based learning and assessment tool for middle school students covering the CCSS and NGSS. It engages students through the game experience; it aims to develop real-world problem-solving skills; and it provides new ways to teach and assess (*www.simcityedu.org*). This GBA, designed to assess middle school science skills, requires players to optimize the pollution and employment levels in a city. The other example is *Cisco Aspire*, a simulation-based educational game, closest in genre to strategic simulation and quest games. It is intended to give users opportunities to develop their technical skills. *Cisco Aspire CCNA Edition* has a medium-fidelity, network-capable, simulation-based learning environment that allows networking novices to design, configure, and troubleshoot computer networks at a Cisco CCNA® level of complexity (*www.youtube.com/watch?v=Lr7hH8DSph0*). Cisco Aspire is designed to assess networking skills for computer engineers, and requires players to bid on and complete contracts to design, implement, and troubleshoot computer networks for simulated clients.

Basic Game Components

The basic components of a game are objects, rules, connections, and states. *Objects* are things in the game environment that have attributes and rules about how they interact with players and other objects. *Rules* define what the connections between objects are (i.e., how they behave and interact). Together they provide an account of the current state of the game and changes to that state. The basic structure of most games revolves around rules that define how the game reacts to player behavior (including inaction), given the current state of the game. *Connections* explicate the relationships among all the objects and their attributes. A vector of game condition variables (just a few in a simple game, thousands in more complicated games), in conjunction with rules that govern possible actions, interactions, and behaviors of objects is called a *state machine*. Patterns of actions under certain game states are also the source of evidence for the assessment aspect of a GBA, such as sequences of actions in states with particular features (e.g., in SimCityEDU: Pollution Challenge!, building a replacement green power plant before bulldozing a coal plant), or attributes of an object (in Cisco Aspire, whether security settings block and allow the desired messages to the PC in the student lounge).

A *game mechanic* combines these elements to produce configurations of kinds of actions that players can take in recurring situations in a game, with certain kinds of outcomes on the game state, to advance play. In GBAs, a designer wants the kind of thinking that game mechanics evoke to advance play to also promote the targeted thinking in the domain. In Cisco Aspire, for example, players configure, replace, and connect network devices.

Game Flow

A game designer determines the kinds of situations players will encounter, how they can interact with them, and what they want to accomplish. Game design concepts here include goals and challenges, complexity and discovery, feedback, and adaptation. Engagement depends in part on their perception of autonomy, competence, and relatedness (Gee, 2007, 2008). Engagement that will keep players near the leading edge of what they can do is one instance where game design, instructional design, and assessment design roughly agree: It is around the cusp of their capabilities that people experience what Csíkszentmihályi (1975) called *flow*, what Vygotsky (1978) called the *zone of proximal development* in learning, and Lord (1970) called *maximum information* in computerized adaptive testing. Engagement is one of the main reasons to consider GBA.

Collaboration

In some games, players collaborate with one another or with a computer agent. The design of the game needs to facilitate the flow of the interactions. This is usually accomplished through a facilitator (system prompt or intelligent facilitator) in SBA or through prompts from the computer agents or the game in GBA. The way the collaborative tasks are designed in SGBA needs to follow the same ECD rules as the other tasks.

The familiar game feature of nonhuman characters, or avatars, is suited to assessing collaboration in digital SGBAs (Liu, von Davier, Hao, Kyllonen, & Zapata-Rivera, 2014; Zapata-Rivera & Bauer, 2011). Avatars appear in the environment as characters to interact with, but their behavior, while displaying some adaptivity, has known styles, knowledge bases, and behavioral patterns—all designed to evoke targeted collaborative capabilities from the human player.

Data

Much excitement about SGBA is generated from its ability to capture fine-grained data about player activity. These data are called *telemetry* in the game world, because they often are captured from a player's actions on a local device, then transmitted over the Internet to a remote site for analysis. We do tend to think that having more data is a good thing, although the key is having more of the *right* data! ECD and research-based theories are paramount for deciding what constitute the "right data"; essentially they are data that provide appropriate evidence for whatever decisions or inferences need to be made, whether by a teacher, the player, or the game itself—valid data, in measurement terminology. Hence one of the challenges in SGBA is to identify the right data from the large amount of data collected (all keystrokes, steps taken, timing, eye-tracking data). As analysts and psychometricians, we identify meaningful patterns through descriptive statistics, visualization, data mining, and (predictive) modeling.

Log Files

A *log file* is a work product that captures, at some level of detail and in some organized form, salient features of the status and activity in a game or simulation (Chung & Kerr, 2012). Log files generally begin from unstructured records of player actions. These often take the form of a time stamp, an identification number, an indicator of location or place in the environment, an indicator of an action, and sometimes detail about that action. More parsimonious log files consist of low-level semantically relevant sequences of actions.

Because evidence inevitably depends on actions in situations, log files are generally supplemented with key contextual game-state variables. In Pollution City, for example, a "heartbeat" was established in the log files. Every 30 seconds of game time, the levels of the primary measures in the city were captured and stored. With this information, it was determined that sufficient context could be established to evaluate actions not just as they contribute to game play, but as they must be interpreted for assessment; for example, "bulldoze in low-pollution scenario" versus "bulldoze in high-pollution scenario."

At Educational Testing Service, we built SGBA Glasspy (Hao, Smith, & Mislevy, 2013), a system for collecting (process) data at the test-taker and system levels (the log file); we also developed a data model for structuring the log file based on ECD principles, and for preliminary data visualization and data analysis. We used an extensible markup language (XML) structure for the log file, and developed a Python (2014) parser to extract the relevant information from the log file. Integrated machine learning tools, cluster analyses, item analyses using classical test theory indices, and item response theory models are included in a modular framework. In addition, natural language processing (NLP) and ECD techniques are used to establish a mapping based on rubrics between the actions set and the skills to be measured. See Hao, von Davier, Liu, Kyllonen, and Zapata-Rivera (2014) for details.

Other examples of similar systems are Assessment Data Aggregator for Game Environments (ADAGE; Owen & Halverson, 2013) and Leverage (Jakl & Gibson,

2013). ADAGE collects and aggregates data; it contains semantic units that are specific to the content domain (determined based on ECD) and data at the test-taker and system levels. Leverage also collects and aggregates clickstream data at the test-taker and system levels, and uses machine learning techniques to identify patterns in the data. Leverage does not use the predetermined semantic units, but does use ECD to determine potential useful features in the data. Chung and Kerr (2012) also developed a software package that structures the data logging and extraction from educational games. Next, the principles of these systems are discussed in more detail.

Data Analysis

The expectation is that the data collected from the rich environments of SGBAs will provide evidence about test takers' knowledge, skills, and capabilities. A primary challenge in fulfilling the potential of log files for making inferences about students thus lies in evidence identification. What are the important features of the work product and how do we apply scoring rules?

The problem of evidence identification in log files is frequently tackled by combining theory-based hypotheses about the relationships between observables and constructs with exploratory data analysis and data mining (Hao, von Davier, et al., 2014; Mislevy, Behrens, DiCerbo, & Levy, 2012). When there are hypotheses about particular actions that are related to the variables of interest, expert tagging of events can be used to train "feature detectors" for these patterns (Gobert, Sao Pedro, Baker, Toto, & Montalvo, 2012). Exploratory data analysis and data-mining techniques can also be used to uncover patterns that provide information about targeted constructs or newly revealed ones.

We mention here the dialectic between theory-based methods and data-driven approaches (data mining). Analyses of SGBA data can start purely by looking at patterns (data-driven methods), but they can also start from experts' input (theory-based approaches). Discovery may involve tagging sequences that experts identify as having important meaning, to serve as targets in "supervised learning" data-mining techniques. Theory-based methods may involve building in some episodes that are more like "tasks" so we know in certain places where to look and what it means—for example, diagramming a system to report to a supervisor.

Then we move from exploratory to confirmatory analyses. Do we have a theory of how the paths or strategies should cluster? For example, the proficient test takers should follow this path to a successful game, whereas the least proficient usually follow that path. Can we quantify the "distance" between these "theoretical" or "expert-based" strategies and the clusters we identified? What methods should we use to express these distances? Can we represent the distances graphically?

Zhu, Shu, and von Davier (2014) used social network analysis to identify the sequence of steps taken by test takers in a simulation. They identified groups of students who used the same strategy and the same path in the simulation. The strategy taken appeared to be relevant for solving the task successfully. Hao, Shu, and von Davier (2014) adapted a distance metric used in NLP, the Levenshtein edit distance that compares strings, to compare the sequences of actions taken by test takers to the sequences that are most efficient and correct as identified by the experts. Similarly, Bergner, Shu, and von Davier (2014) investigated how these sequences of actions clusters across the test takers and compared these clusters with the groups of test takers classified using the scoring rules developed by the experts. Rupp and colleagues (2012) demonstrate how four different indicators in the log files were used to create a measure of the efficiency of a solution to a computer networking problem. The indicators included time, number of commands, proportions of different types of commands, and amount of switching between computer devices. Kerr and Chung (2012) conducted exploratory cluster analyses to identify salient features of student performance in an educational video game targeting rational number addition. DiCerbo and Kidwai (2013) used classification and regression tree (CART) analysis to build a detector of whether game players were pursuing a goal of completing quests (as opposed to other potential goals) in a game environment. Scalise (2013) used Bayes' networks in evidence identification to synthesize information from lower-level features in a learning game. In these applications we see a strong feedback loop between the data-driven approaches and expert-based theory that could lead to building stronger evidence and better scoring rules for the competencies needed for the particular use of the assessment (see again Table 14.1). Ideally, what is learned in such analyses feeds back to improve interfaces, game play, and player affordances.

Psychometric Modeling

This section gives a brief overview of the methodological descriptions and recommendations provided in Mislevy and colleagues (2014, 2015) for extended discussion of a few other promising models.

The goal is to model belief about aspects of what given people know and can do, conditional on everything we learned about them up to that point: for example, what responses they gave to 0/1 quiz items, what path they took in the problem-solving task, what they typed, where they looked, how much time they spent on different items, whether they received hints from the system, and "how far they got" in the game or simulation or how they scored.

Many games already use counts and timing data. We can apply methods from classical test theory (CTT; Lord & Novick, 1968) to more rigorously examine the qualities of evidence that result (Gulliksen, 1950/1987). CTT works well when the multiple measures at issue are similar nuggets of evidence about the same thing—in SGBAs, independent attempts at similar problems, when learning is negligible across those attempts. It does not work as well when the evidence comes in different forms, has dependencies among its pieces, depends on different mixes of skills in different combinations, proficiencies change over the course of observation, or different players contribute different kinds or amounts of evidence.

Latent variable models posit unobservable variables, θ, denoting the construct of interest, and model the relationship between observed variables x and ability θ (both can be vector valued): For situation j, the conditional probability $h_j(x_j|\theta)$ (Moustaki & Knott, 2000) is also known as the link function. Under appropriate conditions, we can estimate the conditional probability distributions, and given a person's observed x's, make inferences back about that person's θ. The forms of the θ's, the x_j's, and the links are determined by the nature and grain size of the inferences about players that are needed, the forms of the observables, and the relationship between them. These are determined by the design of the tasks, the conceptualization of how performance depends on the posited proficiencies, and data to the extent they are available. A basic latent variable model posits conditional independence among the observed variables across J situations, or

$$h(x|\theta) = \prod_j h_j(x_j|\theta)$$ (14.1)

As noted in the following material, conditional dependence due to shared context or serial relationships among actions can be introduced (e.g., Almond, Mulder, Hemat, & Yan, 2009).

Ultimately our interest lies in what can be said about θ given x, given by Bayes' theorem as $g(\theta|x) \propto g(\theta)h(x|\theta)$, where $g(\theta)$ is a prior distribution for θ, based on background information for a student or previous play (Cai, 2013; Mislevy & Gitomer, 1996).

When conditional probabilities are specified by task parameters β_j, which in turn depend on features y_j of the situations, we can write $h_j\left[x_j|\theta,\beta_j(y_j)\right]$ (Adams, Wilson, & Wang, 1997; Geerlings, Glas, & van der Linden, 2011). These y_j's are "data concerning the task" in the assessment argument.

The conditional independence structure of latent variable models is well suited to interactive assessments like SGBAs that allow students to work down different paths. However, the actions of a test taker over the time of the task may be dependent. The student model variables θ in a given student model are of interest for some period of time, perhaps a level or the game as a whole. The conditional probabilities for observations are used to update beliefs about θ as new data x arrive via Bayes' theorem. This procedure holds when different players have different sets of observables, and if the assessment situations have been presented based on a player's previous actions, such as presenting more challenging situations to players who are doing well and easier challenges to players who are struggling. The process takes the form of docking appropriate conditional probability structures, or link functions, to the student model and carrying out Bayesian updating (Almond & Mislevy, 1999; Mislevy, Steinberg, Breyer, Johnson, & Almond, 2002). Often, the initial conditional probabilities in the links are based on the experts' judgment. These prior distributions are assumed to have a large variance so that they do not bias the results. By analyzing sufficient data, the priors are updated using Bayes' theorem. These updated beliefs can then be the basis of selecting activities, modifying features of game situations, providing feedback to students, and reporting summaries to teachers.

Other statistical and psychometric models may be employed in SGBA for different purposes (see Table 14.1). For example, hidden Markov models (HMMs) can be used to identify strategies of solving the tasks. HMMs can be used to describe the sequential actions captured in log files; they also link steps in the data sequence to the past history only through the previous step, and an evolving hidden state, described by a latent variable, is postulated to explain the sequence of observations. An HMM is thus a doubly stochastic process described by the latent transitions and the stochastic distribution of observations at each state.

Another promising model is a Markov decision process (MDP) that can be used for making inferences about test takers' latent traits and to model the cognitive process of the problem solving. An MDP is a model for sequential planning in the presence of uncertainty. It was developed for process optimization in robotics, was used in education to model ideal teacher behavior (Rafferty, LaMar, & Griffiths, 2012), and was applied in cognitive science to model how we infer another person's motivations and beliefs (Baker, Saxe, & Tenenbaum, 2009). Recently, LaMar, Rafferty, and Griffiths (2013) applied the MDP to model data from a GBA.

Psychometric Modeling of Collaboration

How does the inclusion of collaborative tasks impact psychometric modeling? Including collaborative tasks adds dependencies into the data because the test takers' responses will now also depend on the partners' previous responses. One possibility to address these complex dependencies is to model the team performance (at a team level rather than an individual level). The previous discussion about modeling an individual's capabilities applies directly to the modeling of a team *as a unit*. This approach may suffice when the team is of interest in its own right. Discussions of team-level feedback and of individuals' actions within scenarios can still help individuals' learn. Zhu (2014) analyzed the relationships among individuals and among teams using social network analysis.

Modeling the contributions and capabilities of individuals in collaborative units is harder. It is possible to create distinct models for individuals, but it must be noted how each player's actions influence the situations of the other players. Tasks can require noncollaborative work as well as collaborative work, to provide information about players' capabilities as individuals and thus highlight emergent characteristics of joint work.

In collaborative problems, pertinent aspects of log file data can be considered as interacting time series for the players involved. They share situational features. The resulting multivariate time series can be analyzed with a number of modeling strategies used in other fields, such as dynamic linear models, differential equation models, social networks analysis, Bayes' networks, machine learning methods, neural networks, and point processes, which are stochastic processes for discrete events. Soller and Stevens (2008) have applied HMMs (of order 1) to model effective knowledge sharing in collaborative learning tasks, using the hidden state of the HMM to describe the hidden evolving state of the group during the observed discussion process. von Davier and Halpin (2013a, 2013b) describe the use of the Hawkes process to analyze data from collaboration. The Hawkes process is a stochastic model for discrete events (Halpin, 2014) and can describe the interdynamics of the teams. von Davier and Halpin used data from several basketball games to illustrate the method. They also described an extension of item response theory (IRT), in which the probability of a student's response at time t is a function of that student's ability, but also of the event history of the entire process, which includes the actions of the other individuals in the collaborative task. von Davier, Hao, Liu, Kyllonen, and Zapata-Rivera (2014) described the psychometric considerations needed for an assessment that includes collaborative simulated tasks along with traditional MC items. They analyzed the data by obtaining a baseline for the individuals working alone and comparing it to the individuals working in dyads. They considered dynamic linear models, HMM, Bayes' networks, and the Hawkes model in their analyses.

Validity and the Future of SGBAs

At the first sight and under the spell of successful commercial games, the possibilities for SGBAs appear to be endless. Unfortunately, there are constraints that temper the dreams—at least, for now. The surge in the availability of games for learning shows how many possibilities exist. Similarly, the plethora of intelligent tutoring systems (ITS) for individualized learning also show that our conceptions of teaching and learning are changing. However, so far the (validity) research conducted on both games for learning and ITS has been scant and not very rigorous (small and convenient samples, without measurement models), leading Young and colleagues (2012) to conclude from their metaanalysis, "Our Princess Is in Another Castle," that there was no evidence of success.

GBAs that inherently include features from games for learning and ITSs, in addition to assessment design and psychometrics, are bound to be susceptible to the disadvantages of all of these components; hence, the complexity and the challenges associated with designing them. This does not mean that they cannot be done or that they are not useful. The question is not "Do they work or don't they?" as a simple yes–no question, but rather to what use cases (Table 14.1) are they well suited, and in those cases, how do we do the design and modeling to maximize their usefulness?

These issues also mean that we need to invest time, effort, and a high level of expertise in several disciplines to make SGBAs work and to develop them in a thoughtful way. The bolder the claims we make around a sophisticated product such as an SGBA, the less margin of error we have if we need to revise it, and the less tolerance we encounter from our constituents (teachers, school district policymakers, parents, etc.). Moreover, the risk that the constituents will be disappointed with the results and decide to abandon these assessments is quite significant, especially since building this type of assessment is an expensive endeavor (at the time of this writing).

There are still factors that we do not know how to handle in producing fair game-based assessments: (1) how to make the tasks comparable in difficulty over time, (2) how long tasks should be to provide a reliable score, and (3) how to ensure that the game component is not introducing a bias (construct irrelevant variance; see Messick, 1994) either generally or for specific subgroups of test takers. It is important to mention that all of these issues will have meanings and requirements that depend critically on the use case at issue. Our thinking is that the use cases for which GBAs are best suited are generally not the use cases on which testing companies have focused historically. This means that "testing industry intuitions" about these things may need to be recalibrated for less familiar GBA use cases. SBAs are different, though, as nongame simulations in assessments fit more comfortably into the historical use cases in the testing industry.

A few strategies to increase the validity and reliability of the SGBAs include building them according to ECD and supporting scientific theories, administering them to a large and representative sample, adding traditional test components (in forms of "quests"), conducting additional validity research by modifying some of the factors known to impact the performance, and by analyzing the predictive power on external variables. The work conducted by von Davier and colleagues (2014) on building a large-scale collaborative science assessment in a game environment is an example where these assessment issues have been considered and implemented. Riconscente and Vattel (2013) describe the definition of "assessment mechanics" as a way to describe key assessment ideas of work products and observable variables in terms that will be comfortable to game designers. The GlassLab is another good example of such an effort, where experts from different areas worked together to build GBAs such as SimCityEdu: Pollution Challenge! (Mislevy et al., 2014).

The next generation of assessments have several other features that we will need to consider: test security and gaming the game, for example, will have a new meaning for SGBAs. The legal issues could be outstanding: What is the impact on privacy from such a system that collects all types of information about the test takers? However, as mentioned above, the security issues and their impact will have meanings and requirements that depend on the use case at issue.

Collaboration is an engaging aspect of games and learning, and the capabilities that collaboration requires are of current interest in substantive domains. A psychometrics for collaboration, however, is only beginning. A route for further development will continue along formal modeling lines, and low-stakes implementations starting with schemas for which both design configurations and analytic methods have been worked out.

Conclusions

Why do we like SGBAs? They are motivating and entertaining, and can increase validity because they match the way (young) people learn, work, and interact with the world. They allow for richer data to be collected, such as response time, path taken in solving a problem, keystroke and click-level actions, even eye-tracking and facial expression data. They allow for intensive longitudinal data collected over the duration of the game/assessment. If the simulations are complex in the right ways, they can provide evidence about higher-order skills such as strategy, decision making, and inquiry skills that cannot be measured through the traditional item format. They can be supplemented with small quizzes and quests along the way to increase the reliability of measurement.

We neither desire nor expect SGBA to supplant all kinds of existing forms of assessment for all assessment uses. But by leveraging new possibilities to provide richer environments for students to interact with, capturing data of more types and greater volumes, and making sense of patterns in complex performances, SGBA clearly do present exciting new points in the space of assessment design configurations. The job at hand is to integrate the principles and the experience of game design, learning, and assessment and to use them effectively.

REFERENCES

Adams, R. J., Wilson, M., & Wang, W. C. (1997). The multidimensional random coefficients multinomial logit model. *Applied Psychological Measurement, 21,* 1–23.

Almond, R. G., & Mislevy, R. J. (1999). Graphical models and computerized adaptive testing. *Applied Psychological Measurement, 23,* 223–237.

Almond, R. G., Mulder, J., Hemat, L. A., & Yan, D. (2009). Bayesian network models for local dependence among observable outcome variables. *Journal of Educational and Behavioral Statistics, 34,* 491–521.

Baker, C. L., Saxe, R., & Tenenbaum, J. B. (2009). Action understanding as inverse planning. *Cognition, 113*(3), 329–349.

Baker, E. L., & Delacruz, G. C. (2008). What do we know about assessment in games? National Center for Research on Evaluation, Standards, and Student Testing (CRESST). Retrieved from *www.cse.ucla.edu/products/overheads/AERA2008/baker_assessment.pdf.*

Beckett, K., & Shaffer, D. W. (2005). Augmented by reality: The pedagogical praxis of urban planning as a pathway to ecological thinking. *Journal of Educational Computing Research, 33,* 31–52.

Bergner, Y., Shu, Z., & von Davier, A. A. (2014, July). *Visualization and confirmatory clustering of sequence data from a simulation-based assessment task.* Paper presented at the Educational Data Mining Conference, London.

Cai, L. (2013). Potential applications of latent variable modeling for the psychometrics of medical simulation. *Military Medicine, 178*(10), 115–120.

Chung, G. K. W. K., & Kerr, D. (2012). *A primer on data logging to support extraction of meaningful information from educational games: An example from Save Patch* (CRESST Report 814). Los Angeles: University of California, National Center for Research on Evaluation, Standards, and Student Testing.

Csíkszentmihályi, M. (1975). *Beyond boredom and anxiety.* San Francisco: Jossey-Bass.

Darling-Hammond, L., Herman, J., Pellegrino, J., Abedi, J., Aber, J. L., et al. (2013). *Criteria for high-quality assessment.* Stanford, CA: Stanford Center for Opportunity Policy in Education.

DiCerbo, K. E., & Kidwai, K. (2013, July). *Detecting player goals from game log files.* Poster presented at the Sixth International Conference on Educational Data Mining, Memphis, TN.

Dunbar, S. B., Koretz, D. M., & Hoover, H. D. (1991). Quality control in the development and use of performance assessments. *Applied Measurement in Education, 4,* 289–303.

Gee, J. P. (2007). *What video games have to teach us about learning and literacy* (2nd ed.). New York: Palgrave.

Gee, J. P. (2008). Learning and games. In K. Salen (Ed.), *The ecology of games: Connecting youth, games, and learning* (pp. 21–40). Cambridge, MA: MIT Press.

Geerlings, H., Glas, C. A., & van der Linden, W. J. (2011). Modeling rule-based item generation. *Psychometrika, 76,* 337–359.

Gobert, J. D., Sao Pedro, M., Baker, R. S. J. D., Toto, E., & Montalvo, O. (2012). Leveraging educational data mining for real time performance assessment of scientific inquiry skills within microworlds. *Journal of Educational Data Mining, 5,* 153–185.

Gorin, J. S., & Mislevy, R. J. (2013). *Inherent measurement challenges in the Next Generation Science Standards for both formative and summative assessment.* Princeton, NJ: K–12 Center at Educational Testing Service.

Gulliksen, H. (1987). *Theory of mental tests.* New York: Wiley; Reprint: Hillsdale, NJ: Erlbaum. (Original work published 1950)

Halpin, P. F. (2014). An EM algorithm for Hawkes process. In R. E. Millsap, L. A. van der Ark, D. M. Bolt, & C. M. Woods (Eds.), *New developments in quantitative psychology: Presentations from the 77th annual Psychometric Society meeting* (pp. 403–414). New York: Springer.

Hao, J., Shu, Z., & von Davier, A. A. (2014, April). *Scoring a "real world" task: A "real world" way.* Paper presented at the meeting of the National Council of Measurement in Education, Philadelphia.

Hao, J., Smith, L., III, & Mislevy, R. J. (2013). *SGBA Log Safari documentation.* Unpublished manuscript.

Hao, J., von Davier, A. A., Liu, L., Kyllonen, P., & Zapata-Rivera, D. (2014, April). *Investigating collaborative problem solving with extended collaboration tasks.* Paper presented at the meeting of the National Council of Measurement in Education, Philadelphia, PA.

Jakl, P., & Gibson, D. (2013). The Leverage™ approach: Designing virtual performance spaces for data collection, analysis and adaptive applications. Retrieved from *www.pr-sol.com/papers/The%20Leverage%20Approach%20v3.pdf.*

Kerr, D., & Chung, G. K. W. K. (2012). *Using cluster analysis to extend usability testing to instructional content.* CRESST Report 816. Los Angeles: University of California, National Center for Research on Evaluation, Standards, and Student Testing.

Kinect SDK. (2014). Kinect for Windows v2 sensor and software development kit. Retrieved from *www.microsoft.com/en-us/kinectforwindows/discover/features.aspx.*

Kinect for Windows. (2014). Retrieved from *www.microsoft.com/en-us/kinectforwindows.*

LaMar, M., Rafferty, A., & Griffiths, T. (2013, April). *Diagnosing student understanding using Markov decision process models.* Paper presented at the meeting of the National Council on Measurement in Education, San Francisco, CA.

Levy, R. (2012). Psychometric advances, opportunities, and challenges for simulation-based assessment. Princeton, NJ: K–12 Center at ETS. Retrieved from *www.k12center.org/rsc/pdf/session2–levy-paper-tea2012.pdf.*

Linn, R. L. (1994). Performance assessment: Policy promises and technical measurement standards. *Educational Researcher, 23*(9), 4–14.

Liu, L., von Davier, A. A., Hao, J., Kyllonen, P., & Zapata-Rivera, D. (2014, April). *A tough nut to crack: Measuring collaborative problem solving.* Paper presented at the meeting of the National Council on Measurement in Education, Philadelphia, PA.

Lord, F. M. (1970). Some test theory for tailored testing. In W. H. Holtzman (Ed.), *Computer-assisted instruction, testing and guidance* (pp. 139–183). New York: Harper & Row.

Lord, F. M., & Novick, M. R. (1968). *Statistical theories of mental test scores.* Reading, MA: Addison-Wesley.

Malone, T. W. (1981). Towards a theory of intrinsically motivating instruction. *Cognitive Science, 4,* 333–369.

Margolis, M. J., & Clauser, B. E. (2006). A regression-based procedure for automated scoring of a complex medical performance assessment. In D. W. Williamson, I. I. Bejar, & R. J. Mislevy (Eds.), *Automated scoring of complex tasks in computer-based testing* (pp. 123–168). Mahwah, NJ: Erlbaum.

Messick, S. (1994). The interplay of evidence and consequences in the validation of performance assessments. *Educational Researcher, 23*(2), 13–23.

Mislevy, R. J. (2013). Evidence-centered design for simulation-based assessment. *Military Medicine, 178*, 107–114.

Mislevy, R. J., Behrens, J. T., DiCerbo, K. E., Frezzo, D. C., & West, P. (2012). Three things game designers need to know about assessment. In D. Ifenthaler, D. Eseryel, & X. Ge (Eds.), *Assessment in game-based learning: Foundations, innovations, and perspectives* (pp. 59–81). New York, NY: Springer.

Mislevy, R. J., Behrens, J. T., DiCerbo, K. E., & Levy, R. (2012). Design and discovery in educational assessment: Evidence centered design, psychometrics, and data mining. *Journal of Educational Data Mining, 4*, 11–48. Retrieved from *www.educationaldatamining. org/JEDM/images/articles/vol4/issue1/MislevyEtAlVol4Issue1P11_48.pdf*.

Mislevy, R. J., Corrigan, S., Oranje, A., Dicerbo, K., Bauer, M. I., von Davier, A. A., et al. (2015). Psychometrics for game-based assessment. In F. Drasgow (Ed.), *Technology and testing: Improving educational and psychological measurement* (pp. 23–48). Washington, DC: National Council on Measurement in Education.

Mislevy, R. J., Corrigan, S., Oranje, A., Dicerbo, K., John, M., Bauer, M. I., et al. (2014). *Psychometric considerations in game-based assessment.* New York: Institute of Play.

Mislevy, R. J., & Gitomer, D. H. (1996). The role of probability-based inference in an intelligent tutoring system. *User-Modeling and User-Adapted Interaction, 5*, 253–282.

Mislevy, R. J., Steinberg, L. S., & Almond, R. G. (2003). On the structure of educational assessments. *Measurement: Interdisciplinary Research and Perspectives, 1*, 3–67.

Mislevy, R. J., Steinberg, L. S., Breyer, F. J., Johnson, L., & Almond, R. A. (2002). Making sense of data from complex assessments. *Applied Measurement in Education, 15*, 363–378.

Moustaki, I., & Knott, M. (2000). Generalised latent trait models. *Psychometrika, 65*, 391–411.

Owen, V., & Halverson, R. (2013). ADAGE (assessment data aggregator for game environments): A click-stream data framework for assessment of learning in play. In A. Ochsner (Ed.), *Proceedings of the 9th annual Games+Learning+Society conference* (pp. 248–254). Pittsburgh, PA: ETC Press.

Python. (2014). Python 3.4.0 documentation. Retrieved from *https://docs.python.org/3*.

Rafferty, A., LaMar, M., & Griffiths, T. (2012, July). *Diagnosing learners' knowledge from their actions.* Poster presentation at the fifth International Conference on Educational Data Mining.

Riconscente, M. M., & Vattel, L. (2013, April). Extending ECD to the design of learning experiences. In M. M. Riconscente (Chair), *ECD from A to Z: Applying evidence-centered design across the assessment continuum.* Invited session presented at the National Council on Measurement in Education, San Francisco, CA.

Ruiz-Primo, M. A., & Shavelson, R. J. (1996). Rhetoric and reality in science performance assessments: An update. *Journal of Research in Science Teaching, 33*, 1045–1063.

Rupp, A. A., Levy, R., DiCerbo, K. E., Sweet, S., Crawford, A. V., Caliço, T., et al. (2012). Putting ECD into practice: The interplay of theory and data in evidence models within a digital learning environment. *Journal of Educational Data Mining, 4*, 49–110. Retrieved from *www.educationaldatamining.org/JEDM/images/articles/vol4/issue1/RuppEtAl-Vol4Issue1P49_110.pdf*.

Ryans, D. G., & Frederiksen, N. (1951). Performance tests of educational achievement. In E. F. Lindquist (Ed.), *Educational measurement* (pp. 455–494). Washington, DC: American Council on Education.

Salen, K., & Zimmerman, E. (2004). *Rules of play: Game design fundamentals*. Cambridge, MA: MIT Press.

Scalise, K. (2013). *Assessment and games: Potential as learning and assessment tools*. Invitational research symposium on science assessment. Retrieved from *www.k12center.org/rsc/pdf/b2_3_scalise.pdf*.

Shute, V. J. (2011). Stealth assessment in computer-based games to support learning. In S. Tobias & J. D. Fletcher (Eds.), *Computer games and instruction* (pp. 503–524). Charlotte, NC: Information Age.

Shute, V. J., Ventura, M., Bauer, M. I., & Zapata-Rivera, D. (2009). Melding the power of serious games and embedded assessment to monitor and foster learning: Flow and grow. In U. Ritterfeld, M. Cody, & P. Vorder (Eds.), *Serious games: Mechanisms and effects* (pp. 295–321). Mahwah, NJ: Routledge, Taylor & Francis.

Soller, A., & Stevens, R. (2008). Applications of stochastic analyses for collaborative learning and cognitive assessment. In G. R. Hancock & K. M. Samuelson (Eds.), *Advances in latent variable mixture models* (pp. 109–111). Charlotte, NC: Information Age.

von Davier, A. A., & Halpin, P. F. (2013a). *Collaborative problem solving and the assessment of cognitive skills: Psychometric considerations*. Research Report RR-13-41. Princeton, NJ: Educational Testing Service.

von Davier, A. A., & Halpin, P. F. (2013b, May). *Modeling the dynamics in dyadic interactions in collaborative problem solving*. Paper presented at an invited symposium at the meeting of the National Council on Measurement in Education, San Francisco, CA.

von Davier, A. A., Hao, J., Liu, L., Kyllonen, P., & Zapata-Rivera, D. (2014, April). *Considerations on including collaborative problem solving tasks in standardized assessments*. Paper presented at the meeting of the National Council on Measurement in Education, Philadelphia, PA.

Vygotsky, L. S. (1978). *Mind and society: The development of higher psychological processes*. Cambridge, MA: Harvard University Press.

Young, M. F., Slota, S., Cutter, A. B., Jalette, G., Mullin, G., Lai, B., et al. (2012). Our princess is in another castle: A review of trends in serious gaming for education. *Review of Educational Research, 82*(1), 61–89.

Zapata-Rivera, D., & Bauer, M. (2011). Exploring the role of games in educational assessment. In M. C. Mayrath, J. Clarke-Midura, & D. Robinson (Eds.), *Technology-based assessments for 21st century skills: Theoretical and practical implications from modern research* (pp. 149–172). Charlotte, NC: Information Age.

Zhu, M. (2014, April). *Social networks and team performance in large scale online role playing games*. Paper presented at the annual meeting of the National Council on Measurement in Education, Philadelphia.

Zhu, M., Shu, Z., & von Davier, A. A. (2014, February). *Network representation of the process data*. Paper presented at the International Sunbelt Social Network Conference, St. Petersburg Beach, FL.

PART V

Cross-Lingual Assessment

CHAPTER 15

Cross-Lingual Educational Assessment

Avi Allalouf and Pnina Hanani

Cross-lingual assessment, in its simple definition, occurs when a test is constructed and used to assess people across different languages. This chapter focuses on cross-lingual assessment in the educational field. The methodology presented can be applied to any cross-lingual assessment, but it is more relevant to high-stakes testing, where accuracy and fairness are of major importance, and many challenges must be met.

The chapter is divided into three sections. The first discusses the term *cross-lingual assessment* (as distinct from *cross-cultural assessment*) and its importance in educational assessment. The second and main section, which deals with methods and designs used to achieve reliable and valid cross-lingual assessment, begins with considerations and challenges in assessing linguistically diverse populations, and then discusses, in two subsections, how the methods and designs are used *before* and *after* test administration, respectively. The last section presents the standards, guidelines, and frameworks that exist in the area of cross-lingual assessment and explains their importance and use by practitioners. Issues and implications for future directions in cross-lingual assessment are also briefly addressed.

Cross-Lingual and Cross-Cultural Assessment

In recent years, due to the fact that the world is becoming a global village, there is a greater interest in assessments of linguistically and culturally diverse populations of examinees. An increasing number of international studies are dealing with cross-national, cross-cultural, and cross-lingual comparisons of attitudes, traits, abilities, and educational achievement. There is also a growing demand for multiple-language versions of tests and instruments for selection and certification, to be administered to individuals who speak different languages (e.g., for employment purposes). Such assessment tools must therefore be translated and adapted across cultures. There is likewise a need for cross-lingual and cross-cultural personality and intelligence measures, for example, the Wechsler Adult Intelligence Scale that has been translated and adapted for use in many languages (Boake, 2002).

When a psychometric measure (i.e., a measure of personality, intelligence, aptitude, or some other construct) is used to compare people from different cultural backgrounds, we speak of cross-cultural testing and assessment (de Klerk, 2008; see also van de Vijver & Poortinga, Chapter 16, this volume). When a psychometric measure is used to compare people speaking different languages, we speak of cross-lingual testing and assessment. However, cross-lingual assessment and cross-cultural assessment are interrelated: Every cross-lingual assessment is also a cross-cultural assessment. Translations of tests and instruments are never literal translations, as literal translation does not ensure that the same construct is being measured identically in the original and translated instruments. One should also take into account cultural differences between the populations of test takers, and adapt the tests and instruments accordingly. The adaptation process ensures that the same meaning is retained across cultures and languages (Geisinger, 1994; Hambleton, 2005). In other words, the test should not only be *translated* from one language to another but it should also be *adapted* from one language and culture to another language and culture. The term *transadaptation* aptly describes the desired process: Transadaptation consists of closely translating those test items that can be adequately rendered in the target language, and changing other items which, in simple translation, might yield measurement that is linguistically, culturally, or psychometrically inappropriate. The transadaptation process may also involve removing some items and replacing them with others that are more appropriate for the target language test takers.

Testing Examinees in Their Native Language

Generally speaking, unless the aim is to test foreign language proficiency, a test should be administered in the examinee's native language, since examinees can express their ability best in their native tongue. Examinees who take a test in a language other than their native language sometimes cannot fully comprehend instructions, tasks, and questions. They also may not know some of the basic concepts and idioms that are familiar to native speakers of the language. Consequently, they are not able to adequately demonstrate their knowledge and skills. In cases where an examinee is not fully proficient in the language in which the test is administered, the reliability and validity of the measurement instrument might be compromised, and if a score is less reliable and the inferences drawn are not valid, then the test may also be less fair.

Testing organizations and companies should produce preparation materials that are accessible to people who speak different languages. These materials should preferably be available in all of the languages the test has been translated and adapted into, since in many cases, those who use test adaptations are minorities who may not be familiar with various item types, time pressure, and scoring methods. Explanations in the different languages are also needed for score reports that are sent to examinees, parents, educational institutions, or other organizations.

It should be noted, however, that testing in the majority language (and not in the examinee's native language) is, in some cases, the best option from a validity perspective. This is the case, for example, in employment testing, where knowing the local language (dominant language) is a key to functioning and succeeding on the job (Hough, Oswald, & Ployhart, 2001).

Issues to Consider When Constructing Cross-Lingual Tests

When speaking of tests and instruments intended for examinees from different cultural or linguistic backgrounds, the question is whether to provide a new test in the examinee's native language or translate and adapt an existing test. To answer this question, several issues have to be considered (see Allalouf & Hanani, 2010; Stansfield, 2003).

The first issue is the purpose of the test. Sometimes the purpose will dictate that the test be in a language that is not the examinee's native language; for example, when foreign language ability is being assessed, or when tests are constructed for employment purposes in a context where proficiency in the majority language is a work requirement. The second issue is that of cost efficiency. Translating and adapting tests is an expensive undertaking, as there are many steps and extensive reviews built into the process. The budget allocated for the process and the number of examinees taking the test are central issues in the decision of whether to adapt a test. If the number of examinees is small, the cost for each examinee may be too high. Another issue to be considered is the degree to which language impacts the ability to solve test items. Math questions are not always influenced or substantially changed by translation. On the other hand, verbal reasoning questions, which often have connotations that differ across languages and cultures, might change as a result of translation. These considerations should be kept in mind when making a decision about whether to adapt an existing test or construct a new test in the examinee's native language.

There are two main contexts in which translation and adaptation of tests (transadaptation) takes place (International Test Commission, 2010):

1. Translation and adaptation of *existing* tests and instruments. In this case, tests and instruments that were originally developed in a particular language for use in some national context have to be made appropriate for use in one or more other languages or national contexts. The aim of the transadaptation process is to produce a test or instrument with psychometric qualities comparable to those of the original. This practice is employed for the PET (Psychometric Entrance Test), which is used for higher-education admissions in Israel (Beller, Gafni, & Hanani, 2005).

2. Development of *new* tests and instruments for international use. The purpose of new tests is a comparison among examinees from different countries—for example, PISA (Programme for International Student Assessment), TIMSS (Third International

Mathematics and Science Study), and PIRLS (Progress in International Reading Literacy Study). In this instance, tests and instruments are intended for international comparison from the outset, and so versions for use in different languages or different national contexts can be developed simultaneously, which is an advantage. The problem lies in the size of the operation: the large number of versions that need to be developed and the many people who are involved in the development process. Here, too, the aim of the transadaptation process is to produce comparable tests and instruments across languages, so that the comparisons made and the conclusions drawn will be reliable.

Methods and Designs for Cross-Lingual Assessment

Various psychometric challenges arise in the context of assessing linguistically diverse populations of examinees. These challenges affect the design and use of assessments and assessment scores. When translating and adapting tests or instruments from a source language (SL) to a target language (TL), there are three types of bias that may occur: construct bias, method bias, and item bias (van de Vijver & Hambleton, 1996; Yi Hsiu, Chen-Yueh, & Ping-Kun, 2005):

1. *Construct bias* occurs when the construct being measured shows discrepancy across cultures (e.g., items dealing with the connection between social and environmental values, as these concepts differ from culture to culture).

2. *Method bias* occurs when there is a difference in the extent to which certain groups are familiar with the measurement or assessment format (e.g., open-ended or multiple-choice items). Construct bias and method bias are usually caused by cultural factors.

3. *Item bias* occurs when the meaning—and as a result, the psychometric characteristics of an item—are altered by the translation, or when the translation is poor, or when there is inappropriate item content for one or more cultural groups.

The challenge for test developers is to translate and adapt a test so that equivalence is achieved between the original and the adapted test—that is, to create comparable tests in different languages and ensure fair testing. The greater the similarity between the SL and the TL, the greater the number of comparisons that can be made and the more useful are the conclusions that can be drawn.

In order to achieve valid cross-lingual assessment and to minimize any negative effects that linguistic diversity might have on assessment design and use, testing organizations and companies must produce equivalent and comparable test forms. Those involved in the transadaptation process should be aware of the methods and designs that need to be used and consult relevant materials, including the existing standards and guidelines, as well as academic research in relevant journals. The process of translating and adapting should follow a detailed guide that prescribes a series of consecutive stages, the aim of which is to achieve a high degree of similarity between the translated and original items, and at the same time to reduce any form of bias.

The process described below is based both on substantial testing experience and many empirical studies (Angoff & Cook, 1988; Geisinger, 1994; Hambleton, 2005; Hambleton & Patsula, 1999; Stansfield, 2003; Zucker, Miska, Alaniz, & Guzman, 2005). For decades, a lot of research was done regarding cross-cultural comparisons of psychological traits and constructs among members of different cultures, but Israel's National Institute of Testing and Evaluation (NITE) was among the first to undertake the translation and adaptation of high-stakes tests intended for higher-education admissions. Because Arabic is one of Israel's two official languages (alongside Hebrew), and because Israel is home to a considerable number of immigrants from different countries, NITE made it a priority to address the issue of how to process, in a fair and valid manner, applications to higher-education institutions of people who do not have full command of the Hebrew language. As a result, a process of translating and adapting tests was developed (Beller & Gafni, 1995; Beller et al., 2005). This section describes those stages as implemented in two contexts: before and after test administration.

Before Test Administration

Creating a Team of Translators and Reviewers

The first step in the transadaptation process should be the creation of a team of translators and reviewers. A team is much preferable to a single translator, as a team offers a variety of approaches and perspectives, and thus ensures that the right decisions will be made and a good adaptation produced. The team should include:

- A *coordinator* responsible for the whole process of the transadaptation. This person is also responsible for documenting the process, including difficulties that arise and solutions found. This documentation should also include a list of the differences between the items in the translated version and the original one.

- *Professional translators* who are fluent in both languages, familiar with both cultures, and preferably from different backgrounds. They should have knowledge of both the test's subject matter and the principles of test development and also have good writing skills in the TL.

- *Reviewers* who are fluent in both languages and familiar with both cultures. It is important that they be from different backgrounds and countries/regions of origin, as special attention must be given to the different dialects of a language.

- A *psychometrician* who has a good knowledge of test development and other psychometric issues.

A study conducted at the NITE (Gafni, Cohen, & Hanani, 2006) systematically investigated the variance between tests that were transadapted from the same source test by independent teams. The conclusion reached was that for high-stakes tests transadapted by teams of experts working independently, the amount of variance that can be attributed to the transadaptation process is about 6% of the standard deviation of the scores. It is larger for more verbally loaded tests than for tests that are less verbally loaded. Moreover, transadaptation variance is not necessarily smaller when the TL and the SL are closely related.

Ensuring Construct Relevancy and Equivalence

In order to overcome the problem of construct bias mentioned above, persons familiar with both languages and cultures should agree that the same construct exists in the SL and culture and in the TL and culture, and that it is being measured in the same manner in those groups. If the construct being measured shows discrepancy across cultures, test developers should revise the adapted test, so that the same construct will be measured by both tests. If such a revision is not feasible, a decision should be made to either declare that the two tests do not measure the same construct or to discontinue the transadaptation process (see also van de Vijver & Hambleton, 1996).

Checking Sensitivity

Another important step before beginning the transadaptation process is ensuring that none of the item content is provocative or offensive to any of the groups. An item that is offensive to one or more of the groups (e.g., items dealing with political or religious subjects) must be omitted or replaced by appropriate items. For example, an item that deals with wine drinking should not be translated for use in cultural groups where alcohol is prohibited.

Determining the Design of Transadaptation

There are two main models of translation: forward translation and back translation.

Forward translation involves translating from the SL into the TL. When there is one SL, the translation is preferably conducted by two translators, each from a different cultural and scientific background, and working independently. Differences between the two versions of the translation are discussed, the best translation is selected, and the two versions are merged into a single version. The advantage of the double translation is that it achieves a high degree of equivalency between the SL and the TL versions. This method is used, for example, in translating TIMSS instruments (see Maxwell, 1996).

When there are *two parallel source versions* in two different languages, the parallel independent translations are conducted into the TL from each of the SLs. The two translations are merged in the course of the process into a single translation. The advantage of this procedure is that it keeps the translation from being too influenced by the linguistic and cultural properties of one specific SL. This process is in use in a number of international tests, for example, the PISA test (Grisay, 2003; Grisay, de Jong, Gebhardt, Berezner, & Halleux-Monseur, 2007), in which two equivalent source versions (an English one and a French one) that were developed at the same time are translated by every country participating in the research into two target versions— one translated from English, and one translated from French. These two translated versions are merged in the course of the process into a single translation.

Back translation involves translating the original test from the SL into the TL, and then having a different translator translate the TL version back into the SL. The back-translated version and the source version are compared and judged with regard to their equivalency. Discrepancies between the source and the back-translated versions may indicate problems in the initial forward translation. The assumption is that if the initial forward translation was done well, the back-translated version and the source will be similar. The purpose of the back translation is then to identify and correct errors in the forward translation. There are a number of problems with relying solely on back translation to examine the quality of the translated test (Stansfield, 2003). First, this procedure focuses on the source and not on the translated version, since what is being compared are the two versions of the source language. This is why the possibility of finding errors in the translated version is quite small, and consequently the resulting translated version is not equivalent enough to the source version. Secondly, when a translator knows that the initial forward translation will be validated by a back translation procedure, it may influence the quality of the forward translation. By producing a very literal and unnatural forward translation, the translator can ensure that the back translation will produce a document that is highly similar to the source version. However, a literal forward translation is not recommended; natural and fluent language is needed.

The advantage of forward translation—especially when the translation is done by several translators—is that it achieves maximum equivalency between the translated and source versions, because a great deal of attention is given to both throughout the process. The commonly accepted opinion is that back translation can be used as a quality-control tool and as a useful addition to forward translation but cannot be used as the sole tool.

Translating and Adapting (Transadaptation)

When the transadaptation design is determined, the SL(s) version(s) is (are) submitted for translation. In order to ensure that the translated version of the test is clear and fluent, and at the same time equivalent to the SL version, translators must pay attention to the following: that the construct being measured is the same for both the translated and the source versions; that the meaning of each item does not become altered because of the translation; that the difficulty level of the translated items is similar to that of the original items (same difficulty level of vocabulary, syntax, etc.); and that all measurement units, currency units, place names, etc., are familiar to all test takers.

Reviewing

When the translation(s) is (are) completed, the translated version and the source version should be submitted to a number of experts for critical review. The best way of doing such a review is to first check that every item in the translated version stands on its own merits; that is, that the item has one and only one answer, and that there are no hints in the item that point to the correct answer. Solving an item is a good way to conduct a review. If no answer or a wrong answer is given, it suggests that there is a problem with the question that may have been caused by a poor translation. The reviewers need to ensure that the language is fluent, that the wording is clear, that the words being used are not too difficult, and that the meaning of the words used is the same in all dialects of the language. The next step in the review process is to compare the translated version to the source version, ensuring that the translation is accurate and carries the same meaning and difficulty level. A group of translators, experts in the subject area, and psychometricians then discuss the reviewers' comments, and change the translation according to the suggestions made. It must be noted that the transadaptation process typically reveals almost every problem that exists in the source version. Everything that is vague, ambiguous, or unclear in the source version becomes difficult or impossible to translate. In fact, translating is an excellent way of reviewing. Several organizations—especially those that develop international tests—work simultaneously on the source and translated versions, and so problems arising during the translation process may result in changes to the source version.

When the review is completed and recommended changes have been made, a back translation is sometimes done. At this stage, the translated test is translated back (orally or in writing) to the SL, and any inaccuracies found are corrected.

As mentioned above, different organizations use back translation in different ways. Some organizations consider back translation to be the main part of the adaptation and use it in the first stage of the process. Others consider back translation only as another step along the way, as an additional aid to ensuring the quality of the translation.

Key Review

During the stages described above, the translators and reviewers have both the source and the translated versions in front of them. At this final stage, the translated version has to be checked without the "help" of the source version. In other words, the items of the translated test must be solved by qualified reviewers, and if an error is found, the item is checked again to find out whether the error is due to the translation. If this is the case, the item has to be corrected or replaced.

Field Testing and Item and Test Analysis

Even after the process of translating and adapting has been completed, there may still be problems that go unnoticed. Therefore it is recommended that the items (and test forms) be field-tested before being administered operationally. In that way, item analysis can be performed and item statistics used to assess the psychometric quality of the items. Differential item functioning (DIF) analysis should be done to check whether the adapted items have the same psychometric characteristics as the items of the source version (see next section). When the complete adapted test form (and not only each separate item) is field-tested, test characteristics such as difficulty and reliability can be assessed.

Documenting the Transadaptation Process

All of the steps in the transadaptation process should be documented, including translators' decisions, reviewers' comments, and the changes made, so that all considerations taken into account during the process can be reviewed and reconsidered, if need be.

After Test Administration

Once a test has been constructed and administered, a four-step procedure should be implemented to analyze the items and the test, and to ensure a high degree of similarity between forms in different languages and, by extension, in the meaning of the scores from these forms. The four recommended steps are (1) performing item analysis, (2) detecting construct bias by checking that the test versions have equivalent dimensional structure, (3) detecting item bias by applying DIF analysis, and (4) linking the scores of the SL and TL test versions (International Test Commission, 2010; Sireci & Allalouf, 2003). These procedures may need to be compromised if the sample size is small, as is sometimes the case in cross-cultural assessments.

Performing Item Analysis

Following test administration, item analysis is performed. This is, in fact, the first step taken after the administration of any test, but when dealing with translated items, there is a higher chance that some items might lack sufficient psychometric quality (i.e., not be reliable or valid enough). This often happens when items have not been pilot-tested before administration, and also, to a lesser extent, when items have been piloted. If an item does not meet the minimum level of psychometric quality, it should be removed from the scoring process.

Detecting Construct Bias

The data gathered during test administration should be used to ensure that the score calculated for each test version represents the same construct in each language group. In operational terms the purpose is to check whether the relationship *among* the items in each language group is similar. This analysis can be done using factor analysis, weighted multidimensional scaling, or other methods (Georgas, Weiss, van de Vijver,

& Saklofske, 2003; Sireci & Allalouf, 2003). It is expected that tests that are less verbally loaded (e.g., mathematics tests) will be more likely to yield a similar construct after translation.

Detecting Differential Item Functioning

According to the commonly accepted definition of DIF, an item functions differently across groups when examinees of equal ability but from different groups (in this case, different language groups) are not equally likely to respond correctly to that item. When DIF analysis is performed and DIF is detected, the next step is usually to investigate the reasons for it, so as to determine whether the DIF item is also biased against one of the language groups. A comprehensive distinction between the two terms, *DIF* and *item bias*, was made by Zieky (1993): "It is important to realize that DIF is not a synonym for bias . . . judgment is required to determine whether or not the difference in difficulty shown by the DIF index is unfairly related to group membership. The judgment of fairness is based on whether or not the difference in difficulty is believed to be related to the construct being measured" (p. 340). It should be noted that DIF detection can take place before test administration, using a judging-type procedure (Hambleton & Jones, 1995), but is usually carried out statistically, using empirical data, after the test forms have been administered. Among the main methods employed for this purpose are delta plot transformed item difficulty (TID), Mantel–Haenszel, logistic regression, IRT-based, and SIBTEST, each of which has its advantages (see Holland & Wainer, 1993; see also Rogers & Swaminathan, Chapter 8, this volume).

Past studies of DIF in cross-lingual assessment contexts have found that, generally, items translated from an SL tend to vary in terms of the degree of DIF detected. Some item types may have higher DIF than others. Angoff and Cook (1988) analyzed the equivalence between the Scholastic Aptitude Test (SAT; used for admission to higher-education institutions in the United States), and its Spanish-language counterpart, the Prueba de Aptitud Academica (PAA). They found that verbal items containing a large amount of text (e.g., reading comprehension items) have lower DIF than items containing a small amount of text (e.g., verbal analogies). Their explanation was that in short items every word is critical, and every translation problem has a considerable impact on item characteristics. Conversely, no DIF is expected in nonverbal items such as math or figural items, as noted by Gafni and Melamed (1991). Some studies have listed the possible causes for DIF existing across test versions in different languages. For example, Allalouf, Hambleton, and Sireci (1999) studied the translation from Hebrew into Russian of the verbal reasoning domain of the PET. They found that DIF is likely to occur if there are differences between SL and TL in (1) word difficulty, (2) item format, (3) item content, and (4) cultural relevance.

Based on these findings, test constructors and translators should be aware of DIF studies and take them into account when adapting a test from one language to another. This step will enable them to avoid translating items that may have a cultural bias and content that gives an advantage to test takers from one of the language groups. This will also help to identify TL words of comparable difficulty and to preserve original item format.

Scoring and Linking

If the DIF analysis reveals that the psychometric characteristics of certain items have been altered by the translation, an action is needed, but the exact steps to be taken will depend on the assessment's linking design. If common items are used for the linking, the DIF items should not be used for linking. If there is no linking, the no-DIF items should be used for scoring both test versions (source and target). This will make the source and target versions more similar psychometrically, and their scores more comparable. Before the DIF items are omitted, they should be examined carefully for bias by experts in the subject area, since in very rare cases, as pointed out by Ellis (1989), there may be real differences—rooted in experience, knowledge, or culture—in the way a certain language group performs on specific test items. These differences may be considered relevant, and in such cases the DIF items are not to be omitted from the scoring process.

An adapted test can be linked to the SL test even if some items in the TL function differently from the SL items. This linking can be achieved by using only the non-DIF translated items as common items (anchor). However, this should be done carefully since deleting too many DIF items can result in an anchor that is too short for equating (see Sireci, 1997, for a comprehensive discussion, and Rapp & Allalouf, 2003, for ways to evaluate cross-lingual equating). In some cases, when there is no need for cross-lingual or cross-cultural comparisons, linking is not necessary. In other cases, when such comparisons are NEEDED, linking has to be done. This is the case, of course, when the test is a high-stakes test.

Standards, Guidelines, Frameworks, and Future Directions

Researchers and practitioners in the field of testing, and assessment developers in particular, can use existing standards, guidelines, and frameworks to arrive at a valid assessment of linguistically diverse populations. The "Fairness" section of the Standards for Educational and Psychological Testing (2014)—developed by the American Educational Research Association (AERA), the American Psychological Association (APA), and the National Council on Measurement in Education (NCME) in 2014—offers detailed instructions on how to adapt tests from one language and culture to another language and culture. Another important source is Hambleton and Patsula (1999), who offer comprehensive guidelines for adapting tests from SL to TL.

The preeminent source for the translation and adaptation of tests is the International Test Commission (ITC) (2010) Guidelines on Adapting Tests, which was developed by a committee representing a number of international testing organizations (see also Muñiz, Elosua, Padilla, & Hambleton, Chapter 17, this volume). These guidelines are applicable wherever tests need to be adapted from one cultural setting to another, regardless of whether there is a need for translation. The guidelines fall into four main categories: (1) cultural context, (2) technicalities of instrument development and adaptation, (3) test administration, and (4) documentation and interpretation. A new study—"Guidelines Versus Practices in Cross-Lingual Assessment: A Disconcerting Disconnect" by Rios and Sireci (2014)—offers a comprehensive review of articles (published in English from January 1950 to January 1, 2013) and tries to determine whether the methodologies related to test translation process and to evaluation of cross-lingual measurement bias have improved since the initial publication of the ITC Guidelines in 1994. The authors analyze articles published pre- and post-1994, and compare the test translation and validation activities described in the articles to those recommended in the guidelines. Evaluation of method and item bias by post-ITC studies was found to be conducted at similar rates to pre-ITC research. Rios and Sireci conclude that "Results demonstrated that although reporting reliability estimates and statistically analyzing construct equivalence improved since publication of the *Guidelines*, the majority of test development and validation practices in the published literature have not embraced the recommendations put forth by the International Test Commission" (p. 289).

Looking Ahead

Even though, as a rule, a test should be administered in the examinee's native language, sometimes there are instances where for several reasons (e.g., budget restrictions, a group being too small for equating/linking) flexible solutions can be applied while safeguarding the crucial elements of a test. One such solution is providing a glossary of translations (in several languages) of difficult words. The glossary can be changed to accommodate the languages needed. A good example is the combined Hebrew–English version of the PET. In the verbal and quantitative sections of this test, each question is presented in both Hebrew and English, and difficult words are translated into several other languages, such as Russian, Portuguese, Dutch, Italian, German, Hungarian, and Amharic (as of 2014).

Looking ahead to the future, Austermuhl (2001, 2013) has reviewed several information resources, software products, and online services that can help translators. He recommends incorporating machine translation programs into the translation process. Software tools for translation and assessment of translation quality will play an important role in the future, initially as a rough tool for human translators and later as a more sophisticated aid. Automated tools, such as Google Translate, are improving, and in a few years may play a useful role in test adaptations.

*   *   *

Cross-lingual assessment takes place when a test is constructed and used to assess people across different languages. This chapter focused on cross-lingual assessment in the educational field and is more applicable to high-stakes testing, where accuracy and fairness are of major importance. After discussing the term *cross-lingual assessment* and its importance in educational assessment, the chapter dealt with the many methods and designs used to achieve reliable, valid, and fair cross-lingual assessment. The last section reviewed the main standards, guidelines, and frameworks that exist in this area and gave some hints regarding the possible technology that will shape the future of cross-lingual assessment.

REFERENCES

Allalouf, A., Hambleton, R. K., & Sireci, S. G. (1999). Identifying the causes of DIF in translated verbal items. *Journal of Educational Measurement, 36*, 185–198.

Allalouf, A., & Hanani, P. (2010). Test translation and adaptation. In E. Baker, B. McGaw, & P. Peterson (Eds.), *International encyclopedia of education* (3rd ed., pp. 166–169). Oxford, UK: Elsevier

American Educational Research Association, American Psychological Association, & National Council on Measurement in Education. (2014). *Standards for educational and psychological testing.* Washington, DC: Authors.

Angoff, W. H., & Cook, L. L. (1988). *Equating the scores of the Prueba de Aptitud Academica and the Scholastic Aptitude Test* (College Board Report No. 88-2). New York: College Entrance Examination Board.

Austermuhl, F. (2001). *Electronic tools for translators.* Manchester, UK: St. Jerome.

Austermuhl, F. (2013). Future (and not-so-future) trends in the teching of translation technology. *Revista Tradumàtica: Tecnologies de la Traducció, 11*, 326–337. Retrieved from *http://revistas.uab.cat/tradumatica/article/view/46/pdf.*

Beller, M., & Gafni, N. (1995). Equating and validating translated Scholastic Aptitude Tests: The Israeli case. In G. Ben-Shakhar & A. Lieblich (Eds.), *Studies in psychology in honor of Solomon Kugelmass.* Jerusalem: Magnes.

Beller, M., Gafni, N., & Hanani, P. (2005). Constructing, adapting, and validating admissions tests in multiple languages: The Israeli case. In R. K. Hambleton, P. F. Merenda, & C. D. Spielberger (Eds.), *Adapting educational and psychological tests for cross-cultural assessment* (pp. 297–319). Mahwah, NJ: Erlbaum.

Boake, C. (2002). From the Binet–Simon to the Wechsler–Bellevue: Tracing the history of intelligence testing. *Journal of Clinical and Experimental Psychology, 24*, 383–405.

de Klerk, G. (2008). Cross-cultural testing. In M. Born, C. D. Foxcroft, & R. Butter (Eds.), *Online readings in testing and assessment.* International Test Commission. Available at *www.intestcom.org/Publications/ORTA.php.*

Ellis, B. B. (1989). Differential item functioning: Implications for test translation. *Journal of Applied Psychology, 74*, 912–921.

Gafni, N., Cohen, Y., & Hanani, P. (2006, July). *A comparison of parallel test transadaptations.* Paper presented in the Fifth Conference of the International Test Commission, Brussels, Belgium.

Gafni, N., & Melamed, E. (1991). *Equating different language versions of a psychometric test.* Research Report No. 148. Jerusalem: NITE.

Geisinger, K. F. (1994). Cross-cultural normative assessment: Translation and adaptation issues influencing the normative interpretation of assessment instruments. *Psychological Assessment, 6*, 304–312.

Georgas, J., Weiss, L. G., van de Vijver, F. J. R., & Saklofske, D. H. (Eds.). (2003). *Culture and children's intelligence: Cross-cultural analysis of the WISC-III.* New York: Academic Press.

Grisay, A. (2003). Translation procedures in OECD/PISA 2000 international assessment. *Language Testing, 20*(2), 225–240.

Grisay, A., de Jong, J. H. A. L., Gebhardt, E., Berezner, A., & Halleux-Monseur, B. (2007). Translation equivalence across PISA countries. *Journal of Applied Measurement, 8*(3), 249–266.

Hambleton, R. K. (2005). Issues, designs, and technical guidelines for adapting tests in multiple languages and cultures. In R. K. Hambleton, P. Merenda, & C. Spielberger (Eds.), *Adapting educational and psychological tests for cross-cultural assessment* (pp. 3–38). Mahwah, NJ: Erlbaum.

Hambleton, R. K., & Jones, R. W. (1995). Comparison of empirical and judgmental procedures for detecting differential item functioning. *Educational Research Quarterly, 18*, 21–36.

Hambleton, R. K., & Patsula, L. (1999). Increasing the validity of adapted tests: Myths to be avoided and guidelines for improving test adaptation practices. *Applied Testing Technology, 1*, 1–16.

Holland, P., & Wainer, H. (Eds.). (1993). *Differential item functioning.* Hillsdale, NJ: Erlbaum.

Hough, L. M., Oswald, F. L., & Ployhart, R. E. (2001). Determinants, detection and amelioration of adverse impact in personnel selection procedures: Issues, evidence, and lessons learned. *International Journal of Selection and Assessment, 9*(1, 2), 152–194.

International Test Commission. (2010). International Test Commission guidelines for translating and adapting tests. Available at *www.intestcom.org.*

Maxwell, B. (1996). Translation and cultural adaptation of the survey instruments. In M. O. Martin & D. L. Kelly (Eds.), *Third International Mathematics and Science Study (TIMSS) technical report* (Vol. 1, pp. 1–8). Chestnut Hill, MA: Boston College.

Rapp, J., & Allalouf, A. (2003). Evaluating cross-lingual equating. *International Journal of Testing, 3*, 101–117.

Rios, J., & Sireci, S. G. (2014). Guidelines versus practices in cross-lingual assessment: A disconcerting disconnect. *International Journal of Testing, 14*, 289–312.

Sireci, S. G. (1997). Problems and issues in linking tests across languages. *Educational Measurement: Issues and Practice, 16*, 12–19.

Sireci, S. G., & Allalouf, A. (2003). Appraising item equivalence across multiple languages and cultures. *Language Testing, 20*, 148–166.

Stansfield, C. W. (2003). Test translation and adaptation in public education in the USA. *Language Testing, 20*(2), 188–206.

van de Vijver, F. J. R., & Hambleton, R. K. (1996). Translating tests: Some practical guidelines. *European Psychologist, 1*(2), 89–99.

Yi-Hsiu, L., Chen-Yueh, C., & Ping-Kun, C. (2005). Cross-cultural research and back-translation. *Sport Journal, 8*(4), 1–10.

Zieky, M. (1993). Practical questions in the use of DIF statistics in test development. In P. Holland & H. Wainer (Eds.), *Differential item functioning* (pp. 337–347). Hillsdale, NJ: Erlbaum.

Zucker, S., Miska, M., Alaniz, L. G., & Guzman, L. (2005). *Transadaptation: Publishing assessments in world languages.* San Antonio, TX: Harcourt Assessment.

CHAPTER 16

On Item Pools, Swimming Pools, Birds with Webbed Feet, and the Professionalization of Multilingual Assessment

Fons J. R. van de Vijver and Ype H. Poortinga

The first half of this chapter's title refers to striking examples of how meaning can become distorted in translation. "Swimming pools" was the outcome of a translation, followed by a back translation between English and Japanese of the term "pools" (of items). An item asking where birds with "webbed feet" are most likely to live was answered correctly ("in the sea") by a high proportion of Swedish test takers; the Swedish term for *webbed feet*, which is *swimming feet*, made the correct answer virtually a giveaway. These two examples have been taken from Ron Hambleton who, in addition to several other major contributions reported in this book, has become a central figure in the professionalization of multilingual assessment. In the early 1990s he took the initiative to develop *Guidelines for Translating and Adapting Tests* (an updated version can be downloaded from *www.intestcom.org/upload/sitefiles/40.pdf*; see also Hambleton, 1994). These guidelines have become the leading framework for test translation and adaptation, and have made Ron Hambleton the most frequently quoted author on test adaptation, as counted by the number of citations listed by Google Scholar.

In this chapter we examine frameworks that can guide transfer of source instruments to new linguistic contexts. Such a transfer implies the transition to another cultural context. Issues in multilingual assessment and in cross-cultural assessment are closely related (see also Allalouf & Hanani, Chapter 15, this volume). Therefore, we begin with a very brief overview of the history of cross-cultural test use. In the second section we address the development of procedures for transfer of tests and their adaptation across cultures and languages. In the third and final section we provide a perspective on how testing can be further improved by addressing inherent difficulties rather than trying to sidestep them.

Early Approaches to Test Transfer

There are two main reasons why a test developed in one society or group, the source culture (or source language), is to be administered elsewhere, the target culture (or target language). The first reason is to use the test as an instrument to assess the performance of test takers in the target culture. The second reason is to compare the scores of test takers from the source and target cultures. In both instances, transfer makes sense only if the same aspect of behavior is being assessed across cultures and there is equivalence of the underlying constructs. When quantitative comparisons are to be made, there is the additional requirement that a given score has to have the same meaning—that is, there has to be equivalence of score levels. Comparisons of performance among cultural groups on such instruments can be problematic. A Dutch national test of educational achievement, administered yearly to pupils at the end of their primary school period, illustrates how this comparability can be jeopardized. The reading part tends to show more bias (differential item functioning) than the math part in the comparison of mainstream and immigrant Dutch children; items in the math part that use more language are more biased than items using less language (Van Schilt-Mol, 2007).

Psychological measurement was initially aimed at measuring the speed of elementary perceptual and cognitive processes, initiated by Galton (1869) in the 19th century (see also Geisinger & Usher-Tate, Chapter 1, this volume). This kind of measure turned out to be poorly related to performance on everyday cognitive tasks. More success came when tests were developed that consisted of a set of items sampled from a psychological domain; the predecessor of the intelligence test, developed in France by Binet and Simon (1907) in the beginning of the 20th century, became the historical marker point. Most tests of cognitive abilities, and later on questionnaires for personality traits and attitudes, followed the same principle. They consist of a set of items deemed to be representative of the domain of behavior to which the scores are generalized.

Looking at the history of test use, one can only be struck by the optimism of early test developers and users that instruments would show equivalence of score levels across a culturally wide range of (if not all) populations, and could serve as common standards in assessment. This was most evident in the use of intelligence tests to assess group differences ("racial" differences) in intelligence. Especially tests for inductive and deductive reasoning were believed to address the capacity for such processes independent of context (e.g., Porteus, 1937). When the notion of culture-free tests (Cattell, 1940) had been given up as untenable (Frijda & Jahoda, 1966), a more moderate position was taken, asserting that tests could be culture-fair (e.g., Cattell & Cattell, 1963). Requirements for culture fairness amounted to equal exposure to (or opportunity to learn) relevant skills and knowledge, and equal familiarity with item format. As it was difficult to find out in practice whether such conditions had been met, culture fairness came to mean that all test takers should be entirely *un*familiar with the item content and format. Empirically this was best demonstrated by findings of equal test score distributions.

Most of the time, however, expectations of equal or approximately equal test score distributions, preempting any cultural differences in the traits or abilities targeted by a test, are unrealistic; and in fact, this misconception defeated culture fairness as a psychometrically feasible notion. Acknowledging these limitations, Jensen (1980) referred to "culture-reduced tests" to indicate that well-designed tests can capture valid cross-cultural differences in any psychological domain. His evidence was based on finding similar factor structures of intelligence batteries across cultural groups and equal regression lines that link intelligence to school or work outcomes. Both lines of evidence have come under scrutiny. Nowadays identity of factor structures is seen as possibly too weak a criterion for establishing comparability of scores across cultural groups; this line of critique often goes back to structural equation modeling (Dolan, Roorda, & Wicherts, 2004). Equality of regression lines across groups has been widely documented by Schmidt, Hunter, and colleagues (e.g., Schmidt & Hunter, 1998). More recently, this line of evidence has also been challenged by the argument that the regression models used could be biased against minority members (Aguinis, Culpepper, & Pierce, 2010). In addition, doubts have been expressed as to whether criterion scores are always unbiased; criterion scores assigned by supervisors could be suspect because of the potential ethnic bias in such scores. Finally, doubts have been expressed as to whether it is realistic, in societies that are segregated along ethnic lines and in which discrimination is common, to take identity of regression lines as prerequisite for comparability.

Test usage was also attacked from other corners. First, there was a movement criticizing the role of psychological tests in society. The anti-test movement was particularly strong in the United States in the 1970s and 1980s (Gould, 1996). More recently, a similar movement briefly surfaced shortly after the abolishment of apartheid in South Africa, where there was a tendency to prohibit psychological testing because under apartheid. Psychological tests were seen as providing legitimacy to discrimination (the privileged educational and social background of whites ensured that they showed higher scores than other groups, thereby increasing the likelihood of a favorable selection outcome). Second, there were theoretical objections against the use of typically Western-based instruments in other cultural contexts. The most far-reaching challenge to the use of common instruments on theoretical grounds was by proponents of various forms of cultural relativism. Here psychological functioning is seen as inherently shaped by culture and thus behavior as incomparable. In schools of indigenous psychology the use of Western methods and instruments has been criticized widely as Western imposition (Kim, Yang, & Hwang, 2006), and the need for culture-specific methods of assessment has been emphasized. In the world of tests and psychometrics a universalist position remained dominant that presumes a psychological unity of humankind with scope for common traits and abilities (Berry, Poortinga, Breugelmans, Chasiotis, & Sam, 2011). The two positions of universalism and relativism with the associated methodological approaches of qualitative and quantitative research were viewed as incompatible. As a consequence, progress in the field stalled for quite a while. Only lately are there attempts to transcend this dichotomy and to treat the two positions as complementary rather than mutually exclusive (Cheung, van de Vijver, & Leong, 2011).

If equivalence of test scores is neither a given nor ruled out a priori on theoretical grounds, the question can be raised as to how equivalence can be achieved and demonstrated by test users and test developers. Currently we see four partly overlapping approaches: (1) ignoring equivalence issues or assuming that scores are comparable; (2) refining culture-reduced tests; (3) limiting cross-cultural test use to instruments and interpretations with demonstrated equivalence; and (4) adapting tests to new target populations.

Ignoring equivalence issues is rather common in various fields. Intelligence testing is the main area of concern, no doubt because of the social stigma attached to low IQ. Raven's (1989) matrices tests have the reputation of being more or less culture fair, although score levels of national samples are correlated with gross national product (GNP) per capita and even more with school education (Brouwers, van de Vijver, & van Hemert, 2009). Many scales and questionnaires in social psychology were and are being administered and interpreted without any concern about a possible lack of equivalence, even though there is ample evidence to the effect that such scales are not immune to cultural bias. Response styles (He & van de Vijver, 2013) and the reference group effect (i.e., a tendency of respondents to rate themselves against their own social environment; van de Gaer, Grisay, Schulz, & Gebhardt, 2012) are examples of distortions that can affect self-reports. A common problem of ignoring equivalence issues is that observed cross-cultural differences are difficult to interpret, as these may be due to differences in the target construct, measurement issues, or their combination. So, if tests are used across groups or in pools of test takers varying in cultural background, assuming equivalence should not be an option.

We also see problems in the refinement of instruments if the aim is to eliminate the influence of cultural factors on test scores. We acknowledge that the pursuit of such tests is relevant from a test development perspective: Can we improve current tests and come up with a valid evaluation of true cross-cultural similarities and differences? After so many unsuccessful attempts with numerous types of stimuli and responses, it is unrealistic to assume that, in the near future, we will be able to distinguish between variance that is part of the target construct (or domain) and variance that is due to non-target-related sources of variance. Notably when cross-cultural differences in relevant background variables are large, such as educational differences in intelligence testing, the development of culture-reduced tests is beyond our reach. Given the poor viability of these first two approaches, we focus on the third (analysis of equivalence) and fourth (test adaptation) approaches in the next section.

Procedures for Test Transfer and Adaptation

One achievement of the last decades (with Ron Hambleton playing a pivotal role) is the appreciation that test transfer requires the combination of qualitative and quantitative strategies. It amounts to a combination of adequate test design (translation of items and instructions, and the analysis of item content with judgmental methods) and statistical analysis (an analysis of equivalence to check whether scores in the target population meet psychometric conditions for equivalence).

Analysis of Item Content and Translations

Close scrutiny of each item is necessary to identify possible peculiarities in meaning, or other reasons why that item might be inappropriate in a particular culture and should not be used. Experts are asked to give an opinion about the content of stimuli. Usually they evaluate for each item whether or not it belongs to the domain of behavior of interest, and whether or not it presupposes specific knowledge or experiences more readily available in one of the groups to be compared. For a proper evaluation, the judges should have an intimate knowledge of the cultures in a comparative study, as well as of the theory and notions behind an instrument. It has been known for a long time that the opinions of judges often do not match empirical findings on the equivalence of items; it has proven difficult to predict on which items a certain group will show a relatively low performance level (e.g., Tittle, 1982).

There is also an evident need for a careful check on translation quality whenever verbal stimuli or instructions are used cross-culturally (Brislin, 1980, 1986). Usually researchers are satisfied that translation equivalence has been attained when, after translation from the original language in the target language followed by independent back translation, the meaning of the original wording is reproduced more or less precisely. It is questionable whether this is enough; a language has many subtleties that may not be identified in forward–backward translation. The intricate role of language is perhaps best illustrated by the finding that bilinguals, when filling out a questionnaire in either of the two languages, adapt their answers somewhat according to the stereotypes which they hold about the culture concerned (e.g., Yang & Bond, 1980).

In the last 20 years many different procedures to develop and test the adequacy of translations have been proposed (Harkness, 2003); examples include committee approaches (teams of bilingual and bicultural professionals jointly translate an instrument); comparison of independently produced forward translations (followed by an adjudication procedure); and cognitive interviewing (administration of a translated instrument in a nonstandard manner, asking questions about the interpretation of items, and connotations of key words). In addition, standardized approaches to the assessment of translation quality have been proposed; an example can be found in the work by Hambleton and Zenisky (2011). Reviewers of a translated instrument are asked to answer questions about, among other things, language and cultural aspects, such as whether the item has the same or highly similar meaning in the two languages, whether the language of the source and target language version are of comparable difficulty, whether terms have been suitably adapted, and whether there are cultural differences that would have a differential effect on the likelihood of a response being chosen in the source or target language version.

Psychometric Analysis of Equivalence

Among test users it has long been recognized that transferred tests are likely to be biased, implying that test scores cannot be interpreted in the same way across cultural groups. At the same time, well-known Western instruments have been translated for use in non-Western as well as other Western countries, including intelligence batteries, such as the WAIS (Wechsler Adult Intelligence Scale) and the WISC (Wechsler Intelligence Scale for Children; e.g., Georgas, Weiss, van de Vijver, & Saklofske, 2003); personality inventories, such as the NEO PI-R (NEO Personality Inventory—Revised; McCrae & Allik, 2002); and scales for clinical diagnosis, such as the MMPI (Minnesota Multiphasic Personality Inventory; Butcher, 2004; Butcher, Mosch, Tsai, & Nezami, 2006). The success of such translations can be examined with psychometric methods designed to analyze whether scores obtained in various cultural groups are equivalent and can be compared, or are lacking in equivalence due to cultural bias. Here we distinguish four levels of equivalence (Fontaine, 2005; Poortinga, 1989).

Conceptual equivalence pertains to the question as to whether a given construct can be meaningfully defined in both the source group and the target group. A skill such as reading or a domain such as traffic rules does not appear to make sense in any illiterate rural society; as usually understood, these notions are not pertinent to the behavior repertoire of illiterate people. We like to emphasize that impressions are not always adequate to assess conceptual equivalence. For example, among the Rarámuri in Mexico there is no word for the emotion *guilt* as distinct from *shame*. However, differential patterns of reactions to guilt and shame scenarios largely corresponded to the patterns found in an international student sample, suggesting conceptual equivalence of guilt (Breugelmans & Poortinga, 2006).

Structural equivalence has to do with the question as to whether a test reflects the same construct or domain in each of the cultural groups that is being compared. This can be addressed by examining the structure of interrelations between the items. A scale is taken to be structurally equivalent when the factor structure of the items is similar across cultures (van de Vijver & Leung, 1997).

Metric equivalence, or measurement unit equivalence, implies that scaling units or steps on a measurement scale are the same across cultures. (This point can be illustrated with measurements of temperature where one degree of change represents a larger shift in temperature on a Celsius scale than on a Fahrenheit scale, which makes these scales metrically inequivalent.) Patterns of change (e.g., between pretest and posttest measures) can be meaningfully compared if conditions for metric equivalence are satisfied.

Full score (or scalar) equivalence implies that scores on a single variable can be compared at face value. For measures of the Big Five dimensions of the five-factor model, such claims have been made on the basis of both cross-cultural data (McCrae & Terracciano, 2007) and data from a large international set of personality data obtained in employment selection (Bartram, 2013). On the other hand, presumptions of full score equivalence of carefully constructed and analyzed measures in the PISA project have been challenged (Kreiner & Christensen, 2014).

Different traditions to test for equivalence have been developed. First, rooted in domains such as personality and survey research, there has been much interest in the question of whether constructs underlying scales can be compared across cultures. This structural equivalence was often studied using exploratory factor analysis. Agreement of factors obtained in these cultures was then computed (van de Vijver & Leung, 1997). Sufficiently high levels of factorial agreement were taken as evidence that the same underlying constructs were assessed. Second, rooted in education, there has been an emphasis on the application of item response theory (IRT) to identify the occurrence of anomalous items. Is item X biased in favor or against a specific cultural group? Various statistical procedures have been proposed, such as IRT and structural equation modeling (e.g., Hambleton, Swaminathan, & Rogers, 1991). It may be noted that educational tests usually have a much more narrow focus than personality instruments. As a consequence, the focus in education is much less on the establishment of unidimensionality and much more on the understanding of specific items and the comparison of total test scores across cultural groups.

Third, rooted in education but quickly picked up by psychology, a strong interest has developed in identifying items that do not function in the same way across different cultures. This development started with the publication in 1968 by Cleary and Hilton, who used an analysis of variance to identify anomalous items in an educational instrument. Their article led to a prolific development of hundreds of procedures to identify items that do not function in the same way across cultures (e.g., Zumbo, 2007). It is important to note that the statistical yield has not been matched by a substantive yield. The study of differential item functioning (DIF), as this tradition is usually labeled, has not produced a set of guidelines that specifies how items for cross-cultural instruments should be formulated (Linn, 1993).

Fourth, rooted in developments in statistical theory, notably structural equation modeling, procedures have been developed to test the equivalence at different levels together. All the levels of equivalence described above can be tested using structural equation modeling. These procedures are the most statistically advanced currently available. The procedures amount to a hierarchically nested set of statistical tests of the similarity of constructs, the metric to use these constructs, and the origin of the scale used (Vandenberg & Lance, 2000). It may seem preferable to choose the latter procedures, given their statistical superiority. However, practical applications of these procedures have revealed considerable difficulties. For example, when long instruments with complex factorial structures are tested or when equivalence is tested across a large number of cultures, the statistical evaluation of the fit is problematic. Fit statistics often suggest that scalar invariance is not supported, but with no clear indications whether the reason for this poor fit is substantive (i.e., due to misspecifications of the model or real lack of equivalence) or due to numerous small variations in parameters across cultures, which would not challenge the score comparisons across these cultures in any meaningful way. Another problem, also rather common in studies of item bias, is that fit statistics suggest changing the tested model and lifting invariance constraints on intercepts, whereas there is no psychological justification for implementing any specific change. In other words, statistical and substantive considerations often do not go hand in hand.

Types of Adaptations

Transfer of tests can take various forms. A distinction can be made between adoption, adaptation, and assembly (e.g., van de Vijver, 2015; van de Vijver & Poortinga, 2005). With *adoption* the format and content of the test items for a target group stays as close as possible to the original. With verbal tests the focus is on a translation that is as precise as possible. As an example of how translation can be problematic, we refer to the term *race*. In the United States the term is used when asking for biographical information, although this may be controversial. In South Africa the term may also be used, despite its historically very negative connotations. In Europe the term is rather abhorrent and *ethnicity* has to be used. The example clearly shows the limitation of close translations. Such a translation of the term does not necessarily produce the best possible equivalent concept in the target language.

Adaptation refers to adoption of part of the items (or subtests in a battery or multiple scale instrument), and modification of elements that do not transfer well are changed or replaced. Adaptation as a strategy to make a test more suitable for a target culture frequently is based on the belief that cultural norms and values necessitate changes. An example of adaptation, or cultural adaptation, is an item from the Picture Arrangement subtest of the WISC-R (Malda et al., 2008). A pilot study showed that the man in this item, with a small, black mask over the eyes and a black-and-white horizontally striped shirt, was not recognized as a burglar by Kannada children in India and also the sliding window, uncommon in India, created difficulties of understanding. The item was drawn in a somewhat different way to accommodate these difficulties (see Figure 16.1).

Assembly, as a form of test adaptation, requires the new development of parts or an entire instrument for a target culture. The goal may be to assess the same domain or construct, but content and format of items will be largely different. The adaptation of larger chunks of items requires explicit theoretical notions about what is essential in the instrument and how this essence can be best addressed in the target culture. As an example, we refer to the assessment of depression. There has been extensive debate on cross-cultural differences in symptoms, with more somatic expression (e.g., back problems) in some contexts and more mental expressions (e.g., negative mood) in other contexts (Kirmayer & Young, 1998). Obviously, this variation should have implications

FIGURE 16.1. Depiction of a burglar in the Kannada version of a Picture Arrangement item from the WISC-R (Malda et al., 2008).

for the formulation of items. In the case of assembly much of the work involved in original test development has to be carried out. Here test developers have to consider what is to be gained from a connection with the original instrument. The alternative is to construct an entirely new test, which is likely to be geared better to the culture of the client group than a test originally developed for a culturally different group.

Which approach to test adaptation will be followed depends on expectations about the need for changes among test developers. The main factor is the size of the cultural differences of the source and target cultures (known as *cultural distance*; see Torbiörn, 1982). In the case of adoption, the expectation is that a test can consist largely of the same items in the target and source populations. Minor changes may be needed that are a matter of common sense, such as replacement of names of plant and animal species to fit local flora and fauna. Adaptation as a strategy to make a test more suitable for a target culture frequently is based on the belief that cultural practices and conventions that go beyond specific items necessitate changes. Assembly with larger chunks of items or the mode of administration (e.g., less emphasis on speed) requires explicit theoretical notions about construct validity and how this can be best retained in the target culture.

There are various ways in which types of adaptations can be distinguished. Because of the popularity of adaptations in cross-cultural studies, we present a further set of distinctions in five types (see also Malda et al., 2008; van de Vijver, 2015; van de Vijver & Leung, 2011). *Construct-driven adaptations* are related to differences in definitions of psychological concepts across cultures. For example, there are non-Western studies of everyday conceptions of children's intelligence in which obedience and rule compliance are seen as part of intelligence (Goodnow, 2002), unlike what is found in Western studies. *Language-driven adaptations* result from the unavailability of synonyms or similar concepts across languages. For example, the English word *friend* can indicate both a male and a female person, where many other languages use gendered words. *Culture-driven adaptations* result from different cultural norms, values, communication styles, customs, or practices. The translation of the English *you* requires cultural knowledge about appropriate modes of address in tests in languages that have a distinction between a formal and informal mode of address (such as *tu* and *vous* in French). *Theory-driven adaptations* involve changes based on underlying conceptualization or theory. For example, digit span items should ideally have digit names that are all of similar length, which may be lost when the items are translated into another language. Finally, there are *familiarity/recognizability driven adaptations* that are based on differential familiarity with task or item characteristics. For example, drawings of desktop corded phones or of mobile phones with short or long antennas are no longer adequate for the new generation of children who grew up with devices that did not have these features.

A Comprehensive Approach to Test Adaptation

There are numerous sources of information and professional practices that can guide a test adaptation process. As mentioned before, a comprehensive approach was initiated by Hambleton (1994) and has resulted in the *Guidelines for Translating and Adapting Tests*, published by the International Test Commission (ITC), referred to earlier. The first guideline reads as follows: "Effects of cultural differences which are not relevant or important to the main purposes of the study should be minimized to the extent possible" (International Test Commission, 2010, p. 2). This guideline sets the stage by emphasizing a global perspective on test adaptations, in which knowledge of the construct and its theoretical framework, the languages and cultures involved, and psychological assessment are critical for success. A further guideline refers to the need for statistical analysis: "Test developers/publishers should apply appropriate statistical techniques to (1) establish the equivalence of the different versions of the test or instrument, and (2) identify problematic components or aspects of the test or instrument which may be inadequate to one or more of the intended populations" (pp. 2–3). It is a main strength of the ITC Guidelines for test adaptations that they attempt to systematize the process and acknowledge the need to include multiple types of expertise. It is not surprising that large-scale adaptations are nowadays almost always conducted by teams.

Beyond Full Score Equivalence

Each cultural population, however defined, can be said to be unique. When people are socialized in different environments, their behavior repertoire will show differences. Transfer between groups of psychological tools, such as tests, psychotherapies, and intervention programs, implies at least some degree of cultural imposition. After all, such tools were tuned originally to the cultural context and practices of the population for which they were developed.

The alternative to the transfer of a test is to develop a new test for each new target group that differs from the source population. Usually a test developed for a specific group will have a better cultural fit than a transferred test. Still, there are good reasons why test transfer should be considered. First, the development and standardization of an instrument is costly and time-consuming. It makes sense to make use of available tests, provided they are suitable for the target group. Second, transfer of a test comes with research that has already been conducted. If a transferred test meets requirements of equivalence in a target group, it stands to reason that theoretical underpinnings and empirical interrelationships also apply in that group; at least this is a good starting proposition (Poortinga, 1989). Third, transfer of tests adds to an accumulating body of knowledge more than does a string of separate tests that are unrelated to each other. Of course, the points mentioned are not an argument against the construction of new tests, but there should be reasonable expectations that a new instrument will lead to better assessment than an existing one.

At face value the empirical record easily justifies transfer as a strategy for test development. By and large tests travel reasonably well, and there are even remarkable success stories. To emphasize this point we mention a few examples. Schwartz (1992) has reported that across a large number of languages, there was no need to supplement the existing set of 57 items in the Schwartz Values Survey with additional values to cover local values domains. It is common to use translations of the MMPI (and its more recent version, MMPI-2); profiles across countries tend to be similar for well-defined diagnostic categories (e.g., Butcher, 2004). With personality inventories, such as the NEO-PI-R (mapping the so-called Big Five dimensions) and the EPQ (Eysenck Personality Questionnaire, mapping the so-called Giant Three dimensions), there is extensive evidence of structural equivalence across a wide range of countries (e.g., Eysenck, Barrett, & Eysenck, 1985). It even has been argued that the NEO-PI-R can be considered to meet conditions of full score equivalence (McCrae & Terracciano, 2007). In the realm of emotions research there is ample evidence that the structure of dimensions of affective meaning is culturally invariant (Fontaine, Scherer, & Soriano, 2013), and that shades of emotion experience for which there is no expression in a language are recognized readily from descriptions of emotion episodes (Breugelmans & Poortinga, 2006; Frank, Harvey, & Verdun, 2000).

On the other hand, incidental but striking differences have been reported in display rules that control the expression of emotions in specific situations, a famous case being the rule that the widow of a Japanese sword fighter killed in combat should not show regret because of the honorable circumstances of her late husband's death (Klineberg, 1940). For values, large cross-cultural differences can emerge when an event or situation is being categorized differently. For example, in many Western societies children can participate in discussions with their parents and the latter may not be offended when their children express views opposite to their own. In contrast, in many non-Western societies expressing disagreement with parents is considered to be rude and to demonstrate a lack of respect. More systematic challenges have emerged against strong cultural invariance of diagnostic categories and personality structure. Emphasis on the importance of somatic symptoms in depression as argued for non-Western cultures (Kim et al., 2006) or culture-specific syndromes (Guarnaccia & Rogler, 1999) is hardly compatible with the use of common diagnostic scales. With the locally developed Chinese Personality Assessment Inventory (CPAI), an additional factor to the Big Five was identified, Interpersonal Relatedness (IR) (Cheung et al., 1996). This dimension was also found when the CPAI was administered elsewhere (Lin & Church, 2004). Differential relevance across cultures was demonstrated by the finding that the IR dimension predicted significantly more variance for Asian Americans than for European Americans, whereas the opposite was found for scales of the NEO-PI-R (Cheung, Cheung, & Fan, 2013).

Similar results emerged with a personality inventory developed in South Africa from interviews asking for person descriptions in the 11 national languages; also here social–relational aspects of personality were found to be important. An administration of the instrument in mainstream and immigrant groups in The Netherlands revealed stability of the South African factor structure to these groups in The Netherlands (e.g., Valchev et al., 2014). Such findings suggest that the high level of structural equivalence for Western instruments such as the NEO-PI-R cannot be taken to mean that there is equal representation of the entire personality domain across cultures. Rather the available evidence suggests there is a cultural flavor to personality that may easily lead to misrepresentation in assessment instruments of parts of the personality domain that are less salient, or more salient, in the society of origin than in other societies.

The most immediate consequence of this state of affairs is that preferably in the construction of tests meant to be used across certain cultures, members of all those cultures should be involved. This strategy is being followed already in international survey projects such as the European Social Survey. The most advanced form of this strategy is found in the Organisation for Economic Cooperation and Development's (OECD) projects such as PISA (Programme for International Student Assessment) and TALIS (Teaching and Learning International Survey). Here the participating countries are asked to submit items for each test that is being constructed. These items are scrutinized by a panel of experts, and a preliminary version of the test is prepared. Selected items are translated with checks on translation equivalence. The next phase consists of a tryout in all countries, followed by item bias analysis. Only thereafter is the final version of the test administered to assess the performance of national samples of pupils in OECD countries. However, even the PISA studies have not realized the full elimination of bias. For example, an analysis of DIF with reading items showed a systematic advantage for items originating from pupils' own cultural and linguistic contexts (Artelt & Baumert, 2004).

It is important to note that in large-scale cross-cultural studies such as PISA, there is almost never support for scalar invariance. This finding implies that even with a massive investment of resources in the development of a cross-culturally adequate instrument, we are still unable to produce educational achievement tests that are entirely comparable across a wide variety of countries. The same holds for the questionnaires in the PISA studies in which attitudes and motivations are assessed. Given this failure to find scalar invariance in well-designed studies, it stands to reason that obtaining scalar invariance in large-scale psychological studies involving a wider range of cultures is an unrealistic ideal. With our current knowledge of item writing, metric equivalence is the highest level of equivalence that we can reasonably expect to find in such studies. The question then arises how we should proceed and whether we should not reevaluate our implicit goal of reaching scalar invariance in cross-cultural research.

We would argue that, as in many other domains of study, we should settle for the best practical solution rather than the best theoretical solution. Let us give two examples. The first concerns the measurement of internal consistency. Test developers aim for internal consistencies that are as high as possible. However, nobody realistically expects that the internal consistency of a new instrument will be exactly 1.00 or close to 1.00. As a scientific community, we have established rules of thumb in which we settle for considerably lower values as being sufficient for working with an instrument, even in cases of individual assessment. So in the area of psychological assessment, we have found a realistic compromise between what is the theoretical limit and what is practically feasible. Something similar goes for the classification of educational systems, the so-called ISCED (International Standard Classification of Education) system, published by the United Nations Educational, Scientific, and Cultural Organisation (UNESCO) (*www. uis.unesco.org/Education/Pages/international-standard-classification-of-education.*

aspx). Educational systems vary considerably across countries, and the ISCED system is an attempt to map educational systems from different countries on to each other. The system is frequently used in international comparisons of education, although researchers appreciate the limitations. Again, this system is a compromise between what is theoretically possible and practically feasible.

In addition to lowering our expectations with regard to scalar invariance, there are other approaches. First, cross-cultural comparisons could focus more on criterion-referenced testing than on norm-referenced testing (Hambleton, Swaminathan, Algina, & Coulson, 1978). Criterion-referenced testing focuses much more on skill levels or attitudes displayed by a person than on the comparisons between persons. Although criterion-referenced testing has hardly been addressed from a cross-cultural perspective, it has considerable potential because it allows for the combination of both universal and culture-specific operationalizations. A second approach is more statistically oriented. In cross-cultural studies in which equivalence is not supported for the whole instrument, it may well be possible to identify a section of items that approximates the requirements of scalar invariance. If this is the case, tests of the sensitivity of the cross-cultural differences to the lack of scalar invariance can be investigated. Analyses of variance can be conducted in which the effect size of the cross-cultural differences is determined for the items that show scalar invariance and for the entire instrument. It is not uncommon to find that effect sizes are rather similar and that the rank order of cultural groups is rather invariant for the subset and for the entire set of items (e.g., Meiring, van de Vijver, Rothmann, & Barrick, 2005). The failure to find scalar invariance is consequential for conclusions regarding observed cross-cultural differences only when the effect sizes of the two analyses are distinctly different. So, this statistical approach is a pragmatic way of dealing with the lack of scalar invariance by addressing the question of whether the lack has practical implications.

The third way of dealing with a lack of scalar invariance amounts to finding explanations for cross-cultural differences. We have called this approach *peeling the onion called culture* (Poortinga, van de Vijver, Joe, & van de Koppel, 1987; for an update, see Bond & van de Vijver, 2011). In the design stage of the study, researchers should already anticipate potential explanations of cross-cultural differences. For example, personality and attitude questionnaires will presumably have to deal with response styles as alternative explanations of cross-cultural differences. Cross-cultural comparisons of educational performance or intelligence will have to deal with expected differences in educational quality as rival explanations of cross-cultural differences. In most studies it is possible to anticipate the question of how potential explanations of cross-cultural differences in the core variables of a study should be addressed. If measures of these rival explanations are included in a study, statistical analyses, such as analysis of covariance, can be conducted to examine to what extent these rival explanations are successful in reducing or eliminating cross-cultural differences in target variables. It may be noted that, in this approach, finding scalar invariance is not crucial. As long as metric invariance is observed, these analyses of covariance can be conducted and are informative. The crux of this approach is the shift from an emphasis on finding cross-cultural differences to an emphasis on explaining such differences.

In summary, we think that there is enough experience in cross-cultural research to conclude that finding scalar invariance is unlikely to be a realistic expectation. We may need to lower our expectations even if our aim should remain to obtain the highest possible levels of equivalence. A new, more realistic type of thinking about scalar invariance is needed. As described above, approaches in this direction have been developed.

Conclusion

In this chapter we have illustrated how, in the last few decades, test translations have been replaced by test adaptations. We have discussed analyses that can help to evaluate to which extent tests assess the same aspect of behavior across groups of test takers that differ in language and culture. We also have presented taxonomies of adaptations of tests from a source population to a target population. We describe how translatability is related to bias and use of instruments in a new cultural context. Preparing instruments for multilingual and multicultural usage is increasingly seen as a multidisciplinary approach in which expertise in the domain of the instrument and item writing has to be combined with cultural and linguistic expertise. Some best practices from large-scale international projects have been described to illustrate how far we have moved from the use of close translations of Western instruments in new cultures. Finally, we have presented some ideas on how the pernicious problem of bias may be dealt with in the future.

Hambleton's work on this area has been instrumental in advancing the field by linking previously unconnected lines in the literature (linguistic and psychometric approaches to test translation), proposing minimum and best practices, and by his efforts to disseminate this knowledge. More than ever before, test adaptation has become a professional field with specialists and an established body of core knowledge. We also explained that the work is still in progress and that we still have to find better ways to integrate design and analysis (qualitative and quantitative approaches to test adaptations) and to find more realistic ways to deal with the often unattainable ideal of scalar equivalence. The seemingly uninterrupted growth in cross-cultural studies, fueled by globalization and massive international migration (van de Vijver, 2015), provides a solid background for further developments in the field.

REFERENCES

Aguinis, H., Culpepper, S. A., & Pierce, C. A. (2010). Revival of test bias research in preemployment testing. *Journal of Applied Psychology, 95,* 648–680.

Artelt, C., & Baumert, J. (2004). Comparability of students' reading literacy performance measured with items originating from different language backgrounds. *Zeitschrift für Pädagogische Psychologie, 18,* 171–185.

Bartram, D. (2013). Scalar equivalence of OPQ32 Big Five profiles of 31 countries. *Journal of Cross-Cultural Psychology, 44,* 61–83.

Berry, J. W., Poortinga, Y. H., Breugelmans, S. M., Chasiotis, A., & Sam, D. (2011). *Cross-cultural psychology: Research and applications*. Cambridge, UK: Cambridge University Press.

Binet, A., & Simon, T. (1907). *Les enfants anormaux* [Mentally defective children]. Paris: A. Colin.

Bond, M. H., & van de Vijver, F. J. R. (2011). Making scientific sense of cultural differences in psychological outcomes: Unpacking the magnum mysterium. In D. Matsumoto & F. J. R. van de Vijver (Eds.), *Cross-cultural research methods in psychology* (pp. 75–100). New York: Cambridge University Press.

Breugelmans, S. M., & Poortinga, Y. H. (2006). Emotion without a word: Shame and guilt with Rarámuri Indians and rural Javanese. *Journal of Personality and Social Psychology, 91*, 1111–1122.

Brislin, R. W. (1980). Translation and content analysis of oral and written material. In H. C. Triandis & J. W. Berry (Eds.), *Handbook of cross-cultural psychology* (Vol. 1, pp. 389–444). Boston: Allyn & Bacon.

Brislin, R. W. (1986). The wording and translation of research instruments. In W. J. Lonner & J. W. Berry (Eds.), *Field methods in cross-cultural research* (pp. 137–164). Beverly Hills, CA: Sage.

Brouwers, S. A., van de Vijver, F. J. R., & van Hemert, D. A. (2009). Variation in Raven's progressive matrices scores across time and place. *Learning and Individual Differences, 19*, 330–338.

Butcher, J. N. (2004). Personality assessment without borders: Adaptation of the MMPI-2 across cultures. *Journal of Personality Assessment, 83*, 90–104.

Butcher, J. N., Mosch, S. C., Tsai, J., & Nezami, E. (2006). Cross-cultural applications of the MMPI-2. In J. Butcher (Ed.), *MMPI-2: A practitioner's guide* (pp. 505–537). Washington, DC: American Psychological Association.

Cattell, R. B. (1940). A culture free intelligence test, I. *Journal of Educational Psychology, 31*, 176–199.

Cattell, R. B., & Cattell, A. K. S. (1963). *Culture Fair Intelligence Test*. Champaign, IL: Institute for Personality and Ability Testing.

Cheung, F. M., Leung, K., Fan, R. M., Song, W. Z., Zhang, J. X., & Zhang, J. P. (1996). Development of the Chinese Personality Assessment Inventory. *Journal of Cross-Cultural Psychology, 27*, 181–199.

Cheung, F. M., van de Vijver, F. J. R., & Leong, F. T. L. (2011). Toward a new approach to the assessment of personality in culture. *American Psychologist, 66*, 593–603.

Cheung, S. F., Cheung, F. M., & Fan, W. (2013). From Chinese to cross-cultural personality inventory: A combined emic etic approach to the study of personality in culture. In M. J. Gelfand, C. Chiu, & Y. Hong (Eds.), *Advances in culture and psychology* (Vol. 3, pp. 117–179). New York: Oxford University Press.

Cleary, T. A., & Hilton, T. L. (1968). An investigation of item bias. *Educational and Psychological Measurement, 28*, 61–75.

Dolan, C. V., Roorda, W., & Wicherts, J. M. (2004). Two failures of Spearman's hypothesis: The GATB in Holland and the JAT in South Africa. *Intelligence, 32*, 155–173.

Eysenck, H. J., Barrett, P., & Eysenck, S. B. (1985). Indices of factor comparison for homologous and non-homologous personality scales in 24 different countries. *Personality and Individual Differences, 6*, 503–504.

Fontaine, J. R. J. (2005). Equivalence. In K. Kempf-Leonard (Ed.), *Encyclopedia of social measurement* (Vol. 1, pp. 803–813). New York: Academic Press.

Fontaine, J. R. J., Scherer, K. R., & Soriano, C. (Eds.). (2013). *Components of emotional meaning: A sourcebook*. Oxford, UK: Oxford University Press.

Frank, H., Harvey, O. J., & Verdun, K. (2000). American responses to five categories of shame in Chinese culture: A preliminary cross-cultural construct validation. *Personality and Individual Differences, 28*, 887–896.

Frijda, N. H., & Jahoda, G. (1966). On the scope and methods of cross-cultural research. *International Journal of Psychology, 1*, 109–127.

Galton, F. (1869). *Hereditary genius: An inquiry into its laws and consequences*. London: Macmillan.

Georgas, J., Weiss, L., van de Vijver, F. J. R., & Saklofske, D. H. (Eds.). (2003). *Cultures and children's intelligence: A cross-cultural analysis of the WISC-III* (pp. 277–313). New York: Academic Press.

Goodnow, J. J. (2002). Parents' knowledge and expectations: Using what we know. In M. H. Bornstein (Ed.), *Handbook of parenting*: Vol. 3. *Being and becoming a parent* (pp. 439–460). Mahwah, NJ: Erlbaum.

Gould, S. J. (1996). *The mismeasure of man*. New York: Norton.

Guarnaccia, P. J., & Rogler, L. H. (1999). Research on culture-bound syndromes: New directions. *American Journal of Psychiatry, 156*, 1322–1327.

Hambleton, R. K. (1994). Guidelines for adapting educational and psychological tests: A progress report. *European Journal of Psychological Assessment, 10*, 229–244.

Hambleton, R. K., Swaminathan, H., Algina, J., & Coulson, D. B. (1978). Criterion-referenced testing and measurement: A review of technical issues and developments. *Review of Educational Research, 48*, 1–47.

Hambleton, R. K., Swaminathan, H., & Rogers, H. J. (1991). *Fundamentals of item response theory*. Newbury Park, CA: Sage.

Hambleton, R. K., & Zenisky, A. L. (2011). Translating and adapting tests for cross-cultural assessments. Cross-cultural research methods in psychology. In D. Matsumoto & F. J. R. van de Vijver (Eds.), *Cross-cultural research methods in psychology* (pp. 46–70). New York: Cambridge University Press.

Harkness, J. A. (2003). Questionnaire translation. In J. A. Harkness, F. J. R. van de Vijver, & P. P. Mohler (Eds.), *Cross-cultural survey methods* (pp. 19–34). New York: Wiley.

He, J., & van de Vijver, F. J. R. (2013). A general response style factor: Evidence from a multiethnic study in The Netherlands. *Personality and Individual Differences, 55*, 794–800.

International Test Commission. (2010). International Test Commission guidelines for translating and adapting tests. Retrieved from *www.intestcom.org*.

Jensen, A. R. (1980). *Bias in mental testing*. New York: Free Press.

Kim, U., Yang, K.-S., & Hwang, K.-K. (Eds.). (2006). *Indigenous and cultural psychology: Understanding people in context*. New York: Springer.

Kirmayer, L. J., & Young, A. (1998). Culture and somatization: Clinical, epidemiological, and ethnographic perspectives. *Psychosomatic Medicine, 60*, 420–430.

Klineberg, O. (1940). *Social psychology*. New York: Henry Holt.

Kreiner, S., & Christensen, K. B. (2014). Analyses of model fit and robustness: A new look at the PISA scaling model underlying ranking of countries according to reading literacy. *Psychometrika, 79*, 210–231.

Lin, E. J. L., & Church, A. T. (2004). Are indigenous Chinese personality dimensions culturespecific?: An investigation of the Chinese Personality Assessment Inventory in Chinese American and European American samples. *Journal of Cross-Cultural Psychology, 35*, 586–605.

Linn, R. L. (1993). The use of differential item functioning statistics: A discussion of current practice and future implications. In P. W. Holland & H. Wainer (Eds.), *Differential item functioning* (pp. 349–364). Hillsdale, NJ: Erlbaum.

Malda, M., van de Vijver, F. J. R., Srinivasan, K., Transler, C., Sukumar, P., & Rao, K. (2008). Adapting a cognitive test for a different culture: An illustration of qualitative procedures. *Psychology Science Quarterly, 50*, 451–468.

McCrae, R. R., & Allik, J. (Eds.). (2002). *The five-factor model across cultures*. New York: Kluwer Academic/Plenum Press.

McCrae, R. R., & Terracciano, A. (2007). The Five-Factor Model and its correlates in individuals and cultures. In F. J. R. van de Vijver, D. A. Van Hemert, & Y. H. Poortinga (Eds.), *Individuals and cultures in multilevel analysis* (pp. 249–284). Mahwah, NJ: Erlbaum.

Meiring, D., van de Vijver, F. J. R., Rothmann, S., & Barrick, M. R. (2005). Construct, item, and method bias of cognitive and personality tests in South Africa. *South African Journal of Industrial Psychology, 31*, 1–8.

Poortinga, Y. H. (1989). Equivalence of cross-cultural data: An overview of basic issues. *International Journal of Psychology, 24*, 737–756.

Poortinga, Y. H., van de Vijver, F. J. R., Joe, R. C., & van de Koppel, J. M. H. (1987). Peeling the onion called culture: A synopsis. In C. Kagitcibasi (Ed.), *Growth and progress in cross-cultural psychology* (pp. 22–34). Lisse, The Netherlands: Swets & Zeitlinger.

Porteus, S. D. (1937). *Primitive intelligence and environment*. New York: Macmillan.

Raven, J. (1989). The Raven progressive matrices: A review of national norming studies and ethnic and socioeconomic variation within the United States. *Journal of Educational Measurement, 26*, 1–16.

Schmidt, F. L., & Hunter, J. E. (1998). The validity and utility of selection methods in personnel psychology: Practical and theoretical implications of 85 years of research findings. *Psychological Bulletin, 124*, 262–274.

Schwartz, S. H. (1992). Universals in the content and structure of values: Theoretical advances and empirical tests in 20 countries. In M. Zanna (Ed.), *Advances in experimental social psychology* (Vol. 25, pp. 1–65). Orlando, FL: Academic Press.

Tittle, C. K. (1982). Use of judgmental methods in item bias studies. In R. A. Berk (Ed.), *Handbook of methods for detecting bias* (pp. 31–63). Baltimore: Johns Hopkins University Press.

Torbiörn, I. (1982). *Living abroad*. New York: Wiley.

Valchev, V. H., van de Vijver, F. J. R., Meiring, D., Nel, J. A., Laher, S., Hill, C., et al. (2014). Beyond agreeableness: Social–relational personality concepts from an indigenous and cross-cultural perspective. *Journal of Research in Personality, 48*, 17–32.

van de Gaer, E., Grisay, A., Schulz, W., & Gebhardt, E. (2012). The reference group effect: An explanation of the paradoxical relationship between academic achievement and self-confidence across countries. *Journal of Cross-Cultural Psychology, 43*, 1205–1228.

Vandenberg, R. J., & Lance, C. E. (2000). A review and synthesis of the measurement equivalence literature: Suggestions, practices, and recommendations for organizational research. *Organizational Research Methods, 3*, 4–70.

van de Vijver, F. J. R. (2015). Methodological aspects of cross-cultural research. In M. Gelfand, Y. Hong, & C. Y. Chiu (Eds.), *Advances in culture and psychology* (Vol. 5, pp. 101–160). New York: Oxford University Press.

van de Vijver, F. J. R., & Leung, K. (1997). *Methods and data analysis for cross-cultural research*. Newbury Park, CA: Sage.

van de Vijver, F. J. R., & Leung, K. (2011). Equivalence and bias: A review of concepts, models, and data analytic procedures. In D. Matsumoto & F. J. R. van de Vijver (Eds.), *Cross-cultural research methods in psychology* (pp. 17–45). New York: Cambridge University Press.

van de Vijver, F. J. R., & Poortinga, Y. H. (2005). Conceptual and methodological issues in adapting tests. In R. K. Hambleton, P. F. Merenda, & C. D. Spielberger (Eds.), *Adapting educational and psychological tests for cross-cultural assessment* (pp. 39–63). Mahwah, NJ: Erlbaum.

Van Schilt-Mol, T. M. M. L. (2007). *Differential item functioning en itembias in de Cito-Eindtoets Basisonderwijs* [Differential item functioning and item bias in the Cito-Eindtoets Basisonderwijs]. Amsterdam, The Netherlands: Aksant.

Yang, K.-S., & Bond, M. H. (1980). Ethnic affirmation by Chinese bilinguals. *Journal of Cross-Cultural Psychology, 11*, 411–425.

Zumbo, B. D. (2007). Three generations of DIF analyses: Considering where it has been, where it is now, and where it is going. *Language Assessment Quarterly, 4*, 223–233.

CHAPTER 17

Test Adaptation Standards for Cross-Lingual Assessment

José Muñiz, Paula Elosua, José-Luis Padilla, and Ronald K. Hambleton

The adaptation of tests and questionnaires for use in cultural and linguistic contexts that are different from those in which they were developed is a practice that can be traced back to the appearance of Binet and Simon's (1905) first intelligence test at the beginning of the 20th century. The growth of adaptation endeavors in recent decades is a reflection of a social environment that is marked by contact between cultures and languages and in which tests and questionnaires are used every day in educational, social, legal, and clinical settings when making individual or group decisions (Hambleton, Merenda, & Spielberger, 2005; Muñiz & Hambleton, 1996).

The interest in the adaptation of evaluation instruments is not limited to any one unique context or use. For example, a review of the 25 most used tests in Spanish professional practice (clinical, educational, or organizational) clearly shows that 16 are adaptations of instruments created in other languages, mainly in English (Elosua, 2012). The same can be said when it comes to other countries (Elosua & Iliescu, 2012; Evers et al., 2012). A brief glance at recent Spanish publications also reveals this trend (Calvo et al., 2012; Iturbide, Elosua, & Yenes, 2010; Nogueira, Godoy, Romero, Gavino, & Cobos, 2012; Ortiz, Navarro, García, Ramis, & Manassero, 2012; Rodríguez, Martínez, Tinajero, Guisande, & Páramo, 2012). Within the fields of organizational psychology and human resources, multinational corporations and international organizations have an increasing need for accreditation or selection tests that can be used in different countries and in different languages. In the same way, the social impact of educational evaluations—such as the Program for International Student Assessment (PISA) and the Trends in International Mathematics and Science Study (TIMSS), which use tests that have been adapted into more than 40 languages—clearly demonstrates the importance of having a robust adaptation process for the measuring instruments being used.

With this need in mind, the International Test Commission (ITC) began a project in 1992 to create guidelines related to the adaptation of tests and questionnaires. This project (Hambleton, 1994, 1996; Muñiz, Elosua, & Hambleton, 2013; Muñiz & Hambleton, 1996) gave rise to a set of 22 guidelines grouped in four sections (Context, Test Development and Adaptation, Construction and Adaptation, and Administrations and Documentation/Score Interpretation). The ITC Guidelines attempted to anticipate the different sources of error involved in the test adaptation process and offer strategies to control for them. The document has been cited more than 500 times in scientific and professional publications (Hambleton, 2009), which is a clear indication of the guidelines' impact.

One indication of the timeliness of the ITC's efforts in creating guidelines for professionals adapting tests is the inclusion of specific standards dealing with test translation/adaptation in two different chapters of the last edition of the Standards for Educational and Psychological Testing (American Psychological Association, American Educational Research Association, & National Council on Measurement in Education, 2014). In particular, two standards—3.12 and 7.6—are clearly consistent with the new proposals for the last ITC guidelines. Standard 3.12 states:

> When a test is translated and adapted from one language to another, test developers and/or test users are responsible for describing the methods used in establishing the adequacy of the adaptation and documenting empirical or logical evidence for the validity of test score interpretation for intended use. (p. 68)

And standard 7.6 requires that

> When a test is available in more than one language, the test documentation should provide information on the procedures that were employed to translate and adapt the test. Information should also be provided regarding the reliability/precision and validity evidence for the adapted form when feasible. (p. 127)

Efforts to guide professionals in the process of adapting evaluation instruments have not just been limited to the area of psychological or educational assessment but have also been made in fields such as survey methodology. There are many references and proposals that may be cited, but doubtless there would be little argument with referencing the *Guidelines for Best Practice in Cross-Cultural Surveys* (University of Michigan, 2011), which grew out of a collaborative, U.S.-based initiative known as the Comparative Survey Design and Implementation (CSDI; 2014) Guidelines Initiative. In 15 chapters the CSDI guidelines deal with all aspects of the "lifecycle" of an international study survey. The "procedural steps" included in the chapters on questionnaire design, translation, adaptation, and pretesting have had a particular impact on professional practice. The content of these chapters is very similar to the new proposed ITC guidelines.

The New ITC Guidelines: An Integral Framework for Test Adaptation

Recent years have seen significant advances made in the field of test adaptation from both a substantive and a methodological and psychometric point of view (Hambleton et al., 2005; Matsumoto & van de Vijver, 2011; van de Vijver & Tanzer, 1997). The methodological and technical developments in the establishment of intercultural equivalence should be highlighted (Byrne, 2008; Elosua, 2005), as well as the greater awareness of the importance of rational–analytical studies in combination with quantitative methods during the adaptation process in providing more comprehensive evidence of the level of equivalence achieved (Benítez & Padilla, 2014). These, and other advances, have given rise to the need to revise the original guidelines in light of new developments. A multidisciplinary group under the aegis of the ITC was formed to carry out this revision, coordinated by the fourth author of this chapter, Ronald Hambleton, and comprising representatives of various national psychology associations: Dave Bartram (United Kingdom); Giray Berberoglu (Turkey); Jacques Gregoire (Belgium); the first author of this chapter; José Muñiz (Spain); and the first author of the preceding chapter in this volume, on cross-cultural assessment, Fons van de Vijver (The Netherlands).

The coming guidelines offer an integral framework (see Figure 17.1) that addresses the study of previous phases of adaptation, analysis of the adaptation itself, its technical justification, evaluation and interpretation of the scores, and the creation of a final document. There are 20 guidelines, grouped into six categories that are summarized in Table 17.1.

The goal of the guidelines is for the final product of the adaptation process to represent the best possible linguistic, cultural, conceptual, and metric equivalence to the original instrument, and as such, they were designed to be a standard to guide researchers and professionals. The process is comprehensive in nature and covers all of the phases and questions to be considered during the translation process, from legal questions about intellectual property of the original test to formal aspects concerning the editing of a technical manual and the changes made. They are all important and require attention. The main objective of this chapter is to present the new proposed ITC guidelines and at the same time to relate them to the conceptual and methodological advances in the process of adapting evaluation instruments.

Precondition Guidelines

These guidelines focus on two preliminary questions to consider before carrying out any adaptation and are concerned with correct planning, checking intellectual

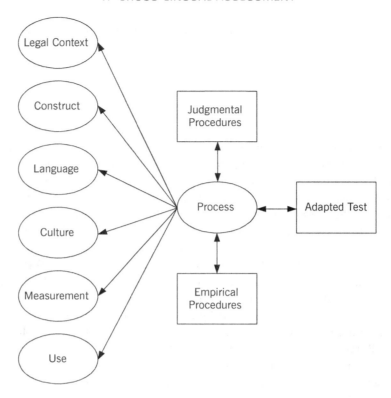

FIGURE 17.1. Components of the test adaptation process.

Categories	Number of guidelines	Areas addressed
TABLE 17.1. Categories and Areas Addressed by the Second Edition of the ITC Guidelines for Test Translation and Adaptation		
Preliminary	5	Legal context (framework) Design Construct assessment
Development	5	Linguistic adaptation Cultural adaptation Pilot studies
Confirmation	4	Data collection Equivalence Reliability Validation
Administration	2	Administration
Scoring and interpretation	2	Scoring and interpretation Comparability
Documentation	2	Differences between versions Correct use

property rights, and ensuring that the design is appropriate. There are five preliminary guidelines:

- PC-1 (1). Obtain the necessary permissions from the holder of the intellectual property rights relating to the test before carrying out any adaptation.
- PC-2 (2). Comply with the laws and professional practice that are pertinent to testing in the country or countries of interest.
- PC-3 (3). Choose the most appropriate test adaptation design.
- PC-4 (4). Appraise the relevance of the construct or constructs measured by the test for the populations of interest.
- PC-5 (5). Evaluate the influence of any incidental, but relevant cultural and linguistic differences in the populations of interest for the test being considered for adaptation.

Checking who has intellectual property rights over the instrument and obtaining relevant legal permissions (PC-1 and PC-2) guarantees the authenticity of the final product and protects the research from using unauthorized adaptations. The regulatory frameworks on intellectual property in each country must be followed and cooperation agreements must be sought between those responsible for the adaptation and the original version's authors or intellectual property rights holders. The second aspect, which has already been addressed in the first edition of the guidelines, refers to studying the characteristics of the construct when measuring the target population (PC-3, PC-4, and PC-5). This point is interesting because it warns of the consequences of simply assuming the universality of constructs across cultures, and it advises the evaluation of the amount of overlap between the construct in the original and the target populations as the only way of estimating and defining the desired level of equivalence (for further discussion on this topic, see van de Vijver and Poortinga, Chapter 16, this volume).

Test Development Guidelines

These guidelines outline the process of developing the adapted version of the evaluation instrument. They offer advice as to how to overcome some of the more common misunderstandings related to the use of literal translation as a guarantee of equivalence or to the excessive weight given to back translation (Brislin, 1986) as a means of verifying the quality of an adaptation. It is usual to think that for a good translation, there will be good equivalence between the original and a version that has been back translated by an independent translator. This method, however, does not guarantee the validity of the adapted version; moreover, with a bad translation, the equivalence between the original and the back translation can be very high. The reason is that often, bad translations make use of literal translations rather than a thorough translation of meaning. For example, the results of automated translations give rise to good back translations, but we would never use them without evaluation and refinement of the version in the target language.

There are five new proposed guidelines to follow during the development of the adapted version of the evaluation instrument:

- TD-1 (6). Ensure that the adaptation process considers linguistic, psychological, and cultural differences in the intended populations through the choice of experts with relevant expertise.

- TD-2 (7). Use appropriate judgmental designs and procedures to maximize the suitability of the test adaptation in the intended populations.

- TD-3 (8). Provide evidence that the test instructions and item content have similar meaning and familiarity for all intended populations.

- TD-4 (9). Provide evidence that the item formats, rating scales, scoring rubrics, test conventions, modes of administration, and other procedures are suitable for all intended populations.

- TD-5 (10). Collect pilot data on the adapted test to enable item analysis and reliability assessment to be carried out, and other small-scale validity studies, as deemed useful, so that any necessary revisions to the adapted test can be made, and decisions made about the validity of the adapted test.

In order to determine which linguistic and cultural factors to consider during the adaptation (TD-1 and TD-2), it is advisable to implement an iterative fine-tuning process beginning with independent translations to be reviewed later by a mixed committee that includes, in addition to translators with cultural knowledge and language skills, specialists in evaluation who can analyze whether the adapted version is suitable. Linguistic correction and suitability in practice are complementary concepts that must be reconciled. The TRAPD (translation, revision, adjudication, pretesting, documentation) model, proposed by Harkness (2002), deals with the linguistic and cultural points referred to in the guidelines in a systematic way. In turn, the iterative fine-tuning processes of independent translations is commonly incorporated into the so-called *translation design by committee* (Harkness, Villar, & Edwards, 2010), which has become the standard design for official statistical institutes and private organizations such as those that provided the quality checks for the PISA study translations (PISA Consortium, 2010).

The evidence required by guidelines TD-3 and TD-4 comes more often nowadays from current qualitative methods such as cognitive interviews (Miller, Chepp, Wilson, & Padilla, 2014; Willis, 2005), or from qualitative methods for the study of sources of bias (van de Vijver & Lung, 2011; van de Vijver & Poortinga, 1997).

The development guidelines also include a section (TD-5) that underscores the importance of pilot testing (Downing, 2006; Downing & Haladyna, 2006; Schmeiser & Welch, 2006; Wilson, 2005). Data from small samples allow for the analysis, study, and correction of aspects related to the adaptation being developed. Pilot studies allow, among other things, (1) the in situ collection of the reactions of test takers, (2) the assurance that test items and instructions are correctly understood, (3) the time the test takes to be appropriately administered, (4) the collection of information about possible content or formatting errors that can be corrected before the operational phase, and (5) the collection of data that permits a preliminary analysis to indicate the results of the more significant psychometric indicators. For example, it is interesting to analyze the arithmetic means of items or difficulty indices, where appropriate, and compare them with results from the original test; then it is possible to compare the quartiles of difficulty for each of the items in the test as a first approximation of later equivalence studies (Elosua, Bully, Mujika, & Almeida, 2012).

In order to assist in the practical application of the guidelines, while also being very useful in complying with the confirmation guidelines, Hambleton and Zenisky (2011) suggested posing 25 questions for each of the items in an adapted test; these questions are especially suitable for evaluating compliance with the development guidelines in an integrated manner. They do not exhaustively cover all of the points in the guidelines, but they do constitute a good first approximation for detecting possible gaps in the quality of the translation–adaptation. The 25 questions are categorized into four sections: general (4), item format (5), grammar and phrasing (6), passages (5), and culture (5). The following are examples of questions for each of the five categories:

- Does the item have the same or highly similar meaning in the two languages?
- Will the format of the item and task required of the examinee be equally familiar in the two language versions?
- Are there any grammatical structures in the source language version of the item that do not have parallels in the target language?
- When the passage is translated from the source language to the target language, do the words and phrases of the translated version convey similar content and ideas to the source version?
- Have terms in the item in one language been suitably adapted to the cultural environment of the second language version? (Hambleton & Zenisky, 2011)

Confirmation Guidelines

This group of guidelines refers to technical aspects that are related to the psychometric properties of the adapted test and its equivalence to the original test. They propose carrying out equivalence studies between the original and adapted versions to determine, for example, the extent to which the relation between each of the items on the test and the dimension it represents is maintained between the different versions of the test. If the functional relationship is not equivalent between the original and adapted versions, the validity of comparisons between the evaluations provided by the different versions will be at risk. There are various theoretical models and methods for conducting equivalence studies, such as structural equation models, item response theory (IRT) models, or the processes for detecting differential item functioning (DIF; see van de Vijver and Poortinga, Chapter 16, this volume, for more discussion on some of these methods). Only equivalence evaluation allows the level of comparability between scores to be understood (Elosua & Hambleton, in press; Elosua & Muñiz, 2010). The confirmation guidelines also propose carrying out reliability and validation studies (Elosua, 2003; Lissitz, 2009; Muñiz, 1997, 2003). There are four proposed confirmation guidelines:

- C-1 (11). Select sample characteristics that are relevant for the intended use of the test and of sufficient size and relevance for the empirical analyses.
- C-2 (12). Provide relevant empirical evidence about the construct equivalence, method equivalence, and item equivalence for all intended populations.
- C-3 (13). Compile evidence regarding the reliability and validity of the adapted version of the test in the intended populations.
- C-4 (14). Establish the level of comparability of scores across cultures using appropriate data analysis procedures or equating designs.

There is a broad consensus about the advantages and disadvantages of the different designs for collecting data (C-1) among those who look at equivalence between versions (e.g., Sireci, 1997). Cook and Schmitt-Cascallar (2005) reviewed thoroughly the pros and cons of the three most common designs for linking tests given in different languages: "separate monolingual group," "bilingual groups," and "matched monolingual." Once the data are obtained, some methods have become the first choice for gathering evidence on the achieved level of equivalence between different versions (C-2) (Sireci, 2011). The method that has been promoted in the literature for carrying out construct equivalence studies from a quantitative perspective is a multigroup confirmatory factor analysis (CFA), which checks for the presence of the same internal test structure in the groups being analyzed (Byrne, 2008; Elosua, 2005). By extending the equivalence condition to the item level, it is possible to measure metric and scalar equivalence. From there one can use mean and covariance structures (Elosua & Muñiz, 2010) or apply any of the procedures for detecting DIF (Holland & Wainer, 1993); DIF procedures analyze whether the response function of an item is equivalent for those people with the same skill level in the measured variable but who are from different groups. There has been an increase in studies with mixed methodology, in which quantitative evidence is complemented by qualitative evidence gained from expert judgment (Elosua & López-Jaúregui, 2007) or cognitive interviews (Benítez & Padilla, 2014; Padilla & Benítez, 2014).

Administration Guidelines

The way in which a test is administered influences the psychometric properties of the scores obtained, such as reliability and validity. The relationships between the test administrators and the test takers (rapport), the method of giving test instructions, and other interactions between the tester and test takers must all be well controlled to avoid introducing bias that might threaten the equivalence between the different versions of the evaluation instrument. As shown by Hambleton (1996), the test administrators (1) must be chosen from the population to be tested, (2) must be familiar with the details of the culture with which they are dealing, and (3) must understand the importance of following procedures to the letter when administering the tests. Rigorous training sessions must be planned for test administrators. This concern with controlling test administration is reflected in these two guidelines:

- A-1 (15). Prepare administration materials and instructions to minimize any culture- and language-related problems that are caused by administration procedures and response modes that can affect the validity of the inferences drawn from the scores.
- A-2 (16). Specify testing conditions that should be followed closely in all populations of interest.

There is a clear need to train test administrators and to avoid conditions that might compromise standardized administration, such as facial expressions or encouraging words (Franco & LeVine, 1985).

Score Scales and Interpretation Guidelines

The guidelines about scores and interpretation warn of the risks of directly comparing scores that have been obtained in different cultural or linguistic contexts through adapted scales. The comparison of scores must extend to the level of psychometric equivalence, which has been empirically demonstrated by the application of the confirmation guidelines. If metric equivalence cannot be demonstrated between the items in the original and adapted scales, the scores obtained cannot be directly compared. The problem of comparing scores is aggravated by their interpretation. As various authors have noted (e.g., Hambleton & Bollwark, 1991; Westbury, 1992), comparative studies should be used to understand the differences and similarities between the groups under analysis but never to solely make comparisons. Making comparisons is inappropriate because it is rare to find two communities that are totally equivalent in such influential aspects as motivation at the time of the test, school curricula, cultural values, standard of living, education policies, access to education, and so on. Two new guidelines warn of these considerations:

- SSI-1 (17). Interpret group score differences taking into account relevant demographic information.
- SSI-2 (18). Make comparisons of scores across populations only at the level of invariance that has been established for the scale on which scores are reported.

Documentation Guidelines

Finally, in order to interpret scores, psychologists and other test score users must have access to comprehensive documentation about how the adaptation process was carried out. The test manual must include all of the details of the adaptation process and the changes and modifications made to the original test, which in some circumstances, may be key for the interpretation of a result (Prieto & Muñiz, 2000).

- Doc-1 (19). • Provide technical documentation of any changes, including an account of the evidence obtained to support equivalence, when a test is adapted for use in another population.

- Doc-2 (20). • Provide documentation for test users that will support good practice in the use of an adapted test with people in the context of the new population.

Discussion and Conclusions

We have presented and commented on the new guidelines for the translation and adaptation of tests, prepared by the ITC. (Note that in the final review of these guidelines, small changes might be expected.) It is already well understood in the scientific community that the adaptation of tests is not merely a linguistic question, but one that demands the incorporation of cultural, linguistic, conceptual, and metric aspects from both analytical–rational and empirical perspectives of analysis. The ITC guidelines bring together, in one simple document, the steps to follow to ensure the highest level of equivalence between original and adapted versions of a test. These steps can be summarized as (1) preliminary legal considerations of intellectual property; (2) evaluation of the construct in the target population; (3) adaptation design that considers linguistic, psychological, and cultural characteristics of the adapted text as well as its practical suitability; (4) the importance of pilot tests; (5) appropriate quantitative and qualitative selection of the adaptation sample; (6) the importance of equivalence studies; (7) the definition of the extent of comparability between scores; (8) the importance of correct conditions of administration and interpretation; and (9) complete information about the changes made to the adapted test. These guidelines are a result of updating and reorganizing the original ones (Hambleton, 1996; Hambleton et al., 2005; Muñiz & Hambleton, 1996), with the intention of making use of experience gained since the publication of the first edition. However, the development of assessment in the scientific field, and in psychology and education in particular, has accelerated significantly in recent years and therefore it can be expected that these new guidelines will have to be revised again in the future in light of further advances.

ACKNOWLEDGMENTS

This work was financed by the Spanish Ministry of Economy and Competitiveness (PSI2011-28638, PSI2011-30256, PSI2014-54020), by the University of the Basque Country (GIU12-32, GIU15-24), and by the Andalusia Regional Government under the Excellent Research Fund (Projects SEJ-6569, SEJ-5188).

REFERENCES

American Psychological Association, American Educational Research Association, & National Council on Measurement in Education. (2014). *Standards for educational and psychological testing.* Washington, DC: Authors.

Benítez, I., & Padilla, J.-L. (2014). Cognitive interviewing in mixed research. In K. Miller, V. Chepp, S. Wilson, & J. L. Padilla (Eds.), *Cognitive interviewing methodology* (pp. 133–152). Hoboken, NJ: Wiley.

Benítez, I., & Padilla, J.-L. (2014). Analysis of nonequivalent assessments across different linguistic groups using a mixed methods approach: Understanding the causes of differential item functioning by cognitive interviewing. *Journal of Mixed Methods Research, 8,* 52–68.

Binet, A., & Simon, T. (1905). Méthodes nouvelles pour le diagnostic du niveau intellectual des anormaux [New methods for the diagnosis of abnormals' intellectual level]. *L'Année Psychologique, 11,* 191–336.

Brislin, R. W. (1986). The wording and translation of research instruments. In W. J. Lonner & J. W. Berry (Eds.), *Field methods in cross-cultural psychology* (pp. 137–164). Newbury Park, CA: Sage.

Byrne, B. (2008). Testing for multigroup equivalence of a measuring instrument: A walk through the process. *Psicothema, 20,* 872–882.

Calvo, N., Gutiérrez, F., Andión, O., Caseras, X., Torrubia, R., & Casas, M. (2012). Psychometric properties of the Spanish version of the self-report Personality Diagnostic Questionnaire–4+ (PDQ-4+) in psychiatric outpatients. *Psicothema, 24*(1), 156–160.

Comparative survey design and implementation (CSDI) guidelines. (2014). Retrieved March 19, 2014, from *http://ccsg.isr.umich.edu.*

Cook, L. L., & Schmitt-Cascallar, A. P. (2005). Establishing score comparability for tests given in different languages. In R. K. Hambleton, P. F. Merenda, & C. D. Spielberger (Eds.), *Adapting educational and psychological tests for cross-cultural assessment* (pp. 139–170). Mahwah, NJ: Erlbaum.

Downing, S. M. (2006). Twelve steps for effective test development. In S. M. Downing & T. M. Haladyna (Eds.), *Handbook of test development* (pp. 3–25). Mahwah, NJ: Erlbaum.

Downing, S. M., & Haladyna, T. M. (Eds.). (2006). *Handbook of test development.* Mahwah, NJ: Erlbaum.

Elosua, P. (2003). Sobre la validez de los tests [About test validity]. *Psicothema, 15*(2), 315–321.

Elosua, P. (2005). Evaluación progresiva de la invarianza factorial entre las versiones original y adaptada de una escala de autoconcepto [Progressive evaluation of factorial invariance between original and adapted versions of a self-concept scale]. *Psicothema, 17*(2), 356–362.

Elosua, P. (2012). Tests published in Spain: Uses, customs and pending matters. *Papeles del Psicólogo, 33*(1), 12–21.

Elosua, P., Bully, P., Mujika, J., & Almeida, L. (2012, July). Practical ways to apply the ITC precondition, and development guidelines in adapting tests. Spanish adaptation of "Bateria de Provas de Raciocinio." Paper presented at the Fifth European Congress on Methodology, Santiago de Compostela, Spain.

Elosua, P., & Hambleton, R. K. (in press). Test score comparability across language and cultural groups in the presence of item bias. *Educational and Psychological Measurement.*

Elosua, P., & Iliescu, D. (2012). Tests in Europe: Where we are and where we should go. *International Journal of Testing, 12,* 157–175.

Elosua, P., & López-Jaúregui, A. (2007). Potential sources of differential item functioning in the adaptation of tests. *International Journal of Testing, 7*(1), 39–52.

Elosua, P., & Muñiz, J. (2010). Exploring the factorial structure of the self-concept: A sequential approach using CFA, MIMIC and MACS models, across gender and two languages. *European Psychologist, 15,* 58–67.

Evers, A., Muñiz, J., Bartram, D., Boben, D., Egeland, J., Fernández-Hermida, J. R., et al. (2012). Testing practices in the 21st century: Developments and European psychologists' opinions. *European Psychologist, 17*(4), 300–319.

Franco, J. N., & LeVine, E. (1985). Effects of examiner variables on reported self-disclosure: Implications for group personality testing. *Hispanic Journal of Behavioral Sciences, 7*(2), 187–197.

Hambleton, R. K. (1994). Guidelines for adapting educational and psychological tests: A progress report. *European Journal of Psychological Assessment, 10*(3), 229–244.

Hambleton, R. K. (1996). Adaptación de tests para su uso en diferentes idiomas y culturas: fuentes de error, posibles soluciones y directrices prácticas [Adapting tests in different languages and cultures: Sources of error, possible solutions, and practical guidelines]. In J. Muñiz (Ed.), *Psicometría* (pp. 207–238). Madrid: Universitas.

Hambleton, R. K. (2009, July). *International Test Commission guidelines for test adaptation, second edition.* Paper presented at the 11th European Congress on Psychology, Oslo, Norway.

Hambleton, R. K., & Bollwark, J. (1991). Adapting tests for use in different cultures: Technical issues and methods. *Bulletin of the International Test Commission, 18,* 3–32.

Hambleton, R. K., Merenda, P., & Spielberger, C. (Eds.). (2005). *Adapting educational and psychological tests for cross-cultural assessment.* Hillsdale, NJ: Erlbaum.

Hambleton, R. K., & Zenisky, A. L. (2011). Translating and adapting tests for cross-cultural assessments. In D. Matsumoto & F. J. R. van de Vijver (Eds.), *Cross-cultural research methods in psychology* (pp. 46–70). New York: Cambridge University Press.

Harkness, J. A. (2002). Questionnaire translation. In J. A. Harkness, F. J. R. van de Vijver, & P. P. Mohler (Eds.), *Cross-cultural survey methods.* Hoboken, NJ: Wiley.

Harkness, J. A., Villar, A., & Edwards, B. (2010). Translation, adaptation, and design. In J. A. Harkness et al. (Eds.), *Survey methods in multinational, multiregional, and multicultural contexts* (pp. 117–140). Hoboken, NJ: Wiley.

Holland, P. W., & Wainer, H. (1993). *Differential item functioning.* Hillsdale, NJ: Erlbaum.

International Test Commission. (2010). International test commission guidelines for translating and adapting tests. Available at *www.intestcom.org.*

Iturbide, L. M., Elosua, P., & Yenes, F. (2010). Medida de la cohesión en equipos deportivos: Adaptación al español del Group Environment Questionnaire (GEQ) [A measure of team cohesion in sport: Spanish adaptation of group environment questionnaire (GEQ)]. *Psicothema, 22,* 482–488.

Lissitz, R. W. (Ed.). (2009). *The concept of validity: Revisions, new directions, and applications.* Charlotte, NC: Information Age.

Matsumoto, D., & van de Vijver, F. J. R. (Eds.). (2011). *Cross-cultural research methods in psychology.* New York: Cambridge University Press.

Miller, K., Chepp, V., Wilson, S., & Padilla, J.-L. (2014). *Cognitive interviewing methodology.* Hoboken, NJ: Wiley.

Muñiz, J. (1997). *Introducción a la teoría de respuesta a los ítems* [Introduction to item response theory]. Madrid: Pirámide.

Muñiz, J. (2003). *Teoría clásica de los tests* [Classical test theory]. Madrid: Pirámide.

Muñiz, J., Elosua, P., & Hambleton, R. K. (2013). Directrices para la traducción y adaptación de los tests, segunda edición [International Test Commission guidelines for test translation and adaptation, second edition]. *Psicothema, 25*(2), 151–157.

Muñiz, J., & Hambleton, R. K. (1996). Directrices para la traducción y adaptación de tests [Guidelines for test translation and adaptation]. *Papeles del Psicólogo, 66,* 63–70.

Nogueira, R., Godoy, A., Romero, P., Gavino, A., & Cobos, M. P. (2012). Propiedades psicométricas de la versión española del Obsessive Belief Questionnaire—Child versión (OBQ-CV) en una muestra no clínica [Psychometric properties of the Spanish version of the Obsessive Belief Questionnaire—Child Version in a non-clinical sample]. *Psicothema, 24*(4), 674–679.

Ortiz, S., Navarro, C., García, E., Ramis, C., & Manassero, M. A. (2012). Validación de la versión española de la escala de trabajo emocional de Frankfurt [Validation of the Spanish version of the Frankfurt Emotion Work Scales]. *Psicothema, 24*(2), 337–342.

Padilla, J.-L., & Benítez, I. (2014). Validity evidence based on response processes. *Psicothema, 26,* 136–144.

PISA Consortium. (2010). Translation and adaptation guidelines for PISA 2012. Retrieved March 31, 2014, from *www.oecd.org/pisa/pisaproducts/49273486.pdf.*

Prieto, G., & Muñiz, J. (2000). Un modelo para evaluar la calidad de los tests utilizados en España [A model to evaluate the quality of tests used in Spain]. *Papeles del Psicólogo, 77,* 65–71.

Rodríguez, M. S., Martínez, Z., Tinajero, C., Guisande, M. A., & Páramo, M. F. (2012). Adaptación española de la escala de aceptación percibida (PAS) en estudiantes universitarios [Spanish adaptation of the Perceived Acceptance Scale (PAS) in university students]. *Psicothema, 24*(3), 483–488.

Schmeiser, C. B., & Welch, C. (2006). Test development. In R. L. Brennan (Ed.), *Educational measurement* (4th ed.). Westport, CT: American Council on Education/Praeger.

Sireci, S. (1997). Technical issues in linking tests across languages. *Educational Measurement: Issues and Practice, 16,* 12–19.

Sireci, S. (2011). Evaluating test and survey items for bias across language and cultures. In D. Matsumoto & F. J. R. van de Vijver (Eds.), *Cross-cultural research methods in psychology* (pp. 216–243). New York: Cambridge University Press.

University of Michigan. (2011). Guidelines for best practice in cross-cultural surveys. Ann Arbor: Survey Research Center, Institute for Social Research, University of Michigan. Retrieved from *http://ccsg.isr.umich.edu/pdf/FullGuidelines1301.pdf.*

van de Vijver, F. J. R., & Lung, K. (2011). Equivalence and bias: A review of concepts, models, and data analytic procedures. In D. Matsumoto & F. J. R. van de Vijver (Eds.),

Cross-cultural research methods in psychology (pp. 17–45). New York: Cambridge University Press.

van de Vijver, F. J. R., & Poortinga, Y. H. (1997). Towards an integrated analysis of bias in cross-cultural assessment. *European Journal of Psychological Assessment, 13*, 29–37.

van de Vijver, F. J. R., & Tanzer, N. K. (1997). Bias and equivalence in cross-cultural assessment: An overview. *European Review of Applied Psychology, 47*(4), 263–279.

Westbury, I. (1992). Comparing American and Japanese achievement: Is the United States really a low achiever? *Educational Researcher, 21*, 10–24.

Willis, G. B. (2005). *Cognitive interviewing.* Thousand Oaks, CA: Sage.

Wilson, M. (2005). *Constructing measures: An item response modeling approach.* Mahwah, NJ: Erlbaum.

PART VI

Accountability Testing and Score Reporting

CHAPTER 18

The History of Accountability in Educational Testing

Robert L. Linn

One of the important uses of educational testing during the last half century has been to meet the many demands for educational accountability. There have been persistent and seemingly growing calls for accountability that have placed heavy demands on educational testing. According to Elmore (2004), the emphasis on test-based accountability as an educational reform policy over the last 50 years is more persistent than any other policy. That conclusion is as well founded today as it was a decade ago when Elmore's chapter was published. The roles that tests play in educational accountability have changed from one decade to the next, but student testing has been a key component of accountability. There is a variety of reasons for the widespread interest in test-based accountability.

Interest in Accountability

The interest in educational accountability during the past half century stems from the dissatisfaction of policymakers and, to a lesser extent, the general public, with student achievement. Early on, when the Elementary and Secondary Education Act (ESEA; 1965) was enacted, attention was directed primarily at the generally low achievement of economically disadvantaged students. Over time, however, the demands for educational accountability expanded to include a broader range of students. Complaints about inadequate student achievement were fueled by the relatively poor performance of American students on international assessments, by the increases in the number of students who need to take non-credit-bearing remedial courses in college, and by complaints of employers about the lack of preparedness of high school graduates for work and job training programs.

Given that policymakers think unsatisfactory student achievement is the educational problem, why do they turn to test-based accountability as the solution? There are several reasons. Compared to other educational reforms such as reduced class size, higher teacher salaries, or a longer school year, testing is relatively inexpensive. Unlike reforms such as improved classroom teaching practices or changes in curriculum, which are hard to implement from afar, testing programs and accountability can be mandated by legislative action.

Test-Based Accountability Systems

Accountability systems have taken on a number of forms since the enactment of ESEA in 1965. The initial emphasis was on program evaluation and was limited to schools receiving Title I funds to improve the education of students from poor families. Accountability was based on norm-referenced interpretations of test results. Although testing requirements have continued under ESEA throughout the various reenactments of the law during the past 50 years, the details and accountability requirements have changed. Those changes are considered later in this chapter.

Minimum-Competency Testing

The minimum-competency testing (MCT) movement was the dominant form of test-based accountability in the 1970s. MCT was an outgrowth of widespread dissatisfaction with the preparation of high school graduates. Over half the states introduced some form of MCT requirement during the 1970s. Unlike the Title I testing requirements, MCT relied on criterion-referenced test interpretation. The question was not how well a student performed in comparison to other students but whether the student's score exceeded the MCT cut score (see also Pitoniak & Cizek, Chapter 3, this volume). The other big shift was that, with MCT, accountability was focused at the individual student level rather than at the program level.

A Nation at Risk

By the 1980s it was recognized that a major limitation of the MCT movement was that the tests measured only low-level knowledge and skills, as would be expected for tests designed to define a minimum performance level. Interest in MCT as an accountability mechanism waned and, with the publication of *A Nation at Risk: The Imperative for Educational Reform* (National Commission on Excellence in Education, 1983) and several other related reports, test-based accountability entered a new era.

A Nation at Risk relied heavily on tests to document shortcomings in student achievement, and also recommended that tests be used as a mechanism of reform.

In combination with several other reports that appeared at about the same time, *A Nation at Risk* had a major impact. Every state implemented some type of educational reform in response, and test-based accountability systems were central to most of these state-initiated reforms. The accountability systems used school and district test results in an effort to make educators more accountable for student achievement.

Many of the newly created school accountability systems relied on the use of off-the-shelf, norm-referenced tests, and the same test forms were used several years in a row. A major flaw in this approach soon became apparent. The use of test preparation materials designed to teach narrowly to the content covered by a single norm-referenced test led to inflated test scores and what came to be known as the "Lake Wobegon effect" after a physician, John Cannell (1987), published a paper in which he noted that almost all states and most districts were reporting that their students were above the national average. Although states and districts had substantial gains in student test scores in the first few years following the adoption of a test (leading to the Lake Woebegon effect), there was almost always a large drop in the average test score the first year that a new norm-referenced test was adopted (Linn, Graue, & Sanders, 1990).

The Lake Wobegon experience, along with other evidence suggesting a narrow teaching to a particular form of a norm-referenced test, clearly demonstrated that the reuse of a single test form led to serious inflation of test results and provided a reason to turn away from reliance on norm-referenced tests for purposes of accountability. The standards-based reform movement (e.g., Smith & O'Day, 1991) provided a second, and possibly more important, reason for the movement away from norm-referenced tests. The standards-based approach called for criterion-referenced tests designed to measure the achievement of specified content standards, and for performance to be judged by comparing student achievement to established performance standards rather than to the performance of other students (for more information on criterion-referenced testing, see Hambleton, Zenisky, & Popham, Chapter 2, this volume).

Since it was recognized that the same form of a test, whether norm-referenced or criterion-referenced, could not be used year after year, the standards-based accountability systems required that a new test form be used each year. To provide comparability across multiple test forms from year to year, each new test was equated to previously used tests or to an item bank using embedded anchor tests and item response theory. Introducing a new form of the test each year that is equated to earlier forms is necessary to avoid inflation in test scores on tests used for accountability, but it is not sufficient. It is also important that the way in which key concepts and understandings are assessed needs to change from year to year in order to avoid the problems caused by teaching to a specific representation of a concept rather than to a broader understanding of it (Koretz, 2008b).

A substantial number of states adopted content standards and developed standards-based accountability systems during the 1990s. Stakes for schools and/or teachers were attached to test results by some states. The use of rewards or sanctions was quite variable, however, from one state to the next. Uniform sanctions across states were introduced with the enactment of the No Child Left Behind (NCLB) law in 2001.

No Child Left Behind

NCLB required states to adopt grade-specific content standards in mathematics and reading or English language arts (ELA), and to develop tests that were aligned with those standards. States also were required to set performance standards on those tests that defined "proficient" performance and at least two other levels. The standards-based tests adopted by states had to be administered each year to students in grades 3–8 and in one grade in high school.

The uses of test results to hold schools accountable required states to establish annual targets that would determine whether or not a school was making "adequate yearly progress" (AYP). The AYP targets had to be set in a way that would culminate in 100% of students scoring at the proficient level or above by 2014. Schools and districts that failed to meet AYP for a given year were designated *needs improvement,* and continued failure to make AYP in subsequent years resulted in increasingly severe sanctions for schools. To avoid being labeled "needs improvement," schools had to make AYP in both mathematics and reading or ELA for each of a variety of subgroups of students defined by race/ethnicity, socioeconomic status, disability, and English learner status, as well as the general population. Moreover, at least 95% of the eligible students in each subgroup had to be assessed in each subject.

Even though most states set lenient proficiency standards (e.g., Linn, 2007), it was apparent from the start that the goal of 100% proficient by 2014 was completely unrealistic and would lead to the vast majority of schools being labeled *needs improvement* as 2014 drew nearer (e.g., Linn, 2003). As predicted, the number of schools failing to make AYP increased from year to year. Faced with that reality, the U.S. Department of Education began granting a variety of waivers, starting in 2011, as part of a new initiative called "Race to the Top" (RTT). To receive RTT grants, states had to agree to make changes in their accountability models that included, among other things, the use of student test results in teacher evaluation.

Teacher Evaluation

It is obvious that it would be unfair to use student test scores from a single point in time to evaluate teachers: The students in one teacher's class differ greatly from their counterparts in another teacher's class in terms of their background and preparedness to learn the material in a given grade. Hence, the teacher evaluation systems developed pursuant to RTT agreements all involved longitudinal results that use changes in student test performance to evaluate teachers. It is believed that such growth measures, in addition to providing a better basis for teacher evaluation, may also enrich school accountability, in comparison to status measures alone, as initially required by NCLB (see Keller, Colvin, and Garcia, Chapter 19, this volume, for a more in-depth discussion of the pros and cons of growth-based accountability models).

States and districts use several different approaches to create teacher evaluation systems that link student test scores, obtained at two or more points in time, to teachers. The two most popular approaches to growth modeling are some form of value-added model (e.g., Kane & Staiger, 2008; Sanders, Saxton, & Horn, 1997) or a norm-based approach based on student growth percentiles (Betebenner, 2008). Both approaches are appealing because they claim a level playing field by taking prior achievement into account. Regardless of approach, teachers are evaluated using scores obtained by students in their classes in a given year after taking into account student test results for the previous year or years. Teachers are considered effective if their students score higher than expected based on their performance in previous years. Similarly, teachers are considered ineffective if their students do worse than expected from their test results in earlier years.

There is evidence at the aggregate level that teacher quality makes a difference in student test scores. A difference of one standard deviation in teacher value-added scores has been found to translate into approximately one-tenth of a standard deviation difference in student test scores (e.g., Chetty, Friedman, & Rockoff, 2011; Kane & Staiger, 2008). In addition to being associated with larger student gains in achievement, value-added estimates of teacher effectiveness have been shown to predict long-term outcomes, such as the likelihood that a student will attend college, the quality of college that a student will attend, the likelihood of a student having a baby when still a teenager, and a student's lifetime earnings (Chetty et al., 2011).

Although these associations of aggregate value-added results are impressive, it does not follow, and is debatable, that value-added scores are adequate for the evaluation of individual teachers. Critics (e.g., Baker et al., 2010) have identified a number of reasons why value-added results alone are not an adequate basis for judging the effectiveness of individual teachers. First, there is substantial volatility in a teacher's value-added scores from one year to the next. Using data from five large Florida school districts, McCaffrey, Sass, Lockwood, and Mihaly (2009) found that year-to-year correlation coefficients in value-added measures ranged from .2 to .5 for elementary teachers and from .3 to .7 for middle school teachers. Such low levels of stability would hardly be considered acceptable for a test used to make high-stakes decisions. To obtain acceptable levels of stability, estimates need to be averaged for at least 2 years.

Another limitation of value-added analyses for teacher evaluation is that they are generally available only for teachers who teach ELA or mathematics in grades 4 through 8. The restriction to these grades is due to the NCLB requirement that tests be administered in reading or ELA and mathematics in grades 3 through 8 and one grade in high school. Since test data are usually not available prior to grade 3 and value-added analyses require test data at two points in time, the typically available test data do not provide a basis for computing value-added scores for teachers who teach grade 3. This limitation also applies at the high school level since testing is required at only one grade in high school. Furthermore, many high school teachers teach subjects other than ELA or mathematics.

Inclusion

NCLB greatly expanded the definition of the population of students who had to be included in test-based accountability. Prior to NCLB, many students were simply excluded from testing either because they had cognitive disabilities or because they were not proficient in English. NCLB changed that and introduced a new emphasis on inclusion.

Students with Disabilities

Most students with disabilities can participate in assessment if appropriate accommodations are made available. A variety of accommodations has been used successfully to enable students with various disabilities to participate in the regular assessment. Some of the more frequently used accommodations include extra time, individual or small-group administration, highlighting of key words, and large-print versions of the test. The choice of a particular accommodation is dictated by each student's individual needs on his or her individualized education program (IEP). The key considerations in choosing accommodations that maintain the validity of the assessment are that they should level the playing field by removing construct-irrelevant barriers to valid measurement, but should not alter the construct being measured.

A small fraction of students with severe cognitive disabilities are not able to participate in the general assessment even with accommodations. In recognition of this group of students, NCLB allows for the inclusion of these students by the administration of an alternate assessment based on alternate content standards. States are not allowed to count the performance of more than 1% of all the students in their accountability results who are administered an alternate assessment. The inclusion of students with severe cognitive disabilities has led to increased attention to the academic preparation of those students. For more information on assessing students with disabilities, readers are referred to Thurlow and Quenemoen (Chapter 24, this volume).

English Learners

Another group of students that was routinely excluded from accountability testing prior to the enactment of NCLB is English learners (ELs).[1] Under NCLB ELs must be included in regular assessment at the same rates as the general population, sometimes with the use of accommodations such as the addition of a dictionary or test forms that are printed in two languages side by side. States are also required to administer English language proficiency tests to measure the degree of English proficiency of their EL students. For more information on this subgroup, see Faulkner-Bond and Forte, Chapter 23, this volume.

---

[1]There are many titles applied to this subgroup of students, including English language learners (ELLs), limited English proficient (LEP), and emergent bilingual students, to name a few. In this chapter, we use the label English learner (EL), which is currently used by the U.S. Department of Education.

Overall, the emphasis under NCLB on inclusion of as many students as possible in mandated tests has led to a substantially larger proportion of students participating in state tests and being counted for purposes of accountability than was true before NCLB.

Future Accountability Systems

Although the reauthorization of NCLB is long overdue,[2] it is not clear when it will be reauthorized. It is evident, however, that there is considerable dissatisfaction with the accountability requirements of the current law. It remains to be seen what implications that dissatisfaction will have for the accountability requirements in the reauthorization, but there are several activities that are likely to help shape the requirements.

Common Core State Standards

The Common Core State Standards (CCSS; *www.corestandards.org*) were developed under the auspices of the Council of Chief State School Officers (CCSSO) and the National Governors Association (NGA). These standards were developed in response to the concerns that state content standards varied substantially from state to state and in many cases lacked rigor.

The developers of the CCSS were informed by the strengths and lessons from state content standards and by the learning expectations in other high-performing countries. The standards are intended to be rigorous and stress higher-order learning and problem-solving skills that may be necessary to be ready for college and the work place. It is intended that students who master the high school level CCSS will be prepared for college and job training programs. Forty-five states and the District of Columbia initially adopted the CCSS when they were released in 2010. Subsequent controversies about the CCSS and the more demanding tests needed to measure them, however, caused a few states to rethink their commitment to these standards.

State Assessment Consortia

Since state tests must be aligned with the state content standards adopted by a state, adoption of the CCSS had direct implications for state testing programs, and required substantial revisions in the tests states use. In 2011, the U.S. Department of Education funded two multistate consortia to develop assessments that aligned with the CCSS: the Partnership for Assessment of Readiness for College and Careers (PARCC; *www.parcconline.org*) and the Smarter Balanced Assessment Consortium (SBAC; *www.k12.wa.us/smarter/default.aspx*). Although membership has fluctuated since 2011, a

---

[2]ESEA was officially reauthorized in December 2015, two days after Dr. Linn passed away. As editors, we chose to publish his comments on future accountability systems without revision, as we believe the points he highlighted remain relevant even after the reauthorization.

majority of states committed to one or both of the consortia, and both consortia completed inaugural administrations of their tests in the 2014–2015 school year.[3]

As the name suggests, PARCC sought to develop an assessment system that will increase the number of high school graduates who are prepared for success in college and in the workplace. To accomplish this goal, PARCC developed assessments that can be used to determine whether students are college- and career-ready or on track. It was intended that the assessments "assess the full range of the CCSS, including standards that are difficult to measure." The assessments intended to measure achievement of both high- and low-performing students. The plan was that the assessment system would provide the data needed for accountability purposes, including the measurement of growth (*www.parcconline.org/parcc-assessment-design*).

To accomplish these ambitious goals, PARCC used computer-administered tests that "include a mix of constructed response items, performance-based tasks and computer-enhanced, computer-scored items" (*www.parcconline.org/parcc-assessment-design*). There are two required summative assessments and three optional nonsummative components, one of which measures speaking and listening skills. Once developed, it was planned that the assessment system would be available to all member states.

The SBAC assessment system plans were equally ambitious. Similar to the PARCC plans, SBAC sought to develop an assessment system comprised of both required summative and optional interim assessments. SBAC also developed an array of formative tools to help teachers assess student acquisition of the CCSS and diagnose student learning needs. Like PARCC, SBAC planned to measure growth with respect to the knowledge and skills required to be college and career ready.

SBAC developed computer-adaptive tests and performance tasks for both the summative and interim assessments. The assessments also included both the computer-adaptive component and performance tasks that would be administered the last 12 weeks of the school year in grades 3–8 and high school for English Language Arts (ELA) and mathematics (*www.k12.wa.us/smarter/pubdocs/SBASSummary.2010. PDF*).

The emphasis on inclusion of all students that is a prominent feature of NCLB continues to be important for new systems developed by PARCC and SBAC. Both of these state consortia planned to provide a system of accommodations to make it possible for students with disabilities to participate in the assessments. Because of the desire to include all students, the U.S. Department of Education also funded two state consortia to develop alternate assessments for students with severe cognitive disabilities and two state consortia to develop English language proficiency tests for ELs. The assessments developed by these consortia are intended to improve the measurement of ELs' English proficiency and the measurement of the degree to which students with

---

[3]Both PARCC and SBAC completed their initial assessment and development work by 2015, as intended. To support continued use and development of the assessments, PARCC has incorporated an independent management organization and SBAC is now housed within the Graduate School of Education and Information at the University of California Los Angeles.

cognitive disabilities have mastered the CCSS. (For a review of the design and development process for one of these consortia, the National Center and State Collaborative [NCSC], see Thurlow & Quenemoen, Chapter 24, this volume.)

Designing Effective Test-Based Accountability Systems

The history of test-based accountability systems reveals that such systems need to be designed with considerable care. The tests need to be designed to measure the knowledge and skills that are important. The validity of the uses of test scores for purposes of accountability needs to be evaluated (American Educational Research Association, American Psychological Association, & National Council on Measurement in Education [AERA, APA, & NCME], 2014; Baker, Linn, Herman, & Koretz, 2002). The tests need to be aligned with high-quality content standards that specify the desired knowledge and skills. It is my opinion that the recently developed CCSS fit that description and provide an excellent framework to guide test development.

High-quality content standards, although critical, are insufficient. They need to be accompanied by tests and instructional materials that are well aligned with each other and with the standards. The tests need to provide broad and representative coverage of the content standards at a depth of knowledge identified by the standards. They need to assess those content standards that are hard to measure as well as those that are more readily measured by a standardized achievement test.

Both the SBAC and PARCC consortia developed tests that are aligned with the CCSS and meet the other characteristics noted above. The consortia goals are ambitious and promised to use technology to make it possible to assess hard-to-measure standards. If the goals of the consortia are finally realized, states will have tests that are substantially better than those in current use. Although promising, it remains to be seen the degree to which the ambitious goals of the consortia will be realized.

Past experience has clearly shown that it is unacceptable to use the same test form from year to year when high stakes are attached to results. A new form of the test that is equated to forms used in previous years must be developed each year. It is also important that the way in which key concepts and understandings are assessed needs to change from year to year to avoid the problems caused by teaching to a specific representation of a concept rather than to a broader understanding of it (Koretz, 2008a, 2008b).

Accountability systems need to stop relying on current status scores, which are fundamental for the current NCLB requirements, and put the emphasis on growth. Learning implies a change in achievement rather than a particular level of achievement at a fixed point in time. Growth may also provide a fairer basis of comparison than current status for comparing schools whose students start at different levels of achievement.

Systems also need to include indicators of the degree to which tests used for accountability provide an inflated impression of achievement gains. This may be done by comparing trends in achievement on the high-stakes accountability tests to trends for low-stakes tests such as the National Assessment of Educational Progress (NAEP). Alternatively, accountability systems could include some form of self-monitoring mechanism such as that suggested by Koretz and Bequin (2010).

It is important that testing systems used for accountability purposes include as many students as possible. Thus, there is a need to provide the accommodations that enable students with disabilities to participate. It is important that the systems include a means of determining when ELs have sufficient proficiency in English to take subject-area tests in English. It is also important to have a system of alternative assessments for students with severe cognitive disabilities so that those students can be included in the overall accountability system.

Conclusion

Test-based accountability has taken a variety of forms during the past 50 years. A great deal has been learned about the design of systems that maximize positive effects and ways to avoid some of the potential unintended negative effects of accountability. The tests and supporting materials being developed by the two multistate consortia are promising. There is pushback, however, by people who do not like the CCSS and those concerned about the increased testing time and cost required by the two consortia. Nevertheless, the demands and concerns about lackluster student achievement and preparedness for college that have fueled demands for test-based accountability for the past 50 years remain strong and seem to be gaining strength. Thus, it seems unlikely that the nation will pull back from heavy reliance on tests to hold schools, teachers, and students accountable.

REFERENCES

American Educational Research Association, American Psychological Association, & the National Council on Measurement in Education. (2014). *Standards for educational and psychological testing.* Washington, DC: Authors.

Baker, E. L., Barton, P. E., Darling-Hammond, L., Haertel, E., Ladd, H. F., Linn, R. L., et al. (2010, August 29). *Problems with the use of student test scores to evaluate teachers.* EPI Briefing Paper #278. Washington, DC: Economic Policy Institute.

Baker, E. L., Linn, R. L., Herman, J. L., & Koretz, D. (2002). *Standards for educational accountability systems.* CRESST Policy Brief 5 (pp. 1–6). Los Angeles: University of California, National Center for Research on Evaluation, Standards, and Student Testing.

Betebenner, D. W. (2008). Toward a normative understanding of student growth. In R. E. Ryan & L. A. Shepard (Eds.), *The future of test-based accountability.* New York: Taylor & Francis.

Cannell, J. J. (1987). *Nationally normed elementary achievement testing in America's public schools: How all 50 states are above the national average* (2nd ed.). Danniels, WV: Friends of Education.

Chetty, R., Friedman, J. N., & Rockoff, J. E. (2011). *The long-term impacts of teachers: Teacher value-added and student outcomes in adulthood.* NBER Working Paper Series. Cambridge, MA: National Bureau of Economic Research.

Elementary and Secondary Education Act of 1965, Public Law 89-10.

Elmore, R. F. (2004). The problem of stakes in performance-based accountability systems. In S. H. Fuhrman & R. F. Elmore (Eds.), *Redesigning accountability systems for education* (pp. 274–296). New York: Teachers College Press.

Kane, T. J., & Staiger, D. O. (2008). *Estimating teacher impacts on student achievement: An experimental evaluation.* NBER Working Paper No. 14607. Cambridge, MA: National Bureau of Economic Research.

Koretz, D. M. (2008a). Further steps toward the development of an accountability-oriented science of measurement. In K. E. Ryan & L. A. Shepard (Eds.), *The future of test-based educational accountability* (pp. 72–91). Mahwah, NJ: Erlbaum.

Koretz, D. M. (2008b). *Measuring up: What educational testing really tells us.* Cambridge, MA: Harvard University Press.

Koretz, D. M., & Bequin, A. (2010). Self-monitoring assessments for educational accountability systems. *Measurement, 8,* 92–109.

Linn, R. L. (2003). Accountability: Responsibility and reasonable expectations. *Educational Researcher, 31*(7), 3–13.

Linn, R. L. (2007). Performance standards: What is proficient performance? In C. E. Sleeter (Ed.), *Facing accountability in education* (pp. 112–131). New York: Teachers College Press.

Linn, R. L., Graue, M. E., & Sanders, N. M. (1990). Comparing state and district test results to national norms: The validity of claims that "everyone is above average." *Educational Measurement: Issues and Practice, 9*(3), 5–14.

McCaffrey, D. F., Sass, T. R., Lockwood, J. R., & Mihaly, K. (2009). The intertemporal variability of teacher effect estimates. *Education Finance and Policy, 4*(4), 572–606.

National Commission on Excellence in Education. (1983). *A nation at risk: The imperative for educational reform.* Washington, DC: U.S. Government Printing Office.

No Child Left Behind Act of 2001, Pub. Law No. 107.110.

Sanders, W. L., Saxton, A. M., & Horn, S. P. (1997). The Tennessee value-added assessment system: A quantitative outcome-based approach to educational assessment. In J. Millman (Ed.), *Grading teachers, grading schools: Is student achievement a valid measure?* (pp. 137–162). Thousand Oaks, CA: Corwin Press.

Smith, M., & O'Day, J. (1991). *Putting the pieces together: Systemic school reform.* CPRE Policy Brief. New Brunswick, NJ: Eagleton Institute Politics.

CHAPTER 19

Growth
Measurement, Meaning, and Misuse

Lisa A. Keller, Kimberly F. Colvin, and Alejandra Garcia

We are living in an information age. Technology has afforded anyone with an Internet connection access to tremendous amounts of information, rather than relying on experts to select and distill information. This access allows users of information to make more informed decisions, and to critically evaluate recommendations made by experts. It has also created a culture in which we rely on data to make decisions. The reach of information and data-based decision making has extended into the educational sphere as well, where teachers and schools are being asked to make decisions based on data.

Access to so much information can be convincing to teachers, parents, administrators, test developers, or researchers that we are making better decisions, since they are based on data. In particular, numerical data are viewed as more accurate, objective, and without bias—and hence, true. Incorporating this information into our decision making only makes sense. However, it is necessary to be sure that the data are *informing* decisions rather than *making* them. The truth is, data have varying degrees of veracity, and the quality of a data-based decision depends directly on the quality of the data we are using. Without recognizing the fallibility of data, especially quantitative, "objective" data, there is the risk of forgetting this distinction; instead of making better decisions, less good decisions are being made. In education, this widespread resurgence of interest in using data to make decisions is likewise creating the situation where the data are making, rather than guiding, decisions. In the second decade of the 21st century, one arena where this risk is perhaps high is the measurement and use of student growth data.

Growth models are used for a variety of purposes, both at the student level and at aggregated levels. The obvious use is to track student progress, and to determine if the student is on track for reaching proficiency. If a student is not making progress, he or she can receive remediation or support services that might be required for him or her to make adequate progress. Students making exceptional gains might be targeted for scholarships or awards. At the aggregate level, inferences about teacher and school effectiveness are made based on some notion of "typical" student growth for a teacher or school. Some of these decisions might be high-stakes (e.g., tenure decisions for teachers) or low-stakes (e.g., flagging teachers who might need extra support).

Why Is It Important to Measure Student Growth?

Starting with No Child Left Behind (2001), there was a great push to be able to identify how well students were learning, and to raise the bar in educational standards to be sure that all students were receiving an adequate education. This movement led to the creation of standards-based assessments that were designed to measure how well students were mastering academic content. These assessments were more or less successful, and provided a snapshot in time of student performance relative to state content standards. The goal was to get all students to reach a level of "proficiency" over time. In such a system, cohorts of students were compared to one another, and "progress" for a school was defined as an increase in the percentage of students in grade X that was classified as proficient. So, if 50% of third graders was proficient in math in Year 1, and 60% of them was proficient in Year 2, then this school has shown progress toward the goal of 100% of students becoming proficient.

There are, of course, flaws to this type of accountability model. One major criticism was that low-performing schools were not getting enough credit for the progress they were making because they weren't making proficiency standards (Hoffer, Hedberg, Brown, Halverson, & McDonald, 2010). In response to this type of concern, the Growth Model Pilot Program (U.S. Department of Education, 2005) was developed to award credit to schools where students were showing improvement in test scores. While this idea seems very logical and intuitively simple, it is actually quite a complex idea to define what is meant by *growth* and how it should be measured.

What Does *Growth* Mean?

This question appears rather simple. If you ask a room full of people what *growth* means in an educational context, you might expect the answer to be straightforward. However, people conceptualize growth in many different ways, and everyone thinks that their own definition is how everyone perceives growth. Taking a step back, when viewed relative to physical phenomena such as height, growth is obvious: Did the person get taller? Also, most people agree on how to measure height, although the choice of unit might vary (feet, inches, centimeters, meters, etc.). If a person is 60 inches at Time 1, and 62 inches at Time 2, then he or she grew 2 inches.

But even in this straightforward case, one might then ponder questions such as "Is 2 inches a lot? A little? Should I have grown more? Less?" And this answer is a bit more complicated, and would usually start with "It depends. . . . " What does it depend on? The age of the person, the sex of the person, the person's genetics, the person's initial height, etc. So to contextualize changes in height, doctors often use a norm group as a base of reference and say things like, "For someone of your age, ethnicity, and sex, we would expect you to have grown 1–3 inches, so you are right on track." Without this contextualizing information, you might not know how to interpret your growth. But we also recognize that the doctor only took into account generic factors such as age, ethnicity, and sex, and could not take into account all possible variables, including genetics. Had you not met the expectation of 1–3 inches (either more or less growth), the doctor would likely consider other variables to help you understand whether there were a cause for concern.

What does this line of thinking have to do with education? The goal is to determine how much growth a student has made in, say, mathematics over 1 year. The first challenge is to determine whether or not the student's skill in mathematics can be measured accurately. Let's assume that standards-based assessments have been able to successfully measure the content domain of interest (e.g., grade-level mathematics skills, as defined by the statewide content standards), and that the definition of mathematics achievement as measured by the statewide large-scale test is agreed upon. Now there is at least a position of agreeing on how to measure the construct to be evaluated; we have our definition of height.

Now it is necessary to agree on what a change in mathematics achievement means. A typical answer would be "You got better at math." But how does one judge "better at math"? It is necessary to think carefully about how to best define that change in achievement, and to agree on a definition that is measureable. Some typical ways of conceptualizing "getting better at math" might be as:

- A higher score on the test compared to last time you took the test.
- A change in proficiency category.
- A greater mastery of the content.
- Doing better than the other students in the class.

Depending on the choice of the definition, how to quantify the change would be different. Therefore, it is essential to be clear about what is meant by the term growth. This term is used quite casually in discussions with educators, as well as psychometricians, and it is necessary to be clearer and more precise in our terminology so that our conversations about students' growth are meaningful. It is most important to be sure that all those involved in the conversation are conceptualizing growth in the same way. Although there are many "growth" models, it is impossible that all of those models conceptualize growth in the same way, so a choice of a model is a choice of a definition of growth, and that must be made explicit.

Even if it is possible to agree on what it means to get better at math, or to grow in the sense of mathematical achievement, there are many obstacles to measuring that change well. Some are technical challenges involving the nature of assessments and statistical models. Some of the most daunting challenges are practical challenges—for example, how do we add in growth measurement without increasing overall time on testing and loss of instructional time? Each of these issues is considered separately.

What Are the Technical Complexities of Measuring Growth?

As mentioned above, the definition of growth dictates how growth gets measured. That means that a measure that is in line with our definition of growth must exist. Ideally, the measure would be designed with that specific purpose in mind. Rarely can this be done, as the resources required to produce an assessment designed solely for the purpose of measuring growth often far exceed what states and schools have to work with in practice. As such, it is natural that states often want to use existing measures, such as their current statewide tests, which were designed to measure achievement relative to the state content standards. However, these assessments were not designed for the purpose of measuring growth, and as a result there are limitations to how they can be used. Some of the technical difficulties that must be taken into account are vertical scaling and floor and ceiling effects.

Vertical Scaling

Vertical scaling refers to having tests from different grades on one continuous scale. That would mean that the third-grade scores of a student could be compared to the fourth-grade scores of the same student. For example, on a vertically scaled test, if a student got a score of 120 in third grade, and a score of 150 in fourth grade, then that student did "grow" by 30 points. This situation sounds like the height example. (It might be desirable to then contextualize that change of 30 points, but that discussion is going to wait for now.) In the absence of a vertical scale, the scores in adjacent grades cannot be compared because they are not on one scale, so it would be like comparing apples to oranges. Often states report scores from all grades on the same numerical scale (e.g., all grades report the scores on the range of 200–300), but that scale is not continuous across grades; a student can obtain a 200 in third grade and a 200 in fourth grade, and those scores mean different things. Similarly, a score of 220 in third grade is *unrelated* to the score in fourth grade; therefore, if that student received a score of 250 in fourth grade, we cannot make any conclusions about the degree of change between third and fourth grades. Many of the statewide tests were designed to *not* have vertical scales specifically so that scores were not comparable across years, which can make it impossible to conceptualize change in this manner.

    Why didn't states want vertical scales? Vertical scales are appealing because scores are comparable across years. However, there are many issues that must be taken into account when creating and maintaining vertical scales. Although it is possible to create a vertical scale using widely applied equating methodologies (see Kolen & Brennan, 2004, for greater detail on equating), it is really the valid inferences that can be made using this scale that are questionable. First, the scale that is obtained is likely not an interval-level scale. That means that a 10-point difference at one part of the scale may not have the same meaning as a 10-point difference in scores at another part of the scale. This limitation would seriously limit the growth inferences that could be made on the basis of a vertical scale.

Second, the construct that is measured by the assessment might not mean the same thing across grade levels. To create a vertical scale, it is necessary to place the same items on adjacent grade-level test forms. For example, the same identical fraction items could appear on test forms for grades 3, 4, and 5. These common items are placed on multiple forms to provide a statistical link between the different grade-level test forms. It would be assumed that the items are most difficult at grade 3, moderately difficult at grade 4, and relatively easy at grade 5, for example. However, part of the change in the difficulty of the item could exist because the concept of a fraction changes in the minds of children between grades 3 and 5. As students become more familiar with the concept over time, their understanding may become deeper and more sophisticated, and in a sense, the idea of a fraction has changed. This change implies that the construct may not be stable over time. However, for the vertical scale to be created, it is typically assumed that the construct does not change across grades. If this assumption is untenable, then the creation of a vertical scale becomes quite complex (see Patz & Yao, 2006; Reckase & Martineau, 2004) and not practical for most testing programs.

An additional concern arises in that the test should measure what is taught in the classroom. Since the content of a given subject changes across grades, the test might, for statistical purposes, need to include content that is not taught; this content could potentially compromise the quality of the assessment and the validity of the use of those test scores. Due to these issues, it is important to be mindful of the inferences you are making using a vertical scale; often, since the scores are on a same scale, we assume that the comparisons we want to make are reasonable, without actually checking.

Floor and Ceiling Effects

In the absence of a vertical scale, a test measures content that is strictly at the grade level being tested. A fourth-grade math test measures fourth-grade content. Although developing a test in this way is sensible, it can provide measurement difficulties for students who are at the low and high ends of the scale. Consider a student who is performing below grade level. The score on a grade-level test would not be a very accurate reflection of that student's achievement because it is likely that the student received the lowest obtainable score. Similarly, for the gifted student who obtains the highest possible score, that score does not adequately reflect the student's level of achievement either. For these students, what would growth look like? Even if the students did learn more (i.e., "grow"), which they likely did, the grade-level test would not be able to reflect that change, since the measurement instrument cannot measure the low and high ends of the scale accurately. Furthermore, scores at either end of the scale are measured less reliably, and changes in scores for these students might also contain more error. As such, although this test may have been constructed well to measure the degree of grade-level mastery, it was not necessarily constructed well to provide insight into how well the student should perform in the next grade level. These examples illustrate some of the problems that arise when tests designed for one purpose are used for alternate purposes. Students at the high and low ends of the scale are not numerous, but the challenges they present for measuring growth must be considered carefully for any growth measure.

Gain Score Measures

Whether using a vertical scale or a within-grade measure, the notion of a pretest–posttest difference score is also an intuitive and appealing option for a measure of growth. In this situation, a student could take a pretest in September (or use the end-of-grade test the previous year), and a posttest in June (or end of grade test in the current year) and the difference in scores could be used to assume growth. Although simple and intuitive, this type of gain score can be highly inaccurate depending on (1) the reliability of the pretest measure, (2) the reliability of the posttest measure, and (3) the correlation of the two scores (Rachor & Cizek, 1996). Therefore, careful attention must be paid to the component measures involved in the computation of gain scores. More information on gain scores is presented in subsequent sections of this chapter.

What Are the Practical Complexities of Measuring Growth?

The technical issues related to measuring growth are quite enormous; however, most daunting might be the practical challenges to measuring growth. Even if the right definition of growth could be agreed upon, and an appropriate model found to measure that definition of growth in a reliable way, the practical limitations might prove too burdensome to overcome. This section provides some of the issues to consider when measuring student growth.

Testing Time

A central issue in all data-based decision models is that collecting data takes time—and typically, it takes time away from instruction. With all of the federal accountability mandates, it is tempting for states to want to use a single assessment for several purposes, whether or not that assessment was designed for all of those purposes. Although this might not be technically appropriate and may violate the *Standards for Educational and Psychological Testing* (American Educational Research Association, American Psychological Association, & National Council on Measurement in Education, [AERA, APA, & NCME], 2014), creating assessments that are appropriate for each need may result in an inordinate amount of testing time. The result of this conflict is the use of tests designed for one purpose to meet multiple purposes. To do this wisely, it is necessary to document the validity of using the test for these multiple purposes (AERA et al., 2014), and ensure that any stakes associated with a particular use are appropriate, given the available validity evidence. In other words, we must understand the limitations placed on the inferences we can make when we employ these compromises.

One-Year Courses

Some courses offered in secondary schools are only 1-year courses, such as economics or psychology. Growth is difficult to measure in these courses since they are only one-semester or 1-year courses. These types of courses would most likely rely on testing multiple times within the course, which raises issues with time spent on testing. The alternative is not to measure growth in these courses.

Change in Construct

This idea is related to that discussed in the section of vertical scales, and also to the idea of a 1-year course. In secondary school, subjects such as mathematics and science often become less of a continuum, and specialized topics are presented in specific grades. For example, a typical math curriculum might include a progression of algebra, geometry, trigonometry, pre-calculus, and calculus. Similarly, a science progression might move from biology to chemistry and then physics. With such differentiated topics across courses, and across grades, what does growth in math and science look like at the higher levels? Do we conceptualize growth within each specialized topic area (e.g., geometry) rather than within the content area (i.e., mathematics)? Thought must be brought to how growth is conceptualized in these contexts.

What Are the Popular Growth Models?

Now that some of the larger issues related to assessing student growth have been discussed, we describe some of the more popular growth models in use today. For each of the growth models presented, we provide (1) a short description of the model, (2) the question the model is designed to answer, (3) the statistical considerations for use, and (4) an example. Comprehensive details are not provided here, in the interest of space. However, relevant resources are provided for interested readers. In particular, Castellano and Ho (2013) provide a comprehensive review of the models presented here. The models are presented based on level of complexity, with the simpler models presented before more complex models.

Simple Gain

This model provides the most basic interpretation of gain scores. The examinee's scores on two administrations are subtracted, and the difference is reported as growth. The advantage to such a model is that it is easy to understand and the results are easy to interpret. One cited disadvantage is that this model ignores the clustering of students within schools, and as a result may lead to biased estimates of school effects (Raudenbush & Willms, 1995).

- *The question the simple gain model attempts to answer.* This model answers the basic question: How much did the student's score change over time?

- *Computational process.* The underlying computational process in this model is quite straightforward: subtraction.

- *Statistical considerations.* This model, although simple in its computation, does require that the scores being subtracted are on the same scale. This could mean that the test scores are on a vertical scale, or that they are scores from parallel test forms administered at two different points in time.

- *Example.* To examine how much growth a student exhibited in math between grades 4 and 5, the scores of the two tests are subtracted. So, consider that the score scale is 100–200, and the student obtained a score of 120 in grade 4, and 150 in grade 5. According to the simple gain model, the student "grew" by 30 points between the 2 years.

The question that is natural to ask now is whether that is a large amount of growth or a small amount of growth. There are various of ways of conceptualizing how much growth was achieved with these 30 points. One basic distinction is whether the contextualization of the growth is norm-referenced or criterion-referenced. Each of these interpretation approaches is described (see also Hambleton, Zenisky, & Popham, Chapter 2, this volume).

   o *Norm-referenced.* One approach that has some appeal is to compare the amount of growth exhibited by a student to the amount of growth obtained on average within a class, school, or state. So, for example, if the average growth for all fifth graders in the state was 25 points, then we would conclude that 30 points is a lot of growth: more than average. This type of information is very straightforward and easy to provide. The disadvantage to this approach is that it does not tell us how much the student has learned relative to the curriculum.

   o *Criterion-referenced.* In the case of criterion-referenced information, we do look at gains relative to the curriculum of interest. In this way, we could provide this kind of information: Students who receive a score of 150 in fifth grade can typically do these types of tasks. When this information is compared to similar information at the score of 120, we can deduce the type of tasks students can do now, that they couldn't do before.

- Often, combining these two types of information provides the most meaning to stakeholders: how students have changed relative to the curriculum, as well as how much change is typical for each student.

Value Tables

The value table model assigns a growth score to each student based on the student's transition from a previous year's performance level to the next. The growth score for a district is simply the average of the student growth scores in the district. A student who moves from a lower proficiency level to a higher level is considered to exhibit growth. Furthermore, the established proficiency categories are often broken down into two levels to get a finer measure of growth (Illinois State Board of Education, 2013). As can be seen in the example that follows, all students who stay in the same performance category from year to year do not receive the same growth score. Students who are in the top performance category and stay there receive a higher growth score than students who remain in the same lower performance categories from year to year.

* *The question value tables attempt to answer.* On average, are students maintaining their current level of performance, improving, or declining?

* *Computational process.* Two computations are necessary in this model. First, a score is assigned to each student, based on his or her proficiency level. Once the scores are assigned to each student, these scores are added. The underlying computation is quite simple.

* *Statistical considerations.* Basing growth estimates on only a student's category loses information when compared to using a student's actual score. Although breaking down each performance category into two subcategories does offer more precision, there is still the issue that some students may be improving from one year to the next, but will still not have grown enough to move to the next subcategory.

Additionally, assigning scores to the various categories of growth—consistent performance, improvement, or decline—is somewhat subjective, and can depend on policies and the perceived value of moving from a specific performance level to another. As Castellano and Ho (2013) address, however, the value table does have the benefit of clearly identifying the value of particular transitions.

* *Example.* In practice, the most critical aspect of a value table model is the assignment of scores to each of the possible patterns for student performance. For example, a state with three performance levels, such as below proficient, proficient, and advanced, would have nine possible transitions and associated growth scores. Considering more levels per performance category would lead to a value table with more cells. Using the sample value table shown in Table 19.1, a student who was advanced in the first year and then went to below proficient in the second year would receive a 0. A student who was in the higher level of the below-proficient category in Year 1 then moved to the low level of the proficient category would receive a growth score of 120. Once the growth values are established, each student is assigned the appropriate growth score, and average growth scores can be computed for classrooms, schools, or districts.

TABLE 19.1. Example of a Value Table

Year 1 performance category		Year 2 performance category				
		Below proficient		Proficient		
		Low	High	Low	High	Advanced
Below proficient	Low	50	100	140	180	200
	High	30	90	120	160	200
Proficient	Low	10	50	100	150	175
	High	0	40	90	120	160
Advanced		0	0	50	100	150

Projection

Using a linear regression model created from a previous group of students, the projection model makes a prediction about how a student will do based on his or her previous test scores.

- *The question projection models attempt to answer.* Based on a linear regression model for a previous cohort of students, what is the predicted, or projected, score for a test this student will achieve in the future?

- *Computational process.* The underlying computations for projection models are based on the results of linear regression.

- *Statistical considerations.* To use linear regression, the usual assumptions of linear regression must be met. As Castellano and Ho (2013) point out, because there is often a strong, linear relationship between scores from year to year, the data often fit the model well. In addition, the variation of the current scores must be relatively consistent across the range of previous years' scores.

An important benefit of the projection model is that the use of linear regression does not require that the scores from year to year be on the same scale. Another benefit of using linear regression is that several years' worth of test scores can be used, in addition to incorporating demographic variables, if desired. This would allow expected scores to be created while taking into account a student's ethnic or socioeconomic status, for example. However, the more data, whether demographic or test scores, in a model, the more students who are likely to have missing data. These students would either be excluded from the model or the use of missing data procedures would need to be employed.

- *Example.* Last year's fifth-grade cohort is used to create a regression model based on 1 year's worth of past test scores, represented by the regression line in Figure 19.1. A prediction can then be made for a student in the next cohort by simply using

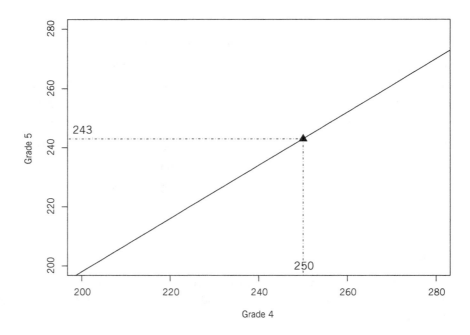

FIGURE 19.1. How to use a projection model.

their fourth-grade score. For example, a student with a score of 250 on the grade 4 assessment would have a predicted score of 243 on the grade 5 assessment.

Residual Gain

In a residual gain model, linear regression is used to create a model regressing this year's scores on last year's scores for the current cohort. This model is not for the purpose of prediction, but for determining an expectation. A student's growth is described by whether or not the student exceeded or fell short of expectations. It should be noted that this is different from the projection model in that regression is used to determine the expected score for the current year, rather than predicting the future score as in the projection model.

• *The question residual gain models attempt to answer.* Based on a linear regression model of this and the previous years' test scores, how much better or worse is the second-year score for a student than the student's predicted score?

• *Computational process.* The underlying computational process in this model is linear regression.

• *Statistical considerations.* Residual gain models are subject to the same restrictions and have the same benefits as projection models, in that both are based on regression models.

• *Example.* As with the projection models, a regression model is constructed, but this model then uses the same students to evaluate whether an individual student is above or below the expected value. Consider Figure 19.2, where the regression line represents the expected grade 5 score for a given grade 4 score. By subtracting Student 1's actual score from the expected score, 257 – 243, we would obtain a residual gain of 6. A student whose actual score fell below the regression line would have a negative residual gain.

Student Growth Percentiles

The student growth percentile (SGP) is one of the most complex models. This model does not assume a vertical scale, and as a result, is attractive to many testing programs. The statistical details of the model can be found in Betebenner (2009). As noted by Goldschmidt, Choi, & Beaudoin (2012), the SGP does not measure absolute growth in performance. Instead, it offers a normative context to compare the results of student test scores to other students with similar score histories. Percentile ranks are assigned to students. For example, a student with an SGP of 60 performed better than 60% of his or her peers that had similar score histories. As such, many students can get an SGP of 60, but it does not mean that they have shown the same changes in performance.

• *The question student growth percentiles attempt to answer.* As noted above, the SGP is a normative measure, and so the question it is designed to answer is about

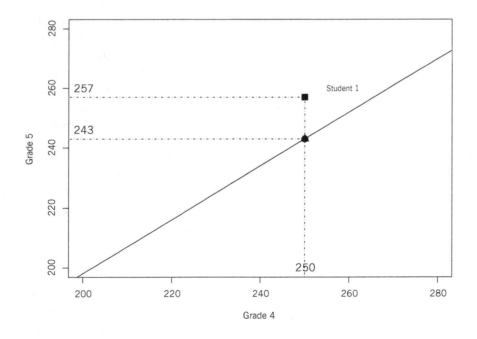

FIGURE 19.2. How to use a residual gain model.

the relative performance of students. In particular, the SGP addresses the question: "How does the student's performance this year compare to other students who performed similarly in the past?"

- *Computational process.* The underlying computational process in this model is quantile regression.

- *Statistical considerations.* This model, although complex in computation, does not have a lot of statistical requirements, making it a very popular model among states. Existing test scores can be used in the model regardless of whether a vertical scale is employed or not.

- *Example.* Consider a test scale that ranges from 300 to 400 in each year. In grade 4, a group of students all attain a score of 350. This is the group of kids that can be considered "academic peers." Their scores in fifth grade are compared to one another, and a percentile rank is assigned to each child. The child who scores highest in this group in fifth grade will receive an SGP of 99, and the child who scores the lowest will receive an SGP of 1. These rankings illustrate only the relative performance of the students and do not distinguish among them in terms of the amount of knowledge gained. Furthermore, the differences in scores of students receiving a 99 and those receiving an SGP of 20 might not vary by much.

Value Added

Value-added models are typically used for measuring teacher or school effectiveness, rather than individual student growth. This class of models is included here, however, because of its popularity and ubiquity in the literature. It does use student achievement data (via test scores) as inputs into the model to determine the effect that the teacher (or school) has had on students. One of the great differentiating factors of value-added models compared to other student growth models is the inclusion of student-level covariates, or background variables. For most measures of student growth, it is customary to exclude demographic variables for students, such as poverty status, ethnicity, gender, English proficiency, or disability status. The exclusion of these variables is explicit, as there is a desire to have the same expectations for all students, regardless of their values on these background variables. However, because we know that many of these variables *do* impact student performance, they are taken into account when evaluating teacher performance. By including these variables in the models, we attempt to "level the playing field" for making comparisons among teachers and their effects on student learning.

There is no one value-added model; rather, it is a class of models, whose goals are to determine what impact a teacher has on student performance, after controlling for student background experience, usually including prior academic achievement. The models are typically hierarchical linear models, with models for the student level, classroom level, and teacher level (the model can be extended to the school level as well, of course).

To compute a value-added score, the expected growth (based on previous achievement and background variables) is computed for each student in a classroom. The actual "growth" of each student is compared to the expected growth, and the difference between the two is the "achievement beyond expectation"; this can be a positive or a negative value. The average value of these differences is computed for a teacher. This is the value-added score for the teacher. It can be conceptualized as the average residual of the students' growth.

- *The question value-added models attempt to answer.* Value-added models are designed to answer questions like: To what degree does the average student in a classroom show improvements beyond expectation, based on previous achievement and background variables?

- *Computational process.* The computational process for this model relies typically on hierarchical, or multilevel, models.

- *Statistical considerations.* This class of models can include a vast amount of data for each student: background variables, previous years' achievement scores (as many years as determined by the user), and achievement data in multiple subject areas. The user of the model determines the specific number of variables. Missing data can become problematic as the number of variables increases. Although the models can typically accommodate missing data, the accuracy of the resulting estimates will be affected by the amount of missingness in the analysis. These models do not require a vertical scale.

- *Example.* The Educational Value Added Assessment System (EVAAS) is the most widely used value-added model. A conceptual overview of the EVAAS is presented here (based on Braun, 2005).
  In a particular year (e.g., grade 4), the student's score on an assessment in a particular subject (e.g., math) is expressed as the sum of three components: the district average math score, the class effect (teacher effect), and systematic and unsystematic variation (error) (see Equation 19.1). The "class effect" is essentially the difference between the students' score and the district average score, and is assumed to be equal across all students in a class, and is thus attributed to the teacher.

$$\text{Year 1} = \text{district average grade 4} + \text{teacher grade 4} \tag{19.1}$$
$$+ \text{ systematic/unsystematic errors (grade 4 errors)}$$

In the next year, for our example, grade 5, the student's score consists of four components: the district average for that year (grade 5), the teacher effect from the previous year (grade 4), the teacher effect from the current year (grade 5), and then the systematic and unsystematic variations (errors) (see Equation 19.2). It is worth noting that the effect of teachers in previous years remains in the model.

$$\text{Year 2} = \text{district average grade 5} + \text{teacher grade 4} + \text{teacher grade 5} \tag{19.2}$$
$$+ \text{ systematic/unsystematic errors (grade 5 errors)}$$

We then subtract these two scores, as in Equation 19.3. If we do so, we get the difference between the 2 years:

$$
\begin{aligned}
\text{Year 2} - \text{Year 1} =\ & (\text{district average grade 5} - \text{district average grade 4}) \\
& + (\text{teacher grade 4} - \text{teacher grade 4}) + \text{teacher grade 5} \\
& + (\text{grade 5 errors} - \text{grade 4 errors}) \\
=\ & \text{average district gain} + \text{teacher grade 5} \\
& + \text{systematic/unsystematic errors}
\end{aligned}
\tag{19.3}
$$

So the difference in the scores is a combination of the average gain in the district, the effect of Year 2 (fifth-grade) teacher, and errors.

The features of the various growth models are summarized in Table 19.2.

Use of Growth Models

Regardless of the particular use of the results from a growth model, it is necessary to be sure that the interpretations of the results support those decisions. Given the

TABLE 19.2. Summary of Growth Model Features

Model	Central question	Computational process	Statistical constraints
Simple gain	How much did the student's score change over time?	Subtraction	Scores on the same scale (could be vertical scale)
Value table	On average, are students maintaining their current level of performance, improving, or declining?	Addition	Size of categories used will have a dramatic influence
Projection	What is the predicted, or projected, score for a test this student will take in the future?	Linear regression	Assumptions of linear regression (usually met)
Residual gain	How much better or worse is the second-year score for a student than the student's predicted score?	Linear regression	Assumptions of linear regression (usually met)
Student growth percentiles	How does the student's performance this year compare to other students who performed similarly in the past?	Quantile regression	Complex statistical models that require expertise Changes in score distributions may cause issues
Value added	To what degree does the average student in classroom show improvements beyond expectation, based on previous achievement and background variables?	Hierarchical linear models	Complex statistical models that require expertise Requires a large amount of data (typically) Missing data often exist and can be problematic

ambiguity and issues raised about growth models in this chapter, it is not always obvious how to appropriately use the results. Therefore, great caution must be exercised before using the results to make any decisions—especially high-stakes decisions.

Conclusions

Measuring student growth seems to be a simple idea, with obvious appeal. However, upon closer examination, because of the inherent complexities in measuring or even defining growth, designing appropriate measures of growth within practical constraints is not always straightforward. Given the complexities of some of the models and the further complexities of appropriately interpreting the results of these models, the decisions made using these results may be flawed due to lack of proper understanding of the issues surrounding the measurement of growth and the proper use of the model results. Thus, although we all have the best intentions when it comes to measuring growth and attributing that growth to various sources, we must remember our responsibility to use the results in a fair, appropriate, and valid way.

REFERENCES

American Educational Research Association, American Psychological Association, & National Council on Measurement in Education. (2014). *Standards for educational and psychological testing.* Washington, DC: Authors.

Betebenner, D. (2009). Norm- and criterion-referenced growth. *Educational Measurement: Issues and Practice, 28*(4), 42–51.

Braun, H. (2005). *Using student progress to evaluate teachers: A primer on value-added models.* Princeton, NJ: Educational Testing Service. Retrieved from *www.ets.org/Media/Research/pdf/PICVAM.pdf.*

Castellano, K. E., & Ho, A. D. (2013). *A practitioner's guide to growth models.* Washington, DC: Council of Chief State School Officers.

Goldschmidt, P., Choi, K., & Beaudoin, J. P. (2012). *A comparison of growth models: Summary of results.* Washington, DC: Council of Chief State School Officers.

Hoffer, T. B., Hedberg, E. C., Brown, K. L., Halverson, M. L., & McDonald, S.-K. (2010). *Interim report on the evaluation of the growth model pilot project.* Chicago: University of Chicago.

Illinois State Board of Education. (2013, August). *Fact sheet: New growth model using value tables.* Division of Public Information, Illinois State Board of Education. Available at *www.isbe.state.il.us/GMWG/pdf/gmvt-fact-sheet-0813.pdf.*

Kolen, M., & Brennan, R. (2004). *Test equating, scaling, and linking: Methods and practices* (2nd ed). New York: Springer-Verlag.

No Child Left Behind Act of 2001, Pub. L. No. 107-110, § 115, Stat. 1425 (2002).

Patz, R. J., & Yao, L. (2006). Vertical scaling: Statistical models for measuring growth and achievement. In S. Sinharay & C. Rao (Eds.), *Handbook of statistics, 26: Psychometrics* (pp. 955–973). Amsterdam: North Holland.

Rachor, R. E., & Cizek, G. J. (1996, April). *Reliability of raw gain, residual gain, and estimated true gain scores: A simulation study.* Paper presented at the annual meeting of the American Educational Research Association, New York.

Raudenbush, S. W., & Willms, J. D. (1995). The estimation of school effects. *Journal of Educational and Behavioral Statistics, 20*(4), 307–335.

Reckase, M. D., & Martineau, J. (2004). *The vertical scaling of science achievement tests.* Paper commissioned by the Committee on Test Design for K–12 Science Achievement. Washington, DC: National Research Council.

U.S. Department of Education, Office of Communications and Outreach. (2005). Secretary Spellings announces Growth Model Pilot, addresses Chief State School Officers' annual policy forum in Richmond [Press release, November 18, 2005]. Retrieved from *www.ed.gov/news/pressreleases/2005/11/11182005.html.*

CHAPTER 20

Toward Improving the Reporting
of Test Score Results

Lessons Learned from the Evolution of Reports
from the National Assessment of Educational Progress

April L. Zenisky, John Mazzeo, and Mary J. Pitoniak

The premise of reporting results of educational tests can be stated quite simply as the responsibility of a testing agency to inform interested constituencies about performance on some measure relative to a construct of interest. This statement holds for reports of performance to individual test takers; summary reports to teachers, schools, and districts; or summative reports of student performance intended for policymakers or the general public. However, this simplicity belies the challenges faced by agencies in effectively communicating details about student achievement, and the importance of high-quality reporting practices. The many resources involved in large-scale assessment, as well as the often considerable stakes associated with testing, mean that test results are receiving greater levels of attention and scrutiny than ever before. Given the high-stakes consequences of test scores and the close scrutiny of the reports that convey them, it is essential that high-quality score reporting principles and practices be developed and implemented to enhance appropriate interpretations and uses of test scores. A "report," of course, is not monolithic, either in structure or in contents; what currently encompasses a report of performance may be paper based or electronically transmitted, may detail the performance of one or of many, and may be intended to address one or more of a range of informational purposes.

Research and development in the area of results reporting, particularly in K–12 education in the United States, have grown a great deal in recent years, and seem to be further increasing as initiatives such as the Common Core State Standards (CCSS) and the assessments to evaluate student learning relative to those standards progress. Because the results from many educational tests are associated with high stakes not

335

only for individuals but also for their teachers, schools, districts, and states, as well as subgroups of students at all levels, the agencies responsible for those assessments are striving to generate materials for results reporting that provide actionable data to users, efficiently and effectively. Of course, what is efficient and effective for some users does not necessarily meet the needs of others, and consequently, much of the work in this area has sought to differentiate the reporting needs of different users. The work of Levine, Rathbun, Selden, and Davis (1998); Simmons and Mwalimu (2000); and Jaeger (2003) is particularly instructive in this regard, as each of these studies highlights the disparate reporting needs and interests among various consumer groups of educational test data (and, in all three cases, work in the context of the National Assessment of Educational Progress [NAEP], National Center for Education Statistics [NCES], n.d.).

The practice of results reporting has been an emerging consideration in recent years, with formal models for report development emerging from Zapata-Rivera and VanWinkle (2010) and Zenisky and Hambleton (2012, 2013). Across both approaches, critical points for report development include the solicitation of user needs and perspectives early in the report development process, as well as the use of field testing to gather data about the understanding and usability of reporting resources prior to final dissemination. Report development also must entail a certain amount of self-reflection, wherein displays and other elements of reporting strategies should be revisited periodically and evaluated for relevance and effectiveness through the years, and should change to reflect evolutions in user needs and interests as warranted.

One large-scale assessment program that has been at the forefront of reporting in education throughout its history is NAEP, which provides the largest nationally representative and continuing assessment of what U.S. students know and can do in various subject areas. It is also important to note that NAEP is a group score assessment, and therefore does not report results for individual students. Of course, NAEP occupies a prominent place in the landscape of educational assessment in the United States by virtue of being the "Nation's Report Card," but the reporting efforts and practices associated with NAEP are especially illustrative of how the reporting of test results can evolve and change over time in response to agency priorities and audience considerations. The focus within this chapter is on three specific areas that NAEP has tried to address over the years: (1) the importance of audience, (2) varied efforts to attach meaning to scale scores, and (3) design and format issues.

The first of these areas, the importance of audience, is a critical aspect of report development as NAEP (and increasingly other testing agencies) has become aware of the differences in data needs among different user groups. The second area, which considers the issues associated with attaching meaning to scale scores, is a topic that in some ways has bedeviled many tests: What does a scale score actually mean? Indeed, for many agencies, the challenge in criterion-referenced testing is to help users understand what knowledge and skills are associated with specific points on the score scale. As shown in the coming pages, it is clear that NAEP has implemented a number of strategies to provide such meaning. The third area—report design and format—encompasses topics ranging from report contents to methods of presentation, and in these respects NAEP also has drawn on both experience and creativity to advance the practice of results reporting.

Throughout this chapter we provide examples from NAEP of displays and reporting strategies relevant to each of these three areas. In our choice of examples, we have attempted to convey a historical perspective of how NAEP reporting has evolved and how, in our view, it now reflects some of the best practices in how to provide stakeholders with test score results. Developments and improvements in NAEP reporting have been informed by the work of Hambleton and colleagues (Hambleton, 2002; Hambleton & Slater, 1997; Wainer, Hambleton, & Meara, 1999). Quotes from those papers are included within the chapter, along with sample displays from current and past NAEP reports.

The Importance of Audience

One key element to consider when designing reports of test score results is that of the intended audience. Recent research on report development processes has suggested that it is necessary to separate out user groups and consider the needs of highly disparate groups separately, because the underlying assumptions and prospective use cases vary considerably (Hambleton & Zenisky, 2013). The idea of being specific to different audiences is echoed by Zapata-Rivera and Katz (2014), who extended the work in this area using audience analysis techniques.

NAEP has a long tradition of focusing on intended audiences in targeting results to specific user groups:

> With various intended audiences, it may be the case that specially-designed reports are needed for each. For example, with policy makers reports might need to be short, with the use of bullets to highlight main points such as conclusions. Tables might be straightforward with focus on only the most important conclusions and implications. Technical data (such as standard errors) and technical discussions along with methodological details of the study should be avoided. Keep the focus on conclusions and significance, and keep the report short. (Hambleton & Slater, 1997, p. 29)

The reports of NAEP results in the 1980s, prepared by the Educational Testing Service (ETS) prior to formation of the National Assessment Governing Board, were relatively brief, focused, and appeared intended for a general audience. They were small—designed to be easily held in the hand—made considerable use of graphics and colors, and confined much statistical detail (such as standard errors) to the appendices. Minus procedural and data appendices, the Reading Report Card published in 1984 (ETS, 1984) was 55 pages, and the report for writing (Applebee, Langer, & Mullis, 1986) was 59 pages.

Beginning around 1990 or so, the explicit audience for NAEP reports—particularly its Report Cards, which typically represent the initial release of results—was defined by policy, with the National Assessment Governing Board policy initially establishing parents, teachers, and principals as key audiences for NAEP reports (Bourque, 2004). (Later, as part of its 1996 redesign of NAEP, the board identified the audience for NAEP reports to be the American public.) It should be noted too that there were a number of other changes made in the NAEP program in 1990 or so, which also presented both opportunities and challenges to NAEP for designing effective reports for its by-policy targeted audience(s).

- The program changed from a grant to a cooperative agreement (and later to a contract). This meant that NAEP reports were National Center for Education Statistics (NCES) reports—not ETS reports—and needed to meet the rigorous standards for impartiality, technical accuracy, and completeness demanded by a federal statistical agency.

- The trial state assessment program was launched, which changed (at least in mathematics, reading, science, and writing) the scope of required reporting. Henceforth, national *and* state results, in particular state-to-state comparisons, needed to be reported *and* to be reported in ways that were statistically rigorous and discouraged inappropriate or invalid comparative inferences.

- Achievement-level reporting was piloted in 1990 and brought on board more officially in the 1992 and 1994 reports. The use of standards-based reporting in NAEP was, at first, somewhat contentious and controversial. Reporting formats needed to take into consideration the various perspectives and concerns of a variety of points of view on standards-based reporting that existed within the NAEP governance structure.

- NAEP bifurcated into Main NAEP (current frameworks and achievement-level reporting) and Long Term Trend NAEP (the old frameworks and anchor-level reporting).

These changes shaped the NAEP assessment program in the last two decades, and hence influenced the development and implementation of a broad-based reporting strategy rooted in research—research that includes the work of Hambleton and Slater (1997)—which clearly advances audience considerations more explicitly in the definition and design of reports.

The impact of these many changes on reporting took some time to work out successfully. In the years between 1990 and 2005, the NAEP report documents became more numerous (individual state reports were generated for each participating jurisdiction) but also went through a technical evolution. At first, reports became considerably longer, their look and feel became less geared to a general audience, and their contents became more statistical and technical than they had been in the 1980s. The area of technical reporting does serve as an example of how the level of detail in the NAEP Report Cards has changed over NAEP's history, such that the technical information that was once included in the main reporting documents is now accessible to researchers and other interested users online.

Later, however, as NAEP experimented with strategies such as "First Look" reports and "Highlights" reports, reporting efforts moved back toward the publication of documents that were designed to be more accessible to the public. In more recent years, "Highlights" reports have evolved to be printed as relatively short, high-level overviews of results (under the headings "First Look" or "Focus on NAEP"), and the Report Cards themselves have undergone redesign and streamlining relative to audience interests and needs, including elements such as Executive Summaries that are intended to focus on key results for general audiences (Figure 20.1). It should also be noted that among the most forward-looking strategies for targeting information to

Executive Summary

Nationally representative samples of 213,100 fourth-graders and 168,200 eighth-graders participated in the 2011 National Assessment of Educational Progress (NAEP) in reading. At each grade, students responded to questions designed to measure their reading comprehension across two types of texts: literary and informational.

Students' reading comprehension unchanged from 2009 at grade 4, and improves at grade 8

At grade 4, the average reading score in 2011 was unchanged from 2009 but 4 points higher than in 1992 (figure A).

- Scores were higher in 2011 than in 2009 for students from both higher-income families (i.e., students not eligible for the National School Lunch Program) and lower-income families (i.e., students eligible for free or reduced-price school lunch).

At grade 8, the average reading score in 2011 was 1 point higher than in 2009, and 5 points higher than in 1992.

- Scores were higher in 2011 than in 2009 for White, Black, and Hispanic students but did not change significantly for Asian/Pacific Islander or American Indian/Alaska Native students. While the White – Hispanic score gap was smaller in 2011 than in 2009, there was no significant change in the White – Black gap over the same period.

Figure A. Trend in fourth- and eighth-grade NAEP reading average scores

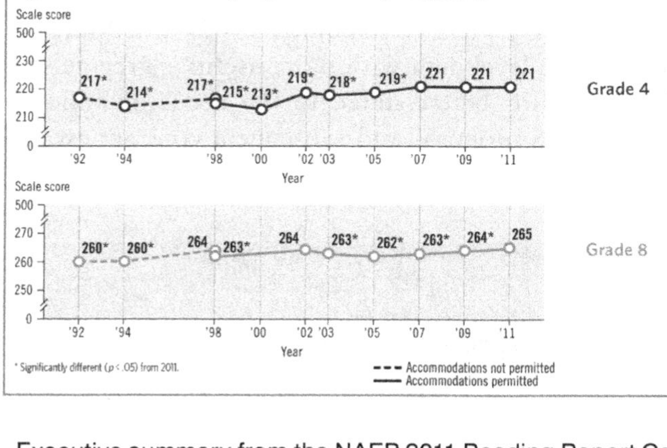

* Significantly different ($p < .05$) from 2011.

– – – Accommodations not permitted
——— Accommodations permitted

FIGURE 20.1. Executive summary from the NAEP 2011 Reading Report Card. From National Center for Education Statistics (2011).

audiences is through the Internet, and indeed the NAEP program has also leveraged its website to provide audience-specific portals into a variety of additional data products and features targeted at specific audiences. NAEP results were first released online as a supplement to the print reports in 1999–2000, and at present the Web is the primary mechanism for release and dissemination of NAEP results, data, and information. Links for different audiences can be found at *http://nces.ed.gov/nationsreportcard/ infofor.asp.*

Attaching Meaning to Scale Scores

Concise, meaningful reporting of assessment results has been a central challenge for the NAEP program from its inception.

> "What is the meaning of a NAEP mathematics score of 220?" "Is the national average of 245 at grade 8 good or bad?" These were two questions from policy makers and educators in a study by Hambleton and Slater (1997) using the executive summary of the 1992 NAEP national and state mathematics results (Mullis, Dossey, Owen, & Phillips, 1993). The fact is that people are more familiar with popular ratio scales, such as those used in measuring distance, time and weight, than they are with educational and psychological test score scales. (Hambleton, 2002, p. 193)

Over the years, the ways in which NAEP provided assessment results has evolved. From 1969 through 1983, for a variety of reasons both substantive and political (Messick, Beaton, & Lord, 1983), NAEP results were reported primarily in terms of average percent correct on individual "exercises" (or *items,* as they are more commonly referred to today) and, somewhat later, as averages over collections of exercises. Table 20.1 illustrates how average percent-correct data were presented for reading items assessing basic comprehension strategies based on simple stories and expository passages.

A 1982 evaluation of NAEP (Wirtz & Lapointe, 1982) called for, among other things, replacing reports of item-level data with more useful aggregate scores of curriculum domains and subdomains better suited to the needs of policymakers and researchers alike. The 1983 ETS proposal and subsequent contract award called for

TABLE 20.1. Sample Collection-Level Percent-Correct Data for the NAEP 1984 Reading Assessment

Basic skills and strategies		
Age 9	Age 13	Age 17
64.2%	94.5%	98.6%

Note. From Applebee et al. (1986).

the introduction of item response theory (IRT) (Hambleton & Swaminathan, 1985) scaling as the basis for summary reporting of NAEP results and as an effective way to allow the pool of assessment exercises to evolve while still reporting trend results. However, as the preceding quotation suggests, an initial and continuing challenge has been how to convey what various levels on the scale mean in an educationally meaningful way, especially given the range of users of NAEP results.

One important attempt from ETS and NAEP to make NAEP scales meaningful involved the use of scale anchoring (Figure 20.2; Beaton & Allen, 1992). *Scale*

Levels of Proficiency   FIGURE 2.3

Rudimentary (150)

Readers who have acquired rudimentary reading skills and strategies can follow brief written directions. They can also select words, phrases, or sentences to describe a simple picture and can interpret simple written clues to identify a common object. *Performance at this level suggests the ability to carry out simple, discrete reading tasks.*

Basic (200)

Readers who have learned basic comprehension skills and strategies can locate and identify facts from simple informational paragraphs, stories, and news articles. In addition, they can combine ideas and make inferences based on short, uncomplicated passages. *Performance at this level suggests the ability to understand specific or sequentially related information.*

Intermediate (250)

Readers with the ability to use intermediate skills and strategies can search for, locate, and organize the information they find in relatively lengthy passages and can recognize paraphrases of what they have read. They can also make inferences and reach generalizations about main ideas and author's purpose from passages dealing with literature, science, and social studies. *Performance at this level suggests the ability to search for specific information, interrelate ideas, and make generalizations.*

Adept (300)

Readers with adept reading comprehension skills and strategies can understand complicated literary and informational passages, including material about topics they study at school. They can also analyze and integrate less familiar material and provide reactions to and explanations of the text as a whole. *Performance at this level suggests the ability to find, understand, summarize, and explain relatively complicated information.*

Advanced (350)

Readers who use advanced reading skills and strategies can extend and restructure the ideas presented in specialized and complex texts. Examples include scientific materials, literary essays, historical documents, and materials similar to those found in professional and technical working environments. They are also able to understand the links between ideas even when those links are not explicitly stated and to make appropriate generalizations even when the texts lack clear introductions or explanations. *Performance at this level suggests the ability to synthesize and learn from specialized reading materials.*

naep

FIGURE 20.2. Proficiency-level descriptions from the NAEP 1984 Reading Report Card. From Educational Testing Service (1984).

anchoring was an approach to describing what students know and can do at several locations along the NAEP scale. The descriptions were arrived at by examining the items that students near these points got correct at a high rate (over the years, either 67% or 80% has been used as the operational definition for a *high rate*), while requiring that students at the anchor point below had a substantially lower probability of getting the item correct (e.g., at least 30% below). These collections of items were presented to expert panels that were charged with examining the substance of the items and crafting interpretive summaries of what students at the different levels knew and were able to do.

Reporting based on scale anchoring appeared in NAEP reports through the remainder of the 1980s. Anchor-level reporting does, however, have its share of critics. The methodological specifics of the scale anchoring approach and the validity of the resulting descriptions have been questioned by some (e.g., Forsyth, 1991). Others, for example, Linn and Dunbar (1992), expressed concerns about the degree to which the presentations of the level results in the report cards from the 1980s—in particular, the information about exemplar items illustrating the levels—were properly interpreted by the press and the general public.

Another strategy from NAEP was to add meaning to scores through the use of item maps, which are displays that attempt to fully exploit the property of IRT models that both items and examinees are located on the same scale. Aimed at a wide range of audiences, these maps provide a condensed look at the particular questions being "successfully" answered by test takers across the scale and offer a continuous perspective on the meaning of scale locations, rather than (1) describing a small subset of points, as is done for anchor levels; or (2) providing descriptions of proficiency that cover the entire interval denoted by an achievement level. However, one obvious limitation is that any synthesis of commonalities or salient features of items that map at various points on the scale is left to the reader.

The basic approach to generating an item map is fairly simple: For each item, find the point on the IRT scale where the probability of successful completion exceeds some predetermined level (for NAEP, the values range from 65 to 74% based on the item type). That scale score location defines the mapping location for that item. Displaying thumbnail descriptions of a substantial collection of items arrayed at their scale score locations provides a visual representation of the meaning of the scale. In practice, the number of items displayed must be tempered by space considerations and the item descriptions kept brief enough to maintain security and to preserve the items for future use.

Figure 20.3 is an example of a grade 8 item map from the 2011 NAEP Reading Report Card (NCES, 2011). Items are arrayed at their composite scale locations, and the achievement level cut point locations are shown as well. Information about the cognitive target (a framework dimension that characterizes the item) is shown, and page numbers are given for the small set of released items that are included in the report in their entirety.

GRADE 8

What Eighth-Graders Know and Can Do in Reading

The item map illustrates a range of reading behaviors associated with scores on the NAEP reading scale. The cut score at the lower end of the range for each achievement level is boxed. The descriptions of selected assessment questions that indicate what students need to do when responding successfully are listed on the right, along with the corresponding cognitive targets. The map on this page shows that eighth-graders performing at the *Basic* level with a score of 263 were likely to be able to recognize the motivation of a narrator in a literary essay. Students performing at the *Proficient* level with a score of 301 were likely to be able to make a connection between a poem and a fable and explain that connection. Students performing at the *Advanced* level with a score of 338 were likely to be able to evaluate the effectiveness of an article's beginning and justify the evaluation with support from the text.

Questions designed to assess the same cognitive target map at different points on the NAEP scale. This is so because the questions are about different passages; thus, an integrate/interpret question may be more or less difficult depending on the passage the question is referring to.

GRADE 8 NAEP READING ITEM MAP

Scale score	Cognitive target	Question description
500		
//		
361	❖ Critique/Evaluate	Evaluate effectiveness of descriptive language and support with specific article references (**see pages 64 and 65**)
356	Critique/Evaluate	Provide an opinion about the persuasiveness of an argument and justify with text support
344	Critique/Evaluate	Evaluate the claims of an argument and justify reasoning with text support
338	Critique/Evaluate	Evaluate the effectiveness of the beginning of an article and justify with text support
327	Integrate/Interpret	Synthesize across a story to provide the theme and support with the text
326	Critique/Evaluate	Provide an opinion about the author's craft and support with information from an expository text
323	Critique/Evaluate	Form an opinion about a central issue in a persuasive text and support with references
323		
315	Locate/Recall	Recognize the major idea of a biographical sketch
313	Integrate/Interpret	Describe the tone of a persuasive essay with a supporting example
310	Integrate/Interpret	Make an inference based on a quotation to explain the supporting idea in an argument text
304	Integrate/Interpret	*Recognize the main purpose of an informative article*
303	Critique/Evaluate	Evaluate how a subheading relates to the passage and provide text support
301	Integrate/Interpret	Explain a cross-text connection between a poem and a fable
293	❖ Locate/Recall	*Locate and recognize a relevant fact in a highly detailed informative article* (**see page 63**)
286	Integrate/Interpret	*Recognize an implicit comparison in a section of a literary essay*
285	Integrate/Interpret	*Recognize the meaning of a word describing a character's action in a story*
281		
278	Integrate/Interpret	Infer the feelings of a narrator in a literary essay
276	Integrate/Interpret	Provide a relevant example from a story that supports a character's description
276	❖ Integrate/Interpret	*Recognize the main purpose of an informative article* (**see page 62**)
273	❖ Locate/Recall	*Recognize the paraphrase of information explicitly stated in an informative article*
263	Locate/Recall	Recognize the motivation of the narrator in a literary essay
255	Integrate/Interpret	*Recognize the meaning of a word as it is used in an expository text*
254	Critique/Evaluate	Use information from an article to provide and support an opinion
243		
242	Locate/Recall	*Recognize an explicitly stated supporting detail in an expository text*
239	Locate/Recall	*Locate and recognize a relevant detail in an expository text*
230	Integrate/Interpret	*Recognize an implicit main idea of a story*
202	Integrate/Interpret	*Recognize character motivation in a fable*
//		
0		

(Scale levels on the left: Advanced, Proficient, Basic)

❖ Indicates a question that pertains to the sample passage "1920: Women Get the Vote."

NOTE: Regular type denotes a constructed-response question. *Italic* type denotes a multiple-choice question. The position of a question on the scale represents the scale score attained by students who had a 65 percent probability of successfully answering a constructed-response question, or a 74 percent probability of correctly answering a four-option multiple-choice question. For constructed-response questions, the question description represents students' performance rated as completely correct. Scale score ranges for reading achievement levels are referenced on the map.

FIGURE 20.3. Item map from the NAEP 2011 Reading Report Card. From National Center for Education Statistics (2011).

The ubiquity and power of the Internet has given NAEP additional opportunities to explore the power of exemplar items and item maps to give meaning to the scale. Motivated users can now go to the NAEP website (*http://nces.ed.gov/nationsreport-card/itemmaps*) and explore a more detailed item map and more extensive collection of exemplar items than could reasonably be provided in a print report.

One potential limitation of anchor-level reporting involves how anchor point locations were determined. As Beaton and Allen (1992) noted, NAEP had chosen anchor points such as 200, 250, 300, and 350 on scales that range from 0 to 500, reflecting in part the fact that the standard deviations of the NAEP scales are typically set to 50 points. Another issue was the language used in the description and how it conveyed information to policymakers, educators, and the general public about whether the reported results were (in some absolute sense) good, bad, or indifferent. Beginning with the 1990 main NAEP assessments, reporting based on scale anchoring was replaced by standards-based reporting on the basis of achievement levels. However, despite differences in meaning, the achievement levels in some ways presented the same sort of reporting challenge as did the anchor levels used with NAEP in the 1980s. In a sense, the achievement levels are nothing more than scale locations established through a standard-setting process (see also Pitoniak & Cizek, Chapter 3, this volume), instead of through selection of anchor points related to the standard deviation of the scale in the scale anchoring approach.

Because of these similarities, the reporting of achievement-level results followed the general approach of what had been done with scale anchoring results—that is, by including tables that showed the percentage of students *at or above* each of the achievement-level cut points. Reporting percentages at or above a given achievement level made a lot of sense to the ETS and NCES statisticians. After all, if there is but a single cut point, the percentage passing (i.e., the percentage of students exceeding the cut score) seems to be what is of interest, and, in the case of multiple cut scores, the percentage at or above each successive cut point is just the natural extension. Moreover, for discrete variables that arise from imposing cut points on a continuous scale, it is often easier for the statistician to work with percents at or above. Increases in these percentages signify improvements in performance, whereas the same cannot be said of percentages at specific achievement levels. For example, an increase in the percentage of students at the Proficient level may be good (if it is due to a decrease in the percentage of students below Proficient) or bad (if accompanied by a decrease in percentage of students at the Advanced level).

The initial presentation of results in the 1992 report cards was largely tabular (Table 20.2) and, judging by the reactions of the interviewees in research carried out by Hambleton and Slater (1997), not readily understood:

> The most confusing point for interviewees was the reporting of students at or above each proficiency category. Interviewees interpreted these cumulative percents as the percent of students in each proficiency category. Then they were surprised and confused when the sum of percentages across any row in Table 8 did not equal 100%. (p. 25)

TABLE 20.2. Scale Score and Achievement-Level Results from the NAEP 1992 Reading Report Card: National Overall Average Reading Proficiency and Achievement Levels, Grades 4, 8, and 12

Grades	Average proficiency	Percentage of Students At or Above			
		Advanced	Proficient	Basic	Below basic
4	218 (1.0)	4 (0.5)	25 (1.1)	59 (1.1)	41 (1.1)
8	260 (0.9)	2 (0.3)	28 (1.1)	69 (1.0)	31 (1.0)
12	291 (0.6)	3 (0.3)	37 (0.8)	75 (0.7)	25 (0.7)

Note. The standard errors of the estimated percentages and proficiencies appear in parentheses. It can be said with 95% certainty that for each population of interest, the value for the whole population is within plus or minus two standard errors of the estimate for the sample. In comparing two estimates, one must use the standard error of the difference. From Mullis et al. (1993).

In the 1994 series of reports an attempt was made to use graphs instead of tables (Figure 20.4), but examining these in retrospect suggests that such presentations probably did little to improve comprehension.

In 1996, with its release of the science achievement-level results, the National Assessment Governing Board experimented with some graphical displays that seemed promising as a step forward in clarity of communication. Essentially, results were shown as bar graphs that were aligned on a particular achievement level. The extension of the bar to the right of the achievement level indicated the percentage at or

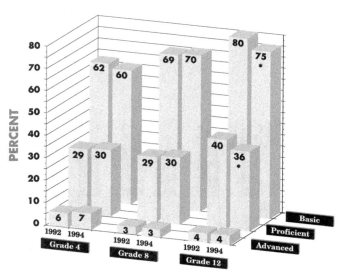

*Significant decrease between 1992 and 1994

FIGURE 20.4. Achievement-level results graph from the NAEP 1994 Reading Report Card. From Campbell, Donahue, Reese, and Phillips (1996).

above. The bars themselves contained the percentages at each of the achievement levels, which in some sense combined both types of information in a single graphic.

From 2000 to 2003, NAEP used a number of variations on the previous attempts, and by 2003 arrived at a stable approach, illustrated in the two displays from the 2011 Report Card Reading Report. The national results (Figure 20.5) make use of a set of nested bar graphs that attempt to convey graphically the nested nature of the cumulative percentages. Figure 20.6 uses the aligned bar graphs that were introduced in the late 1990s as a vehicle for comparatively displaying results by state for the percentage of students at or above Proficient, while also displaying the percentage in each of the achievement-level categories.

The displays and reporting strategies discussed on the preceding pages illustrate the range of approaches used by NAEP over its recent history to provide context to the results for the Nation's Report Card. There are, of course, many challenges in this regard that are quite unique to NAEP, including the lack of results for individuals, which serves to limit the significance of the assessment for any one student or family directly. However, the range of strategies employed by NAEP (and the clear and continuous efforts at improvement) indicate that adding meaning to results for users across audience groups has been (and remains) a priority.

Report Design and Format

The third area of considerable change in NAEP reporting practices over the years has been in the areas of report design and layout. In some ways this area connects to the efforts described in the previous section on how NAEP has sought to add meaning to

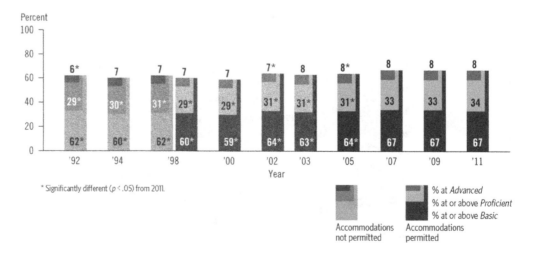

FIGURE 20.5. Achievement-level results from the NAEP 2011 Reading Report Card. From National Center for Education Statistics (2011).

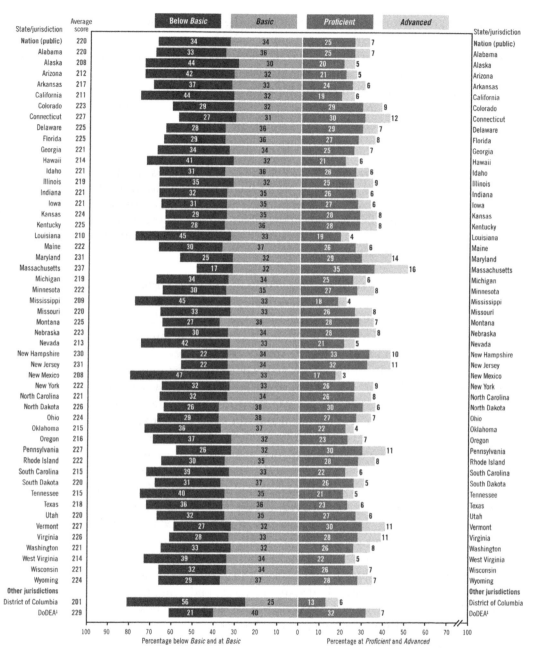

State/jurisdiction	Average score	Below Basic	Basic	Proficient	Advanced
Nation (public)	220	34	34	25	7
Alabama	220	33	36	25	7
Alaska	208	44	30	20	5
Arizona	212	42	32	21	5
Arkansas	217	37	33	24	6
California	211	44	32	19	6
Colorado	223	29	32	29	9
Connecticut	227	27	31	30	12
Delaware	225	28	36	29	7
Florida	225	29	36	27	8
Georgia	221	34	34	25	7
Hawaii	214	41	32	21	6
Idaho	221	31	36	26	6
Illinois	219	35	32	25	9
Indiana	221	32	35	26	6
Iowa	221	31	35	27	6
Kansas	224	29	35	28	8
Kentucky	225	28	36	28	8
Louisiana	210	45	33	19	4
Maine	222	30	37	26	6
Maryland	231	25	32	29	14
Massachusetts	237	17	32	35	16
Michigan	219	34	34	25	6
Minnesota	222	30	35	27	8
Mississippi	209	45	33	18	4
Missouri	220	33	33	26	8
Montana	225	27	38	28	7
Nebraska	223	30	34	28	8
Nevada	213	42	33	21	5
New Hampshire	230	22	34	33	10
New Jersey	231	22	34	32	11
New Mexico	208	47	33	17	3
New York	222	32	33	26	9
North Carolina	221	32	34	26	8
North Dakota	226	26	38	30	6
Ohio	224	29	38	27	7
Oklahoma	215	36	37	22	4
Oregon	216	37	32	23	7
Pennsylvania	227	26	32	30	11
Rhode Island	222	30	35	28	8
South Carolina	215	39	33	22	6
South Dakota	220	31	37	26	5
Tennessee	215	40	35	21	5
Texas	218	36	36	23	6
Utah	220	32	35	27	6
Vermont	227	27	32	30	11
Virginia	226	28	33	28	11
Washington	221	33	32	26	8
West Virginia	214	39	34	22	5
Wisconsin	221	32	34	26	7
Wyoming	224	29	37	28	7
Other jurisdictions					
District of Columbia	201	56	25	13	6
DoDEA[1]	229	21	40	32	7

Percentage below *Basic* and at *Basic*   Percentage at *Proficient* and *Advanced*

[1] Department of Defense Education Activity (overseas and domestic schools).
NOTE: The shaded bars are graphed using unrounded numbers. Detail may not sum to totals because of rounding.

FIGURE 20.6. Graph of achievement-level results by state from the NAEP 2011 Reading Report Card. From National Center for Education Statistics (2011).

scores. Design and format specifically address the choices made about how to display report contents, including the reporting of standard errors and the evolution of strategies for report dissemination focusing on the Internet, which has changed not only what is reported but more fundamentally what constitutes results reporting.

The design and format of reports of test score results affect their usability by various audiences (Goodman & Hambleton, 2004; Hambleton & Zenisky, 2013). NAEP has made considerable efforts in the area of the design and format of certain report elements, specifically tables and displays:

> The tables were more problematic than the text for most of the interviewees. Although most were able to get a general feeling of what the data in the tables meant, many mistakes were made when we asked the interviewees specific questions. The symbols in the tables (e.g., to denote statistical significance) confused some, and others just chose to disregard them. (Hambleton & Slater, 1997, p. 24)

One of the critical activities required to make NAEP reports better suited to a general audience was the redesign of tables, figures, and displays. However, there is a fine line to walk in such simplification activities. As a federal statistical agency, NCES has high and rigorous standards about accurately conveying technical detail regarding the statistical accuracy of all of its survey results. Yet, the statistical/quantitative literacy of a general audience is somewhat limited. The Hambleton and Slater research of the mid-1990s clearly indicated that many of the tables and displays included in the NAEP reports had erred on the side of too much statistical detail and/or had not yet hit upon how to effectively convey that technical and statistical detail to a lay audience.

The NAEP report cards of the 1980s made liberal use of graphics and did not provide standard errors for reported statistics. In contrast, the early transition to NCES published reports in the 1990s was characterized by an attempt to increase the statistical rigor of the reports in general, and also of the tables and displays. The addition of state-by-state reporting complicated matters by making the amount of data to be displayed even greater. Some of the reports of the early 1990s tended to rely largely on tabular presentations and, in the attempt to add rigor, include information about standard errors (Table 20.2).

The work of Hambleton and Slater (1997), when taken with other feedback received, confirmed that including standard errors and using tables were not the best ways to communicate with policymakers or a lay audience. Those audiences frequently did not understand very well what a standard error was, or understand what to do with the information vis-à-vis interpreting results.

Throughout the 1990s, NCES and its contractors were attempting to redesign tables for better public understanding while maintaining a rigorous approach to discussing results based on statistical principles. Figure 20.7 is from the 2002 NAEP Reading Report Card (Grigg, Daane, Ying, & Campbell, 2003). The standard errors have been removed and explicit notations are used to indicate the presence of statistically significant differences between current and prior years. This approach to

Grade 4		Below *Basic*	At *Basic*	At *Proficient*	At *Advanced*	At or above *Basic*	At or above *Proficient*
Accommodations not permitted	1992	38	34	22 *	6	62	29 *
	1994	40 *	31 *	22 *	7	60 *	30
	1998	38	32	24	7	62	31
	2000	37	31	24	8	63	32
Accommodations permitted	1998	40 *	30 *	22 *	7	60 *	29 *
	2000	41 *	30 *	23	7	59 *	29
	2002	36	32	24	7	64	31
Grade 8							
Accommodations not permitted	1992	31 *	40 *	26 *	3	69 *	29 *
	1994	30 *	40 *	27 *	3	70 *	30 *
	1998	26	41 *	31	3	74	33
Accommodations permitted	1998	27 *	41	30	3	73 *	32
	2002	25	43	30	3	75	33
Grade 12							
Accommodations not permitted	1992	20 *	39	36 *	4	80 *	40 *
	1994	25	38	32	4	75	36
	1998	23 *	37	35 *	6 *	77 *	40 *
Accommodations permitted	1998	24 *	36	35 *	6 *	76 *	40 *
	2002	26	38	31	5	74	36

* Significantly different from 2002.
NOTE: Percentages within each reading achievement level range may not add to 100, or to the exact percentages at or above achievement levels, due to rounding.
In addition to allowing for accommodations, the accommodations-permitted results at grade 4 (1998–2002) differ slightly from previous years' results, and from previously reported results for 1998 and 2000, due to changes in sample weighting procedures. See appendix A for more details.

FIGURE 20.7. Achievement-level results from the NAEP 2002 Reading Report Card. From Grigg et al. (2003).

presenting tabular results has been retained fairly intact through to the current generation of reports.[1]

As in many other areas, the potential of the Internet has provided NCES with a more satisfying way of balancing the competing forces of technical rigor and communicating with intended audiences, by offering tremendous flexibility and layout in report design and format. NAEP has developed an Internet-based data tool (*http:// nces.ed.gov/nationsreportcard/naepdata*) that allows users to generate tables of NAEP results on demand and to customize the level of statistical detail contained in these tables. The tool also allows the tables to be exported to applications such as Excel, where they can be further manipulated or converted to graphic displays and exported for use in reports.

---

[1] It should be noted that recent research by Zwick, Zapata-Rivera, and Hegarty (2014) has studied strategies for reporting measurement error, focusing on comparing verbal and graphical methods for communicating those data. The use of a verbal analogy was associated with greater understanding of the results, and variations in experience with statistics was found to impact the kinds of displays of error with which participants in the study were comfortable.

One type of NAEP graphic that had been cited by Hambleton and Slater (1997) as being particularly difficult for a general audience was the so-called *mileage chart*. This chart effectively contained all pairwise comparisons between the jurisdictions assessed in state NAEP. The intention of the mileage chart was to communicate to a report reader interested in a particular jurisdiction which other jurisdictions had higher, similar, or lower NAEP results. (A mileage chart for the jurisdictions in the Trial Urban District Assessments [TUDA] is shown in Figure 20.8 to illustrate this type of display.) The goal of the mileage chart was to encourage readers to treat as different only those jurisdictions whose results were statistically significantly different from the focal jurisdiction of interest.

Research indicated that the mileage chart was perhaps more intimidating (and thus less successful for communication) than intended:

> Several interviewees simply laughed (out of nervousness) when they saw this figure and the next one in the report and indicated a desire to move with

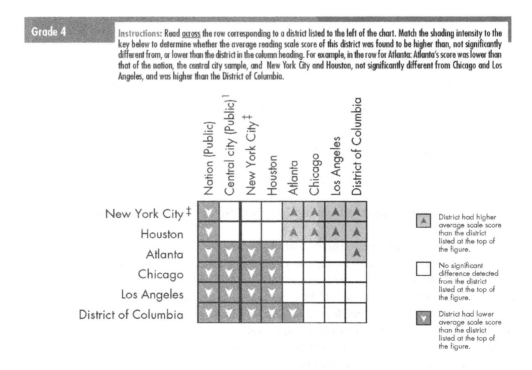

‡ Although deemed sufficient for reporting, the target response rate specified in the NAEP guidelines was not met.
[1] For comparison, at fourth grade 65 percent of students in central city public schools and 40 percent in public schools nationally were non-White. Also, 61 percent of students in central city public schools and 43 percent in public schools nationally were eligible for free/reduced-price school lunch.
NOTE: The between-district comparisons take into account sampling and measurement error and that each district is being compared with every other district shown. Significance is determined by an application of a multiple-comparison procedure.

FIGURE 20.8. Mileage chart from the NAEP TUDA report. From Lutkus, Weiner, Daane, and Jin (2003).

the interview. Perhaps the chart was unclear because the shading was poor. Possibly the problem is that the chart contains a tremendous amount of information, perhaps more than many readers can handle at one time, or handle effectively without clearer directions. (Hambleton & Slater, 1997, p. 19)

Early attempts to improve this display involved the provision of clearer instructions as to how to read the display and better use of shading. Moreover, NCES began to use maps in the individual state reports to convey information to each state regarding which of the other state NAEP participants performed similar, better, or worse. Once again, however, the most satisfactory solution to the problem of how to best display the information in the mileage charts is one that leverages the Internet. NAEP now makes available interactive maps that can be used to convey the same information that was incorporated in the original mileage charts. Now readily available on NCES's website is the State Comparisons tool, which allows the user to create an interactive graphic in the form of a map (Figure 20.9), whereby the user can choose any state or jurisdiction as the focal jurisdiction and the map will instantly configure to show those states with higher, lower, or similar NAEP results (*http://nces.ed.gov/nationsreport-card/statecomparisons*).

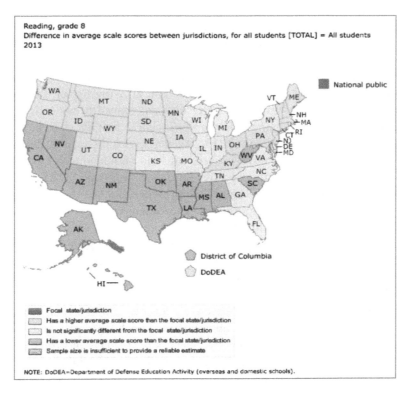

FIGURE 20.9. State comparison map from the NAEP website. From National Center for Education Statistics (2013).

Concluding Thoughts

Improving the reporting of assessment results is an ongoing and evolving enterprise. The goal of this chapter has been to illustrate some of the ways in which NAEP has focused its efforts on three areas of results reporting to better communicate with users about the academic achievement of U.S. schoolchildren. Over its history, NAEP has demonstrated a clear record of continuously reflecting on and striving to improve its communication efforts, and many of the reporting strategies employed have come to represent best practices in results reporting today (Zenisky, Hambleton, & Sireci, 2009). The strides that NAEP has made in terms of audience considerations and differentiation, scale score meaning, and report design and format, described in this chapter, have served to advance the field of reporting not only in terms of report contents but also with respect to how agencies conceptualize reports and how users engage with test data.

An important point to be made in the area of developing reports of test score results is the notion of *process*. Score reporting should not be viewed as a "one-and-done" activity in the broader plan for test development: Rather, it requires investment of time and resources throughout. It must be part of the early conversations on test development and continue through the release of results and beyond, during score interpretation and use by stakeholders. The work NAEP has done to improve its own reporting efforts speaks to the extent to which there is a clear recognition of the importance placed on the results and the necessity of innovation.

Reporting results in educational testing remains an important area for opportunity and growth in both research and practice. The growing use of the Internet as a primary mechanism for dissemination of results, referenced previously, represents a sea change in assessment: It changes how and to what extent agencies have control of the message (Zenisky & Hambleton, 2013). Agencies with the responsibility to report test score results must reflect on how users can and should interact with test data, in light of appropriate (and inappropriate) inferences and uses. NAEP continues to enhance and improve its online tools and Web presence, but the changes in technology are swift and relentless as well, and NAEP and others must continue to adapt their communication strategies accordingly.

Moving forward, as test results take on greater consequences for all levels of stakeholders, the need for quality communication of test results and clear guidance on appropriate score use will only grow. For all testing programs, even those in which considerable resources and effort have already been expended on trying to produce accessible and attractive reports and effectively leverage the Internet, the work must continue. It is the ongoing research on reporting, on both small and large scales, including the systematic study of the effectiveness of displays in targeted audiences, which will provide agencies with the information about their stakeholders' needs for data. Such research will help to foster the development of reports that connect the data from assessments with the intended users, to further promote the responsible use of test results.

ACKNOWLEDGMENT

We wish to thank Katie Faherty for her contributions to an earlier version of this chapter.

REFERENCES

Applebee, A. N., Langer, J. A., & Mullis, I. V. S. (1986). *The Writing Report Card: Writing achievement in American schools.* Princeton, NJ: National Assessment of Educational Progress.

Beaton, A. E., & Allen, N. L. (1992). Interpreting scales through scale anchoring. *Journal of Educational Statistics, 17,* 191–204.

Bourque, M. L. (2004). A history of the National Assessment Governing Board. In L. V. Jones & I. Olkin (Eds.), *The Nation's Report Card: Evolution and perspectives* (pp. 233–249). Bloomington, IN: Phi Delta Kappa Educational Foundation.

Campbell, J. R., Donahue, P. L., Reese, C. M., & Phillips, G. W. (1996). *NAEP 1994 Reading Report Card for the nation and the states: Findings from the National Assessment of Educational Progress and Trial State Assessment.* Washington, DC: National Center for Education Statistics.

Educational Testing Service. (1984). *The Reading Report Card: Progress towards excellence in our schools: Trends in reading over four national assessments, 1971–1984.* Princeton, NJ: Author.

Forsyth, R. A. (1991). Do NAEP scales yield valid criterion-referenced interpretations? *Educational Measurement: Issues and Practice, 10*(3), 3–9.

Goodman, D., & Hambleton, R. K. (2004). Student test score reports and interpretive guides: Review of current practices for future research. *Applied Measurement in Education, 17,* 145–220.

Grigg, W. S., Daane, M. C., Ying, J., & Campbell, J. R. (2003). *The Nation's Report Card: Reading 2002, National Assessment of Educational Progress* (NCES 2003-521). Washington, DC: National Center for Education Statistics, U.S. Department of Education.

Hambleton, R. K. (2002). How can we make NAEP and state test score reporting scales and reports more understandable? In R. W. Lissitz & W. D. Schafer (Eds.), *Assessment in educational reform* (pp. 192–205). Boston: Allyn & Bacon.

Hambleton, R. K., & Slater, S. (1997). *Are NAEP executive summary reports understandable to policy makers and educators?* (CSE Technical Report 430). Los Angeles: National Center for Research on Evaluation, Standards, and Student Teaching. Retrieved from *www.cse.ucla.edu/products/reports/TECH430.pdf.*

Hambleton, R. K., & Swaminathan, H. (1985). *Item response theory: Principles and applications.* Boston: Kluwer.

Hambleton, R. K., & Zenisky, A. L. (2013). Reporting test scores in more meaningful ways: Some new findings, research methods, and guidelines for score report design. In K. F. Geisinger (Ed.), *American Psychological Association handbook of testing and assessment in psychology: Vol. 3. Testing and assessment in school psychology and education* (pp. 479–494). Washington, DC: American Psychological Association.

Jaeger, R. M. (2003). *NAEP validity studies: Reporting the results of the National Assessment of Educational Progress* (Working Paper 2003-11). Washington, DC: U.S. Department of Education, Institute of Education Sciences.

Levine, R., Rathbun, A., Selden, R., & Davis, A. (1998). *NAEP's constituents: What do they want? Report of the National Assessment of Educational Progress Constituents Survey and Focus Groups* (NCES 98–521). Washington, DC: U.S. Department of Education, Office of Educational Research and Improvement.

Linn, R. L., & Dunbar, S. B. (1992). Issues in the design and reporting of the National Assessment of Educational Progress. *Journal of Educational Measurement, 29,* 177–194.

Lutkus, A. D., Weiner, A. W., Daane, M. C., & Jin, Y. (2003). *The Nation's Report Card: Reading 2002, Trial Urban District Assessment* (NCES 2003-523). Washington, DC: Institute of Education Sciences, National Center for Education Statistics, U.S. Department of Education.

Messick, S. J., Beaton, A. E., & Lord, F. M. (1983). *National Assessment of Educational Progress reconsidered: A new design for a new era* (NCES 15-TR-20). Washington, DC: National Center for Education Statistics.

Mullis, I. V. S., Dossey, J. A., Owen, E. H., & Phillips, G. W. (1993). *Executive Summary of the NAEP 1992 Mathematics Report Card for the nation and the states.* Washington, DC: U.S. Department of Education.

National Center for Education Statistics. (n.d.). National Assessment of Educational Progress (NAEP). Retrieved from *http://nces.ed.gov/nationsreportcard.*

National Center for Education Statistics. (2011). *Reading 2011: National Assessment of Educational Progress at grades 4 and 8* (NCES 2012-457). Washington, DC: U.S. Department of Education, Institute of Education Sciences.

National Center for Education Statistics. (2013). *The Nation's Report Card: A first look: 2013 mathematics and reading* (NCES 2014-451). Washington, DC: Institute of Education Sciences, National Center for Education Statistics, U.S. Department of Education.

Simmons, C., & Mwalimu, M. (2000). What NAEP's publics have to say. In M. L. Bourque and S. Byrd (Eds.), *Student performance standards on the National Assessment of Educational Progress: Affirmation and improvements. A study initiated to examine a decade of achievement level setting on NAEP* (pp. 184–219). Washington, DC: National Assessment Governing Board.

Wainer, H., Hambleton, R. K., & Meara, K. (1999). Alternative displays for communicating NAEP results: A redesign and validity study. *Journal of Educational Measurement, 36,* 301–335.

Wirtz, W., & Lapointe, A. (1982). *Measuring the quality of education: A report on assessing educational progress.* Washington, DC: Authors.

Zapata-Rivera, D., & Katz, R. I. (2014). Keeping your audience in mind: Applying audience analysis to the design of interactive score reports. *Assessment in Education: Principles, Policy, and Practice, 21*(4), 442–463.

Zapata-Rivera, D., & VanWinkle, W. (2010). *A research-based approach to designing and evaluating score reports for teachers* (Research Memorandum 10–01). Princeton, NJ: Educational Testing Service.

Zenisky, A. L., & Hambleton, R. K. (2012). Developing test score reports that work: The process and best practices for effective communication. *Educational Measurement: Issues and Practice, 31*(2), 21–26.

Zenisky, A. L., & Hambleton, R. K. (2013). From "Here's the story" to "You're in charge": Developing and maintaining large-scale online test and score reporting resources. In M.

Simon, M. Rousseau, & K. Ercikan (Eds.), *Improving large-scale assessment in education* (pp. 175–185). New York: Routledge.

Zenisky, A. L., Hambleton, R. K., & Sireci, S. G. (2009). Getting the message out: An evaluation of NAEP score reporting practices with implications for disseminating test results. *Applied Measurement in Education, 22*(4), 359–375.

Zwick, R., Zapata-Rivera, D., & Hegarty, M. (2014). Comparing graphical and verbal representations of measurement error in test score reports. *Educational Assessment, 19,* 116–138.

CHAPTER 21

Performance Assessment
and Accountability
Then and Now

Suzanne Lane

Policymakers and educators consider performance assessments to be valuable tools for educational reform (Linn, 1993). The educational reform in the 1980s was based on the premise that too many students were unable to solve meaningful problems requiring critical thinking and reasoning. Proponents of the educational reform contended that assessments needed to better reflect students' competencies in applying their knowledge and skills to solve educationally meaningful tasks. Promising research advances in cognition and learning, and in educational measurement, prompted researchers to think differently about how students process and reason with information, and how assessments can be designed to capture meaningful aspects of students' achievement and learning (Lane & Stone, 2006). Performance assessments were an ideal candidate to measure the types of skills that were at the core of the educational reform movement. As accountability tools, performance assessments then and now are used to make important decisions about students, educators, administrators, schools, and systems. This chapter defines performance assessments in the following way:

> Performance assessments that may be used for high-stakes purposes are designed to closely reflect the performance of interest; require standardized directions, ancillary materials, and administration conditions; allow students to construct or perform an original response that reflects important disciplinary content knowledge and skills, and the student work or performance is evaluated by predetermined scoring criteria and procedures that are applied in a standardized manner.

This chapter begins with a discussion of the argument-based approach to validity that provides the foundation for the design and evaluation of performance assessments for both instructional and accountability purposes. Next, a historical perspective of performance assessments and their use for accountability purposes is summarized, followed by a discussion on their use in state assessment and accountability programs since the 1980s. The design of the next generation of assessments that embody performance assessments is then addressed. The measurement models that can inform the design and evaluation of performance assessments are discussed at the end of the chapter. These discussions address some of the psychometric and practical challenges in the design and use of performance assessments.

Validity of Performance Assessments

To ensure that the multiple and potentially competing purposes of performance assessments are clearly articulated, an argument-based approach to validity should be adopted. It entails an interpretation–use argument (IUA) that explicitly identifies the proposed interpretations and uses of test scores, and a validity argument that provides a structure for evaluating the IUA by requiring an accumulation of evidence to support the appropriateness of the claims (Kane, 2006, 2013). The argument-based approach requires the specification of the score inferences and assessment uses, evaluation of the proposed inferences and their supporting assumptions using evidence, and the consideration of plausible alternative interpretations.

Generalizability of scores is a concern for performance assessments because, typically, only a few performance tasks can be administered. Thus, in the design of performance assessments, attempts should be made to minimize construct underrepresentation and construct-irrelevant variance—two major sources of potential threats to the validity of score inferences (Messick, 1989, 1994). *Construct underrepresentation* occurs when an assessment is not fully representative of its targeted domain. The extent to which the assessment underrepresents the targeted domain will have an impact on the generalizability of the scores—that is, on the extent to which inferences and claims based on scores from the assessment can be applied across other tasks, administration conditions, raters, or over time (Messick, 1989, 1994). *Construct-irrelevant variance* occurs when one or more irrelevant constructs are assessed in addition to the intended construct. Potential sources of construct-irrelevant variance for performance assessments include task wording, response mode, raters' attention to irrelevant features, and students' familiarity with the context of the task (see Clauser & Clauser, Chapter 6, this volume, for a deeper discussion of how to address some of these concerns with generalizability theory).

For both issues, the use of student learning objectives (SLOs), which require establishing an explicit relationship between (1) the targeted domain, (2) the intended learning outcomes within that domain, and (3) the evidence used to determine whether the learning outcomes are attained, can help define and constrain the target domain and the inferences drawn about student performance (Lane & DePascale, in press).

Historical Perspective on Performance Assessment and Accountability

A historical perspective on the treatment of both performance assessment and account-ability from experts can be garnered by examining the four editions of *Educational Measurement* dating back to 1951. In the first edition of *Educational Measurement* (1951), edited by E. F. Lindquist, an entire chapter was devoted to performance tests of educational achievement (Ryans & Frederiksen, 1951) and another to essay tests (Stalnaker, 1951).

In the performance test chapter, Ryans and Frederiksen (1951) indicated that per-formance tests "sometimes are designed to copy or simulate the real-life situations or operations that the test is devised to measure" (p. 459), and they included both simulated tests and work sample tests as examples of performance tests. They pro-vided an example of a work sample test in education as a student playing or singing a musical selection. The third type of test they included was the recognition test that requires students to recognize essential features of a performance or a product of a performance, such as recognizing errors in a played musical selection. The Ryans and Frederiksen (1951) definition is generally consistent with the definition of performance assessments provided in the *Standards for Educational and Psychological Testing* (American Educational Research Association, American Psychological Association, & National Council on Measurement in Education, 2014), which similarly character-izes such assessments as an attempt to emulate the context or conditions in which the intended knowledge or skills are actually applied.

In Stalnaker's (1951) chapter on essays, he expressed concern with the diminish-ing use of essays by testing agencies. Some of these concerns are reminiscent of the psychometric and practical concerns raised in the 1990s, including the cost of rating, insufficient rater and score reliability, limited sample of student performance, lack of a sufficient range of scores, and difficulty in posing prompts so that all students are engaged in the same task. In addition to these chapters in the first edition of *Edu-cational Measurement,* there were chapters on the functions of measurement in the facilitation of learning, in improving instruction, in counseling, and in educational placement. There was no chapter on the use of tests for accountability purposes.

The second edition of *Educational Measurement* (1971), edited by Robert L. Thorndike, similar to the first edition, included a chapter on performance and prod-uct evaluation (Fitzpatrick & Morrison, 1971) and a chapter on essay examinations (Coffman, 1971). Fitzpatrick and Morrison (1971) identified different types of per-formance tests that are still being used in the 21st century or researched for edu-cational assessment and accountability purposes, including simulations, situational tests, work-sample tests, projects, rehearsed performances, and games. In the chapter addressing essays, Coffman (1971) provided data from the 1967 Advanced Placement Exams illustrating variance components for different sources of errors in the rating of student essays. In discussing future research on the use of essays in educational testing, Coffman addressed issues associated with students responding differentially to essays due to the nature of the essay topic and/or context, as well as the concerns related to the consequences (he used the term *side effects*) of eliminating essays from educational tests.

The second edition also included a chapter on the evaluation of educational programs that addressed the use of testing in program evaluations (Astin & Panos, 1971). Although a comprehensive model for educational evaluation was presented, Astin and Panos (1971) indicated that the "task of evaluating educational programs has come to be closely associated with the construction and administration of achievement tests" (p. 741), and they used the National Assessment of Educational Progress (NAEP) as an example of a test-based accountability program.

The third edition of *Educational Measurement* (1989b), edited by Robert L. Linn, had no chapters devoted to performance assessments, essay tests, or educational accountability. However, the use of performance assessments to measure what students know and can do was addressed in many of the chapters, including the chapters on test development, cognitive psychology's implications for measurement, and computer technology and testing. In Ron Hambleton's (1989) chapter on item response theory (IRT), he discussed two promising research directions for scaling essays and performance assessments using IRT: multidimensional IRT models and polytomous IRT models. As he stated, "a merger of these two topics—polychotomously scored, multidimensional item response models—is currently providing a foundation for new types of tests developed from a cognitive perspective" (Hambleton, 1989, p. 195).

In the chapter on administrative uses of school testing programs, Frechtling (1989) addressed the increased use of test scores as a tool for accountability in education within the school effectiveness movement of the time, and merit pay plans for teachers. Linn (1989a) also discussed the increased use of tests for accountability purposes and identified three major testing programs that used tests for accountability: state minimum competency testing (MCT) programs in the 1970s, teacher testing, and NAEP. Although the first example relied exclusively on selected response items, the latter two testing programs included performance tasks.

In the fourth edition of *Educational Measurement* (2006), edited by Robert Brennan, there was a chapter devoted to performance assessments (Lane & Stone, 2006) and one on testing for accountability in grades K–12 (Koretz & Hamilton, 2006). The performance assessment chapter included discussions on the design of performance assessments and scoring systems; validity issues associated with performance assessments; and the use of generalizability theory and IRT in the design, validation, and scaling of performance assessments. In their chapter on accountability, Koretz and Hamilton (2006) discussed the No Child Left Behind (NCLB) Act (NCLB, 2001) that was instituted with the goal of raising academic standards by requiring more challenging content for instruction and student learning. The NCLB Act imposed sanctions on schools if they did not achieve their goals, typically defined as an increase in a given percent of students at or above proficient as measured by state tests.

In Kane's (2006) chapter on validity, he argued for the use of interpretive and validity arguments for NCLB accountability programs, including the evaluation of intended and unintended consequences. The interpretive argument for an assessment and accountability system would include (1) an interpretation of individual student achievement on state content standards, (2) a conversion of the scores to achievement levels, (3) calculation of the percent of students at each achievement level, and then (4) a decision about the school in terms of sanctions and rewards. Evidence related to uses, interpretations, and claims can then be accumulated and organized into a relevant validity argument.

The review of these chapters as well as other chapters in the four editions of *Educational Measurement* are intended to provide the reader with a historical measurement perspective on the use of performance assessments in education in the United States for both instructional and accountability purposes. The general observation is that, although performance assessment has been part of the measurement conversation since at least the 1950s, the use of these types of assessments for the particular purpose of accountability is a relatively recent development, all things considered. For more historical information on the use of performance assessment, the reader is referred to Madaus and O'Dwyer (1999).[1]

Use of Performance Assessments for Accountability Purposes: 1980–2014

Performance assessments that assess complex thinking skills were considered to be valuable tools for educational reform by policymakers and advocates for curriculum reform in the 1980s (Linn, 1993). These assessments were seen as vehicles that could help shape sound instructional practice by modeling for teachers what is important to teach and for students what is important to learn (Lane & Stone, 2006). Beginning in this era, performance assessments were used to hold educators, administrators, schools, and states accountable for improving instruction and student learning. Because a major goal of performance assessments is to improve instruction and student learning, evidence is required of such positive consequences as well as any potentially negative consequences (Messick, 1994). Evidence does suggest that when assessment and accountability systems measure critical thinking and problem solving, teachers engage students in these thinking skills (Borko & Elliott, 1999; Koretz, Barron, Mitchell, & Stecher, 1996; Lane, Parke, & Stone, 2002; Stone & Lane, 2003).

The efficacy of test-based accountability systems, however, depends not only on the capability of assessing critical thinking skills but also on the way the scores and interpretive information are reported to educators, parents, and other stakeholders (Hambleton & Slater, 1997). As an example, based on an evaluation of NAEP score reports that entailed structured interviews with policymakers and educators, Hambleton and Slater (1997) concluded that the score reports were not necessarily leading to

---

[1] As these researchers indicated, the first use of testing as a policy tool was the use of selection tests for civil services in China in 210 B.C.E. These tests consisted of performance tasks, such as composing a poem and demonstrating reasoning by comparing conflicts within the classics. The emphasis on reasoning ability was short-lived, however, because of concerns about the subjectivity of scoring. This concern still prevailed in the 1990s.

appropriate inferences. They recommended that the reports be tailored to particular audiences to improve their understandability, clarity, and usefulness. (See Zenisky, Mazzeo, & Pitoniak, Chapter 20, this volume, for a more in-depth discussion of this study and of score reporting more generally.)

State Assessment and Accountability Systems

The renewed interest in performance assessments in the 1980s led to their use for the purpose of holding schools accountable for improving instruction with attached consequences for schools and, in some cases, students. Maryland was a leader in using performance assessments in its school accountability and educational reform efforts. Prior to NCLB, Maryland designed and implemented a performance assessment program for grades 3, 5, and 8 to measure school performance and provide information on school accountability and improvement (Ferrara, 2010; Maryland State Board of Education, 1995). The Maryland School Performance Assessment Program (MSPAP, 1991–2002) was designed to promote performance-based instruction in an integrated manner in reading, writing, mathematics, science, and social studies. The performance assessment tasks were interdisciplinary, required students to produce both short and extended written responses, and, in some cases, required hands-on activities.

As indicated by Ferrara (2010), by design, MSPAP was the "instructional driver in schools" (p. 13). As an accountability measure, the stakes were high—school report cards were published and sanctions were imposed on poorly performing schools. MSPAP's psychometric characteristics were well documented, including the IRT scaling based on the partial credit model (Yen & Ferrara, 1997). It was considered to be one of the highest-quality large-scale performance assessments during this time, and the design and psychometric features of MSPAP received a favorable review by an expert external committee led by Ron Hambleton (Hambleton et al., 2000).

Other states that used performance assessments in the late 1980s and 1990s provided both student and school scores. In addition to a statewide test in math that included multiple-choice and constructed response items and a test in writing that required students to respond to a prompt, Vermont also used a portfolio-based performance assessment for both instructional and accountability purposes from 1988 through 1996. The portfolio guidelines provided to schools were broad and did not specify the nature of the work to be included, nor the format of the tasks, which raised concerns regarding validity, reliability, and comparability (Koretz, Stecher, Klein, & McCaffrey, 1994). A number of factors could have enhanced the comparability and reliability of scores derived from the portfolios, including standardized guidelines for what should be included in them, standardized directions for the amount of assistance provided by teachers, and detailed rubrics and comprehensive training on rating student products.

The Kentucky Instructional Reporting and Information System (KIRIS; 1990–1999), used for both educational reform and accountability, included a portfolio in writing and mathematics as well as performance tasks that were administered on eight occasions throughout the year and took 1 hour to several hours to complete (Gong &

Reidy, 1996). KIRIS included hands-on performance tasks, portfolios, and extended constructed response items in seven academic areas. Although the reliability of scoring was relatively low initially, with improved training of raters and well-developed rubrics, reliability improved (Koretz, 1998).

The use of performance assessments ended in both Vermont and Kentucky due to issues with their psychometric quality and sustainability as well as due to lack of support by policymakers. In addition to reliability issues, comparability within and across years was a major concern. Thus, concerns about technical quality and costs in providing student-level scores limited the wider use of performance assessments by states (Linn, 1993; Madaus & O'Dwyer, 1999).

Consequential Evidence of State Performance Assessments

During the 1990s, because performance assessments were considered a policy tool for educational change, and therefore the accumulation of evidence of such positive consequences and any potentially negative consequences was warranted (Linn, 1993; Messick, 1994). Adverse impacts bearing on issues of fairness were particularly relevant because it cannot be assumed that a contextualized performance task is equally appropriate for all students. On the other hand, performance assessments that measure complex thinking skills have been shown to have a positive impact on instruction and student learning (Lane et al., 2002; Stecher, Barron, Chun, & Ross, 2000; Stone & Lane, 2003).

Haertel's (2013) framework for classifying mechanisms of intended testing consequences as direct and indirect effects can help illuminate the validity evidence needed for assessment and accountability systems. The direct effects of educational assessments, including instructional guidance for students, informing comparisons among educational approaches, and educational management (e.g., the use of assessments to help evaluate the effectiveness of educators or schools), involve interpretations or uses that rely directly on the information scores provide about the measured constructs. By contrast, indirect effects, which include directing student effort, focusing the curriculum and instruction, and shaping public perceptions that have an impact on actions, have no direct dependence on the information provided by test scores, but are linked closely to the purposes or claims of assessment (Haertel, 2013). These indirect mechanisms of action, which are key components of the interpretive and use argument, are critical in evaluation of the consequences of educational assessments and accountability programs. Haertel's framework provides a foundation for a principled approach to studying both the intended and unintended consequences of assessment and accountability systems.

Positive consequential evidence of Maryland's state performance assessment was provided by examining the relationship between changes in instructional practice and improved school performance on the MSPAP. The results of a set of studies revealed that reform-oriented instructional features accounted for differences in school performance on the MSPAP in reading, writing, mathematics and science, and they accounted for differences in the rate of change in the MSPAP in reading and writing

(Lane et al., 2002; Stone & Lane, 2003). Furthermore, there was no significant relationship between socioeconomic status (SES) and growth on the MSPAP at the school level in four of the five subject areas (Stone & Lane, 2003). This result suggests that improved school performance on performance assessments is not necessarily related to contextual variables such as SES. Positive consequential evidence was also obtained for KIRIS's portfolio system in that teachers reported increasing their emphasis on mathematical problem solving and representation (Koretz et al., 1994).

Decline of Performance Assessments in the Early 2000s

The use of performance assessments in state testing programs declined with the requirements of NCLB. Under NCLB, states were required to annually test all students from grades 3 through 8, as well as students in high school at one grade level, in reading and mathematics. Students also needed to be tested in science at one grade level in elementary, middle, and high school. States needed to document the performance of schools, districts, and student subgroups to determine adequate yearly progress (AYP) toward predetermined benchmarks for student achievement, and consequences were attached to schools that did not make AYP 2 years in a row. Although NCLB required that the tests assess higher-order thinking skills, many states attempted to do so without the use of performance tasks due to a number of constraints, including the need to assess a large number of students each year. Because states were required to provide student-level scores to measure proficiency yearly and in many grades, Maryland's performance-based assessment was no longer tenable given the constraints involved in the design and implementation of large-scale performance assessments.

The Next Generation of State Assessments

The Common Core State Standards (CCSS) initiative (Council of Chief State School Officers & National Governors Association, 2010) and the Race-to-the-Top initiative (U.S. Department of Education, 2009) have led to a renewed interest in using performance assessments that are grounded in academic standards that reflect 21st-century thinking skills. A major goal of the initiatives is to ensure that academic standards are set high for all students. To receive federal funding, evidence is required to show how the assessment system will measure "standards against which student achievement has traditionally been difficult to measure," and include "items that will be varied and elicit complex student demonstrations or applications of knowledge and skills" (U.S. Department of Education, 2009, p. 8). The Race-to-the-Top initiative also calls for a theory of action that specifies the intended benefits of the assessment and accountability system.

Performance assessments are needed to measure the full range of the CCSS and to ensure the validity of the score inferences and actions taken based on these inferences. Two multistate consortia, Partnership for Assessment of Readiness for College and Career (PARCC) and Smarter Balanced Assessment System (SBAC), have been funded by Race to the Top to develop state assessment systems that are aligned with the CCSS. Both assessments are computer-based and include technology-enhanced items as well as performance tasks.

Design of the Next Generation of State Assessments

In the next generation of assessments, performance assessments will be used for making claims about students, educators, administrators, and schools. Each of these claims, and the potential decisions based on them, needs to be considered in the design phase. The design of performance assessments needs to consider their use not only for accountability purposes, but also for informing instruction and for improving student learning. Principled approaches to assessment design, such as evidence-centered design (ECD; Mislevy, Steinberg, & Almond, 1999), will allow for more valid inferences from scores derived from performance assessments. ECD is based on a process of reasoning from the evidence—student performance—to support claims about student skills, knowledge, and competencies (see also Plake et al., Chapter 4, this volume).

The use of task models that allow for the generation of tasks that assess the same skills and knowledge will help promote comparability of tasks across forms and over time. Both PARCC and SBAC are using the ECD approach by first articulating the claims they want to make about student performance, which then serve as the foundation for designing the tasks and scoring rubrics. In an evaluation of the claims proposed by PARCC and SBAC, Herman and Linn (2014) indicated that the claims are "striking in the attention they give to student capabilities that current state tests typically fail to address—particularly the third English language claim, which focuses on research and synthesis, and the third and fourth claims in mathematics, which focus on reasoning, communication, and nonroutine real-world problem solving" (pp. 35–36). They indicated that the consortia's sample performance tasks reach the highest level of Webb's depth-of-knowledge framework—extended thinking and reasoning (Webb, Alt, Ely, & Vesperman, 2005).

One approach adopted by PARCC to enhance domain representation and the validity of score inferences is the use of both extended performance tasks and briefer structured tasks (Messick, 1994). The PARCC English language arts performance-based assessment includes three types of tasks—literary analysis, research simulation, and narrative—and three item types that are aligned with the CCSS and assess critical thinking skills—evidence-based selected response, technology-enhanced constructed response, and prose-constructed response (Dogan, 2014). As an example, for the research simulation task, students read two or more texts to gather information to solve the proposed research problem and write an analytical essay to present their solution. For the literary analysis task, students write a literary analysis after reading two literary texts, demonstrating their close analytic reading ability and their ability to compare and synthesize ideas. In mathematics, some tasks call for written arguments and critiques of reasoning and other tasks call for modeling in real-world scenarios. Scoring for these tasks may include a mix of machine and human scoring

(Dogan, 2014). As an example, a PARCC sample task requires students to read a biography of Abigail Adams and two correspondences between Abigail and John Adams. Below is the prompt:

> Both John and Abigail Adams believed strongly in freedom and independence. However, their letters suggest that each of them understood these terms differently based on their experiences.
>
> Write an essay that explains their contrasting views on the concepts of freedom and independence. In your essay, make a claim about the idea of freedom and independence and how John and Abigail Adams add to that understanding and/or illustrate a misunderstanding of freedom and independence. Support your response with textual evidence and inferences drawn from all three sources. (Dogan, 2014, p. 13)

This English language arts performance task requires students to compare and synthesize information across texts and to provide evidence of their critical thinking skills.

Psychometric Considerations and Measurement Models for Performance Assessments

Psychometrics provides tools for the design of high-quality performance assessments; however, compromises are necessary to achieve the multiple purposes of assessment and accountability systems (Lane & DePascale, in press). Psychometric criteria, such as comparability and reliability, need to be considered in light of design criteria.

Comparability

The comparability of performance assessments can be compromised by the very same features that make them attractive. Comparability of scores is jeopardized when the scores differentially reflect construct-relevant skills, construct-irrelevant skills, and measurement error for subgroups of students or over time (Haertel & Linn, 1996). The use of performance assessments for accountability purposes requires a level of standardization in the construct measured, the forms assembled, test administration, and the scoring of student responses within an administration and across years. Extended time periods, choice of task, and use of ancillary material may pose challenges to the standardization of performance assessments, and consequently, to the comparability of tasks and forms. Comparability is also jeopardized because of the small number of tasks on a performance assessment. Students' individual reactions to specific tasks tend to average out on multiple-choice items because of the relatively large number of them, but such individual reactions to items have a greater effect on scores from performance assessments that are composed of relatively few items (Haertel & Linn, 1996).

Typical equating designs are not applicable to many performance assessments, so it is especially critical to address comparability in the design of tasks and forms. By specifying the set of knowledge and skills to be assessed, careful attention can be paid to potential sources of construct-irrelevant variance and construct underrepresentation, both of which have an impact on comparability. In ECD, a foundation for comparability is provided by the delineation of the claims, evidence, and task and scoring models (Huff, Steinberg, & Matts, 2010).

Modeling Sources of Error with Generalizability Theory

Because performance assessments typically consist of a small number of tasks, the generalizability of the scores to the broader domain needs consideration in the design phase. Generalizability theory provides a conceptual and statistical framework to model multiple sources of error in assessment data that affect the generalizability of score inferences (see Clauser & Clauser, Chapter 6, this volume; also Brennan, 2001; Cronbach, Gleser, Nanda, & Rajaratnam, 1972). Facets that need to be considered when examining the generalizability of scores include task, rater, administration occasion, rater occasion, and rater committee (Lane & Stone, 2006). As an example, error due to tasks occurs because there are usually only a small number of tasks included in a performance assessment. Typically there are task mean differences and an interaction between the student and task indicating that students respond differently across tasks. Error due to raters can occur because raters may differ in their severity as well as in their judgments about whether one student's response is better than another student's response. The former results in rater mean differences and the latter results in an interaction between the student and rater facets. Error due to administration occasion can occur because students respond differently across occasions (resulting in an interaction between student and occasion), and students respond differently on each task from occasion to occasion (resulting in a student by task by occasion interaction).

Task-sampling variability as compared to rater-sampling variability in students' scores on performance assessments is a greater source of measurement error (e.g., Lane, Liu, Ankenmann, & Stone, 1996; Shavelson, Baxter, & Gao, 1993). Using a *person × task × rater* generalizability study design, Lane and her colleagues (Lane et al., 1996) demonstrated that task-sampling variability was the major source of measurement error for a mathematics performance assessment. Between 42 and 62% of the total score variability was accounted for by the *person × task* interaction, indicating that persons were responding differently across tasks. Shavelson and his colleagues (Shavelson et al., 1993; Shavelson, Ruiz-Primo, & Wiley, 1999) conducted a *person × task × rater × occasion* generalizability study for a science performance assessment. The results indicated that the large task-sampling variability was due to variability in both the *person × task* interaction and the *person × task × occasion* interaction. The *person × task* interaction accounted for 26% of the total score variability, whereas the *person × task × occasion* interaction accounted for 31% of the total score variability. The latter suggests that there was a tendency for students to change their approach to each task from occasion to occasion. Although students may have approached the tasks differently on different testing occasions, their aggregated performance did not vary across occasions (Shavelson et al., 1999).

In a recent study, van Rijn and Yoo (2014) investigated the generalizability of scores on forms from eighth-grade writing assessments that were designed to be comparable. The intent was to develop three comparable forms on argumentative writing. The forms had the same layout and prompt type, but they had different scenarios and source texts. The largest variance components were the *person × task* and the *person × task × rater*, which included residual error. The percent of total variance accounted for by the *person × task* interaction ranged from 21 to 30%, and it ranged from 25 to 39% for the three-way interaction. These results highlight the difficulty in creating comparable forms for writing assessments, and have implications for the next generation of state assessments.

Generalizability studies have informed the design of performance assessments as well as scoring rubrics and procedures. Research since the 1990s has demonstrated that increasing the number of tasks, in comparison to increasing the number of raters, has a greater impact on the extent to which one can generalize from the test score to the broader domain. Furthermore, carefully designed scoring rubrics, scoring procedures, and rater training materials were shown to minimize the effects of error due to raters.

Modeling Performance Assessment Data with IRT

Polytomous IRT models that assume an underlying unidimensional construct have been developed and used for scaling performance assessment data. These models account for the multiple score levels by estimating step functions for each item. The graded response model (GRM) developed by Samejima (1969) and clearly described by Hambleton and Swaminathan (1985) can be readily applied to performance assessments that are scored polytomously. The model allows for the estimation of a unique discrimination parameter as well as step functions for each item. The partial credit model (PCM), which belongs to the Rasch family of models, can also be applied to performance assessment data (Masters, 1982). The generalized partial credit model (GPCM), which is based on the PCM, relaxes the assumption of a uniform discriminating power of items (Muraki, 1997). A major difference between the GRM and the models based on the Rasch model is in the estimation and interpretation of the step functions. Examples of the application of these models include scaling responses to a mathematics performance assessment using the GRM (Lane, Stone, Ankenmann, & Liu, 1995) and scaling responses to multiple-choice and constructed response items on NAEP using the GPCM.

As Hambleton (1989) indicated, multidimensional IRT models may be appropriate for modeling performance assessment data that capture complex performances that draw on multiple dimensions such as problem solving and reasoning skills. Multidimensional item response theory (MIRT) models specify multiple latent variables underlying item responses (Ackerman, 1996; Reckase, 1997), and a number of MIRT models have been developed for polytomous responses, including GRMs (de Ayala, 1994) and PCMs (Yao & Schwarz, 2006).

Within the context of ECD, Mislevy, Steinberg, and Almond (2003) discussed an IRT-based Bayesian network modeling approach that can capture multiple, complex features of student proficiency. Another MIRT model, the bifactor model (Gibbons & Hedeker, 1992), is being explored by a number of assessment programs that include performance tasks. In the bifactor model, the responses to each item are a function of a general factor and one specific factor. The specific factor may be due to shared reading passages or a shared context for a set of mathematics tasks. For a test that consists of multiple-choice items and performance tasks that are designed to measure skills that are different from those elicited by the multiple-choice items, one specific factor may be due to the responses to the performance tasks and the second specific factor may be due to the responses to the multiple-choice items.

Although MIRT models have been developed that are appropriate for performance assessments, they are not commonly used in large-scale educational assessment programs. The Cognitively Based Assessment of, for, and as Learning (CBAL) initiative, which includes technology-enhanced assessments based on cognitive competency models that are multidimensional, is exploring the use of the bifactor model to scale the assessment data in reading, writing, and mathematics (e.g., Fu, Chung, & Wise, 2013).

Modeling Rater Effects using IRT

Performance assessments are considered to be "rater-mediated" because they do not provide direct information about the domain of interest, but rather information mediated through raters' interpretations (Engelhard, 2002). Raters bring a variety of potential sources of construct-irrelevant variance to the rating process that may not be controlled for completely in the design of the rubrics and training procedures. Potential sources of construct-irrelevant variance include differential interpretation of score scales, differential assignment of ratings to subgroups, halo effects, and bias in rater interpretation of task difficulty (Engelhard, 2002). These sources of construct-irrelevant variance affect the validity of score inferences.

Rater effects, such as rater severity, rater accuracy, and rater centrality (tendency to assign scores in the middle of the score scale), have been studied using the multifaceted Rasch model (e.g., Englehard, 2002; Wolfe, 2004) as well as multilevel modeling (e.g., Leckie & Baird, 2011). Integrating psychometric, cognitive, and contextual features, Wolfe and McVay (2012) developed procedures to measure four common rater effects: rater severity–leniency, rater centrality, rater inaccuracy, and differential dimensionality. The first three rater effects refer to patterns of ratings that are systematically lower or higher than accurate ratings; more tightly clustered than accurate ratings; and inconsistent, in an unpredictable way, with accurate ratings, respectively. Differential dimensionality occurs when subgroups of raters are influenced by irrelevant features of the response such as handwriting. When modeling rater effects, the effects are considered to be stable within some initial time period, but they may change over time, indicating differential rater functioning over time.

Concluding Thoughts

Similar to the educational reform movement in the 1980s, performance assessments that measure critical thinking skills are considered to be a valuable policy tool for improving instruction and student learning in the 21st century. The Race-to-the-Top initiative called for instruction and assessment to emphasize thinking and reasoning skills that will prepare students for college and careers. Both PARCC and SBAC intend to use performance tasks that are designed to measure such skills. Although important advances have been made in the design and scaling of performance assessments since the 1980s, to fully realize the potential of performance assessments, additional research on the use of computer-based simulation tasks, automated scoring, assessment of learning progressions, and multivariate measurement models in large-scale educational assessment and accountability programs is warranted.

REFERENCES

Ackerman, T. (1996). Graphical representation of multidimensional item response theory analyses. *Applied Psychological Measurement, 20*(4), 113–127.

American Educational Research Association, American Psychological Association, & National Council on Measurement in Education. (2014). *Standards for educational and psychological testing.* Washington, DC: Authors.

Astin, A. W., & Panos, R. J. (1971). The evaluation of educational programs. In R. L. Thorndike (Ed.), *Educational measurement* (2nd ed., pp. 733–751). Washington, DC: American Council on Education.

Borko, H., & Elliott, R. (1999). Hands-on pedagogy versus hands-off accountability, *Phi Delta Kappan, 80*(5), 394–400.

Brennan, R. L. (2001). *Generalizability theory.* New York: Springer-Verlag.

Brennan, R. L. (Ed.). (2006). *Educational measurement* (4th ed.). Westport, CT: American Council on Education/Praeger.

Coffman, W. E. (1971). Essay examinations. In R. L. Thorndike (Ed.), *Educational measurement* (2nd ed., pp. 271–302). Washington, DC: American Council on Education.

Council of Chief State School Officers and National Governors Association. (2010). Common Core Standards for English language arts. Retrieved on June 25, 2010, from *www.corestandards.org.*

Cronbach, L. J., Gleser, G. C., Nanda, H., & Rajaratnam, N. (1972). *The dependability of behavioral measurements: Theory of generalizability of scores and profiles.* New York: Wiley.

De Ayala, R. J. (1994). The influence of multidimensionality on the graded response model. *Applied Psychological Measurement, 18*, 155–170.

Dogan, E. (2014, April). *Design and development of PARCC performance-based assessments and related research.* Paper presented at the annual meeting of the National Council on Measurement in Education, Philadelphia.

Engelhard, G. (2002). Monitoring raters in performance assessments. In G. Tindal & T. M. Haladyna (Eds.), *Large-scale assessment programs for all students: Validity, technical adequacy and implementation* (pp. 261–287). Mahwah, NJ: Erlbaum.

Ferrara, S. (2010). *The Maryland School Performance Assessment Program (MSPAP) 1991–2002: Political considerations*. Paper presented at the National Research Council workshop on best practices for state assessment systems, Washington, DC.

Fitzpatrick, R., & Morrison, E. J. (1971). Performance and product evaluation. In R. L. Thorndike (Ed.), *Educational measurement* (2nd ed., pp. 237–270). Washington, DC: American Council on Education.

Frechtling, J. A. (1989). Administrative uses of school testing programs. In R. L. Linn (Ed.), *Educational measurement* (3rd ed., pp. 475–484). New York: American Council on Education/Macmillan.

Fu, J., Chung, S., & Wise, M. (2013). *Dimensionality analysis of CBAL writing tests* (ETS Research Report 13–10). Princeton, NJ: Educational Testing Service.

Gibbons, R. D., & Hedeker, D. R. (1992). Full-information bi-factor analysis. *Psychometrika, 57*, 423–436.

Gong, B., & Reidy, E. F. (1996). Assessment and accountability in Kentucky's school reform. In J. B. Baron & D. P. Wolf (Eds.), *Performance-based student assessment: Challenges and possibilities* (Vol. 1, pp. 215–233). Chicago: National Society for the Study of Education.

Haertel, E. H. (2013). How is testing supposed to improve schooling? *Measurement: Interdisciplinary Research and Perspectives, 11*(1–2), 1–18.

Haertel, E. H., & Linn, R. L. (1996). Comparability. In G. W. Phillips (Ed.), *Technical issues in large-scale performance assessment* (NCES 96-802, pp. 59–78). Washington, DC: U.S. Department of Education.

Hambleton, R. K. (1989). Principles and selected applications of item response theory. In R. L. Linn (Ed.), *Educational measurement* (3rd ed., pp. 147–200). New York: American Council on Education/Macmillan.

Hambleton, R. K., Impara, J., Mehrens, W., Plake, B. S., Pitoniak, M. J., Zenisky, A. L., et al. (2000). Psychometric review of the Maryland School Performance Assessment (MSPAP). Retrieved March 20, 2014, from *www.abell.org/pubsitems/ed_psychometric_review_1000.pdf*.

Hambleton, R. K., & Slater, S. C. (1997). Are NAEP executive summary reports understandable to policymakers and educators? (CSE Technical Report 430). Los Angeles: Center for the Study of Evaluation, National Center for Research on Evaluation, Standards, and Student Testing.

Hambleton, R. K., & Swaminathan, H. (1985). *Item response theory: Principles and applications*. Boston: Kluwer.

Herman, J., & Linn, R. (2014). New assessments, new rigor. *Educational Leadership, 71*(6), 34–37.

Huff, K., Steinberg, L., & Matts, T. (2010). The promise and challenges of implementing evidence-centered design in large-scale assessment. *Applied Measurement in Education, 23*(4), 310–324.

Kane, M. T. (2006). Validation. In R. L. Brennan (Ed.), *Educational Measurement* (4th ed., pp. 17–64). Westport, CT: American Council on Education/Praeger.

Kane, M. T. (2013). Validating the interpretations and uses of test scores. *Journal of Educational Measurement, 50*(1), 1–73.

Koretz, D. (1998). Large-scale portfolio assessments in the US: Evidence pertaining to the quality of measurement. *Assessment in Education: Principles, Policy and Practice, 5*(3), 309–334.

Koretz, D. M., Barron, S., Mitchell, K., & Stecher, B. M. (1996). *The perceived effects of the*

Kentucky Instructional Results Information System (KIRIS) (MR-792-PCT/FF). Santa Monica, CA: Rand.

Koretz, D. M., & Hamilton, L. S. (2006). Testing for accountability in K–12. In R. L. Brennan (Ed.), *Educational measurement* (4th ed., pp. 531–578). New York: American Council on Education/Praeger.

Koretz, D. M., Stecher, B., Klein, S., & McCaffrey, D. (1994). The Vermont portfolio assessment program: Findings and implications. *Educational Measurement: Issues and Practice, 13*(3), 5–10.

Lane, S., & DePascale, C. (in press). Psychometric considerations for alternative forms of assessments and student learning objectives. In H. Braun (Ed.), *Meeting the challenges to measurement in an era of accountability*. New York: Routledge.

Lane, S., Liu, M., Ankenmann, R. D., & Stone, C. A. (1996). Generalizability and validity of a mathematics performance assessment. *Journal of Educational Measurement, 33*(1), 71–92.

Lane, S., Parke, C. S., & Stone, C. A. (2002). The impact of a state performance-based assessment and accountability program on mathematics instruction and student learning: Evidence from survey data and school performance. *Educational Assessment, 8*(4), 279–315.

Lane, S., & Stone, C. A. (2006). Performance assessments. In B. Brennan (Ed.), *Educational measurement* (4th ed., pp. 387–432). New York: American Council on Education/Praeger.

Lane, S., Stone, C. A., Ankenmann, R. D., & Liu, M. (1995). Examination of the assumptions and properties of the graded item response model: An example using a mathematics performance assessment. *Applied Measurement in Education, 8*, 313–340.

Leckie, G., & Baird, J. (2011). Rater effects on essay scoring: A multilevel analysis of severity drift, central tendency, and rater experience. *Journal of Educational Measurement, 48*(4), 399–418.

Lindquist, E. F. (Ed.). (1951). *Educational measurement*. Washington, DC: American Council on Education.

Linn, R. L. (1989a). Current perspectives and future directions. In R. L. Linn (Ed.), *Educational measurement*. Washington, DC: American Council on Education.

Linn, R. L. (Ed.). (1989b). *Educational measurement* (3rd ed.). New York: American Council on Education/Macmillan.

Linn, R. L. (1993). Educational assessment: Expanded expectations and challenges. *Educational Evaluation and Policy Analysis, 15*, 1–6.

Madaus, G. F., & O'Dwyer, L. M. (1999). Short history of performance assessment: Lessons learned. *Phi Delta Kappan, 80*(9), 688–701.

Maryland State Board of Education. (1995). *Maryland school performance report: State and school systems*. Baltimore: Author.

Masters, G. N. (1982). A Rasch model for partial credit scoring. *Psychometrika, 47*, 149–174.

Messick, S. (1989). Validity. In R. L. Linn (Ed.), *Educational measurement* (3rd ed., pp. 13–104). New York: American Council on Education/Macmillan.

Messick, S. (1994). The interplay of evidence and consequences in the validation of performance assessments. *Educational Researcher, 23*(2), 13–23.

Mislevy, R. J., Steinberg, L. S., & Almond, R. G. (1999). *Evidence-centered assessment design*. Princeton, NJ: Educational Testing Service.

Mislevy, R. J., Steinberg, L. S., & Almond, R. G. (2003). On the structure of educational assessments. *Measurement: Interdisciplinary research and perspectives, 1*(1), 3–62.

Muraki, E. (1997). A generalized partial credit model. In W. J. van der Linden & R. K.

Hambleton (Eds.), *Handbook of modern item response theory* (pp. 153–164). New York: Springer.

No Child Left Behind Act of 2001, 20 U.S.C. 6311 *et seq.*

Reckase, M. D. (1997). A linear logistic multidimensional model. In W. J. van der Linden & R. K. Hambleton (Eds.), *Handbook of modern item response theory* (pp. 271–286). New York: Springer.

Ryans, D. G., & Frederiksen, N. (1951). Performance tests in educational achievement. In E. F. Lindquist (Ed.), *Educational measurement* (pp. 455–494). Washington, DC: American Council on Education.

Samejima, F. (1969). Estimation of latent ability using a response patter of graded scores. *Psychometric Monograph, 17.*

Shavelson, R. J., Baxter, G. P., & Gao, X. (1993). Sampling variability of performance assessments. *Journal of Educational Measurement, 30*(3), 215–232.

Shavelson, R. J., Ruiz-Primo, M. A., & Wiley, E. W. (1999). Note on sources of sampling variability. *Journal of Educational Measurement, 36*(1), 61–71.

Stalnaker, J. M. (1951). The essay type of examination. In E. F. Lindquist (Ed.), *Educational measurement* (pp. 495–532). Washington, DC: American Council on Education.

Stecher, B., Barron, S. E., Chun, T., & Ross, K. (2000, August). *The effects of Washington education reform on schools and classrooms* (CSE Technical Report No. 525). Los Angeles: Center for Research on Evaluation, Standards, and Student Testing, University of California.

Stone, C. A., & Lane, S. (2003). Consequences of a state accountability program: Examining relationships between school performance gains and teacher, student, and school variables. *Applied Measurement in Education, 16*(1), 1–26.

Thorndike, R. L. (Ed.). (1971). *Educational measurement* (2nd ed.). Washington, DC: American Council on Education.

U.S. Department of Education. (2009). *Race to the Top program executive summary.* Retrieved April 15, 2010, from *www.ed.gov/programs/racetothetop/resources.html.*

van Rijn, P., & Yoo, H. (2014, April). *Generalizability of results from parallel forms of next-generation writing assessments.* Paper presented at the annual meeting of the National Council on Measurement in Education, Philadelphia, PA.

Webb, N. L., Alt, M., Ely, R., & Vesperman, B. (2005). *Web alignment tool (WAT): Training manual 1.1.* Madison: University of Wisconsin, Center of Educational Research.

Wolfe, E. W. (2004). Identifying rater effects using latent trait models. *Psychology Science, 46,* 35–51.

Wolfe, E. W., & McVay, A. (2012). Application of latent trait models to identifying substantively interesting raters. *Educational Measurement: Issues and Practice, 31*(3), 31–37.

Yao, L., & Schwarz, R. D. (2006). A multidimensional partial credit model with associated item and test statistic: An application to mixed-format tests. *Applied Psychological Measurement, 30,* 469–492.

Yen, W. M., & Ferrara, S. (1997). The Maryland School Performance Assessment Program: Performance assessments with psychometric quality suitable for high-stakes usage. *Educational and Psychological Measurement, 57*(1), 60–84.

CHAPTER 22

The History of Testing Special Populations
The Evolution of Fairness in Testing

Jennifer Randall and Alejandra Garcia

An ongoing struggle for equity best characterizes the history of education and education testing for special-population students in U.S. schools. Historically, students with disabilities[1] and English learners (ELs) have been excluded from accountability measures, and consequently largely excluded from the curriculum.[2] The introduction of stricter standards-based reform efforts beginning in the 1980s has led to an increased focus on both the participation and performance of all students, including special populations, on state assessments. As a result, participation rates of special populations in large-scale assessments have grown substantially. Currently, 13% of students are diagnosed with a learning or physical disability and receiving services in U.S. schools (U.S. Department of Education, 2013), and the U.S. Census Bureau estimates that as many as 40% of schoolchildren will be ELs[3] in 2030 (Camara & Lane, 2006).

This chapter provides a historical look at the evolution of test practices with respect to special populations in the 20th century—specifically, students with disabilities and ELs. It begins with an overview of the legislative and judicial landmarks associated with special populations, followed by a discussion of the inclusion movement

---

[1] The Individuals with Disabilities Education Act (IDEA) defines a "child with a disability" as a "child . . . with an intellectual disability, hearing impairments (including deafness), speech or language impairments, visual impairments (including blindness), serious emotional disturbance . . . , orthopedic impairments, autism, traumatic brain injury, other health impairments, or specific learning disabilities; AND, who . . . [because of the condition] needs special education and related services."

[2] Shriner and Thurlow (1993) note that most states included fewer than 10% of their students with disabilities on state assessments in the early 1990s.

[3] The federal government uses the term *limited English proficient* (LEP) to describe these students. A student is considered LEP if he or she is unable to communicate effectively in English because his or her primary language is not English, and he or she has not yet developed fluency in English.

that overviews trends in accommodation/modification practices and policies, to that end, beginning in the early 1990s. Special attention is given to the development of policies with respect to alternate assessments (designed for students with the most significant cognitive disabilities). The remainder of the chapter focuses on test development and validity practices related to test fairness, including the history and progression of the *Standards for Psychological and Educational Measurement*. Although this chapter focuses on test fairness with respect to special populations, the narrative mirrors the evolution/treatment of special populations in the United States in general.

Special Populations Legislation

We begin by summarizing the legislative history of how special populations have been educated and assessed. Because students with disabilities and ELs have been affected by different laws and court cases, we address each population separately. All of the major laws, court cases, and judiciary rulings that we describe in this section and the one following it (on litigation) are laid out chronologically in Figure 22.1.

Students with Disabilities

Prior to legislation requiring public education for children with physical, cognitive, and/or emotional disabilities, parents had limited options beyond educating their children at home or paying for private (often expensive) education. In fact, in 1970, only one in five of the 4 million students with disabilities received education services in the

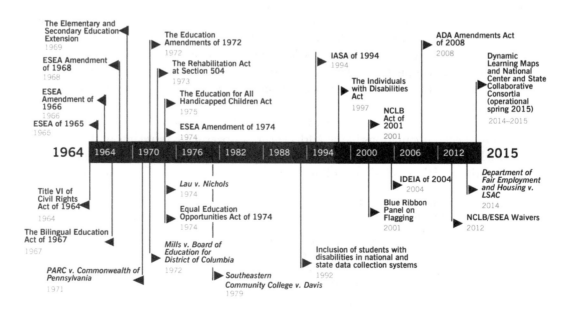

FIGURE 22.1. Timeline of major events.

United States. Moreover, of the students enrolled in public schools, many were placed in inadequate segregated classrooms and/or received insufficient support in general education classrooms. The 1960s and 1970s ushered in a new era with respect to the educational rights of students from special populations. During this time, state governments, federal courts, and the U.S. Senate worked to make the rights of students with disabilities (and other special populations) explicit. Forty-five state legislatures passed laws in favor of special education programs between the mid-1960s and 1975. Perhaps most importantly, the federal courts continued to rule that schools could not discriminate against students based on disability status and that parents had due process rights (under the 14th Amendment Equal Protection clauses) with respect to the education of their children (Martin, Martin, & Terman, 1996).

In 1965, the Elementary and Secondary Education Act (ESEA) was amended to allow grants to state institutions and state-operated schools serving children with disabilities, and was further amended in 1966 to establish the Bureau of Education of the Handicapped (BEH) and the National Advisory Council (now called the National Council on Disability). Congress continued to pass a series of laws and amendments (e.g., Elementary and Secondary Education Amendments of 1968, 1969, 1972, and 1974) over the course of the next decade, gradually increasing educational access for students with disabilities, including the Rehabilitation Act at Section 504 in 1973, which required any recipients of federal funds to end discriminatory practices with respect to providing services for individuals with disabilities. Congress, however, failed to provide funding or monitoring for Section 504, and consequently it went unenforced and ignored by educational agencies for years.

It was the passage of the 1975 Education for All Handicapped Children Act[4] that finally ensured that all students would have access to a free and appropriate public education. Although the language of this act is very similar to that in the Education Amendment of 1974, it is in this act (the Education for All Handicapped Children Act) that some form of testing accommodations is mentioned for the first time. In addition to requiring that "testing and evaluation materials and procedures utilized for the purposes of evaluation and placement of handicapped children will be selected and administered as not to be racially or culturally discriminatory," the act requires that materials and procedures be provided and administered in "the child's native language or mode of communication. . . ." Indeed, by providing unprecedented rights for special populations intended to create equity in education, this law would serve as the basis for many legislative actions and policy decisions that address the need for test development and validation practices that ensure test fairness.

English Learners

In addition to legislation targeted at cementing the educational rights of students with disabilities, the ESEA also addressed, for the first time, the inclusion of educational

---

[4]This act's title would change in 1983 and again into 1990 to become what is now commonly known as the *Individuals with Disabilities Education Act*.

programs designed to support minority-language speakers via Title VII, also known as the Bilingual Education Act of 1967. Although the law did not require bilingual education, Congress did set aside money for school districts to provide such programs. Educational services were extended to include students with limited English-speaking ability with the reauthorization of the Bilingual Education Act in 1974, and expanded even further in 1978 to include students with LEP.

Although not specifically enacted to address the needs of ELs, the Equal Educational Opportunities Act (EEOA) of 1974 provided ELs, in particular, education protection under the law by mandating that "no state shall deny equal educational opportunity to an individual on account of his or her race, color, sex or national origin, by the failure of an educational agency to take appropriate action to overcome language barriers that impede equal participation by its students in its instructional programs." This federal legislation prevented states from blocking the educational rights of ELs and also encouraged states to develop new approaches (e.g., curricula) to educate these students. The EEOA (1974) echoed, in part, the spirit of Title VI of the Civil Rights Act of 1964 and became the foundation for later regulations pertaining to EL education.

Education Reform

The Improving America's Schools Act (IASA) of 1994 reauthorized the ESEA of 1965 and placed an increased focus on improving accountability for all students using state assessments. The law required that each state use multiple measures to assess student performance and provide for:

i. the participation in such assessments of all students
ii. the reasonable adaptations and accommodations for students with diverse learning needs, necessary to measure the achievement of such students relative to state content standards, and
iii. the inclusion of limited English proficient students who shall be assessed, to the extent practicable, in the language and form most likely to yield accurate and reliable information on what such students know and can do, to determine such students' mastery of skills in subjects other than English. (Subpart I. Section 1111. State Plans. [F])

Meanwhile in response to what was perceived as slow implementation of previous laws and low expectations for students with disabilities, in 1997 the Individuals with Disabilities Act (formerly the Education for All Handicapped Children Act) was also heavily amended. The new law (1) expanded the definition of children with disabilities to include developmentally delayed children between 3 and 9 years of age; (2) provided a process by which parents could resolve disputes with local education agencies; and (3) included additional funding for technology, infants and toddlers, and professional development (Public Law 105-17, 111 Stat. 37).

The next reauthorization of ESEA, the No Child Left Behind (NCLB) Act of 2001, included very specific provisions with respect to test practices. State plans for demonstrating annual improvement in schools required 95% of students from each identified subgroup (e.g., students with disabilities, ELs, students of different federally recognized ethnicities) to "take the assessments . . . with accommodations, guidelines, and alternative assessments provided in the same manner as those provided under the Individuals with Disabilities Education Act." The Individuals with Disabilities Education Improvement Act (IDEIA) of 2004 echoed the NCLB legislation, in part, noting that "all students with disabilities must be included in all general State and districtwide assessment programs, including assessments required under the NCLB, with appropriate accommodations and alternate assessments where necessary and as indicated in their respective individualized education programs (IEP)."[5] IDEA 2004 also requires the "State to develop guidelines for the provision of appropriate testing accommodations and, to the extent feasible, use universal design principles in developing and administering State assessments."

NCLB also included new provisions for assessing ELs. First, as mentioned above, it mandated their inclusion in content assessments and required states to disaggregate and report the results of ELs separately from the general population. In support of this goal, it also required states and local educational agencies to expand "the range of accommodations available to students with limited English proficiency and students with disabilities to improve the rates of inclusion of such students. . . ." In addition, and more notably, the law also included, as one of its five central goals, that all ELs would become proficient in English. To accomplish this goal, the law introduced mandatory assessment of ELs' progress and proficiency in English, and tied funding and sanctions to these goals via the new Title III, now called *Language Instruction for Limited English Proficient and Immigrant Students.*

In 2008, the Americans with Disabilities Act (ADA; formerly covered by Section 504 of the Rehabilitation Act of 1973) was amended to reflect requirements for test administration in postsecondary education: "Any person that offers examinations or courses related to applications, licensing, certification, or credentialing for secondary or postsecondary education, professional, or trade purposes shall offer such examinations or courses in a place and manner accessible to persons with disabilities or offer alternative accessible arrangements for such individuals."

The laws discussed in this section provided the legal leverage to call attention to the rights of students from special populations in the courts. The subsequent legal victories, in turn, provided the social and legal push for more comprehensive legislation. In the following section, we highlight the important judicial victories secured for students from special populations.

---

[5]The IEP is the cornerstone of a student's educational program. It specifies the services to be provided and how often, describes the student's present levels of performance and how the student's disabilities affect academic performance, and specifies accommodations and modifications to be provided for the student.

Special-Populations Litigation

Students with Disabilities

There have been many legislative victories won for students with disabilities since the 1960s, with Section 504 and the ADA serving as the basis for most judicial remedies for these populations. In *Pennsylvania Association for Retarded Children (PARC) v. Commonwealth of Pennsylvania* (1971), PARC contested a public school policy that allowed schools to specifically deny services to any "child that had not attained a mental age of five years" at the time of first-grade enrollment. Under a consent decree, the state agreed to provide free public education to all children, including children with mental retardation, until the age of 21. Moreover, this case would establish the standard of appropriateness that included a preference for the least restrictive environment and access to an education that was appropriate for the child's learning capacity. A year later, in *Mills v. Board of Education for District of Columbia* (1972), the district was sued for the expulsion and/or refusal to admit approximately 12,340 students with disabilities during the 1971–1972 academic year due to budget constraints. In this case, the district courts ruled such a practice unconstitutional, noting that the burden of insufficient funding could not be the sole responsibility of students with disabilities. *PARC* and *Mills* are the most widely cited and discussed cases with respect to the rights of students from special populations, and by 1973 the rulings in these two cases were upheld more than 30 times in federal courts (Martin et al., 1996). Indeed, *PARC* and *Mills* established a precedent for the inclusion of (or educational access for) students with disabilities. Since that time, several cases have had implications for the testing of students from special populations.

In 1979, the Supreme Court ruled in *Southeastern Community College v. Davis* that Section 504 did not require "an educational institution to lower or to effect substantial modifications of standards to accommodate a handicapped person." A 1983 federal circuit court, in *Brookhart v. Illinois State Board of Education*, interpreted Section 504 to mean that "an otherwise qualified student who is unable to disclose the degree of learning he actually possesses because of the test format or environment would be the object of discrimination solely on the basis of his handicap." The court went so far as to provide examples of mandated accommodations, for the purposes of providing an appropriate format or environment, which included Braille and the use of small quiet rooms. The Brookhart court went on to say, however, that "Altering the content of the test to accommodate an individual's inability to learn the tested material because of his handicap would be a substantial modification as well as a perversion of the diploma requirement. A student who is unable to learn because of his handicap is surely not an individual who is qualified in spite of his handicap." In summary, the courts began to make the distinction—perhaps unknowingly—between test *modifications* and test *accommodations*.

Still, students with disabilities won an important victory in 1990 when a mother sued the state of Hawaii for not allowing her child—diagnosed as learning disabled with a specific disability in writing—a "reader" accommodation when the state superintendent ordered that *all* nonblind students be denied the use of readers for the graduation exam. The federal Office of Civil Rights (OCR) ruled that decisions regarding the allowance or nonallowance of testing accommodations for students must be made on a case-by-case basis.

English Learners

A parallel story exists for ELs with respect to judicial battles and victories with EL proponents relying heavily on the 14th Amendment and/or Title VI of the Civil Rights Act for judicial relief. In *Lau v. Nichols* (1974), perhaps the most influential decision with respect to EL education, a class-action lawsuit was brought against the San Francisco school system on behalf of non-English-speaking Chinese students. The students argued that the school system had failed to provide them with additional instruction in English, yet required that they be proficient in order to graduate. Citing a violation of their rights under the 14th Amendment, the plaintiffs argued that the school system's policy was tantamount to withholding equal educational opportunities. The Supreme Court, relying on Section 601 of the Civil Rights Act of 1964, ruled that the San Francisco Unified School District received considerable federal funding and, as such, was prohibited from discrimination based on race, color, or national origin in any program or activity receiving federal financial assistance. The court wrote:

> Under these state-imposed standards there is no equality of treatment merely by providing students with the same facilities, textbooks, teachers, and curriculum; for students who do not understand English are effectively foreclosed from any meaningful education. . . . We know that those who do not understand English are certain to find their classroom experiences wholly incomprehensible and in no way meaningful.

The system was required to ensure that students of a particular race, color, or national origin not be denied the same opportunities to receive/obtain an education as generally available to other students. The *Lau* decision would eventually lead to what is referred to as the *Lau Remedies*. Unlike Title VII of the Bilingual Education Act, which applied only to federally funded programs, the Lau Remedies applied to all school districts and, in essence, required schools to provide bilingual and/or English as a second language instruction to students.

The court's ruling in *Lau v. Nichols* (1974) would lead to a series of state-level judicial battles regarding bilingual education across the United States. In New York, for example, a lawsuit filed by Puerto Rican parents, *Aspira v. New York* (1975), resulted in the Aspira Consent Decree, which continues to require transitional bilingual programs for Spanish-surnamed students who are more proficient in Spanish than English. This decree remains a model for school districts across the United States. This victory was echoed and tremendously strengthened in 1978 in *Rios v. Reed* when the court, under Title VI of the Civil Rights Act and the EEOA, ruled that simply having a bilingual program was not sufficient. It found the city's bilingual programs were inadequate and dispatched the federal Office of Civil Rights to ensure that improvements were made.

Of course, not all judicial battles have resulted in victories for ELs. In *San Antonio Independent School District v. Rodriguez* (1973), the plaintiffs argued, under the Equal Protection Clause of the 14th Amendment, that predominately minority schools received less funding than schools that served predominately white students. The U.S. Supreme Court ruled that there is no fundamental right to an education guaranteed by the Constitution, which in turn implies no fundamental right to a bilingual education (Del Valle, 2003). This decision would later become the basis for several anti-bilingual education initiatives (e.g., *Otero v. Mesa County Valley School District* [1980] and *Keyes v. School District No. 1* [1973]).

Still, perhaps the most important decision with respect to EL students since *Lau* was in the case of *Castañeda v. Pickard* (1981). In its decision, the Fifth Circuit Court established the three-pronged test, referenced earlier for evaluating programs serving ELs: (1) Schools must base their program on sound educational theory, (2) the program must be implemented with the appropriate amount of resources required, and (3) schools must evaluate the effectiveness of any programs and make adjustments accordingly [648 F. 2d 989 (Fifth Circuit, 1981)].

The legislative and judicial histories of students from special populations reflect an evolving public consciousness toward those students. Still, the transition from legislative policy to operational practice can be complicated. In the next section, we briefly describe the inclusion and (consequently) test accommodation movement in the United States.

History of Inclusion

In 1993, Algozzine described full inclusion as circumstances in which "all children are educated in supported, heterogeneous, age-appropriate, dynamic, natural, child-focused classroom, school, and community environments . . . [with] open doors, accessibility, proximity, friends, support, and valuing diversity. . . . Schools that practice full inclusion take responsibility for the learning of all students" (p. 6). In this section we describe how advocates for students with disabilities and ELs have defined, fought for, won, and improved these students' right to full inclusion over time.

Students with Disabilities

Despite legislative initiatives such as IDEA and ADA designed to guarantee, or foster, the inclusion of students with disabilities, significant numbers of students with disabilities were still not being included in state reports of academic performance or national databases (McGrew, Thurlow, Shriner, & Spiegel, 1992). For example, Ysseldyke, Thurlow, McGrew, and Shriner (1994) reported that the exclusion rates of students with disabilities from the 1990 trial state National Assessment of Educational Progress (NAEP) ranged from 33 to 87%. Historically, decisions about inclusion of students were made at the local level with varying criteria and their interpretations. A 1993 report indicated that the most common criteria were (1) time spent in general education settings, (2) courses for which the student is mainstreamed, and (3) the match between instructional objectives and assessment objectives (National Center on Education Outcomes [NCEO]). Still, little consensus existed, and students were consistently excluded.

In 1994 a working conference was held in Washington, DC, to discuss the inclusion of students with disabilities in large-scale assessments. This conference convened, in large part, in response to the exclusion rates of students from large-scale assessments. The committee outlined several underlying factors for the exclusion of students from special populations, which included:

- the use of vague guidelines that allow local decisions to be made about the participation of students who are on Individualized Educational Plans (IEPs)
- the differential implementation of guidelines
- the failure to monitor the extent to which the intent of the guidelines is followed
- sampling plans that systematically exclude students who are in separate schools and students who are not in graded programs
- an unwillingness to make accommodations in assessment materials and procedures that will enable some individuals to participate
- an altruistic motivation to lessen the emotional distress to the student who is not expected to perform well (Ysseldyke & Thurlow, 1994, p. 2)

Based on key assumptions (e.g., assessment should make clear that the same high standards are expected of all students) for making inclusion decisions, this working group put forth three primary recommended guidelines:

1. The inclusion of students with disabilities in the initial stages of test development when trying out items.
2. The inclusion of all students with disabilities in taking some form of the assessment by allowing partial participation in an assessment or the use of an alternative assessment for some students if necessary.
3. The inclusion of students with disabilities in the reporting of results.

With respect to making accommodation decisions, the committee recommended using modifications that (1) provide students with a comfortable setting that (2) does not adversely affect the validity of the measures. Furthermore, and perhaps most importantly, the committee recommended the need for additional research on the impact of presentation, response, setting, and time/scheduling alternatives. To that end, considerable research (Fuchs & Fuchs, 2001; Randall & Engelhard, 2010; Zuriff, 2000) has focused on the impact of test modifications/accommodations, as the inclusion of students with disabilities and ELs in large-scale assessments and accountability measures continues to present some measurement challenges. Nonetheless, as more federal statutes seek to prevent the exclusion of students from special populations in accountability practices and policies, the need for testing accommodations that compensate for the unique needs and disabilities of these students has become increasingly apparent and unavoidable, despite these challenges.

As already mentioned, some accommodations (e.g., Braille) have been available for students since the 1970s, whereas many students with special needs were still being excluded from large-scale assessments in the 1990s. Also mentioned was the beginning of a distinction between test accommodations and test modifications by the courts. Specifically, any change in the standardized administration of a test is considered an accommodation if it provides "equitable instructional and assessment access for students with disabilities and ELLs (English learners) in the areas of presentation, response, timing, scheduling, setting, and linguistics" (Thurlow et al., 2006, p. 658). On the other hand, a *modification* refers to test changes for which there is insufficient evidence to determine whether these changes in administration alter the underlying construct being measured. Modifications are also referred to as *adaptations, alternates, nonstandard accommodations*, or *nonallowable accommodations* (Lazarus et al., 2006; Thurlow et al., 2006). In the following section, we outline the progression of accommodation use.

English Learners[6]

The inclusion of ELs with respect to both instruction and assessment involves a history of challenges, particularly with respect to testing. Indeed, ELs must acquire a second language to participate in a school setting while simultaneously mastering content knowledge through that second language. Federal policy regarding ELs has vacillated since the early 1970s from policies that accommodate students with flexible approaches to education by taking into consideration their home language, to far more rigid policies that reflect English-only attitudes about instruction for ELs. Garcia et al. (2008) described six types of educational programs intended for use with ELs, each with specific, perhaps competing, goals: (1) submersion, (2) EL pullout—submersion plus EL, (3) structured immersion—sheltered English, (4) traditional bilingual education—early exit, (5) developmental bilingual education—late exit, and (6) Two-Way Bilingual Education—Dual Immersion. To be sure, the Bilingual Education Act of 1968 (reauthorized in 1974, 1978, 1984, and 1988; and 1994 with the ESEA) may account for some of the diversity in EL education policy in many districts. The original law focused more on providing ELs the language support they needed

---

[6]ELs, also referred to as LEP students, are "students who speak a language other than English and are acquiring English in school" (Garcia, Kleifgen, & Falch, 2008, p. 7).

to acquire English, but as the years progressed we begin to see a shift of federal support to English-language-only programs. By 1988, the Bilingual Education Act had imposed a 3-year limit on student participation in any transitional bilingual education programs.

Moreover, the use of bilingual instruction came under fire in several states in the 1990s. In 1998, Proposition 227 in California—referred to as the *English for the Children Initiative*—prohibited the use of native language instruction, instead requiring the use of sheltered content programs for no more than 1 year (California Education Code, Sec. 300–311). A similar initiative in 2000 banned bilingual education in the state of Arizona, as did a proposition in Massachusetts in 2002. Perhaps the end of bilingual education is best marked by No Child Left Behind (2002) legislation, which required that all states provide evidence that several student subgroups—including ELs—meet annual targets. Consequently, the focus for many local education agencies (LEAs) became less about supporting or leveraging bilingualism, and more about improving the English proficiency of ELs and reducing/shrinking the achievement gap between these students and their English-speaking counterparts.

History of Accommodations

The primary purpose of any test accommodation is to promote equity and improve the validity of assessments results. In doing so, both ELs and students with disabilities are better able to demonstrate what they know and to do so with the same accuracy as their nondisabled and non-EL counterparts. This goal is achieved by eliminating, or at least reducing, the construct-irrelevant variance from an assessment. As a result of both legislative imperatives and focused research in the area, the progression of accommodation use is, indeed, an interesting one mirroring the progression of educational inclusion, with some states doing as little as legally possible and/or finding it difficult to adequately evaluate and meet the needs of their special populations, including students with disabilities and ELs. As late as 1993, the variability across states was still remarkable. An accommodation that was expressly recommended in one state could have been expressly forbidden in another. The most commonly allowed accommodations involved alterations in the presentation and/or response format. Other common accommodations included setting changes and timing/scheduling modifications. This lack of consistency, or uniformity, could be linked primarily to the lack of research at the time on the impact of testing modifications/accommodations.

Assessment accommodations are typically grouped into one of five categories based on the type of change required: (1) presentation (e.g., read aloud, Braille); (2) equipment and material (e.g., calculator, thesaurus); (3) response (e.g., scribe records response); (4) timing/scheduling (e.g., extended time, frequent breaks); and (5) setting (e.g., separate room, small group). Presentation accommodations are typically reserved for students whose disabilities make it difficult for them to visually decode standard print (i.e., print disabilities). These accommodations afford students the opportunity to access test content and/or directions in an alternate format.

Both response and equipment/material accommodations, unlike presentation accommodations that modify the way in which test content is presented to the students, adjust the manner in which students are allowed to respond to the test content. These accommodations generally allow students to record responses to test questions in alternate ways. Included within these categories also are accommodations that allow students to solve/organize a response using some type of material or device (e.g., calculator).

Timing/scheduling accommodations typically modify the allowable length of testing time and may also change the way the time is organized. The extended time accommodation, which falls within this category, is one of the most frequently requested and granted accommodations. Students requiring this type of accommodation range from those with specific learning disabilities to ELs (who may read or write more slowly than English-proficient students) to students with attention-deficit/hyperactivity disorder (ADHD) or even more profound physical and cognitive disabilities. Timing/scheduling accommodations are also often used in combination with other accommodation types.

Finally, setting accommodations simply change either the location or the conditions in which an assessment is given. These accommodations are most often reserved for students who become easily distracted (as a by-product of their disabilities) or for students for whom their primary accommodation (e.g., read-aloud) would be considered a distraction to students completing the assessment under standardized conditions. As seen in Tables 22.1–22.5, which highlight state-allowed accommodations in 1997 and 2009, the number of state-/district-allowed accommodations has increased with the advent of additional research and legislation regarding accommodations for special populations. Indeed, current federal law requires states to identify, through IEP teams, appropriate accommodations (i.e., accommodations that do not invalidate test scores) for students with disabilities. Although there is no comparable requirement or system for ELs, some states have adopted a similar approach to assigning accommodations for ELs. Kopriva (2011) has also developed a framework (selection taxonomy for English learner accommodations [STELLA]) for this purpose.

Flagging

A discussion of the progression of test accommodations must be accompanied by a discussion of flagging. *Flagging* refers to the practice of notifying schools that a test score was achieved under nonstandard testing conditions. This practice began at least as early as the early 1970s when students with disabilities began receiving accommodated versions of admissions tests. In fact, the 1985 *Standards for Educational and Psychological Testing* encouraged the practice noting, that "until tests have been validated for people who have specific handicapping conditions, test publishers should issue cautionary statements in manuals and elsewhere regarding confidence in interpretations based on such test scores" (American Educational Research Association, American Psychological Association, & National Council on Measurement in Education, [AERA, APA, & NCME], 1985, p. 79). A decade later, the standards (AERA,

TABLE 22.1. Evolution of Presentation Accommodations Allowed by State Policy: A Count of States

Accommodation	1997		2009	
	Allow in some configuration	Explicitly prohibit	Allow in some configuration	Explicitly prohibit
Large print	32		50	
Braille	31		50	
Read aloud	25	3		
Read aloud directions			42	
Read aloud questions			51	
Read aloud passages			23	9
Sign language	27			
Sign interpret directions			47	1
Sign interpret questions			39	
Sign interpret passages			12	3
Native language translation of directions			21	2
Native language translation of questions			11	4
Native language translation of passages			10	2
Repeat/clarify directions	13	1	34	
Visual cues			24	
Administration by others	11		4	
Familiar examiner			19	
Additional examples			4	
Teacher highlighting			21	
Student highlighting			16	
Student reads test aloud			14	
Increased space between items			5	
Simplify/paraphrase directions			21	1
Tactile graphics			15	
Prompt/encourage student			15	
Page turner			6	
With assistance (e.g., aide)	5			
Equipment	30			

Note. In Tables 22.1–22.5, 1997 data are from Thurlow, Seyfarth, Scott, and Ysseldyke (1997); 2009 data are from Christensen, Braam, Scullin, and Thurlow (2011).

TABLE 22.2. Evolution of Equipment and Materials Accommodations: A Count of States

Accommodation	1997 Allow in some configuration	1997 Explicitly prohibit	2009 Allow in some configuration	2009 Explicitly prohibit
Magnification equipment	22		49	
Amplification equipment	16	1	48	
Light/acoustics	11		35	
Calculator	20	2	43	4
Templates	17		39	
Audio/video equipment	9		23	
Noise buffer	8		34	
Adaptive/special furniture			34	
Abacus	9		33	1
Manipulatives			26	2
Adaptive writing tools			24	
Slant board/wedge			10	
Secure paper to work area			12	
Visual organizers			17	
Color overlay			24	
Assistive technology			28	
Special paper			23	
Math tables/numberline			22	3
Dictionary/glossary			35	1
Thesarus			6	1
Keyboard			11	
Graphic organizers			14	1
Computer/machine	15			

TABLE 22.3. Evolution of Response Accommodations: A Count of States

Accommodation	1997 Allow in some configuration	1997 Explicitly prohibit	2009 Allow in some configuration	2009 Explicitly prohibit
Proctor/scribe	29		51	
Computer or machine	22		47	1
Write in test booklets	20		41	
Tape recorder	13		26	
Communication device	12		29	
Spell checker/assistance	1		21	16
Brailler	12		41	
Sign responses to sign language interpreter			20	
Pointing	11		26	
Speech/text device			26	1
Monitor placement of student responses			8	

TABLE 22.4. Evolution of Scheduling: Timing Accommodations: A Count of States

Accommodation	1997 Allow in some configuration	1997 Explicitly prohibit	2009 Allow in some configuration	2009 Explicitly prohibit
Extended time	26	2	46	
With breaks	22		45	
Multiple sessions	14	1	21	
Time beneficial to student	11		39	
Over multiple days	12		20	2
Flexible scheduling			18	
Student can no longer sustain activity	5			

TABLE 22.5. Evolution of Setting Accommodations: A Count of States

Accommodation	1997 Allow in some configuration	1997 Explicitly prohibit	2009 Allow in some configuration	2009 Explicitly prohibit
Individual	26		47	
Small group	27		48	
Carrel	13		37	
Separate room	17		33	
Seat location/proximity	13		35	
Minimize distractions			25	
Student's home	10		21	
Special ed. classroom	8		6	
Increase/decrease opportunity for movement			10	
Physical support			2	
Hospital	6		14	
Non-school setting			8	

APA, & NCME, 1999) provided a little more context regarding the practice of flagging, noting:

> the inclusion of a flag on a test score where an accommodation for a disability was provided may conflict with legal and social policy goals promoting fairness in the treatment of individuals with disabilities. If a score from a modified administration is comparable to a score from a non-modified administration, there is no need for a flag. Similarly, if a modification is provided for which there is no reasonable basis for believing that the modification would affect score comparability, there is no need for a flag. Further, reporting practices that use asterisks or other nonspecific symbols to indicate that a test's administration has been modified provide little useful information to test

users. When permitted by law, if a non-standardized administration is to be reported because evidence does not exist to support score comparability, then this report should avoid referencing the existence or nature of the test taker's disability and should instead report only the nature of the accommodation provided, such as extended time for testing, the use of a reader, or the use of a tape recorder. (p. 108)

The 2014 standards (AERA, APA, & NCME) echoed these recommendations and note that "there is little agreement in the field on how to proceed when credible evidence on comparability does not exist" (pp. 61–62).

In 2001, a blue ribbon panel on flagging[7] was convened to consider the issues related to the flagging of standardized test scores administered to students who used an extended time accommodation. The panel voted to discontinue the process of flagging Scholastic Aptitude Test (SAT) scores because the bias against applicants with flagged scores outweighed any other benefits of the practice. After the College Board discontinued its flagging policy, American College Testing (ACT) soon followed. Other testing organizations have since considered revising their policies, but not all have eliminated the practice. Most recently, in the *Department of Fair Employment and Housing v. Law School Admission Council (LSAC), Inc.* (2014), the U.S. District Court entered a permanent injunction against the LSAC, banning the flagging, or annotation, of test scores for students who are administered the exam under extended time conditions.

Legislation and court cases have provided an impetus for the creation and availability of testing accommodations for students with special needs. The awareness provided by these actions has also supported the generation of guidelines about the types of acceptable accommodations and how or when to inform others when someone has taken a test with an accommodation. Beyond the inclusion of students from special populations in large-scale assessment and the increased availability of testing accommodations, legislation and court cases regarding these special populations have led to assessments created specifically for students in these populations.

History of Alternate Assessments

In this section of our chapter we highlight the short history of alternative assessments for students with disabilities. Unlike the history of legislative actions, judicial decisions, and test accommodations/modifications, no parallel story exists for ELs. Alternate assessments exist primarily to mitigate the impact of acute cognitive deficits on student performance. In EL populations—assuming ELs do not also have a profound physical or cognitive disability—the issue is one of English language proficiency only. Indeed, the acknowledgment in the Lau Remedies that low English proficiency is *not*

---

[7]This panel was convened as part of the settlement of the *Breimhorst v. ETS* litigation (N.D. Cal, March 27, 2001). It consisted of a nonvoting chair and six members (two of whom were designated as the psychometric committee).

a cognitive disability and should not be treated as such was a major victory for ELs. Thus, in large-scale assessments of academic content, ELs are expected to be included in the general assessment (with test accommodations to address their language needs, if appropriate); recent trends in legislation have expressly focused on ensuring that this is the case. Consequently, ELs are absent from our discussion here.

For students with disabilities, three kinds of large-scale assessments are possible: general state tests, general state tests with accommodations (discussed in the previous section), and alternate assessments (typically reserved for students with more profound disabilities). As late as 1990, large-scale academic assessments for students with significant cognitive disabilities did not exist. With the passage of NCLB legislation and the federal requirement that 95% of all students and all subgroups participate in accountability assessment systems, the use of alternative assessments has seen exponential growth. Ysseldyke, Olsen, and Thurlow (1997) outlined four critical/foundational assumptions in the development of alternative assessments:

1. Focus on authentic skills and on assessing experiences in community/real life environments.
2. Measure integrated skills across domains.
3. Use continuous documentation methods if at all possible.
4. Include, as criteria, the extent to which the system provides the needed supports and adaptations and trains the student to use them. (pp. 5–6)

In 1999, a survey conducted by the NCEO revealed that only two states—Kentucky in 1997 and Maryland soon thereafter—had operational alternative assessments, though 20 states reported that they were in the process of developing such an assessment. By 2003, however, most states had at least one operational alternative assessment in place (Quenemoen, 2008), and by the 2005–2006 academic year, all states had alternative assessments.

Still, the extent to which each state sought to include students with more profound disabilities and the quality of the assessments varied considerably. Kentucky, the first state to implement alternative assessments in 1997, required a totally inclusive assessment with identical academic expectations and no exemptions. Other states, however, adopted less inclusive policies. Table 22.6 summarizes the guiding principles of four states that Thompson and Thurlow (2000) compared.

The principles of these four states represent the vast differences in the policies/approaches to assessment of students with profound/significant disabilities. Regardless, however, of each state's underlying principles, stakeholders have been left to struggle with two issues: (1) whether these assessments should focus on functional or academic content, and (2) how to appropriately score and report the results. Although initial attempts to assess these students with significant cognitive disabilities moved slowly from adapting infant/early childhood curricula (early 1970s) to a functional skills model in the 1980s, the IDEA legislation in 1997 (which required that all students have access to the general curriculum) and NCLB Act in 2001 (which required that at least 95% of the student population be included in accountability measures)

TABLE 22.6. Guiding Policies for Inclusion and Assessment from Four States

State 1	State 2
• All children can learn. • All children are full participants in the school experience. • All children will participate in the statewide assessment system.	• Expectations for all students should be high, regardless of the existence of any disability. • The goals for an educated student must be applicable to all students, regardless of disability. • Special education programs must be an extension and adaptation of general education programs rather than an alternate or separate system.

State 3	State 4
• All children have value, can learn, and are expected to be full participants in the school experience. • School personnel, parents, local and state policymakers, and the students themselves are responsible for ensuring this full participation.	• Meet the law. • Nonabusive to students, staff, and parents. • Inexpensive. • Easy to do and take little time.

have led to an increased focus on academic outcomes (Browder & Spooner, 2006). Moreover, the development of high-quality and meaningful alternate assessments continues to garner more support and attention. In 2010, the U.S. Department of Education offered competitive grants to aid in the development of quality alternate assessments. Consequently, two consortia—Dynamic Learning Maps Alternate Assessment Consortium and National Center and State Collaborative (NCSC)—have designed assessments to be launched in 2014–2015 in 43 states. The assessment development process for one of these consortia, NCSC, is described in detail by Thurlow and Quenemoen (Chapter 24, this volume).

Special Populations: *Standards for Educational and Psychological Testing*

Although the history of testing special populations can be well told using legislative/ judicial and state policies, the role of the *Standards for Educational and Psychological Testing* (the *Standards*) must also be included in the narrative. It is the *Standards* that both reflect and dictate the influence of the psychometric community in this evolution. Indeed, the *Standards* have provided test developers, administrators, and interpreters with criteria for developing and evaluating tests and testing practices. The most recent *Standards* (AERA, APA, & NCME, 2014) were preceded by six earlier documents: *Technical Recommendations for Psychological Tests and Diagnostic Techniques* (APA, 1954), *Technical Recommendations for Achievement Tests* (AERA & NCME, 1955), *Standards for Educational and Psychological Tests* (APA, AERA,

NCME, 1966), *The Standards for Educational and Psychological Tests* (APA, AERA, & NCME, 1974), *The Standards for Educational and Psychological Testing* (AERA et al., 1985), and *The Standards for Educational and Psychological Testing* (AERA et al., 1999). To a large extent, the evolution of the *Standards* with respect to special populations parallels the legislative and judicial evolutions of these populations as well.

Though *The Standards for Educational and Psychological Tests* (APA et al., 1974) did make a fleeting reference about attending to test bias ("A test user should investigate the possibility of bias in tests or in test items. Wherever possible, there should be an investigation of possible differences in criterion-related validity for ethnic, sex, or other subsamples that can be identified when the test is given. The manual or research report should give the results for each subsample separately or report that no differences were found" [p. 43]), it was the 1985 *Standards* (AERA et al., 1985) that first mentioned students with disabilities (at the time referred to as "people who have handicapping conditions") and linguistic minorities. For example, with respect to linguistic minorities the *Standards* (AERA et al., 1985) noted that "when it is intended that the two versions of dual-language tests be comparable, evidence of test comparability should be reported" (p. 75). When developing and administering tests to students with disabilities, the *Standards* (AERA et al., 1985), which focused primarily on test modifications related to physical (e.g., hearing, visually impaired) disabilities, mandated that "people who modify tests for handicapped people should have available to them psychometric expertise for so doing" (p. 79); and that, "when feasible, the validity and reliability of tests administered to people with various handicapping conditions should be investigated and reported by the agency or publisher that makes the modification. Such investigations should examine the effects of modifications made for people with various handicapping conditions on resulting scores, as well as the effects of administering standard unmodified tests to them" (p. 80).

The 1999 *Standards* (AERA et al., 1999) included a considerable increase in attention to individuals with disabilities (from eight to 12 standards) and learners with diverse linguistic backgrounds (from seven to 11 standards). The most recent *Standards* (AERA et al., 2014) echoed this attention to students from special populations.

Whereas legislation and court cases have served to highlight meaningful gains in education for students from special populations, guidelines developed by testing professionals such as the *Standards* have served to provide some direction and consistency in the development of assessments in a manner meant to support the populations served and prevent the need for legal action. Together, the laws, lawsuits, and the *Standards* developed in the past few decades have worked to provide increased opportunities and valid assessments for ELs and students from other special groups.

In Summary

The struggle for equity, which was first conceived as academic inclusion (i.e., integration into general education classrooms) and/or academic skills acqisition (regardless of the type/kind of classroom), developed into concerns about the academic outcomes and post K–12 opportunities for students with disabilities and ELs. Although the meaning of educational equity and what that represents in action remains open to some limited extent, the increased consideration—as a direct result of these equity efforts—of students from special populations regarding standards, assessments, and accountability policies has led to an increasingly extensive research literature on the impact of testing/assessment on students from special populations.

Indeed, developing an assessment program that can provide meaningful and useful information about a group of students, any group, is a challenge. Doing so for special populations is particularly challenging. These challenges are exacerbated when the assessments serve as the primary source of data about student outcomes for state and national entities. In particular, when addressing the assessment of students from special populations, historically two issues arose: inclusion and accommodations. Decisions must be made about who should be included (or excluded) from assessment and what psychometrically sound modifications, if any, can be made for these students. The next two chapters in this volume provide more current and specific examples of how large-scale assessments can be designed and administered effectively to ensure the fair and valid inclusion of ELs (see Faulkner-Bond & Forte, Chapter 23) and students with disabilities (see Thurlow & Quenemoen, Chapter 24).

In this chapter we highlighted the evolution of testing special populations from two perspectives: (1) legislative and judicial wins and losses, and (2) the influence and role of testing professionals. Whereas the legislative and judicial acts and cases have aimed at equity by addressing injustices that have already occurred, guidelines and standards aim at preventing future injustices and providing a standard direction that ensures the validity of the created assessments. Through the combination of both perspectives, the inclusion and manner of assessing students from special groups has improved. Still, given the variation in priorities about the assessment of special populations across states and the fact that lawsuits regarding testing accommodations and flagging have been ongoing up to the year this chapter was written, the history of testing special populations is not yet complete.

REFERENCES

Algozzine, B. (1993). Including students with disabilities in systemic efforts to measure outcomes: Why ask why? In National Center on Educational Outcomes (Ed.), *Views on inclusion and testing accommodations for students with disabilities* (pp. 5–10). Minneapolis, MN: National Center on Educational Outcomes.

American Educational Research Association, American Psychological Association, & National Council on Measurement in Education. (1985). *Standards for educational and psychological testing.* Washington, DC: Authors.

American Educational Research Association, American Psychological Association, & National Council on Measurement in Education. (1999). *Standards for educational and psychological testing.* Washington, DC: Authors.

American Educational Research Association, American Psychological Association, & National

Council on Measurement in Education. (2014). *Standards for educational and psychological testing.* Washington, DC: Authors.

American Psychological Association. (1954). *Recommendations for psychological tests and diagnostic techniques.* Washington, DC: Author.

American Psychological Association, American Educational Research Association, & National Council on Measurement in Education. (1966). *Standards for educational and psychological tests.* Washington, DC: Authors.

American Psychological Association, American Educational Research Association, & National Council on Measurement in Education. (1974). *Standards for educational and psychological testing.* Washington, DC: Authors.

American Psychological Association & National Council on Measurements Used in Education. (1955). *Technical recommendations for psychological tests and diagnostic techniques.* Washington, DC: Authors.

Aspira of New York, Inc. v. Board of Education of the City of New York, 394 F. Supp. 1161 (1975).

Breimhorst et al. v. Educational Testing Service, District Court of Northern California, Case No. C-99-3387.

Brookhart v. Illinois State Board of Educationm 697 F2d 179 (1983).

Browder, D., & Spooner, F. (Eds). (2006). *Teaching language arts, math, and science to students with significant cognitive disabilities.* Baltimore: Brookes.

Camara, W., & Lane, S. (2006). A historical perspective and current views on the Standards for Educational and Psychological Testing. *Educational Measurement: Issues and Practice, 25,* 35–41.

Castañeda et al. v. A. M. Billy Pickard. U.S. Court of Appeals, Fifth Circuit. Unit A 648 F.2d 989 U.S. App. Lexis 12 063.

Christensen, L., Braam, M., Scullin, S., & Thurlow, M. (2011). *2009 state policies on assessment participation and accommodations for students with disabilities* (Synthesis Report 83). Minneapolis: University of Minnesota, National Center on Educational Outcomes.

Del Valle, S. (2003). *Language rights and the law in the United States: Finding our voices.* Clevedon, UK: Multilingual Matters.

Department of Fair Employment and Housing v. LSAC, Inc. (2014). District Court of Northern California, Case No. CV 12-1830-EMC.

Fuchs, L. S., & Fuchs, D. (2001). Helping students formulate sound test accommodation decisions for students with learning disabilities. *Learning Disabilities Research and Practice, 16,* 174–181.

Garcia, O., Kleifgen, J., & Falch, L. (2008). From English learners to emergent bilinguals: Equity matters (Research Review No. 1). Columbia University, Teachers College. Retrieved December 12, 2014, from *www.equitycampaign.org/i/a/document/6532_Ofelia_ELL__ Final.pdf.*

Keyes v. School District No. 1, Denver, Colorado, 413 U.S. 189 (1973).

Kopriva, R. (2011). *Improving testing for English learners.* New York: Routledge.

Lau v. Nichols, 414 U.S. 563 (1974).

Lazarus, S. S., Thurlow, M. L., Lail, K. E., Eisenbraun, K. D., & Kato, K. (2006). 2005 state policies on assessment participation and accommodations for students with disabilities (Synthesis Report 64). Minneapolis: University of Minnesota, National Center on Educational Outcomes.

Martin, E., Martin, R., & Terman, D. (1996). The legislative and litigation history of special education. *The Future of Children, 6*(1), 25–39.

McGrew, K. S., Thurlow, M. L., Shriner, J. G., & Spiegel, A. (1992). *Inclusion of students with disabilities in national and state data collection systems*. Minneapolis: University of Minnesota, National Center on Educational Outcomes.

Mills v. Board of Education for District of Columbia, 348 F. Supp. 866 (1972).

Otero v. Mesa County Valley School District No. 51, 628 F2d 1271 (1980).

PARC v. Commonwealth of Pennsylvania, 343 F. Supp. (1972).

Quenemoen, R. (2008). *A brief history of alternate assessments based on alternate achievement standards* (Synthesis Report 68). Minneapolis: University of Minnesota National Center on Educational Outcomes.

Randall, J., & Engelhard, G. (2010). Performance of students with and without disabilities under modified conditions. *Journal of Special Education, 44*(2), 79–93.

San Antonio Independent School District v. Rodriguez, 411 U.S. 1 (1973).

Shriner, J. G., & Thurlow, M. (1993). *State special education outcomes: A report on state activities at the end of the century*. Minneapolis: University of Minnesota, National Center on Educational Outcomes.

Southeastern Community College v. Davis, 442 U.S. 397 (1979).

Thompson, S. J., & Thurlow, M. (2000). *State alternate assessments: Status as IDEA alternate assessment requirements take effect* (Synthesis Report 35). Minneapolis: University of Minnesota, National Center on Educational Outcomes.

Thurlow, M. L., Seyfarth, A., Scott, D., & Ysseldyke, J. (1997). *State assessment policies on participation and accommodations for students with disabilities: 1997 update* (Synthesis Report 29). Minneapolis: University of Minnesota, National Center on Educational Outcomes.

Thurlow, M. L., Thompson, S. J., & Lazarus, S. S. (2006). Considerations for the administration of tests to special needs students: Accommodations, modifications, and more. In S. M. Downing & T. M. Haladyna (Eds.), *Handbook of test development* (pp. 653–673). Mahwah, NJ: Erlbaum.

U.S. Department of Education, National Center for Educational Statistics. (2013). Digest of Education Statistics, 2012 (NCES 2014–2015), Chapter 2. Retrieved July 14, 2014, from *http://nces.ed.gov/fastfacts/display.asp?id=64*.

Ysseldyke, J. E., Olsen, K. R., & Thurlow, M. L. (1997). Issues and considerations in alternate assessments (Synthesis Report 27). Minneapolis: University of Minnesota, National Center on Educational Outcomes.

Ysseldyke, J., & Thurlow, M. (1994). Guidelines for inclusion of students with disabilities in largescale assessments (Policy Directions No. 1). Minneapolis: University of Minnesota, National Center on Educational Outcomes. Retrieved January 31, 2016, from *http://education.unm.edu/NCEO/OnlinePubs/Policy1.html*.

Ysseldyke, J. E., Thurlow, M. L., McGrew, K. S., & Shriner, J. G. (1994). *Recommendations for making decisions about the participation of students with disabilities in statewide assessment programs: A report on a working conference to develop guidelines for statewide assessments and students with disabilities* (Synthesis Report 15). Minneapolis: University of Minnesota, National Center for Educational Outcomes.

Zuriff, G. (2000). Extra examination time for students with learning disabilities: An examination of the maximum potential thesis. *Applied Measurement in Education, 13*(1), 99–117.

CHAPTER 23

English Learners and Accountability
The Promise, Pitfalls, and Peculiarity of Assessing Language Minorities via Large-Scale Assessment

Molly Faulkner-Bond and Ellen Forte

Overview: English Learners and Large-Scale Assessment

Approximately 9% of the U.S. K–12 population consists of students who are learning the English language in addition to learning academic content in areas such as English language arts (ELA) and mathematics. These students, whom we refer to as *English learners* (ELs),[1] are entitled to special instructional services to help them learn English as quickly as possible so that they can participate in academic settings where English is the language of instruction. In the interim, however—that is, while these students are mastering English—they still must participate in the same assessments of ELA and mathematics that are required of all students for federal accountability. As we argue in this chapter, this participation mandate is a response to a history of exclusion and is, overall, a positive development for ELs' educational opportunities.

Nonetheless, assessing ELs' content knowledge, as well as judging when and whether their language proficiency no longer poses a barrier to their academic achievement, are both fraught psychometric tasks. As noted in the *Standards for Educational and Psychological Testing,* "Proficiency in English not only affects interpretation of an English language learner's test scores on tests administered in English but, more important, also may affect the individual's development and academic progress" (American Educational Research Association, American Psychological Association, & National Council on Measurement in Education, 2014, p. 53). Extracting "clean"

---

[1] There are many labels or terms applied to this subgroup of students, including *English language learners* (ELLs), *limited English proficient* (LEP), and *emergent bilingual students*, to name a few. The label *English learner* (EL) is currently used by the U.S. Department of Education.

samples of ELs' content knowledge and skills is a nearly impossible task, as their language skills will inevitably introduce some construct-irrelevant variance (Messick, 1990) that complicates interpretations of their performance, often in negative ways. This construct-irrelevant variance can also mean, in turn, that the meaning and reliability of ELs' ELA and math scores are not comparable to the meaning and reliability of scores for native speakers.

In this chapter, we attempt to accomplish two concurrent tasks. First, we specifically summarize the context and challenges of validly assessing ELs in K–12 settings in the United States. We begin with a brief overview of the evolving policy context in which ELs are assessed and their assessment scores used, after which we list and briefly discuss some important additional characteristics of ELs that are important to consider from a psychometric standpoint to ensure fair and valid measurement on large-scale assessments. In the final two sections, we consider specific validity concerns related to content and language assessment, respectively, as well as checks and actions that test developers can employ to minimize these risks proactively. Our approach is designed to emphasize the fact that the specific validity threats or concerns for a given EL examinee population are context-dependent and will vary from test to test and use to use.

Second, although this chapter focuses on assessing ELs in U.S. K–12 schools, we also wish to emphasize that neither the challenges nor the process described here are unique to this context. In the current day and era, nearly any assessment or assessment system will include linguistic minorities (LMs) who, like ELs, are entitled to fair assessment opportunities and interpretations. For any assessment in which such examinees participate, the validity and fairness of the resulting scores depend on the ability of test developers and users to show that LMs have not been unfairly disadvantaged, and that their scores have comparable meaning and quality to those of non-LMs. Failure to ensure these safeguards can undermine the meaning and validity of scores for all examinees, not solely LMs.

To achieve these dual purposes, our discussion of assessing K–12 ELs is organized using a general three-step framework that test developers and users can implement to identify and address validity threats for any LM population in any context. These steps, as illustrated by the EL example, are:

1. *Establish a strong understanding of the assessment context* and intended uses of the scores. A related task in this step is to establish a thoughtful articulation of the intended testing construct(s), including the role that language should or should not play in its definition and in interpretations of student performance.

2. *Identify relevant characteristics of the LM population* that could affect fairness or score validity. The particular characteristics that may be of interest will be driven, in part, by the testing construct and purpose and, in general, will go beyond the simple binary of LM versus non-LM.

3. *Systematically identify and address specific validity threats or concerns* that are likely to stem from the interactions among the testing construct and score uses identified in Step 1, and the characteristics identified in Step 2.

Appropriate response actions may affect test development, score reporting, score use, or a combination of these.

Thus, although we limit our particular discussion to U.S. ELs, we believe that the general approach we describe has broader applications. We also encourage readers to consult the chapters in the "Cross-lingual Assessment" section of this volume (Allalouf & Hanani, Chapter 15; van de Vijver & Poortinga, Chapter 16; and Muñiz et al., Chapter 17), for additional information and considerations that are relevant to this practice.

Step 1: Understanding the Assessment Context

In this section, we summarize the policy context driving EL assessment in the United States. We describe the reasons we assess ELs' academic knowledge and skills and how we use these students' scores. In particular, we address:

1. *Stated educational goals for ELs*: What are we ultimately trying to accomplish for these students?
2. *Assessment mandates under various laws*: Why do these students have to be assessed? When do they have to be assessed? How are the scores used?

For the example of K–12 ELs in the United States, we answer these questions by first tracing the initial aims of federal policy related to assessing ELs, then turn to the mandates of that policy in its most recent manifestation. A different LM assessment context—for example, one in which LMs must participate in a mandated certification assessment as part of their job training—might require looking in different places to answer these questions, but the exercise of asking the same questions remains central to articulating a clear sense of the purpose and context for assessment.

Stated Educational Goals for ELs: The Federal Policy Background

Although ado over its current reach has clouded understanding of its actual purpose, the Elementary and Secondary Education Act (ESEA) of 1965 has always targeted the lowest performing students in schools serving the highest poverty communities. ELs have always been among our most challenged students in those communities, and therefore our educational services to them are an inextricable component of federal education policy implementation. More fundamentally, however, ELs' access to high-quality educational opportunities is a civil right, protected by the Equal Protection Clause of the 14th Amendment to the U.S. Constitution and § 601 of the Civil Rights Act of 1964, upheld by a number of civil verdicts across the country and clarified in a series of memoranda published by the Office of Civil Rights (OCR) in the U.S. Department of Education.

Neither the civil rights arguments nor the initial ESEA legislation points to the assessment of ELs, per se. In fact, ESEA had no assessment requirement for any students until the 1970s. Rather, the civil rights arguments and ESEA mandates are about legitimate access to instruction in academic content areas. This position was expressed unambiguously by Justice William O. Douglas in his majority opinion in the 1974 *Lau v. Nichols* U.S. Supreme Court decision (*Lau v. Nichols*, 414 U.S. 563 [1974]):

> There is no equality of treatment merely by providing students with the same facilities, textbooks, teachers, and curriculum; for students who do not understand English are effectively foreclosed from any meaningful education. Basic English skills are at the very core of what these public schools teach. Imposition of a requirement that, before a child can effectively participate in the educational program, he must already have acquired those basic skills is to make a mockery of public education. We know that those who do not understand English are certain to find their classroom experiences wholly incomprehensible and in no way meaningful.

The Lau case involved a class suit brought by 1,800 Chinese American students in the San Francisco Unified School District who did not speak English and were provided with equal access to academic settings as their English-speaking peers but no access to the language support services necessary for them to learn in those settings. The decision in the Lau case reversed a Court of Appeals decision that had denied relief to these students and invoked § 601 of the Civil Rights Act of 1964, which bans discrimination based "on the ground of race, color, or national origin," in "any program or activity receiving federal financial assistance."

Essentially foreshadowing this decision, OCR issued a memorandum on May 25, 1970, stating that "where inability to speak and understand the English language excludes national-origin-minority group children from effective participation in the educational program offered by a school district, the district must take affirmative steps to rectify the language deficiency in order to open the instructional program to the students." Among other expectations, the May 25th memorandum prohibits public school districts from placing ELs in special education programs based on their language support needs and from operating language support programs as separate, permanent tracks to academic nowhere.

As can be seen from these few examples, ELs' right to academic instruction is the fundamental principle underlying programs and services for these students; support for becoming proficient in English is a means to accessing that instruction. Likewise, mandates for ELs' inclusion in English language proficiency assessments and academic content assessments under the most recent authorization of ESEA (through 2015), the No Child Left Behind (NCLB) Act of 2001, are meant to ensure that ELs are (1) acquiring proficiency in the academic English they need to participate fully in their academic contexts, and, at the same time, (2) receiving instruction on the same academic standards that apply to their non-EL peers. Participation in assessments and the use of assessment results in accountability systems are merely means for targeting the instruction access goal.

Assessment Mandates

Under NCLB, Title I of ESEA, including as "augmented" by the ESEA Federal Flexibility Waiver, required states to administer annual academic assessments in ELA and mathematics in grades 3 through 8 and at least once in the 9–12 grade range. States had to administer annual academic assessments in science at least once in each of the 3–5, 6–8, and 9–12 grade ranges. All students, including all ELs, must participate in these assessments in their enrolled grades.[2] States, districts, and schools must report results for all students and, separately, for each of several student groups, including ELs.

ELs' scores on these academic assessments are used for accountability purposes in two ways. First, in a form of informal accountability, scores must be reported in the context of scores for all students and for other student groups such that differences in overall performance are apparent to those who wish to see them. The logic behind this requirement is that merely seeing the differences could lead to action by those who are concerned by them and what such differences (or low scores for ELs) may mean about ELs' access to high-quality academic instruction. Although this may be true, we note that these scores are usually not reported in association with information about error or the statistical significance of the differences.

In the formal version of accountability for academic achievement, NCLB mandated that at least 95% of ELs in each school and district must participate in each of the annual academic assessments and that an increasing proportion (to 100% in the 2013–2014 school year[3]) of ELs score in the proficient or above performance levels. (These same targets applied to all other student groups as well.) Under the ESEA flexibility, states were not required to report scores or establish performance targets for ELs on academic assessments, per se, but did have to use scores for ELs and other student groups in some way to evaluate achievement gaps. Failure to reach these goals resulted in consequences that were assumed to be serious enough to incentivize local educators to take reform steps to avoid them.

In addition to these academic assessment requirements, NCLB Title I required that states annually administer English language proficiency (ELP) assessments to measure "students' oral language, reading, and writing skills in English" (NCLB §1111[b][7]), and Title III further required that states provide evidence that ELs are learning to "speak, read, write, and comprehend the English language" (NCLB §3116[d]). (Comprehension scores are typically based on some combination of reading and listening items.) Title III also included accountability requirements related to ELs' ELP status and their progress toward achieving ELP. Each state determined its own definitions of proficiency and progress; districts (or consortia of districts if they jointly operate

---

[2] There is only one exception to this full participation rule: ELs in their first year of enrollment in a U.S. school may be exempted from participation in the ELA assessment for that year as long as they participate in the state's English language proficiency assessments.

[3] Although the 2013–2014 school year has come and gone (and the 100% proficiency goal was not reached), NCLB remained enshrined as law through December 10, 2015, when it was replaced by the Every Student Succeeds Act. States' inability to reach the 100% proficiency benchmark was one of many reasons the U.S. Department of Education began offering states waivers from NCLB in the form of the Federal Flexibility waiver system in 2010.

a Title III–funded program) had to meet targets for proportions of students meeting these definitions.

The logic underlying the assessment of ELs and the use of their scores in formal accountability systems stems from the notion that inclusion in accountability-related assessment will drive educators to serve these students' academic and linguistic needs. Although some may argue that it is inappropriate to include ELs with very limited English reading and writing skills in academic assessments administered in English, we suggest that the "policy argument" for using assessment to drive inclusion in instruction may trump the validity argument for excluding students from testing (Forte, 2010). That is, although we recognize that ELs' academic assessment scores may not always be as meaningful as such scores are for other students, excluding ELs from testing poses a greater threat to ELs' achievement than does including them.

Step 2: Knowing the Population

The NCLB definition for an EL, referred to in the law as an LEP student, is reproduced in Figure 23.1. Two points are notable about this definition: First, it is conjunctive, meaning that students must meet some aspect of clause A through D to qualify as LEP. Second, relatedly, clause D is the most relevant consideration from an assessment perspective. This clause specifically requires evidence that language in some way poses a barrier to the individual, either in school or in society more generally. As discussed in the preceding section, the purpose of identifying students as ELs at all is to remove such barriers through instruction and support.

---

(25) LIMITED ENGLISH PROFICIENT.—The term 'limited English proficient,' when used with respect to an individual, means an individual

    (A) who is aged 3 through 21;

    (B) who is enrolled or preparing to enroll in an elementary school or secondary school;

    (C)   (i) who was not born in the United States or whose native language is a language other than English;

        (ii) (I) who is a Native American or Alaska Native, or a native resident of the outlying areas; and

            (II) who comes from an environment where a language other than English has had a significant impact on the individual's level of English language proficiency; or

        (iii) who is migratory, whose native language is a language other than English, and who comes from an environment where a language other than English is dominant; and

    (D) whose difficulties in speaking, reading, writing, or understanding the English language may be sufficient to deny the individual—

        (i) the ability to meet the State's proficient level of achievement on State assessments described in section 1111(b)(3);

        (ii) the ability to successfully achieve in classrooms where the language of instruction is English; or

        (iii) the opportunity to participate fully in society.

FIGURE 23.1. Federal definition for LEP students (NCLB §9101 [25]).

Nationwide, there are roughly 5 million students who, by meeting this definition, are identified as ELs (U.S. Department of Education, 2011). Although these students are distributed across all 50 states and all grade levels, there are definite trends within the population: First, nearly two-thirds of the entire U.S. population (62%) reside in the five states with the largest EL populations: California, Texas, Florida, New York, and Illinois (U.S. Department of Education, 2011). Second, the EL population is largest in early grades (e.g., K–3), although it is not uncommon to see a small spike in new EL enrollment at the high school level (e.g., Massachusetts Department of Elementary and Secondary Education & DePascale, 2012); these students are sometimes referred to as "newcomers," based on the fact that they often are recent immigrants or refugees (Boyson & Short, 2003; Francis, Rivera, Lesaux, Kieffer, & Rivera, 2006). An important related point is that, nationwide, a majority of ELs are actually not immigrants (Swanson, 2009).

Third, over three-quarters of all ELs (77%) are Spanish speakers (U.S. Department of Education, 2011), and they are more likely than the general population to come from a low-socioeconomic status (SES) background (e.g., see Grissom, 2004; Kim & Herman, 2009; Lakin & Young, 2013; Massachusetts Department of Elementary and Secondary Education & DePascale, 2012; Parrish et al., 2006; Robinson, 2011).

Beyond these points, however, it is equally important to note that great diversity also exists among the individuals who meet the federal LEP definition. Most notably, ELs may vary from one another in terms of their actual English proficiency, which could range from very low to nearly proficient. Although it has repeatedly been shown that language does generally play a role in the content performance of ELs (Martiniello, 2008; Parker, Louie, & O'Dwyer, 2009; Wolf & Leon, 2009; Young et al., 2008), the extent to which it does so, and possibly the ways in which it does, could vary for students based on their level of ELP. Wolf and Leon (2009) found, for example, that the presence of technical academic vocabulary in science items considered easy from a content standpoint caused differential item functioning (DIF) specifically for ELs with low levels of ELP compared both to native speakers and to ELs with a high level of ELP.

Similarly, given the wide age range for LEP identification (ages 3–21), ELs also may face different challenges or perform differently based on their age or grade-level. Studies have found that the students who remain ELs through later elementary and middle school years often have a harder time transitioning out of EL status (American Institutes for Research, 2013; Massachusetts Department of Elementary and Secondary Education & DePascale, 2012; Slama, 2014; Thompson, 2012), and also may be less likely to meet academic content standards after having done so (Robinson, 2011). Opportunity to learn may play a role in these types of trends, as can the increased language demands of middle school academics, where students are expected to have mastered basic literacy and to start demonstrating more complex critical thinking and expression skills.

Despite the prevalence of Spanish among ELs, it is also important to remember that (1) hundreds of other languages are also spoken (in some cases, even within a single state) (O'Conner, Abedi, & Tung, 2012; Swanson, 2009; U.S. Department of

Education, 2011), and (2) great dialectical diversity is also present within the Spanish-speaking subgroup (Solano-Flores & Li, 2009; Swanson, 2009). Given this diversity, test developers should also consider whether and how students' home language could play a role in their linguistic performance, content performance, or both. Students who speak "high-incidence" languages such as Spanish or Arabic may have access to better resources or more instructional options, which could in turn affect their performance relative to students who speak languages that are not widely represented in their schools or communities.

On a related note, although it is still relatively uncommon for schools to collect information about students' native language proficiency or education, such information could also be valuable for assessing students' "true" content knowledge and making instructional decisions. Two students who speak the same language could still perform very differently and have different instructional needs based on their level of literacy and proficiency in the home language in question.

Finally, when it comes to demographic variables such as immigration or refugee status, SES, parental education, or parental ELP, it is important to note that many of these may *not* be relevant considerations for ELs, or may only be relevant for certain types of EL populations. Numerous studies have found, for example, that SES is not a significant predictor or correlate of performance within the EL subgroup (Grissom, 2004; Kim & Herman, 2012; Massachusetts Department of Elementary and Secondary Education & DePascale, 2012), which is not surprising since, as mentioned previously, ELs tend to be very homogeneous on this front as a group. Similarly, although some studies have found that ELs' length of time in the United States is a relevant performance predictor (Francis & Rivera, 2007), this variable is unlikely to be helpful in an EL population of primarily native-born students, rather than immigrants or refugees.

Given the many ways in which ELs may differ from one another, an important step for assessment developers or users is to understand their particular EL (or LM) population with regard to traits such as those listed in the preceding paragraphs. As we discuss in subsequent sections, different variables may be relevant for different kinds of assessment (e.g., language proficiency vs. academic content performance), or the same variables may be relevant in different ways for different assessments. Ultimately, the exact characteristics that are relevant will depend on (1) the construct being measured, (2) the intended uses for the assessment scores, and (3) any political or legal factors to which the test developer or user is bound.

Step 3: Specific Validity Concerns and Considerations

In the next sections, we describe the third and final step of our process, which involves identifying and neutralizing validity concerns for LMs based on assessment context, score use, and population characteristics. As indicated above, NCLB mandates that K–12 ELs in the United States participate in regular assessments of both their content knowledge and their language proficiency. This context is relatively unique; in many other assessment contexts where developers must consider the rights of LMs, only one type of assessment is used—for example, foreign students may need to demonstrate proficiency on a language exam to gain entry to a university, or, as suggested above, LMs may need to demonstrate content knowledge in a different language as part of a job certification.

In any context, the validity concerns stemming from language assessment and content assessment are likely to be different. Because these two types of assessment serve different purposes and scores are used in different ways, we separate our discussion of specific validity concerns for ELs according to the two types of assessment: content and language.

Content Assessment

To support interpretations that content assessment scores reflect ELs' knowledge and skills in relation to the domains the assessments are intended to measure, as well as the accountability and evaluation uses to which these scores are put, test developers must establish a body of evidence that addresses three issues:

1. *Identification and inclusion of relevant linguistic demands.* What are the relevant linguistic demands of the target domain and how are these reflected in the test items?

2. *Identification and minimization of irrelevant linguistic demands.* How are irrelevant demands, which may interfere with ELs' accessing and responding to items, minimized?

3. *Accommodations.* How do the conditions under which ELs experience tests and test items minimize the effects of remaining barriers to allow ELs to demonstrate their knowledge and skills in relation to the measurement targets?

In the next sections, we address each of these questions in turn for the particular context of K–12 ELs in United States public schools.

Identification and Inclusion of Relevant Linguistic Demands

At or very near the heart of any validity evaluation is the discrimination between score variance that is relevant to the construct/measurement target and score variance that is irrelevant to that target. Good test development maximizes the former and minimizes the latter. With regard to relevant variance, every academic domain comprises a conceptual network of knowledge and skills as well as language that represents and communicates the knowledge and skills. For example, there is physics as a domain within science, and there is the language of physics. A student of physics must learn the concepts as well as the language to become proficient in that domain. If that student is in a context where English is the language of instruction (or the lingua franca for the domain), then that student must learn "physics English."

"Physics English" is more than vocabulary such as *mass, motion,* and *momentum*. It includes academic language functions such as *synthesize, hypothesize, postulate,* and *prove* as well as the grammatical- and discourse-level skills necessary to engage in those functions. Ideally, students learn the language of the domain as part of their instruction, although many students, including many ELs, need direct instruction on the academic language in addition to their incidental exposure to it in the classroom (DiCerbo, Anstrom, Baker, & Rivera, 2014).

When it comes time to assess what students know and can do, test developers should determine what aspects of "physics English" are relevant to that domain so that they can reflect them in the test items. At present, this is handled more implicitly than explicitly; the standards or framework on which a test is based naturally encompasses domain language that finds its way into test and item specifications and items themselves, and test items are always reviewed by content experts that include educators who teach courses in the domain. One assumes that any misuses of the academic language would be avoided or caught. However, we know of no academic test development efforts that include specific and direct consideration of domain language other than through items meant to measure vocabulary. Although it is unlikely that tests include errors of commission (i.e., of inclusion) with regard to domain language, there is currently no rigorous attempt to ensure that key domain language features are included—that there are no errors of omission (i.e., exclusion) in domain language.

Test developers should make no attempt to reduce the relevant language demands of a test for ELs, per se, but may need to address potential frailties in domain language knowledge and skills via embedded accommodations (discussed in the next section). This does not mean that relevant domain language demands should not be evaluated. Some students participating in a recent study using cognitive labs methods struggled with the word *numerator*; once they learned that this meant the "number on top," in most cases they were able to solve the problem (Chambers, Kerbel, Rivera, & Forte, 2011). These students were taking tests in their dominant language, which was also the language of instruction, but the study revealed that instruction may not adequately support academic language acquisition even when it supports the acquisition of academic knowledge and skills. Unfortunately, without the language, there can be no proficiency in a domain.

We recommend that test developers directly articulate the domain language that is relevant to the intended interpretations of test scores. If one claims that test scores reflect a student's knowledge and skills in physics, then one should provide evidence that students can talk the talk as well as walk the walk.

Identification and Minimization of Irrelevant Linguistic Demands

Now for the construct/measurement target irrelevant variance. The flip side of the relevant domain language coin involves language that is not an intrinsic component of an academic domain. For example, the preceding sentence invokes a coin, which has nothing to do with the topic at hand. Although colorful and helpful in breaking up the monotony of a book chapter, such imagery can be out of place in test questions because it can distract and confuse students whose linguistic sophistication is somewhat fragile. In a more pedestrian example, but one that is far more important to test development endeavors, an EL taking a part in another study of state test questions using cognitive labs methods revealed that the use of the word *one*, as in "which one of the following," led her to answer the question incorrectly (Martiniello, 2008). That item included a graphic of a circle broken into several pie wedges, each with a number indicated on it. One of those numbers was "1." One of the incorrect response choices was "1." To the student, "which one of the following . . . ?" meant "which of the following is one . . . ?" From that item, we learned nothing about her math skills, which were the measurement target.

The moral of this story is that test developers must look high and low to help ensure that test items do not include language that could get in a student's way. Avoiding vocabulary that is unnecessarily sophisticated (i.e., not domain relevant) is one obvious step, but it is far from enough. Language demands also come in the form of grammatical structures; "which one of the following" is a common test item structure that may pose a challenge for some students if they do not encounter this structure in their classrooms.

To avoid inappropriate lexical and grammatical demands on a test, we recommend that test developers include guidance in item writing specifications on linguistic complexity at these levels. Item writers are typically adept at recognizing and evaluating the complexity of passages, but may need to be directed to the word and sentence levels as sources of complexity, as well. In addition to item writing guidance, test developers may need to revise item review protocols to direct panelists' attention to the words and sentence structures of individual items (e.g., "Is this how you ask questions in your classroom?"). Here, it is particularly helpful to include educators with expertise in second-language acquisition on item review panels and to allow discussion among panelists about language demands. This is not an issue to constrain to item reviews that target bias and sensitivity issues, which typically are separated in time and place and include completely separate sets of panelists from the content reviews. Language demands are content concerns even if they disproportionately affect ELs.

Accommodations

When all else fails, accommodate. This is our cheeky way of saying that the issues that cannot be or are not addressed during the item and test development process must be addressed while a student is taking the test. As discussed by Randall and Garcia (Chapter 22, this volume), accommodations are changes to the standard model for how items are presented, the conditions under which a student takes the test, or how a student responds to test questions (Thurlow, Thompson, & Lazarus, 2006).

Excellent and comprehensive discussions of accommodations use among ELs are available elsewhere (Abedi & Ewers, 2013; Kieffer, Lesaux, Rivera, & Francis, 2009; Pennock-Roman & Rivera, 2011); for the present purposes, we only highlight key issues in this area. Most notably, reliance on accommodations is not an ideal means for minimizing construct-irrelevant variance among ELs. Although some accommodations appear to help some ELs demonstrate what they know and can do (e.g., glossaries of domain-relevant terms used on the test), test items are generally not developed with accommodations in mind. This point is well understood among those developing tests that must be accessible for students who are blind, for example, and those creating Brailled forms must identify items that can be Brailled rather than use the same set of items that other students encounter. This means that not all items on a test will lend themselves to accommodation and that selected accommodations may not address the issues that arise in a given item. Consider the item described in the previous section, in which the use of the word *one* caused a problem for some ELs. None of the common accommodations, such as extra time or a glossary, would have helped in that case.

This points to two other issues with accommodations. First, accommodations are selected for ELs at the test level, not the item level. This one-size-fits-all-items approach may introduce more problems than it solves by distracting students with extra documents or confusing them with translations that don't correspond to the language they know from their academic or English as a second language (ESL) classroom, or frustrating them with extra time they neither want nor need. Fortunately, some recent innovations in technology-enhanced item development may allow for "embedded" accommodations such as hypertext options that may prove helpful for some ELs, in part by allowing students to self-determine when and how to accommodate themselves (Kopriva, Emick, Hipolito-Delgado, & Cameron, 2007).

Second, the process by which accommodations are selected for students is inconsistent across students, locations, and time, and is very often not informed by research on what works for whom. Although this can also be the case in the selection of accommodations for students with disabilities, there is at least a defined decision-making group (a student's individualized education program or IEP team) and a requirement under NCLB and the Individuals with Disabilities Education Act (IDEA) that testing accommodations correspond to the accommodations used in the classroom. It's unclear who makes most decisions about ELs' accommodations or on what evidence they base those decisions.

Our strong recommendation with regard to how test developers can (1) include language that is domain relevant, (2) exclude language that is domain irrelevant, and (3) allow for appropriate accommodations, when necessary, is to clearly articulate the measurement targets in terms of both content and skill features *and* linguistic features. If done early in the development and design process, this more evidence-centered approach to development can inform item and test reviews as well as enable presentation and format decisions that render post hoc accommodations unnecessary. Furthermore, we recommend that test developers examine how ELs interact with individual items, using cognitive labs or cognitive interview methods, to evaluate formatively how substantive and incidental language influences ELs' receptive and response processes.

Language Assessment

ELP assessment scores have multiple uses in the U.S. K–12 context, but the most critical and unique use is to make decisions for individual students about their linguistic needs and abilities, and particularly whether they should remain as ELs or be reclassified as former ELs. This classification decision may, in turn, affect (1) the supports and accommodations an individual student receives in class or on assessments, (2) the makeup of that student's instructional time, and even (3) the particular classes or teachers in or with which the student is eligible to enroll. Obviously, any of these factors can have direct and considerable consequences for an individual student's future academic performance. This scenario is unique to ELs, as the scores from academic content assessments are not put to such direct individual uses for the general population.

Because of the high individual stakes associated with reclassification decisions, validation of ELP scores for this particular use is of critical importance. As Kane (2013) has repeatedly argued regarding validation of test score interpretations and uses, "more ambitious claims require more support than less ambitious claims" (p. 3). In this case, the central "ambitious" claim test users would wish to make is that a student's score on an ELP assessment is a valid and reliable indicator of whether that student has mastered English to the point that language is unlikely to create further barriers to his or her access to or success in academic settings where English is the language of instruction. Put differently, the judgment being made is whether, based on a student's performance this year, it is reasonable to conclude that the student can succeed next year without receiving additional language support.

As one can imagine, determining whether this is the case is a complex process that requires information about (1) current proficiency in both language and content, (2) future expectations and demands in both language and content, and (3) the relationships between language and content at both time points. As a result, test users should prioritize the investigation and collection of information on these fronts, to ensure that ELs are not being subjected to highly consequential decisions based on erroneous or incomplete information. The previous section outlined specific checks that test developers and users can use to maximize the quality and utility of content assessment scores for this and other purposes. In the remainder of this section, we provide recommendations about particular types of validity evidence that test developers and users could collect to support the validity of using ELP scores for redesignation decisions.

ELP Standards: Content Validity and "Alignment"

ELP standards form the foundation on which ELP assessments are built, scored, and reported to stakeholders. As such, the validity of ELP assessment scores rests in part on the quality and validity of the ELP standards on which they are based. The quality of those standards, in turn, depends generally on how well they represent their intended domain (in this case, ELP), and, in the particular context of K–12 ELP assessment, on how well that domain reflects the actual language demands of academic content and achievement standards (e.g., *physics English*, as described in the previous section).

NCLB specifically required that states develop ELP standards that are "derived from the four recognized domains of speaking, listening, reading, and writing, and that are aligned with achievement of the challenging State academic content and student academic achievement standards" (NCLB §3113[b][2]). In plain language, this means that states were expected to define ELP in terms of the four linguistic domains, and that ELP standards should reflect the linguistic knowledge and skills necessary to meet academic content and achievement standards.

The first generation of ELP standards and assessments under NCLB focused particularly on the first of these two ideas—the domain-based framework. Thus, not surprisingly, a 2009 survey of states' ELP standards found that 20 sets of ELP standards (out of 32 reviewed sets, which represented 47 states in total) were organized into separate sections by domain (Forte, Kuti, & O'Day, 2012), and a 2012 survey of ELP score reports found that nearly all ELP assessments in use at that time were built and reported according to the four language domains of reading, writing, listening, and speaking (Faulkner-Bond, Shin, Wang, Zenisky, & Moyer, 2013).

Arguably, however, the second aspect of the NCLB definition—that of "alignment" between language and content standards—may be the more important criterion from a validity perspective.[4] Since proficient performance relative to the ELP standards is assumed to be a valid indicator of a student's preparedness to meet academic content standards without further language support, it is critically important that states gather evidence to support the assertion that their ELP standards are in fact "aligned" with their content standards. If students who have met language proficiency standards for their state (i.e., redesignated ELs) continue to lag behind peers who have never been ELs in their performance on academic content assessments, this would suggest that the state has not defined linguistic proficiency in a way that supports ELs' ability to meet content and achievement standards.

On a positive note in this regard, an evaluation report issued by the Office of Planning, Evaluation and Policy Development, Policy and Program Studies Service reported that, by 2009–2010, 45 states had established alignment between their ELP standards and their academic content standards in at least one subject area, most commonly ELA (in 41 of the 45 states) (Tanenbaum et al., 2012). There are two important caveats to such findings, however: First, in addition to evaluating the language demands of academic content standards, it is also important to evaluate the language demands of academic content assessments (i.e., the language demands of the items themselves, the reading passages, the graphics), as these may differ from the standards and can affect ELs' performance. Studies have found mismatches in the linguistic complexity of ELP and content assessments (Stevens, Butler, & Castellon-Wellington, 2000), and have found evidence that linguistic complexity in assessment items may differentially affect ELs (as in the Martiniello, 2008, example discussed above). Procedures for evaluating

---

[4]Since "alignment" typically refers to the relationship between a set of standards and an assessment that is built to measure them, there has been some debate over whether "alignment" is an appropriate term to use for the relationship between ELP standards or assessments and content standards. Technically, *alignment* should refer to the relationship between ELP standards and ELP assessments. To this end, some experts have recommended using the term "correspondence" to refer to the relationship between ELP content and performance standards and academic content and performance standards (Bailey, Butler, & Sato, 2007; Council of Chief State School Officers, 2013).

the linguistic complexity of content standards and assessments have been proposed in numerous papers (e.g., Bailey & Butler, 2007; Bailey et al., 2007; Wolf & Leon, 2009).

Second, a critical factor for establishing linkages between language and content standards is a clear articulation of the language skills and knowledge necessary for—or targeted by—academic content and performance standards (to continue the example from above, this would mean clearly defining *physics English,* among other things). On this front, NCLB-era content and language standards—which we define as those standards used from NCLB's implementation up until the widespread adoption of the Common Core State Standards (CCSS) in 2009—were somewhat mixed. For instance, the same 2009 survey of ELP standards (Forte et al., 2012) found that although 19 sets included explicit references to the academic content areas such as ELA, mathematics, or science, states varied considerably in the depth and specificity of these references. In another study about linkages between science and ELP standards, Bailey and colleagues (2007) found that barely a third of the science standards included enough information about language demands to even be ratable for subsequent evaluations of linkage to ELP standards.

In this sense, the shift for most states to the CCSS and to next-generation ELP standards (starting in 2011) reflects some important progress on this front. For better or worse, the CCSS include many language-specific standards and references (e.g., about students' expression of ideas in writing, in spoken language), making them generally a more language-heavy set of content standards compared to many of the state-developed content standards that came before them. Although this emphasis on language does have some experts concerned about fairness for ELs (Abedi & Linquanti, 2012; Bailey & Wolf, 2012), the presence of specific linguistic skills and knowledge will make the task of identifying language demands and linking ELP and academic content standards more achievable and straightforward than it may have been in the past.

Also, relatedly, new ELP standards that have been released since 2012 (California Department of Education, 2012; Council of Chief State School Officers, 2013; WIDA Consortium, 2012) generally include more explicit and intentional linkages and references to the language of school, and the CCSS in particular. In addition, tools have been developed specifically to help states identify (1) the linguistic knowledge and skills necessary to meet CCSS standards, and (2) the extent to which their own ELP standards reflect similar knowledge and skills (Council of Chief State School Officers, 2013). These developments should make it easier for states to identify and evaluate clear and specific connections between language and content standards, thereby providing more and better information by which to determine when students' language proficiency suggests they no longer need the supports associated with EL status.

ELP Assessment Standard Setting and Redesignation

Generally speaking, all states use ELP assessment scores as the sole or primary criterion for redesignation (Ragan & Lesaux, 2006). Beyond this commonality, however, states vary in whether they use overall ELP proficiency scores (usually signifying a compensatory proficiency model) or a set of unique domain scores (signifying a conjunctive model) as the final criterion. They also vary in whether (and how) they use content performance in addition to ELP performance. On all these points, there can also be variation within states (i.e., at the district level) as well. Not surprisingly, studies have found that differences on all of these variables can affect students' classification and subsequent academic performance (Carroll & Bailey, 2016; Grissom, 2004; Kim & Herman, 2009; Robinson, 2011). Given the consequences of this cut score, the standard-setting process to determine the redesignation threshold for ELs is perhaps the most important aspect of ensuring valid score use for ELP assessments.

Because EL status is defined based on language-related consequences for academic content learning and performance, it is critical to provide evidence showing that the performance level associated with the redesignation signifies that language no longer poses a barrier for students who have met it. As the preceding sections should hopefully make clear, there are numerous ways for states to build in and furnish this evidence. First, as we discussed in the section about alignment, the ELP/D[5] standards the assessment is designed to measure should reflect some kind of concordance or alignment with the language demands of grade-level academic content, so that mastery of the ELP/D standards bears some relation to mastery of the language skills and knowledge necessary to succeed in academic settings the students will go on to face.

Second, as we suggested in the discussion about domain definition, the construct of *English language proficiency,* as well as the performance levels associated with it, should be articulated in ways that explicitly reflect these ELP/D standards. This domain definition will drive an ELP assessment's specifications and design, which will in turn affect the quality and utility of the scores it produces for the purpose of redesignation. Thus, a test that has been designed based on a carefully defined and well-articulated language framework should produce scores (or at least, be capable of producing scores) that can be interpreted as indicative of a student's mastery of language as it is used in academic settings.

Third, states may wish to consider both content and language performance when setting standards and cut scores on the ELP test. This final point can be tricky, as studies have found that misplaced content criteria can lead either to an "overprotected" subgroup of ELs who meet content standards but not language standards (Grissom, 2004; Robinson, 2011), or to an underprepared subgroup of former ELs who struggle to meet content standards after redesignation (Kim & Herman, 2009, 2012; Robinson, 2011). The key for standard setters is to thread the needle between these two undesirable consequences.

To accomplish this feat, Cook, Linquanti, Chinen, & Jung (2012) have proposed three quantitative methods—decision consistency, logistic regression, and descriptive box plots—that all seek to identify the level of ELP performance that minimizes the number of students who are proficient in language or content but not both. Perhaps

---

[5] Some states refer to these as English Language Development (ELD) standards.

counterintuitively, these authors note that the true sign that a student is ready for redesignation may actually be a *decrease* in the relationship between the student's language proficiency and content performance—this would suggest that language no longer plays a significant role in the student's content performance, which is the implied goal based on the law's definition of ELs in the first place.

Questions without Answers: Future Research

NCLB marked an important shift for the inclusion of ELs in assessment and accountability, and helped to draw the attention of more teachers and policymakers to these students' access to and opportunity for high-quality instruction. During the first 10 years after NCLB, scholars and practitioners made tremendous progress toward understanding attitudes, access, and assessment for ELs, and the new era of accountability and assessment ushered in by the CCSS reflects many of the findings and improvements furnished by these activities. That said, however, more work is needed, and the shift to the new standards and assessments in both language and content will undoubtedly introduce new challenges that will require further study in the next decade and beyond.

Chief among these is continued study and articulation of the relationships between language and content performance. Given the high language demands of the CCSS and other next-generation standards, it will be important for researchers to study the actual observed relationships between language and content performance on the new assessments, as well as how these relationships may vary across students, schools, or states. It may be particularly enlightening to attempt to derive measures of how and how much language skills affect the performance of non-ELs, as such skills may be more important and more construct-relevant on measures of the CCSS.

Growth is another topic that has taken on outsize importance in the era of the CCSS (see Keller, Colvin, & Garcia, Chapter 19, this volume, for a more in-depth discussion on this point). Given that preliminary studies have found differences in how commonly used growth models perform for ELs versus non-ELs (Lakin & Young, 2013), it will be important for states that insist on using these models to establish comparability and validity for ELs relative to other students. If this cannot be done, states may need to consider using different models or indicators for ELs to ensure that the models applied to these students produce meaningful and appropriate results.

Clearly, in contexts beyond the U.S. K–12 example, considerations for future research may differ. In all cases, however, we believe that the framework presented in this chapter can help test developers and users to ensure that LMs participating in any type of assessment are given fair opportunities to demonstrate their knowledge and skills in valid ways given a particular assessment's purpose. We encourage the users of any assessment system to consider and revisit these themes regularly and iteratively to ensure that LMs continue to be included fairly. Ensuring this fact is critical for the validity and utility of scores for all examinees.

REFERENCES

Abedi, J., & Ewers, N. (2013). *Accommodations for English language learners and students with disabilities: A research-based decision algorithm.* Davis, CA: Smarter Balanced Assessment Consortium.

Abedi, J., & Linquanti, R. (2012, January). Issues and opportunities in improving the quality of large scale assessment systems for ELLs. Presented at the Understanding Language Conference, Palo Alto, CA. Retrieved from *http://ell.stanford.edu/publication/issues-and-opportunities-improving-quality-large-scale-assessment-systems-ells.*

American Educational Research Association, American Psychological Association, & National Council on Measurement in Education. (2014). *Standards for educational and psychological testing.* Washington, DC: Authors.

American Institutes for Research. (2013). *ELPA-to-ELPA look back.* Washington, DC: Author. Retrieved from *www.ode.state.or.us/teachlearn/standards/contentperformance/elpa-to-elpa_look-back_report_02052013.pdf.*

Bailey, A. L., & Butler, F. (2007). A conceptual framework for academic English language for broad application to education. In A. L. Bailey (Ed.), *The language demands of school: Putting academic English to the test* (pp. 68–102). New Haven, CT: Yale University Press.

Bailey, A. L., Butler, F., & Sato, E. (2007). Standards-to-standards linkage under Title III: Exploring common language demands in ELD and science standards. *Applied Measurement in Education, 20*(1), 53–78.

Bailey, A. L., & Wolf, M. K. (2012). *The challenge of assessing language proficiency aligned to the Common Core State Standards and some possible solutions.* Paper presented at the Understanding Language Conference, Palo Alto, CA. Retrieved from *http://ell.stanford.edu/publication/issues-and-opportunities-improving-quality-large-scale-assessment-systems-ells.*

Boyson, B., & Short, D. (2003). *Secondary school newcomer programs in the United States* (Research No. 12, pp. 1–33). Santa Cruz, CA: University of California, CREDE/CAL.

California Department of Education. (2012, November). Overview of the California English language development standards and proficiency level descriptors. California Department of Education. Retrieved from *www.cde.ca.gov/sp/el/er/documents/sbeoverviewpld.pdf.*

Carroll, P. E., & Bailey, A. L. (2016). Do decision rules matter?: A descriptive study of English language proficiency assessment classifications for English-language learners and native English speakers in fifth grade. *Language Testing, 33,* 23–52.

Chambers, D., Kerbel, A., Rivera, A., & Forte, E. (2011). *Cognitive process study report for the Pruebas Puertorriqueñas de Aprovechamiento Académico (PPAA).* San Juan: Puerto Rico Department of Education.

Cook, H. G., Linquanti, R., Chinen, M., & Jung, H. (2012). *National evaluation of Title III implementation supplemental report: Exploring approaches to setting English language proficiency performance criteria and monitoring English learner progress.* Washington, DC: Office of Planning, Evaluation and Policy Development, U.S. Department of Education.

Council of Chief State School Officers. (2013). *English language proficiency (ELP) standards with correspondences to K–12 English language arts (ELA), mathematics, and science practices, K–12 ELA standards, and 6–12 literacy standards.* Washington, DC: Council of Chief State School Officers. Retrieved from *www.elpa21.org/sites/default/files/Final%204_30%20ELPA21%20Standards_1.pdf.*

DiCerbo, P. A., Anstrom, K. A., Baker, L. L., & Rivera, C. (2014). A review of the literature on teaching academic English to English language learners. *Review of Educational Research, 84*(3), 446–482.

Faulkner-Bond, M., Shin, M., Wang, X., Zenisky, A. L., & Moyer, E. (2013, April). *Score reports for English proficiency assessments: Current practices and future directions.* Paper presented at the National Council on Measurement in Education, San Francisco.

Forte, E. (2010). Examining the assumptions underlying the NCLB federal accountability policy on school improvement. *Educational Psychologist, 45*(2), 76–88.

Forte, E., Kuti, L., & O'Day, J. (2012). *National evaluation of Title III implementation: A survey of states' English language proficiency standards.* Office of Planning, Evaluation and Policy Development, U.S. Department of Education.

Francis, D. J., & Rivera, M. O. (2007). Principles underlying English language proficiency tests and academic accountability for ELLs. In J. Abedi (Ed.), *English language proficiency assessment in the nation: Current status and future practice* (pp. 13–32). Davis, CA: Regents of the University of California.

Francis, D. J., Rivera, M. O., Lesaux, N. K., Kieffer, M. J., & Rivera, H. (2006). *Research-based recommendations for serving adolescent newcomers* (pp. 1–40). Houston, TX: Center on Instruction.

Grissom, J. B. (2004). Reclassification of English learners. *Education Policy Analysis Archives, 12*, 36.

Kane, M. T. (2013). Validating the interpretations and uses of test scores. *Journal of Educational Measurement, 50*(1), 1–73.

Kieffer, M. J., Lesaux, N. K., Rivera, M., & Francis, D. J. (2009). Accommodations for English language learners taking large-scale assessments: A meta-analysis on effectiveness and validity. *Review of Educational Research, 79*(3), 1168–1201.

Kim, J., & Herman, J. L. (2009). A three-state study of English learner progress. *Educational Assessment, 14*(3–4), 212–231.

Kim, J., & Herman, J. L. (2012). *Understanding patterns and precursors of ELL success subsequent to reclassification* (CRESST Report No. 818). Los Angeles: University of California, National Center for Research on Evaluation, Standards, and Student Testing (CRESST).

Kopriva, R. J., Emick, J. E., Hipolito-Delgado, C. P., & Cameron, C. (2007). Do proper accommodations assignments make a difference?: Examining the impact of improved decision making on scores for English language learners. *Educational Measurement: Issues and Practice, 26*(3), 11–20.

Lakin, J. M., & Young, J. W. (2013). Evaluating growth for ELL students: Implications for accountability policies. *Educational Measurement: Issues and Practice, 32*(3), 11–26.

Lau v. Nichols, 414 U.S. 563. (1974). Certiorari to the United States Court of Appeals for the Ninth Circuit, No. 72–6520. Retrieved August 1, 2014, from *http://caselaw.lp.findlaw.com/scripts/getcase.pl?court=US&navby=case&vol=414&invol=563.*

Martiniello, M. (2008). Language and the performance of English-language learners in math word problems. *Harvard Educational Review, 78*(2), 333–368.

Massachusetts Department of Elementary and Secondary Education, & DePascale, C. (2012). *Transitioning English language learners in Massachusetts: An exploratory data review.* Malden, MA: Massachusetts Department of Elementary and Secondary Education. Retrieved from *www.nciea.org/publication_PDFs/Transitioning%20ELL_CD12.pdf.*

Messick, S. (1990). *Validity of test interpretation and use.* Princeton, NJ: Educational Testing Service.

O'Conner, R., Abedi, J., & Tung, S. (2012). *A descriptive analysis of enrollment and achievement among English language learner students in Pennsylvania* (Issues and Answers Report, REL 2012-No. 127). Washington, DC: U.S. Department of Education, Institute of Educational Sciences, National Center for Education Evaluation and Regional Assistance, Regional Educational Laboratory Mid-Atlantic. Retrieved from *http://ies.ed.gov/ncee/edlabs*.

Parker, C., Louie, J., & O'Dwyer, L. (2009). *New measures of English language proficiency and their relationship to performance on large-scale content assessments* (Issues & Answers Report REL 2009–No. 066). Washington, DC: U.S. Department of Education, Institute of Education Sciences, National Center for Education Evaluation and Regional Assistance, Regional Educational Laboratory Northeast and Islands. Retrieved from *http://ies.ed.gov/ncee/edlabs*.

Parrish, T. B., Merickel, A., Perez, M., Linquanti, R., Socias, M., Spain, A., et al. (2006). *Effects of the implementation of Proposition 227 on the education of English learners, K–12: Findings from a five-year evaluation* (Final Report No. AB 56 and AB 1116). Palo Alto, CA: American Institutes for Research.

Pennock-Roman, M., & Rivera, C. (2011). Mean effects of test accommodations for ELLs and non-ELLs: A meta-analysis of experimental studies. *Educational Measurement: Issues and Practice, 30*(3), 10–28.

Ragan, A., & Lesaux, N. K. (2006). Federal, state, and district level English language learner program entry and exit requirements: Effects on the education of language minority learners. *Education Policy Analysis Archives, 14*(20), 1–32.

Robinson, J. P. (2011). Evaluating criteria for English learner reclassification: A causal-effects approach using a binding-score regression discontinuity design with instrumental variables. *Educational Evaluation and Policy Analysis, 33*(3), 267–292.

Slama, R. B. (2014). Investigating whether and when English learners are reclassified into mainstream classrooms in the United States: A discrete-time survival analysis. *American Educational Research Journal, 51*(2), 220–252.

Solano-Flores, G., & Li, M. (2009). Language variation and score variation in the testing of English language learners, native Spanish speakers. *Educational Assessment, 14*(3–4), 180–194.

Stevens, R., Butler, F., & Castellon-Wellington, M. (2000). *Academic language and content assessment: Measuring the progress of ELLs* (Technical Report No. 552). Los Angeles: University of California, National Center for Research on Evaluation, Standards, and Student Testing (CRESST). Retrieved from *www.cse.ucla.edu/products/reports/TR552.pdf*.

Swanson, C. B. (2009). *Perspectives on a population: English-language learners in American schools*. Bethesda, MD: Editorial Projects in Education Research Center.

Tanenbaum, C., Boyle, A., Soga, K., Floch, L., Carlson, K., Golden, L., et al. (2012). *National evaluation of Title III implementation: Report on state and local implementation*. Office of Planning, Evaluation and Policy Development, U.S. Department of Education. Retrieved from *www2.ed.gov/rschstat/eval/title-iii/state-local-implementation-report.pdf*.

Thompson, K. D. (2012, June). *Are we there yet?: Exploring English learners' journey to reclassification and beyond*. Doctoral dissertation, Stanford University, Stanford, CA. Retrieved from *http://purl.stanford.edu/qd054zq1735*.

Thurlow, M. L., Thompson, S. J., & Lazarus, S. S. (2006). Considerations for the administration of tests to special needs students: Accommodations, modifications, and more. In S. M. Downing & T. M. Haladyna (Eds.), *Handbook of test development* (pp. 653–673). Mahwah, NJ: Erlbaum.

U.S. Department of Education. (2011). *Consolidated state performance reports: Parts I and II school years 2009–10*. Office of Elementary and Secondary Education. Retrieved from *www2.ed.gov/admins/lead/account/consolidated/sy09-10part1/index.html*

WIDA Consortium. (2012). *2012 Amplificaton of the English language development standards, kindergarten–grade 12*. Madison: Board of Regents of the University of Wisconsin System.

Wolf, M. K., & Leon, S. (2009). An investigation of the language demands in content assessments for English language learners. *Educational Assessment, 14*(3–4), 139–159.

Young, J. W., Cho, Y., Ling, G., Cline, F., Steinberg, J., & Stone, E. (2008). Validity and fairness of state standards-based assessments for English language learners. *Educational Assessment, 13*(2–3), 170–192.

CHAPTER 24

Alternate Assessments
for Students with Disabilities
Lessons from the National Center and State Collaborative

Martha L. Thurlow and Rachel F. Quenemoen

In the 1994 reauthorization of the Elementary and Secondary Education Act (ESEA), Congress formalized the sweeping standards-based reform movement of the time into federal law. This movement, which continues today, has been well documented since the beginning (e.g., National Commission on Excellence in Education, 1983; National Governors Association, 1986). By all accounts, the movement was meant to address issues of equity and excellence in publicly funded elementary and secondary education.

Public education is meant, in part, to ensure the quality of our democratic processes by providing a high-quality education for all the children of all of the people, regardless of their circumstances. In the late 1980s and early 1990s, a groundswell of concern had arisen based on ample evidence that the United States was not achieving that goal. Thus, the 1994 ESEA reauthorization (Improving America's Schools Act) refocused federal support toward a free and universal public education by funding state and local educational standards-based reform targeting students who were not achieving at the levels necessary for carrying out the essential roles of citizenship. This funding from the federal level was accompanied by data-based reporting requirements built on the assumption that all students should be taught and learn to the same content and achievement expectations. It was up to states to define those content and achievement expectations, as well as to develop assessment systems to generate the data to measure and report how *all* students were doing, not just those students for whom intervention was required.

Although civil rights reforms in the 1960s had been spurred on by a court decision that a separate education is inherently unequal in terms of race (*Brown v. Board of Education of Topeka*, 1954), and reforms in the 1970s resulted in case law (e.g., *Pennsylvania Association for Retarded Children [PARC] v. Commonwealth of Pennsylvania*, 1972; *Mills v. Board of Education of District of Columbia*, 1972) and Congressional legislation (Public Law 94-142, Education for All Handicapped Children Act) that opened the schoolhouse doors to students with disabilities, achievement data demonstrated persistent and troubling achievement gaps between white, more affluent students and students of color, students of lower economic status, students with disabilities, and students who were English language learners. (See Randall and Garcia, Chapter 22, this volume, for a more in-depth discussion of the history of legislation and litigation with respect to students with disabilities.)

Based on this overarching goal of closing persistent achievement gaps, the Individuals with Disabilities Education Act (IDEA) amendments in 1997 clarified what students with disabilities should know and be able to do. IDEA 1997 also included the first federal requirement for alternate assessments. In the preamble to IDEA 1997, Congress noted that historically

> the implementation of this Act has been impeded by low expectations, and an insufficient focus on applying replicable research on proven methods of teaching and learning for children with disabilities. Over 20 years of research and experience has demonstrated that the education of children with disabilities can be made more effective by having high expectations for such children and ensuring their access to the general curriculum to the maximum extent possible. (Preamble to Individuals with Disabilities Education Act, 1997)

Not everyone recognized the magnitude of the shift at the time as states began operationalizing what was meant by "the maximum extent possible" noted in the IDEA preamble. Researchers and others documented the systematic exclusion of students with disabilities from state achievement data (Kantrowitz & Springen, 1997; Shriner, Spande, & Thurlow, 1994; Ysseldyke, Algozzine, & Thurlow, 1992; Ysseldyke, Thurlow, & Linn, 1999; Zlatos, 1994) and the implications of these exclusions on the transparency of data for closing the achievement gap. The exclusion of students with disabilities also masked systematic interactions with students of color and low-income students, both disproportionately overidentified for special education services.

Thus, researchers exposed a back door to the federal requirements for all of the children of all the people to be given a quality public education through standards-based reform: The most vulnerable students—those with disabilities—were being systematically excluded from reform efforts. The research findings indicated a need for a renewed focus to ensure that students with disabilities were fully included in standards-based reform. Closing these loopholes would, in part, improve the overall quality of data on student achievement. Just as important, if not more so, was to ensure that students with disabilities were included in the benefits of standards-based reform.

With the closing of the measurement loopholes and full inclusion of students with disabilities, the fields of special education and measurement had to rethink a century of assumptions underlying standardization as a gold standard (American Educational

Research Association, American Psychological Association, & National Council on Measurement in Education, 1999; McDonnell, McLaughlin, & Morison, 1997; Phillips, 1994). Students with disabilities had often been excluded in the past based on limited measurement models to assess them well. In many cases, accommodations might be required to be able to show what they did indeed know (Bielinski, Sheinker, & Ysseldyke, 2003; Sireci, 2005). Including these students in assessments meant that these old measurement models had to be revisited to determine how to ensure the validity of the measurement model for students with disabilities.

As measurement, special education, and policy experts joined forces to resolve some of these issues, another major measurement challenge emerged: How can we fully include students with the most significant cognitive disabilities (e.g., typically those with the federal disability category label of *intellectual disabilities*, formerly known as *mental retardation*)? These students were generally acknowledged to be about 10% of all students with disabilities, or about 1% of the total student population. Here, again, a back door to inclusion of all students was identified, and additional students who could benefit from standards-based reform were being excluded (Thompson & Thurlow, 1999; Thurlow, Elliott, & Ysseldyke, 1998; Ysseldyke, Thurlow, McGrew, & Shriner, 1994). Federal legislation addressed the need to include these students in standards-based reform by requiring alternate assessments in 1997.

Although alternate assessments based on alternate achievement standards (AA-AAS) have been used in large-scale assessment systems for fewer than 25 years, their development and implementation represent a dramatic increase in knowledge about how to assess students with very different educational needs and, in turn, about the educational outcomes possible for these students. In addition, the development of alternate assessments has contributed to the understanding and development of assessments beyond alternate assessments so that they are accessible for all students, including those with disabilities and those who are English learners.

Alternate Assessments: AA-AAS and Beyond

AA-AAS represents just one option among several for the participation of students with disabilities in large-scale assessment systems. Most students with disabilities participate in general assessments, with accommodations as needed, and are held to the same academic achievement standards as their peers. It is also possible for students to be held to the same grade-level academic achievement standards via alternate assessments—that is, alternate assessments based on grade-level achievement standards (AA-GLAS), although only two states have provided this kind of assessment for their students with disabilities.

Between 2007 and 2015, some states developed alternate assessments based on modified achievement standards (AA-MAS). These assessments, which were to be based on the same grade-level content standards as other assessments, but which held students to less difficult achievement standards, were phased out by 2015, and students who participated in them now are expected to take the general assessment (Lazarus,

Thurlow, Christensen, & Shyyan, 2014). Thus, by 2015, all students with disabilities were participating in either an AA-GLAS or the AA-AAS for ESEA accountability.

The purpose of this chapter is to focus on AA-AAS and the tremendous changes that have occurred in the field's understanding of the students who participate in AA-AAS. It also addresses the implications of student characteristics for the development of an appropriate assessment. We start by clarifying the purpose of AA-AAS and what we know about the students who participate in these assessments. We follow this with a brief history of the development of AA-AAS, as well as highlight some of the lessons learned about AA-AAS that apply to the development of assessments in general. We conclude by identifying the challenges that remain in the development and implementation of high-quality AA-AAS.

First, we need to clarify how AA-AAS differ in one specific way from general assessments and from other alternate assessments. Alternate achievement standards are different standards from grade-level achievement standards (Rigney, 2009). Federal guidance for the 2003 ESEA regulation defined an *alternate achievement standard* as "an expectation of performance that differs in complexity from a grade-level achievement standard" (U.S. Department of Education, 2003, p. 20). This alternate achievement standard was meant for very narrow application, for students who met specific criteria, and for whom the alternate achievement standard raised expectations significantly from what had been true in the past. The students were part of a small group for which there was little to no debate on whether an alternate expectation was warranted, estimated as less than 1% of the total student population.

Students Who Participate in AA-AAS

The federal regulation that provided for students with significant cognitive disabilities to be held to alternate achievement standards (U.S. Department of Education, 2003) indicated that the provision was for those students with the most significant cognitive disabilities. Describing the students who have the "most significant cognitive disabilities" has been a focus of research.

Kearns, Towles-Reeves, Kleinert, Kleinert, and Thomas (2011) conducted a seven-state study in 2006–2007 of the characteristics of students participating in the states' AA-AAS. The following are the general conclusions they reached about the characteristics of the students participating in states' AA-AAS:

- The majority of students have the IDEA disability categories of intellectual disabilities, multiple disabilities, and autism.
- Most students communicate at a symbolic level of expressive and receptive language development, using either oral speech or augmentative assistive communication (AAC).
- Percentages vary, but typically around 15% of these students are able to read fluently with basic understanding in print or Braille; percentages varied considerably across states.

- Percentages vary, but typically around 50% of these students are able to do computational procedures with or without a calculator.
- Most students have vision and hearing within normal limits with or without correction, and no significant motor dysfunction (although this percentage, at 80%, is somewhat lower than the approximately 90% for vision and hearing).
- Most students (about 90%) respond to social interactions.

The picture painted by these data, which have been confirmed by other studies (e.g., Towles-Reeves et al., 2012; Towles-Reeves, Kearns, Kleinert, & Kleinert, 2009), obscures, to some extent, the tremendous variability in the population of students with significant cognitive disabilities. As described by Kearns et al. (2011), students cover the range in each of the areas. A small percentage has very significant disabilities, perhaps up to 10% of the students with significant cognitive disabilities, given the current quality of educational interventions and supports. Kearns et al. noted these characteristics of this small percentage of students:

- Expressive communication is at a presymbolic level via cries, facial expressions, and body movements; the intent of this communication has to be interpreted by the listener/observer.
- Receptive communication involves alerting to sensory information; some have low levels of these behaviors and others have inconsistent responses.

This small population of students who represents less than 10% of the total 1% who participate in AA-AAS have, on occasion, been assumed to be the total population of students who participate in the AA-AAS. They are instead a very small percentage of the students who appropriately participate in AA-AAS. This type of erroneous assumption was highlighted by Quenemoen, Kearns, Quenemoen, Flowers, and Kleinert (2010) as they addressed this and other misconceptions about students with significant cognitive disabilities.

Another misconception about these students addressed by Quenemoen and colleagues (2010) was that many students who take the AA-AAS function more like infants or toddlers than their actual age. The implication of this misperception was that it made no sense for schools to be held accountable for their academic performance. Quenemoen et al. dispelled this myth by noting that historical notions of "mental age" determining what types of educational materials a student should use were outdated and replaced by documentation that all students can benefit from age-appropriate materials and activities (Browder & Spooner, 2006; Brown, Nietupski, & Hamre-Nietupski, 1976) and by participating with grade-level peers (McDonnell, Mathot-Buckner, Thorson, & Fister, 2001; Roach & Elliott, 2006; Ryndak, Morrison, & Sommerstein, 1999). Most experts today agree that the notion of developmental stages should not prohibit students from working on age-appropriate academic skills (Hughes & Carter, 2008; Kleinert, Browder, & Towles-Reeves, 2009; Spooner & Browder, 2006).

How AA-AAS Has Evolved over Time

In 1999, just 20 states indicated that they were developing some type of alternate assessment (Thompson & Thurlow, 1999). Although severe disability experts were beginning to see the value of academic instruction for students with significant cognitive disabilities, most states' alternate assessments at that time still primarily reflected a functional approach (Kleinert & Kearns, 1999). Brown and colleagues (1976) defined *functional skills* as those needed to function in daily life in the community, vocation, domestic, and recreational areas. The focus on functional skills has diminished dramatically over time, as documented by Quenemoen (2009). By 2001, all states indicated that they had some form of alternate assessment (Thompson & Thurlow, 2001), and the nature of states' alternate assessments has changed significantly since then. Quenemoen portrayed the scope of changes in format, content, scoring criteria and procedures, achievement-level descriptors and standard setting, and reporting and accountability. These changes are highlighted briefly here.

Format

In 1999, more than half of all alternate assessments were portfolios or some form of a body of evidence collection. This percentage stayed pretty much the same, dropping slightly over time through the mid-2000s. A few states used rating scales or checklists and a few relied on individualized education programs (IEPs) to define assessment targets. It became clear as time progressed that there was a trend toward increased numbers of states using some type of standardized set of performance tasks, as well as a blending of approaches (e.g., a portfolio that included evidence from a standardized set of performance tasks) (Altman et al., 2010).

Content

The content focus of the AA-AAS, similar to the content focus of curriculum and instruction for students with significant cognitive disabilities, has changed dramatically since the first AA-AAS was produced. In 1999 the content of most states' AA-AAS was either "extended" versions of the state content standards or only functional skills with no link to the state content standards. This has changed over time with a steady decrease in the number of states with any content related to functional skills in their AA-AAS (Quenemoen, 2009). By the late 2000s, most states focused on the state content standards, either through grade-level academic content standards or through extended academic content standards.

The documentation of the connection to the content standards has evolved over time. Researchers at the University of North Carolina at Charlotte created an alternative to the commonly used Webb (1997) approach for quantifying alignment between an assessment and the content standards on which it was based. The Links for Academic Learning (Flowers, Wakeman, Browder, & Karvonen, 2009; Wakeman, Flowers, & Browder, 2007) is the primary approach that is now used for checking the alignment of the AA-AAS with academic content standards.

Scoring Criteria and Procedures

With the reauthorization of ESEA in 2001 and the regulation (U.S. Department of Education, 2003) that allowed for AA-AAS proficient scores to be counted for school accountability purposes, the scoring criteria and procedures for AA-AAS gained heightened importance. Early scoring criteria included many areas beyond a measure of the student's skill or competence in a content area. For example, a 2005 survey of states (Thompson, Johnstone, Thurlow, & Altman, 2005) indicated that 40% or more of state rubrics for assessing students' performance on AA-AAS included (1) the level of assistance that was given to the student, (2) the degree of progress made by the student, or (3) the number or variety of settings in which the student performed. When surveyed again in 2009, fewer states were using a rubric to measure achievement (although it was still the most frequent approach at that time), and more were counting the number of items correct (Altman et al., 2010).

Procedures for scoring also have changed over time. As noted by Quenemoen (2009), between 2001 and 2003 some states shifted from having teachers score their own students to centralized scoring. Over time there continued to be shifts toward more oversight of scoring, including increased requirements for evidence of student work to support ratings or checklist scores (when those were used), random sampling for verification of evidence, and videotaping for later review by a neutral trained second scorer. Altman and colleagues (2010) documented that by 2009, almost half of the states had a test company contractor scoring the AA-AAS, and nearly one-fourth had teachers from other districts doing the scoring. Still, one-fourth of the states had the students' special education teachers scoring their students' performance on the AA-AAS.

Achievement-Level Descriptors and Standard Setting

Considerable confusion surrounding the concept of achievement-level descriptors (ALDs) and standard setting existed among the special education personnel who were generally responsible for the development and implementation of AA-AAS in the early 2000s. Quenemoen (2009) described the steep learning curve that surrounded the understanding of content standards for AA-AAS, and even more confusion about the setting of performance standards. By 2009, most states had a grasp of what it meant to engage in the development of ALDs and to set standards for performance. At that time, the primary standard-setting method was *body of work* (Kingston & Tiemann, 2012), followed closely by *bookmarking* (Lewis, Mitzel, Mercado, & Schulz, 2012). Pitoniak and Cizek (Chapter 3, this volume) provide more information about how these and other standard-setting procedures typically work.

Reporting and Accountability

Requirements for reporting and accountability heightened awareness of the AA-AAS and the role that it could play in school accountability. Several researchers documented the positive consequences of greater access to the general curriculum and higher expectations for students with significant cognitive disabilities that followed from their participation in the AA-AAS (Cameto et al., 2010; Kleinert, Kennedy, & Kearns, 1999; Schafer & Lissitz, 2009). Reporting and accountability heightened the awareness of the importance of developing technically adequate AA-AAS.

Next-Generation Assessments and the Common Core State Standards: New Developments in AA-AAS

In 2010, two consortia of states were funded to develop next generation AA-AAS. These assessments were to be based on the Common Core State Standards (CCSS) for groups of states, and to make more and better use of technology. The Dynamic Learning Maps (DLM) Consortium and the National Center and State Collaborative (NCSC) both initiated the development of technically adequate AA-AAS (Center for K–12 Assessment, 2013). DLM allowed for either the administration of instructionally relevant testlets as part of day-to-day instructional activities or a stand-alone summative assessment that was adapted based on mastery of concepts in a DLM-developed learning map. NCSC provided comprehensive curriculum and instruction resources as well as a technology-based summative assessment. Both of these assessments were operational in spring 2015.

Closer examination of the NCSC alternate assessment as an example shows the steps that were taken to develop next-generation AA-AAS. This assessment was developed on the foundation of lessons learned over the past two decades, but pushed the development toward the future to be a "next-generation" AA-AAS. The sections that follow provide brief descriptions of key NCSC development activities that reflect this progress.

Framework

The most promising potential measurement solutions for how to design assessments for the small, unique group of students who participate in an AA-AAS emerge from the concept of the *assessment triangle*, first presented in Pellegrino, Chudowsky, and Glaser (2001), then modified under the New Hampshire Enhanced Assessment Initiative (NHEAI), and ultimately documented in Marion and Pellegrino (2006). Pellegrino and colleagues suggested that every assessment must rest on three foundations: "a model of how students represent knowledge and develop competence in the subject domain, tasks or situations that allow one to observe students' performance, and an interpretation method for drawing inferences from the performance evidence thus obtained" (p. 2). Given the unique population being assessed in AA-AAS, and the limited utility of traditional measurement models for the unusual measurement challenges of this diverse population, using the assessment triangle in design, development, and evaluation of the large-scale AA-AAS provides an unusual opportunity to rethink traditional assumptions.

NCSC used these foundations to support improved achievement for students with the most significant cognitive disabilities. It built a system of curriculum, instruction, and assessments based on an informed articulation of the content model, an understanding of the learner characteristics, and a model of learning that brings the content and learner together.

Development

In implementing the concept of the assessment triangle, NCSC specifically made use of principled-design strategies based on evidence-centered design (ECD; Mislevy, Almond, & Lukas, 2003) to guide the development of assessments and assessment items. In NCSC's principled-design approach knowledge, skills, and abilities that are to be assessed are identified first, along with detailed content specifications based on a hypothesized model of learning and what evidence of student learning is observed as students build their skills and knowledge (Browder et al., 2009, 2012; Hess, 2011a, 2011b; National Center and State Collaborative, 2014). Through development of design patterns and related task templates, assessment developers provide examples of what tasks or items look like and how they are to be presented and scored, and these then are replicated and refined through item development procedures.

Use of these procedures strengthens system alignment and integrity from the beginning, and results in clarity of construct by item to ensure that accessibility features for students who need them do not inadvertently challenge the construct. In most traditional methods, item developers and implementers are guessing at the construct as they go, and often either overprotect items at the risk of limiting access for students who actually do know the content, or alternatively give away the content through misinterpretation or misguided assumptions that accessibility trumps content.

In the NCSC item development process, once the design patterns and task templates were developed and tested with small tryouts of students and teachers across the diversity of the target population, the item bank was built to ensure the full range of difficulty for each of the prioritized content targets. That is, a family of items is built to assess each targeted focal knowledge, skill, and ability (FKSA) across a range of performances, essential to measure a small population that is widely diverse in academic achievement. This process results in an item bank that can accommodate some level of adaptivity to ensure that all students can show what they know in the context of the eventual test blueprint.

Connections to Instruction

The development of coherent, aligned, and rigorous curriculum, instruction, and assessment resources is key to building a high-quality measurement opportunity for the diverse group of students who participate in AA-AAS. The NCSC project goal was to ensure that students with significant cognitive disabilities achieve increasingly higher academic outcomes and leave high school ready for postsecondary options. A well-designed summative assessment alone is insufficient to achieve this goal. The NCSC AA-AAS system also required curricular and instructional frameworks and teacher resources and professional development in a common domain-based model of learning and understanding. This model includes within-year classroom assessments and progress monitoring tools embedded in curricular materials, as well as professional development through on-demand modules for teachers to learn to develop their own curricular materials using model content, curriculum, and instruction tools (see *https://wiki.ncscpartners.org/mediawiki/index.php/Main_Page*).

In the NCSC system, companion curricular and instructional materials were built at the same time as the AA-AAS items, using the same content model, understanding of learner characteristics, and model of student learning. Thus, the consortium fostered explicit connections between best practice in both teaching and assessing content, all built purposively on a common model of student cognition in the academic content areas. Professional development, content-knowledge supports and tools for teachers, and collegial networking through communities of practice provided the glue that holds the system of curriculum, instruction, and assessment together.

Administration

NCSC's summative assessment itself, as part of the overall system of curriculum, instruction, and assessment, is more similar to general assessments in design than are most previous AA-AAS. The NCSC summative math and ELA tests for grades 3–8 and 11 are administered in a 6-week window in the spring. Each includes approximately 30–35 items that require about 1.5–2 hours per content area for most students to complete, with flexibility to permit smaller time slots across the testing window, based on student needs. The tests are delivered via online technology, with the test administrator providing support to ensure that the student can enter responses appropriately. Universal design features and accommodations guidelines for administration are derived from the principled design components of design patterns and task templates, and are provided at the item level. Test administrators complete and certify online training and quizzes prior to administering the NCSC assessment.

Most students interact with the test administrator during the administration of the NCSC assessment, though some respond to the test items directly via the computer presentation. Test administrators have prior access to summative content to permit preparation for accommodations, approved manipulatives or paper versions, and appropriate testing environments. All answers are entered into the online system.

Some students who participate in the NCSC assessment qualify to take a shorter assessment based on evidence collected before and during the assessment. Most of the items are machine-scored, selected-response items. A small number of the items are open-response activities with correct answers that the test administrator marks as correct or incorrect based on the test directions. Writing prompts were field tested during the spring 2015 administration, and scored by the test vendor using third-party scoring procedures. Selected response writing items were included in the operational test in 2015.

Outcomes of the NCSC assessment include a total score and performance level for mathematics and for English language arts (ELA), which combines reading and writing. Separate information for writing prompts will be provided once the prompts are operational, including a narrative description of student performance. Total scores for each content area are comparable within year and across years. Additional descriptive information is provided in parent-friendly language, describing what skills and knowledge the student demonstrated on the assessment.

Evaluation of the Next-Generation AA-AAS

NCSC, like all other CCSS assessment consortia, is completing the full complement of technical documentation to support defense of the assessment for the defined purposes and uses. These include studies that demonstrate alignment to standards, adherence to test blueprint, bias and sensitivity results, and psychometric analyses. Still, additional research questions must be asked about this large-scale assessment that assesses the diverse and unique population that participates in AA-AAS, especially given the short history of assessing this group and the documented challenges of balancing the flexibility needed to include all students with the standardization needed to defend the technical qualities of the assessment (Gong & Marion, 2006). For example, given the heavy investment in principled design work in the front end of test development, and the application of principled design to development of the item bank, key questions include: To what extent are the hypothesized progressions in difficulty/complexity designed into the item bank specifications borne out by the item data? To what extent does performance vary by skill/context? Which item/presentation features promote access and which features compromised access, specifically for students who are blind, deaf, deaf-blind, or who have complex and multiple disabilities?

For NCSC, these questions were answered through a two-phase pilot/field test. In Phase I, items were administered broadly in a matrix design for the primary purpose of evaluating item performance and developing item bank calibrations, along with a family of smaller student interaction studies and accessibility studies. Then, in Phase II, based on item calibrations from Phase I, intact forms were constructed and administered that targeted the blueprint coverage with appropriate levels of challenge, based on item statistics from Pilot I. The full operational NCSC assessment was conducted in spring 2015 based on minor adjustments to the Phase II forms, followed by standard setting, reporting, and technical documentation of the system.

Member states are moving forward with the NCSC system of assessments with all the information necessary to move into year 2 of operational testing consistent with the test specifications, blueprints, and psychometric targets for the assessment, including algorithms, rules, or tables necessary to produce overall scale scores and performance levels and rubrics for all human-scored items. There are protocols for training scorers and implementing the scoring process and design specifications for all static reports produced, including individual student reports. Ancillary material to support administration of the summative assessment includes test administration manuals and resources to support the training of test examiners. A score interpretation guide; detailed technical documentation of process, procedures, and results from all test development activities; and all test items developed for the NCSC assessments (i.e., the item bank) are available in a format that meets industry standards for interoperability. Specifications for certification and implementation of the technology system and training resources are also available, along with the release of open source code for the NCSC technology platform, based on the TAO open-source software but tailored for use in the NCSC system.

Lessons Learned

The path to the development of the NCSC AA-AAS is lined with lessons that have been learned about assessment development. These lessons apply to all assessment development endeavors.

1. The principles of the National Research Council's work on the assessment triangle (Pellegrino et al., 2001) and the three foundations for assessment design of the model of domain learning, observations, and inferences can effectively guide development of large-scale assessments, especially for populations for whom traditional test development procedures may inadvertently mask what the students actually do know (i.e., many underserved populations). An assessment system should be comprehensive and coherent, including formative assessments, interim/benchmark assessments, and summative assessments (Quenemoen, Flowers, & Forte, 2014; Thurlow et al., 2008).

2. A principled approach to assessment development (Mislevy et al., 2003) should be used to ensure system alignment and integrity from the beginning, and result in clarity of construct by item to ensure that accessibility features for students who need them do not inadvertently challenge the construct.

3. A model of domain learning that includes hypothesized learning progressions— evidence of how students develop literacy and numeracy, should be identified and articulated (e.g., Browder, Ahlgrim-Delzell, Courtade, Gibbs, & Flowers, 2008; Browder et al., 2009, 2012; Browder & Spooner, 2014; Jimenez, Browder, Spooner, & DiBiase, 2012).

4. Curriculum, instruction, and assessment need to be aligned. More curriculum materials are needed for students with significant cognitive disabilities (Quenemoen et al., 2014; also see *https://wiki.ncscpartners.org/mediawiki/index. php/Main_Page*).

5. Administrators and teachers need to better understand how to provide access to the general curriculum for students with significant cognitive disabilities

(Flowers, Ahlgrim-Delzell, Browder, & Spooner, 2005; Towles-Reeves, Kleinert, & Anderman, 2008).

Continuing Challenges in the Development and Implementation of AA-AAS

The genesis of AA-AAS has been swift, involving dramatic changes in not only development and implementation, but also huge shifts in the beliefs and knowledge of those developing and implementing the assessments. Dramatic changes in the beliefs and knowledge of those responsible for educating the students who participate in these assessments have also been required. There continue to be challenges, just as there are for the large consortia of states developing regular assessments and those consortia developing assessments of English language proficiency.

The example of the NCSC project approach illustrates bold steps forward toward a next-generation AA-AAS, but key challenges remain. They include (1) continuing efforts to scale up use of the model curriculum and instruction materials, leveraging the work being done in the field through collegial networks; (2) building capacity in the field to improve quality of educational services for students with the most complex, challenging disabilities, including those sometimes considered the 10% of the 1%, not only to improve the quality of their lives, but so that we can accurately measure and support their achievement; and (3) the continued need to counter the belief that students with significant cognitive disabilities cannot learn—or benefit from—academic content. The opportunities that result from building a system of curriculum, instruction, and assessment based on how these students learn and then demonstrate what they know can contribute to the "existence proof" to improve outcomes for these students long into the future.

REFERENCES

Altman, J. R., Lazarus, S. S., Quenemoen, R. F., Kearns, J., Quenemoen, M., & Thurlow, M. L. (2010). *2009 survey of states: Accomplishments and new issues at the end of a decade of change.* Minneapolis: University of Minnesota, National Center on Educational Outcomes.

American Educational Research Association, American Psychological Association, & National Council on Measurement in Education. (1999). *Standards for educational and psychological testing.* Washington, DC: Authors.

Bielinski, J., Sheinker, A., & Ysseldyke, J. (2003). *Varied opinions on how to report accommodated test scores: Findings based on CTB/McGraw-Hill's framework for classifying accommodations* (Synthesis Report 49). Minneapolis: University of Minnesota, National Center on Educational Outcomes.

Browder, D. M., Ahlgrim-Delzell, L., Courtade, G., Gibbs, S. L., & Flowers, C. (2008). Evaluation of the effectiveness of an early literacy program for students with significant developmental disabilities. *Exceptional Children, 75*, 33–52.

Browder, D. M., Gibbs, S., Ahlgrim-Delzell, L., Courtade, G. R., Mraz, M., & Flowers, C. (2009). Literacy for students with severe developmental disabilities: What should we teach and what should we hope to achieve? *Remedial and Special Education, 30*(5), 269–282.

Browder, D. M., Jimenez, B. A., Spooner, F., Saunders, A., Hudson, M., & Bethune, K. S. (2012). Early numeracy instruction for students with moderate and severe developmental disabilities. *Research and Practice for Persons with Severe Disabilities, 37,* 1–13.

Browder, D. M., & Spooner, F. (Eds.). (2006). *Teaching language arts, math and science to students with significant cognitive disabilities.* Baltimore: Brookes.

Browder, D. M., & Spooner, F. (2014). More content, more learning, more inclusion. In D. M. Browder & F. Spooner (Eds.), *More language arts, math, and science for students with severe disabilities* (pp. 3–14). Baltimore: Brookes.

Brown v. Board of Education of Topeka, 347 U.S. 483, 74 S. Ct. 686, 98 L. Ed. 873 (1954).

Brown, L., Nietupski, J., & Hamre-Nietupski, S. (1976). Criterion of ultimate functioning. In M. A. Thomas (Ed.), *Hey, don't forget about me!: Education's investment in the severely, profoundly, and multiply handicapped* (pp. 2–15). Reston, VA: Council for Exceptional Children.

Cameto, R., Bergland, F., Knokey, A.-M., Nagle, K. M., Sanford, C., Kalb, S. C., et al. (2010). *Teacher perspectives of school-level implementation of alternate assessments for students with significant cognitive disabilities.* A report from the National Study on Alternate Assessments (NCSER 2010-3007). Menlo Park, CA: SRI International.

Center for K–12 Assessment. (2013, June). *Coming together to raise achievement: New assessments for the Common Core State Standards.* Princeton, NJ: ETS, Center for K–12 Assessment & Performance Management.

Education for All Handicapped Children Act of 1975, PL 94–142, 20 U.S.C., 89 Stat. 773.

Elementary and Secondary Education Act of 1965, PL 89–10, 20 U.S.C. §§ 241 *et seq.*

Flowers, C., Ahlgrim-Delzell, L., Browder, D., & Spooner, F. (2005). Teachers' perceptions of alternate assessments. *Research and Practice for Persons with Severe Disabilities, 30,* 81–92.

Flowers, C., Wakeman, S., Browder, D., & Karvonen, M. (2009). Links for academic learning (LAL): A conceptual model for investigating alignment of alternate assessments based on alternate achievement standards. *Educational Measurement: Issues and Practice, 28*(1), 25–37.

Gong, B., & Marion, S. (2006). *Dealing with flexibility in assessments for students with significant cognitive disabilities* (Synthesis Report 60). Minneapolis: University of Minnesota, National Center on Educational Outcomes.

Hess, K. K. (2011a). E-x-p-a-n-d-e-d learning progressions frameworks for K–12 mathematics: A companion document to the learning progressions frameworks designed for use with the Common Core State Standards in mathematics K–12. Lexington, KY: University of Kentucky, National Alternate Assessment Center. Available at *www.naacpartners.org/publications/MathExpandedLPF.pdf.*

Hess, K. K. (2011b). Learning progressions frameworks designed for use with the Common Core State Standards in English language arts and literacy K–1. Lexington, KY: University of Kentucky, National Alternate Assessment Center. Available at *www.naacpartners.org/publications/ELA_LPF_12.2011_final.pdf.*

Hughes, C., & Carter, E. W. (2008). *Peer buddy programs for successful secondary school inclusion.* Baltimore: Brookes.

Improving America's Schools Act of 1994, PL 103–382, 20 U.S.C. §§ 630 *et seq.*

Individuals with Disabilities Education Act (IDEA) of 1997 amendments, PL 105-17, 20 U.S.C. §§ 1400 *et seq.*

Individuals with Disabilities Education Act (IDEA) of 1997. Preamble 20 U.S.C. § 1400 *et seq.*

Jimenez, B. A., Browder, D. M., Spooner, F., & DiBiase, W. (2012). Inclusive inquiry science using peer-mediated embedded instruction for students with moderate intellectual disabilities. *Exceptional Children, 78,* 301–317.

Kantrowitz, B., & Springen, K. (1997, Oct 6). Why Johnny stayed home: On test days, some schools encourage absences. *Newsweek, 130*(14), 60.

Kearns, J. F., Towles-Reeves, E., Kleinert, H. L., Kleinert, J. O., & Thomas, M. (2011). Characteristics of and implications for students participating in alternate assessments based on alternate academic achievement standards. *Journal of Special Education, 45*(1), 3–14.

Kingston, N. M., & Tiemann, G. C. (2012). Setting performance standards on complex assessments: The body of work method. In G. J. Cizek (Ed.), *Setting performance standards: Foundations, methods, and innovations* (pp. 201–223). New York: Routledge.

Kleinert, H., Browder, D., & Towles-Reeves, E. (2009). Models of cognition for students with significant cognitive disabilities: Implications for assessment. *Review of Educational Research, 79,* 301–326.

Kleinert, H., & Kearns, J. (1999). A validation study of the performance indicators and learner outcomes of Kentucky's alternate assessment for students with significant disabilities. *Journal of the Association for Persons with Severe Handicaps, 24*(2), 100–110.

Kleinert, H., Kennedy, S., & Kearns, J. (1999). Impact of alternate assessments: A statewide teacher survey. *Journal of Special Education, 33*(2), 93–102.

Lazarus, S., Thurlow, M., Christensen, L., & Shyyan, V. (2014). *Successfully transitioning from the AA-MAS to the general assessment* (Policy Directions 22). Minneapolis: University of Minnesota, National Center on Educational Outcomes.

Lewis, D. M., Mitzel, H. C., Mercado, R. L., & Schulz, E. M. (2012). The bookmark standard setting procedure. In C. J. Cizek (Ed.), *Setting performance standards: Foundations, methods, and innovations* (pp. 225–254). New York: Routledge.

Marion, S., & Pellegrino, J. (2006). A validity framework for evaluating the technical quality of alternate assessments. *Educational Measurement: Issues and Practice, 25*(4), 47–57.

McDonnell, J., Mathot-Buckner, C., Thorson, N., & Fister, S. (2001). Supporting the inclusion of students with moderate and severe disabilities in junior high school general education classes: The effects of classwide peer tutoring, multi-element curriculum, and accommodations. *Education and Training of Children, 24,* 141–160.

McDonnell, L. M., McLaughlin, M. J., & Morison, P. (1997). *Educating one and all: Students with disabilities and standards-based reform.* Washington, DC: National Academy Press.

Mills v. Board of Education of District of Columbia, 348 F. Supp. 866 (1972).

Mislevy, R. J., Almond, R. G., & Lukas, J. (2003). *A brief introduction to evidence-centered design* (CSE Technical Report 632). Los Angeles: National Center for Research on Evaluation, Standards, and Student Testing (CRESST).

National Center and State Collaborative. (2014). *The NCSC model for a comprehensive system of curriculum, instruction, and assessment.* Available at *www.ncscpartners.org/Media/Default/PDFs/Resources/Parents/NCSC%20Model%20for%20a%20Comprehensive%20System%20of%20Curriculum%20Instruction%20and%20Assessment%201-6-14%20.pdf.*

National Commission on Excellence in Education. (1983). *Time for results: The imperative for educational reform.* Washington, DC: Author.

National Governors Association. (1986). *Time for results: The governors' 1991 report.* Washington, DC: Author.

Pellegrino, J. W., Chudowsky, N., & Glaser, R. (2001). *Knowing what students know: The science and design of educational assessment.* Washington, DC: National Academy of Sciences.

Pennsylvania Association for Retarded Children (PARC) v. Commonwealth of Pennsylvania, 343 Fed. Supp. 279 (1972).

Phillips, S. E. (1994). High-stakes testing accommodations: Validity versus disabled rights. *Applied Measurement in Education, 7*(2), 93–120.

Quenemoen, R. F. (2009). The long and winding road of alternate assessments: Where we started, where we are now, and the road ahead. In W. D. Schafer & R. W. Lissitz (Eds.), *Alternate assessments based on alternate achievement standards: Policy, practice, and potential* (pp. 127–153). Baltimore: Brookes.

Quenemoen, R. F., Flowers, C., & Forte, E. (2014). The curriculum, instruction, and assessment pieces of the student achievement puzzle. In D. M. Browder & F. Spooner (Eds.), *More language arts, math, and science* (pp. 237–254). Baltimore: Brookes.

Quenemoen, R. F., Kearns, J., Quenemoen, M., Flowers, C., & Kleinert, H. (2010). *Common misperceptions and research-based recommendations for alternate assessment based on alternate achievement standards* (Synthesis Report 73). Minneapolis: University of Minnesota, National Center on Educational Outcomes.

Rigney, S. L. (2009). Public policy and the development of alternate assessments for students with cognitive disabilities. In W. D. Schafer & R. W. Lissitz (Eds.), *Alternate assessments based on alternate achievement standards: Policy, practice, and potential* (pp. 41–59). Baltimore: Brookes.

Roach, A. T., & Elliott, S. N. (2006). The influence of access to the general education curriculum on the alternate assessment performance of students with severe cognitive disabilities. *Educational Evaluation and Policy Analysis, 28,* 181–194.

Ryndak, D. L., Morrison, A. P., & Sommerstein, L. (1999). Literacy before and after inclusion in general education settings: A case study. *Journal of the Association for Persons with Severe Handicaps, 24,* 5–22.

Schafer, W. D., & Lissitz, R. W. (2009). *Alternate assessments based on alternate achievement standards: Policy, practice, and potential.* Baltimore: Brookes.

Shriner, J. G., Spande, G. E., & Thurlow, M. L. (1994). *1993: A report on state activities in the assessment of educational outcomes for students with disabilities.* Minneapolis: University of Minnesota, National Center on Educational Outcomes.

Sireci, S. G. (2005). Unlabeling the disabled: A perspective on flagging scores from accommodated test administrations. *Educational Researcher, 34*(1), 3–12.

Spooner, F., & Browder, D. (2006). Why teach the general curriculum? In D. Browder & F. Spooner (Eds.), *Teaching language arts, math and science to students with significant cognitive disabilities* (pp. 1–13). Baltimore: Brookes.

Thompson, S. J., Johnstone, C. J., Thurlow, M. L., & Altman, J. R. (2005). *2005 state special education outcomes: Steps forward in a decade of change.* Minneapolis: University of Minnesota, National Center on Educational Outcomes.

Thompson, S. J., & Thurlow, M. L. (1999). *1999 state special education outcomes: A report on state activities at the end of the century.* Minneapolis: University of Minnesota, National Center on Educational Outcomes.

Thompson, S. J., & Thurlow, M. L. (2001). *2001 state special education outcomes: A report on state activities at the beginning of a new decade.* Minneapolis: University of Minnesota, National Center on Educational Outcomes.

Thurlow, M. L., Elliott, J. L., & Ysseldyke, J. E. (1998). *Testing students with disabilities: Practical strategies for complying with district and state requirements.* Thousand Oaks, CA: Corwin.

Thurlow, M. L., Quenemoen, R. F., Lazarus, S. S., Moen, R. E., Johnstone, C. J., Liu, K. K., et al. (2008). *A principled approach to accountability assessments for students with disabilities* (Synthesis Report 70). Minneapolis: University of Minnesota, National Center on Educational Outcomes.

Towles-Reeves, E., Kearns, J., Flowers, C., Hart, L., Kerbel, A., Kleinert, H., et al. (2012). *Learner characteristics inventory project report (A product of the NCSC validity evaluation).* Minneapolis: University of Minnesota, National Center and State Collaborative.

Towles-Reeves, E., Kearns, J., Kleinert, H., & Kleinert, J. (2009). An analysis of the learning characteristics of students taking alternate assessments based on alternate achievement standards. *Journal of Special Education, 42*(4), 241–254.

Towles-Reeves, E., Kleinert, H., & Anderman, L. (2008). Alternate assessments based on alternate achievement standards: Principals' perceptions. *Research and Practice for Persons with Severe Disabilities, 33,* 122–133.

U.S. Department of Education. (2003, December). *Standards and assessments: Non-regulatory guidance.* Washington, DC: Author.

Wakeman, S., Flowers, C., & Browder, D. (2007). *Aligning alternate assessments to grade level content standards: Issues and considerations for alternates based on alternate achievement standards* (NCEO Policy Directions No. 19). Minneapolis: University of Minnesota, National Center on Educational Outcomes.

Webb, N. L. (1997). Determining alignment of expectations and assessment in mathematics and science education: NISE Brief 1(2). Available at *www.wcer.wisc.edu/archive/nise/ publications/briefs/vol_1_no_2.*

Ysseldyke, J. E., Algozzine, B., & Thurlow, M. L. (1992). *Critical issues in special education.* Boston: Houghton-Mifflin.

Ysseldyke, J. E., Thurlow, M. L., & Linn, D. (1999). *NGA Brief: Including students with disabilities in statewide assessments and accountability systems.* Washington, DC: National Governors Association.

Ysseldyke, J. E., Thurlow, M. L., McGrew, K. S., & Shriner, J. G. (1994). *Recommendations for making decisions about the participation of students with disabilities in statewide assessment programs* (Synthesis Report 15). Minneapolis: University of Minnesota, National Center on Educational Outcomes.

Zlatos, B. (1994). Don't test, don't tell: Is "academic red-shirting" skewing the way we rank our schools? *American School Board Journal, 181*(11), 24–28.

PART VII

Ongoing Debates and Future Directions

The Times They Are A-Changing, but the Song Remains the Same
Future Issues and Practices in Test Validation

Stephen G. Sireci and Molly Faulkner-Bond

Come gather 'round people
Wherever you roam
And admit that the waters
Around you have grown
And accept it that soon
You'll be drenched to the bone
If your time to you, Is worth savin'
Then you better start swimmin'
Or you'll sink like a stone
For the times they are a-changin.'
—BOB DYLAN, "The Times They Are A-Changin'"[1]

A s we write this Chapter 15 years into the 21st century, the world of educational assessment is full of change. It is the first year the new Race to the Top assessment consortia (groups of states and jurisdictions in the United States that have come together to develop tests that measure new K–12 curriculum standards) administered their tests. The new standards measured by these tests focus on getting students ready for 21st-century colleges and careers, and involve "on-track" or "readiness" benchmarks for students from third through 11th grade. In addition, these consortia tests, like assessments used in licensure and certification, are incorporating technology in exciting ways. The consortia assessments are also being used, or considered for use, to hold public schools accountable in the United States, which may lead to rewards and sanctions for teachers, educational administrators, schools, districts, and

---

[1] "The Times They Are A-Changin'" lyrics copyright © 1963, 1964 by Warner Bros. Inc., renewed 1991, 1992 by Special Rider Music.

states. Clearly, the waters around us have grown, and it appears the times are certainly a-changin' in educational measurement.

But how new and different are these "changes"? One can only answer that question by knowing what has come before. Fortunately, in this book there are several chapters on the history of educational assessment, and others that describe current practices and projections of future practice. Thus, this book provides a unique opportunity for us to review the history of our field through the lens of the present. In this chapter, we relate the current, and somewhat frenetic, trends in educational assessment to the most pressing issues and important developments that have occurred since educational tests came into vogue over 100 years ago. Our motivation behind this inquiry is to learn from the past so that it can inform our future. A key question we ask is, "Are the times really a-changin', or is what we are experiencing essentially the same as what has occurred in the past?" We are hopeful that our field is not an example of what George Santayana envisioned when he wrote, "Those who cannot remember the past are condemned to repeat it" (1905, p. 284).

Current Trends in Educational Assessment: A Look Forward or Backward?

A review of the chapters in this book, current measurement journals, and the popular press uncovers several current "hot topics" in educational assessment. These topics include:

- Using students' performances on tests to evaluate teachers, schools, and others involved in public education.
- Measuring "growth."
- Providing more diagnostic information regarding students' proficiencies.
- Improving the assessment of students with disabilities and English learners.
- Using tests for international comparisons of educational achievement.
- Embedding assessments into instruction for more formative purposes.
- Using technology to improve educational assessments.

A theme across these topics is the desire to have educational tests do more than they have traditionally been called to do. We want to use tests not only to say something about a student, but also to infer something about that student's teacher, principal, school, and district. We want tests to tell us not only how well a student is doing overall in a subject area; we want details about his or her strengths and weaknesses. We want tests to be standardized so that they provide a level playing field for everyone, but we also want them to be flexible enough to accommodate the needs of students who are English learners or who have disabilities. We want to use tests to compare and evaluate students not only within a classroom, but also across states and countries. We want tests not only to measure how well students learn, but also to help them to learn. We want tests to be an interactive experience for students, so we can measure skills beyond those that are measurable in a paper-based format. Clearly, the demands on 21st-century educational tests are daunting.

However, before concluding that we will get "drenched to the bone" by these "waters of change," it is important to remember there are several fundamental constants in educational testing that will not change. For example, although the way we build tests or the way we use their scores may change, the criteria of validity and fairness with which we evaluate such use remains an important constant. In the next section of this chapter, we sort these "hot topics" into five current trends to discuss both current issues and historical constancies within each topic area.

Current Trend 1: Accountability Testing

As Linn (Chapter 18, this volume), Geisinger and Usher-Tate (Chapter 1, this volume) and many others have pointed out, the No Child Left Behind (NCLB) Act of 2001 elevated the role of tests in education reform movements. NCLB originally required all states receiving federal funds for K–12 education to develop math and reading tests aligned with statewide curriculum frameworks in grades 3 through 8, and in one grade in high school. By 2007, science assessments in at least one grade in each of three grade spans (3–5, 6–9, and 10–12) had to be implemented as well. States were also required to establish at least three standards of performance on the assessments, one of which needed to signify "proficient" in the subject area for that grade. Students were classified into proficiency categories based on their test scores, and schools were evaluated for "adequate yearly progress" (AYP) based on how well they were meeting the goal of attaining 100% proficiency for all students by the year 2014. Schools could be rewarded or sanctioned based on their yearly progress. Districts had a similar accountability process.[2] Thus, the inferences from these assessments were generalized beyond the individual student level to support inferences about schools and school districts.

Subsequent federal initiatives increased the use of tests for generalizing from student inferences to inferences at a larger system level. "Flexibility waivers" allowed states to avoid the NCLB requirements if they adopted rigorous curriculum standards (e.g., the Common Core State Standards) and used students' test scores to evaluate teachers (typically by using changes in students' test performance across years as a measure of "growth"; see Keller, Colvin, & Garcia, Chapter 19, this volume). The Race-to-the-Top initiative funded two consortia of states to develop common assessments to measure whether students were "on-track" (below grade 11) or "ready" for college and career. Again, it was implicit that the performance of students on these consortium assessments would be used to evaluate teachers, schools, and school districts.

---

[2] The details of AYP under NCLB are beyond the scope of this chapter; interested readers are referred to Chudowsky and Chudowsky (2005) and the White House (2002).

Test-based accountability systems have been criticized for using test scores beyond the purposes for which they have been validated. The *Standards for Educational and Psychological Testing* (American Educational Research Association [AERA], American Psychological Association [APA], & National Council on Measurement in Education [NCME], 2014) define validity as "the degree to which evidence and theory support the interpretations of test scores for proposed uses of tests" (p. 11). Most, if not all, validity evidence for NCLB assessments focuses on interpreting the proficiency of individual students. Little to no evidence has focused on using aggregations of students' performance, such as "value-added estimates" of teaching effectiveness or "median student growth percentiles" to evaluate teachers, schools, or districts.

This lack of validation of educational tests for accountability purposes is troubling and puts many statewide educational testing programs in violation of the AERA, APA, and NCME (2014) *Standards*, which state:

> An index that is constructed by manipulating and combining test scores should be subjected to the same validity, reliability, and fairness investigations that are expected for the test scores that underline the index. (p. 210)

and:

> Users of information from accountability systems might assume that the accountability indices provide valid indicators of the intended outcomes of education . . ., that the differences among indices can be attributed to differences in the effectiveness of the teacher or school, and that these differences are reasonably stable over time and across students and items. These assumptions must be supported by evidence. (p. 206)

Unfortunately, there is little research to support value-added estimates of teachers' effectiveness (Braun, 2013) or aggregations of student "growth" percentiles (Wells, Sireci, & Bahry, 2014).

The use of tests beyond the individual student level for which they have been validated has amplified traditional criticisms of educational tests. Critics rightly claim that evaluating teachers and schools based on students' test performance does not control for preexisting differences across students assigned to teachers (because the assignment of students to teachers is not random) and does not control for differences in many variables that are known to be associated with achievement, such as socioeconomic status, parental education, and school and community resources. Interestingly, however, the use of tests to evaluate teaching, and criticisms of the practice, are not new developments. The practice itself, and criticisms of it, can be traced to the earliest days of modern educational testing.

Ruch (1929), for example, remarked that the use of tests for evaluating teaching seemed like a good idea at the outset, but was quickly criticized by the National Education Association for not accounting for differences across the students assigned to teachers (p. 12). On determining the causes of differences across teachers, Pressey and Pressey (1922) wrote:

First to be considered is the possibility that the work in one school may be poor because the children in the school are unusually dull and consequently, even with the best of instruction, do not learn readily. . . . A supervisor will do a large injustice to the teachers in a "poor" district of a city if she fails to take account of this factor and attributes to poor teaching what is really due to the poor . . . capacity of the children who are being taught. (p. 28)

The excerpt was written almost 100 years ago, which suggests the times aren't a-changin' as much as we aren't a-learnin'. Pressey and Pressey also advised, "Test results must be used along with, not to the exclusion of, other sources of information" (p. 69). This sounds like sage advice to us, and also sounds remarkably similar to the AERA (2000) "Position Statement; High-Stakes Testing," which relayed the same cautions regarding student testing. We believe, in addition to reminding policymakers and others of the limitations of a single test score, research is needed on sensible and practical methods for combining multiple measures into an accountability system in a manner that takes into account the unique characteristics of each individual, school, and classroom. If student progress based on educational tests is to be a major component of the system, more research is needed on better ways for measuring student progress. Keller, Colvin, and Garcia (Chapter 19, this volume) present some promising ideas in this area.

Current Trend 2: Making Assessments More Accessible

The most recent version of the AERA and colleagues (2014) *Standards* features a much larger chapter on "Fairness" that focuses on issues regarding testing special populations such as examinees with disabilities and linguistic minorities (e.g., English learners). The *Standards* acknowledge fairness can be defined in different ways and state:

This chapter interprets fairness as responsiveness to individual characteristics and testing contexts so that test scores will yield valid interpretations for intended uses. . . . A test that is fair within the meaning of the *Standards* reflects the same construct(s) for all test takers, and scores from it have the same meaning for all individuals in the intended population; a fair test does not advantage or disadvantage some individuals because of characteristics irrelevant to the intended construct. (p. 50)

An important component of fairness is *accessibility*, which the *Standards* define as "the notion that all test takers should have an unobstructed opportunity to demonstrate their standing on the construct(s) being measured" (p. 49). Accessibility is an important issue for many populations of examinees, such as those with disabilities or those who are not fully proficient in the language in which the test is administered [in the United States, this second group is referred to as *English learners* (ELs) (Forte & Faulkner-Bond, 2010)].

A positive recent trend in educational assessment is considering the unique needs of ELs and examinees with disabilities in test development and administration (Thurlow

& Quenemoen, Chapter 24, this volume). The concept of *universal test design* informs test development by minimizing any features of the test that may present barriers to certain groups of examinees (e.g., overly linguistically complex items that may hinder ELs). Universal design can also be applied to testing conditions to make them more flexible so that accommodations are not needed for certain groups. Traditionally, examinees with disabilities applied for and received accommodations to test administration conditions such as extra time, oral administration, or increased font size. Universal design in test administration would involve (1) setting time limits under which virtually all examinees would have sufficient time to complete the test and (2) making other options, such as larger print or oral administration, available for all examinees.

Even with universal design in test development and administration, some examinees may still need accommodations. However, the ubiquitous presence of universal test design and the provision of test accommodations illustrate the serious efforts undertaken by testing agencies to ensure fairness in educational testing. We believe that these *practices* are new, relative to testing in the 20th century, and we appreciate their contribution to fairness in testing. However, it is interesting to note that the *concerns* are not new. For example, Likert (1932), in his famous introduction of survey development that became known as Likert scaling, remarked, "Because a series of statements form a unit or cluster when used with one group of subjects which justifies combining the reactions to the different statements into a single score, it does not follow that they will constitute a unit on all other groups of persons with the same or different cultural backgrounds" (pp. 51–52). Likert's insight was impressive in that he was essentially concerned with measurement invariance across subpopulations of students during a time when racism was more common than fairness. Today, measurement invariance is a fundamental aspect of fairness for educational and psychological assessments (AERA et al., 2014).

Concerns regarding the construct-irrelevant effects of language proficiency have also been around a long time. For example, Pressey and Pressey (1922) cautioned, "The possibility of a language handicap should always be considered in interpreting test results" (p. 67). These excerpts from Likert, and from Pressey and Pressey, were written over 80 years ago, but if the dates beside the citation were missing, most would guess they were far more recent writings. Thus, concerns over fairness are a hallmark of these a-changin' times in educational assessment, as they have been for over 80 years. Happily, the difference now is that practitioners have begun to heed the call, and improvements in test development, test administration, and test validation have made many educational assessments fairer.

Current Trend 3: International and Cross-Lingual Assessment

As the chapters by Allalouf and Hanani (Chapter 15, this volume), van de Vijver and Poortinga (Chapter 16, this volume), and Muñiz, Elosua, Padilla, and Hambleton (Chapter 17, this volume) illustrate, testing people who operate in different languages is becoming increasingly common. The world is becoming smaller, but cultural identity remains strong. Given that language is intimately linked with culture, a global community necessitates a multilingual community. For educational assessments to be useful in a global society, they must, in some sense, transcend language. The need for cross-lingual assessment has made test translation (adaptation) popular, but as the aforementioned chapters attest, it is difficult to ensure that we are measuring the same constructs with equal precision and utility across languages. The *Guidelines* proposed by the International Test Commission (ITC), described by Muñiz and colleagues (Chapter 17, this volume), are extremely helpful in identifying the issues in test development, administration, and validation to be considered in cross-lingual assessment. Emerging adaptation tools, such as those described by Allalouf and Hanani (Chapter 15, this volume) are also encouraging. However, as van de Vijver and Poortinga (Chapter 16, this volume) remind us, we need to be aware of what is lost in cross-lingual assessment relative to assessing examinees within a single language. In our view, the hard work comes in providing cautions with respect to interpretations of cross-lingual test results, and making policymakers and others who interpret the results aware of their limitations.

Rios and Sireci (2014) pointed out that although the ITC *Guidelines* are helpful, they are not enforced, and much of the published literature in cross-lingual assessment makes no reference to them. Thankfully, international educational assessment practices seem better, with the major assessment programs (e.g., Programme for International Student Assessment [PISA], Progress in International Reading Literacy Study [PIRLS], Third International Mathematics and Science Study [TIMSS]) devoting considerable time and resources to test adaptation. Nevertheless, comparisons across countries' performance on these assessments are often made without considering their limitations (Ercikan, Roth, & Asil, 2015). With respect to cross-lingual assessments, it appears the practices are outpacing the validation to support them. Like the use of educational tests for accountability, the lack of balance across use and validation is troubling.

Current Trend 4: Using Technology to Improve Assessment

Way and Robin (Chapter 11, this volume) provided a comprehensive review of the history of computer-based assessment, and Mills and Breithaupt (Chapter 12, this volume), von Davier and Mislevy (Chapter 14, this volume), and Zenisky and Luecht (Chapter 13, this volume) described exciting new developments in this area. It is hard to keep up with developments in computer-based testing because the technology evolves faster than we can write about it. Currently, technology is being used to determine the most appropriate sets of items to administer to individual examinees (i.e., computerized-adaptive testing), to expand what we can measure beyond what is possible in a paper-based environment (e.g., research skills; Mills & Breithaupt, Chapter 12, this volume); to embed video and other media into assessments; and to engage, motivate, and accommodate specific subpopulations of examinees (e.g., students with disabilities).

Technology has always been a big part of large-scale educational assessment. In fact, Reynold Johnson's invention of the scanner that could read and score "bubble sheets" in 1931 made large-scale assessment possible and popularized the multiple-choice item. However, of the five current trends we identified, using technology to improve assessment stands out as the one that is most a-changin'. Educational assessments may lag far behind the use of technology in other areas—such as entertainment or surveillance—but current tests that incorporate technology are very different from 20th-century tests. A key development in technology-enhanced assessments is the ability of the computer to "learn" something about an examinee. Adaptive testing is one example, whereby the test adjusts its difficulty to best match the estimated proficiency of an examinee. But the computer can also be used to provide supports such as encouragement or accommodations, if it "senses" that the examinee needs them. We are impressed with current developments in computer-based assessments (e.g., see Mills & Breithaupt, Chapter 12, this volume), and we anticipate further benefits of incorporating technology into assessments, such as integrating instruction and assessment, and making tests more "fun" for examinees by giving them more control over the assessment experience (e.g., choosing avatars to represent themselves, pausing the assessment to access tutorials; see Drasgow, 2015, for further descriptions of technology-enhanced assessment).

Current Trend 5: Improved Score Reporting and Diagnostic Assessment

As the use of testing increases, focus has also increased on how scores from assessments are interpreted and reported for consumption by various audiences. This interest has been driven by examinees and test users (e.g., institutions, professional organizations, educators) alike, all of whom have a vested interest in a clear understanding of what test scores mean about examinee ability. As Zenisky, Mazzeo, and Pitoniak (Chapter 20, this volume) discuss, the practice of score reporting matured considerably in the last quarter of the 20th century, with assessment developers attending increasingly to design and audience as they sought to report test information in ways that are clearer, more useful, and more tailored for a variety of users.

Like assessment, score reporting also stands to benefit from the transition to digital platforms, where navigation tools and dynamic presentation methods make it possible for users to call up additional information to help them understand and interact with scores in real time based on their particular interests. Zenisky and colleagues (Chapter 20, this volume) also documented how the National Assessment of Educational Progress (NAEP) program took advantage of digital and online functionalities to enhance the breadth, depth, and utility of information reported from those assessments. In this century, online score reporting is likely to become increasingly common, as more K–12 summative and formative assessments are administered and scored on digital platforms.

A related area of interest is extracting and communicating more meaning from test scores about examinees' strengths and weaknesses. Particularly for examinees who score poorly, this type of diagnostic information is often cited as an important tool to help them improve their future performance. Providing such information touches on not only score interpretation and report design, but also on assessment design itself. As Ackerman and Henson (Chapter 9, this volume) note, diagnostic classification models (DCMs) typically require an assessment that taps multiple abilities or dimensions, which could be built and scored using advanced techniques such as multidimensional item response theory (MIRT). These types of models have garnered increasing interest and research in the 21st century as psychometricians work to develop assessments that can produce reliable, valid, and usable diagnostic information that can be reported to students, instructors, parents, examinees, and other stakeholders. However, it should be noted that the "new" idea of MIRT dates back at least 40 years to the work of Mulaik (1972) and Reckase (1972), and has its origins in the work of Spearman (1904) and Thurstone (1935).

Current Trend 6: Embedded and Formative Assessment

In the first quarter of the 21st century, one of the most "futuristic" phrases one can utter is *stealth assessment*. This approach, in which assessment items are embedded within a nontest context (e.g., a game, a lesson, a simulation) allows test users to collect information about examinees in ways that purport to be authentic and noninvasive. Such assessments are often presented as a promising tool for instructors and learners alike, as they may be able to provide finer-grained details about an examinee's progress and ability in a shorter time frame, and via means that are more instructionally relevant and actionable.

As with score reporting and diagnostic assessment, technological advances have made stealth assessment seem like a plausible reality only recently. In particular, computers offer a convenient way to surreptitiously collect examinee process and response information without announcing that this is happening—thereby creating the potential to reduce testing time and anxiety, and boost examinee engagement and task authenticity.

Stealth assessment does present a number of measurement challenges, but advances in these areas have also proliferated since the turn of the 21st century, as von Davier and Mislevy discuss (Chapter 14, this volume). The vast amounts of process data produced by stealth assessment require new and more flexible measurement models that, in particular, are flexible or agnostic with respect to dimensionality and error distribution. Even prior to the use of such models, examinee actions in simulation- and game-based assessments must be meaningfully parceled and assigned with values; this process also requires advanced measurement and computing, as von Davier and Mislevy discuss.

Stealth assessment sounds, in many ways, like one area of assessment that truly is new and futuristic. Without the technological and methodological bells and whistles of the 21st century, however, stealth assessment is really a combination of two relatively "old" ideas in assessment: formative assessment and embedded assessment.

Constancies

Aside from technology-enhanced assessment, the other trends we identified as "current" have historical roots that, once realized, make them seem long-standing. Thus, with respect to using tests for accountability purposes, for cross-lingual/cross-cultural assessment purposes, and for improving instruction, it may seem more like the assessment song has remained the same, rather than the testing times are a-changin'. One reason for these constancies is that the fields of education and psychology, from which the science of psychometrics emerged, have long histories of concern over validity.

Since the earliest days of modern testing there has been a great awareness of the limitations of tests and the need to be explicit about what test scores represent, and what they do not represent. There have been debates for sure, with some proclaiming that tests can do more than what validity evidence might suggest, and others who claim that test scores held little utility. But these debates led to progress. For example, due to debates over what *validity* means and how tests should be validated, the three major professional associations most involved in testing practices and research came together to create standards for test development, administration, and interpretation.

The first version of the joint testing standards (APA, 1954) stated, "Validity information indicates to the test user the degree to which the test is capable of achieving certain aims" (p. 13)—which is similar to the AERA and colleagues (2014) edition (which represents the sixth version of these joint *Standards*) that describes validity as the degree to which evidence and theory support the use of a test for a particular purpose. A review of the evolution of these *Standards* indicates that the educational and psychometric professions have consistently demanded evidence that a test measures what it purports to measure and that the use of test scores is justified based on evidence that the test scores are appropriate for that use (Sireci, 2009). To illustrate this constant concern regarding the need to justify test use with evidence, we present two quotes on this topic. These two quotes were written about 60 years apart. We challenge readers to identify which is the more recent writing.

> Validity is not a property of the test. Rather, it is a property of the proposed interpretations and uses of the test scores. Interpretations and uses that make sense and are supported by appropriate evidence are considered to have high validity (or for short, to be valid). . . .

> No [technical] manual should report that "this test is valid." . . . The manual should report the validity of each type of inference for which a test is recommended. If validity of some recommended interpretation has not been tested, that fact should be made clear.

The first quote is from Kane (2013, p. 3); the second is from APA (1954, p. 19). A review of the history of validity reveals fundamental constants (Sireci, 2009, 2015) that apply not only to traditional test score interpretations that pertain to individuals, but also to aggregations of test scores that are used for accountability purposes.

Another constancy in the field of educational testing is criticism of that very testing. It is important for the testing community to embrace criticisms because they may point to deficiencies in tests or in testing policies that could be addressed, and thereby improve educational assessments. However, like the other "current events" in educational testing, criticisms of tests are not new. What might the most common criticisms be? We could review current newspapers and education blogs, or perhaps revisit this list of criticisms put together by Odell (1928):

   I. Examinations are injurious to the health of those taking them, causing overstrain, nervousness, worry, and other undesirable physical and mental results.

  II. The content covered by examination questions does not agree with the recognized objectives of education, but instead encourages cramming, mere factual memorizing, and acquiring items of information rather than careful and conscientious study, reasoning, and other higher thought processes.

 III. Examinations too often become objectives in themselves, the pupils believing the chief purpose of study is to pass examinations rather than to master the subject or gain mental power.

  IV. Examinations encourage bluffing and cheating.

   V. Examinations develop habits of careless use of English and poor handwriting.

  VI. The time devoted to examinations can be more ably used otherwise, for more study, recitation, review, and so forth.

 VII. The results of instruction in the field of education are intangible and cannot be measured as can products in industry.

VIII. Examinations are unnecessary. Capable instructors handling classes which are not too large are able to rate the work of their pupils without employing examinations.

Current critics may use newer terms such as *teaching to the test,* but it is remarkable how the spirit of the criticisms raised in 1928 is essentially the same as those raised in 2015.

Concluding Remarks

In this chapter, we reviewed current trends in educational testing and illustrated that many of them have roots deep into the earliest days of modern testing. Our review brings the adage "The more things change, the more they stay the same" to mind.

However, as the collection of chapters in this book illustrates, great progress has been made in the science and practice of educational measurement. On the science side, new measurement models such as developments in IRT and cognitive modeling have improved the precision and efficiency of our measures and enhanced test score interpretations. On the practice side, concerns for testing fairness are now incorporated into test development, and are manifested through statistical procedures such as differential item functioning (DIF) analysis, quality-control procedures such as sensitivity review, and through validation efforts such as differential predictive validity and measurement invariance studies. In addition, test administration conditions have become more flexible, and great strides have been made in the area of providing test accommodations to examinees who need them, while maintaining fidelity to the construct measured (Abedi & Ewers, 2013).

Although we acknowledge the great strides made in measurement theory and practices, our historical review also points to areas greatly in need of improvement. First, the use of tests for multiple purposes has far outpaced validity studies to evaluate or justify such use. Therefore, we recommend that (a) much more research be conducted on derivative measures such as value-added estimates and "growth" percentiles used for accountability purposes, and (b) these and other newer metrics *not* be used until there is a substantial research base to support such use. Although the amount of research in this area may seem daunting, Cronbach (1988) noted that if we all work together, we can make great progress. As he put it:

> Fortunately, validators are also a community. That enables members to divide up the investigative and educative burden according to their talents, motives, and political ideals. Validation will progress in proportion as we collectively do our damnedest—no holds barred—with our minds and our hearts. (p. 14)

Another area where more progress is needed is in measuring the academic progress of students. Twenty-first century educational tests should be able to quantify how much a student has learned over the course of a school year, but we seem to have great trouble doing so. Keller, Colvin, and Garcia (Chapter 19, this volume) provide one example of research needed in this area, but clearly more needs to be done.

A third area where we anticipate greater progress in the near future is using technology not only to improve educational assessments, but also to make the assessment experience more enjoyable for examinees. Although a "fun test" may presently seem like an oxymoron, technology can be used to make tests more personal for examinees (e.g., choose an avatar, scene, decide when to pause), and the opportunity for gamification to make tests more engaging, and to integrate them with instruction, is strong.

In closing, we note that the field of educational measurement has an interesting history that is founded on a concern for the legitimacy of what we are measuring, appropriate due process for examinees, and evaluation of the degree to which the goals of the assessment are met. Much progress has been made, critical aspects of validity and fairness have endured, and the field remains one with many interesting problems to tackle. Thankfully, as the contributors to this volume and those who attended the

Ronference illustrate, there are many creative and talented people in our community to move this field forward. We thank our friend and colleague, Professor Ron Hambleton, for enlightening us on the important problems in educational measurement, and encouraging us to solve them. One "song" that has remained the same over the last 40 years is Ron's commitment not only to educational measurement, but also to the mentorship of us all. For that, we remain grateful.

REFERENCES

Abedi, J., & Ewers, N. (2013). *Accommodations for English learners and students with disabilities: A research based decision algorithm.* Smarter Balanced Assessment Consortium.

American Educational Research Association. (2000, July). AERA position statement: High-stakes testing in preK–12 education. Retrieved February 19, 2015, from *www.aera.net/AboutAERA/AERARulesPolicies/AssociationPolicies/PositionStatementonHighStakesTesting/tabid/11083/Default.aspx.*

American Educational Research Association, American Psychological Association, & National Council on Measurement in Education. (2014). *Standards for educational and psychological testing.* Washington, DC: Authors.

American Psychological Association. (1954). Technical recommendations for psychological tests and diagnostic techniques. *Psychological Bulletin, 51*(2, Suppl.).

Braun, H. (2013). Value-added modeling and the power of magical thinking. *Applied Measurement in Education, 21,* 115–130.

Chudowsky, N., & Chudowsky, V. (2005, March). *Identifying school districts for improvement and corrective action.* Washington, DC: Center for Education Policy. Retrieved January 28, 2006, from *www.ctredpol.org/nclb.*

Cronbach, L. J. (1988). Five perspectives on the validity argument. In H. Wainer & H. I. Braun (Eds.), *Test validity* (pp. 3–17). Hillsdale, NJ: Erlbaum.

Dragow, F. (Ed.). (2015). *Technology and testing.* New York: Routledge.

Ercikan, K., Roth, W.-M., & Asil, M. (2015). Cautions about inferences from international assessments: The case of PISA 2009. *Teachers College Record, 117*(1), 1–28. Retrieved March 3, 2015, from *www.tcrecord.org.*

Forte, E., & Faulkner-Bond, M. (2010). *The administrators' guide to federal programs for English learners.* Washington, DC: Thompson.

Kane, M. (2013). Validating the interpretations and uses of test scores. *Journal of Educational Measurement, 50,* 1–73.

Likert, R. (1932). A technique for the measurement of attitudes. *Archives of Psychology, 140,* 44–53.

Mulaik, S. A. (1972, July). *A mathematical investigation of some multidimensional Rasch models for psychological tests.* Paper presented at the annual meeting of the Psychometric Society, Princeton, NJ.

Odell, C. W. (1928). *Traditional examinations and new-type tests.* New York: Century.

Pressey, S. L., & Pressey, L. C. (1922). *Introduction to the use of standard tests: A brief manual in the use of tests of both ability and achievement in the school subjects.* Yonkers-on-Hudson, NY: World Book.

Reckase, M. D. (1972). *Development and application of a multivariate logistic latent trait model.* Unpublished doctoral dissertation, Syracuse University, Syracuse, NY.

Rios, J. A., & Sireci, S. G., (2014). Guidelines versus practices in cross-lingual assessment: A disconcerting disconnect. *International Journal of Testing, 14,* 289–312.

Ruch, G. M. (1929). *The objective or new type examination.* Chicago: Scott Foresman.

Santayana, G. (1905). *The life of reason: Reason in common sense.* New York: Scribner's.

Sireci, S. G. (2009). Packing and upacking sources of validity evidence: History repeats itself again. In R. Lissitz (Ed.), *The concept of validity: Revisions, new directions and applications* (pp. 19–37). Charlotte, NC: Information Age.

Sireci, S. G. (2015). On the validity of useless tests. *Assessment in Education: Principles, Policy, and Practice.*

Spearman, C. (1904). General intelligence: Objectively determined and measured. *American Journal of Psychology, 15,* 201–293.

Thurstone, L. L. (1935). *The vectors of mind: Multiple-factor analysis for the isolation of primary traits.* Chicago: University of Chicago Press.

Wells, C. S., Sireci, S. G., & Bahry, L. (2014, April). *Estimating the amount of error in student growth percentiles.* Paper presented at the annual meeting of the National Council on Measurement in Education, Philadelphia.

White House. (2002). *No child left behind.* Retrieved January 30, 2006, from *www.whitehouse.gov/news/reports/no-child-left-behind.html.*

Epilogue
A History of Ronald K. Hambleton

Else Hambleton

The conference program at the 2012 "Ronference" to honor Ronald K. Hambleton included a long, heartfelt personal history by "the other Doctor Hambleton," Ron's wife, Else. Through 50 years of marriage (the couple's 50th anniversary is June 2016, shortly after this book's initial publication), Else has accompanied Ron to conferences, workshops, and awards ceremonies around the world, and she counts as personal friends some of our field's most preeminent and influential scholars. In addition to revealing some little-known secrets about Ron (such as his early plans to play professional hockey), Else's personal history also helps to put a face on Ron and many other individuals who have shaped and led the development and implementation of modern testing over the past half century. We include an excerpt of Else's history here in an effort both to honor her contribution to Ron's life and the measurement field, and to share her warm and personal depictions of Ron and his colleagues over the years. Psychometricians, as it turns out, are people too.—THE EDITORS

My version of Ron's life is unabashedly biased, selective, impressionistic, affectionate, and nontechnical. Everyone who attended the Ronference knows more about Ron's research contributions to the field of educational and psychological testing than I do, but 48 years of marriage have given me some insight into his character and a ringside seat to his career. (Ron suggested I add here that I wouldn't know how to use the phrase "item response theory" in a sentence—but I would.) I am going to focus on his early years as a professor because they are the least known and the most formative of his career.

Ronald K. Hambleton, pictured in his office at the University of Massachusetts Amherst.

Ron was born June 27, 1943, in Hamilton, Ontario, Canada. His mother, Ethel Ralph, immigrated to Canada from Scotland with her family when she was a child. Ron's father, Kenneth Hambleton, was an English airman, who trained with the Royal Air Force at Mount Hope, near Hamilton. In 1944, Ron, his sister Carol, and his mother boarded a ship filled with Canadian war brides and sailed to wartime England in a military convoy. In 1948 they returned to Hamilton where Ethel's parents and sisters lived. When Ron was in grade 9, his father, who worked as an auto mechanic, died. As I am writing this history of Ron, Ethel is 95 years old, still feisty, lucid, and very proud of her son. Not that she would tell him, but she tells strangers on airplanes, the way I do, about her son, the professor. Watching her with our sons, I have gained insight into the origin of Ron's strong work ethic. When our sons were toddlers and built a house of blocks, I would say to them, "What a wonderful house!" Ethel would say, "You can do better than that," and they would start building again. Ron was educated in the Hamilton public schools from kindergarten through grade 13.

Ron and I met as undergraduates at the University of Waterloo, which recruited mathematics students like Big Ten universities recruit football players. The university administered a grade 13 high school mathematics competition that enabled Waterloo to identify the most talented high school graduates. As undergraduates, Ron and his classmates had their own office in the university library where they played bridge, wrote the Waterloo Fortran compiler (WatFor), published papers in math journals, and, in general, epitomized 1960s nerd-dom. Most of his classmates went on to Ph.D. programs in pure mathematics. Ron was a good student, but had trouble equaling many of his classmates in mathematics, who besides being amazingly good students, all seemed disconnected from reality.

When Ron was a senior he started to think seriously about graduate school. He was recruited by the University of Toronto, which offered him a summer position after graduation and an assistantship for the fall to study psychometrics with a new professor whom they had just hired from McGill University: Ross Traub. He was also interested in computer science, and the University of Waterloo had a very strong program. That he chose psychometrics, I attribute partially to the fact that I didn't get the teaching job I applied for in the Waterloo area—although the school principal who interviewed me, when he learned that my fiancé was about to graduate from Waterloo with a BA in mathematics, accompanied me back to the waiting room and offered Ron a job teaching high school math!

We graduated from the University of Waterloo in May 1966 and were married in June. Ron started work with his graduate advisor, Ross Traub. Dr. Traub, as we called him for the 3 years Ron spent at the University of Toronto (Canadians were formal in the sixties), was the best possible mentor for Ron. Ross was, and still is, a creative thinker, a hard worker, and kind. Ross modeled professorial virtues in a way that reinforced Ron's work ethic, creativity, and desire to serve as a mentor himself. For Ross's retirement party, Ron's graduate students developed a psychometric genealogy with Harold Gulliksen of Princeton who had taught Ross—and through Ross, Ron and Hariharan Swaminathan (better known as Swami)—a connection the students enjoyed being able to make. Ross taught Ron to write, too. He made Ron write, rewrite, and write again until Ron learned to string words together to journal standards. Ross's first wife, Irene, died far too young from breast cancer, but in the same way that Ron admired and sought to emulate Ross Traub, I wanted to be the kind of person Irene Traub was.

Hariharan Swaminathan arrived at the University of Toronto in September 1966, and he and Ron began their long collaboration, first as students, then as faculty together at the University of Massachusetts (UMass) Amherst. You could say that 1966 was a formative year for Ron: He met Ross Traub and Swami and he married me. In 1967 the Toronto Maple Leafs won the Stanley Cup and it was all downhill after that for them. Fortunately, we went the other direction.

The University of Toronto met and exceeded all of Ron's expectations. One of his strengths is his ability to see practical applications for abstract formulations, and the university was a good fit for his talents. He did most of his work with Ross Traub, but he also studied with Rod McDonald, Les McLean, Glen Evans (who later returned to Australia), and Shizuhiko Nishisato. Of the students, I remember Swami, of course, Bikkar (Randy) Randawa, Stan Halliwell, Martin Herbert, Michel Trahan, Wilfred Futcher, and Paul Barbuto. Swami and Randy introduced the rest of the students to Indian food, and Ron and Swami began their lifelong competition to see who could eat the hottest food. They also golfed. The students and Ross sometimes played 81 holes on summer Fridays, Saturdays, and Sundays with much macho wringing of blood from socks due to blisters. I think Ross was the only one who knew how to play.

Ron worked very hard in graduate school. I can't remember an evening we didn't go by the University of Toronto computer center to pick up or drop off a box of computer cards. Then it was back to the university computing center the next morning to pick up completed jobs. For two summers we took 2-week holidays after the Labor Day weekend camping in Canada's Maritime Provinces and New England. Ron was never able to stay away from his work for that length of time. There would come a day, usually after about a week, when Ron just couldn't relax a moment longer, when he needed to get back to his work because he missed it, and we'd take down the tent and pack the car in Halifax, or Charlottetown, or Newfoundland, and start a marathon drive home.

It was always fun going to his office in the evening because it was located a few blocks from the University of Toronto in Yorkville, the Haight Ashbury of Toronto. Neil Young and Joni Mitchell had played in Yorkville coffee clubs prior to 1964 and The Band had played with Rockin' Ronnie Hawkins in a club up the street from Ron's building until they left to back up Bob Dylan when he went electric. By 1966, however, when we arrived, all but Rockin' Ronnie Hawkins had moved on and most weekend nights while Ron worked, Yorkville was clogged with flower children, wannabe hippies, teenage runaways, draft dodgers, and gawking suburbanites cruising by slowly taking in the scene or looking for their teenagers.

In the spring of 1969 Ron started job hunting. Watching today's graduate students choose among an array of amazing options, from certification groups, state departments of education, and universities, I realize with surprise that it never occurred to us that Ron would do anything other than teach. We had always assumed that it would be at the University of Alberta in Edmonton, which at that time housed Canada's other major psychometric program after the University of Toronto. Alberta offered Ron a job, but so did UMass. That first trip to UMass in the spring of 1969 is still very clear in my mind. UMass offered Ron a job the day we visited, and as we drove away from the School of Education, Ron told me, in awed tones, that they had offered him the munificent sum of $13,400. I think it was $900 more than the University of Alberta offered. That seemed like a huge amount of money to us. We were stunned by the value they were assigning to Ron. UMass courted Ron with phone calls most Sundays for the next month. We were seduced by the friendliness of the people in the dean's office and the idea of living in a New England college town for a few years, after which we planned to return to Canada and the University of Alberta.

Immigrating to the United States during the Vietnam War was not simple. Since Canada provided a welcome refuge for draft dodgers, the United States responded by closing the border to incoming Canadians. In late August, with no Green Card in sight, and me pregnant and having left my job with the Ontario government, UMass came up with a plan. Senator Ted Kennedy's office got Ron a Social Security number. He was a legal employee of UMass at the same time as we were residing illegally in the United States. This situation made for some difficult border crossings. The following summer Ron was given a Green Card. By then our first son, Kenneth, had been born.

If push had come to shove, we decided our 1-year-old son could sponsor our immigration! Remembering our travails makes me sympathetic to the illegal immigrants of today. We met with only kindness; faculty loaned us furniture because we were afraid to draw attention to ourselves by bringing our furniture across the border, and L & H Electronics, a Northampton store, gave us a television set, trusting us to come back to pay for it when Ron got his first paycheck!

If we had grandiose notions of what being a university professor meant, they were quickly deflated. Ron was given an office but it was empty. He foraged for a metal desk (which he still uses), and found a file cabinet and some book shelves in one of the halls. Dr. Traub had not become "Ross" to Ron until he defended his dissertation, but Ron was "Ron" from the first day with his American graduate students.

Shortly before Ron graduated from the University of Toronto, we were invited to dinner at Ross and Irene's apartment to meet Mel Novick. That was an exercise in terror for me. I was very nervous, and I hope I have never inspired the same feeling in any of Ron's students' significant others. Ron was so attached to Lord and Novick's *Statistical Theories of Mental Test Scores* that he had two copies. He kept one at home and one at school so he would never be without it. Two years later, Dr. Novick (calling him *Mel* was always hard for me) phoned Ron. At that time we lived in Townhouse of Amherst, on Meadow Street. It was home to many junior faculty who were saving to buy their first house, including Swami and David Berliner. Now it is a locally notorious party spot for UMass undergraduates. Ron was almost as nervous as I had been those 2 years prior. Dr. Novick invited him to spend time in the summers of 1971 and 1972 with him at American College Testing (ACT) in Iowa City, and together they produced one of the first papers in which anyone other than Jim Popham had tried to describe measurement principles for criterion-referenced testing. This paper was a huge boost to Ron's career and led to many opportunities to publish other work.

It is not well-known now, but Ron's thesis topic and first publications were about the Rasch model. Since he was rather critical of the Rasch model, his publications did not win him many friends. In the early years of his career, attending the National Council on Measurement in Education (NCME) meetings were not much fun because of the resulting controversy. But he put up a good fight, and for the second time in his career, post-Dr. Novick, his research generated many invitations to publish papers, attend meetings, and do consulting. Now we number many Rasch modelers among our friends.

In 1973, the summer after our second son, Charles, was born, I was hospitalized in Toronto with congestive heart failure. A virus had eaten much of my heart muscle, and at that time the only cure was bed rest—years of it. Ron found himself with a wife in uncertain health and two young sons. We didn't know when I would be strong enough to travel back to Amherst. Ron didn't have tenure, and Dean Dwight Allen could have cut him loose. Instead, Dean Allen told Ron to take the fall semester off, not to worry about his salary—it would be paid—and to bring his family back to Amherst when he could. Dean Allen's thoughtfulness at a difficult time meant the world to Ron. He was back in the classroom in October with a new dimension to his work. Teaching and research became his refuge. It was a safe place where he could control the outcome, where hard work would be rewarded, and where he could lose himself in his work.

In 2003, 30 years later, we learned I needed a heart transplant. As part of the heart transplant protocol, we had to undergo psychological testing together to prove our marriage could withstand the stress. After we were accepted into the program, we learned of an experimental machine, a cardioverter, which had just become available. I am on my second cardioverter now. Not many people can say they have a stronger heart at 69 than they had at 29, but I can. You all know Ron's prodigious work output. I know the number of times I've woken up in a hospital and he has been there—working, but always there. Bob Linn has been helpful many times in Ron's career, and he has provided Ron with much needed medical advice and assurance over the years.

Swami joined Ron at UMass when he graduated from the University of Toronto in 1971. Each reinforced the other's strengths, and they worked well together because they liked and respected each other and had complementary personalities. Swami was the thinker of the two; Ron was more energetic; both were committed teachers. Swami seemed to be natural at teaching; Ron worked every weekend to prepare his classes. Together they built a strong program in measurement and statistics at UMass—the Research in Educational Measurement and Psychometrics (REMP) concentration. As well as teaching together for 30 years at UMass, they roomed together at NCME and other conferences for many years. Ron was always impressed by Swami's skill with an iron and his desire to press his pants. Swami saved Ron a lot of money too. He lived in a beautiful and carefully planned house and had a Mercedes with a sunroof before sunroofs became standard. When I had a yen for luxury, we would sit in Swami's house and ride in his car. I still remember clearly driving back from dinner in Northampton on a warm summer night with the sunroof open, looking at the stars. His daughter, Anitra, and son, Hamenth, were the closest thing to relatives our sons had in town, and we spent many happy times together.

Ron and Swami were joined at UMass by Steve Sireci in 1994. Any fears that Swami's retirement would leave an irreplaceable gap in the program have been assuaged by the arrival of first Steve, and then Lisa Keller, Craig Wells, Jennifer Randall, and April L. Zenisky. Steve is creative, committed, and very hard working. I think Ron now works sometimes simply to try and keep up with Steve and the other faculty. Lisa and April, of course, were formerly students in the program, and it has been rewarding to watch them grow from graduate students to respected professionals, wives, and mothers. It is different without Swami, but the growth in the program has been exponential. It is bigger—and younger, equally vital. I still enjoy watching Ron and Swami together at NCME.

In the 1990s I decided to go to graduate school. I think I put it to Ron as, "I'm going to buy a sports car and become a graduate student." This meant I had to take the Graduate Record Examination (GRE). I had managed to convince Ron that I was clever—but if I wasn't, I would be exposed. Not many husbands are as uniquely qualified to interpret a GRE score. Fortunately, my verbal score was very good. I was impressed with myself. It might not have gotten me into REMP; I have no quantitative skills, but it got me into the history department at UMass, where I gained a reputation as a "quant," merely because I could compute a mean and a median and make a frequency diagram. During my years in the history department I gained a greater appreciation for the family atmosphere and esprit de corps that Ron and Swami and later, Steve, had created. I had taken for granted that professors and students collaborated on research, that students worked together cooperatively, that lifelong friendships were created, and that former students took an active role in mentoring and helping to find employment for current students.

The history department was different. The professors were writing books, not papers, there were few jobs available for newly minted PhDs, and students worked on dissimilar research in isolation. This was fine for me; I didn't need a lot of guidance, and I had wonderful professors, but it didn't have the family atmosphere I like to think existed and still exists in REMP. While I was a graduate student I enjoyed visiting with Ron's students at their parties. We could grouse together about how unreasonable our professors' expectations were or about how many assignments and readings we had to do, but I got the feeling that they thought their lot was pretty good. The day I defended my dissertation, Swami had a party at his house. There was so much good feeling there, I like to think my committee who attended the party realized there was something lacking in the history department model for graduate training.

While I was a graduate student I had a teaching assistantship. As such, I was responsible for writing and grading undergraduate exams. This was both good and bad. The good was the exam that Jay Millman and Ron wrote for me one weekend when we were visiting Jay and Meredith in Ithaca, New York. Part essay questions, part multiple-choice questions, I think it was probably the best exam ever constructed and administered in the history department. The bad was the professor who wanted me to grade on the curve. A median student in his class, he said, would be a C-minus student. I was into criterion-referenced testing.[1] I told the students what I expected them to know by the end of the course and said that if they knew it, they would get an A. Compromise was required. I think the professor, who should remain unnamed, looked the other way when I submitted the grades. Jay Millman and Jim Popham would have been proud of me. Ron was, and he had been prepared to throw around his new title as Distinguished University Professor, if that was needed.

Ron has always been very secretive about sabbaticals because he likes Amherst. He's most happy moving from home office to school office and keeping busy at the university with his teaching, research, and advising. He has only spent two semesters away from UMass in 43 years of teaching. We spent a fall semester at the University of Leiden in the Netherlands when our sons were 8 and 10. The faculty in Leiden took morning and afternoon coffee breaks to discuss their research with each other. On the weekends, the university was closed. Ron had a special key to his office building so he could go into work on the weekends. The only problem was that the University of

---

[1] I have learned a great deal about psychometrics from Ron and his colleagues and friends. For example, I have bored countless strangers on planes by explaining the difference between norm-referenced tests and criterion-referenced tests. I tell them that a norm-referenced test can rank surgeons from best to worst, but a criterion-referenced test can provide a range of surgeons all eminently qualified to take out their appendix. I learned this from Jim Popham and Jay Millman.

Leiden would not heat the building on the weekend, and it got too cold even for him. Fortunately that coincided with the start of our sons' Dutch hockey season.

In the fall of 1991 we spent a spring semester at the University of Ottawa. In a sense, this was our consolation prize, because it came as our sons had finished high school, and although we were very happy at UMass, there had always been a part of us that saw a Canadian university as our ultimate future. Ottawa is our favorite Canadian city. Marvin Boss was retiring from the University of Ottawa, and he encouraged Ron to accept a position. Decision time coincided with NCME's annual meeting. It met in Boston that year, and it was Ron's presidential year. Ron's graduate students, past and present, arranged a dinner in which approximately 50 students and spouses attended, and we were reminded of all that we would have to leave behind. On the drive back to Amherst, we decided that we weren't leaving UMass for longer than a semester. We spent the next spring in Ottawa, but every second week we drove back to Amherst so Ron could meet with his students, and that semester he taught both at the University of Ottawa and UMass. He isn't very good at sabbaticals.

He manages shorter periods away from UMass better. We enjoyed many visits with Wim and Tonneke van der Linden at the University of Twente in the Netherlands over the years. Now we enjoy seeing them in Monterey, California. José Muñiz, of the University of Oviedo, introduced us to Spain, to Spanish psychometricians, but most especially to Spanish food and wine. It is with José that Ron is most able to live in the moment, not making mental lists in his head or worrying about how many papers, reviews, or letters of recommendation are overdue. It helps that José takes us to Rioja, and we drink a lot of very good wine together.

We have made frequent visits to the University of Umea in Sweden, although it is telling that our favorite restaurant there is a tapas bar. For years we worried that it wouldn't be there on our next visit; now we worry whether or not we'll be able to get a table. Ingemar Wedman, who headed the measurement program in Umea, was a very good friend of Ron. He visited Amherst with Sten Henyrssen, in the late 70s, and they, along with the graduate students of the time, and Swami and some of our graduate students, drank so much wine midafternoon that no one was fit to drive them to the airport afterward. It was one of our happiest moments. I think Linda Cook, Dan Eignor, and Leah Hutten were part of the festivities. Later Ingemar and his wife Anita spent a sabbatical year in Amherst. Their son, Jonathan, whom we knew well as a child, is now a graduate student in psychometrics at the University of Umea, and we enjoy seeing him (as I am writing this Epilogue, it seems important to me to add that Jonathan is visiting UMass). In more recent years we have come to know many people at the University of Umea. One summer, they humored Ron by taking him fishing—he caught a very big fish. Christine Stage and her husband Jorn have been especially good friends over the years. Ron continues to conduct research with faculty at the university and as recently as last year, he was teaching there.

I would be remiss if I did not mention Ron's relationship with hockey. He planned to play professional hockey for the Toronto Maple Leafs. He was too short, however, and he couldn't skate. Unrealistically, he thinks that if his parents had been Canadian born, they would have known to get him on skates by the age of 3, and they would have known how to build a backyard rink. Craig Mills humored him when Craig was a graduate student at UMass. Craig and Ron played street hockey—no skating ability required. Craig was the goaltender. Later, Ron coached our sons' hockey teams. To ensure that he could make all the practices and games, he agreed to schedule all 12 teams in the Amherst program to gain more flexible ice times for his teams. He prided himself on matching the opponents' lines so that each of his skaters got the same amount of ice time. He had no ego—winning was a matter of scheduling your team against a weaker team, and Ron had no patience for that. His teams played the state champions of Rhode Island, New Hampshire, and Connecticut, and he thought that better competition made his teams work harder. It wasn't if you won, it was how you played the game—an attitude perhaps instilled by his training as a Queen's Scout, the Canadian equivalent of an Eagle Scout.

In Ontario, where we are from, there are two status symbols that say you have arrived. One is a summer cottage, the other is season tickets to the Maple Leafs. We have the summer cottage, but it is a 12-hour drive from Amherst. I love it; Ron thinks it is a money pit. We had season tickets to the Hartford Whalers. By Ontario standards, we had it made. Then the Whalers left for North Carolina. The day after the move was announced, Dick Jaeger called and offered Ron a job at UNC Greensboro. Even the prospect of a local hockey team was not enough to move Ron from UMass, but we have enjoyed many hockey games in Raleigh with Ric and Vickie Luecht, and often Terry and Debbie Ackerman. The innovative part of hockey in the South is year-round tailgating. There is something special about a glass of wine and sausage and peppers grilled by Ric in an arena parking lot surrounded by little boys playing street hockey in their Hurricanes shirts.

We have been very lucky. Ron found a profession he could love and in which intelligence and hard work are rewarded. There are so many more people I would like to mention and thank. Sadly, there are three who are no longer with us. Frank Stetz, a graduate from REMP, was a good friend of mine. I think he was the only student who ever came to visit me when I was in the hospital. He was very easy to talk to. Dean Arrasmith is gone too. The loss of Dan Eignor in the summer of 2012 was very difficult because we have been so close to both Dan and Linda. Her grief doubled the sadness. On the happy side, there is one constant. Peg Lorraine has been at the center of REMP since she arrived about 1984. She has given students good advice and helped with housing and other problems. What she does with them she does not share with Ron. She maintains very strict hours. While she is always in early, working from 9:00 A.M. to noon and from 1:00 to 4:00 P.M. She told Ron early on that her work day ended at 4:00 P.M. She knew that if she didn't, her workday would stretch on ambiguously. She and I share the burden of trying to keep Ron on schedule. If he is really overdue on something and she is getting frantic calls from a book editor for Ron's paper that is so overdue it is holding up publication, she lets me know it is time for a combined nag. She makes Ron look good.

I've covered a lot of very old ground in this Epilogue. I've tried to show you the Ron I know. He loves his job. He likes to say he can't believe he gets paid to have so much fun. He is genuinely modest. And here is one last anecdote to illustrate it. When he was told that he would receive the NCME Career Achievement Award in Atlanta about 1993, he was dismayed. Honored and thrilled, yes, but also embarrassed. He didn't think he had reached the stage in his career when he deserved the award. At that point, I did not usually go to the NCME meeting. He and Swami did NCME together. I told him I wanted to see him receive his award. He told me I couldn't come because if I did, he would appear to be attaching too much importance to the award. I said this would put our marriage in jeopardy—a hollow threat—and Ron agreed I could fly into Atlanta the night before the NCME breakfast, but I should leave again afterward. I came to Atlanta, stayed, and I think I have been to every NCME meeting since. I look forward to seeing former students and old friends at the UMass party and to seeing the wives and husbands with whom I've built friendships. I always want to stay at the conference hotel so I can see everyone. We stay at another hotel, though, because Ron is embarrassed by the fuss and hates the thought that he might not remember the name or the face of someone who knows him and inadvertently hurt their feelings.

Glossary of Abbreviations

AA-AAS	Alternate assessments based on alternate achievement standards
AA-GLAS	Alternate assessments based on grade-level achievement standards
AIG	Automated item generation
ALD	Achievement-level descriptor
ATA	Automated test assembly
AYP	Adequate yearly progress
CAT	Computer/ized-adaptive test
CBT	Computer-based test
CCSS	Common Core State Standards
CDA	Cognitive diagnostic assessment
CFA	Confirmatory factor analysis
CFI	Comparative fit index
CR	Constructed response
CRT	Criterion-reference test/ing
CTT	Classical test theory
DC	Decision consistency
DCM	Diagnostic cognitive model
DIF	Differential item functioning
DINA	Noncompensatory diagnostic model
ECD	Evidence-centered design
EFA	Exploratory factor analysis
EL	English learner
ELP	English language proficiency
ESEA	Elementary and Secondary Education Act
GBA	Game-based assessment
GPCM	Generalized partial credit model
GRM	Graded response model
ICC	Item characteristic curve
IDEA	Individuals with Disabilities Education Act

IEP	Individualized education program
IRT	Item response theory
JMLE	Join maximum likelihood estimation
KSAs	Knowledge, skills, and ability
LEP	Limited English proficiency/proficient
LMs	Language minorities
LOFT	Linear on the fly test
MC	Multiple choice
MCMC	Markov chain Monte Carlo
MCT	Minimum-competency testing
MDT	Measurement decision theory
MG-CFA	Multigroup confirmatory factor analysis
MH	Mantel–Haenszel
MIMIC	Multiple-indicator, multiple-cause
MIRT	Multidimensional item response theory
MLE	Maximum likelihood estimation
MMLE	Marginal maximum likelihood estimation
MST	Multistage test
NAEP	National Assessment of Educational Progress
NCLB	No Child Left Behind
NLP	Natural language processing
OIB	Ordered item booklet
PARCC	Partnership for Assessment of Readiness for College and Careers
PBT	Paper-based test
PCM	Partial credit model
PIRLS	Progress in International Reading Literacy Study
PISA	Programme for International Student Assessment
PLD	Performance-level descriptor
PLL	Performance-level label
RMSEA	Root mean square error of approximation
RP	Response probability
RTT	Race to the Top
SBA	Simulation-based assessment

SBAC	Smarter Balanced Assessment Consortium
SGBA	Simulation- and game-based assessment
SGP	Student growth percentile
SLO	Student learning objective
SME	Subject-matter expert
SR	Selected response
SRMR	Standardized root mean square residual
SWD	Student with disabilities
TEI	Technology-enhanced item
TIMSS	Trends in International Mathematics and Science Study
TLI	Tucker–Lewis index
WLS	Weighted least squares
1PL model	One-parameter logistic
2PL model	Two-parameter logistic
3PL model	Three-parameter logistic

GLOSSARY OF ABBREVIATIONS

Author Index

Abedi, J., 401, 405, 409, 446
Ackerman, T. A., 109n, 112, 121, 130, 143, 148, 151, 154, 169, 367, 443
Adams, A., 365
Adams, J., 365
Adams, R. J., 249
Agger, C. A., 42
Aguinis, H., 275
Ahlgrim-Delzell, L., 427, 428
Aitkin, M., 119, 120
Alagoz, C., 130
Alaniz, L. G., 263
Albus, D., 199, 231
Aldrich, J., 5
Algina, J., 26, 75, 130, 285
Algozzine, B., 380, 417
Allalouf, A., 127, 259, 261, 267, 268, 269, 273, 397, 440, 441
Allen, D., 23
Allen, D. G., 167
Allen, M. J., 74
Allen, N. L., 66, 198, 341, 344
Allik, J., 278
Almeida, L., 297
Almond, R., 228
Almond, R. G., 63, 223, 244, 249, 364, 368, 424
Alt, M., 364
Altman, J. R., 421, 422
Alves, C., 64
Amrein, A. L., 15
Anastasi, A., 15
Anderman, L., 428
Anderson, G. S., 195, 223
Anderson, L. W., 223

Anderson G., 211
Angoff, W. H., 29, 43, 45, 48, 49, 50, 65, 127, 263, 268
Ankenmann, R. D., 366, 367
Anstrom, K. A., 404
Anthony, J. C., 132
Applebee, A. N., 337, 340t
Arean, P., 129
Ariel, A., 196
Artelt, C., 284
Asil, M., 441
Astin, A. W., 359
Auerbach, M. A., 48
Austermuhl, F., 270
Azevedo, R., 228
Azocar, F., 129

Bahry, L., 438
Bailey, A. L., 408n, 409, 410
Baird, J., 368
Baker, C. L., 250
Baker, E. L., 240, 311, 315
Baker, L. L., 404
Baker, R. S. J. D., 247
Balogh, J., 231
Banks, K., 131
Baranowski, R. A., 226
Barbier, I., 231
Baron, P. A., 41
Barrett, P., 283
Barrick, M. R., 285
Barron, S., 15, 360
Barron, S. E., 362
Barton, M. A., 120

Bartram, D., 192, 278, 293
Bauer, M., 227, 245
Bauer, M. I., 244
Baumert, J., 284
Baxter, G. P., 366
Bay, L., 51
Beaton, A. E., 66, 340, 341, 344
Beaudoin, J. P., 329
Beavers, A. S., 168
Becker, K. A., 7
Beckett, K., 241
Behrens, J. T., 227n, 243, 247
Beimers, J., 55
Bejar, I. I., 44, 53, 162, 186, 197, 198, 216, 224, 225,
    227, 229
Beller, M., 261, 263
Benítez, I., 293, 298
Benjamin, L. T., 187
Bennett, R. E., 195, 196, 198, 216, 217, 222, 225,
    228, 229
Bentler, P. M., 164, 166
Bequin, A., 316
Berberoglu, G., 293
Beretvas, S. N., 135
Berezner, A., 265
Bergner, Y., 248
Berk, R. A., 25, 76, 126
Berliner, D. C., 15
Bernstein, J., 231, 232
Berry, J. W., 275
Best, N., 122
Betebenner, D. W., 311, 329
Betz, N. E., 187
Bhola, D. S., 197
Bielinski, J., 418
Binet, A., 6, 7, 8, 185, 187, 274, 291
Birnbaum, A., 114, 118, 119, 187
Bishop, Y. M. M., 170
Biswas, G., 232
Bloom, B. S., 223
Boake, C., 260
Bock, R. D., 108, 114, 115, 118, 119, 120, 121
Boekkooi-Timminga, E., 193, 222
Bohrnstedt, G., 49
Bollen, K. A., 164
Bollwark, J., 299
Bolt, D. M., 129, 133, 162, 173, 175, 176
Bond, M. H., 277, 285
Borko, H., 360
Bormuth, J. R., 226
Bouchet, F., 228
Bourque, M. L., 30, 48, 338
Box, G. E. P., 163
Boyson, B., 401
Braam, M., 385n
Bradlow, E. T., 134
Bradshaw, L., 122
Brandon, P. R., 48
Braun, H., 186, 198, 438
Braun, H. I., 44, 229

Breithaupt, K. J., 191, 196, 208, 209, 210, 211, 212,
    214, 441, 442
Brennan, R. L., 12, 15, 28, 30, 77, 78, 79, 80, 83, 97,
    99, 103, 223, 321, 359, 366
Breugelmans, S. M., 275, 278, 283
Breyer, F. J., 229, 249
Bridgeman, B., 190
Brigham, C., 9
Brislin, R. W., 277, 295
Brouwers, S. A., 276
Browder, D., 390, 420, 422, 428
Browder, D. M., 420, 424, 427
Brown, K. L., 319
Brown, L., 420, 421
Brown, T. A., 163
Buckendahl, C. W., 50
Bully, P., 297
Bunch, M., 38, 42, 49
Bunch, M. B., 14
Bunderson, C. V., 185
Burg, S. S., 168
Burke, M., 225
Burstein, J., 197, 229, 230
Burstein, L., 132
Bush, G. W., 15
Busuttil-Reynaud, G., 186
Butcher, J. N., 278, 283
Butler, F., 408, 408n, 409
Buzick, H., 199
Byrne, B., 293, 298

Cai, L., 121, 170, 249
Calvo, N., 291
Camara, W., 373
Cameron, C., 406
Cameto, R., 423
Camilli, G., 99, 126, 127, 128, 130
Campbell, J. R., 345f, 348
Cannell, J. J., 309
Cardall, C., 127
Carlson, J. E., 189
Carlson, S., 190
Carr, N., 185
Carroll, P. E., 410
Carter, E. W., 420
Carver, C. S., 165
Case, S., 210, 224, 226
Castellano, K. E., 324, 326, 327
Castellon-Wellington, M., 408
Cattell, A. K. S., 274
Cattell, J., 4, 5, 6
Cattell, R. B., 167, 274
Cella, D., 16
Chajewski, M., 62, 67, 68
Chambers, D., 404
Chang, H., 129, 156
Chasiotis, A., 275
Chen, F. F., 165
Chen, W. H., 163, 170
Cheng, J., 231

Chen-Yueh, C., 262
Chepp, V., 296
Chernyshenko, O. S., 132
Chetty, R., 311
Cheung, F. M., 275, 283
Cheung, G. W., 165
Cheung, S. F., 283
Chinen, M., 410
Chodorow, M., 229, 230
Choi, K., 329
Choi, S., 16
Chon, K. H., 171
Christensen, K. B., 278
Christensen, L., 385n, 419
Christoffersson, A., 131
Chudowsky, N., 423, 437n
Chudowsky, V., 437n
Chun, T., 362
Chung, G. K. W. K., 228, 246, 247, 248
Chung, S., 368
Church, A. T., 283
Cizek, G. J., 14, 25, 29, 30, 31, 38, 39, 40, 41, 42,
   46, 48, 49, 57, 63, 65, 90, 99, 308, 323, 344,
   422
Clark, A., 64
Clark, C. K., 188
Clark, D. B., 232
Clauser, B. E., 12, 46, 89, 91, 93, 99, 100, 103, 126,
   127, 186, 196, 210, 222, 243, 357, 366
Clauser, J. C., 12, 89, 99, 100, 101, 357, 366
Cleary, T. A., 279
Cline, F., 190
Clyman, S. G., 93, 222
Cobos, M. P., 291
Coffman, W. E., 127, 358
Cohen, A. S., 130, 173, 175, 176, 215
Cohen, J., 75
Cohen, Y., 264
Cohn, D. L., 81
Cole, N. S., 126, 127
Colvin, K. F., 311, 318, 411, 437, 439, 446
Conant, J., 9
Congdon, P., 130
Cook, H. G., 410
Cook, L., 26
Cook, L. L., 263, 268, 298
Copella, J., 42
Copella, J. M., 99
Coscarelli, W. C., 25
Costello, A. B., 167
Coulson, D., 26
Coulson, D. B., 285
Courtade, G., 427
Cronbach, L. J., 12, 81, 97, 101, 103, 224, 366, 446
Csíkszentmihályi, M., 245
Culpepper, S. A., 275

Daane, M. C., 348, 350f
Dalton C. M., 81
Darling-Hammond, L., 240

Darwin, C., 4
Davey, T., 186, 195, 196, 209, 222
Davidson, C., 4
Davis, A., 336
Davis, L. L., 199, 217
Davis-Becker, S. L., 50
Dayton, C. M., 135
de Ayala, R. J., 109, 135, 168, 170, 367
de Jong, J. H. A. L., 265
de Klerk, G., 260
de Leeuw, J., 131
Dean, V., 198, 216
Deane, P., 228
Del Valle, S., 380
Delacruz, G. C., 240
DeMars, C. E., 135
Dempster, A. P., 119
DePascale, C., 357, 365, 401, 402
Devore, R. N., 222
DiBiase, W., 427
DiCerbo, K. E., 227n, 243, 247, 248
DiCerbo, P. A., 404
Dick, W., 188
Dillingham, A., 50
Dodeen, H., 171
Dogan, E., 364, 365
Dolan, C. V., 275
Donahue, P. L., 345f
Donoghue, J. R., 129
Dorans, N. J., 128, 129, 130
Dossey, J. A., 340
Douglas, J., 131, 156, 169, 173, 174, 175, 176
Douglas, J. A., 10
Douglas, W. O., 398
Downing, S. M., 296
Draper, N. R., 163
Drasgow, F., 132, 188, 195, 214, 217, 222, 442
du Toit, S. H. C., 121
DuBois, P. H., 3, 4, 5, 6, 8
Dunbar, S. B., 243, 342
Duncan, A., 15
Dylan, B., 435

Ebel, R., 29
Edwards, B., 296
Edwards, M. C., 170
Egan, K. L., 41, 44, 66
Eignor, D. E., 26, 190
Elliott, J. L., 418
Elliott, R., 360
Elliott, S. N., 420
Ellis, B. B., 269
Elmore, R. F., 307
Elosua, P., 269, 291, 292, 293, 297, 298, 440
Ely, R., 364
Embretson, S. E., 162, 224, 226, 227
Emick, J. E., 406
Engelhard, G., 368, 382
Engelhard, G., Jr., 115, 117
Engelhart, M. D., 223

Ercikan, K., 441
Eubank, R. L., 174
Evers, A., 291
Ewers, N., 405, 446
Ewing, M., 64
Eysenck, H. J., 283
Eysenck, S. B., 283

Fabrigar, L. R., 167
Fagan, R. L., 188
Falch, L., 382
Fan, W., 283
Faulkner-Bond, M., 13, 107, 110, 113, 162, 313, 392, 395, 408, 435, 439
Ferdous, A. A., 170
Ferrara, S., 66, 170, 361
Ferrara, S. F., 41
Fienberg, S. E., 170
Finch, H., 169
Finch, W. H., 132, 133
Finney, D. J., 118
Fisher, R., 4, 5, 10, 119
Fisher, R. A., 118
Fisher, W. M., 232
Fister, S., 420
Fitzpatrick, A. R., 109, 209
Fitzpatrick, R., 358
Flaugher, J., 189
Flaugher, R., 195
Fleer, P. F., 131
Flowers, C., 420, 422, 427, 428
Folk, V. G., 186
Foltz, P. W., 229
Fontaine, J. R. J., 278, 283
Forsyth, R. A., 342
Forte, E., 313, 392, 395, 400, 404, 408, 409, 427, 439
Foster, D., 216
Fowles, M., 230
Francis, D. J., 401, 402, 405
Franco, J. N., 299
Frank, H., 283
Frechtling, J. A., 359
Frederiksen, N., 243, 358
Fremer, J. J., 195
Frezzo, D. C., 243
Frick, T., 81
Friedman, J. N., 311
Frijda, N. H., 274
Frye, D., 229
Fu, J., 228, 368
Fuchs, D., 382
Fuchs, L. S., 382
Fukuhara, H., 134
Furst, E. J., 223

Gafni, N., 261, 263, 264, 268
Gaines, M., 66
Gallo, J. J., 132

Galton, F., 3, 4, 5, 6, 7, 10, 274
Gamerman, D., 136
Gao, J., 214, 215
Gao, X., 366
Garcia, A., 311, 318, 373, 405, 411, 417, 437, 439, 446
García, E., 291
Garcia, O., 382
Gavino, A., 291
Gebhardt, E., 265, 276
Gee, J. P., 245
Geerlings, H., 225, 227, 249
Geisinger, K. F., 3, 4, 14, 260, 263, 274, 437
Georgas, J., 267, 278
Gerritz, K., 130
Gerrow, J., 50
Gershon, R., 16
Gibbons, R. D., 368
Gibbs, S. L., 427
Gibson, D., 241n, 246
Gierl, M. J., 122, 130, 151, 169, 217, 224, 227
Gifford, J., 26
Gifford, J. A., 120
Gitomer, D. H., 249
Glas, C. A. W., 195, 225, 249
Glaser, R., 24, 25, 26, 49, 423
Glass, G. V., 29
Gleser, G. C., 12, 81, 101, 366
Gobert, J. D., 247
Godoy, A., 291
Gold, R., 227
Goldschmidt, P., 329
Gomez, P. G., 66
Gonçalves, F. B., 136
Gong, B., 361, 426
Goodman, D., 348
Goodman, D. P., 32
Goodnow, J. J., 281
Gorin, J. S., 224, 226, 227, 241, 242
Gould, S. J., 8, 275
Graue, M. E., 309
Green, B. F., 224
Green, D. R., 49
Green, J. R., 231
Gregoire, J., 293
Griffiths, T., 250
Grigg, W. S., 348, 349f
Grima, A., 129
Grimm, K. J., 133
Grisay, A., 265, 276
Grissom, J. B., 401, 402, 410
Guarnaccia, P. J., 283
Guilford, J. P., 11
Guisande, M. A., 291
Gulliksen, H., 11, 96, 248
Guo, F., 197
Guttman, I., 177
Guttman, L., 13
Guzman, L., 263

Haberman, S. J., 27, 171, 172
Habing, B., 169
Habon, M. W., 223
Haertel, E. H., 28, 55, 97, 362, 365
Haertel, G. D., 186, 196
Hakkinen, M., 199
Haladyna, T. M., 217, 223, 224, 226, 296
Halleux-Monseur, B., 265
Halpin, P. F., 250
Halverson, M. L., 319
Halverson, R., 242, 244, 246
Hambleton, R. K., 13, 14, 23, 24, 25, 26, 27, 28, 29,
     30, 31, 32, 33, 41, 42, 43, 44, 47, 48, 49, 51, 75,
     76, 80, 81, 99, 109, 114, 115, 118, 121, 122, 126,
     127, 131, 144, 147, 161, 162, 163, 173, 186, 188,
     192, 193, 221, 223, 232, 233, 260, 262, 263, 264,
     268, 269, 273, 276, 277, 279, 282, 285, 286, 291,
     292, 293, 297, 298, 299, 300, 309, 325, 336, 337,
     338, 340, 341, 344, 348, 350, 351, 352, 359, 360,
     361, 367, 440, 447
Hamen, C., 64
Hamilton, L. S., 359
Hamre-Nietupski, S., 420
Han, K. (C.) T., 28, 74
Hanani, P., 259, 261, 264, 273, 397, 440, 441
Haney, W., 189
Hansen, D. N., 188
Hansen, E., 199
Hansen, M. A., 171
Hanson, B. A., 78, 79, 80, 83, 197
Hao, J., 245, 246, 247, 251
Harada, Y., 231
Hardin, E., 51
Hardle, W., 174
Hare, D. R., 196, 211, 214
Hare, R. D., 129
Harik, P., 100, 103
Harkness, J. A., 277, 296
Harley, J. M., 228
Harmes, J. C., 186, 196, 222
Harrison, D., 163
Harvey, O. J., 283
Hattie, J., 163, 169
Hayes, A., 165
Hays, R. D., 16
Hayton, J. C., 167
He, J., 276
Hedberg, E. C., 319
Hedeker, D. R., 368
Hegarty, M., 349n
Heilman, M., 229, 230
Hemat, L. A., 249
Hendrickson, A., 15, 44, 53, 195
Henri, V., 6, 7
Henson, R., 156
Henson, R. A., 109n, 112, 121, 122, 143, 443
Herman, J., 364
Herman, J. L., 315, 401, 402, 410
Hess, K. K., 424

Hetter, R. D., 193
Hicks, M. M., 188
Higgins, D., 229, 230
Hill, W. H., 223
Hilton, T. L., 279
Hipolito-Delgado, C. P., 406
Ho, A. D., 324, 326, 327
Hodgson, J., 199, 231
Hoffer, T. B., 319
Hoijtink, H., 175
Holland, P. W., 126, 128, 130, 170, 268, 298
Hoover, H. D., 129, 243
Horkay, N., 198
Horn, J. L., 167
Horn, S. P., 311
Hornke, L. F., 223
Hosom, J.-P., 231
Hough, L. M., 261
Houser, R. L., 191
Hoyt, C., 12
Hsu, Y. C., 170
Hu, L. T., 164
Huff, K. L., 44, 62, 64, 66, 366
Hughes, C., 420
Hulin, C. L., 188
Hunter, J. E., 275
Hurtz, G. M., 48
Husek, T., 14, 24, 27
Huynh, H., 28, 77, 78, 81, 170
Hwang, K.-K., 275

Iliescu, D., 291
Impara, J. C., 32, 48
Inouye, D. K., 185
Irvine, S. H., 223, 225, 227
Iturbide, L. M., 291
Izsák, A., 122

Jackson, D. N., 167
Jacobson, E., 122
Jaeger, R. M., 30, 54, 336
Jahoda, G., 274
Jakl, P., 241n, 246
Jasper, F., 169
Jennrich, R. I., 166
Jensen, A. R., 275
Jeon, M., 135
Jiao, H., 135
Jimenez, B. A., 427
Jin, Y., 350f
Jodoin, M. G., 130
Joe, R. C., 285
Johnson, B. F., 188
Johnson, L., 249
Johnson, M., 177
Johnson, R., 442
Johnstone, C. J., 422
Jones, L. R., 30, 49
Jones, R. W., 80, 126, 268

Jung, H., 410
Junker, B., 145, 169

Kahl, S. R., 51
Kaiser, H. F., 167
Kaliski, P. K., 62, 64, 67, 68
Kalohn, J. C., 209
Kamata, A., 134
Kane, M., 28, 30, 43, 47, 445
Kane, M. T., 65, 90, 99, 223, 357, 359, 407
Kane, T. J., 311
Kant, I., 4
Kantrowitz, B., 417
Kao, C., 132
Kaplan, B., 198
Kaplan, S. H., 189
Karantonis, A., 50
Karvonen, M., 422
Katz, I. R., 43
Katz, R. I., 337
Kaur, P., 232
Kearns, J. F., 419, 420, 421, 423
Keller, L. A., 162, 311, 318, 411, 437, 439, 446
Kelly, E., 66
Kelly, F., 4
Keng, L., 55, 199, 217
Kennedy, S., 423
Kerbel, A., 66, 404
Kerr, D., 228, 246, 247, 248
Kidwai, K., 248
Kieckhaefer, W. F., 188
Kieffer, M. J., 401, 405
Kim, D., 170
Kim, E. S., 132
Kim, J., 401, 402, 410
Kim, S., 130, 135
Kim, S.-H., 130
Kim, U., 275, 283
Kingsbury, G. C., 213
Kingsbury, G. G., 81, 191
Kingston, N. M., 51, 422
Kirkpatrick, 217
Kirmayer, L. J., 280
Kleifgen, J., 382
Klein, S., 361
Kleine-Kracht, M., 419
Kleinert, H., 419, 420, 421, 423, 428
Kleinert, J., 419, 420
Kline, R. B., 163
Kline, R. G., 189
Klineberg, O., 283
Knott, M., 248
Koch, D. A., 222
Kolen, M., 15, 80, 223, 321
Kopriva, R. J., 384, 406
Koretz, D. M., 243, 309, 315, 316, 359, 360, 361, 362, 363
Kraepelin, E., 4
Krakowski, K., 169

Krathwohl, D. R., 223
Kreiner, S., 278
Kuder, G. F., 12, 23
Kuhn, T. S., 114
Kukich, K., 229, 230
Kulick, E., 128, 129, 196
Kuo, B. C., 16
Kuti, L., 408
Kyllonen, P., 245, 246, 251

LaDuca, A., 226
Laham, D., 229
LaHart, C., 228
Lai, H., 227
Lai, J. S., 16
Laird, N. M., 119
Laitusis, C., 199
Lakin, J. M., 401, 411
Lam, T. C. M., 129
LaMar, M., 250
Lance, C. E., 279
Landauer, T. K., 229
Lane, S., 356, 357, 359, 360, 362, 363, 365, 366, 367, 373
Langer, J. A., 337
Lapointe, A., 340
Lathrop, Q., 80
Lau, A., 135
Laurenceau, J.-P., 165
Lautenschlager, G. J., 132
Lawless, R. R., 225
Layman, H., 216
Lazarfeld, P. F., 13, 118
Lazarus, S. S., 199, 231, 382, 405, 418
Leckie, G., 368
Lee, W., 77, 80, 83
Lehr, C. A., 199
Leighton, J. P., 122, 169
Lemann, N., 9, 10
Lenke, J. M., 188
Leon, S., 401
Leong, F. T. L., 275
Lesaux, N. K., 401, 405, 409
Leung, K., 278, 281
LeVine, E., 299
Levine, R., 336
Levy, R., 163, 169, 170, 244, 247
Lewis, C., 28, 78, 79, 81, 83, 189, 192, 193n, 195, 211, 212, 213
Lewis, D. M., 49, 422
Li, H., 130
Li, M., 402
Liang, L., 195
Liang, T., 173, 175, 176
Lieberman, M., 119, 120
Likert, R., 440
Lin, E. J. L., 283
Linacre, J. M., 120, 169
Lindquist, E. F., 10, 358

Linn, D., 417
Linn, R. L., 49, 97, 243, 279, 307, 309, 310, 315, 342, 356, 359, 360, 362, 364, 365, 437
Linnaeus, C., 4
Linquanti, R., 409, 410
Lissitz, R. W., 129, 135, 298, 423
Liu, L., 245, 246, 251
Liu, M., 366, 367
Liu, O. L., 230
Liu, Y., 170
Livingston, S., 38
Livingston, S. A., 27, 28, 29, 47, 50, 76, 78, 79, 83
Lockwood, J. R., 311
Lohman, D. F., 3, 6, 7, 8, 10, 223
Loomis, S. C., 44, 48
López-Jaúregui, A., 298
Lord, F. M., 13, 17, 74, 77, 78, 79, 80, 107, 114, 116, 117, 118, 119, 120, 121, 122, 128, 173, 174, 188, 193, 212, 245, 248, 340
Louie, J., 401
Lu, C., 229
Lu, R., 135
Luecht, R. M., 34, 41, 44, 186, 195, 196, 208, 212, 213, 217, 221, 222, 223, 224, 225, 227, 232, 441
Lugg, C. A., 99
Lukas, J., 424
Lung, K., 296
Lunn, D. J., 122
Lutkus, A. D., 350f

MacCallum, R. C., 167
Macready, G., 81
Madaus, G. F., 360, 362
Malda, M., 280, 281
Malone, T. W., 240
Manassero, M. A., 291
Margolis, M., 100
Margolis, M. J., 46, 91, 103, 210, 243
Marion, S., 423, 426
Marshall, G. N., 129
Martin, C., 15
Martin, E., 375, 378
Martin, R., 375
Martineau, J., 198, 216, 322
Martínez, Z., 291
Martinez-Garza, M., 232
Martiniello, M., 401, 405, 408
Marzano, R. J., 223
Masters, G. N., 115, 121, 367
Mathot-Buckner, C., 420
Matsumoto, D., 293
Matts, T., 64, 366
Mavronikolas, E., 228
Maxwell, B., 264
Maydeu-Olivares, A., 170
Mayfield, K., 190
Mazor, K. M., 126, 127, 129
Mazzeo, J., 32, 129, 171, 196, 335, 361, 442

McBride, J. R., 188
McCaffrey, D., 361
McCaffrey, D. F., 311
McClarty, K. L., 192
McCrae, R. R., 278, 283
McDonald, R. P., 121
McDonald, S.-K., 319
McDonnell, J., 420
McDonnell, L. M., 418
McGrew, K. S., 380, 418
McHorney, C. A., 130
McKinley, R. L., 151
McLaughlin, M. J., 418
McPeek, W. M., 130
McVay, A., 368
Mead, R., 51
Mead, R. J., 120
Meade, A. W., 132
Meara, K., 32, 337
Mee, J., 46
Meiring, D., 285
Meisner, R., 227
Melamed, E., 268
Melican, G., 191, 209, 212
Mellenbergh, D., 26
Mellenbergh, G. J., 26, 81, 128
Melnick, D. E., 186, 222
Melsa, J. L., 81
Mercado, R. L., 49, 422
Merenda, P., 291
Meskauskas, J. A., 54
Messick, S., 224, 251, 357, 340, 360, 362, 364, 396
Metropolis, N., 122
Mihaly, K., 311
Miles, J., 55
Miller, K., 296
Mills, C. N., 31, 189, 190, 191, 195, 208, 209, 212, 441, 442
Minton, H. L., 6
Miranda, J., 129
Miska, M., 263
Mislevy, R. J., 63, 121, 170, 171, 194, 196, 197, 216, 223, 239, 241, 242, 243, 244, 246, 247, 248, 249, 252, 364, 368, 424, 427, 441, 443
Mitchell, K. J., 30, 49, 360
Mitzel, H. C., 49, 422
Molenaar, I. W., 175
Monahan, P. O., 130
Montalvo, O., 247
Moore, M., 199
Moreno, K. E., 188
Morgan, D. L., 42, 43, 51
Morison, P., 418
Morley, M. E., 225
Morrison, A. P., 420
Morrison, E. J., 358
Mortimer, T., 226
Mosch, S. C., 278
Mosier, C. I., 11, 13

Moss, P. A., 126
Moustaki, I., 248
Moyer, E., 408
Mujika, J., 297
Mulaik, S. A., 443
Mulder, J., 249
Muller, E. S., 134
Mullis, I. V. S., 337, 340, 345t
Muñiz, J., 269, 291, 292, 293, 298, 300, 397, 440, 441
Munoz, R. F., 129
Muraki, E., 121, 367
Muthén, B. O., 131, 132
Muthén, L. K., 132
Mwalimu, M., 336

Nanda, H., 12, 101, 366
Nandakumar, R., 169
Navarro, C., 291
Nedelsky, L., 29
Nering, M. L., 112, 170, 195
Newman, J. P., 129
Nezami, E., 278
Nichols, P., 223
Nietupski, J., 420
Nitko, A. J., 25
Noah, A., 66
Nogueira, R., 291
Novick, M. R., 13, 26, 27, 28, 75, 76, 79, 81, 114, 121, 248

Obama, B., 15
O'Conner, R., 401
O'Day, J., 309, 408
Odell, C. W., 445
O'Dwyer, L. M., 360, 362, 401
Olsen, J. B., 185
Olsen, K. R., 389
Olson, B., 51
O'Malley, J. W., 4
O'Malley, K., 55, 56
O'Neill, K. A., 130
Oranje, A., 196
Orlando, M., 129, 171, 172
Ortiz, S., 291
Osborne, J. W., 167
Osterlind, S. J., 226
Ostini, R., 112
Oswald, F. L., 261
Otis, A., 8
Owen, E. H., 340
Owen, R. J., 187
Owen, V., 242, 244, 246

Packman, S., 64
Padilla, J.-L., 269, 291, 293, 296, 298, 440
Page, E. B., 197, 229
Page, S. H., 226
Pagliaro, L. A., 187
Pallett, D. S., 232

Panchepakesan, N., 13
Panos, R. J., 359
Páramo, M. F., 291
Parke, C. S., 360
Parker, C., 401
Parkerson, D. H., 208
Parkerson, J. A., 208
Parrish, T. B., 401
Parshall, C. G., 186, 196, 209, 222
Parsons, C. K., 188
Pashley, P. J., 196, 222
Patelis, T., 50
Patsula, L., 263, 269
Patterson, D. G., 8
Patterson, H. L., 226
Patz, R. J., 49, 322
Pausch, R., 227
Payne, D., 51
Pearson, K., 4, 5, 10
Pellegrino, J. W., 30, 48, 49, 64, 423, 427
Penfield, R. D., 126, 128, 129, 130
Peng C.-Y. J., 78
Pennock-Roman, M., 405
Perie, M., 38, 44, 66
Perkins, A. J., 130
Phillips, G. W., 55, 340, 345f
Phillips, S. E., 418
Pierce, C. A., 275
Ping-Kun, C., 262
Pinter, R., 8
Pitoniak, M. J., 14, 25, 31, 32, 38, 41, 42, 43, 47, 48, 63, 65, 90, 99, 308, 335, 344, 361, 422, 442
Plake, B. S., 44, 48, 53, 62, 64, 66, 364
Ployhart, R. E., 261
Poortinga, Y. H., 131, 260, 273, 275, 278, 279, 282, 283, 285, 295, 397, 440, 441
Pope, G., 210
Popham, W. J., 14, 23, 24, 25, 26, 27, 29, 30, 309, 325
Potenza, M. T., 129, 195
Powers, D., 230
Pressey, L. C., 438, 439, 440
Pressey, S. L., 187, 438, 439, 440
Price, P., 232
Prieto, G., 300
Puhan, G., 27

Quenemoen, M., 420
Quenemoen, R. F., 199, 312, 315, 389, 390, 392, 416, 420, 421, 422, 427, 440
Quinlan, T., 228

Rabe-Hesketh, S., 135
Rabiner, L. R., 231
Rachor, R. E., 323
Rafferty, A., 250
Ragan, A., 409
Rajaratnam, N., 12, 101, 366
Raju, N. S., 128, 131

Ramis, C., 291
Ramsay, J. O., 174
Randall, J., 373, 382, 405, 417
Rapp, J., 269
Rasch, G., 13, 116, 117, 120, 121
Rathbun, A., 336
Raudenbush, S. W., 325
Raven, J., 276
Raymond, M. R., 41, 44
Reagan, R., 14
Reckase, M. D., 13, 43, 46, 49, 81, 112, 151, 170, 227, 322, 367, 443
Reese, C. M., 345f
Reid, J. B., 44
Reidy, E. F., 362
Reise, S. P., 162, 166
Ren, X., 168
Rensvold, R. B., 165
Rentz, R. R., 188
Reshetar, R., 44, 62, 64
Revuelta, J., 225
Richardson, M. W., 12, 23
Riconscente, M. M., 252
Rigney, S. L., 419
Rijmen, F., 135
Rios, J., 110, 113, 162, 270, 441
Rivera, A., 404
Rivera, C., 404, 405
Rivera, H., 401
Rivera, M. O., 401, 402, 405
Rizavi, S., 50
Roach, A. T., 420
Robin, F., 50, 127, 185, 195, 196, 441
Robinson, J. P., 401, 410
Robustelli, S. L., 41
Rock, D. A., 228
Rockoff, J. E., 311
Rodriguez, G., 50
Rodriguez, M. C., 226
Rodríguez, M. S., 291
Rogers, H. J., 14, 109, 126, 128, 129, 130, 132n, 133, 136, 162, 169, 193, 268, 279
Rogers, J., 49
Rogler, L. H., 283
Romero, P., 291
Roorda, W., 275
Rosen, Y., 228
Rosenbluth, A. W., 122
Rosenbluth, M. N., 122
Ross, K., 362
Roth, W.-M., 441
Rothmann, S., 285
Roussos, L. A., 129, 130, 131, 169
Rubin, D. B., 119
Ruch, G. M., 438
Rudner, L. M., 28, 74, 79, 80, 81n
Ruiz-Primo, M. A., 243, 366
Rupp, A. A., 122, 143, 145, 248
Ryans, D. G., 243, 358

Ryndak, D. L., 420

Saini, P., 232
Saklofske, D. H., 268, 278
Salen, K., 244
Sam, D., 275
Samejima, F., 116, 121, 122
Samuelsen, K. M., 135
Sanders, N. M., 309
Sanders, W. L., 311
Santayana, G., 436
Sao Pedro, M., 247
Sass, T. R., 311
Sato, E., 408n
Saxe, R., 250
Saxton, A. M., 311
Scalise, K., 216, 228, 248
Scarpello, V., 167
Schaeffer, G. A., 190
Schafer, W. D., 423
Schedl, M., 66
Scherer, K. R., 283
Scheuneman, J. D., 127, 128, 129, 130
Schmeiser, C. B., 193, 223, 296
Schmidt, F. L., 275
Schmitt, A. J., 129, 130
Schmitt, A. P., 130
Schmitt-Cascallar, A. P., 298
Schneider, M. C., 41, 66
Schnipke, D. L., 197
Schulz, E. M., 49, 422
Schulz, W., 276
Schwartz, S. H., 282
Schwarz, R. D., 367
Schweizer, K., 168
Scott, D., 385n
Scrams, D. J., 197
Scullin, S., 385n
Segall, D. O., 188
Selden, R., 336
Sen, R., 136
Sengupta, P., 232
Serici S., 216
Seyfarth, A., 385n
Shaffer, D. W., 241
Shavelson, R. J., 12, 243, 366, 367
Shealy, R., 128, 130, 131
Sheehan, K., 81, 189
Sheinker, A., 418
Shepard, L. A., 49, 126, 127, 128
Shermis, M. D., 197
Shin, M., 408
Shindoll, R. R., 226
Short, D., 401
Shriberg, L., 231
Shriner, J. G., 373n, 380, 417, 418
Shrock, S. A., 25
Shu, Z., 225, 227, 247, 248
Shute, V. J., 227, 241, 244

Shyyan, V., 419
Sijtsma, K., 145, 169
Simmons, C., 336
Simon, T., 7, 187, 274, 291
Sinharay, S., 27, 129, 170, 171, 177
Sireci, S. G., 50, 127, 186, 195, 196, 208, 212, 222,
    267, 268, 269, 270, 298, 352, 418, 435, 438, 441,
    444, 445
Skaggs, G., 129, 135
Skelly, T., 227
Skinner, B. F., 187
Skorupski, W., 44
Slama, R. B., 401
Slater, S., 337, 338, 340, 344, 348, 350, 351
Slater, S. C., 32, 190, 360
Smith, J., 148
Smith, L., III, 246
Smith, M., 309
Smith, R. L., 186
Snow, R. E., 223
Soares, T. M., 136
Solano-Flores, G., 402
Soller, A., 250
Soloway, E., 229
Sommerstein, L., 420
Soriano, C., 283
Spande, G. E., 417
Spearman, C., 5, 10, 443
Speigelhalter, D., 122
Spiegel, A., 380
Spielberger, C., 291
Spooner, F., 390, 420, 427, 428
Spray, J. A., 81, 209
Springen, K., 417
Srain-Seymour, E., 217
Staiger, D. O., 311
Stalnaker, J. M., 358
Stansfield, C. W., 261, 263, 265
Stapleton, L. M., 135
Stark, S., 132
Stecher, B., 360, 361, 362
Steffan, M., 211
Steffen, M., 190, 195, 223
Steinberg, L., 64, 128, 130, 366
Steinberg, L. S., 63, 223, 244, 249, 364, 368
Stern, H. S, 177
Stevens, R., 250, 408
Stockford, I., 80
Stocking, M. L., 189, 193, 193n, 194, 195, 208, 211, 213
Stone, C. A., 171, 356, 359, 360, 362, 363, 366, 367
Stone, E., 199
Stone, M. H., 13
Stout, W. F., 128, 130, 131, 133, 168, 169
Strahan, E. J., 167
Strain-Seymour, E., 199
Strecher, B. M., 15
Stroulia, E., 226
Stump, T. E., 130
Subkoviak, M. J., 28, 77, 78

Suen, H. K., 3
Suzuki, M., 231
Svetina, D., 163, 169, 170
Swaminathan, H., 13, 26, 28, 75, 76, 109, 120, 126,
    128, 129, 130, 132n, 133, 136, 147, 162, 169, 188,
    193, 268, 279, 285, 341, 367
Swaminathan, H. R., 49
Swanson, C. B., 401, 402
Swanson, D., 224, 226
Swanson, D. B., 91, 93, 100
Swanson, L., 189, 193, 194, 195
Sweeney, K., 51
Sydorenko, T., 228
Sympson, J. B., 193

Takane, Y., 131
Tan, P., 188
Tan, X., 169
Tanenbaum, C., 408
Tannenbaum, R. J., 41, 43, 44
Tanzer, N. K., 293
Tate, R., 163, 168, 169
Tatsuoka, K. K., 122
Tay, L., 214
Teller, A. H., 122
Teller, E., 122
Templin, J., 122, 143
Tenenbaum, J. B., 250
Terman, D., 375
Terman, L. M., 7, 8, 9
Terracciano, A., 278, 283
Thayer, D. T., 126, 128, 130
Theunissen, T. J. J. M., 193
Thiel, D., 227
Thissen, D., 121, 128, 130, 131, 163, 170, 171, 172
Thomas, A., 122
Thompson, K. D., 401
Thompson, S. J., 199, 389, 405, 418, 421, 422
Thorndike, E. L., 3, 4
Thorndike, R. L., 358
Thorndike, R. M., 3, 6, 7, 8, 10
Thorson, N., 420
Thurlow, M. L., 199, 231, 312, 315, 373n, 380, 382,
    385n, 389, 390, 392, 405, 416, 417, 418, 419, 421,
    422, 427, 439
Thurstone, L. L., 114, 115, 116, 117, 119, 443
Tiemann, G. C., 51, 422
Tinajero, C., 291
Tittle, C. K., 277
Toffler, A., 17
Torbiörn, I., 281
Toto, E., 247
Towles-Reeves, E., 419, 420, 428
Trevors, G. J., 5, 228
Trotter, A., 191
Tsai, J., 278
Tsai, T. H., 170
Tucker, L. R., 116
Tung, S., 401

Ulam, S., 122
Usher-Tate, B. J., 3, 274, 437

Valchev, V. H., 283
van Abswoude, A. A., 169
van de Gaer, E., 276
van de Koppel, J. M. H., 285
van de Vijver, F. J. R., 131, 260, 262, 264, 267, 273, 275, 276, 278, 279, 281, 285, 286, 293, 295, 296, 397, 440, 441
van der Ark, L. A., 169
van der Linden, W. J., 25, 26, 81, 109, 131, 144, 193, 195, 196, 197, 211, 213, 214, 222, 223, 225, 249
van Hemert, D. A., 276
van Rijn, P., 367
Van Schilt-Mol, T. M. M. L., 274
Vandenberg, R. J., 279
VanWinkle, W., 336
Vattel, L., 252
Veldkamp, B. P., 196, 214
Velicer, W. F., 167
Ventura, M., 227, 244
Verdun, K., 283
Vesperman, B., 364
Vicino, F. L., 188
Villar, A., 296
Vitale, J. E., 129
Voltaire, 4
von Davier, A. A., 192, 212, 239, 245, 246, 247, 248, 250, 251, 252, 441, 443
von Davier, M., 189
Von Mayrhauser, R. T., 8
Vos, H. J., 81
Vygotsky, L. S., 245

Wagner, M., 228
Wagner, M. E., 225
Wainer, H., 32, 126, 128, 134, 172, 190, 194, 268, 298, 337
Wakeman, S., 422
Wald, A., 81
Walker, C., 151
Walker, C. M., 135
Wallack J. A., 215
Wan, L., 77
Wang, T., 197
Wang, W. C., 249
Wang, X., 134, 136, 408
Ward, W. C., 189, 195, 196, 228
Way, D., 185, 217, 441
Way, W. D., 192, 195, 196, 199, 211, 223
Webb, N., 223
Webb, N. L., 364, 421
Webb, N. M., 12
Wegener, D. T., 167
Weiner, A. W., 350f
Weiss, D. J., 13, 81, 186, 187, 188
Weiss, L., 278

Weiss, L. G., 267
Welch, C., 129, 296
Welch, C. J., 193, 223
Welch, R. E., 81
Wells, C. S., 13, 107, 109, 110, 113, 162, 173, 175, 176, 438
Wesman, A. G., 223
West, P., 243
Westbury, I., 299
Wheadon, C., 80
Whitely, S. E., 223
Wicherts, J. M., 275
Wiggins, G., 229
Wiley, E. W., 366
Williamson, D. M., 197, 216, 229
Willis, G. B., 296
Willms, J. D., 325
Wilson, M., 214, 224, 249, 296
Wilson, S., 296
Wingersky, M. S., 76, 80, 120
Winkley, J., 186
Wirtz, W., 340
Wise, M., 368
Wise, S. L., 197
Wolf, M. K., 401, 409
Wolfe, E. W., 368
Wolff, S., 229
Woods, C. M., 133
Wright, B. D., 13, 115, 120, 121
Wright, C., 66
Wu, H. M., 16
Wu, Q., 3
Wundt, W., 4, 6

Xi, X., 229
Xu, X., 196

Yan, D., 192, 212, 249
Yan, F., 198
Yang, J. M., 16
Yang, K.-S., 275, 277
Yang, S., 197
Yang, X., 224, 226, 227
Yao, L., 322, 367
Yates, F., 118
Yazdchi, M. V., 226
Yen, W. M., 74, 109, 170, 171, 188, 209, 361
Yenes, F., 291
Yerkes, R., 8
Yi-Hsiu, L., 262
Ying, J., 348
Ying, Z., 156
Yocom, P., 225, 227
Yoes, M. E., 13
Yolkut, A., 66
Yoo, H., 367
Yoon, M., 132
Young, A., 280
Young, J. W., 401, 411

Young, M. F., 251
Ysseldyke, J. E., 380, 385n, 389, 417, 418

Zapata-Rivera, D., 227, 228, 244, 245, 246, 251,
　　336, 337, 349n
Zara, A., 213
Zara, A. R., 187, 191, 208
Zenisky, A. L., 23, 32, 33, 34, 127, 196, 216, 221,
　　222, 277, 297, 309, 325, 335, 336, 337, 348, 352,
　　361, 408, 441, 442
Zhang, B., 171
Zhang, J., 168, 169
Zhang, M., 216

Zhang, O., 214
Zhang, O. Y., 196
Zhang, Z., 165
Zhu, M., 247, 250
Zieky, M. J., 29, 38, 46, 47, 50, 51, 130, 268
Zimmerman, E., 244
Zlatos, B., 417
Zucker, S., 263
Zumbo, B. D., 127, 130, 210, 279
Zuriff, G., 382
Zwick, R., 129, 349n
Zwick, W. R., 167

Subject Index

Page numbers followed by *f* indicate figure; *n*, note; and *t*, table

Absolute error, 93–94, 94*f*, 95*f*
Absolute standards, 54–55
Academic language, 403–404
Academic outcomes, 391–392
Accessibility of assessments, 439–440
Accommodations. *See* Testing accommodations
Accountability
  accountability systems, 313–315
  alternative assessments based on alternative
    achievement standards (AA-AAS) and, 423
  computer-based testing (CBT) and, 215
  current trends in assessment and, 437–439
  designing test-based accountability systems,
    315–316
  English learners (ELs) and, 395–397, 398,
    399–400
  growth measuring and, 319
  historical perspective of, 358–360
  inclusion, 312–313
  minimum-competency testing (MCT) and, 308
  A Nation at Risk (National Commission on
    Excellence in Education, 1983), 308–310
  No Child Left Behind (NCLB) and, 310
  overview, 307–308, 316
  psychometric considerations and, 365–368
  simulation- and game-based assessments and, 242*t*
  state assessment and, 361–363
  teacher evaluations and, 310–312
  test-based accountability systems, 308
  use of performance assessments for, 360–363
  See also Growth; Performance assessments;
    Reporting test results; Standards
ACCUPLACER, 221
Accuracy of measurement, 186, 209, 270–271

Achievement levels
  alternative assessments based on alternative
    achievement standards (AA-AAS) and, 419
  contrasting groups method and, 50
  cut scores and, 39
  English learners (ELs) and, 399–400
  performance assessments and accountability and,
    360
  performance-level descriptors and, 63
  reporting test results and, 31–32, 344–346, 345*f*,
    346*f*, 347*f*
  standard setting and, 30
  See also Advanced achievement level; Basic
    achievement level; Below Basic achievement
    level; Proficient achievement level; Standards
Achievement-level descriptors (ALDs). *See*
  Performance-level descriptors (PLDs)
ACT (American College Testing), 10, 11, 26
Adaptive testing
  comprehensive approach to, 281–282
  computer-based testing (CBT) and, 211–212, 221
  cross-cultural and cross-lingual assessments and,
    261–262, 263
  evolution of CBT and, 187–188
  ITC Guidelines on Adapting Tests (2010),
    292–300, 294*f*
  overview, 273, 291–293, 300
  procedures for, 276–282, 280*f*
  test transfer and, 282–286
  types of adaptations, 279–281, 280*f*
  See also Computerized adaptive testing (CAT);
    Transadaption; Translation of testing material
Adequate yearly progress (AYP), 310, 363, 437
Administration models, 210–215, 267–269, 425–426

Advanced achievement level, 39, 50, 63. *See also* Achievement levels

Advanced Placement (AP) program
  developing performance-level descriptors and, 63–65
  overview, 62
  performance assessments and accountability and, 358–359
  test score interpretations, 65–71, 69*f*, 70*t*

Advanced simulations, 227–229. *See also* Simulation-based assessments (SBAs)

Age as a scaling factor, 115–116

Alignment, 408, 408*n*

Alternative assessments, 388–390, 390*t*, 416–418. *See also* Special populations

Alternative assessments based on alternative achievement standards (AA-AAS)
  evolution of, 421–423
  future of, 423–427
  overview, 418–420, 427–428

American College Testing (ACT). *See* ACT (American College Testing)

American Educational Research Association (AERA), 269

American Institute of Certified Public Accountants (AICPA), 191, 210

American Psychological Association (APA), 8, 269

American Recovery and Reinvestment Act of 2009, 192

Americans with Disabilities Act (ADA), 377, 378, 380–381

Analysis of variance (ANOVA) method
  development of, 10
  differential item functioning of test items (DIF) and, 127–128
  generalizability and, 12
  test transfer and, 285

Anchoring, 341–342. *See also* Scale anchoring/item mapping

AP Environmental Science (APES) examination, 65–71, 69*f*, 70*t*. *See also* Advanced Placement (AP) program

AP Examination Program. *See* Advanced Placement (AP) program

Architect Registration Examination (ARE), 208, 227, 229

Area method, 128–129

Armed Services Vocational Aptitude Batter (ASVAB), 188, 208, 221

Army Alpha, 11

Artificial intelligence, 216

Assembly form of test adaptation, 280–281. *See also* Adaptive testing

Assessment, 198, 210, 436–444

Assessment Data Aggregator for Game Environments (ADAGE), 246–247

Assessment design
  alternative assessments based on alternative achievement standards (AA-AAS) and, 423–424
  cross-cultural and cross-lingual assessments and, 262–269

simulation- and game-based assessments and, 240, 243
  test transfer and, 276
  See also Evidence-centered design (ECD)

Assessment engineering (AE), 223–225, 225*f*

Assessment format, 421

Assessment framework, 64

Assessment mandates, 399–400

Assessment subtest (AT), 169

Assessment triangle, 423–424

Assumptions of the IRT models
  dimensionality assumption, 163–170, 166*f*
  item characteristic curve (ICC) and, 170–176, 173*f*
  local independence assumption, 109–110, 163–170, 166*f*
  overview, 162–163, 177
  See also Item response theory (IRT)

Audience, 337–340, 339*f*

Authentic assessment, 228–229

AutoCAD, 198

Automated item generation (AIG), 217

Automated scoring, 197, 216, 229–231. *See also* Computer-based testing (CBT); Scoring

Automated speech recognition (ASR) technology, 231–232

Automated test assembly (ATA) mechanisms, 214, 221–222, 223. *See also* Test assembly

Automated translations, 295–296. *See also* Translation of testing material

Automatic item generation (AIG), 225–227, 225*f*

Back translation, 264–265, 266. *See also* Translation of testing material

Backward procedures, 132

Bar plots, 154

Basic achievement level, 39, 50, 63. *See also* Achievement levels

Bayesian estimation
  collaboration and, 250–251
  criterion-referenced testing and, 26–27
  differential item functioning of test items (DIF) and, 135
  item response theory (IRT) and, 122
  maximum likelihood estimation (MLE) and, 120
  measurement decision theory (MDT) and, 81–82
  simulation- and game-based assessments and, 249

Bayesian framework, 117, 368

Bayesian *p*-value, 136. *See also p*-values

Behavioral objectives, 33, 34

Below Basic achievement level, 39, 50, 63. *See also* Achievement levels

Beta-binomial distributions, 77, 83–85, 84*f*, 85*f*

Bias
  cross-cultural and cross-lingual assessments and, 262–263, 264, 267–268, 274
  differential item functioning of test items (DIF) and, 126–127, 128
  test transfer and, 277–278
  See also Item bias; Test bias

BICAL software, 120–121

Bifactor model, 165–166, 166f, 368
Big Five dimensions, 278, 283
Bilingual education, 379–380, 382–383. *See also* English learners (ELs)
Bilingual Education Act, 376, 383
BILOG software, 121
Binary-scored test items, 34
Binet, Alfred, 6–8, 185, 187
Board games in assessment, 240
Body of work (BoW) method, 51, 422
Bookmark method, 48, 49–50, 422
Borderline examinee, 42, 45, 53. *See also* Minimally competent examinee; Minimally qualified candidate; Target examinee
Branched testing, 187–188
BUGS software, 122
Bureau of Education of the Handicapped (BEH), 375

Calibration, 216–217
CAT version of the Armed Services Vocational Aptitude Battery (CAT-ASVAB), 188. *See also* Armed Services Vocational Aptitude Batter (ASVAB)
Cattell, James McKeen, 5–6
Ceiling effects, 322–323
Centroid plot, 159, 159f
Certified Public Accountants (CPA) Examination, 221
Cheating, 215
Chinese Personality Assessment Inventory (CPAI), 283
Chi-square method, 127–129
Cisco Aspire game, 244–245
Civil Rights Act of 1964, 376, 379–380, 397–398
Civil rights reform, 416–417
Clamshell plot, 155, 155f
Class effect, 331
Classical test theory (CTT)
    decision consistency indices and, 76–80, 83–85, 84f, 85f
    development of, 10–11
    generalizability and, 12
    measurement decision theory (MDT) and, 81–83
    overview, 74, 85, 89, 107
    performance-level descriptors and, 67–71
    p-values, 23*n*
    reliability and, 11–12
    simulation- and game-based assessments and, 248
    See also Correlational statistics
Classification and regression tree (CART) analysis, 248
Classification consistency, 74–75
Classification model, 8, 28–29, 99
Classify software, 80
Coefficient alpha, 12
Cognitive diagnostic assessment (CDA), 122. *See also* Item response theory (IRT)
Cognitive diagnostic models, 143–144. *See also* Diagnostic classification models (DCM)

Cognitively Based Assessment of, for, and as Learning (CBAL) initiative, 368
Cohen's kappa coefficient, 28, 75–76, 82
Collaboration
    game-based assessments (GBAs) and, 245
    psychometric modeling of, 250–251
    simulation- and game-based assessments and, 250–251, 252
College admission tests, 9–10
College Board, 189, 221. *See also* Advanced Placement (AP) program
College Entrance Examination Board, 9
College-level placement, 189
Combined loss function, 193, 193*n*
Common Core State Standards (CCSS)
    accountability and, 313, 313–314
    alternative assessments based on alternative achievement standards (AA-AAS) and, 423–427
    automated scoring and, 230
    computer-based testing (CBT) and, 198–199, 218
    English learners (ELs) and, 409, 411
    performance assessments and accountability and, 363–365
    reporting test results and, 335–336
    simulation- and game-based assessments and, 241
    standard setting and, 57
Comparability of performance assessments, 365–366. *See also* Performance assessments
Comparative fit index (CFI), 164–165
Comparative Survey Design and Implementation (CSDI) Guidelines Initiative, 292–293
Comparisons, 274
Compensatory items, 149–153, 149f, 150f, 151f, 152f
Compensatory logistic model (DINA)
    conditional estimation for, 159, 159f
    item information and, 154–156, 155f
    overview, 143, 145, 160
    true score representation and, 157–158, 158f
    two-dimensional MIRT models and, 153–154, 153f
Compensatory model, 144–145, 153–154, 153f, 160
Compensatory RUM, 145
Complex skills assessment, 210
Computational process
    projection growth model and, 327
    residual gain growth model and, 328
    simple gain growth model and, 325
    student growth percentile (SGP) and, 330
    value tables growth model and, 326
    value-added growth model and, 331
Computer software
    decision consistency indices and, 77, 80
    generalizability theory and, 99
    item response theory (IRT) and, 120–121
    See also individual software programs
Computer-assisted instruction (CAI), 187
Computer-based assessments, 16–17, 34, 441–442. *See also* Computer-based testing (CBT)

Computer-based testing (CBT)
  administration models, 210–215
  alternative assessments based on alternative
    achievement standards (AA-AAS) and, 426
  assessment engineering and principled test design,
    223–225, 225f
  automated scoring and, 229–231
  automated speech recognition technology, 231–232
  automatic item generation and, 225–227, 225f
  current trends in assessment and, 441–442,
    443–444
  developments and challenges in, 215–218
  evolution of, 187–192, 195–196
  gaming and advanced simulations, 227–229
  methodological implications and, 192–197
  overview, 16–17, 185–186, 200, 208, 218,
    221–223, 232–233
  policy implications of, 197–199
  reasons to implement, 208–210
  See also Game-based assessments (GBAs);
    Simulation-based assessments (SBAs)
Computerized adaptive testing (CAT)
  administration models, 212–215
  evolution of CBT and, 187–191
  game-based assessments (GBAs) and, 245
  large-scale assessment and, 192–195
  overview, 16–17, 186, 221–223
  See also Adaptive testing; Computer-based testing
    (CBT)
Computerized sequential testing (CST), 195–196
Conceptual equivalence, 278. See also Equivalence
  issues
Concordant CR score, 67–68. See also Constructed
  response (CR)
Conditional analysis, 160, 160f, 249
Conditional estimation, 159, 159f
Conditional probabilities, 249
Confirmation guidelines, 297–298
Confirmatory factor analysis (CFA)
  dimensionality and local independence and, 163–165
  dimensionality assumption and, 168
  exploratory factor analysis and, 167
  simulation- and game-based assessments and, 247
  test adaptation and, 298
Consistency, 27–29, 30
Constraints, 193, 193n, 194, 194n, 212–213
Construct, 324
Construct bias, 262–263, 264, 267–268. See also Bias
Construct map, 224, 225f
Construct relevancy, 264
Construct underrepresentation, 357
Construct-driven adaptations, 281. See also Adaptive
  testing
Constructed response (CR)
  body of work (BoW) method and, 51
  bookmark method and, 49
  choosing a standard-setting method and, 43
  computer-based testing (CBT) and, 222
  gaming and advanced simulations and, 228
  performance-level descriptors and, 67–71, 69f, 70t

test score interpretations, 67–68
  See also Item formats
Construct-irrelevant variance, 357
Content assessment, 403–406, 411, 421–422
Content standards, 40–41, 421–422
Content-referenced standard setting, 55–56, 56f. See
  also Standard setting
Continuous scale, 74
Continuous variables, 137t
Contour plots
  compensatory and noncompensatory models and,
    150–151, 150f
  diagnostic models and, 153–154
  true score representation and, 157–158, 158f
Contrasting groups method, 50–51
Control Data Cooperation (CDC), 187
Convenience, 209
Coordinator role, 263
Correction, 228
Correlated error, 101–103, 102t
Correlational statistics, 10. See also Classical test
  theory (CTT)
Council of Chief State School Officers (CCSSO), 313
Covariances, 101–103, 102t
C-rater, 230
Credentialing, 39–40, 40–41, 41
Criterion-referenced domain scores, 31–32
Criterion-referenced testing (CRT)
  accountability and, 309
  consistency and, 27–29
  developments in, 13–14, 25–27
  overview, 23–25, 33–34, 74–76
  reporting test results, 31–33
  simple gain growth model and, 325
  standard setting and, 29–31
  test transfer and, 285
  See also Standard setting; Validity
Criticism of testing, 445
Cross-cultural assessment
  current trends in assessment and, 440–441
  early approaches to, 274–276
  ITC Guidelines on Adapting Tests (2010),
    292–300, 294f
  methods and designs for, 262–269
  overview, 259–262, 269–271, 273
  scalar invariance and, 285–286
  test transfer and, 282–286
  See also Cross-lingual assessment; English learners
    (ELs); Multilingual assessment
Cross-lingual assessment
  current trends in assessment and, 440–441
  early approaches to, 274–276
  ITC Guidelines on Adapting Tests (2010),
    292–300, 294f
  methods and designs for, 262–269
  overview, 259–262, 269–271, 273, 300
  test transfer and, 282–286
  See also Cross-cultural assessment; English
    learners (ELs); Multilingual assessment;
    Translation of testing material

Cultural adaptation, 280–281. *See also* Adaptive
    testing
Cultural difference, 281
Curriculum, 241, 424–425, 427–428
Cut scores
    generalizability theory and, 99
    overview, 41
    standard setting and, 39–40, 54
    steps for setting performance standards, 46
    training panelists and, 45

D studies, 96–99, 98*t*
Darwin, Charles, 4
Data analysis, 243, 247–248
Data collection, 241–243, 243, 246
Data management, 243
Data mining, 247
Data-driven approaches to data analysis, 247
Decision accuracy, 83–85, 84*f*, 85*f*
Decision consistency
    classical test theory and, 76–79
    examples of, 83–85, 84*f*, 85*f*
    item response theory (IRT) and, 79–80
    measurement decision theory (MDT) and, 81–83
    overview, 74–75, 85
Decision making, 38, 318
Decision theory, 26, 27–28
Declarative knowledge, 224
Degrees of freedom, 171–172
Delta plot transformed item difficulty (TID), 268
Dependability coefficient, 97
DETECT procedure, 169
Diagnostic assessments, 442–443
Diagnostic classification models (DCM)
    conditional analysis and, 160, 160*f*
    current trends in assessment and, 443
    overview, 143–144
    See also Multidimensional item response theory
        (MIRT) models
Diagnostic cognitive models (DCM)
    diagnostic models and, 156
    overview, 122
    theoretical background, 145–147, 146*f*
    See also Item response theory (IRT)
Diagnostic information, 240, 436, 443
Diagnostic modeling, 153–154, 153*f*, 156, 157*f*
Diagnostic testing, 283
Dichotomous items, 111, 169, 174
Differential bundle functioning (DBF), 131
Differential functioning of items and tests (DFIT),
    131
Differential item functioning of test items (DIF)
    cross-cultural and cross-lingual assessments and,
        267, 268–269, 274, 279
    English learners (ELs) and, 401
    history of research on, 127–137, 133*f*, 134*f*, 137*f*
    models, 144–145
    overview, 126–127, 128, 137, 446
    test adaptation and, 297–298
Dimensionality. *See* Test dimensionality

Dimensionality assumption, 163–169, 166*f*, 177
Dimensionality evaluation to enumerate contributing
    traits (DETECT), 168–169
DIMTEST software program, 168–169, 169
Disabilities, 197–198, 199, 312
Discrete interval scale, 74
Discrete variables, 137*t*
Distributed online scoring, 222
Documentation, 267, 300
Domain model, 64, 427
Dynamic Learning Maps Alternative Assessment
    Consortium, 390, 423

E-assessment, 186. *See also* Computer-based testing
    (CBT)
Education for All Handicapped Children Act, 375, 376.
    See also Individuals with Disabilities Act (IDEA)
Educational achievement, 436
Educational reform
    developments in testing and, 14–17
    legislative history pertaining to, 376–377
    A Nation at Risk (National Commission on
        Excellence in Education, 1983), 308–310
    performance assessments and accountability and,
        361–363
    students with disabilities and, 416
Educational surveys, 242*t*
Educational Testing Service (ETS)
    differential item functioning of test items (DIF)
        and, 129
    evolution of CBT and, 189–191
    history of, 9–10
    instruction and, 198
    reporting test results and, 337, 341–342
    simulation- and game-based assessments and, 246
    See also National Assessment of Educational
        Progress (NAEP)
Educational Value Added Assessment System
    (EVAAS), 331–332
EDUG software, 99
Effect size measures, 129–130
Effective test length, 77–78
Efficiency of measurement, 186
Eigenvalue-greater-than-1 rule (K1), 167
Electronic assessment, 186. *See also* Computer-based
    testing (CBT)
Elementary and Secondary Education Act (ESEA)
    accountability and, 307
    alternative assessments based on alternative
        achievement standards (AA-AAS) and, 418–419,
        422
    educational reform and, 15, 376–377
    English learners (ELs) and, 375–376, 397–398,
        399–400
    overview, 416–417
    students with disabilities and, 375
    See also Improving America's Schools Act (IASA)
Embedded assessment, 240, 443–444. *See also*
    Game-based assessments (GBAs); Simulation-
    based assessments (SBAs)

Emergent bilingual students, 395n. *See also* English
    learners (ELs)
End-of-course assessment, 242t
Enemy constraints, 193, 193n
Engagement, 245
English as a second language (ESL) classroom, 406.
    See also English learners (ELs)
English Language Arts (ELA) standards, 314
English Language Development (ELD) standards,
    410–411, 410n
English language proficiency (ELP) assessments,
    399–400, 406–411, 409–411
English learners (ELs)
    accessibility and, 439–440
    accommodations and, 383–388, 385f–387f
    accountability and, 312–313
    alternative assessments and, 388–390, 390t
    current trends in assessment and, 436
    federal definition for, 400–402, 400f
    future of, 411
    inclusion and, 382–383
    large-scale assessment and, 395–397
    legislative history pertaining to, 374, 374f, 375–376
    litigation and, 379–380
    overview, 373–374, 391–392, 400–402, 400f
    standards and, 390–391
    understanding of the assessment content, 397–400
    validity concerns and, 402–411
    See also Cross-cultural assessment; Cross-lingual
        assessment; Multilingual assessment; Special
        populations
Equal Educational Opportunities Act (EEOA), 376,
    379–380
Equal Protection Clause of the 14t Amendment to the
    U.S. Constitution, 397–398
Equipment accommodations, 383, 384, 386t. *See also*
    Testing accommodations
Equity, 240
Equivalence issues, 275–276, 277–279, 297–298
Error, 102–103, 366–367
Essays in educational testing, 358–359
Essential dimensionality, 168. *See also*
    Dimensionality assumption
Estimation methods, 117–120
Ethnicity, 280
ETS (Educational Testing Service). *See* Educational
    Testing Service (ETS)
Evaluating teachers. *See* Teacher evaluations
Evaluation, 230
Evidence-based standard setting, 55–56, 56f, 65–71,
    69f, 70t. *See also* Standard setting
Evidence-centered design (ECD)
    alternative assessments based on alternative
        achievement standards (AA-AAS) and, 424
    developing performance-level descriptors and,
        63–65
    overview, 72
    performance assessment and, 364, 368
    simulation- and game-based assessments and,
        244–248

Examinee-centered method, 47–48
Examinees, 89–93, 91t, 92t, 95, 210. *See also* Object
    of measurement
Expectation-maximization (EM) algorithm, 119–120.
    See also Maximum likelihood estimation (MLE)
Expected mean squares, 98–99, 98t
Exploratory factor analysis (EFA), 166–168, 247
EXPLORATORY procedure, 169
Extended Angoff method, 48. *See also* Modified
    Angoff method
Eysenck Personality Questionnaire (EPQ), 283

Factor analysis, 267–268
Factor retention, 167–168
Fairness
    accessibility and, 439–440
    cross-cultural and cross-lingual assessments and,
        270–271
    English learners (ELs) and, 396
    performance assessments and, 362
    simulation- and game-based assessments and, 240
Familiarity/recognizability driven adaptations, 281.
    See also Adaptive testing
Feedback, 42, 46
Field testing, 266–267
Fit statistics, 279
Five-factor model, 278, 283
Fixed-length computerized adaptive testing, 213–214.
    See also Computerized adaptive testing (CAT)
Flagging, 384, 387–388
Flexibility, 216, 218, 437
Flexilevel testing, 188
FlexMIRT software, 121
Floor effects, 322–323
Flow, 245
Focal knowledge, skill, and ability (FKSA), 424
Format of assessments, 421
Formative assessments
    current trends in assessment and, 436, 443–444
    simulation- and game-based assessments and, 240,
        242t
    standard setting and, 30
Forward procedures, 132
Forward translation, 264–265. *See also* Translation
    of testing material
Full score (or scalar) equivalence, 278. *See also*
    Equivalence issues
Future-referenced standard setting, 56–57. *See also*
    Standard setting

G studies, 96–99, 98t
Gain score measures, 323
Galton, Sir Francis, 4, 5, 6, 7
Game-based assessments (GBAs)
    computer-based testing (CBT) and, 227–229
    current trends in assessment and, 443–444
    future of, 251–252
    overview, 239–243, 242t, 252–253
    psychometric modeling, 248–251
    structure of, 243–248

validity and, 251–252
See also Computer-based testing (CBT)
Gaussian kernal function, 174–175
General Test, 196
Generalizability
  absolute and relative error, 93–94, 94f, 95f
  correlated error and, 101–103, 102t
  evaluating standard-setting results within, 99–101,
    100t
  G studies and D studies and, 96–99, 98t
  multivariate generalizability analysis, 101–103,
    102t
  nested designs, 95
  overview, 12, 89–93, 91t, 92t, 103
  performance assessments and, 357, 359, 366–367
  See also Reliability; Score interpretations
Generalizability coefficients, 96–97
Generalized partial credit model (GPCM), 67–68,
  367
Glaser, Robert, 24–25
GlassLab, 252
Globalization, 286
Golden Rule settlement, 128
Goodness-of-fit indices, 164–165
Grade levels, 322–323, 418–419
Graded response model (GRM), 367
Graduate Management Admission Test (GMAT),
  190, 208, 221
Graduate Record Examination (GRE)
  computer-based testing (CBT) and, 193–194, 196,
    221
  evolution of CBT and, 189–190
Graphical representations (GR)
  assessing the shape of ICCs and, 172, 173f
  overview, 143
  report design and format, 348–351, 349f, 350f,
    351f
  theoretical background, 145–146
Gross national product (GNP), 276
Group administered intelligence tests, 8. *See also*
  Intelligence measures
Growth
  accountability and, 438
  current trends in assessment and, 436
  English learners (ELs) and, 411
  importance of measuring, 319
  models of, 324–332, 327t, 328f, 329f, 332f
  overview, 318–321, 333, 446
  practical complexities in measuring, 323–324
  technical complexities in measuring, 321–323
  use of growth models, 332–333
  See also Accountability

Hambleton, Ron, 232–233, 449–457
Hawkes process, 250–251
Heuristic models, 213
Hidden Markov models (HMMs), 249–250,
  250–251
High school exit examinations, 56–57
High-stakes CAT programs, 194, 215

High-stakes testing
  accountability and, 309–310, 315–316
  cross-cultural and cross-lingual assessments and,
    270–271
  performance assessments and, 356
  reporting test results and, 335–336
  simulation- and game-based assessments and, 240
History of testing
  accommodations and, 383–388, 385t–387t
  alternative assessments and, 388–390, 390t
  computer-based testing (CBT) and, 187–192
  criterion-referenced testing and, 23–27
  development of IRT, 114–121
  developments in psychometrics, 10–13
  developments in testing, 13–17
  differential item functioning of test items (DIF)
    and, 127–137, 133f, 134f, 137f
  early history of psychometrics, 4–8
  large-scale assessment, 8–10
  multilingual assessment and, 274–276
  overview, 3–4, 17, 444
  performance assessments and accountability and,
    358–360
Hypothesis, 168–169, 230

ICC shape assumption. *See* S-shape curve assumption
Identification response, 228
IGOR program, 226
Impact feedback, 42, 46, 55. *See also* Feedback
Improving America's Schools Act (IASA), 376, 416.
    See also Elementary and Secondary Education
    Act (ESEA)
Inclusion
  accountability and, 312–313
  overview, 391–392
  special populations and, 380–383
  students with disabilities and, 417–418
Individualized Education Plans (IEPs), 381
Individualized education program (IEP)
  accountability and, 312
  alternative assessments based on alternative
    achievement standards (AA-AAS) and, 421
  educational reform and, 377
  overview, 377n
Individualized measurement, 187–188
Individually prescribed instruction (IPI), 25
Individuals with Disabilities Act (IDEA)
  alternative assessments and, 389–390
  educational reform and, 376–377
  English learners (ELs) and, 406
  inclusion and, 380–381
  overview, 417
  See also Education for All Handicapped Children
    Act; Individuals with Disabilities Education Act
    (IDEA)
Individuals with Disabilities Education Act (IDEA),
  373n. *See also* Individuals with Disabilities Act
  (IDEA)
Individuals with Disabilities Education Improvement
  Act (IDEIA), 377

Information and communication technology, 186. *See also* Computer-based testing (CBT)

Information representation, 154–156, 155*f*, 157*f*

Infrastructure, 197, 198–199

Inquiry strategies, 242–243

Instruction
  alternative assessments based on alternative achievement standards (AA-AAS) and, 424–425, 427–428
  computer-based testing (CBT) and, 198
  inclusion and, 381–383
  litigation and, 378–380
  performance assessments and accountability and, 361–363
  simulation- and game-based assessments and, 240–241
  technology and, 197

Instructional design, 240, 243

Intellectual disabilities, 418. *See also* Students with disabilities (SWDs)

Intelligence measures
  computer-based testing (CBT) and, 187
  early history of psychometrics and, 5–6, 7
  large-scale assessment of, 8–9

Intelligent tutoring systems (ITS), 251. *See also* Game-based assessments (GBAs)

Internal consistency reliability, 12, 284–285. *See also* Reliability

Internal evidence, 47

International assessment, 440–441

International comparisons, 436

International Standard Classification of Education (ISCED) system, 284–285

International Test Commission (ITC) Guidelines on Adapting Tests (2010)
  comprehensive approach to adaptation and, 281–282
  cross-cultural and cross-lingual assessments and, 269–270
  current trends in assessment and, 441
  overview, 292–300, 294*f*

Internet-based testing (iBT), 196, 216. *See also* Computer-based testing (CBT)

Interoperability, 217–218

Interpretation-use argument (IUA), 357

Invariance, 111–112, 285–286

IRT-CLASS software, 80

IRTPRO software, 121

ITC Guidelines on Adapting Tests (2010). *See* International Test Commission (ITC) Guidelines on Adapting Tests (2010)

Item analysis, 267

Item bank
  computer-adaptive testing (CAT) and, 192–193
  computer-based testing (CBT) and, 194–195, 224, 225*f*
  overview, 192*n*

Item bias, 126–127, 262–263, 268. *See also* Bias

Item characteristic curve (ICC)
  assessing the shape of, 170–176, 173*f*
  diagnostic models and, 153–154, 153*f*, 156

dimensionality assumption and, 168–169
  kernel smoothing and, 174–175
  nonparametric approach and, 173–176, 176*f*
  overview, 13, 146–147
  two-dimensional MIRT models and, 149–150, 149*f*

Item characteristic surface
  true score representation and, 157–158, 158*f*
  two-dimensional MIRT models and, 148, 148*f*, 149–150, 149*f*, 150*f*, 151*f*

Item cloning, 226–227. *See also* Automatic item generation (AIG)

Item content, 277

Item development, 216–217

Item discrimination, 111

Item formats
  choosing a standard-setting method and, 43
  computer-based testing (CBT) and, 196, 224–225
  gaming and advanced simulations and, 228
  test score interpretations, 67
  See also Constructed response (CR); Selected response (SR)

Item generation, 224–227, 225*f*

Item information, 154–156, 155*f*, 157*f*

Item inventory management, 216–217

Item pool
  computer-adaptive testing (CAT) and, 192–193
  computer-based testing (CBT) and, 194–195, 196
  overview, 192*n*, 273

Item representation
  diagnostic models and, 153–154, 153*f*
  two-dimensional MIRT models and, 148–154, 149*f*, 150*f*, 151*f*, 152*f*, 153*f*

Item response surface (IRS), 147–148, 148*f*

Item response theory (IRT)
  assessing the shape of ICCs and, 172
  bookmark method and, 49–50
  choosing a standard-setting method and, 43
  collaboration and, 251
  computer-based testing (CBT) and, 193–194, 209, 223
  cross-cultural and cross-lingual assessments and, 268, 279
  decision consistency indices and, 79–80, 83–85, 84*f*, 85*f*
  development of, 114–121
  diagnostic models and, 156
  differential item functioning of test items (DIF) and, 127–128, 130, 131–132, 134, 136, 137*t*
  evolution of CBT and, 188
  measurement decision theory (MDT) and, 81–83
  nonparametric approach and, 170–176, 173*f*, 176*f*
  overview, 13, 17, 85, 107–113, 121–123, 162–163, 446
  performance assessments and, 359, 367–368
  performance-level descriptors and, 67, 71
  reporting test results and, 342
  test adaptation and, 297–298
  test score interpretations, 66
  See also Assumptions of the IRT models

Item response time, 197
Item score string estimation method, 48
Item selection, 212–213
Item trace line, 13
Item-level reporting, 31–32
Item's difficulty, 111

Joint maximum likelihood estimation (JMLE), 119, 120–121. *See also* Maximum likelihood estimation (MLE)

K–12 testing, 191–192, 198–199, 218
Kaplan test preparation company, 189–190, 194
Kentucky Instructional Reporting and Information System (KIRIS), 361–362, 363
Kernel smoothing, 174–175, 176*f*
Kinect for Windows, 240
Kinect Software Development Kit (SDK), 240
Knowledge, 224
Knowledge, skills, and abilities (KSAs)
    alternative assessments based on alternative achievement standards (AA-AAS) and, 424
    content standards and, 40–41
    standard setting and, 56–57
    steps for setting performance standards, 43, 44, 45
KR-20 formula, 27–28, 34
Kullback-Liebler information (KLI), 156, 157*f*

Lake Wobegon effect, 309
Language, 260–261. *See also* Cross-lingual assessment; Multilingual assessment
Language assessment, 406–411
Language-driven adaptations, 281. *See also* Adaptive testing
Large-scale assessment
    computer-based testing (CBT) and, 192–195
    English learners (ELs) and, 395–397
    history of, 8–10
    Internet-based testing (iBT), 196
    item response theory (IRT) and, 107–108
    reporting test results and, 336
    simulation- and game-based assessments and, 242*t*
    special populations and, 382
Latent class models, 137*t*
Latent profile analysis, 137*t*
Latent semantic analysis, 229
Latent trait theory
    evolution of CBT and, 187–188
    item response theory (IRT) and, 116, 118
    overview, 13
    See also Item response theory (IRT)
Latent variables
    differential item functioning of test items (DIF) and, 131–135, 133*f*, 134*f*, 136, 137*t*
    dimensionality assumption and, 163–170, 166*f*
    performance assessment data and, 367–368
    simulation- and game-based assessments and, 248–249
Lau Remedies, 379, 388–389
Law School Admissions Test (LSAT), 190

Learning
    alternative assessments based on alternative achievement standards (AA-AAS) and, 427
    environment, 242
    learning abilities, 8
    performance assessments and, 362
    simulation- and game-based assessments and, 241
Learning outcomes, 33, 335–336
Legislative history
    alternative assessments and, 389–390
    litigation and, 378–380
    students with disabilities and English learners and, 374–377, 374*f*
Licensure and certification, professional, 39–40, 40–41, 190–192
Likelihood ratio test, 128–129, 131–132
Limited English proficient (LEP), 373*n*, 395*n*, 400–402, 400*f*. *See also* English learners (ELs)
Linear fixed form administration model, 210–211. *See also* Administration models
Linear on the fly tests (LOFTs), 195–196, 211, 214, 222
Linear regression
    differential item functioning of test items (DIF) and, 137*t*
    projection growth model and, 327–328, 328*f*
    residual gain growth model and, 328–329, 329*f*
Linear tests, 196
Linguistic minorities (LMs), 396–397, 402–403, 411. *See also* English learners (ELs)
Links for Academic Learning, 421–422
Litigation, 378–379, 398
Local average, 174
Local independence assumption, 109–110, 170, 177. *See also* Item response theory (IRT)
Location CR score, 67–68. *See also* Constructed response (CR)
Log files, 246–247, 250–251
LOGIST software, 120–121
Logistic regression procedure
    cross-cultural and cross-lingual assessments and, 268
    differential item functioning of test items (DIF) and, 128–129, 130, 137*t*

Mantel-Haenszel (MH) procedure
    cross-cultural and cross-lingual assessments and, 268
    differential item functioning of test items (DIF) and, 128–129, 130, 133, 137*t*
Marginal maximum likelihood estimation (MMLE), 119–120, 121, 122. *See also* Maximum likelihood estimation (MLE)
Markov chain Monte Carlo (MCMC), 122, 136, 177
Markov decision process (MDP), 250
Maryland School Performance Assessment Program (MSPAP), 361–362, 362–363
Massively open online course (MOOC) offerings, 216
Mastery, 13–14, 320

Material accommodations, 383, 384, 386t. *See also* Testing accommodations
Mathematics standards, 314
Maximum information, 245
Maximum likelihood estimation (MLE)
    computer-based testing (CBT) and, 193–194
    item response theory (IRT) and, 117, 119–120
    nonparametric approach and, 175
MDISC, 151–152
Mean estimation method, 48. *See also* Modified Angoff method
Measurable objectives, 26
Measurement decision theory (MDT), 74, 81–83, 84–85, 85t
Measurement error, 90, 99–101, 100t
Mental modeling approaches, 229
Method bias, 262–263. *See also* Bias
Methods
    choosing a standard-setting method and, 43
    cross-cultural and cross-lingual assessments and, 262–269
    setting performance standards and, 47–51
    standard setting and, 30
Metric equivalence, 278. *See also* Equivalence issues
mGENOVA software, 99
Mileage chart, 350–351, 350f
MIMIC (multiple-indicator, multiple-cause) model, 132–134, 133f, 133f
Minimally competent examinee, 42. *See also* Borderline examinee
Minimally qualified candidate, 42. *See also* Borderline examinee
Minimum average partial (MAP) test, 167
Minimum-competency testing (MCT), 308. *See also* Accountability
MMPI and MMPI-2, 283
Models, 117–120
Modified Angoff method, 48–49
Mozilla's Open Badge initiative, 216
Mplus software, 132, 135
MULTI-CLASS software, 77
Multidimensional item response theory (MIRT) models
    bifactor model and, 165–166, 166f
    current trends in assessment and, 443
    overview, 109t, 121–122, 143–145, 160
    performance assessments and accountability and, 359, 367–368
    See also Diagnostic cognitive models (DCM); Item response theory (IRT); Two-dimensional MIRT models
Multidimensional scaling, 267–268
Multifaceted Rasch model, 368
Multigroup confirmatory factor analysis (MG-CFA), 131–133
Multilingual assessment
    current trends in assessment and, 440–441
    early approaches to, 274–276
    overview, 273
    procedures for, 276–282, 280f

test transfer and, 282–286
See also Cross-cultural assessment; Cross-lingual assessment; English learners (ELs); Translation of testing material
Multinomial approaches, 77
Multiparameter IRT models, 116. *See also* Three-parameter logistic (3PL) IRT model; Two-parameter logistic (2PL) IRT model
Multiple-choice tests
    computer-based testing (CBT) and, 222
    criterion-referenced testing and, 34
    gaming and advanced simulations and, 228
    performance-level descriptors and, 67–71, 69f, 70t
    simulation- and game-based assessments and, 241
    test score interpretations, 67–68
    See also Selected response (SR)
Multistage testing (MST), 17, 195–196, 196n, 211–212, 214, 221–222
Multivariate generalizability analysis, 101–103, 102t. *See also* Generalizability

NAEP Reading Report Card (NCES, 2011), 342, 343f
A Nation at Risk (National Commission on Excellence in Education, 1983), 14–15, 308–310
National Advisory Council. *See* National Council on Disability
National Assessment Governing Board (NAGB), 30, 337, 345–346
National Assessment of Educational Progress (NAEP)
    accountability and, 316
    computer-based testing (CBT) and, 196, 198
    current trends in assessment and, 442–443
    inclusion and, 381
    modified Angoff method and, 48–49
    NAEP Reading Report Card (NCES, 2011), 342, 343f
    performance-level descriptors and, 63
    standard setting and, 30–31
    test score interpretations, 66
    See also Educational Testing Service (ETS); Reporting test results
National Center and State Consortium (NCSC)
    accountability and, 315
    alternative assessments and, 390
    alternative assessments based on alternative achievement standards (AA-AAS) and, 423, 424, 425–428
    computer-based testing (CBT) and, 218
National Center for Education Statistics (NCES), 30, 338
National Center on Education Outcomes (NCEO), 381, 389
National Council of Architects Registration Boards (NCARB), 191, 222
National Council on Disability, 375
National Council on Measurement in Education (NCME), 269, 438
National Council on Nursing Licensure's Examinations for Registered and Practical Nurses (NCLEX-RN), 190–191

National Council on Nursing Licensure's
Examinations (NCLEX), 208, 213–214, 221
National Institute of Testing and Evaluation (NITE),
263, 264
Natural language processing (NLP), 246
NCLB (No Child Left Behind). *See* No Child Left
Behind (NCLB)
NEO Personality Inventory—Revised (NEO PI-R),
278, 283–284
Nested models, 164–165
New Hampshire Enhanced Assessment Initiative
(NHEAI), 423–424
Next Generation Science Standards (NGSS), 241
No Child Left Behind (NCLB)
accountability and, 310, 311–312, 314–315,
437–438
alternative assessments and, 389–390
educational reform and, 15, 377
English learners (ELs) and, 312–313, 398,
399–402, 400*f*, 407–409, 411
evolution of CBT and, 191
growth measuring and, 319
history of, 10
inclusion and, 312
performance assessments and accountability and,
359–360, 363
Noncompensatory diagnostic model (CRUM/GDM),
143, 145, 153*f*, 154, 160
Noncompensatory items, 149–153, 149*f*, 150*f*, 151*f*,
152*f*
Noncompensatory MIRT model, 144–145, 160
Nonparametric conditional covariance-based
procedures, 168–169
Nonparametric IRT technique, 173–176, 176*f*
Nonuniform differential item functioning, 128
Normative feedback, 42, 46. *See also* Feedback
Norm-referenced standard setting, 54–55, 309, 325.
See also Standard setting
Norm-referenced testing, 13–14, 31
Null hypothesis, 169
Number plot, 155, 155*f*

Object of measurement, 90–91. *See also* Examinees
Objectives, 26, 29–31
Oblique rotation method, 167. *See also* Rotation
methods
Observed proportion, 170–172, 173*f*
Observed variables, 137*t*
Office of Civil Rights (OCR), 379, 397–398
One-parameter logistic (1PL) IRT model, 110–111.
See also Item response theory (IRT)
One-year courses, 324
Online scoring networks (OSN), 222
Open Assessment Technologies (TAO), 218
Open Badge initiative, 216
Open-source platforms, 217–218
Optimization, 230
Oral assessment, 231
Ordered item booklet (OIB), 49–50
Ordinal logistic regression, 130

Orthogonal rotation method, 167. *See also* Rotation
methods
Otis, Arthur, 8

Panelists
body of work (BoW) method and, 51
challenges in standard setting and, 51–54
collecting ratings, 45–46
contrasting groups method and, 50
discussion and, 46
feedback from, 46
overview, 41
performance-level descriptors and, 67–71, 69*f*, 70*t*
steps for setting performance standards, 44
training, 44–45
Parallel analysis (PA), 167
Parallel source versions, 264–265
Parameter invariance, 111–112
Parametric bootstrapping procedure, 176
Parametric IRT models, 172
Parametric linear factor analytic procedures, 168
PARSCALE software, 121
Partial credit model (PCM), 367
Partially compensatory model, 150–151
Partitioning test (PT), 169
Partnership for Assessment of Readiness for College
and Careers (PARCC)
accountability and, 313–315
computer-based testing (CBT) and, 217–218
performance assessments and accountability and,
363–365, 369
Path analysis, 137*t*
Pearson Assessment, 6
Pennsylvania Association for Retarded Children
(PARC), 378
Performance assessments
future of state assessments and, 363–365
generalizability theory and, 102–103
historical perspective of, 358–360
item response theory (IRT) and, 107–108
overview, 356–357, 369
psychometric considerations and, 365–368
simulation- and game-based assessments and, 243
use of for accountability, 360–363
validity and, 357
See also Accountability; Performance standards
Performance levels, 30
Performance standards
Advanced Placement (AP) program and, 65–66
challenges in setting, 51–54
criterion-referenced testing and, 34
cut scores and, 39–40, 40*f*
future of, 54–57, 56*f*
methods for setting, 47–51
overview, 38–39, 41
steps for setting, 42–47
See also Performance assessments; Standard
setting; Standards
Performance tasks, 30, 34
Performance-based tasks, 240

Performance-level descriptors (PLDs)
  alternative assessments based on alternative
    achievement standards (AA-AAS) and, 422
  challenges in standard setting and, 53–54
  contrasting groups method and, 50
  developing, 44, 63–65
  overview, 41, 63
  reporting test results and, 31–32
  test score interpretations, 65–71, 69f, 70t
  training panelists and, 45
  validity and, 62, 71–72
Performance-level labels (PLLs), 41, 44
Pilot testing, 296–297
PLATO (Programmed Logic for Automatic Teaching
  Operations), 187, 188
Policy implications
  accountability and, 308
  computer-based testing (CBT) and, 197–199
  English learners (ELs) and, 396
  students with disabilities and, 418
Policy-referenced standard setting, 55–56, 56f. See
  also Standard setting
Polytomous items
  dimensionality assumption and, 169
  item response theory (IRT) and, 111
  performance assessment and, 359, 367–368
Portfolio-based performance assessment, 361, 421.
  See also Performance assessments
Posterior predictive model checking (PPMC), 177
Posterior probability, 82
Poverty, 401
Praxis Professional Assessments for Beginning
  Teachers, 190
Preknowledge, 214–215
Presentation, 228
Presentation accommodations, 383, 384, 385t. See
  also Testing accommodations
Present-referenced standard setting, 56–57. See also
  Standard setting
Pressey, Sidney, 187
Principle of essential local independence, 168
Principled test design, 223–225, 225f
Probability structures, 249
Procedural evidence, 47
Proficiency goals, 399–400
Proficient achievement level
  contrasting groups method and, 50
  cut scores and, 39
  English learners (ELs) and, 408
  performance-level descriptors and, 63
  reporting test results and, 341–342, 341f
  See also Achievement levels
Programme for International Student Assessment
  (PISA)
  computer-based testing (CBT) and, 218
  cross-cultural and cross-lingual assessments and,
    261–262, 265, 278
  current trends in assessment and, 441
  test adaptation and, 291–292
  test transfer and, 284

Programmed testing, 187–188
Progress in International Reading Literacy Study
  (PIRLS), 262, 441
Progress monitoring, 318–319, 320, 335–336
Project Essay Grade, 229
Projection growth model, 327–328, 328f, 332t. See
  also Growth
Prometric and Pearson VUE, 191
Proportional scoring, 190
Prueba de Aptitud Academica (PAA), 268
Psychological Corporation, 6
Psychometric Entrance Test (PET), 261
Psychometric measures, 260–262
Psychometricians, 263
Psychometrics
  developments in, 10–13
  early history of, 4–8
  performance assessments and, 365–368
  simulation- and game-based assessments and,
    248–251
  test transfer and, 277–279
Purpose of the test, 261
p-values, 23n, 136

Q weights, 174
Qualitative strategies, 276
Quality control (QC), 222, 224, 225
Quantitative strategies, 276, 410–411
Question and test interoperability (QTI), 217–218

R programming language, 121
Race, 280
Race to the Top assessment consortia, 435–436
Race to the Top (RTT)
  accountability and, 310, 437
  educational reform and, 15
  performance assessments and accountability and,
    363, 369
Random sampling, 98, 101
Rasch modeling software package, 120–121, 191
Rater effects, 368
Rater-sampling variability, 366–367
Ratings, 45–46
Reading Report Card (ETS, 1984)
  report design and format, 348–349, 349f
  reporting test results and, 337–338, 346, 346f
Reality feedback, 42, 46, 55. See also Feedback
Real-life activities in assessment, 240
Reform, education. See Educational reform
Regression lines, 275
Rehabilitation Act, 375, 377
Relative error, 93–94, 94f, 95f
Relative standards, 54
Reliability
  classical test theory and, 89–90
  criterion-referenced testing and, 27–29, 34
  overview, 11–12, 74
  simulation- and game-based assessments and, 252
  See also Score interpretations; Test reliability
Reordering items, 228

Reporting test results
   alternative assessments based on alternative
     achievement standards (AA-AAS) and, 423, 426
   audience and, 337–340, 339f
   computer-based testing (CBT) and, 209
   criterion-referenced testing and, 31–33
   current trends in assessment and, 442–443
   flagging of scores and, 384, 387–388
   gaming and advanced simulations and, 228
   inclusion and, 381
   overview, 335–337, 352
   report design and format, 346, 348–351, 349f,
     350f, 351f
   scale scores and, 340–346, 340t, 341f, 343f, 345f,
     346f, 347f
   See also National Assessment of Educational
     Progress (NAEP)
Residual gain growth model, 328–329, 329f, 332t.
   See also Growth
Resource materials, 209–210
Response accommodations, 383, 384, 386t. *See also*
   Testing accommodations
Response format, 276, 383
Response variable, 136–137, 137t, 241
Response-contingent testing, 187–188
Response-type systems, 229
Review process, 266
Reviewers, 263
Right–wrong items, 111. *See also* Dichotomous items
Root integrated squared error (RISE), 176
Root mean square error of approximation (RMSEA),
   164
Rotation methods, 167

SAT (Scholastic Aptitude Test)
   classical test theory and, 11
   criterion-referenced testing and, 24
   cross-cultural and cross-lingual assessments and,
     268
   evolution of CBT and, 190
   history of, 9–10
Scalar invariance, 285–286. *See also* Invariance
Scale anchoring/item mapping, 31–32, 66, 341–342
Scaling factors
   growth measuring and, 321–322
   item response theory (IRT) and, 115–116
   reporting test results and, 340–346, 341f, 343f,
     345f, 346f, 347f
Scheduling accommodations, 383, 387t. *See also*
   Testing accommodations
Scholastic Aptitude Test (SAT). *See* SAT (Scholastic
   Aptitude Test)
School districts, 437
School evaluations, 436, 437
School reform. *See* Educational reform
Schools interoperability framework (SIF), 217–218
Score interpretations
   absolute and relative error and, 93–94
   alternative assessments based on alternative
     achievement standards (AA-AAS) and, 422

computer-based testing (CBT) and, 223–224
evidence-centered design (ECD) and, 65–71, 69f,
   70t
generalizability theory and, 89–93, 91t, 92t, 100,
   101t
overview, 62
test adaptation and, 299
See also Reliability; Scoring; Validity
Score report development model, 32–33
Scores, 31–33, 34
Scoring
   alternative assessments based on alternative
     achievement standards (AA-AAS) and, 422,
     425–426
   computer-adaptive testing (CAT) and, 192,
     193–194
   computer-based testing (CBT) and, 197, 216, 222,
     229–231
   cross-cultural and cross-lingual assessments and,
     269
   evolution of CBT and, 190
   flagging of scores and, 384, 387–388
   gaming and advanced simulations and, 228
   performance assessments and accountability and,
     364–365
   standard setting and, 29–31
   test adaptation and, 299
   See also Classical test theory (CTT); Item response
     theory (IRT); Score interpretations
Scree plot, 167
Section 504 of the Rehabilitation Act, 375, 377, 378
Secure test delivery, 211, 214–215, 223. *See also* Test
   delivery
Selected response (SR)
   bookmark method and, 49
   choosing a standard-setting method and, 43
   computer-based testing (CBT) and, 222
   gaming and advanced simulations and, 228
   See also Item formats; Multiple-choice tests
Sequential testing, 187–188
Serious games, 227. *See also* Computer-based testing
   (CBT); Game-based assessments (GBAs)
Setting accommodations, 383, 387t. *See also* Testing
   accommodations
Sharable content object reference model (SCORM),
   217–218
Short-answer (SA) item type, 222
SIBTEST procedure, 130, 133–135, 137t, 268
Significance tests, 129
SimCityEDU: Pollution Challenge! game, 244–245,
   252
Simple gain growth model, 324–325, 332t. *See also*
   Growth
Simulation studies, 171–172
Simulation-based assessments (SBAs)
   automated scoring and, 230
   computer-based testing (CBT) and, 186, 227–229
   current trends in assessment and, 443–444
   future of, 251–252
   overview, 239–243, 242t, 252–253

Simulation-based assessments (SBAs) *(cont.)*
  psychometric modeling, 248–251
  structure of, 243–248
  validity and, 251–252
  See also Advanced simulations; Computer-based
    testing (CBT)
Single-administration estimation method, 28–29
Skinner, B. F., 187
Smarter Balanced Assessment Consortium (SBAC)
  accountability and, 314–315
  computer-based testing (CBT) and, 217–218
  performance assessments and accountability and,
    363–365, 369
Socioeconomic status, 401
Software. *See* Computer software; *individual*
    software programs
Special education, 417–418. *See also* Special
    populations; Students with disabilities (SWDs)
Special populations
  accessibility and, 439–440
  accommodations and, 383–388, 385*f*–387*t*
  alternative assessments and, 388–390, 390*t*
  overview, 391–392
  standards and, 390–391
  See also English learners (ELs); Students with
    disabilities (SWDs)
Speech recognition. *See* Automated speech
    recognition (ASR) technology
S-shape curve assumption
  assessing the shape of ICCs and, 170–176, 173*f*
  overview, 110, 177
  See also Item response theory (IRT)
Standard error of estimation (SEE), 79–80
Standard error of measurement (SEM), 80, 175–176
Standard setting
  Advanced Placement (AP) program and, 65–66
  alternative assessments based on alternative
    achievement standards (AA-AAS) and, 418–419,
    422
  challenges in, 51–54
  concepts in, 40–42
  criterion-referenced testing and, 29–31
  English learners (ELs) and, 409–411
  evaluating results from within a generalizability
    theory framework, 99–101, 100*t*
  future of, 54–57, 56*f*
  methods for setting performance standards, 47–51
  overview, 38–40, 40*f*, 57
  steps for setting performance standards, 42–47
  See also Criterion-referenced testing (CRT);
    Standards
Standardization (STD) procedure, 128–129, 130, 137*t*
Standardized assessments, 107–108
Standardized residual (SR), 171, 172, 173*f*
Standardized root mean square residual (SRMR), 164
Standards
  alternative assessments based on alternative
    achievement standards (AA-AAS) and, 418–419
  cross-cultural and cross-lingual assessments and,
    262–263

developments in testing and, 14–17
English learners (ELs) and, 406–411
growth measuring and, 320
performance assessments and accountability and,
  360
reporting test results and, 335–336
students with disabilities and, 416
test adaptation and, 291–293
See also Accountability; Standard setting;
  Standards for Educational and Psychological
  Testing (AERA, APA, & NCME, 2014)
Standards for Educational and Psychological Testing
  (AERA, APA, & NCME, 2014)
  accessibility and, 439–440
  accountability and, 438
  English learners (ELs) and, 395–396
  growth measuring and, 323–324
  overview, 38–39
  performance assessments and accountability and,
    358–360
  special populations and, 390–391
  testing accommodations and, 384, 387–388
  See also Standards
Standards-referenced standard setting, 54–55. *See*
  also Standard setting
Standards-referenced tests (SRTs), 41
Stanford–Binet Intelligence Scales, 7
Stanford–Binet test of children's intelligence, 115
State assessment consortia, 313–315
State assessments
  accountability and, 361–363
  consequential evidence of, 362–363
  developments in testing and, 14–17
  future of, 363–365
State content standards, 360. *See also* Standards
Statistical modeling, 135
Statistical procedures
  absolute and relative error and, 93–94, 94*f*, 95*f*
  classical test theory and, 76–79
  cross-cultural and cross-lingual assessments and, 279
  differential item functioning of test items (DIF)
    and, 127–129
  early history of psychometrics and, 6
  examples of, 83–85, 84*f*, 85*f*
  measurement decision theory (MDT) and, 81–83
  nested designs and, 95
  overview, 74–76, 75*f*, 446
  projection growth model and, 327
  residual gain growth model and, 328
  simple gain growth model and, 325
  simulation- and game-based assessments and,
    248–251
  student growth percentile (SGP) and, 330
  test transfer and, 276
  value tables growth model and, 326
  value-added growth model and, 331–332
Stealth assessment approach, 443–444. *See also*
  Game-based assessments (GBAs); Simulation-
  based assessments (SBAs)
Stopping rules, 213–214

Strict dimensionality, 168. *See also* Dimensionality assumption
Structural equation modeling (SEM), 131–135, 133*f*, 134*f*, 137*t*
Structural equivalence, 278. *See also* Equivalence issues
Student growth percentile (SGP), 329–330, 332*t*. *See also* Growth
Student learning objectives (SLOs), 357
Students with disabilities (SWDs)
    accessibility and, 439–440
    accommodations and, 383–388, 385*f*–387*t*
    accountability and, 312
    alternative assessments and, 388–390, 390*t*, 416–418
    alternative assessments based on alternative achievement standards (AA-AAS) and, 418–428
    computer-based testing (CBT) and, 199
    current trends in assessment and, 436
    inclusion and, 380–382
    legislative history pertaining to, 374–377, 374*f*
    litigation and, 378–379
    overview, 373–374, 391–392
    standards and, 390–391
    See also Disabilities; Special populations
Subject-matter experts (SMEs), 223
Substitution, 228
Summary statistic, 171–172
Summative assessments, 30, 240
Sums of squares, 98–99, 98*t*
Supervised learning, 247
Surface plot, 157–158, 158*f*

Tailored testing, 187–188
Target examinee, 42. *See also* Borderline examinee
Task model grammar (TMG), 224, 225*f*
Task model map (TMM), 224, 225*f*
Task-sampling variability, 366–367
Teacher evaluations, 310–312, 436, 437, 438–439
Teaching and Learning International Survey (TALIS), 284
Teamwork, 240
Technical documentation, 47
Technology
    alternative assessments based on alternative achievement standards (AA-AAS) and, 426
    current trends in assessment and, 436, 441–442, 443–444
    instruction and, 197
    Internet-based testing (iBT), 196
    National Assessment of Educational Progress (NAEP), 344
    overview, 185, 318
    See also Computer-based testing (CBT); Game-based assessments (GBAs); Simulation-based assessments (SBAs)
Technology-enhanced items (TEI), 216, 222
Terman, Lewis M., 7
Test adaptation. *See* Adaptive testing; Cross-cultural assessment; Cross-lingual assessment; Multilingual assessment

Test administration, 262–269, 298–299, 446. *See also* Administration models
Test analysis, 266–267
Test assembly, 192, 193–194, 214
Test bias, 126–127. *See also* Bias
Test delivery, 192, 195
Test design, 276, 440. *See also* Assessment design
Test development, 403–405, 427
Test dimensionality, 167–168, 168. *See also* Dimensionality assumption
Test modifications, 378–379
Test of English as a Foreign Language (TOEFL), 190, 211
Test reliability, 74–76. *See also* Reliability
Test score distributions, 274–275
Test security, 53, 223
Test statistic (*T*), 168–169
Test theory research, 26
Test transfer
    early approaches to, 274–276
    overview, 282–286
    procedures for, 276–282, 280*f*
    See also Cross-lingual assessment; Multilingual assessment; Translation of testing material
Test validation. *See* Validity
Test-based accountability systems, 308, 360–361, 438. *See also* Accountability
Test-centered method, 47–48, 48–49
Testing, 13–17
Testing accommodations
    English learners (ELs) and, 403, 405–406
    history of, 383–388, 385*t*–387*t*
    inclusion and, 381–382
    litigation and, 378–379
    students with disabilities and, 375
Testing locations, 216
Testing time, 323–324
Testlets, 211–212
Theory-based methods to data analysis, 247
Theory-driven adaptations, 281. *See also* Adaptive testing
Third International Mathematics and Science Study (TIMSS), 261–262, 441
Three-parameter logistic (3PL) IRT model, 67, 111, 116, 162. *See also* Item response theory (IRT)
Three-parameter logistic (3PL) MIRT model, 144–145
Timing accommodations, 383, 387*t*. *See also* Testing accommodations
Training of scorers, 425–426
Transadaption
    considerations regarding, 261–262
    early approaches to, 274–276
    methods and designs and, 262–269
    overview, 261–262
    See also Adaptive testing; Cross-cultural assessment; Cross-lingual assessment; Multilingual assessment; Translation of testing material
Transformed item difficulty (TID), 268

Translation of testing material
  analysis of item content and, 277
  considerations regarding, 261–262
  early approaches to, 274–276
  ITC Guidelines on Adapting Tests (2010),
     292–300, 294*f*
  methods and designs and, 262–269
  models of translation, 264–265
  overview, 261–262, 273
  procedures for, 276–282, 280*f*
  See also Cross-lingual assessment; Multilingual
     assessment
Translators, 263
TRAPD (translation, revision, adjudication,
     pretesting, documentation) model, 296
Trends in International Mathematics and Science
     Study (TIMSS), 291–292
True negative probability, 79–80
True score (T), 74, 157–158, 158*f*
Tucker-Lewis index (TLI), 164
TUTOR language, 188
Two-dimensional compensatory model, 144–145
Two-dimensional MIRT models
  item information, 154–156, 155*f*, 157*f*
  item representation and, 148–154, 149*f*, 150*f*, 151*f*,
     152*f*, 153*f*
  overview, 143–144
  theoretical background, 145–147, 146*f*
  two-dimensional extension, 147–148, 148*f*
  See also Multidimensional item response theory
     (MIRT) models
Two-parameter logistic (2PL) IRT model
  development of IRT and, 116, 118
  nonparametric approach and, 175
  overview, 111, 144–145
  theoretical background, 145–146
  See also Item response theory (IRT)
Type I errors, 171–172

Undesired multidimensionality, 130
Unidimensional IRT model, 165–166
Unidimensionality assumption
  DIMTEST and, 168–169
  item response theory (IRT) and, 162–163
  null hypothesis and, 169
  overview, 109
  See also Item response theory (IRT)
Uniform CPA Exam, 196, 222, 227, 229
Uniform differential item functioning, 128
Uniform kernal function, 174–175
United Nations Educational, Scientific, and Cultural
     Organisation (UNESCO), 284–285
United States Medical Licensing Examination
     (USMLE), 191

Universal test design, 440. *See also* Test design
Universe score, 96–97, 101–102
U.S. Medical Licensing Examination (USMLE), 210,
     222, 229

Validity
  accountability and, 438
  automated scoring and, 229–230
  computer-based testing (CBT) and, 223
  developing performance-level descriptors and,
     63–65
  English learners (ELs) and, 396–397, 402–411
  generalizability theory and, 99–101, 100*t*
  overview, 62, 71–72, 444–445
  performance assessments and, 357, 359–360
  performance-level descriptors and, 65–71, 69*f*, 70*t*
  simulation- and game-based assessments and,
     251–252
  test score interpretations, 65–71, 69*f*, 70*t*
  validity evidence, 47
  See also Criterion-referenced testing (CRT); Score
     interpretations
Value tables growth model, 326, 327*t*, 332*t*. *See also*
     Growth
Value-added growth model, 330–332, 332*t*. *See also*
     Growth
Variability, 93–94
Variable-length computerized adaptive testing,
     213–214. *See also* Computerized adaptive
     testing (CAT)
Variance components
  generalizability theory and, 91–93, 91*t*, 92*t*,
     97–99, 98*t*, 100–101, 100*t*
  test transfer and, 285
Vector plots, 154
Vertical articulation, 42
Vertical scaling, 321–322
Virtual environments, 227. *See also* Computer-based
     testing (CBT); Game-based assessments (GBAs)

Wechsler Adult Intelligence Scale (WAIS), 260, 278
Wechsler Intelligence Scales for Children (WISC),
     278, 280, 280*f*
Weighted deviations model, 213
Weighted least squares (WLS), 168
Weighted multidimensional scaling, 267–268
WinBUGS software, 135
WinSteps software, 120–121
Writing samples, 30, 34

Yerkes, Robert, 8
Yes–no method, 48

Zone of proximal development, 245

About the Editors

Craig S. Wells, PhD, is Associate Professor in the Department of Educational Policy, Research, and Administration and Associate Director of the Center for Educational Assessment at the University of Massachusetts Amherst, where he teaches courses in statistical and psychometric methods. Dr. Wells's research interests pertain to the application of item response theory models specifically for examining the effects and detection of item parameter drift, differential item functioning, and model misfit. He also has a keen interest in the philosophy of science and its applications to behavioral and social science research.

Molly Faulkner-Bond, PhD, studied under Ron Hambleton at the University of Massachusetts Amherst and earned her doctorate in Research, Educational Measurement, and Psychometrics in 2016. She has published in prominent national and international journals such as the *Review of Research in Education*, the *International Journal of Testing*, and *Educational Measurement: Issues and Practice*. Her research focuses on validity issues and evaluation in large-scale K–12 testing systems, with a particular focus on policies and assessments for English learners.

Contributors

Terry A. Ackerman, PhD, Department of Educational Research Methodology, University of North Carolina at Greensboro, Greensboro, North Carolina

Avi Allalouf, PhD, National Institute for Testing and Evaluation, Jerusalem, Israel

Krista J. Breithaupt, MA, Medical Council of Canada, Ottawa, Ontario, Canada

Michael Chajewski, PhD, The College Board, New York, New York

Gregory J. Cizek, PhD, School of Education, University of North Carolina at Chapel Hill, Chapel Hill, North Carolina

Brian E. Clauser, EdD, National Board of Medical Examiners, Philadelphia, Pennsylvania

Jerome C. Clauser, EdD, American Board of Internal Medicine, Philadelphia, Pennsylvania

Kimberly F. Colvin, EdD, Research in Learning, Assessing, and Tutoring Effectively, Massachusetts Institute of Technology, Cambridge, Massachusetts

Paula Elosua, PhD, Department of Social Psychology and Methodology, University of the Basque Country, San Sebastian, Spain

Molly Faulkner-Bond, PhD, College of Education, University of Massachusetts Amherst, Amherst, Massachusetts

Ellen Forte, PhD, edCount LLC, Washington, DC

Alejandra Garcia, MS, College of Education, University of Massachusetts Amherst, Amherst, Massachusetts

Kurt F. Geisinger, PhD, Buros Center for Testing, University of Nebraska–Lincoln, Lincoln, Nebraska

Else Hambleton, PhD, Department of History, University of Massachusetts Amherst, Amherst, Massachusetts

Ronald K. Hambleton, PhD, Department of Educational Policy, Research, and Administration, University of Massachusetts Amherst, Amherst, Massachusetts

Kyung (Chris) T. Han, EdD, Graduate Management Admission Council, Reston, Virginia

Pnina Hanani, MA, National Institute for Testing and Evaluation, Jerusalem, Israel

Robert A. Henson, PhD, School of Education, University of North Carolina at Greensboro, Greensboro, North Carolina

Kristen Huff, PhD, ACT Inc., Iowa City, Iowa

Pamela Kaliski, PhD, The College Board, Yardley, Pennsylvania

Lisa A. Keller, EdD, Department of Educational Policy, Research, and Administration, University of Massachusetts Amherst, Amherst, Massachusetts

Suzanne Lane, PhD, School of Education, University of Pittsburgh, Pittsburgh, Pennsylvania

Robert L. Linn, PhD (deceased), School of Education, University of Colorado Boulder, Boulder, Colorado

Richard M. Luecht, PhD, School of Education, University of North Carolina at Greensboro, Greensboro, North Carolina

John Mazzeo, PhD, Educational Testing Service, Princeton, New Jersey

Craig N. Mills, EdD, National Board of Medical Examiners, Philadelphia, Pennsylvania

Robert J. Mislevy, PhD, Educational Testing Service, Princeton, New Jersey

José Muñiz, PhD, Faculty of Psychology, University of Oviedo, Oviedo, Spain

José-Luis Padilla, PhD, Faculty of Psychology, University of Granada, Granada, Spain

Mary J. Pitoniak, PhD, Educational Testing Service, Princeton, New Jersey

Barbara S. Plake, BA, Buros Center for Testing, University of Nebraska–Lincoln, Lincoln, Nebraska

Ype H. Poortinga, PhD, Tilburg School of Social and Behavioral Sciences, Tilburg University, Tilburg, The Netherlands

W. James Popham, PhD, Graduate School of Education, University of California, Los Angeles, Los Angeles, California

Rachel F. Quenemoen, MS, National Center on Educational Outcomes, University of Minnesota, Minneapolis, Minnesota

Jennifer Randall, PhD, Department of Educational Policy, Research, and Administration, University of Massachusetts Amherst, Amherst, Massachusetts

Rosemary R. Reshetar, EdD, The College Board, Yardley, Pennsylvania

Joseph Rios, MA, Educational Testing Service, Princeton, New Jersey

Frederic Robin, EdD, Educational Testing Service, Princeton, New Jersey

H. Jane Rogers, PhD, Department of Educational Psychology, University of Connecticut, Storrs, Connecticut

Lawrence M. Rudner, PhD, The Arcturus Group, Easton, Maryland

Stephen G. Sireci, PhD, Department of Educational Policy, Research, and Administration, University of Massachusetts Amherst, Amherst, Massachusetts

Hariharan Swaminathan, PhD, Department of Educational Psychology, University of Connecticut, Storrs, Connecticut

Martha L. Thurlow, PhD, National Center on Educational Outcomes, University of Minnesota, Minneapolis, Minnesota

Betty Jean Usher-Tate, MA, Buros Center for Testing, University of Nebraska–Lincoln, Lincoln, Nebraska

Fons J. R. van de Vijver, PhD, Tilburg School of Social and Behavioral Sciences, Tilburg University, Tilburg, The Netherlands

Alina A. von Davier, PhD, Educational Testing Service, Princeton, New Jersey

Walter D. Way, PhD, Pearson, Iowa City, Iowa

Craig S. Wells, PhD, Department of Educational Policy, University of Massachusetts Amherst, Amherst, Massachusetts

April L. Zenisky, EdD, Department of Educational Policy, Research, and Administration, University of Massachusetts Amherst, Amherst, Massachusetts